What's New in this Edition

Teach Yourself C Programming in 21 Days, Premier Edition, is a new edition of the international bestseller, *Teach Yourself C in 21 Days*. This premier edition offers you more than just 21 days of learning C. You'll not only learn C programming in 21 days, but you will learn even more by continuing on through a bonus week—an additional seven days of topics have been added.

The bonus days are not required reading. They present advanced topics that build on what you learn during the standard 21-day course and provide you with valuable information for creating more sophisticated programs.

Bonus Day 1

"Coding Styles," describes the importance of adopting a coding style. Included in this discussion is a description of standard styles, such as Hungarian notation. Tips for writing clear, maintainable code are emphasized.

Bonus Day 2

"Portability," covers issues you should consider if you plan to make your code portable across different computer systems or compilers.

Bonus Day 3

"Working with Bits," is an expansion of material presented in the previous edition's earlier chapters. You gain a better understanding of bit-manipulation within C programs today.

Bonus Day 4

"Working with Different Number Systems," expands on what the previous edition of this book covered in three pages. It explains the importance of working with different number systems, such as Binary and Hexadecimal. Several code listings help to illustrate this point.

Bonus Day 5

"Advanced Structures: Linked Lists," focuses on one of the most confusing topics in C, linked lists. Few C programming books contain a complete working listing of a linked-list program. This book does! Not only do you learn to work with a linked list, but you also learn to work with stacks and queues. Additionally, double-linked lists and binary trees are covered at a high level.

Bonus Day 6

"Variable-Length Structures," is a topic that will come in handy when you start working with storage-efficient programs. You learn how to use only the space necessary to save information.

Bonus Day 7

"What Is C++?" you learn the basics about C++ and how it differs from C. Many C programmers move on to program in C++, or they use C++ compilers. This chapter provides an overview of the differences between what you've learned about C and what C++ can do.

Note: Even though there are 28 days of material presented in this book, you still learn C in 21 days. In fact, you are entering programs on the first day. By the end of the first week, you should be able to create your own simple programs. At the end of 21 days, you will know the C language.

Teach
Yourself
C Programming
in 21 Days

Teach Yourself
C Programming
in 21 Days

Peter Aitken
Bradley L. Jones

SAMS
PUBLISHING

201 West 103rd Street
Indianapolis, Indiana 46290

Trademarks

Overview

Contents

Acknowledgments

First and foremost, my thanks go to my co-author Brad Jones for his hard work and dedication. I also am greatly indebted to all the people at Sams Publishing, unfortunately too many to mention by name, who helped bring this book from concept to completion. The text and programs in this book have been thoroughly edited and tested, and we believe the book to be largely, if not completely, error free. Should you encounter an error, we would like to know about it. You can contact me through the publisher at the address on the disk order form at the back of the book, via CompuServe (76367,136), or via the Internet (76367.136@COMPUSERVE.COM).

Peter Aitken

I would like to acknowledge all the people who have taken the time to provide comments and feedback on this book. By incorporating their feedback, I hope that we have made this an even better book.

Bradley L. Jones

Reviewed by the Indianapolis Computer Society

About the Authors

Peter Aitken

Peter Aitken is an Associate Professor at Duke University Medical Center, where he uses PCs extensively in his research on the nervous system. He is an experienced author on microcomputer subjects, with some 70 magazine articles and 16 books to his credit. Aitken's writing covers both applications and programming topics; his books include *QuickBasic Advanced Techniques* (Que), *Learning C* (Sams Publishing), and *The First Book of 1-2-3 for Windows* (Alpha Books). He is a Contributing Editor at *PC Techniques* magazine.

Bradley L. Jones

Bradley L. Jones is a professional C Programmer. He has helped in the development of systems for several national and international corporations and is an active member of the Indianapolis Computer Society, where he heads the teaching of C and C++ as the leader of the C/C++ SIG. He also wrote *Even You Can Soup Up and Fix PC's* (Sams Publishing) and is a regular writer in the *Indy PC News* magazine.

Introduction

As you can guess from the title, this book is set up so that you can teach yourself the C programming language in 21 days. Of the various programming languages available, more professional programmers choose C because of its power and flexibility. For reasons we detail on Day 1, you can't go wrong in selecting C as your programming language.

We think you've made a wise decision selecting this book as your means for learning C. Although there are many books on C, we believe this book presents C in the most logical and easy-to-learn sequence. We designed this book for you to work through the chapters in order on a daily basis. We do not assume any previous programming experience on your part, although experience with another language, such as BASIC, might help you learn faster. We also make no assumptions about your computer or compiler; this book concentrates on teach C, regardless of your compiler.

Special Features of This Book

The book contains some special features to aid you on your path to C enlightenment. Syntax boxes show you how to use a specific C item. Each box provides concrete examples and a full explanation of the C command or concept. To get a feel for the style of the syntax boxes, look at the following example. (Don't try to understand the material; you haven't even reached Day 1!)

```
#include <stdio.h>
printf( format-string[,arguments,...]);
```

Syntax

printf() is a function that accepts a series of *arguments*, each applying to a *conversion specifier* in the given format string. It prints the formatted information to the standard output device, usually the display screen. When using printf(), you need to include the standard input/output header file. STDIO.H.

The format-string is required; however, arguments are optional. For each argument, there must be a conversion specifier. Table 7.2 lists the most commonly needed conversion specifiers. The format string also can contain escape sequences. Table 7.1 lists the most frequently used escape sequences. The following are examples of calls to printf() and their output:

Example 1

```
#include <stdio.h>
main()
{
    printf( "This is an example of something printed!");
}
```

Displays

```
This is an example of something printed!
```

Example 2

```
printf( "This prints a character, %c\na number, %d\na floating point, %f", 'z',
123, 156.789 );
```

Displays

```
This prints a character, z
a number, 123
a floating point, 456.789
```

Another feature of this book is DO/DON'T boxes, which give you pointers on what to do and what not to do.

DO	DON'T

DO read the rest of this section. It provides an explanation of the workshop section at the end of each day.

DON'T skip any of the quiz questions or exercises. If you can finish the day's workshop, you are ready to move on to new material.

You'll encounter Tip, Note, and Warning boxes as well. Tips provide useful shortcuts and techniques for working with C. Notes provide special details that enhance the explanations of C concepts. Warnings help you avoid common problems.

Numerous sample programs are provided throughout the book to illustrate C features and concepts so that you can apply them in your own programs. Each program's discussion is divided into three different components: the program itself, the input required and the output generated by it, and a line-by-line analysis of how the program works. The components are indicated by special icons for easy reference.

Each day ends with a Q&A section containing answers to common questions relating to that day's material. There is also a workshop at the end of each day. The workshop contains quiz questions and exercises. The quiz tests your knowledge of the concepts presented that day. If you want to check your responses, or in case you're stumped, the answers are in Appendix F, "Answers."

You won't learn C by just reading this book, however. If you want to be a programmer, you've got to write programs. Following each set of quiz questions is a set of exercises. We recommend that you attempt each exercise. Writing C code is the best way to learn the C programming language.

We consider the BUG BUSTER exercises most beneficial. A bug is a program error in C. BUG BUSTER exercises are code listings that contain common problems (bugs). It is your job to locate and fix the errors.

As you progress through the book, some of the exercise answers tend to get long. Other exercises have a multitude of answers. As a result, later chapters might not provide answers for all the exercises.

Making a Better Book

Nothing is perfect, but we do believe in striving for perfection. This Premier Edition has some new features. The most notable is that this book has been checked twice to insure the ultimate in technical accuracy for a book. This is in addition to the checks made by both authors and the suggested changes from readers of the previous two editions and over eight printings of this book.

This Premier Edition gives you more than the 21 days of the original editions. All the concepts necessary to learn C are presented in the first 21 Days. Once you are done with the first 21 days, you will have taught yourself C. A Bonus Week has been added following these 21 days.

There are several topics that many people ask about once they have learned C. In addition, there are several advanced topics that are simply different ways of using the topics covered in the 21 days of this book. Many C programmers want to know about issues such as portability and they want to know how C++ differs from C. It is to provide answers about these additional areas that we have included the bonus week. While these extra seven days are not necessary for learning C, we believe they you will find they are well worth the extra time to read!

Where You Can Obtain This Book's Code

For your convenience, the code listings in this book are available on the Internet and CompuServe.

Internet: World Wide Web

```
http://www.mcp.com/sams
```

Internet: Anonymous FTP

```
ftp.mcp.com
/pub/sams/books/TYC/tyc.zip
```

Remember that directory names on the Internet are case-sensitive.

CompuServe

"GO" keyword: SAMS
Library 9, Programming
File: TYC.ZIP

Conventions Used in This Book

This book uses different typefaces to help you differentiate between C code and regular English, and also to help you identify important concepts. Actual C code is typeset in a special monospace font. In examples of the input and output for a C program presented in this book, the user input is typeset in **bold monospace**. Placeholders—terms used to represent what you actually type within the code—are typeset in an *italic monospace* font. New or important terms are typeset in *italic*.

> **Note:** The source code in this book has been tested on many different platforms. It was compiled and tested on the following platforms; DOS, Windows, System 7.*x* (Macintosh), UNIX, and OS/2. Additionally, readers of this book have used the code on virtually every platform that supports C!

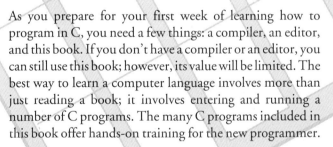

As you prepare for your first week of learning how to program in C, you need a few things: a compiler, an editor, and this book. If you don't have a compiler or an editor, you can still use this book; however, its value will be limited. The best way to learn a computer language involves more than just reading a book; it involves entering and running a number of C programs. The many C programs included in this book offer hands-on training for the new programmer.

This book is set up so that each day ends with a workshop containing a quiz and some exercises. At the end of each day, you should be able to answer all the quiz questions and complete the exercises. At first, answers to all questions and exercises are provided in Appendix F, "Answers." On later days, answers are not provided for all exercises because there is a multitude of possible solutions. We strongly suggest that you take advantage of the exercises and check your answers.

Where You're Going

The first week covers basic material that you need to know to understand C fully. On Day 1, "Getting Started," and Day 2, "The Components of a C Program," you learn how to create a C program and recognize the basic elements of a simple program. Day 3, "Numeric Variables and Constants," builds on the first two days by defining the variable types. Day 4, "Statements, Expressions, and Operators," takes the variables and adds simple expressions so that new values can be created. The day also provides information on how to make decisions and change the program flow using if statements. Day 5, "Functions: The Basics," covers C functions and structured programming. Day 6, "Basic Program Control," introduces more commands that enable you to control the flow of your programs. The week ends on Day 7, "Basic Input/Output," with a discussion on printing information and help on making your programs interact with your keyboard and screen.

This is a large amount of material to cover in just one week, but if you take the information one chapter a day, you should have no problems.

Note: This book covers the ANSI Standard C. This means that it doesn't matter which C compiler you use as long as it follows the ANSI Standard.

Getting Started

Welcome to *Teach Yourself C Programming in 21 Days!* This chapter starts you toward becoming a proficient C programmer. Today, you learn

- Why C is the best choice among programming languages
- The steps in the program development cycle
- How to write, compile, and run your first C program
- About error messages generated by the compiler and linker

A Brief History of the C Language

You may be wondering about the origin of the C language, and where it got its elegant name. C was created by Dennis Ritchie at the Bell Telephone Laboratories in 1972. The language was not created for the fun of it, but for a specific purpose: designing the UNIX operating system (which is used on many computers). From the beginning, C was intended to be useful: to allow busy programmers to get things done.

Because C is such a powerful and flexible language, its use quickly spread beyond Bell Labs. Programmers everywhere began using it to write all sorts of programs. Soon, however, different organizations began utilizing their own versions of C, and subtle differences between implementations started to cause programmers headaches. In response to this problem, the American National Standards Institute (ANSI) formed a committee in 1983 to establish a standard definition of C, which became known as *ANSI Standard C*. With few exceptions, every modern C compiler adheres to this standard.

Now, what about the name? The C language is so named because its predecessor was called B. The B language was developed by Ken Thompson, who was also at Bell Labs. You might guess easily why it was called B.

Why Use C?

In today's world of computer programming, there are many high-level languages to choose from, such as C, Pascal, BASIC, and Modula. These are all excellent languages suited for most programming tasks. Even so, there are several reasons why many computer professionals feel that C is on top of the list:

- C is a powerful and flexible language. What you can accomplish with C is limited only by your imagination. The language itself places no constraints on you. C is used for projects as diverse as operating systems, word processors, graphics, spreadsheets, and even compilers for other languages.
- C is a popular language, preferred by professional programmers. As a result, a wide variety of C compilers and helpful accessories are available.

- C is a portable language. *Portable* means that a C program written for one computer system (an IBM PC, for example) can be compiled and run on another system (a DEC VAX system perhaps) with little or no modification. Portability is enhanced by the ANSI standard for C, the set of rules for C compilers discussed earlier.

- C is a language of few words, containing only a handful of terms, called *keywords,* which serve as a base on which the language's functionality is built. You might think that a language with more keywords (sometimes called reserved words) would be more powerful. This is not true. As you program with C, you will find it can be programmed to do any task.

- C is modular. C code can (and should) be written in routines called *functions.* These functions can be reused in other applications or programs. By passing pieces of information to the functions, you can create useful, reusable code.

As these features show, C is an excellent choice for your first programming language. What about this new language called *C++* (pronounced *C plus plus*)? You may have heard already about C++ and a new programming technique called *object-oriented programming.* Perhaps you're wondering what the differences are between C and C++ and whether you should be teaching yourself C++ instead of C.

Not to worry! C++ is a *superset* of C, which means that C++ contains everything C does, plus new additions for object-oriented programming. If you do go on to learn C++, almost everything you learn about C will still apply to the C++ superset. In learning C, you are not only learning today's most powerful and popular programming language, but you also are preparing yourself for object-oriented programming.

Note: Bonus Day 7, "What is C++?," has been added to explain what C++ is and how it differs from C.

Preparation for Programming

You should take certain steps when you are solving a problem. First, you must define the problem. If you don't know what the problem is, you can't find a solution! Once the problem is known, you can devise a plan to fix it. Once there is a plan, usually you can implement it easily. Finally, once the plan is implemented, you must test the results to see whether the problem is solved. This same logic can be applied to many other areas, too, including programming.

When creating a program in C (or for that matter, a computer program in any language), you should follow a similar sequence of steps:

1. Determine the objective(s) of the program.
2. Determine the methods you want to use in writing the program.
3. Create the program to solve the problem.
4. Run the program to see the results.

An example of an objective (see step one) might be to write a word processor or database program. A much simpler objective is to display your name on the screen. If you did not have an objective, you would not be writing a program, so you already have the first step done.

The second step is to determine the method you want to use to write the program. Do you need a computer program to solve the problem? What information needs to be tracked? What formulas are going to be used? During this step, you should try to determine what you need to know and in what order the solution should be implemented.

As an example, assume that someone asks you to write a program to determine the area inside a circle. Step one is complete because you know your objective: determine the area inside a circle. Step two is to determine what you need to know to ascertain the area. In this example, assume that the user of the program will provide the radius of the circle. Knowing this, you can apply the formula πr^2 to obtain the answer. Now you have the pieces you need, so you can continue to steps three and four, which are called the Program Development Cycle.

The Program Development Cycle

The Program Development Cycle has its own steps. In the first step, you use an editor to create a disk file containing your *source code*. In the second step, you compile the source code to create an *object file*. In the third step, you link the compiled code to create an *executable file*. Finally, the fourth step is to run the program to see whether it works as originally planned.

Creating the Source Code

Source code is a series of statements or commands that are used to instruct the computer to perform your desired tasks. As mentioned, the first step in the Program Development Cycle is to enter source code into an editor. For example, here is a line of C source code:

```
printf("Hello, Mom!");
```

This statement instructs the computer to display the message Hello, Mom! on the screen. (For now, don't worry about how this statement works.)

Using an Editor

Some compilers come with an editor that can be used to enter source code and some do not. Consult your compiler manuals to see whether your compiler came with an editor. If not, many editors are available.

Most computer systems include a program that can be used as an editor. If you are using a UNIX system, you can use such editors as ed, ex, edit, emacs, or vi. If you are using Microsoft Windows, Notepad is available. If you are using MS/DOS 5.0 or later, you can use edit. If you are using a version of DOS before 5.0, you can use edlin. If you are using PC/DOS 6.0 or later, you can use E. If you are using OS/2, you can use the E and EPM editors.

Most word processors use special codes to format their documents. These codes can't be read correctly by other programs. The American Standard Code for Information Interchange (ASCII) has specified a standard text format that nearly any program, including C, can use. Many word processors, such as WordPerfect, AmiPro, Word, and WordStar, are capable of saving source files in ASCII form (as a text file rather than a document file). When you want to save a word processor's file as an ASCII file, select the ASCII or text option when saving.

If none of these editors is what you want to use, you can always buy a different editor. There are packages, both commercial and shareware, that have been designed specifically for entering source code.

When you save a source file, you must give it a name. What should a source file be called? The name you give it should describe what the program does. In addition, when you save C program source files, name the file with a .C extension. Although you could give your source file any name and extension you want, .C is recognized as the appropriate extension to use.

Note: This book covers the ANSI Standard C. This means that it doesn't matter which C compiler you use as long as it follows the ANSI Standard.

Compiling the Source Code

Although you may be able to understand C source code (at least, after reading this book, you will be able to), your computer cannot. A computer requires digital, or binary, instructions in what is called *machine language*. Before your C program can run on a computer, it must be translated from source code to machine language. This translation, the second step in program development, is performed by a program called a *compiler*. The compiler takes your source code file as input and produces a disk file containing the machine language instructions that correspond to your source code statements. The machine language instructions created by the compiler are called *object code*, and the disk file containing them is called an *object file*.

Each compiler needs its own command to be used to create the object code. To compile, you typically use the command to run the compiler followed by the source filename. The following are examples of the commands issued to compile a source file called RADIUS.C using various DOS compilers:

Compiler	Command
Microsoft C	cl radius.c
Borland's Turbo C	tcc radius.c
Borland C	bcc radius.c
Zortec C	ztc radius.c

To compile RADIUS.C on a UNIX machine, use the following command. Consult the compiler manual to determine the exact command for your compiler.

```
cc radius.c
```

After you compile, you have an object file. If you look at a list of the files in the directory in which you compiled, you should find a file with the same name as your source file, but with an .OBJ (rather than a .C) extension. The .OBJ extension is recognized as an object file and is used by the linker. On UNIX systems, the compiler creates object files with the .o extension instead of the .OBJ extension.

Linking to Create an Executable File

One more step is required before you can run your program. Part of the C language is a *function library* that contains object code (that is, code that has already been compiled) for predefined functions. A *predefined function* contains C code that has already been written and is supplied in a ready-to-use form with your compiler package. The printf() function used in the previous example is a library function.

These library functions perform frequently needed tasks, such as displaying information on-screen and reading data from disk files. If your program uses any of these functions (and hardly a program exists that doesn't use at least one), the object file produced when your source code was compiled must be combined with object code from the function library to create the final executable program. (*Executable* means that the program can be run, or executed, on your computer.) This process is called *linking* and is performed by a program called (you guessed it) a *linker*.

The progression from source code to object code to executable program is diagrammed in Figure 1.1.

Figure 1.1.
The C source code that you write is converted to object code by the compiler and then to an executable file by the linker.

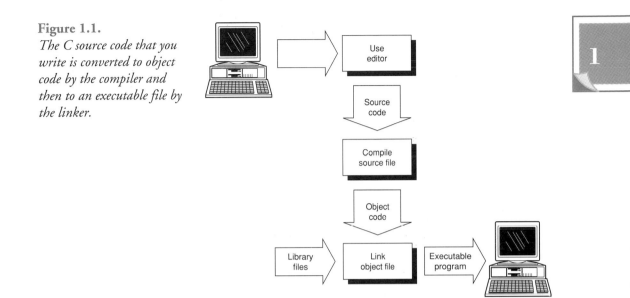

Completing the Development Cycle

Once your program is compiled and linked to create an executable file, you can run it by entering its name at the system prompt, just like you would any other program. If you run the program and receive results different from what you believed you should, you need to go back to the first step. You must identify what caused the problem and correct it in the source code. When a change is made to the source code, you need to recompile and relink the program to create a corrected version of the executable file. You keep following this cycle until you get the program to execute exactly as you intended.

One final note on compiling and linking. Although compiling and linking are mentioned as two separate steps, many compilers, such as the DOS compilers mentioned earlier, do both as one step. Regardless of the method by which compiling and linking are accomplished, understand that these two processes, even when done with one command, are two separate actions.

C Development Cycle

Step 1 Use an editor to write your source code. By tradition, C source code files have the extension .C (for example, MYPROG.C, DATABASE.C, and so on).

Step 2 Compile the program using a compiler. If the compiler does not find any errors in the program, it produces an object file. The compiler produces object files with the .OBJ extension and the same name as the source code file (for example, MYPROG.C compiles to MYPROG.OBJ). If the compiler finds errors, it reports them. You must return to step one to make corrections in your source code.

Step 3   Link the program using a linker. If no errors occur, the linker produces an executable program located in a disk file with the .EXE extension and the same name as the object file (for example, MYPROG.OBJ is linked to create MYPROG.EXE).

Step 4   Execute the program. You should test to determine whether it functions properly. If not, start again with step one and make modifications and additions to your source code.

Program development steps are presented schematically in Figure 1.2. For all but the simplest programs, you may go through this sequence many times before finishing your program. Even the most experienced programmers can't sit down and write a complete, error-free program in just one step! Because you'll be running through the edit-compile-link-test cycle many times, it's important to become familiar with your tools: the editor, compiler, and linker.

Your First C Program

You probably are eager to try your first program in C. To help you become familiar with your compiler, here's a quick demonstration for you to work through. You may not understand everything at this point, but you should get a feel for the process of writing, compiling, and running a real C program.

This demonstration uses a program named HELLO.C, which does nothing more than display the words Hello, World! on your screen. This program, a traditional introduction to C programming, is a good one for you to learn. The source code for HELLO.C is in program Listing 1.1. When entering this listing, don't include the line numbers or colons.

Type   **Listing 1.1. HELLO.C.**

```
1: #include <stdio.h>
2:
3: main()
4: {
5:     printf("Hello, World!");
6: }
```

Figure 1.2.
*The steps involved in C
program development.*

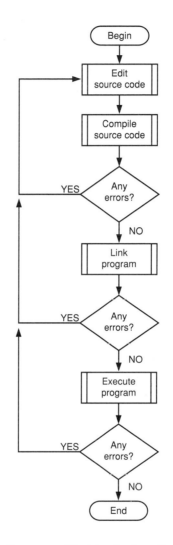

Make certain you have installed your compiler as specified in the installation instructions
provided with the software. Whether you are working with UNIX, DOS, or any other operating
system, make sure you understand how to use the compiler and editor of your choice. Once your
compiler and editor are ready, follow these steps to enter, compile, and execute HELLO.C.

Warning: When you compile Listing 1.1 you may receive a warning similar to `Function must return a value`. You may also get this warning in several of the listings in the first few days of this book. For now you can ignore this warning or you can add the following line just before the closing } of your programs. For the HELLO.C program, this is between lines 5 and 6.

```
return 0;
```

When you reach Day 5, "Functions: The Basics," you will learn why you get this warning.

Entering and Compiling HELLO.C

To enter and compile the HELLO.C program, follow these steps:

1. Make active the directory your C programs are in and start your editor. As mentioned previously, any text editor can be used, but most C compilers (such as Borland's Turbo C++ and Microsoft's Visual C/C++) come with an integrated development environment (IDE) that enables you to enter, compile, and link your programs in one convenient setting. Check the manuals to see whether your compiler has an IDE available.

2. Use your keyboard to type the HELLO.C source code exactly as shown in Listing 1.1. Press Enter at the end of each line of the code.

Note: Don't enter the line numbers to the left of the listing. The line numbers are for reference only.

3. Save the source code. You should name the file HELLO.C.

4. Verify that HELLO.C is on disk by listing the files in the directory. You should see HELLO.C within this listing.

5. Compile and link HELLO.C. Execute the appropriate command specified by your compiler's manuals. You should get a message stating that there were no errors or warnings.

6. Check the compiler messages. If you receive no errors or warnings, everything should be okay.

But what if you made an error typing the program? The compiler catches it and displays an error message on your screen. For example, if you misspelled the word printf as prntf, a message similar to the following is displayed:

```
Error: undefined symbols:_prntf in hello.c (hello.OBJ)
```

7. Go back to step two if this or any other error message is displayed. Open the HELLO.C file in your editor. Compare your file's contents carefully with Listing 1.1, make any necessary corrections, and then continue with step three.

8. Your first C program should now be compiled and ready to run. If you display a directory listing of all files named HELLO (having any extension), you should see the following:

   - HELLO.C (which is the source code file you created with your editor).
   - HELLO.OBJ or HELLO.O (which contains the object code for HELLO.C).
   - HELLO.EXE (which is the executable program created when you compiled and linked HELLO.C).

9. To run, or execute, HELLO.EXE, simply enter hello. The message Hello, World! is displayed on your screen.

Congratulations! You have just entered, compiled, and run your first C program. Admittedly, HELLO.C is a simple program that doesn't do anything useful, but it's a start. In fact, you should remember that most of today's expert C programmers started learning C in this same way—by compiling HELLO.C—so you're in good company.

Compilation Errors

A *compilation error* occurs when the compiler finds something in the source code that it can't compile. A misspelling, typographical error, or any of a dozen other things can cause the compiler to choke. Fortunately, modern compilers don't just choke, they tell what they're choking on and where it is! This makes it easier to find and correct errors in your source code.

This can be illustrated by introducing a deliberate error into HELLO.C. If you worked through that example (and you should have), you now have a copy of HELLO.C on your disk. Using your editor, move the cursor to the end of the line containing the call to printf(), and erase the terminating semicolon. HELLO.C should now look like Listing 1.2.

Type **Listing 1.2. HELLO.C with an error.**

```
1: #include <stdio.h>
2:
3: main()
4: {
5:     printf("Hello, World!")
6: }
```

Next, save the file. You're now ready to compile the file. Do so by entering the command for your compiler. Because of the error you introduced, the compilation is not completed. Rather, the compiler displays a message on the screen similar to the following:

```
hello.c(6) : Error: ';' expected
```

Looking at this line, you can see that it has three parts:

`hello.c`	The name of the file where the error was found
`(6) :`	The line number where the error was found
`Error: ';' expected`	A description of the error

This is quite informative, telling you that in line 6 of HELLO.C the compiler expected to find a semicolon but did not. Yet, you know the semicolon was actually omitted from line 5, and that there is a discrepancy. You're faced with the puzzle of why the compiler reports an error in line 6 when in fact, a semicolon was omitted from the end of line 5. The answer lies in the fact that C doesn't "care" about things like breaks between lines. The semicolon that belongs after the `printf()` statement could have been placed on the next line (although doing so would be bad programming practice). Only after coming upon the brace in line 6 is the compiler sure that the semicolon is missing. Therefore, the compiler reports that the error is in line 6.

This points out an undeniable fact about C compilers and error messages. Although the compiler is very clever about detecting and localizing errors, it is no Einstein. You, using your knowledge of the C language, must interpret the compiler's messages and determine the actual location of any errors that are reported. They are often found on the line reported by the compiler and if not, they are almost always on the preceding line. At first, you may have a bit of trouble finding errors, but you should soon get better at it.

> **Note:** The errors given may differ depending on the compiler. In most cases, the error should give you an idea of what or where the problem is.

Before leaving this topic, take a look at another example of a compilation error. Load HELLO.C into your editor again and make the following changes:

1. Replace the semicolon at the end of line 5.
2. Delete the double quotation mark just before the word `Hello`.

Save the file to disk and compile the program again. This time, the compiler should display error messages similar to the following:

```
hello.c(5) : Error: undefined identifier 'Hello'
hello.c(6) : Lexical error: unterminated string
Lexical error: unterminated string
```

```
Lexical error: unterminated string

Fatal error: premature end of source file
```

The first error message finds the error correctly, locating it in line 5 at the word Hello. The error message unidentified identifier means that the compiler does not know what to make of the word Hello, because it is no longer enclosed in quotes. What, however, about the other four errors that are reported? These errors, the meaning of which you don't need to worry about now, illustrate the fact that a single error in a C program can sometimes cause multiple error messages.

The lesson to learn from all this is as follows: If the compiler reports multiple errors, and you can find only one, go ahead and fix that error and recompile. You may find that your single correction is all that's needed, and the program now compiles without errors.

Linker Error Messages

Linker errors are relatively rare and usually result from misspelling the name of a C library function. In this case, you get an Error: undefined symbols: error message, followed by the misspelled name (preceded by an underscore). Once you correct the spelling, the problem should go away.

Summary

After reading this chapter, you should feel confident that selecting C as your programming language is a wise choice. C offers an unparalleled combination of power, popularity, and portability. These factors, together with C's close relationship to the new C++ object-oriented language, make C unbeatable.

This chapter has explained the various steps involved in writing a C program—the process known as program development. You should have a clear grasp of the edit-compile-link-test cycle, as well as the tools to use for each step.

Errors are an unavoidable part of program development. Your C compiler detects errors in your source code and displays an error message, giving both the nature and the location of the error. Using this information, you can edit your source code to correct the error. Remember, however, that the compiler cannot always report accurately the nature and location of an error. Sometimes you need to use your knowledge of C to track down exactly what is causing a given error message.

Q&A

Q If I want to give someone a program I wrote, which files do I need to give them?

A One of the nice things about C is that it is a compiled language. This means that after the source code is compiled, you have an executable program. This executable

program is a self-standing program. If you wanted to give HELLO to all your friends with computers, you could. All you need to give them is the executable program, HELLO.EXE. They don't need the source file, HELLO.C, or the object file, HELLO.OBJ. They don't need to own a C compiler either.

Q **After I create an executable file, do I need to keep the source file (.C) or object file (.OBJ)?**

A If you get rid of the source file, you have no way to make changes to the program in the future, therefore you should keep this file. The object files are a different matter. There are reasons to keep object files; however, they are beyond the scope of what you are doing now. For now, you can get rid of your object files once you have your executable file. If you need the object file, you can recompile the source file.

Q **If my compiler came with an editor, do I have to use it?**

A Definitely not. You can use any editor as long as it saves the source code in text format. If the compiler came with an editor, you should try to use it. If you like a different editor better, use it. I (Brad) use an editor that I purchased separately even though all my compilers have their own editors. The editors that are coming with compilers are getting better. Some of them automatically format your C code. Others color-code different parts of your source file to make it easier to find errors.

Q **Can I ignore warning messages?**

A Some warning messages don't affect how the program runs. Some do. If the compiler gives you a warning message, it's a signal that something is not quite right. Most compilers let you set the warning level. By setting a warning level you can get only the most serious warnings, or you can get all the warnings including the most minute. Some compilers even give various levels in between. In your programs, you should look at each warning and make a determination. It is always best to try to write all your programs with absolutely no warnings or errors. (With an error, your compiler won't create the executable file.)

Workshop

The Workshop provides quiz questions to help you solidify your understanding of the material covered and exercises to provide you with experience in using what you've learned. Try to understand the quiz and exercise answers before continuing to the next chapter. Answers are provided in Appendix F, "Answers."

Quiz

1. Give three reasons why C is the best choice of programming languages.
2. What does the compiler do?

3. What are the steps in the program development cycle?

4. What command do you need to enter to compile a program called PROGRAM1.C with your compiler?

5. Does your compiler do both the linking and compiling with just one command, or do you have to enter separate commands?

6. What extension should you use for your C source files?

7. Is FILENAME.TXT a valid name for a C source file?

8. If you execute a program that you have compiled and it does not work as you expected, what should you do?

9. What is machine language?

10. What does the linker do?

Exercises

1. Use your text editor to look at the object file created by Listing 1.1. Does the object file look like the source file? (Don't save this file when you exit the editor.)

2. Enter the following program and compile it. What does this program do? (Don't include the line numbers.)

```
1: #include <stdio.h>
2:
3: int radius, area;
4:
5: main()
6: {
7:     printf( "Enter radius (i.e. 10): " );
8:     scanf( "%d", &radius );
9:     area = 3.14159 * radius * radius;
10:    printf( "\n\nArea = %d", area );
11:    return 0;
12: }
```

3. Enter and compile the following program. What does this program do?

```
1: #include <stdio.h>
2:
3: int x,y;
4:
5: main()
6: {
7:     for ( x = 0; x < 10; x++, printf( "\n" ) )
8:         for ( y = 0; y < 10; y++ )
9:             printf( "X" );
10:
11:    return 0;
12: }
```

4. **BUG BUSTER:** The following program has a problem. Enter it in your editor and compile it. What lines generate error messages?

```
1: #include <stdio.h>
2:
3: main();
4: {
5:     printf( "Keep looking!" );
6:     printf( "You\'ll find it!" );
7:     return 0;
8: }
```

5. **BUG BUSTER:** The following program has a problem. Enter it in your editor and compile it. What lines generate problems?

```
1: #include <stdio.h>
2:
3: main()
4: {
5:     printf( "This is a program with a " );
6:     do_it( "problem!");
7:     return 0;
8: }
```

6. Add the following changes to the program in exercise three. Recompile and rerun this program. What does the program now do?

```
9: printf( "%c", 1 );
```

7. Enter and compile the following program. This program can be used to print your listings. If you get any errors, make sure you entered the program correctly.

The usage for this program is PRINT_IT *filename.ext*, where *filename.ext* is the source filename along with the extension. Note that this program adds line numbers to the listing. (Don't let this program's length worry you; you're not expected to understand it yet. It's included here to help you compare printouts of your programs with the ones given in the book.)

```
1: /* PRINT_IT.C--This program prints a listing with line numbers! */
2: #include <stdlib.h>
3: #include <stdio.h>
4:
5: void do_heading(char *filename);
6:
7: int line, page;
8:
9: main( int argv, char *argc[] )
10:{
11:    char buffer[256];
12:    FILE *fp;
13:
14:    if( argv < 2 )
15:    {
16:        fprintf(stderr, "\nProper Usage is: " );
17:        fprintf(stderr, "\n\nPRINT_IT filename.ext\n" );
```

```
18:      exit(1);
19:    }
20:
21:    if (( fp = fopen( argc[1], "r" )) == NULL )
22:    {
23:        fprintf( stderr, "Error opening file, %s!", argc[1]);
24:        exit(1);
25:    }
26:
27:    page = 0;
28:    line = 1;
29:    do_heading( argc[1]);
30:
31:    while( fgets( buffer, 256, fp ) != NULL )
32:    {
33:      if( line % 55 == 0 )
34:         do_heading( argc[1] );
35:
36:        fprintf( stdprn, "%4d:\t%s", line++, buffer );
37:    }
38:
39:    fprintf( stdprn, "\f" );
40:    fclose(fp);
41:    return 0;
42:}
43:
44:void do_heading( char *filename )
45:{
46:    page++;
47:
48:    if ( page > 1)
49:        fprintf( stdprn, "\f" );
50:
51:    fprintf( stdprn, "Page: %d, %s\n\n", page, filename );
52:}
```

Note: This listing uses a value that is available within many PC compilers, but not necessarily in all other compilers. Although stdout is an ANSI-defined value, stdprn is not. You need to check your compiler for specifics on sending output to the printer.

One option for getting around this is to change the stdprn statements to stdout statements. This causes the output to go to the screen. Using your operating system's redirection features (or by piping if you are using UNIX), you should be able to redirect the output from the screen to the printer.

On Day 14, "Working with the Screen, Printer, and Keyboard," you will learn more about how this program works.

The Components
of a C Program

Every C program consists of several components combined in a certain way. Most of this book is devoted to explaining these various program components and how you use them. To get the overall picture, however, you should begin by seeing a complete (though small) C program with all its components identified. Today, you learn

- About a short C program with its components identified
- The purpose of each program component
- To compile and run a sample program

A Short C Program

Listing 2.1 presents the source code for MULTIPLY.C. This is a very simple program; all it does is input two numbers from the keyboard and calculate their product. At this stage, don't worry about understanding the details of the program's workings. The point is to gain some familiarity with the parts of a C program so that you can better understand the listings presented later in the book.

Before looking at the sample program, you need to know what a function is, because functions are central to C programming. A *function* is an independent section of program code that performs a certain task and has been assigned a name. By referencing a function's name, your program can execute the code in the function. The program also can send information, called *arguments,* to the function, and the function can return information to the program. The two types of C functions are *library functions,* which are a part of the C compiler package, and *user-defined functions,* which you, the programmer, create. You learn about both types of functions in this book.

Note that the line numbers in Listing 2.1, as with all the listings in this book, are not part of the program. They are included only for identification purposes.

Type **Listing 2.1. MULTIPLY.C.**

```
1: /* Program to calculate the product of two numbers. */
2: #include <stdio.h>
3: int a,b,c;
4: int product(int x, int y);
5: main()
6: {
7:     /* Input the first number */
8:     printf("Enter a number between 1 and 100: ");
9:     scanf("%d", &a);
10:
11:     /* Input the second number */
12:     printf("Enter another number between 1 and 100: ");
13:     scanf("%d", &b);
14:
```

```
15:     /* Calculate and display the product */
16:     c = product(a, b);
17:     printf ("\n%d times %d = %d", a, b, c);
18: }
19:
20: /* Function returns the product of its two arguments */
21: int product(int x, int y)
22: {
23:     return (x * y);
24: }
```

Input Output

```
Enter a number between 1 and 100: 35
Enter another number between 1 and 100: 23

35 times 23 = 805
```

The Program Components

The following sections describe the various components of the preceding sample program. Line numbers are included so you can easily identify the program parts being discussed.

The *main()* Function (Lines 5–18)

The only component that is required in every C program is the main() function. In its simplest form, the main() function consists of the name main followed by a pair of empty parentheses (()) and a pair of braces ({}). Within the braces are statements that make up the main body of the program. Under normal circumstances, program execution starts at the first statement in main() and terminates with the last statement in main().

The *#include* Directive (Line 2)

The #include directive instructs the C compiler to add the contents of an include file into your program during compilation. An *include* file is a separate disk file that contains information needed by the compiler. Several of these files (sometimes called *header files*) are supplied with your compiler. You never need to modify the information in these files; that's why they are kept separate from your source code. Include files should all have the .H extension (for example, STDIO.H).

You use the #include directive to instruct the compiler to add a specific include file to your program during compilation. The #include directive in this sample program means "Add the contents of the file STDIO.H." Most C programs require one or more include files. More information about include files is presented on Day 21, "Taking Advantage of Preprocessor Directives and More."

Variable Definition (Line 3)

A *variable* is a name assigned to a data storage location. Your program uses variables to store various kinds of data during program execution. In C, a variable must be defined before it can be used. A *variable definition* informs the compiler of the variable's name and the type of data it is to hold. In the sample program, the definition on line 3, `int a,b,c;`, defines three variables—named a, b, and c—that are each going to hold an *integer* value. More information about variables and variable definitions is presented on Day 3, "Numeric Variables and Constants."

Function Prototype (Line 4)

A *function prototype* provides the C compiler with the name and arguments of the functions contained in the program and must appear before the function is used. A function prototype is distinct from a *function definition* that contains the actual statements which make up the function. (Function definitions are discussed in more detail later in this chapter.)

Program Statements (Lines 8, 9, 12, 13, 16, 17, and 23)

The real work of a C program is done by its *statements*. C statements display information on the screen, read keyboard input, perform mathematical operations, call functions, read disk files, and all the other operations that a program needs to perform. Most of this book is devoted to teaching you the various C statements. For now, remember that in your source code, C statements are written one per line and always end with a semicolon. The statements in MULTIPLY.C are explained briefly in the following sections.

printf()

The `printf()` statement (lines 8, 12, and 17) is a library function that displays information on the screen. The `printf()` statement can display a simple text message (as in lines 8 and 12) or a message and the value of one or more program variables (as in line 17).

scanf()

The `scanf()` statement (lines 9 and 13) is another library function. It reads data from the keyboard and assigns that data to one or more program variables.

The program statement on line 16 *calls* the function named `product()`. That is, it executes the program statements contained in the function `product()`. It also sends the *arguments* a and b to the function. After the statements in `product()` are completed, `product()` returns a value to the program. This value is stored in the variable named c.

The `return` statement on line 23 is part of the function `product()`. It calculates the product of the variables `x` and `y` and returns the result to the program that called `product()`.

Function Definition (Lines 21–24)

A *function* is an independent, self-contained section of code that is written to perform a certain task. Every function has a name, and the code in each function is executed by including that function's name in a program statement. This is known as *calling* the function.

The function named `product()`, in lines 21–24 of Listing 2.1, is a *user-defined* function. As the name implies, user-defined functions are written by the programmer during program development. This function is simple; all it does is multiply two values and return the answer to the program that called it. On Day 5, "Functions: The Basics," you learn that the proper use of functions is an important part of good C programming practice.

Note that in a real C program, you would probably not use a function for a task as simple as multiplying two numbers. It is done here for demonstration purposes only.

C also includes *library functions* that are a part of the C compiler package. Library functions perform most of the common tasks (such as screen, keyboard, and disk input/output) that your program needs. In the sample program, `printf()` and `scanf()` are library functions.

Program Comments (Lines 1, 7, 11, 15, and 20)

Any part of your program that starts with `/*` and ends with `*/` is called a *comment*. The compiler ignores all comments, and so they have absolutely no effect on how a program works. You can put anything you want into a comment and it will not modify the way your program operates. A comment can span part of a line, an entire line, or multiple lines. Here are three examples:

```
/* A single-line comment */

int a,b,c; /* A partial-line comment */

/* a comment
spanning
multiple lines */
```

You should not, however, use nested comments (which means you should not include one comment within another). Most compilers would not accept the following:

```
/*
/* Nested comment */
*/
```

Some compilers, however, do allow nested comments. Although this feature might be tempting to use, you should avoid doing so. Because one of the benefits of C is portability, using a feature such as nested comments may limit the portability of your code. Nested comments also may lead to hard-to-find problems.

Many beginning programmers view program comments as unnecessary and a waste of time. This is a mistake! The operation of your program may be quite clear while you are writing it—particularly when writing simple programs. As your programs become larger and more complex, however, or when you need to modify a program you wrote six months ago, you'll find comments invaluable. Now is the time to develop a habit of using comments liberally to document all your programming structures and operations.

Note: Many people have started using a new style of comments in their C programs. Within C++, you can use double forward slashes for signaling a comment. Following are two examples:

```
// This entire line is a comment
int x;  // Comment starts with slashes.
```

The two forward slashes signal that the rest of the line is a comment. Although many C compilers support this form of comment, you should avoid them if you are interested in portability. The newer ANSI C Standard may support the double-slash comments, but older compilers most likely will not.

DO   DON'T

DO add abundant comments to your program's source code, especially near statements or functions that could be unclear to you or to someone who might have to modify it later.

DON'T add unnecessary comments to statements that are already clear. For example, entering

```
/* The following prints Hello World! on the screen */
printf("Hello World!);
```

may be going a little too far, at least once you're completely comfortable with the `printf()` function and how it works.

DO learn to develop a style that will be helpful. A style that's too lean or cryptic doesn't help, nor does one that's so verbose you're spending more time commenting than programming!

Braces (Lines 6, 18, 22, and 24)

You use braces ({}) to enclose the program lines that make up every C function—including the `main()` function. A group of one or more statements enclosed within braces is called a *block*. As you will see in later chapters, C has many uses for blocks.

Running the Program

Take the time to enter, compile, and run MULTIPLY.C now. It provides additional practice using your editor and compiler. Recall these steps from Day 1, "Getting Started:"

1. Make your programming directory current.

2. Start your editor.

3. Enter the source code for MULTIPLY.C exactly as shown in Listing 2.1, but be sure to omit the line numbers and colons.

4. Save the program file.

5. Compile and link the program by entering the appropriate command(s) for your compiler. If no error messages are displayed, you can run the program by entering `multiply` at the command prompt.

6. If one or more error messages are displayed, return to step 2 and correct the errors.

A Note on Accuracy

A computer is fast and accurate, but it also is completely literal. It doesn't know enough to correct your simplest mistake; it takes everything you enter exactly as you entered it, and not as you meant it!

This goes for your C source code as well. A simple typographical error in your program can cause the C compiler to choke, gag, and collapse. Fortunately, although the compiler is not smart enough to correct your errors (and you'll make errors—everyone does!), it is smart enough to recognize them as errors and report them to you. How the compiler reports error messages and how you interpret them is covered on Day 1.

The Parts of a Programming Review

Now that all the parts of a program have been described, you should be able to look at any program and find some similarities. Look at Listing 2.2 and see whether you can identify the different parts.

Type

Listing 2.2. LIST_IT.C.

```
1:  /* LIST_IT.C  This program displays a listing with line numbers! */
2:  #include <stdio.h>
3:
4:  void display_usage(void);
5:
6:  int line;
7:
8:  main( int argc, char *argv[] )
9:  {
10:     char buffer[256];
11:     FILE *fp;
12:
13:     if( argc < 2 )
14:     {
15:        display_usage();
16:        exit(1);
17:     }
18:
19:     if (( fp = fopen( argv[1], "r" )) == NULL )
20:     {
21:         fprintf( stderr, "Error opening file, %s!", argv[1] );
22:         exit(1);
23:     }
24:
25:     line = 1;
26:
27:     while( fgets( buffer, 256, fp ) != NULL )
28:        fprintf( stdout, "%4d:\t%s", line++, buffer );
29:
30:     fclose(fp);
31:     return 0;
32: }
33:
34: void display_usage(void)
35: {
36:         fprintf(stderr, "\nProper Usage is: " );
37:         fprintf(stderr, "\n\nLIST_IT filename.ext\n" );
38: }
```

Input Output

```
C:\>list_it list_it.c
1:    /* LIST_IT.C - This program lists out a listing with line numbers! */
2:    #include <stdio.h>
3:
4:    void display_usage(void);
5:
6:    int line;
7:
8:    main( int argc, char *argv[] )
9:    {
10:       char buffer[256];
11:       FILE *fp;
```

```
12:
13:        if( argc < 2 )
14:        {
15:            display_usage();
16:            exit(1);
17:        }
18:
19:        if (( fp = fopen( argv[1], "r" )) == NULL )
20:        {
21:            fprintf( stderr, "Error opening file, %s!", argv[1] );
22:            exit(1);
23:        }
24:
25:        line = 1;
26:
27:        while( fgets( buffer, 256, fp ) != NULL )
28:            fprintf( stdout, "%4d:\t%s", line++, buffer );
29:
30:        fclose(fp);
31:        return 0;
32:    }
33:
34:    void display_usage(void)
35:    {
36:        fprintf(stderr, "\nProper Usage is: " );
37:        fprintf(stderr, "\n\nLIST_IT filename.ext\n" );
38:    }
```

Analysis LIST_IT.C is similar to PRINT_IT.C, which you entered in exercise seven of Day 1. Listing 2.2 displays saved C program listings on the screen instead of printing them on the printer.

Looking at the listing, you can summarize where the different parts are. The required main() function is in lines 8–32. In line 2, you have a #include directive. Lines 6, 10, and 11 have variable definitions. A function prototype, void display_usage(void), is in line 4. This program has many statements (lines 13, 15, 16, 19, 21, 22, 25, 27, 28, 30, 31, 36, and 37). A function definition for display_usage() fills lines 34–38. Braces enclose blocks throughout the program. Finally, only line 1 has a comment. In most programs, you should probably include more than one comment line.

LIST_IT.C calls many functions. It calls only one user-defined function, display_usage(). The library functions that it uses are exit() in lines 16 and 22, fopen() in line 19, fprintf() in lines 21, 28, 36, and 37, fgets() in line 27, and fclose() in line 30. These library functions are covered in more detail throughout this book.

Summary

This chapter is short, but it's important because it introduces you to the major components of a C program. You learned that the single required part of every C program is the `main()` function. You also learned that the program's real work is done by program statements that instruct the computer to perform your desired actions. This chapter also introduced you to variables and variable definitions, and it showed you how to use comments in your source code.

In addition to the `main()` function, a C program can use two types of subsidiary functions: library functions supplied as part of the compiler package and user-defined functions created by the programmer.

Q&A

Q   **What effect do comments have on a program?**

A   Comments are for the programmer. When the compiler converts the source code to object code, it throws the comments and the whitespace away. This means that they have no effect on the executable program. Comments do make your source file bigger, but this is usually of little concern. To summarize, you should use comments and whitespace to make your source code as easy to understand and to maintain as possible.

Q   **What is the difference between a statement and a block?**

A   A block is a group of statements enclosed within braces (`{}`). A block can be used in most places that a statement can be used.

Q   **How can I find out what library functions are available?**

A   Many compilers come with a manual dedicated specifically to documenting the library functions. They are usually in alphabetical order. Another way to find out what library functions there are is to buy a book that lists them. Appendix D, "Function Prototypes and Header Files," and Appendix E, "Common C Functions," list functions by category and alphabetically, respectively. After you begin to understand more of C, it is a good idea to read these appendixes so that you don't rewrite a library function. (No use in reinventing the wheel!)

Workshop

The Workshop provides quiz questions to help you solidify your understanding of the material covered and exercises to provide you with experience in using what you've learned.

Quiz

1. What is the term for a group of one or more C statements enclosed within braces?
2. What is the one component that must be present in every C program?
3. How do you add program comments, and why are they used?
4. What is a function?
5. C offers two types of functions. What are they and how are they different?
6. What is the #include directive used for?
7. Can a comment be nested?
8. Can comments be longer than one line?
9. What is another name for an include file?
10. What is an include file?

Exercises

1. Write the smallest program possible.
2. Consider the following program:

```
1: /* EX2-2.C */
2: #include <stdio.h>
3:
4: void display_line(void);
5:
6: main()
7:     {
8:     display_line();
9:     printf("\n Teach Yourself C In 21 Days!\n");
10:    display_line();
11:
12:    return 0;
13: }
14:
15: /* print asterisk line */
16: void display_line(void)
17: {
18:    int counter;
19:
20:    for( counter = 0; counter < 21; counter++ )
21:        printf("*" );
22: }
23: /* end of program */
```

   a. What line(s) contains statements?
   b. What line(s) contains variable definitions?
   c. What line(s) contains function prototypes?
   d. What line(s) contains function definitions?
   e. What line(s) contains comments?

3. Write an example of a comment.

4. What does the following program do? (Enter, compile, and run it.)

```
1: /* EX2-4.C */
2: #include <stdio.h>
3:
4: main()
5: {
6:     int ctr;
7:
8:     for( ctr = 65; ctr < 91; ctr++ )
9:         printf("%c", ctr );
10:
11:     return 0;
12: }
13: /* end of program */
```

5. What does the following program do? (Enter, compile, and run it.)

```
1: /* EX2-5.C */
2: #include <stdio.h>
3: #include <string.h>
4: main()
5: {
6:     char buffer[256];
7:
8:     printf( "Enter your name and press <Enter>:\n");
9:     gets( buffer );
10:
11:     printf( "\nYour name has %d characters and spaces!",
12                      strlen( buffer ));
13:
14:     return 0;
15: }
```

Numeric Variables
and Constants

Computer programs usually work with different types of data and need a way to store the values being used. These values can be numbers or characters. C has two ways of storing number values—variables and constants—with many options for each. A *variable* is a data storage location that has a value that can change during program execution. In contrast, a *constant* has a fixed value that cannot change. Today, you learn

- How to create variable names in C
- The use of different types of numeric variables
- The differences and similarities between character and numeric values
- How to declare and initialize numeric variables
- C's two types of numeric constants

Before you get to variables, however, you need to know a little about the operation of your computer's memory.

Computer Memory

If you already know how a computer's memory operates, you can skip this section. If you're not sure, however, please read on. This information will help you better understand certain aspects of C programming.

A computer uses *random-access memory* (RAM) to store information while it is operating. RAM is located in integrated circuits, or *chips,* inside your computer. RAM is *volatile,* which means it is erased and replaced with new information as often as needed. Being volatile also means that RAM "remembers" only while the computer is turned on and loses its information when you turn off the computer.

Each computer has a certain amount of RAM installed. The amount of RAM in a system is usually specified in kilobytes (KB) or megabytes (MB), such as 512KB, 640KB, 2MB, 4MB, or 8MB. One kilobyte of memory consists of 1,024 bytes. Thus, a system with 640KB of memory actually has 640 times 1,024, or 65,536, bytes of RAM. One megabyte is 1,024 kilobytes. A machine with 4MB of RAM would have 4,096KB or 4,194,304 bytes of RAM.

A *byte* is the fundamental unit of computer data storage. Day 20, "Working with Memory," has more information about bytes. For now, though, to get an idea of how many bytes it takes to store certain kinds of data, you can refer to Table 3.1.

Table 3.1. Memory space required to store data.

Data	Bytes Required
The letter *x*	1
The number *100*	2

Data	Bytes Required
The number *120.145*	4
The phrase Teach Yourself C	17
One typewritten page	3,000 (approximately)

The RAM in your computer is organized sequentially, one byte following another. Each byte of memory has a unique *address* by which it is identified—an address that also distinguishes it from all other bytes in memory. Addresses are assigned to memory locations in order, starting at zero and increasing to the system limit. For now, you don't need to worry about addresses; it's all handled automatically for you by the C compiler.

What is your computer's RAM used for? It has several uses, but only data storage need concern you as a programmer. *Data* is the information with which your C program works. Whether your program is maintaining an address list, monitoring the stock market, keeping a household budget, or tracking the price of hog bellies, the information (names, stock prices, expense amounts, or hog futures) is kept in your computer's RAM while the program is running.

Now that you understand a little about the nuts and bolts of memory storage, you can get back to C programming and how C uses memory to store information.

Variables

A *variable* is a named data storage location in your computer's memory. By using a variable's name in your program, you are, in effect, referring to the data stored there.

Variable Names

To use variables in your C programs, you must know how to create variable names. In C, variable names must adhere to the following rules:

- The name can contain letters, digits, and the underscore character (_).
- The first character of the name must be a letter. The underscore is also a legal first character, but its use is not advised.
- Case matters (that is, upper- and lowercase letters). Thus, the names count and Count refer to two different variables.
- C keywords cannot be used as variable names. A keyword is a word that is part of the C language. (A complete list of 33 C keywords can be found in Appendix B, "Reserved Words.")

The following code contains some examples of legal and illegal C variable names:

```
percent            /* legal */
y2x5__fg7h         /* legal */
annual_profit      /* legal */
_1990_tax          /* legal but not advised */
savings#account    /* illegal: contains illegal character # */
double             /* illegal: is a C  keyword */
9winter            /* illegal: first character is a digit */
```

Because C is case-sensitive, the three names percent, PERCENT, and Percent are considered to refer to three distinct variables. C programmers commonly use only lowercase letters in variable names although it's not required. Uppercase letters are usually reserved for the names of constants (which are covered later in this chapter).

For many compilers, a C variable name can be up to 31 characters long. (It can actually be longer than that, but the compiler looks only at the first 31 characters of the name.) With this flexibility, you can create variable names that reflect the data being stored. For example, a program that calculates loan payments could store the value of the prime interest rate in a variable named interest_rate. The variable name helps make its usage clear. You could as well have created a variable named x or even johnny_carson; it doesn't matter to the C compiler. The use of the variable, however, would not be nearly as clear to someone else looking at the source code. Although it may take a little more time to type descriptive variable names, the improvements in program clarity make it worthwhile.

Many naming conventions are used for variable names created from multiple words. You've been shown one style: interest_rate. Using an underscore to separate words in a variable name makes it easy to interpret. The second style is called *camel notation*. Instead of using spaces, the first letter of each word is capitalized. Instead of interest_rate, the variable would be named InterestRate. Camel notation is gaining popularity because it is easier to type a capital letter than an underscore. We use the underscore in this book because it is easier for most people to read. You should decide which style you wish to adopt. Bonus Day 1, "Coding Styles," contains more information on coding styles.

DO	DON'T

DO use variable names that are descriptive.

DO adopt and stick with a style for naming your variables.

DON'T start your variable names with an underscore unnecessarily.

DON'T name your variables with all capitals unnecessarily.

Numeric Variable Types

C provides several different types of numeric variables. Why do you need different types of variables? Different numeric values have varying memory storage requirements and differ in the ease with which certain mathematical operations can be performed on them. Small integer numbers (for example, 1, 199, – 8) require less memory space for storage, and mathematical operations (addition, multiplication, and so on) with such numbers can be performed by your computer very quickly. In contrast, large integers and floating-point values (123,000,000 or 0.000000871256, for example) require more storage space and more time for mathematical operations. By using the appropriate variable types, you ensure that your program runs as efficiently as possible.

C's numeric variables fall into the following two main categories:

- *Integer variables* hold values that have no fractional part (that is, whole numbers only). Integer variables come in two flavors: signed integer variables can hold positive or negative values, whereas unsigned integer variables can hold only positive values (and 0, of course).

- *Floating-point variables* hold values that have a fractional part (that is, real numbers).

Within each of these categories are two or more specific variable types. These are summarized in Table 3.2, which also shows the amount of memory, in bytes, required to hold a single variable of each type when you use a microcomputer with 16-bit architecture.

Table 3.2. C's numeric data types.

Variable Type	Keyword	Bytes Required	Range
Character	`char`	1	–128 to 127
Integer	`int`	2	–32768 to 32767
Short integer	`short`	2	–32768 to 32767
Long integer	`long`	4	–2,147,483,648 to 2,147,438,647
Unsigned character	`unsigned char`	1	0 to 255
Unsigned integer	`unsigned int`	2	0 to 65535
Unsigned short integer	`unsigned short`	2	0 to 65535
Unsigned long integer	`unsigned long`	4	0 to 4,294,967,295
Single-precision floating-point	`float`	4	1.2E–38 to 3.4E38[1]
Double-precision floating-point	`double`	8	2.2E–308 to 1.8E308[2]

[1] Approximate range; precision = 7 digits.
[2] Approximate range; precision = 19 digits.

Approximate range (see Table 3.2) means the highest and lowest values a given variable can hold. (Space limitations prohibit listing exact ranges for the values of these variables.) *Precision* means the accuracy with which the variable is stored. (For example, if you evaluate 1/3, the answer is 0.33333… with 3s going to infinity. A variable with a precision of 7 stores seven 3s.)

Looking at Table 3.2, you may notice that the variable types int and short are identical. Why then have two different types? The int and short variable types are indeed identical on 16-bit IBM PC-compatible systems, but they may be different on other types of hardware. On a VAX system, a short and an int are not the same size. Instead, a short is 2 bytes, whereas an int is 4. Remember that C is a flexible, portable language, so it provides different keywords for the two types. If you're working on a PC, you can use int and short interchangeably.

No special keyword is needed to make an integer variable signed; integer variables are signed by default. You can, however, include the signed keyword if you wish. The keywords in Table 3.2 are used in variable declarations, discussed in the next section of this chapter.

Listing 3.1 will help you determine the size of variables on your particular computer. Don't be surprised if your output doesn't match the output presented after the listing.

Type

Listing 3.1. A program that displays the size of variable types.

```
1:   /* SIZEOF.C--Program to tell the size of the C variable */
2:   /*            type in bytes */
3:
4:   #include <stdio.h>
5:
6:   main()
7:   {
8:
9:       printf( "\nA char        is %d bytes", sizeof( char ));
10:      printf( "\nAn int        is %d bytes", sizeof( int ));
11:      printf( "\nA short       is %d bytes", sizeof( short ));
12:      printf( "\nA long        is %d bytes", sizeof( long ));
13:      printf( "\nAn unsigned char  is %d bytes", sizeof( unsigned char ));
14:      printf( "\nAn unsigned int   is %d bytes", sizeof( unsigned int ));
15:      printf( "\nAn unsigned short is %d bytes", sizeof( unsigned short ));
16:      printf( "\nAn unsigned long  is %d bytes", sizeof( unsigned long ));
17:      printf( "\nA float       is %d bytes", sizeof( float ));
18:      printf( "\nA double      is %d bytes", sizeof( double ));
19:
20:      return 0;
21:   }
```

Output

```
A char       is 1 bytes
An int       is 2 bytes
A short      is 2 bytes
A long       is 4 bytes
An unsigned char  is 1 bytes
An unsigned int   is 2 bytes
An unsigned short is 2 bytes
An unsigned long  is 4 bytes
A float      is 4 bytes
A double     is 8 bytes
```

Analysis

As the preceding output shows, Listing 3.1 tells you exactly how many bytes each variable type on your computer takes. If you are using a 16-bit PC, your numbers should match those in Table 3.2.

Don't worry about trying to understand all the individual components of the program. Although some items are new, such as sizeof(), others should look familiar. Lines 1 and 2 are comments about the name of the program and a brief description. Line 4 includes the standard input/output header file to help print the information on the screen. This is a simple program, in that it contains only a single function, main() (lines 7–21). Lines 9–18 are the bulk of the program. Each of these lines prints a textual description with the size of each of the variable types, which is done using the sizeof operator. Day 19, "Exploring the Function Library," covers the sizeof operator in detail. Line 20 of the program returns the value of 0 to the operating system before ending the program.

C does make some guarantees, thanks to the ANSI Standard. There are five things that you can count on.

- The size of a char is one byte.
- The size of a short is less than or equal to the size of an int.
- The size of an int is less than or equal to the size of a long.
- The size of an unsigned is equal to the size of an int.
- The size of a float is less than or equal to the size of a double.

Variable Declarations

Before you can use a variable in a C program, it must be declared. A *variable declaration* informs the compiler of the name and type of a variable and optionally initializes the variable to a specific value. If your program attempts to use a variable that has not been declared, the compiler generates an error message. A variable declaration has the following form:

typename varname;

typename specifies the variable type and must be one of the keywords given in Table 3.2. `varname` is the variable name, which must follow the rules mentioned earlier. You can declare multiple variables of the same type on one line by separating the variable names with commas.

```
int count, number, start;    /* three integer variables */
float percent, total;        /* two float variables */
```

On Day 12, "Variable Scope," you learn that the location of variable declarations in the source code is important, because it affects the ways in which your program can use the variables. For now, you can place all the variable declarations together just before the start of the `main()` function.

The *typedef* Keyword

The `typedef` keyword is used to create a new name for an existing data type. In effect, `typedef` creates a synonym. For example, the statement

```
typedef int integer;
```

creates `integer` as a synonym for `int`. You then can use `integer` to define variables of type `int`, as in this example:

```
integer count;
```

Note that `typedef` does not create a new data type, but only enables you to use a different name for a predefined data type. The most common use for `typedef` concerns *aggregate data types,* as explained on Day 11, "Structures." An aggregate data type consists of a combination of data types presented in this chapter.

Initializing Numeric Variables

When you declare a variable, you instruct the compiler to set aside storage space for the variable. However, the value stored in that space—the value of the variable—is not defined. It may be zero, or it may be some random "garbage" value. Before using a variable, you should always initialize it to a known value. This can be done independent of the variable declaration by using an assignment statement, as in this example:

```
int count;    /* Set aside storage space for count */
count = 0;    /* Store 0 in count */
```

Note that this statement uses the equal sign (=), which is C's assignment operator and is discussed further on Day 4, "Statements, Expressions, and Operators." For now, you need to be aware that the equal sign in programming is not the same as the equal sign in algebra. If you write

```
x = 12
```

in an algebraic statement, you are stating a fact: "*x* equals 12." In C, however, it means something quite different: "Assign the value 12 to the variable named x."

You also can initialize a variable when it is declared. To do so, follow the variable name in the declaration statement with an equal sign and the desired initial value:

```
int count = 0;
double percent = 0.01, taxrate = 28.5;
```

Be careful not to initialize a variable with a value outside the allowed range. Here are two examples of out-of-range initializations:

```
int weight = 100000;
unsigned int value = -2500;
```

The C compiler does not catch such errors. Your program may compile and link, but you may get unexpected results when the program is run.

DO	DON'T

DO understand the number of bytes that variable types take for your computer.

DO use typedef to make your programs more readable.

DO initialize variables when you declare them whenever possible.

DON'T use a variable that has not been initialized. Results can be unpredictable.

DON'T use a float or double variable if you are only storing integers. Although they will work, using them is inefficient.

DON'T try to put numbers into variable types that are too small to hold them.

DON'T put negative numbers into variables with an unsigned type.

Constants

Like a variable, a *constant* is a data storage location used by your program. Unlike a variable, the value stored in a constant cannot be changed during program execution. C has two types of constants, each with its own specific uses.

Literal Constants

A *literal constant* is a value that is typed directly into the source code wherever it is needed. Here are two examples:

```
int count = 20;
float tax_rate = 0.28;
```

The 20 and the 0.28 are literal constants. The preceding statements store these values in the variables count and tax_rate. Note that one of these constants contains a decimal point whereas the other does not. The presence or absence of the decimal point distinguishes floating-point constants from integer constants.

A literal constant written with a decimal point is a *floating-point constant* and is represented by the C compiler as a double-precision number. Floating-point constants can be written in standard decimal notation, as shown in these examples:

```
123.456
0.019
100.
```

Note that the third constant, `100.`, is written with a decimal point even though it is an integer (that is, it has no fractional part). The decimal point causes the C compiler to treat the constant as a double-precision value. Without the decimal point, it is treated as an integer constant.

Floating-point constants also can be written in *scientific notation*. You may recall from high school math that scientific notation represents a number as a decimal part multiplied by 10 to a positive or negative power. Scientific notation is particularly useful for representing extremely large and extremely small values. In C, scientific notation is written as a decimal number followed immediately by an E or e and the exponent:

1.23E2	1.23 times 10 to the 2nd power, or 123
4.08e6	4.08 times 10 to the 6th power, or 4,080,000
0.85e−4	0.85 times 10 to the −4th power, or 0.000085

A constant written without a decimal point is represented by the compiler as an integer number. Integer constants can be written in three different notations:

- A constant starting with any digit other than 0 is interpreted as a *decimal* integer (that is, the standard base 10 number system). Decimal constants can contain the digits 0–9 and a leading minus or plus sign. (Without a leading sign, a constant is assumed to be positive.)

- A constant starting with the digit 0 is interpreted as an *octal* integer (the base 8 number system). Octal constants can contain the digits 0–7 and a leading minus or plus sign.

- A constant starting with 0x or 0X is interpreted as a *hexadecimal* constant (the base 16 number system). Hexadecimal constants can contain the digits 0–9, the letters A–F, and a leading minus or plus sign.

Note: See Bonus Day 4, "Working with Different Number Systems," for a more complete explanation of decimal and hexadecimal notation.

Symbolic Constants

A *symbolic constant* is a constant that is represented by a name (symbol) in your program. Like a literal constant, a symbolic constant cannot change. Whenever you need the constant's value in your program, you use its name as you would use a variable name. The actual value of the symbolic constant needs to be entered only once, when it is first defined.

Symbolic constants have two significant advantages over literal constants, as the following example shows. Suppose that you are writing a program that performs a variety of geometrical calculations. The program frequently needs the value π (3.14) for its calculations. (You may recall from geometry class that π is the ratio of a circle's circumference to its diameter.) For example, to calculate the circumference and area of a circle with a known radius you could write

```
circumference = 3.14 * (2 * radius);
area = 3.14 * (radius)*(radius);
```

The asterisk (*) is C's multiplication operator and is covered on Day 4. Thus, the first of the previous statements means "Multiply 2 times the value stored in the variable radius, and then multiply the result by 3.14. Finally, assign the result to the variable named circumference."

If, however, you define a symbolic constant with the name PI and the value 3.14, you could write

```
circumference = PI * (2 * radius);
area = PI * (radius)*(radius);
```

The resulting code is clearer. Rather than puzzling over what the value 3.14 is for, you can see immediately that the constant PI is being used.

The second advantage of symbolic constants becomes apparent when you need to change a constant. Continuing the preceding example, you may decide that for greater accuracy your program needs to use a value of PI with more decimal places: 3.14159 rather than 3.14. If you had used literal constants for PI, you would have to go through your source code and change each occurrence of the value from 3.14 to 3.14159. With a symbolic constant, you would need to make a change only in the place where the constant is defined.

C has two methods for defining a symbolic constant, the #define directive and the const keyword. The #define directive is one of C's preprocessor directives, discussed fully on Day 21, "Taking Advantage of Preprocessor Directives and More." The #define directive is used as follows:

```
#define CONSTNAME literal
```

This program line creates a constant named CONSTNAME with the value of literal. literal represents a numeric constant, as described earlier today. CONSTNAME follows the same rules described for variable names earlier today. By convention, the names of symbolic constants are uppercase. This makes them easy to distinguish from variable names, which by convention are lowercase. For the previous example, the required #define directive would be

```
#define PI 3.14159
```

Note that #define lines do not end with a semicolon (;). #defines can be placed anywhere in your source code, but are in effect only for the portions of the source code that follow the #define directive. Most commonly, programmers group all #defines together, near the beginning of the file and before the start of main().

The precise action of the #define directive is to instruct the compiler, "In the source code, replace CONSTNAME with literal." The effect is exactly the same as if you had used your editor to go through the source code and make the changes manually. Note that #define does not replace instances of its target that occur as parts of longer names, within double quotes, or as part of a program comment:

```
#define PI 3.14
/* You have defined a constant for PI. */ not changed
#define PIPETTE 100                         not changed
```

The second way to define a symbolic constant is with the const keyword. const is a modifier that can be applied to any variable declaration. A variable declared to be const can't be modified during program execution—only initialized at the time of declaration. Here are some examples:

```
const int count = 100;
const float pi = 3.14159;
const long debt = 12000000, float tax_rate = 0.21;
```

const affects all variables on the declaration line. In the last example, debt and tax_rate are symbolic constants. If your program tries to modify a const variable, the compiler generates an error message, as illustrated by this example:

```
const int count = 100;
count = 200;         /* Does not compile! Cannot reassign or alter
the value of a constant. */
```

What are the practical differences between symbolic constants created with the #define directive and those created with the const keyword? The differences have to do with pointers and variable scope. Pointers and variable scope are two very important aspects of C programming and are covered on Day 9, "Pointers," and Day 12, "Variable Scope."

Look now at a program that demonstrates variable declarations and the use of literal and symbolic constants. The code in Listing 3.2 prompts the user to input his or her weight and year of birth. It then calculates and displays a user's weight in grams and his or her age in the year 2000. You can enter, compile, and run this program using the procedures explained on Day 1.

Listing 3.2. A program that demonstrates the use of variables and constants.

```
1:    /* Demonstrates variables and constants */
2:    #include <stdio.h>
3:    /* Define a constant to convert from pounds to grams */
4:    #define GRAMS_PER_POUND 454
5:    /* Define a constant for the start of the next century */
```

```
 6:    const int NEXT_CENTURY = 2000;
 7:    /* Declare the needed variables */
 8:    long weight_in_grams, weight_in_pounds;
 9     int year_of_birth, age_in_2000;
10:
11:
12:    main()
13:    {
14:        /* Input data from user */
15:
16:        printf("Enter your weight in pounds: ");
17:        scanf("%d", &weight_in_pounds);
18:        printf("Enter your year of birth: ");
19:        scanf("%d", &year_of_birth);
20:
21:        /* Perform conversions */
22:
23:        weight_in_grams = weight_in_pounds * GRAMS_PER_POUND;
24:        age_in_2000 = NEXT_CENTURY - year_of_birth;
25:
26:        /* Display results on the screen */
27:
28:        printf("\nYour weight in grams = %ld", weight_in_grams);
29:        printf("\nIn 2000 you will be %d years old", age_in_2000);
30:        return 0;
31:    }
```

Input Output

```
Enter your weight in pounds: 175
Enter your year of birth: 1960

Your weight in grams = 79450
In 2000 you will be 40 years old
```

Analysis The program declares the two types of symbolic constants in lines 4 and 6. In line 4, a constant is being used to make the value 454 more understandable. Because it uses GRAMS_PER_POUND, line 23 is easy to understand. Lines 8 and 9 declare the variables used in the program. Notice the use of descriptive names such as weight_in_grams. By reading its name, you see what this variable is used for. Lines 16 and 18 print prompts on the screen. The printf() function is covered in greater detail later. To allow the user to respond to the prompts, lines 17 and 19 use another library function scanf() that is covered later. scanf() gets information from the screen. For now, accept that this works as shown in the listing. Later, you will learn exactly how it works. Lines 23 and 24 calculate the user's weight in grams and his or her age in the year 2000. Those statements and others are covered in detail tomorrow. To finish the program, lines 28 and 29 display the results for the user.

Numeric Variables and Constants

<table>
<tr><td>**DO**</td><td>**DON'T**</td></tr>
</table>

DO use constants to make your programs easier to read.

DON'T try to assign a value to a constant after it has already been initialized.

Summary

This chapter has explored numeric variables, which are used by a C program to store data during program execution. You've seen that there are two broad classes of numeric variables, integer and floating point. Within each class are specific variable types. Which variable type—int, long, float, or double—you use for a specific application depends on the nature of the data to be stored in the variable. You've also seen that in a C program, you must declare a variable before it can be used. A variable declaration informs the compiler of the name and type of a variable.

This chapter has also covered C's two constant types, literal and symbolic. Unlike variables, the value of a constant cannot change during program execution. You type literal constants into your source code whenever the value is needed. Symbolic constants are assigned a name that is used wherever the constant value is needed. Symbolic constants can be created with the #define directive or with the const keyword.

Q&A

Q long int variables hold bigger numbers, so why not always use them instead of int variables?

A A long int variable takes up more RAM than the smaller int. In smaller programs, this doesn't pose a problem. As programs get bigger, however, try to be efficient with the memory you use.

Q What happens if I assign a number with a decimal to an integer?

A You can assign a number with a decimal to an int variable. If you are using a constant variable, your compiler probably will give you a warning. The value assigned will have the decimal portion truncated. For example, if you assign 3.14 to an integer variable called pi, pi will only contain 3. The .14 will be chopped off and thrown away.

Q What happens if I put a number into a type that is not big enough to hold it?

A Many compilers will allow this without signaling any errors. The number is wrapped to fit, however, and it isn't correct. For example, if you assign 32768 to a two-byte signed integer, the integer really contains the value -32768. If you assign the value 65535 to this integer, it also really contains the value -1. Subtracting the maximum value the field will hold generally gives you the value that will be stored.

Q What happens if I put a negative number into an unsigned variable?

A As the previous answer indicated, your compiler may not signal any errors if you do this. The compiler does the same wrapping as if you assigned a number that was too big. For instance, if you assign -1 to an unsigned int variable that is two bytes long, the compiler will put the highest number possible in the variable (65535).

Q What are the practical differences between symbolic constants created with the #define directive and those created with the const keyword?

A The differences have to do with pointers and variable scope. Pointers and variable scope are two very important aspects of C programming and are covered on Days 9 and 12. For now, know that by using #define to create constants, you can make your programs much easier to read.

Workshop

The Workshop provides quiz questions to help you solidify your understanding of the material covered and exercises to provide you with experience in using what you've learned.

Quiz

1. What's the difference between an integer variable and a floating-point variable?

2. Give two reasons for using a double-precision, floating-point variable (type double) instead of a single-precision, floating-point variable (type float)?

3. What are five rules that the ANSI Standard states are always true when allocating size for variables?

4. What are the two advantages of using a symbolic constant instead of a literal constant?

5. Show two methods for defining a symbolic constant named MAXIMUM that has a value of 100.

6. What characters are allowed in C variable names?

7. What guidelines should you follow in creating names for variables and constants?

8. What's the difference between a symbolic and a literal constant?

9. What's the minimum value that a type int variable can hold?

Exercises

1. In what variable type would you best store the following values?

   a. A person's age to the nearest year.

   b. A person's weight in pounds.

   c. The radius of a circle.

   d. Your annual salary.

   e. The cost of an item.

   f. The highest grade on a test (assume it is always 100).

   g. The temperature.

   h. A person's net worth.

   i. The distance to a star in miles.

2. Determine appropriate variable names for the values in exercise 1.

3. Write declarations for the variables in exercise 2.

4. Which of the following variable names are valid?

   a. `123variable`

   b. `x`

   c. `total_score`

   d. `Weight_in_#s`

   e. `one`

   f. `gross-cost`

   g. `RADIUS`

   h. `Radius`

   i. `radius`

   j. `this_is_a_variable_to_hold_the_width_of_a_box`

Statements, Expressions, and Operators

C programs consist of statements, and most statements are composed of expressions and operators. You need an understanding of these three topics to be able to write C programs. Today, you learn

- What a statement is
- What an expression is
- C's mathematical, relational, and logical operators
- What operator precedence is
- The `if` statement

Statements

A *statement* is a complete direction instructing the computer to carry out some task. In C, statements are usually written one per line, although some statements span multiple lines. C statements always end with a semicolon (except for preprocessor directives such as `#define` and `#include`, which are discussed on Day 21, "Taking Advantage of Preprocessor Directives and More"). You've already been introduced to some of C's statement types. For example,

```
x = 2 + 3;
```

is an *assignment statement.* It instructs the computer to add 2 to 3 and assign the result to the variable x. Other types of statements are introduced as needed throughout the book.

Statements and Whitespace

The term *whitespace* refers to spaces, tabs, and blank lines in your source code. The C compiler is not sensitive to whitespace. When the compiler is reading a statement in your source code, it looks for the characters in the statement and for the terminating semicolon, but it ignores the whitespace. Thus, the statement x=2+3; is exactly equivalent to this statement:

```
x = 2 + 3;
```

It also is equivalent to this:

```
x       =
2
+
3;
```

This gives you a great deal of flexibility in formatting your source code. You shouldn't use formatting like the previous example, however. Statements should be entered one per line with a standardized scheme for spacing around variables and operators. If you follow the formatting conventions used in this book, you should be in good shape. As you become more experienced, you may discover that you prefer slight variations. The point is to keep your source code readable.

The rule that C doesn't care about whitespace has, however, one exception. Within literal string constants, tabs and spaces are not ignored, but are considered part of the string. A *string* is a series of characters. *Literal string* constants are strings that are enclosed within quotes and interpreted literally by the compiler, space for space. Although it's extremely bad form, the following is legal:

```
printf(
"Hello, world!"
);
```

This, however, is not legal:

```
printf("Hello,
world!");
```

To break a literal string constant line, you must use the backslash character (\) just before the break. Thus, the following is legal:

```
printf("Hello,\
world");
```

If you place a semicolon by itself on a line, you create a *null statement,* that is, a statement that doesn't perform any action. This is perfectly legal in C. Later in the book, you will learn how the null statement can be useful at times.

Compound Statements

A *compound statement,* also called a *block,* is a group of two or more C statements enclosed in braces. Here's an example of a block:

```
{
printf("Hello, ");
printf("world!");
}
```

In C, a block can be used anywhere a single statement can be used. Many examples of this appear throughout the book. Note that the enclosing braces can be positioned in different ways. The following is equivalent to the previous example:

```
{printf("Hello, ");
printf("world!");}
```

It's a good idea to place braces on their own lines, making the beginning and end of blocks clearly visible. Placing braces on their own lines also makes it easier to see whether you've left one out.

DO	DON'T

DO stay consistent with how you use whitespace in statements.

DO put block braces on their own lines. This makes the code easier to read.

DO line up block braces so that it is easy to find the beginning and end of a block.

DON'T spread a single statement across multiple lines if there is no need. Limit statements to one line, if possible.

Expressions

In C, an *expression* is anything that evaluates to a numeric value. C expressions come in all levels of complexity.

Simple Expressions

The simplest C expression consists of a single item: a simple variable, literal constant, or symbolic constant. Here are four expressions:

```
PI      /* a symbolic constant (defined in the program) */
20      /* a literal constant. */
rate    /* a variable */
-1.25   /* Another literal constant. */
```

A literal constant evaluates to its own value. A symbolic constant evaluates to the value it was given when you created it with the `#define` directive. A variable evaluates to the value assigned to it by the program.

Complex Expressions

More *complex expressions* consist of simpler expressions connected by operators. For example,

```
2 + 8
```

is an expression consisting of the subexpressions 2 and 8 and the addition operator +. The expression 2 + 8 evaluates, as you know, to 10. You can write C expressions of great complexity:

```
1.25 / 8 + 5 * rate + rate * rate / cost
```

When an expression contains multiple operators, the evaluation of the expression depends on operator precedence. This concept, as well as details about all of C's operators, are covered later in this chapter.

C expressions get even more interesting. Look at the following assignment statement:

```
x = a + 10;
```

This statement evaluates the expression a + 10 and assigns the result to x. In addition, the entire statement x = a + 10 is itself an expression that evaluates to the value of the variable on the left side of the equal sign. This is shown in Figure 4.1.

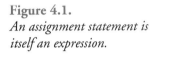

Figure 4.1.
An assignment statement is itself an expression.

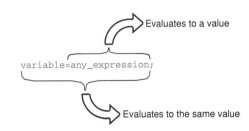

Thus, you can write statements such as the following, which assigns the value of the expression a + 10 to both variables, x and y:

```
y = x = a + 10;
```

You can also write statements such as

```
x - 6 + (y - 4 + 5);
```

The result of this statement is that y has the value 9 and x has the value 15. Note the parentheses, which are required for the statement to compile. The use of parentheses is covered later in this chapter.

Operators

An *operator* is a symbol that instructs C to perform some operation, or action, on one or more operands. An *operand* is something that an operator acts on. In C, all operands are expressions. C operators fall into several categories:

- The assignment operator
- Mathematical operators
- Relational operators
- Logical operators

The Assignment Operator

The assignment operator is the equal sign (=). Its use in programming is somewhat different from its use in regular math. If you write

```
x = y;
```

in a C program, it does not mean "x is equal to y." It means rather, "assign the value of y to x." In a C assignment statement, the right side can be any expression and the left side must be a variable name. Thus, the form is as follows. When executed, *expression* is evaluated, and the resulting value is assigned to *variable*.

```
variable = expression;
```

Mathematical Operators

C's mathematical operators perform mathematical operations such as addition and subtraction. C has two unary mathematical operators and five binary mathematical operators.

The Unary Mathematical Operators

The *unary* mathematical operators are so named because they take a single operand. C has two unary mathematical operators, listed in Table 4.1.

Table 4.1. C's unary mathematical operators.

Operator	Symbol	Action	Example
Increment	++	Increments operand by one	++x, x++
Decrement	--	Decrements operand by one	--x, x--

The increment and decrement operators can be used only with variables, not with constants. The operation performed is to add one to or subtract one from the operand. In other words, the statements

```
++x;
--y;
```

are the equivalent of these statements:

```
x = x + 1;
y = y - 1;
```

You should note from Table 4.1 that either unary operator can be placed before its operand (*prefix mode*) or after its operand (*postfix mode*). These two modes are not equivalent. They differ in terms of when the increment or decrement is performed:

- When used in prefix mode, the increment and decrement operators modify their operand before it is used.
- When used in postfix mode, the increment and decrement operators modify their operand after it is used.

An example should make this clearer. Look at these two statements:

```
x = 10;
y = x++;
```

After these statements are executed, x has the value 11 and y has the value 10: the value of x was assigned to y, and then x was incremented. In contrast, the following statements result in both y and x having the value 11: x is incremented, and then its value is assigned to y.

```
x = 10;
y = ++x;
```

Remember that = is the assignment operator and not a statement of equality. As an analogy, think of = as the "photocopy" operator. The statement y = x means to copy x into y. Subsequent changes to x, after the copy has been made, have no effect on y.

The program in Listing 4.1 illustrates the difference between prefix mode and postfix mode.

4

Type

Listing 4.1. UNARY.C demonstrates prefix and postfix modes.

```
1:    /* Demonstrates unary operator prefix and postfix modes */
2:
3:    #include <stdio.h>
4:
5:    int a, b;
6:
7:    main()
8:    {
9:        /* Set a and b both equal to 5 */
10:
11:       a = b = 5;
12:
13:       /* Print them, decrementing each time. */
14:       /* Use prefix mode for b, postfix mode for a */
15:
16:       printf("\n%d    %d", a--, --b);
17:       printf("\n%d    %d", a--, --b);
18:       printf("\n%d    %d", a--, --b);
19:       printf("\n%d    %d", a--, --b);
20:       printf("\n%d    %d", a--, --b);
21:
22:       return 0;
23:    }
```

```
5    4
4    3
3    2
2    1
1    0
```

This program declares two variables, a and b, in line 5. In line 11, the variables are set to the value of 5. With the execution of each printf() statement (lines 16–20), both a and b are decremented by one. After a is printed, it is decremented, whereas b is decremented before it is printed.

The Binary Mathematical Operators

C's *binary operators* take two operands. The binary operators, which include the common mathematical operations found on a calculator, are listed in Table 4.2.

Table 4.2. C's binary mathematical operators.

Operator	Symbol	Action	Example
Addition	+	Adds its two operands	x + y
Subtraction	-	Subtracts the second operand from the first operand	x - y
Multiplication	*	Multiplies its two operands	x * y
Division	/	Divides the first operand by the second operand	x / y
Modulus	%	Gives the remainder when the first operand is divided by the second operand	x % y

The first four operators in Table 4.2 should be familiar to you, and you should have little trouble using them. The fifth operator, modulus, may be new. *Modulus* returns the remainder when the first operand is divided by the second operand. For example, 11 modulus 4 equals 3 (that is, 4 goes into 11 two times with 3 left over). Here are some more examples:

```
100 modulus 9 equals 1
10 modulus 5 equals  0
40 modulus 6 equals 4
```

The program in Listing 4.2 illustrates how you can use the modulus operator to convert a large number of seconds into hours, minutes, and seconds.

Type

Listing 4.2. SECONDS.C demonstrates the modulus operator.

```
1:  /* Illustrates the modulus operator. */
2:  /* Inputs a number of seconds, and converts to hours, */
3:  /* minutes, and seconds. */
4:
5:  #include <stdio.h>
6:
7:  /* Define constants */
8:
9:  #define SECS_PER_MIN 60
10: #define SECS_PER_HOUR 3600
11:
12: unsigned seconds, minutes, hours, secs_left, mins_left;
13:
14: main()
15: {
16:     /* Input the number of seconds */
17:
18:     printf("Enter number of seconds (< 65000): ");
19:     scanf("%d", &seconds);
20:
21:     hours = seconds / SECS_PER_HOUR;
22:     minutes = seconds / SECS_PER_MIN;
23:     mins_left = minutes % SECS_PER_MIN;
24:     secs_left = seconds % SECS_PER_MIN;
25:
26:     printf("%u seconds is equal to ", seconds);
27:     printf("%u h, %u m, and %u s", hours, mins_left, secs_left);
28:
29:     return 0;
30: }
```

4

Input Output

```
C:\>seconds
Enter number of seconds (< 65000): 60
60 seconds is equal to 0 h, 1 m, and 0 s

C:\>seconds
Enter number of seconds (< 65000): 10000
10000 seconds is equal to 2 h, 46 m, and 40 s
```

Analysis

SECONDS.C follows the same format that all the previous programs have followed. Lines 1–3 provide some comments to state what the program is going to do. Line 4 is whitespace to make the program more readable. Just like the whitespace in statements and expressions, blank lines are ignored by the compiler. Line 5 includes the necessary header file for this program. Lines 9 and 10 define two constants, SECS_PER_MIN and SECS_PER_HOUR, that are used to make the statements in the program easier to read. Line 12 declares all the variables that will be used. Some people choose to declare each variable on an individual line rather than all on one as shown previously. As with many elements of C, this is a matter of style. Either method is correct.

Line 14 is the main() function, which contains the bulk of the program. To convert seconds to hours and minutes, the program must first get the values it needs to work with. To do this, line 18 uses the printf() function to display a statement on the screen followed by line 19, which uses the scanf() function to get the number entered by the user. The scanf() statement then stores the number of seconds to be converted into the variable seconds. The printf() and scanf() functions are covered in more detail on Day 7, "Basic Input/Output." Line 21 contains an expression to determine the number of hours by dividing the number of seconds by the constant SECS_PER_HOUR. Because hours is an integer variable, the remainder value is ignored. Line 22 uses the same logic to determine the total number of minutes for the seconds entered. Because the total number of minutes figured in line 22 also contains minutes for the hours, line 23 uses the modulus operator to divide out the hours and keep the remaining minutes. Line 24 does a similar calculation for determining the number of seconds that are left. Lines 26 and 27 are reflective of what you have seen before. They take the values that have been calculated in the expressions and display them. Line 29 finishes the program by returning 0 to the operating system before exiting.

Operator Precedence and Parentheses

In an expression that contains more than one operator, what is the order in which operations are performed? The importance of this question is illustrated by the following assignment statement:

```
x = 4 + 5 * 3;
```

If the addition is performed first, you have the following, and x is assigned the value 27:

```
x = 9 * 3;
```

In contrast, if the multiplication is performed first, you have the following, and x is assigned the value 19:

```
x = 4 + 15;
```

Clearly, some rules are needed about the order in which operations are performed. This order, called *operator precedence,* is strictly spelled out in C. Each operator has a specific precedence. When an expression is evaluated, operators with higher precedence are performed first. The precedence of C's mathematical operators are listed in Table 4.3. Number 1 is the highest precedence.

Table 4.3. The precedence of C's mathematical operators.

Operators	Relative Precedence
++ --	1
* / %	2
+ -	3

Looking at Table 4.3, you can see that in any C expression, operations are performed in the following order:

- Unary increment and decrement
- Multiplication, division, and modulus
- Addition and subtraction

If an expression contains more than one operator with the same precedence level, the operators are performed in left-to-right order as they appear in the expression. For example, in the following expression the % and * have the same precedence level, but the % is the leftmost operator, so it is performed first:

```
12 % 5 * 2
```

The expression evaluates to 4 (12 % 5 evaluates to 2; 2 times 2 is 4).

Returning to the previous example, you see that the statement x = 4 + 5 * 3; assigns the value 19 to x because the multiplication is performed before the addition.

What if the order of precedence does not evaluate your expression as needed? Using the previous example, what if you wanted to add 4 to 5 and then multiply the sum by 3? C uses parentheses to modify the evaluation order. A subexpression enclosed in parentheses is evaluated first, without regard to operator precedence. Thus, you could write

```
x = (4 + 5) * 3;
```

The expression 4 + 5 inside the parentheses is evaluated first and so the value assigned to x is 27.

You can use multiple and nested parentheses in an expression. When parentheses are nested, evaluation proceeds from the innermost expression outward. Look at the following complex expression:

```
x = 25 - (2 * (10 + (8 / 2)));
```

The evaluation of this expression proceeds as follows:

1. The innermost expression, 8 / 2, is evaluated first, yielding the value 4.

   ```
   25 - (2 * (10 + 4))
   ```

2. Moving outward, the next expression, which becomes 10 + 4, is evaluated, yielding the value 14.

   ```
   25 - (2 * 14)
   ```

3. The last, or outermost, expression becomes 2 * 14 and is evaluated, yielding the value 28.

   ```
   25 - 28
   ```

4. The final expression, 25 - 28, is evaluated, assigning the value -3 to the variable x.

   ```
   x = -3
   ```

You may want to use parentheses in some expressions for the sake of clarity, even when they are not needed for modifying operator precedence. Parentheses must always be in pairs, or the compiler generates an error message.

Order of Subexpression Evaluation

As was mentioned in the previous section, if C expressions contain more than one operator with the same precedence level, they are evaluated left to right. For example, in the expression

```
w * x / y * z
```

w is first multiplied by x, the result of the multiplication is then divided by y, and the result of the division is then multiplied by z.

Across precedence levels, however, there is no guarantee of left-to-right order. Look at this expression:

```
w * x / y + z / y
```

Because of precedence, the multiplication and division are performed before the addition. C does not specify, however, whether the subexpression w * x / y is to be evaluated before or after z / y. It may not be clear to you why this matters. Look at another example:

```
w * x / ++y + z / y
```

If the left subexpression is evaluated first, y is incremented when the second expression is evaluated. If the right expression is evaluated first, y isn't incremented, and the result is different. You should, therefore, avoid this sort of indeterminate expression in your programming.

Appendix C, "Operator Precedence," lists the precedence of all of C's operators.

DO	DON'T

DO use parentheses to make the order of expression evaluation clear.

DON'T overload an expression. It is often more clear to break an expression into two or more statements. This is especially true when using the unary operators (- -) or (++).

Relational Operators

C's *relational operators* are used to compare expressions, "asking" questions such as, "Is *x* greater than 100?" or "Is *y* equal to 0?" An expression containing a relational operator evaluates as either true (1) or false (0). C's six relational operators are listed in Table 4.4.

See Table 4.5 for some examples of how relational operators might be used. These examples use literal constants, but the same principles hold with variables.

Table 4.4. C's relational operators.

Operator	Symbol	Question Asked	Example
Equal	==	Is operand 1 equal to operand 2?	x == y
Greater than	>	Is operand 1 greater than operand 2?	x > y
Less than	<	Is operand 1 less than operand 2?	x < y
Greater than or equal to	>=	Is operand 1 greater than or equal to operand 2?	x >= y
Less than or equal to	<=	Is operand 1 less than or equal to operand 2?	x <= y
Not equal	!=	Is operand 1 not equal to operand 2?	x != y

Table 4.5. Relational operators in use.

Expression	Evaluates As	Read As
5 == 1	0 (false)	Is 5 equal to 1?
5 > 1	1 (true)	Is 5 greater than 1?
5 != 1	1 (true)	Is 5 not equal to 1?
(5 + 10) == (3 * 5)	1 (true)	Is (5 + 10) equal to (3 * 5)?

DO	DON'T

DO learn how C interprets true and false. When working with relational operators, true is equal to 1, and false is equal to 0.

DON'T confuse ==, the relational operator, with =, the assignment operator. This is one of the most common errors that C programmers make.

The *if* Statement

Relational operators are used mainly to construct the relational expressions used in `if` and `while` statements, covered in detail on Day 6, "Basic Program Control." For now, it is useful to explain the basics of the `if` statement to show how relational operators are used to make program control statements.

You may be wondering what a program control statement is. Statements in a C program normally execute from top to bottom, in the same order as they appear in your source code file. A *program control statement* modifies the order of statement execution. Program control statements can cause other program statements to execute multiple times or to not execute at all, depending on the circumstances. The `if` statement is one of C's program control statements. Others, such as `do` and `while`, are covered on Day 6.

In its basic form, the `if` statement evaluates an expression and directs program execution depending on the result of that evaluation. The form of an `if` statement is as follows:

```
if (expression)
    statement;
```

If `expression` evaluates as true, `statement` is executed. If `expression` evaluates as false, `statement` is not executed. In either case, execution then passes to whatever code follows the `if` statement. You can say that execution of `statement` depends on the result of `expression`. Note that both the line `if (expression)` and the line `statement;` are considered to make up the complete `if` statement; they are not separate statements.

DO	DON'T

DO remember that if you program too much in one day, you'll get C sick.

DON'T make the mistake of putting a semicolon at the end of an `if` statement. An `if` statement should end with the conditional statement that follows it. In the following, `statement1` executes whether x equals 2 or not, because each line is evaluated as a separate statement, not together as intended:

```
if( x == 2 );          /* semicolon does not belong!  */
    statement1;
```

An `if` statement can control the execution of multiple statements through the use of a compound statement, or block. As defined earlier in this chapter, a block is a group of two or more statements enclosed in braces. A block can be used anywhere a single statement can be used. You could therefore write an `if` statement as follows:

```
if (expression)
{
    statement1;
    statement2;
    /* additional code goes here */
    statementn;
}
```

In your programming, you will find that `if` statements are used most often with relational expressions; in other words, "execute the following statement(s) only if such-and-such a condition is true." Here's an example:

```
if (x > y)
    y = x;
```

This code assigns the value of x to y only if x is greater than y. If x is not greater than y, no assignment takes place. Listing 4.3 illustrates the use of if statements.

Listing 4.3. LIST0403.C demonstrates if statements.

```
1:    /* Demonstrates the use of if statements */
2:
3:    #include <stdio.h>
4:
5:    int x, y;
6:
7:    main()
8:    {
9:        /* Input the two values to be tested */
10:
11:       printf("\nInput an integer value for x: ");
12:       scanf("%d", &x);
13:       printf("\nInput an integer value for y: ");
14:       scanf("%d", &y);
15:
16:       /* Test values and print result */
17:
18:       if (x == y)
19:           printf("x is equal to y");
20:
21:       if (x > y)
22:           printf("x is greater than y");
23:
24:       if (x < y)
25:           printf("x is smaller than y");
26:
27:       return 0;
28:   }
```

```
C:\>list0403

Input an integer value for x: 100

Input an integer value for y: 10
x is greater than y

C:\>list0403

Input an integer value for x: 10

Input an integer value for y: 100
x is smaller than y

C:\>list0403

Input an integer value for x: 10

Input an integer value for y: 10
x is equal to y
```

4

Analysis LIST0403.C shows three `if` statements in action (lines 18–25). Many of the lines in this program should be familiar. Line 5 declares two variables, x and y, and lines 11–14 prompt the user for values to be placed into these variables. Lines 18–25 use `if` statements to determine whether x is greater than, less than, or equal to y. Note that line 18 uses an `if` statement to see whether x is equal to y. Remember ==, the equal operator, is the same as "is equal to" and should not be confused with =, the assignment operator. After the program checks to see whether the variables are equal, in line 21 it checks to see whether x is greater than y, followed by a check in line 24 to see whether x is less than y. You might think that this is inefficient, and you are right. In the next program, you will see how to avoid this inefficiency. For now, run the program with different values for x and y to see the results.

> **Note:** You will notice that the statements within an `if` clause are indented. This is a common practice for readability.

The *else* Clause

An `if` statement can optionally include an `else` clause. The `else` clause is included as follows:

```
if (expression)
    statement1;
else
    statement2;
```

If *expression* is true, *statement1* is executed. If *expression* is false, *statement2* is executed. Both *statement1* and *statement2* can be compound statements, or blocks.

Listing 4.4 shows the program in Listing 4.3 rewritten to use an `if` statement with an `else` clause.

Type **Listing 4.4. if statement with an else clause.**

```
1:  /* Demonstrates the use of if statement with else clause */
2:
3:  #include <stdio.h>
4:
5:  int x, y;
6:
7:  main()
8:  {
9:      /* Input the two values to be tested */
10:
11:     printf("\nInput an integer value for x: ");
12:     scanf("%d", &x);
13:     printf("\nInput an integer value for y: ");
```

```
14:     scanf("%d", &y);
15:
16:     /* Test values and print result */
17:
18:     if (x == y)
19:         printf("x is equal to y");
20:     else
21:         if (x > y)
22:             printf("x is greater than y");
23:         else
24:             printf("x is smaller than y");
25:
26:     return 0;
27: }
```

```
C:\>list0404

Input an integer value for x: 99

Input an integer value for y: 8
x is greater than y

C:\>list0404

Input an integer value for x: 8

Input an integer value for y: 99
x is smaller than y

C:\>list0404

Input an integer value for x: 99

Input an integer value for y: 99
x is equal to y
```

Lines 18–24 are slightly different from the previous listing. Line 18 still checks to see whether x equals y. If x does equal y, x is equal to y is printed just as in IF.C; however, the program then ends. Lines 20–24 are not executed. Line 21 is executed only if x is not equal to y , or to be more accurate, if the expression "x equals y" is false. If x does not equal y, line 21 checks to see whether x is greater than y. If so, line 22 prints x is greater than y, otherwise (else) line 24 is executed.

The program in Listing 4.4 uses a nested if statement. *Nesting* means to place (nest) one or more C statements inside another C statement. In the case of Listing 4.4, an if statement is part of the first if statement's else clause.

The *if* Statement

Form 1

```
if( expression )
    statement1;
next_statement;
```

This is the if statement in its simplest form. If *expression* is true, then *statement1* is executed. If *expression* is not true, then *statement1* is ignored.

Form 2

```
if( expression )
    statement1;
else
    statement2;
next_statement;
```

This presents the most common form of the if statement. If the first *expression* is true, then *statement1* is executed; otherwise *statement2* is executed.

Form 3

```
if( expression )
    statement1;
else if( expression )
    statement2;
else
    statement3;
next_statement;
```

This presents a nested if. If the first *expression* is true, then *statement1* is executed, otherwise the second *expression* is checked. If the first *expression* is not true, and the second is true, then *statement2* is executed. If both expressions are false, then *statement3* is executed. Only one of the three statements is executed.

Example 1

```
if( salary > 45,0000 )
    tax = .30;
else
    tax = .25;
```

Example 2

```
if( age < 18 )
    printf("Minor");
else if( age < 65 )
    printf("Adult");
else
    printf( "Senior Citizen");
```

Evaluation of Relational Expressions

Remember that expressions using relational operators are true C expressions that evaluate, by definition, to a value. Relational expressions evaluate to a value of either false (0) or true (1). Although the most common use for relational expressions is within `if` statements and other conditional constructions, they can be used as purely numeric values. This is illustrated by the program in Listing 4.5.

Listing 4.5. Demonstrating the evaluation of relational expressions.

```
1:   /* Demonstrates the evaluation of relational expressions */
2:
3:   #include <stdio.h>
4:
5:   int a;
6:
7:   main()
8:   {
9:       a = (5 == 5);             /* Evaluates to 1 */
10:      printf("\na = (5 == 5)\na = %d", a);
11:
12:      a = (5 != 5);             /* Evaluates to 0 */
13:      printf("\na = (5 != 5)\na = %d", a);
14:
15:      a = (12 == 12) + (5 != 1); /* Evaluates to 1 + 1 */
16:      printf("\na = (12 == 12) + (5 != 1)\na = %d", a);
17:      return 0;
18:  }
```

```
a = (5 == 5)
a = 1
a = (5 != 5)
a = 0
a = (12 == 12) + (5 != 1)
a = 2
```

The output from this listing may seem a little confusing at first. Remember, the most common mistake people make when using the relational operators is to use a single equal sign—the assignment operator—instead of a double equal sign. The following expression evaluates as 5 (and also assigns the value 5 to x):

```
x = 5
```

In contrast, the following expression evaluates as either 0 or 1 (depending on whether x is equal to 5) and does not change the value of x:

```
x == 5
```

If by mistake you write

```
if (x = 5)
    printf("x is equal to 5");
```

the message always prints because the expression being tested by the `if` statement always evaluates as true, no matter what the original value of x happens to be.

Looking at Listing 4.5, you can begin to understand why a takes on the values that it does. In line 9, the value 5 does equal 5, therefore true (1) is assigned to a. In line 12, the statement "5 does not equal 5" is false, so 0 is assigned to a.

To reiterate, the relational operators are used to create relational expressions that ask questions about relationships between expressions. The answer returned by a relational expression is a numeric value of either 1 (representing true) or 0 (representing false).

Precedence of Relational Operators

Like the mathematical operators discussed earlier in the day, the relational operators each have a precedence that determines the order in which they are performed in a multiple-operator expression. Similarly, you can use parentheses to modify precedence in expressions that use relational operators. Remember, Appendix C lists the precedence of all C's operators.

First, all the relational operators have a lower precedence than the mathematical operators. Thus, if you write the following, 2 is added to x, and the result is compared to y:

```
if (x + 2 > y)
```

This is the equivalent of the following line, which is a good example of using parentheses for the sake of clarity:

```
if ((x + 2) > y)
```

Although not required by the C compiler, the parentheses surrounding (x + 2) make it clear that it is the sum of x and 2 that is to be compared with y.

There is also a two-level precedence within the relational operators. This is shown in Table 4.6.

Thus, if you write

```
x == y > z
```

it is the same as

```
x == (y > z)
```

because C first evaluates the expression y > z, resulting in a value of 0 or 1. Next, C determines whether x is equal to the 1 or 0 obtained in the first step. You rarely, if ever, use this sort of construction, but you should know about it.

DO	DON'T

DON'T put assignment statements in `if` statements. This can be confusing to other people who look at your code. They may think it is a mistake and change your assignment to the logical equal statement.

DON'T use the "not equal to" operator (`!=`) in an `if` statement containing an `else`. It is almost always clearer to use the "equal to" operator (`==`) with an `else`. For instance, the following code:

```
if ( x != 5 )
    statement1;
else
    statement2;
```

would be better written as this:

```
if (x == 5 )
    statement2;
else
    statement1;
```

4

Table 4.6. C's relational operators' precedence order.

Operator	Relative Precedence
< <= > >=	1
!= ==	2

Logical Operators

At times, you may need to ask more than one relational question at the same time. For example, "If it's 7:00 AM and a weekday and not your vacation, ring the alarm." C's logical operators enable you to combine two or more relational expressions into a single expression that evaluates as either true or false. C's three logical operators are listed in Table 4.7.

Table 4.7. C's logical operators.

Operator	Symbol	Example
AND	&&	*exp1* && *exp2*
OR	||	*exp1* || *exp2*
NOT	!	!*exp1*

The way these logical operators work is explained in Table 4.8.

Table 4.8. C's logical operators in use.

Expression	Evaluates As
(exp1 && exp2)	True (1) only if both *exp1* and *exp2* are true; false (0) otherwise.
(exp1 ¦¦ exp2)	True (1) if either *exp1* or *exp2* is true; false (0) only if both are false.
(!exp1)	False (0) if *exp1* is true; true (1) if *exp1* is false.

You can see that expressions which use the logical operators evaluate as either true or false depending on the true/false value of their operand(s). Table 4.9 shows some actual code examples.

Table 4.9. Code examples of C's logical operators.

Expression	Evaluates As
(5 == 5) && (6 != 2)	True (1) because both operands are true.
(5 > 1) ¦¦ (6 < 1)	True (1) because one operand is true.
(2 == 1) && (5 == 5)	False (0) because one operand is false.
!(5 == 4)	True (1) because the operand is false.

You can create expressions that use multiple logical operators. For example, to ask the question "Is x equal to 2, 3, or 4?" you would write

```
(x == 2) ¦¦ (x == 3) ¦¦ (x == 4)
```

The logical operators often provide more than one way to ask a question. If x is an integer variable, the previous question also could be written in either of the following ways:

```
(x > 1) && (x < 5)
```

```
(x >= 2) && (x <= 4)
```

More on True/False Values

You've seen that C's relational expressions evaluate to 0 to represent false and to 1 to represent true. It's important to be aware, however, that any numeric value is interpreted as either true or false when it is used in a C expression or statement that is expecting a logical (that is, a true or false) value. The rules for this are as follows:

- A value of zero represents false.
- Any nonzero value represents true.

This is illustrated by the following example, in which case the value of x is printed:

```
x = 125;
if (x)
    printf("%d", x);
```

Because x has a nonzero value, the expression (x) is interpreted as true by the if statement. You can further generalize this because, for any C expression, writing

```
(expression)
```

is equivalent to writing

```
(expression != 0)
```

Both evaluate as true if *expression* is nonzero, and as false if *expression* is 0. Using the not (!) operator, you can also write

```
(!expression)
```

which is equivalent to

```
(expression == 0)
```

Precedence of Logical Operators

As you may have guessed, C's logical operators also have a precedence order, both among themselves and in relation to other operators. The ! operator has a precedence equal to the unary mathematical operators ++ and --. Thus, ! has a higher precedence than all the relational operators and all the binary mathematical operators.

In contrast, the && and ¦¦ operators have much lower precedence, lower than all the mathematical and relational operators, although && has a higher precedence than ¦¦. As with all of C's operators, parentheses can be used to modify evaluation order when using the logical operators. Look at the following example.

You want to write a logical expression that makes three individual comparisons:

- Is a less than b?
- Is a less than c?
- Is c less than d?

You want the entire logical expression to evaluate as true if condition 3 is true and either condition 1 or condition 2 is true. You might write

```
a < b ¦¦ a < c && c < d
```

This does not, however, do what you intended. Because the && operator has higher precedence than ¦¦, the expression is equivalent to

```
a < b ¦¦ (a < c && c < d)
```

and evaluates as true if (a < b) is true, whether or not the relationships (a < c) and (c < d) are true. You need to write

```
(a < b ¦¦ a < c) && c < d
```

which forces the ¦¦ to be evaluated before the &&. This is shown in Listing 4.6, which evaluates the expression written both ways. The variables are set so that, if written correctly, the expression should evaluate as false (0).

Type   **Listing 4.6. Logical operator precedence.**

```
1:   #include <stdio.h>
2:
3:   /* Initialize variables. Note that c is not less than d, */
4:   /* which is one of the conditions to test for. */
5:   /* Therefore the entire expression should evaluate as false.*/
6:
7:   int a = 5, b = 6, c = 5, d = 1;
8:   int x;
9:
10:  main()
11:  {
12:      /* Evaluate the expression without parentheses */
13:
14:      x = a < b ¦¦ a < c && c < d;
15:      printf("\nWithout parentheses the expression evaluates as %d", x);
16:
17:      /* Evaluate the expression with parentheses */
18:
19:      x = (a < b ¦¦ a < c) && c < d;
20:      printf("\nWith parentheses the expression evaluates as %d", x);
21:      return 0;
22:  }
```

Output   Without parentheses the expression evaluates as 1
          With parentheses the expression evaluates as 0

Analysis   Enter and run this listing. Note that the two values printed for the expression are different. This program initializes four variables, in line 7, with values to be used in the comparisons. Line 8 declares x to be used to store and print the results. Lines 14 and 19 use the logical operators. Line 14 does not use the parentheses, so the results are determined by operator precedence. In this case, the results are not those you desired. Line 19 uses parentheses to change the order in which the expressions are evaluated.

Compound Assignment Operators

C's *compound assignment operators* provide a shorthand method for combining a binary mathematical operation with an assignment operation. For example, say you want to increase the value of x by 5, or in other words, add 5 to x and assign the result to x. You could write

```
x = x + 5;
```

Using a compound assignment operator, which you can think of as a shorthand method of assignment, you would write

```
x += 5;
```

In more general notation, the compound assignment operators have the following syntax (where op represents a binary operator):

```
exp1 op= exp2
```

This is equivalent to writing

```
exp1 = exp1 op exp2;
```

You can create compound assignment operators with the five binary mathematical operators discussed earlier in this chapter. Table 4.10 lists some examples.

Table 4.10. Examples of compound assignment operators.

When You Write This...	It Is Equivalent To This
x *= y	x = x * y
y -= z + 1	y = y - z + 1
a /= b	a = a / b
x += y / 8	x = x + y / 8
y %= 3	y = y % 3

The compound operators provide a convenient shorthand, the advantages of which are particularly evident when the variable on the left side of the assignment operator has a long name. As with all other assignment statements, a compound assignment statement is an expression and evaluates to the value assigned to the left side. Thus, executing the following statements results in both x and z having the value 14:

```
x = 12;
z = x += 2;
```

The Conditional Operator

The *conditional operator* is C's only *ternary operator,* meaning that it takes three operands. Its syntax is

```
exp1 ? exp2 : exp3;
```

If `exp1` evaluates as true (that is, nonzero), the entire expression evaluates as the value of `exp2`. If `exp1` evaluates as false (that is, zero), the entire expression evaluates as the value of `exp3`. For example, the following statement assigns the value 1 to x if y is true and assigns `100` to x if y is false.

```
x = y ? 1 : 100;
```

Likewise, to make z equal to the larger of x and y, you could write

```
z = (x > y) ? x : y;
```

Perhaps you've noticed that the conditional operator functions somewhat like an `if` statement. The previous statement could also be written

```
if (x > y)
    z = x;
else
    z = y;
```

The conditional operator can't be used in all situations in place of an `if...else` construction, but the conditional operator is more concise. The conditional operator can also be used in places you can't use an `if` statement, such as inside a single `printf()` statement.

The Comma Operator

The *comma* is frequently used in C as a simple punctuation mark, serving to separate variable declarations, function arguments, and so on. In certain situations the comma acts as an operator rather than just as a separator. You can form an expression by separating two subexpressions with a comma. The result is as follows:

- Both expressions are evaluated, with the left expression being evaluated first.
- The entire expression evaluates as the value of the right expression.

For example, the following statement assigns the value of b to x, then increments a, and then increments b:

```
x = (a++ , b++);
```

Because the ++ operator is used in postfix mode, the value of b—before it is incremented—is assigned to x. Using parentheses is necessary because the comma operator has a low precedence, even lower than the assignment operator.

As you'll learn in the next chapter, the most common use of the comma operator is in `for` statements.

DO	DON'T

DO use (`expression == 0`) instead of (`!expression`). When compiled, these two expressions evaluate the same; however, the first is more readable.

DO use the logical operators `&&` and `¦¦` instead of nesting `if` statements.

DON'T confuse the assignment operator (`=`) with the equal to (`==`) operator.

Summary

This chapter covered a lot of material. You have learned what a C statement is, that whitespace does not matter to a C compiler, and that statements always terminate with a semicolon. You've also learned that a compound statement (or block), which consists of two or more statements enclosed in braces, can be used anywhere a single statement can be used.

Many statements are made up of some combination of expressions and operators. Remember that an expression is anything that evaluates to a numeric value. Complex expressions can contain many simpler expressions, which are called subexpressions.

Operators are C symbols that instruct the computer to perform an operation on one or more expressions. Some operators are unary, which means that they operate on a single operand. Most of C's operators are binary, however, operating on two operands. One operator, the conditional operator, is ternary. C's operators have a defined hierarchy of precedence that determines the order in which operations are performed in an expression that contains multiple operators.

The C operators covered by this chapter fall into three categories:

- Mathematical operators perform arithmetic operations on their operands (for example, addition).
- Relational operators perform comparisons between their operands (for example, greater than).
- Logical operators operate on true/false expressions. Remember that C uses `0` and `1` to represent false and true, respectively, and that any nonzero value is interpreted as being true.

You've also been introduced to C's `if` statement, which enables you to control program execution based on the evaluation of relational expressions.

Q&A

Q What effect do spaces and blank lines have on how a program runs?

A Whitespace (lines, spaces, tabs) makes the code listing more readable. When the program is compiled, whitespace is stripped and thus has no effect on the executable program. For this reason, whitespace should be used to make your program easier to read.

Q Is it better to code a compound `if` statement or to nest multiple `if` statements?

A You should make your code easy to understand. If you nest `if` statements, they are evaluated as shown in the chapter. If you use a single compound statement, the expressions are evaluated only until the entire statement is evaluated as false.

Q What is the difference between unary and binary operators?

A As the names imply, unary operators work with one variable and binary operators work with two.

Q Is the subtraction operator (-) binary or unary?

A It's both! The compiler is smart enough to know which you are using. It knows which form to use based on the number of variables in the expression that is used. In the following statement, it is a unary:

```
x = -y;
```

versus the following binary use:

```
x = a - b;
```

Q Are negative numbers considered to be true or false?

A Remember 0 is false, and any other value is true. This includes negative numbers.

Workshop

The Workshop provides quiz questions to help you solidify your understanding of the material covered and exercises to provide you with experience in using what you've learned.

Quiz

1. What is the following C statement called, and what is its meaning?

   ```
   x = 5 + 8;
   ```

2. What is an expression?

3. In an expression that contains multiple operators, what determines the order in which operations are performed?

4. If the variable x has the value 10, what are the values of x and a after each of the following statements is executed separately?

```
a = x++;
a = ++x;
```

5. To what value does the expression `10 % 3` evaluate?

6. To what value does the expression `5 + 3 * 8 / 2 + 2` evaluate?

7. Rewrite the expression in question 6, adding parentheses so that it evaluates to 16.

8. If an expression evaluates to false, what value does the expression have?

9. Which has higher precedence?

    a. `== or <`

    b. `* or +`

    c. `!= or ==`

    d. `>= or >`

10. What are the compound assignment operators and how are they useful?

Exercises

1. The following code is not well written. Enter and compile it to see whether it works.

```
#include <stdio.h>
int x,y;main(){ printf(
"\nEnter two numbers");scanf(
"%d %d",&x,&y);printf(
"\n\n%d is bigger",(x>y)?x:y);return 0;}
```

2. Rewrite the code in exercise one to be more readable.

3. Change Listing 4.1 to count upward instead of downward.

4. Write an `if` statement that assigns the value of x to the variable y only if x is between 1 and 20. Leave y unchanged if x is not in that range.

5. Use the conditional operator to perform the same task as in exercise 4.

6. Rewrite the following nested `if` statements using a single `if` statement and compound operators.

```
if (x < 1)
  if ( x > 10 )
    statement;
```

7. To what value do each of the following expressions evaluate?

    a. `(1 + 2 * 3)`

    b. `10 % 3 * 3 - (1 + 2)`

    c. `((1 + 2) * 3)`

    d. `(5 == 5)`

    e. `(x = 5)`

8. If x = 4, y = 6, and z = 2, determine whether each of the following evaluates to true or false.

    a. `if( x == 4)`

    b. `if(x != y - z)`

    c. `if(z = 1)`

    d. `if(y)`

9. Write an if statement that determines whether someone is legally an adult (age 21), but not a senior citizen (age 65).

10. **BUG BUSTER:** Fix the following program so that it runs correctly.

```
/* a program with problems... */
#include <stdio.h>
int x= 1:
main()
{
    if( x = 1);
         printf(" x equals 1" );
    otherwise
        printf(" x does not equal 1");

    return;
}
```

5

Functions:
The Basics

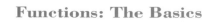

Functions are central to C programming and to the philosophy of C program design. You've already been introduced to some of C's library functions, which are complete functions supplied as part of your compiler. This chapter covers user-defined functions which, as the name implies, are functions that you, the programmer, create. Today, you learn

- What a function is and what its parts are
- About the advantages of structured programming with functions
- How to create a function
- About the declaration of local variables in a function
- How to return a value from a function to the program
- How to pass arguments to a function

What Is a Function?

This chapter approaches the question "What is a function?" in two ways. First, it tells you what functions are and then shows you how they're used.

A Function Defined

First the definition: a *function* is a named, independent section of C code that performs a specific task and optionally returns a value to the calling program. Now, look at the parts of this definition.

- *A function is named.* Each function has a unique name. By using that name in another part of the program, you can execute the statements contained in the function. This is known as calling the function. A function can be called from within another function.
- *A function is independent.* A function can perform its task without interference from or interfering with other parts of the program.
- *A function performs a specific task.* This is the easy part of the definition. A task is a discrete job that your program must perform as part of its overall operation, such as sending a line of text to a printer, sorting an array into numerical order, or calculating a cube root.
- *A function can return a value to the calling program.* When your program calls a function, the statements it contains are executed. These statements, if desired, can pass information back to the calling program.

That's all there is to the "telling" part. Keep the previous definition in mind as you look at the next section.

A Function Illustrated

The program in Listing 5.1 contains a user-defined function. The line numbers are not part of the program.

Listing 5.1. A program that uses a function to calculate the cube of a number.

```
1:   /* Demonstrates a simple function */
2:   #include <stdio.h>
3:
4:   long cube(long x);
5:
6:   long input, answer;
7:
8:   main()
9:   {
10:     printf("Enter an integer value: ");
11:     scanf("%d", &input);
12:     answer = cube(input);
13:     /* Note: %ld is the conversion specifier for */
14:     /* a long integer */
15:     printf("\nThe cube of %ld is %ld.", input, answer);
16:   }
17:
18:   long cube(long x)
19:   {
20:     long x_cubed;
21:
22:     x_cubed = x * x * x;
23:     return x_cubed;
24:   }
```

Input/Output

```
Enter an integer value: 100

The cube of 100 is 1000000.

Enter an integer value: 9

The cube of 9 is 729.

Enter an integer value: 3

The cube of 3 is 27.
```

Note: This analysis focuses on the components of the program that relate directly to the function rather than explain the entire program.

Line 4 contains the *function prototype,* a model for a function that will appear later in the program. A function's prototype contains the name of the function, a list of variables that must be passed to it, and the type of variable it returns, if any. Looking at line 4 you can tell that the function is named cube, that it requires a variable of the type long, and that it will return a value of type long. The list of variables to be passed to the function are called arguments and appear between the parentheses following the function's name. In this example, the function's argument is long x. The keyword before the name of the function indicates the type of variable the function returns. In this case, a type long variable is returned.

Line 12 calls the function cube and passes the variable input to it as the function's argument. The function's return value is assigned to the variable answer. Notice that both input and answer are declared on line 6 as long variables, in keeping with the function prototype on line 4.

The function itself is called the *function definition.* In this case, it's called cube and is contained on program lines 18–24. Like the prototype, the function definition has several parts. The function starts out with a function header on line 18. The *function header* is at the start of a function and gives the function's name (in this case, the name is cube). The header also gives the function's return type and describes its arguments. Note that the function header is identical to the function prototype (minus the semicolon).

The body of the function, lines 19–24, is enclosed in braces. The body contains statements, such as shown on line 22, that are executed whenever the function is called. Line 20 is a variable declaration that looks like the declarations you have seen before, with one difference: it is local. *Local* variables are those that are declared within a function body. (Local declarations are discussed further on Day 12, "Variable Scope.") Finally, the function concludes with a return statement on line 23, which signals the end of the function. A return statement also passes a value back to the calling program. In this case, the value of the variable x_cubed is returned.

If you compare the structure of the cube() function with that of the main() function, you see that they are the same. main() is also a function. Other functions that you already have used are printf() and scanf(). Although printf() and scanf() are library functions (as opposed to user-defined functions) they are functions that can take arguments and return values just like the functions you create.

How a Function Works

A C program does not execute the statements in a function until the function is called by another part of the program. When a function is called, the program can send the function information in the form of one or more arguments. An argument is program data needed by the function to perform its task. The statements in the function then execute, performing whatever task each was designed to do. When the function's statements have finished, execution passes back to the same location in the program that called the function. Functions can send information back to the program in the form of a return value.

Figure 5.1 shows a program with three functions, each of which is called once. Each time a function is called, execution passes to that function. When the function is finished, execution passes back to the place from which the function was called. A function can be called as many times as needed, and functions can be called in any order.

Figure 5.1.

When a program calls a function, execution passes to the function and then back to the calling program.

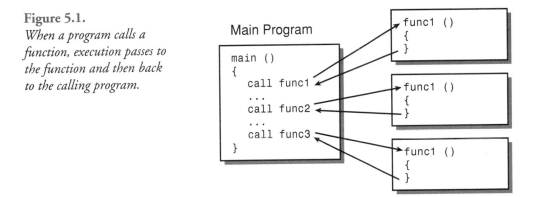

You now know what a function is and the importance of functions. Lessons on how to create and use your own functions follow.

Functions

Function Prototype

```
return_type function_name( arg-type name-1,…,arg-type name-n);
```

Function Definition

```
return_type function_name( arg-type name-1,…,arg-type name-n)
{
    statements;
}
```

A *function prototype* provides the compiler with the description of a function that will be defined at a later point in the program. The prototype includes a return type indicating the type of variable that the function will return. It also includes the function name, which should describe what the function does. The prototype also contains the variable types of the arguments (arg type) that will be passed to the function. Optionally, it can contain the names of the variables that will be passed. A prototype always should end with a semicolon.

A *function definition* is the actual function. The definition contains the code that will be executed. The first line of a function definition, called the *function header,* should be identical to the function prototype, with the exception of the semicolon. A function header should not end with a semicolon. In addition, although the argument variable names were optional in the

Syntax

5

83

prototype, they must be included in the function header. Following the header is the function body, containing the statements that the function will perform. The function body should start with an opening bracket and end with a closing bracket. If the function return type is anything other than void, a return statement should be included, returning a value matching the return type.

Function Prototype Examples

```
double squared( double number );
void print_report( int report_number );
int get_menu_choice( void );
```

Function Definition Examples

```
double squared( double number )        /* function header */
{                                      /* opening bracket */
    return( number * number );         /* function body   */
}                                      /* closing bracket */
void print_report( int report_number )
{
    if( report_number == 1 )
        puts( "Printing Report 1" );
    else
        puts( "Not printing Report 1" );
}
```

Functions and Structured Programming

By using functions in your C programs, you can practice *structured programming* in which individual program tasks are performed by independent sections of program code. "Independent sections of program code" sounds just like part of the definition of functions given earlier, doesn't it? Functions and structured programming are closely related.

The Advantages of Structured Programming

Why is structured programming so great? There are two important reasons:

- It's easier to write a structured program because complex programming problems are broken into a number of smaller, simpler tasks. Each task is performed by a function in which code and variables are isolated from the rest of the program. You can make progress faster dealing one at a time with these relatively simple tasks.

- It's easier to debug a structured program. If your program has a *bug* (something that causes it to work improperly), a structured design makes it easy to isolate the problem to a specific section of code (a specific function).

A related advantage of structured programming is the time you can save. If you write a function to perform a certain task in one program, you quickly and easily can use it in another program that needs to execute the same task. Even if the new program needs to accomplish a slightly different task, you often find that modifying a function you created earlier is easier than writing a new one from scratch. Consider how much you've used the two functions printf() and scanf() even though you probably haven't seen the code they contain. If your functions have been created to do a single task, using them in other programs is much easier.

Planning a Structured Program

If you're going to write a structured program, you need to do some planning first. This planning should take place before you write a single line of code, and usually can be done with nothing more than pencil and paper. Your plan should be a list of the specific tasks that your program performs. Begin with a global idea of the program's function. If you were planning a program to manage your name and address list, what would you want the program to do? Here are some obvious things:

- Enter new names and addresses.
- Modify existing entries.
- Sort entries by last name.
- Print mailing labels.

With this list, you've divided the program into four main tasks, each of which can be assigned to a function. Now you can go a step further, dividing these tasks into subtasks. For example, the "Enter new names and addresses" task can be subdivided into these subtasks:

- Read the existing address list from disk.
- Prompt the user for one or more new entries.
- Add the new data to the list.
- Save the updated list to disk.

Likewise, the "Modify existing entries" task can be subdivided as follows:

- Read the existing address list from disk.
- Modify one or more entries.
- Save the updated list to disk.

You might have noticed that these two lists have two subtasks in common—the ones dealing with reading from and saving to disk. You can write one function to "Read the existing address list from disk," and that function can be called by both the "Enter new names and addresses" function and the "Modify existing entries" function. The same is true for "Save the updated list to disk."

Already, you should see at least one advantage of structured programming. By carefully dividing the program into tasks, you can identify parts of the program that share common tasks. You can write "double-duty" disk access functions, saving yourself time and making your program smaller and more efficient.

This method of programming results in a hierarchical, or layered, program structure. Figure 5.2 illustrates hierarchical programming for the address list program.

Figure 5.2.
A structured program is organized hierarchically.

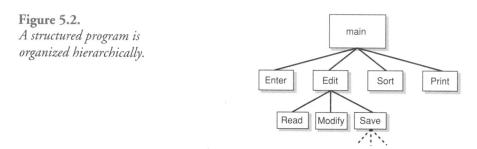

When you follow this planned approach, you quickly make a list of discrete tasks that your program needs to perform. Then you can tackle the tasks one at a time, giving all your attention to one relatively simple task. When that function is written and working properly, you can move on to the next task. Before you know it, your program starts to take shape.

The Top-Down Approach

By using structured programming, C programmers take the *top-down approach*. You saw this illustrated in Figure 5.2, where the program's structure resembles an inverted tree. Many times, most of the real work of the program is performed by the functions at the "tips of the branches." The functions closer to the "trunk" primarily direct program execution among these functions.

As a result, many C programs have a small amount of code in the main body of the program, that is, in main(). The bulk of the program's code is found in functions. In main(), all you may find are a few dozen lines of code that direct program execution among the functions. Often, a menu is presented to the person using the program, with program execution branched according to the user's choices.

This is a good approach to program design. Day 13, "More Program Control," shows how you can use the switch statement to create a versatile menu-driven system.

Now that you know what functions are and why they're so important, the time has come for you to learn how to write your own functions.

<table>
<tr><td>DO</td><td>DON'T</td></tr>
</table>

DO plan before starting to code. By determining your program's structure ahead of time, you can save time writing the code and debugging it.

DON'T try to do everything in one function. A single function should do a single task, such as reading information from a file.

Writing a Function

The first step in writing a function is knowing what you want the function to do. Once you know that, the actual mechanics of writing the function are not particularly difficult.

The Function Header

The first line of every function is the function header, which has three components, each serving a specific function. They are diagrammed in Figure 5.3 and explained in the following subsections.

Figure 5.3.
The three components of a function header.

```
                              Function name
          Function return type        Parameter list
                     ↓          ↓        ↓
              type funcname(parm1,...)
```

The Function Return Type

The function return type specifies the data type that the function returns to the calling program. The return type can be any of C's data types: char, int, long, float, or double. You also can define a function that doesn't return a value, a return type of void. Here are some examples:

```
int func1(...)          /* Returns a type int.   */
float func2(...)        /* Returns a type float. */
void func3(...)         /* Returns nothing.      */
```

The Function Name

You can name a function anything you like, as long as you follow the rules for C variable names (given in Day 3, "Numeric Variables and Constants"). A function name must be unique (not assigned to any other function or variable). It's a good idea to assign a name that reflects what the function does.

The Parameter List

Many functions use *arguments,* which are values passed to the function when it is called. A function needs to know what kinds of arguments to expect—the data type of each argument. You can pass a function any of C's data types. Argument type information is provided in the function header by the parameter list.

For each argument that is passed to the function, the parameter list must contain one entry. This entry specifies the data type and the name of the parameter. For example, here's the header from the function in Listing 5.1:

```
long cube(long x)
```

The parameter list reads long x, specifying that this function takes one type long argument, represented by the parameter x. If there is more than one parameter, each must be separated by a comma. The function header

```
void func1(int x, float y, char z)
```

specifies a function with three arguments: a type int named x, a type float named y, and a type char named z. Some functions take no arguments, in which case, the parameter list should read void like this:

```
void func2(void)
```

> **Note:** You do not place a semicolon at the end of a function header. If you mistakenly include one, the compiler generates an error message.

Sometimes confusion arises about the distinction between a parameter and an argument. A *parameter* is an entry in a function header; it serves as a "place holder" for an argument. A function's parameters are fixed; they do not change during program execution.

An argument is an actual value passed to the function by the calling program. Each time a function is called, it can be passed different arguments. A function must be passed the same number and type of arguments each time it is called, but the argument values can be different. In the function, the argument is accessed by using the corresponding parameter name.

An example makes this clearer. Listing 5.2 presents a very simple program with one function that is called twice.

Listing 5.2. The difference between arguments and parameters.

```
1:   /* Illustrates the difference between arguments and parameters. */
2:
3:   #include <stdio.h>
4:
5:   float x = 3.5, y = 65.11, z;
6:
7:   float half_of(float k);
8:
9:   main()
10:  {
11:      /* In this call, x is the argument to half_of(). */
12:      z = half_of(x);
13:      printf("The value of z = %f\n", z);
14:
15:      /* In this call, y is the argument to half_of(). */
16:      z = half_of(y);
17:      printf("The value of z = %f\n", z);
18:  }
19:
20:  float half_of(float k)
21:  {
22:      /* k is the parameter. Each time half_of() is called, */
23:      /* k has the value that was passed as an argument. */
24:
25:      return (k/2);
26:  }
```

```
The value of z = 1.750000
The value of z = 32.555000
```

Figure 5.4 shows the relationship between arguments and parameters schematically.

Figure 5.4.
Each time a function is called, the arguments are passed to the function's parameters.

First function call   `z=half_of(x);`
                                    3.5
`float half_of(float k)`

Second function call   `Z=half_of(y);`
                                    65.11
`float half_of(float k)`

Looking at Listing 5.2, you can see that the `half_of()` function prototype is declared on line 7. Lines 12 and 16 call `half_of()` and lines 20–26 contain the actual function. Lines 12 and 16 each send a different argument to `half_of()`. Line 12 sends x, which contains a value of 3.5, and line 16 sends y, which contains a value of 65.11. When the program runs, it prints the correct number for each. The values in x and y are passed into the argument k of `half_of()`. This is like copying the values from x to k, and then y to k. `Half_of()` then returns this value after dividing it by 2 (line 25).

DO	DON'T

DO use a function name that describes the purpose of the function.

DON'T pass values to a function that it doesn't need.

DON'T try to pass fewer (or more) arguments to a function than there are parameters.

The Function Body

The *function body* is enclosed in braces and follows immediately after the function header. It's here that the real work is done. When a function is called, execution begins at the start of the function body and terminates (returns to the calling program) when a `return` statement is encountered or when execution reaches the closing brace.

Local Variables

You can declare variables within the body of a function. Variables declared in a function are called *local variables.* The term *local* means the variables are private to that particular function and are distinct from other variables of the same name declared elsewhere in the program. This is explained shortly; for now, you should learn how to declare local variables.

A local variable is declared like any other variable, using the same variable types and rules for names that you learned on Day 3. Local variables can also be initialized when they are declared. You can declare any of C's variable types in a function. Here is an example of four local variables being declared within a function:

```
int func1(int y)
{
    int a, b = 10;
    float rate;
    double cost = 12.55;
    ...
}
```

The preceding declarations create local variables a, b, rate, and cost that can be used by the code in the function. Note that the function parameters are considered to be variable declarations, so the variables, if any, in the function's parameter list also are available.

When you declare and use a variable in a function, it is totally separate and distinct from any other variables that are declared elsewhere in the program. This is true even if the variables have the same name. The program in Listing 5.3 demonstrates this independence.

Type **Listing 5.3. Demonstration of local variables.**

```
1:   /* Demonstrates local variables. */
2:
3:   #include <stdio.h>
4:
5:   int x = 1, y = 2;
6:
7:   void demo(void);
8:
9:   main()
10:  {
11:    printf("\nBefore calling demo(), x = %d and y = %d.", x, y);
12:    demo();
13:    printf("\nAfter calling demo(), x = %d and y = %d.", x, y);
14:  }
15:
16:  void demo(void)
17:  {
18:      /* Declare and initialize two local variables. */
19:
20:      int x = 88, y = 99;
21:
22:      /* Display their values. */
23:
24:      printf("\nWithin demo(), x = %d and y = %d.", x, y);
25:  }
```

```
Before calling demo(), x = 1 and y = 2.
Within demo(), x = 88 and y = 99.
After calling demo(), x = 1 and y = 2.
```

Analysis Listing 5.3 is similar to the previous programs in this chapter. Line 5 declares variables x and y. These are declared outside of any functions and therefore are considered global. Line 7 contains the prototype for our demonstration function, named demo(). It is a function that does not take any parameters, and therefore has void in the prototype. It also does not return any values, giving it a type of void. Line 9 starts our main() function, which is very simple. First, printf() is called on line 11 to display the values of x and y, and then the demo() function is called. Notice that demo() declares its own local versions of x and y on line 20. Line 24 shows that the local variables take precedence over any others. After the demo function is called, line 13 again prints the values of x and y. Because you are no longer in demo(), the original global values are printed.

As you can see, local variables x and y in the function are totally independent from the global variables x and y declared outside the function. Three rules govern the use of variables in functions:

- To use a variable in a function, you must declare it in the function header or the function body (except for global variables, which are covered on Day 12).
- For a function to obtain a value from the calling program, the value must be passed as an argument.
- For a calling program to obtain a value from a function, the value must be explicitly returned from the function.

To be honest, these "rules" are not strictly applied because you learn how to get around them later in the book. However, follow these rules for now, and you should stay out of trouble.

Keeping the function's variables separate from other program variables is one way in which functions are independent. A function can perform any sort of data manipulation you want, using its own set of local variables. There's no worry that these manipulations have an unintended effect on another part of the program.

Function Statements

There is essentially no limitation on the statements that can be included within a function. The only thing you can't do inside a function is define another function. You can, however, use all other C statements, including loops (these are covered on Day 6, "Basic Program Control"), if statements, and assignment statements. You can call library functions and other user-defined functions.

What about function length? C places no length restriction on functions, but as a matter of practicality, you should keep your functions relatively short. Remember that in structured programming, each function is supposed to perform a relatively simple task. If you find a function getting long, perhaps you are trying to perform a task too complex for one function alone. It probably can be broken into two or more smaller functions.

How long is too long? There's no definite answer to that question, but in practical experience it's rare that you find a function longer than 25 to 30 lines of code. You have to use your own judgment. Some programming tasks require longer functions, whereas many functions are only a few lines. As you gain programming experience, you will become more adept at determining what should and should not be broken into smaller functions.

Returning a Value

To return a value from a function, you use the return keyword, followed by a C expression. When execution reaches a return statement, the expression is evaluated, and execution passes the value back to the calling program. The return value of the function is the value of the expression. Look at this function:

```
int func1(int var)
{
    int x;
    ...
    ...
    return x;
}
```

When this function is called, the statements in the function body execute up to the return statement. The return terminates the function and returns the value of x to the calling program. The expression that follows the return keyword can be any valid C expression.

A function can contain multiple return statements. The first return executed is the only one that has any effect. Multiple return statements are an efficient way to return different values from a function, as demonstrated in Listing 5.4.

Type

Listing 5.4. Demonstration of using multiple return statements in a function.

```
1:  /* Demonstrates using multiple return statements in a function. */
2:
3:  #include <stdio.h>
4:
5:  int x, y, z;
6:
7:  int larger_of( int , int );
8:
9:  main()
10: {
11:     puts("Enter two different integer values: ");
12:     scanf("%d%d", &x, &y);
13:
14:     z = larger_of(x,y);
15:
16:     printf("\nThe larger value is %d.", z);
17: }
18:
19: int larger_of( int a, int b)
20: {
21:     if (a > b)
22:         return a;
23:     else
24:         return b;
25: }
```

5

```
Enter two different integer values:
200 300

The larger value is 300.

Enter two different integer values:
300
200

The larger value is 300.
```

As in other examples, Listing 5.4 starts with a comment to describe what the program does (line 1). The STDIO.H header file is included for the standard input/output functions that enable the program to display information to the screen and get user input. Line 7 is the function prototype for larger_of(). Notice that it takes two int variables for parameters and returns an int. Line 14 calls larger_of() with x and y. The function larger_of() has the multiple return statements. Using an if statement, the function checks to see whether a is bigger than b on line 21. If it is, line 22 executes a return statement and the function immediately ends. Lines 23 and 24 are ignored in this case. If a is not bigger than b, line 22 is skipped, the else clause is instigated, and the return on line 24 executes. You should be able to see that, depending on the arguments passed to the function larger_of(), either the first or the second return statement is executed, and the appropriate value is passed back to the calling function.

One final note on this program. Line 11 is a new function that you have not seen before. puts()—read *put string*—is a simple function that displays a string to the standard output, usually the computer screen. (Strings are covered on Day 10, "Characters and Strings"; for now, know that they are just quoted text.)

Remember that a function's return value has a type that is specified in the function header and function prototype. The value returned by the function must be of the same type or the compiler generates an error message.

The Function Prototype

A program must include a prototype for each function that it uses. You saw an example of a function prototype on line 4 of Listing 5.1, and there have been function prototypes in the other listings as well. What is a function prototype, and why is it needed?

You can see from the earlier examples that the prototype for a function is identical to the function header, with a semicolon added at the end. Like the function header, the function prototype includes information about the function's return type, name, and parameters. The prototype's job is to tell the compiler about the function's return type, name, and parameters. With this information, the compiler can check every time your source code calls the function and verify that you are passing the correct number and type of arguments to the function and using the return value correctly. If there's a mismatch, the compiler generates an error message.

Strictly speaking, a function prototype need not exactly match the function header. The parameter names can be different, as long as they are the same type, number, and in the same order. There's no reason for the header and prototype not to match; having them identical makes source code easier to understand. Matching the two also makes writing a program easier. When you complete a function definition, use your editor's cut-and-paste feature to copy the function header and create the prototype. Be sure to add a semicolon at the end.

Where should function prototypes be placed in your source code? They must be placed before the start of `main()` or before the first function is defined. For readability, it's best to group all prototypes together in one location.

DO	DON'T

DON'T try to return a value that has a different type than the function's type.

DO use local variables whenever possible.

DON'T let functions get too long. If a function starts getting long, try to break it into separate, smaller tasks.

DO limit each function to a single task.

DON'T have multiple `return` statements if they are not needed. You should try to have one `return` when possible; however, sometimes having multiple `return` statements is easier and clearer.

Passing Arguments to a Function

To pass arguments to a function, you list them in parentheses following the function name. The number of arguments and the type of each argument must match the parameters in the function header and prototype. For example, if a function is defined to take two type `int` arguments, you must pass it exactly two `int` arguments—no more, no less—and no other type. If you try to pass a function an incorrect number and/or type of arguments, the compiler detects it, based on the information in the function prototype.

If the function takes multiple arguments, the arguments listed in the function call are assigned to the function parameters in order: the first argument to the first parameter, the second argument to the second parameter, and so on, as illustrated in Figure 5.5.

Each argument can be any valid C expression: a constant, a variable, a mathematical or logical expression, or even another function (one with a return value). For example, if `half()`, `square()`, and `third()` are all functions with return values, you could write

```
x = half(third(square(half(y))));
```

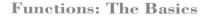
Figure 5.5.

Multiple arguments are assigned to function parameters in order.

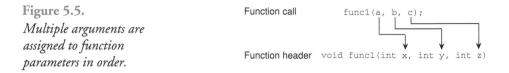

The program first calls `half()`, passing it y as an argument. When execution returns from `half()`, the program calls `square()`, passing `half()`'s return value as an argument. Next, `third()` is called with `square()`'s return value as the argument. Then, `half()` is called again, this time with `third()`'s return value as an argument. Finally, `half()`'s return value is assigned to the variable x. The following is an equivalent piece of code:

```
a = half(y);
b = square(a);
c = third(b);
x = half(c);
```

Calling Functions

There are two ways to call a function. Any function can be called by simply using its name and argument list alone in a statement, as in the following example. If the function has a return value, it is discarded.

```
wait(12);
```

The second method can be used only with functions that have a return value. Because these functions evaluate to a value (that is, their return value), they are valid C expressions and can be used anywhere a C expression can be used. You've already seen an expression with a return value used as the right side of an assignment statement. Here are some more examples.

In this example, `half_of()` is a parameter of a function:

```
printf("Half of %d is %d.", x, half_of(x));
```

First, the function `half_of()` is called with the value of x, and then `printf()` is called using the values x and `half_of(x)`.

For this second example, multiple functions are being used in an expression:

```
y = half_of(x) + half_of(z);
```

Although `half_of()` is used twice, the second call could have been any other function. The following code shows the same statement, but not all on one line:

```
a - half_of(x);
b = half_of(z);
y = a + b;
```

The final two examples show effective ways to use the return values of functions. Here a function is being used with the `if` statement:

```
if ( half_of(x) > 10 )
{
    statements;                /* this could be any statements! */
}
```

If the return value of the function meets the criteria (in this case, if `half_of()` returns a value greater than 10), the `if` statement is true, and its statements are executed. If the returned value does not meet the criteria, the `if`'s statements are not executed.

The following example is even better:

```
if ( do_a_process() != OKAY )
{
    statements;                   /* do error routine */
}
```

Again, I have not given the actual statements, nor is `do_a_process()` a real function; however, this is an important example that checks the return value of a process to see whether it did not run all right. If it didn't, the statements take care of any error handling or cleanup. This is used commonly with accessing information in files, comparing values, and allocating memory.

If you try to use a function with a `void` return type as an expression, the compiler generates an error message.

DO	DON'T
DO pass parameters to functions in order to make the function generic and thus reusable.	
DO take advantage of the ability to put functions into expressions.	
DON'T make an individual statement confusing by putting a bunch of functions in it. Only put functions into your statements if they don't make the code more confusing.	

Recursion

The term *recursion* refers to a situation where a function calls itself either directly or indirectly. *Indirect recursion* occurs when one function calls another function that then calls the first function. C allows recursive functions, and they can be useful in some situations.

For example. recursion can be used to calculate the factorial of a number. The factorial of a number x is written x!, and is calculated as follows:

```
x! = x * (x-1) * (x-2) * (x-3) .... * (2) * 1
```

However, you also can calculate x! like this:

```
x! = x * (x-1)!
```

Going one step further, you can calculate (x-1)! by the same procedure:

```
(x-1)! = (x-1) * (x-2)!
```

You can continue calculating recursively until you're down to a value of 1, in which case, you're finished. The program in Listing 5.5 uses a recursive function to calculate factorials. Because the program uses unsigned integers, it's limited to an input value of 8; the factorial of 9 and larger values are outside the allowed range for integers.

Type

Listing 5.5. Using a recursive function to calculate factorials.

```
1:   /* Demonstrates function recursion. Calculates the */
2:   /* factorial of a number. */
3:
4:   #include <stdio.h>
5:
6:   unsigned int f, x;
7:   unsigned int factorial(unsigned int a);
8:
9:   void main()
10:  {
11:      puts("Enter an integer value between 1 and 8: ");
12:      scanf("%d", &x);
13:
14:      if( x > 8 ¦¦ x < 1)
15:      {
16:          printf("Only values from 1 to 8 are acceptable!");
17:      }
18:      else
19:      {
20:          f = factorial(x);
21:          printf("%u factorial equals %u", x, f);
22:      }
23:  }
24:
25:  unsigned int factorial(unsigned int a)
26:  {
27:      if (a == 1)
28:          return 1;
29:      else
30:      {
31:          a *= factorial(a-1);
32:          return a;
33:      }
34:  }
```

Input Output

```
Enter an integer value between 1 and 8:
6
6 factorial equals 720
```

Analysis

The first half of this program is like many of the other programs you have worked with so far. It starts with comments on lines 1 and 2. On line 4, the appropriate header file is included for the input/output routines. Line 6 declares a couple of unsigned integer values. Line 7 is a function prototype for the factorial function. Notice that it takes an unsigned int as its parameter and returns an unsigned int. Lines 9–23 are the main() function. Lines 11 and 12 print a message asking for a value from 1 to 8, and then accept an entered value.

Lines 14–22 show an interesting if statement. Because a value greater than 8 causes a problem, this if statement checks the value. If it is greater than 8, an error message is printed; otherwise, the program figures the factorial on line 20 and prints the result on line 21. When you know there could be a problem, such as a limit on the size of a number, add code to detect the problem and prevent it.

Our recursive function, factorial(), is located on lines 14–22. The value passed is assigned a. On line 27, the value of a is checked. If it is 1, the program returns the value of 1. If the value is not 1, a is set equal to itself times the value of factorial(a-1). The program calls the factorial function again, but this time the value of a is (a-1). If (a-1) is not equal to 1, factorial() is called again with ((a-1)-1), which is the same as (a-2). This process continues until the if statement on line 27 is true. If the value of the factorial is 3, the factorial is evaluated to the following:

```
3 * (3-1) * ((3-1)-1)
```

DO	DON'T
DO understand and work with recursion before you use it. **DON'T** use recursion if there will be several iterations. (An iteration is the repetition of a program statement.) Recursion uses many resources because the function has to remember where it is.	

5

Where Functions Belong

You may be wondering where in your source code you should place your function definitions. For now, they should go in the same source code file as main() and after the end of main(). The basic structure of a program that uses functions is shown in Figure 5.6.

Figure 5.6.

*Place your function proto-
types before* main() *and your
function definitions after*
main().

```
/*  start of source code *
    ...
    prototypes here
    ...
    main()
    {
        ...
        ...
    }
    func1()
    {
        ...
    }
    func2()
    {
        ...
    }
/*  end of source code *
```

You can keep your user-defined functions in a separate source-code file, apart from main(). This technique is useful with large programs, and when you want to use the same set of functions in more than one program. This technique is discussed on Day 21, "Taking Advantage of Preprocessor Directives and More."

Summary

This chapter introduced you to functions, an important part of C programming. Functions are independent sections of code that perform specific tasks. When your program needs a task performed, it calls the function that performs that task. The use of functions is essential for structured programming—a method of program design that emphasizes a modular, top-down approach. Structured programming creates more efficient programs and also is much easier for you, the programmer, to use.

You learned, too, that a function consists of a header and body. The header includes information about the function's return type, name, and parameters. The body contains local variable declarations and the C statements that are executed when the function is called. Finally, you saw that local variables—those declared within a function—are totally independent from any other program variables declared elsewhere.

Q&A

Q What if I need to return more than one value from a function?

A Many times you will need to return more than one value from a function, or more commonly, you will want to change a value you send to the function and keep the change after the function ends. This is covered on Day 18, "Getting More from Functions."

Q How do I know what a good function name is?

A A good function name describes as specifically as possible what the function does.

Q When variables are declared at the top of the listing, before main(), they can be used anywhere, but local variables can only be used in the specific function. Why not just declare everything before main()?

A On Day 12, "Variable Scope," variable scope is discussed in more detail.

Q What other ways are there to use recursion?

A The factorial function is a prime example of using recursion. In many statistical calculations, the factorial number is needed. Recursion is just a loop; however, it has one difference from other loops. With recursion, each time a recursed function is called, a new set of variables is created. This is not true of the other loops that you will learn about in the next chapter.

Q Does main() have to be the first function in a program?

A No. It is a standard in C that the main() function is the first function to execute; however, it can be placed anywhere in your source file. Most people place it first so that it is easy to locate.

5

Workshop

The Workshop provides quiz questions to help you solidify your understanding of the material covered and exercises to provide you with experience in using what you've learned.

Quiz

1. Are you going to use structured programming when writing your C programs?
2. How does structured programming work?
3. How do C functions fit into structured programming?

4. What must be the first line of a function definition, and what information does it contain?

5. How many values can a function return?

6. If a function does not return a value, what type should it be declared?

7. What's the difference between a function definition and a function prototype?

8. What is a local variable?

9. How are local variables special?

Exercises

1. Write a header for a function named do_it() that takes three type char arguments and returns a type float to the calling program.

2. Write a header for a function named print_a_number() that takes a single type int argument and does not return anything to the calling program.

3. What type value do the following functions return?

   a. `int print_error( float err_nbr);`

   b. `long read_record( int rec_nbr, int size );`

4. **BUG BUSTER:** What is wrong with the following listing?

```
#include <stdio.h>
void print_msg( void );
main()
{
    print_msg( "This is a message to print" );
}

void print_msg( void )
{
    puts( "This is a message to print" );
    return 0;
}
```

5. **BUG BUSTER:** What is wrong with the following function definition?

```
int twice(int y);
{
    return (2 * y);
}
```

6. Rewrite Listing 5.4 so that it needs only one return statement.

7. Write a function that receives two numbers as arguments and returns the value of their product.

8. Write a function that receives two numbers as arguments. The function should divide the first number by the second. Don't divide by the second number if it is zero. (Hint: use an `if` statement.)

9. Write a function that calls the functions in exercises seven and eight.

10. Write a program that uses a function to find the average of five type `float` values entered by the user.

11. Write a recursive function to take the value 3 to the power of another number. For example, if 4 is passed, the function will return 81.

6

Basic Program
Control

Day 4, "Statements, Expressions, and Operators," covered the `if` statement, which gives you some control over the flow of your programs. Many times, though, you need more than just the ability to make true and false decisions. This chapter introduces three new ways to control the flow of the program. Today you learn

- How to use simple arrays
- How to use `for`, `while`, and `do...while` loops to execute statements multiple times
- How you can nest program control statements

This chapter is not intended to be a complete treatment of these topics, but we hope to provide enough information for you to be able to start writing real programs. These topics are covered in greater detail on Day 13, "More Program Control."

Arrays: The Basics

Before we cover the `for` statement, let's take a short detour and learn the basics of arrays. (See Day 8, "Numeric Arrays," for a complete treatment of arrays.) The `for` statement and arrays are closely linked in C, so it is difficult to define one without explaining the other. To help you understand the arrays used in the `for` statement examples to come, a quick treatment of arrays follows.

An *array* is an indexed group of data storage locations that have the same name and are distinguished from each other by a *subscript*, or *index*—a number following the variable name, enclosed in brackets. (This will become clearer as you continue.) Like other C variables, arrays must be declared. An array declaration includes both the data type and the size of the array (the number of elements in the array). For example, the following statement declares an array named `data` that is type `int` and has 1,000 elements:

```
int data[1000];
```

The individual elements are referred to by subscript as `data[0]` through `data[999]`. The first element is `data[0]`—not `data[1]`. In other languages, such as BASIC, the first element of an array is 1; this is not true in C.

Each element of this array is equivalent to a normal integer variable and can be used the same way. The subscript of an array can be another C variable, such as in this example:

```
int data[1000];
int count;
count = 100;
data[count] = 12;      /* The same as data[100] = 12 */
```

This has been a quick introduction to arrays. However, you now should be able to understand how arrays are used in the program examples later in this chapter. If every detail of arrays is not clear to you, don't worry. You can find more about arrays on Day 8.

DO	**DON'T**

DON'T declare arrays with subscripts larger than you will need; it wastes memory.

DON'T forget that in C, arrays are referenced starting with subscript 0, not 1.

Controlling Program Execution

The default order of execution in a C program is top-down. Execution starts at the beginning of the main() function and progresses, statement by statement, until the end of main() is reached. However, this order is rarely encountered in real C programs. The C language includes a variety of program control statements that enable you to control the order of program execution. You have already learned how to use C's fundamental decision operator, the if statement, so let's explore three additional control statements you will find useful.

The *for* Statement

The for statement is a C programming construct that executes a block of one or more statements a certain number of times. It is sometimes called the for *loop* because program execution typically loops through the statement more than one time. You've seen a few for statements used in programming examples earlier in this book. Now you're ready to see how the for statement works.

A for statement has the following structure:

```
for(initial; condition; increment)
    statement
```

initial, *condition*, and *increment* are all C expressions, and *statement* is a single or compound C statement. When a for statement is encountered during program execution, the following events occur:

1. The expression *initial* is evaluated. *initial* is usually an assignment statement that sets a variable to a particular value.

2. The expression *condition* is evaluated. *condition* is typically a relational expression.

3. If *condition* evaluates as false (that is, as zero), the for statement terminates, and execution passes to the first statement following *statement*.

6

4. If `condition` evaluates as true (that is, as nonzero), the C statement(s) in `statement` are executed.

5. The expression `increment` is evaluated, and execution returns to step 2.

The operation of a `for` statement is shown schematically in Figure 6.1. Please note that `statement` never executes if `condition` is false the first time it is evaluated.

Figure 6.1.
Schematic representation of a `for` *statement.*

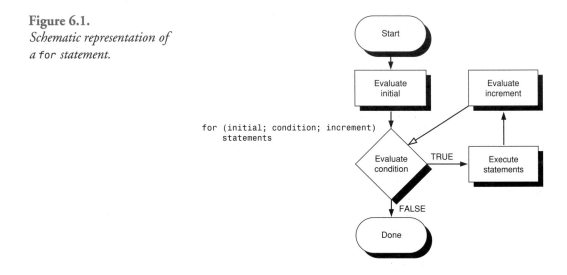

Here is a simple example. The program in Listing 6.1 uses a `for` statement to print the numbers 1 through 20. You can see that the resulting code is much more compact than it would be if a separate `printf()` statement were used for each of the 20 values.

Type

Listing 6.1. Demonstration of a simple for statement.

```
 1:   /* Demonstrates a simple for statement */
 2:
 3:   #include <stdio.h>
 4:
 5:   int count;
 6:
 7:   main()
 8:   {
 9:       /* Print the numbers 1 through 20 */
10:
11:       for (count = 1; count <= 20; count++)
12:           printf("\n%d", count);
13:   }
```

Output

```
1
2
3
4
5
6
7
8
9
10
11
12
13
14
15
16
17
18
19
20
```

Analysis

The diagram in Figure 6.2 illustrates the operation of the for loop in Listing 6.1.

Figure 6.2.
How the for loop in Listing 6.1 operates.

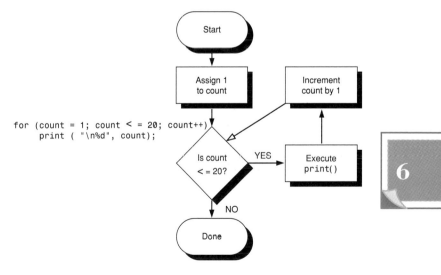

```
for (count = 1; count < = 20; count++)
    print ( "\n%d", count);
```

6

Line 3 includes the standard input/output header file. Line 5 declares a type int variable, named count, that will be used in the for loop. Lines 11 and 12 are the for loop. When the for statement is reached, the initial statement is executed first. In this listing, the initial statement is count = 1. This initializes count so that it can be used by the rest of the loop. The second step

in executing this `for` statement is the evaluation of the condition `count <= 20`. Because `count` was just initialized to 1, you know that it is less than 20, so the statement in the `for` command, the `printf()`, is executed. After executing the printing function, the increment expression, `count++`, is evaluated. This adds 1 to `count`, making it 2. Now the program loops back and checks the condition again. If it is true, the `printf()` reexecutes, the increment adds to `count` (making it 3), and the condition is checked. This loop continues until the condition evaluates to false, at which point the program exits the loop and continues to the next line (line 13), which in this listing ends the program.

The `for` statement is frequently used, as in the previous example, to "count up," incrementing a counter from one value to another. You also can use it to "count down," decrementing, rather than incrementing, the counter variable.

```
for (count = 100; count > 0; count--)
```

You also can "count by" a value other than 1, as in this example:

```
for (count = 0; count < 1000; count += 5)
```

The `for` statement is quite flexible. For example, you can omit the initialization expression if the test variable has been initialized previously in your program. (You still must use the semicolon separator, however, as shown.)

```
count = 1;
for ( ; count < 1000; count++)
```

The initialization expression need not be an actual initialization; it can be any valid C expression. Whatever it is, it is executed once when the `for` statement is first reached. For example, the following prints a statement, `Now sorting the array...`:

```
count = 1;
for (printf("Now sorting the array...") ; count < 1000; count++)
    /* Sorting statements here */
```

You also can omit the increment expression, performing the updating in the body of the `for` statement. The semicolon, again, must be included. To print the numbers from 0 to 99, for example, you could write

```
for (count = 0; count < 100; )
    printf("%d", count++);
```

The test expression that terminates the loop can be any C expression. As long as it evaluates as true (nonzero), the `for` statement continues to execute. You can use C's logical operators to construct complex test expressions. For example, the following `for` statement prints the elements of an array named `array[]`, stopping when all elements have been printed or an element with a value of 0 is encountered.

```
for (count = 0; count < 1000 && array[count] != 0; count++)
    printf("%d", array[count]);
```

You could simplify the previous `for` loop even further, writing it as follows. (If you don't understand the change made to the test expression, you need to review Day 4, "Statements, Expressions, and Operators.")

```
for (count = 0; count < 1000 && array[count]; )
    printf("%d", array[count++]);
```

You can follow the `for` statement with a null statement, enabling all the work to be done in the `for` statement itself. Remember, the null statement is a semicolon alone on a line. For example, to initialize all elements of a 1,000-element array to the value 50, you could write

```
for (count = 0; count < 1000; array[count++] = 50)
    ;
```

In this `for` statement, 50 is assigned to each member of the array by the increment part of the statement.

Day 4 mentioned that C's comma operator is most often used in `for` statements. You can create an expression by separating two subexpressions with the comma operator. The two subexpressions are evaluated (in left-to-right order), and the entire expression evaluates to the value of the right subexpression. By using the comma operator, you can make each part of a `for` statement perform multiple duty.

Imagine that you have two 1,000-element arrays, `a[]` and `b[]`. You want to copy the contents of `a[]` to `b[]` in reverse order so that after the copy operation, `b[0]` = `a[999]`, `b[1]` = `a[998]`, and so on. The following `for` statement does the trick:

```
for (i = 0, j = 999; i < 1000; i++, j--)
    b[j] = a[i];
```

The comma operator is used to initialize two variables, `i` and `j`. It also is used to increment part of these two variables with each loop.

Syntax

The *for* Statement

```
for (initial; condition; increment)
    statement(s)
```

initial is any valid C expression. It is usually an assignment statement that sets a variable to a particular value.

condition is any valid C expression. It is usually a relational expression. When *condition* evaluates to false (zero), the `for` statement terminates and execution passes to the first statement following *statement(s)*; otherwise, the C *statement(s)* in *statement(s)* are executed.

increment is any valid C expression. It is usually an expression that increments a variable initialized by the initial expression.

statement(s) are the C statements that are executed as long as the condition remains true.

6

A `for` statement is a looping statement. It can have an initialization, test condition, and increment as parts of its command. The `for` statement executes the initial expression first. It then checks the condition, and if the condition is true, the statements execute. Once the statements are completed, the increment expression is evaluated. The `for` statement then rechecks the condition and continues to loop until the condition is false.

Example 1

```
/* Prints the value of x as it counts from 0 to 9 */
int x;
for (x = 0; x <10; x++)
    printf( "\nThe value of x is %d", x );
```

Example 2

```
/*Obtains values from the user until 99 is entered */
int nbr = 0;
for ( ; nbr != 99; )
    scanf( "%d", &nbr );
```

Example 3

```
/* Enables user to enter up to 10 integer values      */
/* Values are stored in an array named value. If 99 is */
/* entered, the loop stops                             */

int value[10];
int ctr,nbr=0;
for (ctr = 0; ctr < 10 && nbr != 99; ctr++)
{
    puts("Enter a number, 99 to quit ");
    scanf("%d", &nbr);
    value[ctr] = nbr;
}
```

Nesting *for* Statements

A `for` statement can be executed within another `for` statement. This is called *nesting*. (You saw this on Day 4 with the `if` statement.) By nesting `for` statements, some complex programming can be done. Listing 6.2 is not a complex program, but it illustrates the nesting of two `for` statements.

Type **Listing 6.2. Demonstration of nested `for` statements.**

```
1:    /* Demonstrates nesting two for statements */
2:
3:    #include <stdio.h>
4:
5:    void draw_box( int, int);
6:
7:    main()
8:    {
```

```
9:      draw_box( 8, 35 );
10: }
11:
12: void draw_box( int row, int column )
13: {
14:     int col;
15:     for ( ; row > 0; row--)
16:     {
17:         for (col = column; col > 0; col--)
18:             printf("X");
19:
20:         printf("\n");
21:     }
22: }
```

```
XXXXXXXXXXXXXXXXXXXXXXXXXXXXXXXXXXXXX
XXXXXXXXXXXXXXXXXXXXXXXXXXXXXXXXXXXXX
XXXXXXXXXXXXXXXXXXXXXXXXXXXXXXXXXXXXX
XXXXXXXXXXXXXXXXXXXXXXXXXXXXXXXXXXXXX
XXXXXXXXXXXXXXXXXXXXXXXXXXXXXXXXXXXXX
XXXXXXXXXXXXXXXXXXXXXXXXXXXXXXXXXXXXX
XXXXXXXXXXXXXXXXXXXXXXXXXXXXXXXXXXXXX
XXXXXXXXXXXXXXXXXXXXXXXXXXXXXXXXXXXXX
```

Analysis The main work of this program is accomplished on line 18. When you run this program, 280 Xs are printed on the screen, forming an 8-by-35 square. The program has only one command to print an X, but it is nested in two loops.

In this listing, a function prototype for draw_box() is declared on line 5. This function takes two type int variables, row and column, which contain the dimensions of the box of Xs to be drawn. In line 9, main() calls draw_box() and passes the value 8 as the row and the value 35 as the column.

Looking closely at the draw_box() function, you might see a couple things you don't readily understand. The first is why the local variable col was declared. The second is why the second printf() in line 20 was used. Both of these will become clearer after looking at the two for loops.

Line 15 starts the first for loop. The initialization is skipped because the initial value of row was passed to the function. Looking at the condition, you see that this for loop is executed until the row is 0. On first executing line 15, row is 8; therefore, the program continues to line 17.

Line 17 contains the second for statement. Here the passed parameter, column, is copied to a local variable, col, of type int. The value of col is 35 initially (the value passed via column), and column retains its original value. Because col is greater than 0, line 18 is executed, printing an X. col is then decremented and the loop continues. When col is 0, the for loop ends and control goes to line 20. Line 20 causes the printing on the screen to start on a new line. (On Day 7, "Basic Input/Output," printing is covered in detail.) After moving to a new line on the screen, control reaches the end of the first for loop's statements, thus executing the increment expression, which subtracts 1 from row, making it 7. This puts control back at line 17. Notice

6

that the value of col was 0 when last used. If column had been used instead of col, it would fail the condition test because it will never be greater than 0. Only the first line would be printed. Take the initializer out of line 17 and change the two col variables to column to see what actually happens.

<table>
<tr><td>**DO**</td><td>**DON'T**</td></tr>
</table>

DON'T put too much processing in the for statement. Although you can use the comma separator, it is often clearer to put some of the functionality into the body of the loop.

DO remember the semicolon if you use a for with a null statement. Put the semicolon placeholder on a separate line or place a space between it and the end of the for statement.

```
for (count = 0; count < 1000; array[count] = 50) ;
    /* note space! */
```

The *while* Statement

The while statement, also called the while *loop,* executes a block of statements as long as a specified condition is true. The while statement has the following form:

```
while (condition)
    statement
```

This *condition* is any C expression, and *statement* is a single or compound C statement. When program execution reaches a while statement, the following events occur:

1. The expression *condition* is evaluated.
2. If *condition* evaluates as false (that is, as zero), the while statement terminates and execution passes to the first statement following *statement*.
3. If *condition* evaluates as true (that is, as nonzero), the C statement(s) in *statement* are executed.
4. Execution returns to step 1.

The operation of a while statement is diagrammed in Figure 6.3.

Listing 6.3 is a simple program that uses a while statement to print the numbers 1–20. (This is the same task that is performed by a for statement in Listing 6.1.)

Figure 6.3.

Schematic representation of the operation of a while *statement.*

```
while (condition)
    statements;
```

Listing 6.3. Demonstration of a simple while statement.

```
1:  /* Demonstrates a simple while statement */
2:
3:  #include <stdio.h>
4:
5:  int count;
6:
7:  int main()
8:  {
9:      /* Print the numbers 1 through 20 */
10:
11:     count = 1;
12:
13:     while (count <= 20)
14:     {
15:         printf("\n%d", count);
16:         count++;
17:     }
18:     return 0;
19: }
```

Output

```
1
2
3
4
5
6
7
8
9
10
11
12
13
14
15
```

115

```
16
17
18
19
20
```

Analysis

Examine Listing 6.3 and compare it with Listing 6.1, which uses a for statement to perform the same task. In line 11, count is initialized to 1. Because the while statement does not contain an initialize section, you must take care of initializing any variables before starting the while. Line 13 is the actual while statement, and it contains the same condition statement from Listing 6.1, count <= 20. In the while loop, line 16 takes care of incrementing count. What do you think would happen if you forgot to put line 16 in this program? Your program would not know when to stop because count would always be 1, which is always less than 20.

You might have noticed that a while statement is essentially a for statement without the initialization and increment components. Thus,

```
for ( ; condition ; )
```

is equivalent to

```
while (condition)
```

Because of this equivalence, anything that can be done with a for statement can also be done with a while statement. When you use a while statement, any needed initialization must first be performed in a separate statement, and the updating must be performed by a statement that is part of the while loop.

When initialization and updating are required, most experienced C programmers prefer to use a for statement rather than a while statement. This preference is based primarily on source code readability. When you use a for statement, the initialization, test, and increment expressions are located together and are easy to find and modify. With a while statement, the initialization and update expressions are located separately and may be less obvious.

The *while* Statement

```
while (condition )
    statement(s)
```

condition is any valid C expression, usually a relational expression. When condition evaluates to false (zero), the while statement terminates and execution passes to the first statement following statement(s); otherwise, the first C statement in statement(s) is executed.

statement(s) is the C statement(s) that is executed as long as condition remains true.

A while statement is a C looping statement. It enables repeated execution of a statement or block of statements as long as the condition remains true (nonzero). If the condition is not true when the while command is first executed, the statement(s) is never executed.

Example 1

```
int x = 0;
while (x < 10)
{
    printf("\nThe value of x is %d", x );
    x++;
}
```

Example 2

```
/* get numbers until you get one greater than 99 */
int nbr=0;
while (nbr <= 99)
    scanf("%d", &nbr );
```

Example 3

```
/* Enables user to enter up to 10 integer values    */
/* Values are stored in an array named value. If 99 is */
/* entered, the loop stops                 */
int value[10];
int ctr = 0;
int nbr;
while (ctr < 10 && nbr != 99)
{
    puts("Enter a number, 99 to quit ");
    scanf("%d", &nbr);
    value[ctr] = nbr;
    ctr++;
}
```

Nesting *while* Statements

Just like the for and if statements, while statements can also be nested. Listing 6.4 shows an example of nested while statements. Although this is not the best use of a while statement, the example does present some new ideas.

Type

Listing 6.4. Demonstration of nested while statements.

```
1:    /* Demonstrates nested while statements */
2:
3:    #include <stdio.h>
4:
5:    int array[5];
6:
7:    main()
8:    {
9:       int ctr = 0,
10:          nbr = 0;
11:
```

6

continues

Listing 6.4. continued

```
12:        printf("This program prompts you to enter 5 numbers\n");
13:        printf("Each number should be from 1 to 10\n");
14:
15:        while ( ctr < 5 )
16:        {
17:            nbr = 0;
18:            while (nbr < 1 ¦¦ nbr > 10)
19:            {
20:                printf("\nEnter number %d of 5: ", ctr + 1 );
21:                scanf("%d", &nbr );
22:            }
23:
24:            array[ctr] = nbr;
25:            ctr++;
26:        }
27:
28:        for (ctr = 0; ctr < 5; ctr++)
29:            printf("\nValue %d is %d", ctr + 1, array[ctr] );
30:    }
```

```
This program prompts you to enter 5 numbers
Each number should be from 1 to 10

Enter number 1 of 5: 3

Enter number 2 of 5: 6

Enter number 3 of 5: 3

Enter number 4 of 5: 9

Enter number 5 of 5: 2

Value 1 is 3
Value 2 is 6
Value 3 is 3
Value 4 is 9
Value 5 is 2
```

Analysis As in previous listings, line 1 contains a comment with a description of the program, and line 3 contains a #include statement for the standard input/output header file. Line 5 contains a declaration for an array (named array) that can hold 5 integer values. The function main() contains two additional local variables, ctr and nbr (lines 9 and 10). Notice that these variables are initialized to zero at the same time they are declared. Also notice that the comma operator is used as a separator at the end of line 9, enabling nbr to be declared as an int without restating the int type command. Stating declarations in this manner is a common practice for many C programmers. Lines 12 and 13 print messages stating what the program does and what is expected of the user. Lines 15–26 contain the first while command and its statements. Lines 18–22 also contain a nested while loop with its own statements that are all part of the outer while.

This outer loop continues to execute while `ctr` is less than 5 (line 15). As long as `ctr` is less than 5, line 17 sets `nbr` to 0, lines 18–22 (the nested `while` statement) gather a number in variable `nbr`, line 24 places the number in `array`, and line 25 increments `ctr`. Then the loop starts again. Therefore, the outer loop gathers five numbers and places each into `array`, indexed by `ctr`.

The inner loop is a good use of a `while` statement. Only the numbers from 1 to 10 are valid, so until the user enters a valid number, there is no point continuing the program. Lines 18–22 prevent continuation. This `while` statement states that while the number is less than 1 or while it is greater than 10, the program should print a message to enter a number, and then get the number.

Lines 28 and 29 print the values that are stored in `array`. Notice that because the `while` statements are done with the variable `ctr`, the `for` command can reuse it. Starting at zero and incrementing by one, the `for` loops five times, printing the value of `ctr` plus one (because the count started at zero), and printing the corresponding value in `array`.

For additional practice, there are two things you can change in this program. The first is the values that are accepted by the program. Instead of 1 to 10, try making it accept from 1 to 100. You can also change the number of values that it accepts. Currently it allows for five numbers. Try making it accept 10.

DO	DON'T

DON'T use the following convention if it is not necessary:

```
while (x)
```

Instead, use this convention:

```
while (x != 0)
```

Although both work, the second is clearer when debugging the code. When compiled, these produce virtually the same code.

DO use the `for` statement instead of the `while` statement if you need to initialize and increment within your loop. The `for` statement keeps the initialization, condition, and increment statements all together. The `while` statement does not.

The *do...while* Loop

C's third loop construct is the `do...while` loop, which executes a block of statements as long as a specified condition is true. The `do...while` loop tests the condition at the end of the loop rather than at the beginning as is done by the `for` loop and the `while` loop.

The structure of the `do...while` loop is as follows:

```
do
    statement
while (condition);
```

`condition` is any C expression, and `statement` is a single or compound C statement. When program execution reaches a `do...while` statement, the following events occur:

1. The statements in `statement` are executed.

2. `condition` is evaluated. If it is true, execution returns to step one. If it is false, the loop terminates.

The operation of a `do...while` loop is shown schematically in Figure 6.4.

Figure 6.4.
The operation of a
`do...while` *loop.*

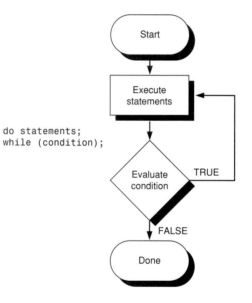

```
do statements;
while (condition);
```

The statements associated with a `do...while` loop are always executed at least once. This is because the test condition is evaluated at the end, instead of the beginning, of the loop. In contrast, `for` loops and `while` loops evaluate the test condition at the start of the loop, and so the associated statements are not executed at all if the test condition is initially false.

The `do...while` loop is used less frequently than `while` and `for` loops. It is most appropriate when the statement(s) associated with the loop must be executed at least once. You could, of course, accomplish the same thing with a `while` loop by making sure that the test condition is true when execution first reaches the loop. A `do...while` loop probably would be more straightforward, however.

Listing 6.5 shows an example of a `do...while` loop.

Type
Listing 6.5. Demonstration of a simple do...while loop.

```c
1:  /* Demonstrates a simple do...while statement */
2:
3:  #include <stdio.h>
4:
5:  int get_menu_choice( void );
6:
7:  main()
8:  {
9:      int choice;
10:
11:     choice = get_menu_choice();
12:
13:     printf("You chose Menu Option %d", choice );
14: }
15:
16: int get_menu_choice( void )
17: {
18:     int selection = 0;
19:
20:     do
21:     {
22:         printf("\n" );
23:         printf("\n1 - Add a Record" );
24:         printf("\n2 - Change a record");
25:         printf("\n3 - Delete a record");
26:         printf("\n4 - Quit");
27:         printf("\n" );
28:         printf("\nEnter a selection: " );
29:
30:         scanf("%d", &selection );
31:
32:       }while ( selection < 1 || selection > 4 );
33:
34:       return selection;
35: }
```

6

Input Output

```
1 - Add a Record
2 - Change a record
3 - Delete a record
4 - Quit

Enter a selection: 8


1 - Add a Record
2 - Change a record
3 - Delete a record
4 - Quit

Enter a selection: 4
You chose Menu Option 4
```

This program provides a menu with four choices. The user selects one of the four choices, and then the program prints the number selected. Programs later in this book use and expand on this concept. For now, you should be able to follow most of the listing. The main() function (lines 7–14) adds nothing to what you already know.

> **Note:** All of main() could have been written into one line, like this:
>
> ```
> printf( "You chose Menu Option %d", get_menu_option() );
> ```
>
> If you were to expand this program and act on the selection, you would need the value returned by get_menu_choice(), so it is wise to assign the value to a variable (such as choice).

Lines 16–35 contain get_menu_choice(). This function displays a menu on the screen (lines 22–28), and then gets a selection. Because you have to display a menu at least once to get an answer, it is appropriate to use a do...while loop. In the case of this program, the menu is displayed until a valid choice is entered. Line 32 contains the while part of the do...while statement and validates the value of the selection, appropriately named selection. If the value entered is not between 1 and 4, the menu is redisplayed and the user is prompted for a new value. When a valid selection is entered, the program continues to line 34, which returns the value in the variable selection.

The *do_while* Statement

```
do
{
    statement(s)
}while (condition);
```

condition is any valid C expression, usually a relational expression. When *condition* evaluates to false (zero), the while statement terminates and execution passes to the first statement following the while statement; otherwise, the program loops back to the do, and the C statement(s) in *statement(s)* are executed.

statement(s) is either a single C statement or a block of statements that are executed the first time through the loop and then as long as *condition* remains true.

A do...while statement is a C looping statement. It allows repeated execution of a statement or block of statements as long as the condition remains true (nonzero). Unlike the while statement, a do...while loop executes its statements at least once.

Example 1

```
/* prints even though condition fails! */
int x = 10;
do
{
    printf("\nThe value of x is %d", x );
}while (x != 10);
```

Example 2

```
/* gets numbers until the number is greater than 99 */
int nbr;
do
{
    scanf("%d", &nbr );
}while (nbr <= 99);
```

Example 3

```
/* Enables user to enter up to 10 integer values     */
/* Values are stored in an array named value. If 99 is */
/*    entered, the loop stops                          */
int value[10];
int ctr = 0;
int nbr;
do
{
    puts("Enter a number, 99 to quit ");
    scanf( "%d", &nbr);
    value[ctr] = nbr;
    ctr++;
}while (ctr < 10 && nbr != 99);
```

Nested Loops

The term *nested loop* refers to a loop that is contained within another loop. You have seen examples of some nested statements. C places no limitations on the nesting of loops except that each inner loop must be enclosed completely in the outer loop; you cannot have overlapping loops. Thus, the following is not allowed:

```
for ( count = 1; count < 100; count++)
{
    do
    {
        /* the do...while loop */
} /* end of for loop */
    }while (x != 0);
```

If the do...while loop is placed entirely in the for loop, there is no problem.

```
for (count = 1; count < 100; count++)
{
    do
    {
        /* the do...while loop */
    }while (x != 0);
} /* end of for loop */
```

When you use nested loops, remember that changes made in the inner loop might affect the outer loop as well. Note, however, that the inner loop may be independent from any variables in the outer loop; in this example, they are not. In the previous example, if the inner do...while loop modifies the value of count, the number of times the outer for loop executes is affected.

Good indenting style makes code with nested loops easier to read. Each level of loop should be indented one step farther than the last level. This clearly labels the code associated with each loop.

DO	DON'T

DON'T try to overlap loops. You can nest them, but they must be entirely within each other.

DO use the do...while loop when you know that a loop should be executed at least once.

Summary

Now you are almost ready to start writing real C programs on your own.

C has three loop statements that control program execution: for, while, and do...while. Each of these constructs enables your program to execute a block of statements zero, one, or more than one time, based on the condition of certain program variables. Many programming tasks are well served by the repetitive execution allowed by these loop statements.

Although all three can be used to accomplish the same task, each is different. The for statement enables you to initialize, evaluate, and increment all in one command. The while statement operates as long as a condition is true. The do...while statement always executes its statements at least once and continues to execute them until a condition is false.

Nesting is the placing of one command within another. C allows for the nesting of any of its commands. Nesting the if statement was demonstrated on Day 4, "Statements, Expressions, and Operators." In this chapter, the for, while, and do...while statements were nested.

Q&A

Q How do I know which programming control statement to use, the `for`, the `while`, or the `do...while`?

A If you look at the syntax boxes provided, you can see that any of the three can be used to solve a looping problem. Each has a small twist to what it can do, however. The `for` statement is best when you know that you need to initialize and increment in your loop. If you only have a condition that you want to meet, and you are not dealing with a specific number of loops, `while` is a good choice. If you know that a set of statements needs to be executed at least once, a `do...while` might be best. Because all three can be used for most problems, the best course is to learn them all and then evaluate each programming situation to determine which is best.

Q How deep can I nest my loops?

A You can nest as many loops as you want. If your program requires you to nest more than two loops deep, consider using a function instead. You might find sorting through all those braces difficult, and a function is easier to follow in code.

Q Can I nest different loop commands?

A You can nest `if`, `for`, `while`, `do...while`, or any other command. You will find that many of the programs you try to write will require that you nest at least a few of these.

Workshop

The Workshop provides quiz questions to help you solidify your understanding of the material covered, and exercises to provide you with experience in using what you've learned.

Quiz

1. What is the index value of the first element in an array?
2. What is the difference between a `for` statement and a `while` statement?
3. What is the difference between a `while` statement and a `do...while` statement?
4. Is it true that a `while` statement can be used and still get the same results as coding a `for` statement?
5. What must be remembered when nesting statements?
6. Can a `while` statement be nested in a `do...while` statement?

Exercises

1. Write a declaration for an array that will hold 50 type `long` values.

2. Show a statement that assigns the value of 123.456 to the 50th element in the array from exercise 1.

3. What is the value of x when the following statement is complete?

   ```
   for (x = 0; x < 100, x++) ;
   ```

4. What is the value of `ctr` when the following statement is completed?

   ```
   for (ctr = 2; ctr < 10; ctr += 3) ;
   ```

5. How many `X`s does the following print?

   ```
   for (x = 0; x < 10; x++)
       for (y = 5; y > 0; y--)
           puts("X");
   ```

6. Write a `for` statement to count from 1 to 100 by 3s.

7. Write a `while` statement to count from 1 to 100 by 3s.

8. Write a `do...while` statement to count from 1 to 100 by 3s.

9. **BUG BUSTER:** What is wrong with the following code fragment?

   ```
   record = 0;
   while (record < 100)
   {
       printf( "\nRecord %d ", record );
       printf( "\nGetting next number..." );
   }
   ```

10. **BUG BUSTER:** What is wrong with the following code fragment? (`MAXVALUES` is not the problem!)

    ```
    for (counter = 1; counter < MAXVALUES; counter++);
        printf("\nCounter = %d", counter );
    ```

Basic Input/Output

In most programs you create, you will need to display information on the screen or read information from the keyboard. Many of the programs presented in earlier chapters performed these tasks, but you might not have understood exactly how. Today, you learn

- Something about C's input and output statements
- How to display information on the screen with the `printf()` and `puts()` library functions
- How to format the information that is displayed on the screen
- How to read data from the keyboard with the `scanf()` library function

This chapter is not intended to be a complete treatment of these topics, but provides enough information so that you can start writing real programs. These topics are covered in greater detail later in the book.

Displaying Information on the Screen

You will need most programs to display information on the screen. The two most frequently used ways to do this are with C's library functions `printf()` and `puts()`.

The *printf()* Function

The `printf()` function, part of the standard C library, is perhaps the most versatile way for a program to display data on the screen. You've already seen `printf()` used in many of the examples in this book. Now you need to see how `printf()` works.

Printing a text message on the screen is simple. Call the `printf()` function, passing the desired message enclosed in double quotation marks. For example, to display An error has occurred! on the screen, you write

```
printf("An error has occurred!");
```

In addition to text messages, however, you frequently need to display the value of program variables. This is a little more complicated than displaying only a message. For example, suppose you want to display the value of the numeric variable x on the screen, along with some identifying text. Furthermore, you want the information to start at the beginning of a new line. You could use the `printf()` function as follows:

```
printf("\nThe value of x is %d", x);
```

The resulting screen display, assuming the value of x is 12, would be

```
The value of x is 12
```

In this example, two arguments are passed to `printf()`. The first argument is enclosed in double quotation marks and is called the *format string*. The second argument is the name of the variable (x) containing the value to be printed.

A `printf()` format string specifies how the output is formatted. The three possible components of a format string are as follows:

- Literal text is displayed exactly as entered in the format string. In the example, characters starting with the T (in The) and up to, but not including, the % comprise a literal string.

- An *escape sequence* provides special formatting control. An escape sequence consists of the backslash (\) followed by a single character. In the previous example, \n is an escape sequence. It is called the *newline* character and means "move to the start of the next line." Escape sequences are also used to print certain characters. More escape sequences are listed in Table 7.1.

- A *conversion specifier* consists of the percent sign followed by a single character. In the example, the conversion specifier is %d. A conversion specifier tells `printf()` how to interpret the variable(s) being printed. The %d tells `printf()` to interpret the variable x as a signed decimal integer.

Table 7.1. The most frequently used escape sequences.

Sequence	Meaning
\a	Bell (alert)
\b	Backspace
\n	Newline
\t	Horizontal tab
\\	Backslash
\?	Question mark
\'	Single quotation

The *printf()* Escape Sequences

Now look at the format string components in more detail. Escape sequences are used to control the location of output by moving the screen cursor. They are also used to print characters that would otherwise have a special meaning to `printf()`. For example, to print a single backslash character, include a double backslash (\\) in the format string. The first backslash tells `printf()`

that the second backslash is to be interpreted as a literal character, not the start of an escape sequence. In general, the backslash tells `printf()` to interpret the next character in a special manner. Here are some examples:

Sequence	Meaning
n	The character *n*
\n	Newline
\"	The double quotation character
"	The start or end of a string

Table 7.1 lists C's most commonly used escape sequences. A full list can be found on Day 15, "More on Pointers."

Listing 7.1 is a program that demonstrates some of the frequently used escape sequences.

Type

Listing 7.1. Using `printf()` escape sequences.

```
1:  /* Demonstration of frequently used escape sequences */
2:
3:  #include <stdio.h>
4:
5:  #define QUIT   3
6:
7:  int  get_menu_choice( void );
8:  void print_report( void );
9:
10: main()
11: {
12:     int choice = 0;
13:
14:     while (choice != QUIT)
15:     {
16:         choice = get_menu_choice();
17:
18:         if (choice == 1)
19:             printf("\nBeeping the computer\a\a\a" );
20:         else
21:         {
22:             if (choice == 2)
23:                 print_report();
24:         }
25:     }
26:     printf("You chose to quit!");
27: }
28:
29: int get_menu_choice( void )
30: {
31:     int selection = 0;
32:
33:     do
34:     {
```

```
35:         printf( "\n" );
36:         printf( "\n1 - Beep Computer" );
37:         printf( "\n2 - Display Report");
38:         printf( "\n3 - Quit");
39:         printf( "\n" );
40:         printf( "\nEnter a selection:" );
41:
42:         scanf( "%d", &selection );
43:
44:     }while ( selection < 1 ¦¦ selection > 3 );
45:
46:     return selection;
47: }
48:
49: void print_report( void )
50: {
51:     printf( "\nSAMPLE REPORT" );
52:     printf( "\n\nSequence\tMeaning" );
53:     printf( "\n=========\t=======" );
54:     printf( "\n\\a\t\tbell (alert)" );
55:     printf( "\n\\b\t\tbackspace" );
56:     printf( "\n...\t\t...");
57: }
```

```
1 - Beep Computer
2 - Display Report
3 - Quit

Enter a selection:1

Beeping the computer

1 - Beep Computer
2 - Display Report
3 - Quit

Enter a selection:2

SAMPLE REPORT
Sequence        Meaning
=========       =======
\a              bell (alert)
\b              backspace
...             ...

1 - Beep Computer
2 - Display Report
3 - Quit

Enter a selection:3

You chose to quit!
```

7

Analysis Listing 7.1 seems long compared with previous examples, but it offers some additions that are worth noting. The STDIO.H header was included in line 3 because printf() is used in this listing. In line 5, a constant named QUIT is defined. From Day 3, "Numeric Variables and Constants," you know that #define makes using the constant QUIT equivalent to using the value 3. Lines 7 and 8 are function prototypes. This program has two functions, get_menu_choice() and print_report(). get_menu_choice() is defined in lines 29–47. This is similar to the menu function in Listing 6.5. Lines 35 and 39 contain calls to printf() that print the newline escape sequence. Lines 36, 37, 38, and 40 also use the newline escape character, and they print text. Line 35 could have been eliminated by changing line 36 to the following:

```
printf( "\n\n1 - Beep Computer" );
```

However, leaving line 35 makes the program easier to read.

Looking at the main() function, you see the start of a while loop on line 14. The while loop's statements are going to keep looping as long as choice is not equal to QUIT. Because QUIT is a constant, you could have replaced it with 3; however, the program would not be as clear. Line 16 gets the variable choice, which is then analyzed in lines 18–25 in an if statement. If the user chooses 1, line 19 prints the newline character, a message, and then three beeps. If the user selects 2 on the menu, line 23 calls the function print_report().

print_report() is defined on lines 49–57. This simple function shows the ease of using printf() and the escape sequences to print formatted information to the screen. You've already seen the newline character. Lines 52 to 56 also use the tab escape character, \t. It lines the columns of the report vertically. Lines 54 and 55 might seem confusing at first, but if you start at the left and work right, they make sense. Line 54 prints a newline (\n), then a backslash (\), then the letter a, followed by two tabs (\t\t). The line ends with some descriptive text, (bell (alert)). Line 55 follows the same format.

This program prints the first two lines of Table 7.1, along with a report title and column headings. In exercise 9 at the end of the day, you will complete this program by making it print the rest of the table.

The *printf()* Conversion Specifiers

The format string must contain one conversion specifier for each printed variable. printf() then displays each variable as directed by its corresponding conversion specifier. You learn more about this process on Day 15. For now, be sure to use the conversion specifier that corresponds to the type of variable being printed.

What exactly does this mean? If you're printing a variable that is a *signed decimal integer* (types int and long), use the %d conversion specifier. For an *unsigned decimal integer* (types unsigned int and unsigned long), use %u. For a *floating-point variable* (types float and double), use the %f specifier. The conversion specifiers you need most often are listed in Table 7.2.

Table 7.2. The most commonly needed conversion specifiers.

Specifier	Meaning	Types Converted
%c	Single character	char
%d	Signed decimal integer	int, short, long
%f	Decimal floating-point number	float, double
%s	Character string	char arrays
%u	Unsigned decimal integer	unsigned int, unsigned short, unsigned long

The literal text of a format specifier is anything that doesn't qualify as either an escape sequence or a conversion specifier. Literal text is simply printed as is, including all spaces.

What about printing the values of more than one variable? A single `printf()` statement can print an unlimited number of variables, but the format string must contain one conversion specifier for each variable. The conversion specifiers are paired with variables in left-to-right order. If you write

```
printf("Rate = %f, amount = %d", rate, amount);
```

the variable `rate` is paired with the `%f` specifier, and the variable `amount` is paired with the `%d` specifier. The positions of the conversion specifiers in the format string determine the position of the output. If there are more variables passed to `printf()` than there are conversion specifiers, the unmatched variables are not printed. If there are more specifiers than variables, the unmatched specifiers print "garbage."

You are not limited to printing the value of variables with `printf()`. The arguments can be any valid C expression. For example, to print the sum of x and y you could write

```
z = x + y;
printf("%d", z);
```

You also could write

```
printf("%d", x + y);
```

Any program that uses `printf()` should include the header file STDIO.H. Listing 7.2 demonstrates the use of `printf()`. Day 15 gives more details on `printf()`.

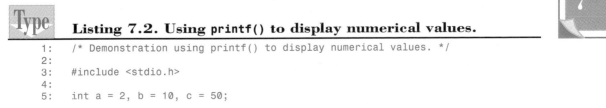

Type

Listing 7.2. Using `printf()` to display numerical values.

```
1:   /* Demonstration using printf() to display numerical values. */
2:
3:   #include <stdio.h>
4:
5:   int a = 2, b = 10, c = 50;
```

continues

Listing 7.2. continued

```
 6:    float f = 1.05, g = 25.5, h = -0.1;
 7:
 8:    main()
 9:    {
10:        printf("\nDecimal values without tabs: %d %d %d", a, b, c);
11:        printf("\nDecimal values with tabs: \t%d \t%d \t%d", a, b, c);
12:
13:        printf("\nThree floats on 1 line: \t%f\t%f\t%f", f, g, h);
14:        printf("\nThree floats on 3 lines: \n\t%f\n\t%f\n\t%f", f, g, h);
15:
16:        printf("\nThe rate is %f%%", f);
17:        printf("\nThe result of %f/%f = %f", g, f, g / f);
18:    }
```

```
Decimal values without tabs: 2 10 50
Decimal values with tabs:       2       10      50
Three floats on 1 line: 1.050000 25.500000 -0.100000
Three floats on 3 lines:
        1.050000
        25.500000
        -0.100000
The rate is 1.050000%
The result of 25.500000/1.050000 = 24.285715
```

Listing 7.2 prints six lines of information. Lines 10 and 11 each print three decimals, a, b, and c. Line 10 prints them without tabs, and line 11 prints them with tabs. Lines 13 and 14 each print three `float` variables, f, g, and h. Line 13 prints them on one line, and line 14 prints them on three lines. Line 16 prints out a `float` variable, f, followed by a percentage sign. Because a percentage sign is normally a message to print a variable, you must place two in a row to print a single percent sign. This is exactly like the backslash escape character. Line 17 shows one final concept. When printing values in conversion specifiers, you do not have to use variables. You can also use expressions such as g / f, or even constants.

DO	DON'T

DON'T try to put multiple lines of text into one `printf()` statement. In most instances, it is clearer to print multiple lines with multiple print statements than it is to use just one with several newline (\n) escape characters.

DON'T forget to use the newline escape character when printing multiple lines of information in separate `printf()` statements.

DON'T misspell `stdio.h`. Many C programmers accidentally type `studio.h`; however, there is no u.

Sams Learning Center

The *printf()* Function

```
#include <stdio.h>
printf( format-string[,arguments,...]);
```

printf() is a function that accepts a series of arguments, each applying to a *conversion specifier* in the given format string. printf() prints the formatted information to the standard output device, usually the display screen. When using printf(), you need to include the standard input/output header file, STDIO.H.

The *format-string* is required; however, arguments are optional. For each argument, there must be a conversion specifier. Table 7.2 lists the most commonly needed conversion specifiers.

The *format-string* also can contain escape sequences. Table 7.1 lists the most frequently used escape sequences.

The following are examples of calls to printf() and their output:

Example 1 Input

```
#include <stdio.h>
main()
{
    printf("This is an example of something printed!");
}
```

Example 1 Output

```
This is an example of something printed!
```

Example 2 Input

```
printf("This prints a character, %c\na number, %d\na floating \
point, %f", 'z', 123, 456.789 );
```

Example 2 Output

```
This prints a character, z
a number, 123
a floating point, 456.789
```

Displaying Messages with *puts()*

The puts() function also can be used to display text messages on the screen, but it cannot display numeric variables. puts() takes a single string as its argument and displays it, automatically adding a newline at the end. For example, the statement

```
puts("Hello, world.");
```

performs the same action as

```
printf("Hello, world.\n");
```

7

You can include escape sequences (including \n) in a string passed to puts(). They have the same effects as when they are used with printf() (see Table 7.1).

Any program that uses puts() should include the header file STDIO.H. Note that STDIO.H should be included only once in any program.

DO	**DON'T**

DO use the puts() function instead of the printf() function whenever you want to print text but don't need to print any variables.

DON'T try to use conversion specifiers with the puts() statement.

The *puts()* Function

```
#include <stdio.h>
puts( string );
```

puts() is a function that copies a string to the standard output device, usually the display screen. When you use puts(), include the standard input/output header file (STDIO.H). puts() also appends a newline character to the end of the string that is printed. The format string can contain escape sequences. Table 7.1, shown previously, lists the most frequently used escape sequences.

The following are examples of calls to puts() and their output:

Example 1 Input

```
puts("This is printed with the puts() function!");
```

Example 1 Output

```
This is printed with the puts() function!
```

Example 2 Input

```
puts("This prints on the first line. \nThis prints on the second line.");
puts("This prints on the third line.");
puts("If these were printf()s, all four lines would be on two lines!");
```

Example 2 Output

```
This prints on the first line.
This prints on the second line.
This prints on the third line.
If these were printf()s, all four lines would be on two lines!
```

Inputting Numeric Data with *scanf()*

Just as most programs need to output data to the screen, so also do they need to input data from the keyboard. The most flexible way your program can read numeric data from the keyboard is by using the scanf() library function.

The scanf() function reads data from the keyboard according to a specified format and assigns the input data to one or more program variables. Like printf(), scanf() uses a format string to describe the format of the input. The format string utilizes the same conversion specifiers as the printf() function. For example, the statement

```
scanf("%d", &x);
```

reads a decimal integer from the keyboard and assigns it to the integer variable x. Likewise, the following statement reads a floating-point value from the keyboard and assigns it to the variable rate:

```
scanf("%f", &rate);
```

What is the ampersand (&) doing before the variable's name? The & symbol is C's *address of* operator, which is fully explained on Day 9, "Pointers." For now, all you need to remember is that scanf() requires the & symbol before each numeric variable name in its argument list (unless the variable is a *pointer,* which is also explained on Day 9).

A single scanf() can input more than one value if you include multiple conversion specifiers in the format string and variable names (again, each preceded by & in the argument list). The following statement inputs an integer value and a floating point value and assigns them to the variables x and rate, respectively:

```
scanf("%d %f", &x, &rate);
```

When multiple variables are entered, scanf() uses whitespace to separate input into fields. Whitespace can be spaces, tabs, or new lines. Each conversion specifier in the scanf() format string is matched with an input field; the end of each input field is identified by whitespace.

This gives you considerable flexibility. In response to the previous scanf(), you could enter

```
10 12.45
```

You also could enter this:

```
10                12.45
```

or this:

```
10
12.45
```

As long as there's some whitespace between values, scanf() can assign each value to its variable.

As with the other functions discussed in this chapter, programs that use scanf() must include the STDIO.H header file. Although Listing 7.3 gives an example of using scanf(), a more complete description is presented on Day 15.

Type

Listing 7.3. Using scanf() to obtain numerical values.

```
 1:    /* Demonstration on using scanf() */
 2:
 3:    #include <stdio.h>
 4:
 5:    #define QUIT 4
 6:
 7:    int get_menu_choice( void );
 8:
 9:    main()
10:    {
11:        int    choice   = 0;
12:        int    int_var  = 0;
13:        float float_var = 0.0;
14:        unsigned unsigned_var = 0;
15:
16:        while (choice != QUIT)
17:        {
18:            choice = get_menu_choice();
19:
20:            if (choice == 1)
21:            {
22:                puts("\nEnter a signed decimal integer (i.e. -123)");
23:                scanf("%d", &int_var);
24:            }
25:            if (choice == 2)
26:            {
27:                puts("\nEnter a decimal floating-point number\
28                 (i.e. 1.23)");
29:                scanf("%f", &float_var);
30:            }
31:            if (choice == 3)
32:            {
33:                puts("\nEnter an unsigned decimal integer \
34                 (i.e. 123)" );
35:                scanf( "%u", &unsigned_var );
36:            }
37:        }
38:        printf("\nYour values are: int: %d  float: %f  unsigned: %u ",
39:                               int_var, float_var, unsigned_var );
40:    }
41:
42:    int get_menu_choice( void )
43:    {
44:        int selection = 0;
45:
46:        do
47:        {
```

```
48:            puts( "\n1 - Get a signed decimal integer" );
49:            puts( "2 - Get a decimal floating-point number" );
50:            puts( "3 - Get an unsigned decimal integer" );
51:            puts( "4 - Quit" );
52:            puts( "\nEnter a selection:" );
53:
54:            scanf( "%d", &selection );
55:
56:        }while ( selection < 1 || selection > 4 );
57:
58:        return selection;
59:  }
```

```
1 - Get a signed decimal integer
2 - Get a decimal floating-point number
3 - Get an unsigned decimal integer
4 - Quit

Enter a selection:
1

Enter a signed decimal integer (i.e. -123)
-123

1 - Get a signed decimal integer
2 - Get a decimal floating-point number
3 - Get an unsigned decimal integer
4 - Quit

Enter a selection:
3

Enter an unsigned decimal integer (i.e. 123)
321

1 - Get a signed decimal integer
2 - Get a decimal floating-point number
3 - Get an unsigned decimal integer
4 - Quit

Enter a selection:
2

Enter a decimal floating point number (i.e. 1.23)
1231.123

1 - Get a signed decimal integer
2 - Get a decimal floating-point number
3 - Get an unsigned decimal integer
4 - Quit

Enter a selection:
4


Your values are: int: -123   float: 1231.123047 unsigned: 321
```

Listing 7.3 uses the same menu concepts that were used in Listing 7.1. The differences in get_menu_choice() (lines 42–59) are minor, but should be noted. First, puts() is used instead of printf(). Because no variables are printed, there is no need to use printf(). Because puts() is being used, the newline escape characters have been removed from lines 49–51. Line 56 was also changed to allow values from 1 to 4 because there are now four menu options. Notice that line 54 has not changed; however, now it should make a little more sense. scanf() gets a decimal value and places it in the variable selection. The function returns selection to the calling program in line 58.

Listings 7.1 and 7.3 use the same main() structure. An if statement evaluates choice, the return value of get_menu_choice(). Based on choice's value, the program prints a message, asks for a number to be entered, and reads the value with scanf(). Notice the difference between lines 23, 29, and 35. Each is set up to get a different type of variable. Lines 12–14 declare variables of the appropriate types.

When the user selects quit, the program prints the last-entered number for all three types. If the user did not enter a value, 0 is printed because lines 12, 13, and 14 initialized all three types. One final note on lines 20 through 36: The if statements used here are not structured well. If you are thinking that an if...else structure would have been better, you are correct. On Day 14, "Working with the Screen, Printer, and Keyboard," a new control statement, switch, is introduced. This statement would have been the best option.

DO	DON'T

DON'T forget to include the *address of* operator (&) when using scanf() variables.

DO use printf() or puts() in conjunction with scanf(). Use the printing functions to display a prompting message for the data you want scanf() to get.

Syntax

The *scanf()* Function

```
#include <stdio.h>
scanf( format-string[,arguments,...]);
```

scanf() is a function that uses a *conversion specifier* in a given *format-string* to place values into variable arguments. The arguments should be the addresses of the variables rather than the actual variables. For numeric variables, you can pass the address by adding the *address of* (&) operator at the beginning of the variable name. When using scanf(), you should include the STDIO.H header file.

scanf() reads input fields from the standard input stream, usually the keyboard. It places each of these read fields into an argument. When it places the information, it converts it to the format of the corresponding specifier in the format string. For each argument, there must be a conversion specifier. Table 7.3, shown previously, lists the most commonly needed conversion specifiers.

Example 1

```
int x, y, z;
scanf( "%d %d %d", &x, &y, &z);
```

Example 2

```
#include <stdio.h>
main()
{
    float y;
    int x;

    puts( "Enter a float, then an int" );
    scanf( "%f %d", &y, &x);
    printf( "\nYou entered %f and %d ", y, x );
}
```

Summary

With the completion of this chapter, you are ready to write your own C programs. By combining the printf(), puts(), and scanf() functions and the programming control you learned in earlier chapters, you have the tools needed to write simple programs.

Screen display is performed with the printf() and puts() functions. The puts() function can display text messages only, whereas printf() can display text messages and variables. Both functions use escape sequences for special characters and printing controls.

The scanf() function reads one or more numeric values from the keyboard and interprets each one according to a conversion specifier. Each value is assigned to a program variable.

Q&A

Q Why should I use puts() if printf() does everything puts() does and more?

A Because printf() does more, it has additional overhead. When you are trying to write a small efficient program or when your programs get big and resources are valuable, you will want to take advantage of the smaller overhead of puts(). In general, use the simplest available resource.

Q Why do I need to include STDIO.H when I use `printf()`, `puts()`, or `scanf()`?

A STDIO.H contains the prototypes for the standard input/output functions. `printf()`, `puts()`, and `scanf()` are three of these standard functions. Try running a program without the STDIO.H header and see the errors and warnings you get.

Q What happens if I leave the address of operator (&) off a `scanf()` variable?

A This is an easy mistake to make. Unpredictable results can occur if you forget the address of operator. When you read about pointers on Days 9 and 13, "Pointers" and "More Program Control," you will understand this better. For now know that if you omit the address of operator, `scanf()` doesn't place the entered information in your variable, but in some other place in memory. This could do anything from apparently having no effect at all to locking up your computer so that you have to reboot.

Workshop

The Workshop provides quiz questions to help you solidify your understanding of the material covered, and exercises to provide you with experience in using what you've learned.

Quiz

1. What is the difference between `puts()` and `printf()`?
2. What header file should be included when using `printf()`?
3. What do the following escape sequences do?

   a. `\\`

   b. `\b`

   c. `\n`

   d. `\t`

   e. `\a`

4. What conversion specifiers should be used to print the following?

   a. A character string

   b. A signed decimal integer

   c. A decimal floating-point number

5. What is the difference between using each of the following in the literal text of `puts()`?

   a. `b`

   b. `\b`

   c. `\`

   d. `\\`

Exercises

Note: Starting with this chapter, some of these exercises ask you to write complete programs that perform a particular task. Because there is always more than one way to do things in C, the answers provided at the back of the book should not be interpreted as the only correct ones. If you can write your own code that performs what's desired, that's great! If you have trouble, refer to the answer example for help. Those answers are presented with minimal comments; it's good practice for you to figure out how they operate.

1. Write both a `printf()` and a `puts()` statement to start a new line.

2. Write a `scanf()` statement that could be used to get a character, an unsigned decimal integer, and another single character.

3. Write the statements to get an integer value and print it.

4. Modify exercise 3 so that it accepts only even values (2, 4, 6, and so on).

5. Modify exercise 4 so that it returns values until the number 99 is entered, or until six even values have been entered. Store the numbers in an array. (Hint: You need a loop.)

6. Turn exercise 5 into an executable program. Add a function that prints the values, separated by tabs, in the array on a single line. (Print only the values that were entered into the array.)

7. **BUG BUSTER:** Find the error(s) in the following code fragment:

```
printf( "Jack said, "Peter Piper picked a peck of pickled
peppers."");
```

8. **BUG BUSTER:** Find the error(s) in the following program:

```
int get_1_or_2( void )
{
    int answer = 0;

    while (answer < 1 ¦¦ answer > 2)
    {
        printf(Enter 1 for Yes, 2 for No);
        scanf( "%f", answer );
    }
    return answer;
}
```

9. Using Listing 7.1, complete the `print_report()` function so that it prints the rest of Table 7.1.

10. Write a program that inputs two floating-point values from the keyboard, and then displays their product.

11. Write a program that inputs 10 integer values from the keyboard, and then displays their sum.

12. Write a program that inputs integers from the keyboard, storing them in an array. Input should stop when a zero is entered or when the end of the array is reached. Then, find and display the array's largest and smallest values. (Note: This is a tough problem because arrays haven't been completely covered yet. If you have difficulty, try to solve it again after reading Day 8, "Numeric Arrays.")

After finishing your first week of learning how to program in C, you should feel comfortable entering programs and using your editor and compiler. The following program pulls together many of the topics from the previous week.

Note: The numbers to the left of the line numbers indicate the chapter that covers the concept presented on that line. If you are confused by the line, refer to the referenced chapter for more information.

Listing R1.1. Week one's review listing.

```
CH02    1: /* Program Name: week1.c                                    */
        2: /*              program to enter the ages and incomes of up */
        3: /*              to 100 people.  The program prints a report */
        4: /*              based on the numbers entered.               */
        5: /*---------------------------------------------------------*/
        6: /*-------------------*/
        7: /* included files    */
        8: /*-------------------*/
CH02    9: #include <stdio.h>
       10:
CH02   11: /*-------------------*/
       12: /* defined constants */
       13: /*-------------------*/
       14:
CH03   15: #define MAX    100
       16: #define YES    1
       17: #define NO     0
       18:
CH02   19: /*-------------------*/
       20: /* variables         */
       21: /*-------------------*/
       22:
CH03   23: long   income[MAX]; /* to hold incomes      */
       24: int    month[MAX], day[MAX], year[MAX]; /* to hold birthdays */
       25: int    x, y, ctr;   /* For counters         */
       26: int    cont;  /* For program control */
       27: long   month_total, grand_total;  /* For totals       */
       28:
CH02   29: /*-------------------*/
       30: /* function prototypes*/
       31: /*-------------------*/
       32:
CH05   33: void main(void);
       34: int display_instructions(void);
       35: void get_data(void);
       36: void display_report(void);
       37: int continue_function(void);
       38:
       39: /*-------------------*/
       40: /* start of program  */
       41: /*-------------------*/
       42:
CH02   43: void main(void)
       44: {
CH05   45:    cont = display_instructions();
```

```
       46:
CH04   47:    if ( cont == YES )
       48:    {
CH05   49:        get_data();
CH05   50:        display_report();
       51:    }
CH04   52:    else
CH07   53:        printf( "\nProgram Aborted by User!\n\n");
       54: }
CH02   55: /*------------------------------------------------------------*
       56:  *  Function:  display_instructions()                         *
       57:  *  Purpose:   This function displays information on how to    *
       58:  *             use this program and asks the user to enter 0   *
       59:  *             to quit, or 1 to continue.                      *
       60:  *  Returns:   NO  - if the user enters 0                      *
       61:  *  YES - if the user enters any number other than 0          *
       62:  *------------------------------------------------------------*/
       63:
CH05   64: int display_instructions( void )
       65: {
CH07   66:    printf("\n\n");
       67:    printf("\nThis program enables you to enter up to 99 people\'s ");
       68:    printf("\nincomes and birthdays.  It then prints the incomes by");
       69:    printf("\nmonth along with the overall income and overall average.");
       70:    printf("\n");
       71:
CH05   72:    cont = continue_function();
       73:
CH05   74:    return( cont );
       75: }
CH02   76:  /*-----------------------------------------------------------*
       77:  *  Function:  get_data() *
       78:  *  Purpose: This function gets the data from the user. It     *
       79:  *           continues to get data until either 100 people are *
       80:  *           entered, or until the user enters 0 for the month.*
       81:  *  Returns: nothing *
       82:  *  Notes:   This allows 0/0/0 to be entered for birthdays in   *
       83:  *           case the user is unsure.  It also allows for 31    *
       84:  *           days in each month.                               *
       85:  *-----------------------------------------------------------*/
       86:
CH05   87: void get_data(void)
       88: {
CH06   89:    for ( cont = YES, ctr = 0; ctr < MAX && cont == YES; ctr++ )
       90:    {
CH07   91:        printf("\nEnter information for Person %d.", ctr+1 );
       92:        printf("\n\tEnter Birthday:");
       93:
CH06   94:        do
       95:        {
CH07   96:            printf("\n\tMonth (0 - 12): ");
CH07   97:            scanf("%d", &month[ctr]);
```

continues

Listing R1.1. continued

```
CH06    98:            }while (month[ctr] < 0 || month[ctr] > 12 );
        99:
CH06    100:      do
        101:      {
CH07    102:          printf("\n\tDay (0 - 31): ");
CH07    103:          scanf("%d", &day[ctr]);
CH06    104:      }while ( day[ctr] <  0 || day[ctr] > 31 );
        105:
CH06    106:      do
        107:      {
CH07    108:          printf("\n\tYear (0 - 1994): ");
CH07    109:          scanf("%d", &year[ctr]);
CH06    110:      }while ( year[ctr] < 0 || year[ctr] > 1994 );
        111:
CH07    112:      printf("\nEnter Yearly Income (whole dollars): ");
CH07    113:      scanf("%ld", &income[ctr]);
        114:
CH05    115:      cont = continue_function();
        116:   }
CH07    117:   /* ctr equals the number of people that were entered.   */
        118: }
CH02    119: /*-----------------------------------------------------------*
        120:  *  Function: display_report()                               *
        121:  *  Purpose:  This function displays a report to the screen  *
        122:  *  Returns:  nothing                                        *
        123:  *  Notes:    More information could be printed.             *
        124:  *-----------------------------------------------------------*/
        125:
CH05    126: void display_report()
        127: {
CH04    128:    grand_total = 0;
CH07    129:    printf("\n\n\n");                    /* skip a few lines    */
        130:    printf("\n         SALARY SUMMARY");
        131:    printf("\n         ==============");
        132:
CH06    133:    for( x = 0; x <= 12; x++ )   /* for each month, including 0*/
        134:      {
        135:          month_total = 0;
CH04    136:      for( y = 0; y < ctr; y++ )
CH06    137:      {
        138:          if( month[y] == x )
CH04    139:              month_total += income[y];
CH04    140:      }
        141:      printf("\nTotal for month %d is %ld", x, month_total);
CH07    142:      grand_total += month_total;
CH04    143:    }
        144:    printf("\n\nReport totals:");
CH07    145:    printf("\nTotal Income is %ld", grand_total);
        146:    printf("\nAverage Income is %ld", grand_total/ctr );
        147:
        148:    printf("\n\n* * * End of Report * * *");
        149: }
CH02    150: /*-----------------------------------------------------------*
        151:  * Function: continue_function()                             *
```

```
152:  * Purpose:  This function asks the user if they wish to continue.*
153:  * Returns:  YES - if user wishes to continue               *
154:  *           NO - if user wishes to quit                    *
155:  *---------------------------------------------------------------*/
156:
157: int continue_function( void )
158: {
159:     printf("\n\nDo you wish to continue? (0=NO/1=YES): ");
160:     scanf( "%d", &x );
161:
162:     while( x < 0 || x > 1 )
163:         {
164:         printf("\n%d is invalid!", x);
165:         printf("\nPlease enter 0 to Quit or 1 to Continue: ");
166:         scanf("%d", &x);
167:         }
168:     if(x == 0)
169:         return(NO);
170:     else
171:         return(YES);
172: }
```

CH05 157:
CH07 159:
CH06 162:
CH07 164:
CH04 168:
CH05 169:
CH04 170:
CH05 171:

Analysis After completing the quizzes and exercises on Day 1, "Getting Started," and Day 2, "The Components of a C Program," you should be able to enter and compile this program. This program contains more comments than other listings throughout this book. These comments are typical of a "real-world" C program. In particular, you should notice the comments at the beginning of the program and before each major function. The comments on lines 1–5 contain an overview of the entire program, including the program name. Some programmers also include information such as the author of the program, the compiler used, its version number, the libraries linked into the program, and the date the program was created. The comments before each function describe the purpose of the function, possible return values, the function's calling conventions, and anything relating specifically to that function.

The comments on lines 1–5 specify that you can enter information in this program for up to 100 people. Before you can enter the data, the program calls display_instructions() (line 45). This function displays instructions for using the program, asking you whether you want to continue or quit. On lines 66–70, you can see that this function uses the printf() function from Day 7, "Basic Input/Output," to display the instructions.

On lines 157–172, continue_function() uses some of the features covered at the end of the week. The function asks whether you want to continue (line 159). Using the while control statement from Day 6, "Basic Program Control," the function verifies that the answer entered was a 0 or a 1. As long as the answer is not one of these two values, the function keeps prompting for a response. Once the program receives an appropriate answer, an if...else statement (Day 4, "Statements, Expressions, and Operators") returns a constant variable of either YES or NO.

The heart of this program lies in two functions: get_data() and display_report(). The get_data() function prompts you to enter data, placing the information into the arrays declared near the beginning of the program. Using a for statement on line 89, you are prompted to enter data until cont is not equal to the defined constant YES (returned from continue_function()) or the counter, ctr, is greater than or equal to the maximum number of array elements, MAX. This program checks each piece of information entered to ensure that it is appropriate. For example, lines 94–98 prompt you to enter a month. The only values that the program accepts are 0–12. If you enter a number greater than 12, the program prompts for the month again. Line 115 calls continue_function() to check whether you want to continue adding data.

When you respond to the continue function with a 0, or the maximum number of sets of information is entered (MAX sets), the program returns to line 50 in main() where it calls display_report(). The display_report() function on lines 119–149 prints a report to the screen. This report uses a nested for loop to total incomes for each month and a grand total for all the months. This report might seem complicated; if so, review Day 6 for coverage of nested statements. Many of the reports that you create as a programmer are more complicated than this one.

This program uses what you learned in your first week of teaching yourself C. This was a large amount of material to cover in just one week, but you did it! If you use everything you learned this week, you can write your own programs in C. However, there are still limits to what you can do.

You have finished your first week of learning how to program in C. By now you should feel comfortable entering programs and using your editor and compiler.

Where You're Going

This week covers a large amount of material. You will learn many of the features that make up the heart of the C language. You will learn how to use numeric and character arrays, expand character variable types into arrays and strings, and group together different variable types by using structures.

The second week builds on subjects you learned in the first week, introduces additional program control statements, provides detailed explanations of functions, and presents alternative functions.

Days 9, "Pointers," and 12, "Variable Scope," focus on concepts that are extremely important to capitalizing on C's assets. You should spend extra time working with pointers and their basic functions.

At the end of the first week you learned to write many simple C programs. By the time you finish the second week, you should be able to write complex programs that can accomplish almost any task.

Numeric Arrays

Arrays are a type of data storage that you often use in C programs. You had a brief introduction to arrays on Day 6, "Basic Program Control." Today, you learn

- What an array is
- The definition of single- and multidimensional numeric arrays
- How to declare and initialize arrays

What Is an Array?

An *array* is a collection of data storage locations, each having the same data type and the same name. Each storage location in an array is called an *array element*. Why do you need arrays in your programs? This question can be answered with an example. If you are keeping track of your business expenses for 1996, and filing your receipts by month, you could have a separate folder for each month's receipts, but it would be more convenient to have a single folder with twelve compartments.

Extend this example to computer programming. Imagine that you are designing a program to keep track of your business expense totals. The program could declare twelve separate variables, one for each month's expense total. This approach is analogous to having twelve separate folders for your receipts. Good programming practice, however, would utilize an array with twelve elements, storing each month's total in the corresponding array element. This approach is comparable to filing your receipts in a single folder with twelve compartments. Figure 8.1 illustrates the difference between using individual variables and an array.

Figure 8.1.
Variables are like individual folders, whereas an array is like a single folder with many compartments.

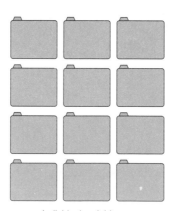
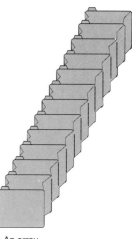

Individual variables   An array

Single-Dimensional Arrays

A *single-dimensional* array is an array that has only a single subscript. A *subscript* is a number in brackets following an array's name. This number can identify the number of individual elements in the array. An example should make this clear. For the business expenses program, you could use the following program line to declare an array of type `float`:

```
float expenses[12];
```

The array is named `expenses`, and contains twelve elements. Each of the twelve elements is the exact equivalent of a single `float` variable. All of C's data types can be used for arrays. C array elements are always numbered starting at 0, so the twelve elements of expenses are numbered 0–11. In the preceding example, January's expense total would be stored in `expenses[0]`, February's in `expenses[1]`, and so on.

When you declare an array, the compiler sets aside a block of memory large enough to hold the entire array. Individual array elements are stored in sequential memory locations, as illustrated in Figure 8.2.

Figure 8.2.

Array elements are stored in sequential memory locations.

```
int array[10];
```

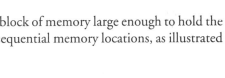

The location of array declarations in your source code is important. As with nonarray variables, the declaration's location affects how your program can use the array. The effect of a declaration's location is covered in more detail on Day 12, "Variable Scope." For now, place your array declarations with other variable declarations, just before the start of `main()`.

An array element can be used in your program anywhere a nonarray variable of the same type can be used. Individual elements of the array are accessed by using the array name followed by the element subscript enclosed in square brackets. For example, the following statement stores the value 89.95 in the second array element (remember, the first array element is `expenses[0]`, not `expenses[1]`):

```
expenses[1] = 89.95;
```

Likewise, the statement

```
expenses[10] = expenses[11];
```

assigns the value that is stored in array element `expenses[11]` to array element `expenses[10]`. When you refer to an array element, the array subscript can be a literal constant, as in these examples. Your programs may, however, frequently use a subscript that is a C integer variable or expression, or even another array element. Here are some examples:

```
float expenses[100];
int a[10];
/* additional statements go here */
expenses[i] = 100;       /* i is an integer variable */
expenses[2 + 3] = 100;   /* equivalent to expenses[5] */
expenses[a[2]] = 100;    /* a[] is an integer array */
```

That last example may need an explanation. If, for instance, you have an integer array named a[] and that the value 8 is stored in element a[2], writing

```
expenses[a[2]]
```

has the same effect as writing

```
expenses[8];
```

When you use arrays, keep the element numbering scheme in mind: In an array of n elements, the allowable subscripts range from 0 to $n-1$. If you use the subscript value n, you may get program errors. The C compiler does not recognize whether your program uses an array subscript that is out of bounds. Your program compiles and links, but out-of-range subscripts generally produce erroneous results.

Sometimes you might want to treat an array of n elements as if its elements were numbered $1-n$. For instance, in the previous example, a more natural method might be to store January's expense total in expenses[1], February's in expenses[2], and so on. The simplest way to do this is to declare the array with one more element than needed, and ignore element 0. In this case, you would declare the array as follows. You also could store some related data in element 0 (the yearly expense total, perhaps).

```
float expenses[13];
```

The program EXPENSES.C in Listing 8.1 demonstrates the use of an array. This is a simple program with no real practical use; it's for demonstration purposes only.

Type

Listing 8.1. EXPENSES.C demonstrates the use of an array.

```
1:    /* EXPENSES.C--Demonstrates use of an array */
2:
3:    #include <stdio.h>
4:
5:    /* Declare an array to hold expenses, and a counter variable */
6:
7:    float expenses[13];
8:    int count;
9:
10:   main()
11:   {
12:       /* Input data from keyboard into array */
13:
14:       for (count = 1; count < 13; count++)
15:       {
16:           printf("Enter expenses for month %d: ", count);
17:           scanf("%f", &expenses[count]);
```

```
18:     }
19:
20:     /* Print array contents */
21:
22:     for (count = 1; count < 13; count++)
23:     {
24:         printf("\nMonth %d = $%.2f", count, expenses[count]);
25:     }
26: }
```

```
Enter expenses for month 1: 100
Enter expenses for month 2: 200.12
Enter expenses for month 3: 150.50
Enter expenses for month 4: 300
Enter expenses for month 5: 100.50
Enter expenses for month 6: 34.25
Enter expenses for month 7: 45.75
Enter expenses for month 8: 195.00
Enter expenses for month 9: 123.45
Enter expenses for month 10: 111.11
Enter expenses for month 11: 222.20
Enter expenses for month 12: 120.00

Month 1 = $100.00
Month 2 = $200.12
Month 3 = $150.50
Month 4 = $300.00
Month 5 = $100.50
Month 6 = $34.25
Month 7 = $45.75
Month 8 = $195.00
Month 9 = $123.45
Month 10 = $111.11
Month 11 = $222.20
Month 12 = $120.00
```

When you run EXPENSES.C, the program prompts you to enter expenses for months 1–12. The values you enter are stored in an array. You must enter some value for each month. After the twelfth value is entered, the array contents are displayed on the screen.

The flow of the program is similar to listings you have seen before. Line 1 starts with a comment that describes what the program is going to do. Notice that the name of the program is included, EXPENSES.C. By including the name of the program in a comment, you know which program you are viewing. This is helpful when you print the listings, and then want to make a change.

Line 5 contains an additional comment explaining the variables that are being declared. In line 7, an array of 13 elements is declared. In this program, only 12 elements are needed, one for each month, but 13 have been declared. The for loop in lines 14–18 ignores element 0. This enables the program to use elements 1–12, which relate directly to the 12 months. Going back to line 8, a variable, count, is declared and is used throughout the program as a counter and an array index.

The program's `main()` function begins on line 10. As stated earlier, the program uses a `for` loop to print a message and accept a value for each of the 12 months. Notice that in line 17, the `scanf()` function uses an array element. In line 7, the expenses array was declared as `float`, so `%f` is used. The *address-of* operator (`&`) also is placed before the array element, just as if it were a regular type `float` variable and not an array element.

Lines 22–25 contain a second `for` loop that prints the values just entered. An additional formatting command has been added to the `printf()` function so that the expenses values print in a more orderly fashion. For now, know that `%.2f` prints a floating number with two digits to the right of the decimal. Additional formatting commands are covered in more detail on Day 14, "Working with the Screen, Printer, and Keyboard."

DO	DON'T

DON'T forget that array subscripts start at element `0`.

DO use arrays instead of creating several variables that store the same thing. (For example, if you want to store total sales for each month of the year, create an array with 12 elements to hold sales rather than creating a sales variable for each month.)

Multidimensional Arrays

A multidimensional array has more than one subscript. A two-dimensional array has two subscripts, a three-dimensional array has three subscripts, and so on. There is no limit to the number of dimensions a C array can have. (There is a limit on total array size, which is discussed later in the chapter.)

For example, you might write a program that plays checkers. The checkerboard contains 64 squares arranged in eight rows and eight columns. Your program could represent the board as a two-dimensional array, as follows:

```
int checker[8][8];
```

The resulting array has 64 elements: `checker[0][0]`, `checker[0][1]`, `checker[0][2]` ...`checker[7][6]`, `checker[7][7]`. The structure of this two-dimensional array is illustrated in Figure 8.3.

Similarly, a three-dimensional array could be thought of as a cube. Four-dimensional arrays (and higher) are probably best left to your imagination. All arrays, no matter how many dimensions they have, are stored sequentially in memory. More detail on array storage is presented on Day 15, "More on Pointers."

Figure 8.3.
A two-dimensional array has a row and column structure.

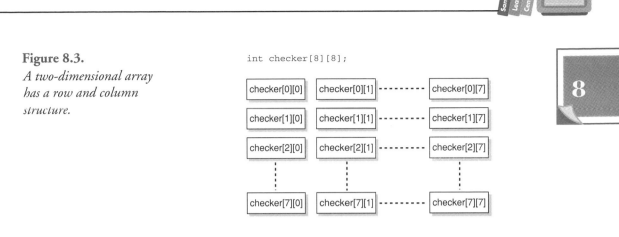

```
int checker[8][8];
```

Naming and Declaring Arrays

The rules for assigning names to arrays are the same as for variable names, covered on Day 3, "Numeric Variables and Constants." An array name must be unique. It can't be used for another array or for any other identifier (variable, constant, and so on). As you have probably realized, array declarations follow the same form as declarations of nonarray variables, except that the number of elements in the array must be enclosed in square brackets immediately after the array name.

When you declare an array, you can specify the number of elements with a literal constant (as was done in the earlier examples) or with a symbolic constant created with the #define directive. Thus the following:

```
#define MONTHS 12
int array[MONTHS];
```

is equivalent to this statement:

```
int array[12];
```

With most compilers, however, you cannot declare an array's elements with a symbolic constant created with the const keyword.

```
const int MONTHS = 12;
int array[MONTHS];          /* Wrong! */
```

Listing 8.2, GRADES.C, is another program demonstrating the use of a single-dimensional array. GRADES.C uses an array to store 10 grades.

 Listing 8.2. GRADES.C stores 10 grades in an array.

```
1:  /*GRADES.C--Example program with array */
2:  /* Get 10 grades and then average them */
3:
4:  #include <stdio.h>
5:
```

continues

Listing 8.2. continued

```
6:    #define MAX_GRADE 100
7:    #define STUDENTS   10
8:
9:    int grades[STUDENTS];
10:
11:   int idx;
12:   int total = 0;            /* used for average */
13:
14:   main()
15:   {
16:       for( idx=0;idx< STUDENTS;idx++)
17:       {
18:           printf( "Enter Person %d's grade: ", idx +1);
19:           scanf( "%d", &grades[idx] );
20:
21:           while ( grades[idx] > MAX_GRADE )
22:           {
23:               printf( "\nThe highest grade possible is %d",
24:                       MAX_GRADE );
25:               printf( "\nEnter correct grade: " );
26:               scanf( "%d", &grades[idx] );
27:           }
28:
29:           total += grades[idx];
30:       }
31:
32:       printf( "\n\nThe average score is %d", ( total / STUDENTS) );
33:
34:       return (0);
35:   }
```

**Input
Output**

```
Enter Person 1's grade: 95
Enter Person 2's grade: 100
Enter Person 3's grade: 60
Enter Person 4's grade: 105

The highest grade possible is 100
Enter correct grade: 100
Enter Person 5's grade: 25
Enter Person 6's grade: 0
Enter Person 7's grade: 85
Enter Person 8's grade: 85
Enter Person 9's grade: 95
Enter Person 10's grade: 85


The average score is 73
```

 Analysis

Like EXPENSES.C, this listing prompts the user for input. It prompts for 10 people's grades. Instead of printing each grade, it prints the average score.

As you learned earlier, arrays are named like regular variables. On line 9, the array for this program is named grades. It should be safe to assume that this array holds grades. On lines 6 and 7, two constants are defined, MAX_GRADE and STUDENTS. These constants can be changed

160

easily. Knowing that STUDENTS is defined as 10, you then know that the grades array has 10 elements. In the listing, there are two other variables declared, idx and total. An abbreviation for index, idx is used as a counter and array subscript. A running total of all grades is kept in total.

The heart of this program is the for loop on lines 16–30. The for statement initializes idx to 0, the first subscript for an array. It then loops as long as idx is less than the number of students. Each time it loops, it increments idx by 1. For each loop, the program prompts for a person's grade (lines 18 and 19). Notice that in line 18, 1 is added to idx in order to count the people from 1 to 10 instead of from 0 to 9. Because arrays start with subscript 0, the first grade is put in grade[0]. Instead of confusing users by asking for Person 0's grade, they are asked for Person 1's grade.

Lines 21–27 contain a while loop nested within the for loop. This is an edit check that ensures the grade is not higher than the maximum grade, MAX_GRADE. Users are prompted to enter a correct grade if they enter a grade that is too high. You should check program data whenever you can.

Line 29 adds the entered grade to a total counter. On line 32, this total is used to print the average score (total/STUDENTS).

DO	DON'T

DO use #define statements to create constants that can be used when declaring arrays. Then you can change easily the number of elements in the array. In GRADES.C, you could change the number of students in the #define and you wouldn't have to make any other changes in the program.

DO avoid multidimensional arrays with more than three dimensions. Remember, multidimensional arrays can get very big, very quickly.

Initializing Arrays

You can initialize all or part of an array when you first declare it. Follow the array declaration with an equal sign and a list of values enclosed in braces and separated by commas. The listed values are assigned in order to array elements starting at number 0. For example, the following code assigns the value 100 to array[0], 200 to array[1], 300 to array[2], and 400 to array[3]:

```
int array[4] = { 100, 200, 300, 400 };
```

If you omit the array size, the compiler creates an array just large enough to hold the initialization values. Thus, the following statement would have exactly the same effect as the previous array declaration statement:

```
int array[] = { 100, 200, 300, 400 };
```

You can, however, include too few initialization values, as in this example:

```
int array[10] = { 1, 2, 3 };
```

If you do not explicitly initialize an array element, you cannot be sure what value it holds when the program runs. If you include too many initializers (more initializers than array elements), the compiler detects an error.

Multidimensional arrays also can be initialized. The list of initialization values is assigned to array elements in order, with the last array subscript changing first. For example,

```
int array[4][3] = { 1, 2, 3, 4, 5, 6, 7, 8, 9, 10, 11, 12 };
```

results in the following assignments:

```
array[0][0] is equal to 1
array[0][1] is equal to 2
array[0][2] is equal to 3
array[1][0] is equal to 4
array[1][1] is equal to 5
array[1][2] is equal to 6
...
array[3][1] is equal to 11
array[3][2] is equal to 12
```

When you initialize multidimensional arrays, you can make your source code clearer by using extra braces to group the initialization values and also by spreading them over several lines. The following initialization is equivalent to the one given previously:

```
int array[4][3] = { { 1, 2, 3 } , { 4, 5, 6 } ,
{ 7, 8, 9 } , { 10, 11, 12 } };
```

Remember, initialization values must be separated by a comma—even when there is a brace between them. Also, be sure to use braces in pairs—a closing brace for every opening brace—or the compiler becomes confused.

Now look at an example that demonstrates the advantages of arrays. The program in Listing 8.3, RANDOM.C, creates a 1000-element, three-dimensional array and fills it with random numbers. The program then displays the array elements on the screen. Imagine how many lines of source code you would need to perform the same task with nonarray variables.

You see a new library function, getch(), in this program. The getch() function reads a single character from the keyboard. In Listing 8.3, getch() pauses the program until the user presses a key. The getch() function is covered in detail on Day 14.

Type

Listing 8.3. RANDOM.C creates a multidimensional array.

```
1:   /* RANDOM.C--Demonstrates using a multidimensional array */
2:
3:   #include <stdio.h>
4:   #include <stdlib.h>
5:   /* Declare a three-dimensional array with 1000 elements */
6:
7:   int random_array[10][10][10];
8:   int a, b, c;
9:
10:  main()
11:  {
12:      /* Fill the array with random numbers. The C library */
13:      /* function rand() returns a random number. Use one */
14:      /* for loop for each array subscript. */
15:
16:      for (a = 0; a < 10; a++)
17:      {
18:          for (b = 0; b < 10; b++)
19:          {
20:              for (c = 0; c < 10; c++)
21:              {
22:                  random_array[a][b][c] = rand();
23:              }
24:          }
25:      }
26:
27:      /* Now display the array elements 10 at a time */
28:
29:      for (a = 0; a < 10; a++)
30:      {
31:          for (b = 0; b < 10; b++)
32:          {
33:              for (c = 0; c < 10; c++)
34:              {
35:                  printf("\nrandom_array[%d][%d][%d] = ", a, b, c);
36:                  printf("%d", random_array[a][b][c]);
37:              }
38:              printf("\nPress a key to continue, CTRL-C to \
                        quit.");
39:              getch();
40:          }
41:      }
42:  }          /* end of main() */
```

Output

```
random_array[0][0][0] = 346
random_array[0][0][1] = 130
random_array[0][0][2] = 10982
random_array[0][0][3] = 1090
random_array[0][0][4] = 11656
random_array[0][0][5] = 7117
random_array[0][0][6] = 17595
random_array[0][0][7] = 6415
```

```
random_array[0][0][8] = 22948
random_array[0][0][9] = 31126
Press a key to continue, CTRL-C to quit.
random_array[0][1][0] = 9004
random_array[0][1][1] = 14558
random_array[0][1][2] = 3571
random_array[0][1][3] = 22879
random_array[0][1][4] = 18492
random_array[0][1][5] = 1360
random_array[0][1][6] = 5412
random_array[0][1][7] = 26721
random_array[0][1][8] = 22463
random_array[0][1][9] = 25047
Press a key to continue, CTRL-C to quit
...         ...
random_array[9][8][0] = 6287
random_array[9][8][1] = 26957
random_array[9][8][2] = 1530
random_array[9][8][3] = 14171
random_array[9][8][4] = 6951
random_array[9][8][5] = 213
random_array[9][8][6] = 14003
random_array[9][8][7] = 29736
random_array[9][8][8] = 15028
random_array[9][8][9] = 18968
Press a key to continue, CTRL-C to quit.
random_array[9][9][0] = 28559
random_array[9][9][1] = 5268
random_array[9][9][2] = 20182
random_array[9][9][3] = 3633
random_array[9][9][4] = 24779
random_array[9][9][5] = 3024
random_array[9][9][6] = 10853
random_array[9][9][7] = 28205
random_array[9][9][8] = 8930
random_array[9][9][9] = 2873
Press a key to continue, CTRL-C to quit.
```

Analysis

On Day 6 you saw a program that used a nested `for` statement; this program has two `for` loops nested. Before you look at the `for` statements in detail, note that lines 7 and 8 declare four variables. The first is an array named `random_array`, used to hold random numbers. `random_array` is a three-dimensional type `int` array that is 10 by 10 by 10 giving a total of 1,000 type `int` elements (10×10×10). Imagine coming up with 1,000 unique variable names if you couldn't use arrays. Line 8 then declares three variables, a, b, and c, used to control the `for` loops.

This program also includes a the header file, STDLIB.H (for standard library), in line 4. This is included to provide the prototype for the `rand()` function used on line 22.

The bulk of the program is contained in two nests of `for` statements. The first is on lines 16–25, the second on lines 29–41. Both `for` nests have the same structure. They work just like the loops in Listing 6.2, but they go one level deeper. In the first set of for statements, line 22 is executed repeatedly. Line 22 assigns the return value of a function, rand(), to an element of the random_array array, where rand() is a library function that returns a random number.

Going backward through the listing, you can see that line 20 changes variable c from 0 to 9. This loops through the farthest right subscript of the random_array array. Line 18 loops through b, the middle subscript of the random array. Each time b changes, it loops through all the c elements. Line 16 increments variable a, which loops through the farthest left subscript. Each time this subscript changes, it loops through all 10 values of subscript b, which in turn loop through all 10 values of c. This loop initializes every value in the random array to a random number.

Lines 29–41 contain the second nest of for statements. These work like the previous for statements, but this loop prints each of the values assigned previously. After 10 are displayed, line 38 prints a message and waits for a key to be pressed. Line 39 takes care of the keypress. getch() returns the value of a key that has been pressed. If a key has not been pressed, getch() waits until one is. Run this program and watch the displayed values.

Maximum Array Size

Because of the way memory models work, you should not try to create more than 64KB of data variables for now. An explanation of this limitation is beyond the scope of this book, but there's no need to worry; none of the programs in this book exceed this limitation. To understand more, or to get around this limitation, consult your compiler manuals. Generally, 64KB is enough data space for programs, particularly the relatively simple programs you write as you work through this book. A single array can take up the entire 64KB of data storage if your program uses no other variables. Otherwise, you need to apportion the available data space as needed.

Note: Some operating systems don't have a 64KB limit. DOS does.

The size of an array in bytes depends on the number of elements it has, as well as each element's size. Element size depends on the data type of the array and your computer. The sizes for each numeric data type, given in Table 3.2, are repeated here in Table 8.1 for your convenience. These are the data type sizes for most PCs.

Table 8.1. Storage space requirements for numeric data types for many PCs.

Element Data Type	Element Size (Bytes)
int	2 or 4
short	2
long	4
float	4
double	8

To calculate the storage space required for an array, multiply the number of elements in the array by the element size. For example, a 500-element array of type `float` requires storage space of `(500) * (4) = 2000` bytes.

Storage space can be determined within a program by using C's `sizeof()` operator; `sizeof()` is a unary operator and not a function. It takes as its argument a variable name or the name of a data type and returns the size, in bytes, of its argument. The use of `sizeof()` is illustrated in Listing 8.4.

Listing 8.4. Using the `sizeof()` operator to determine storage space requirements for an array.

```
1:   /* Demonstrates the sizeof() operator */
2:
3:   #include <stdio.h>
4:
5:   /* Declare several 100 element arrays */
6:
7:   int intarray[100];
8:   float floatarray[100];
9:   double doublearray[100];
10:
11:  main()
12:  {
13:      /* Display the sizes of numeric data types */
14:
15:      printf("\n\nSize of int = %d bytes", sizeof(int));
16:      printf("\nSize of short = %d bytes", sizeof(short));
17:      printf("\nSize of long = %d bytes", sizeof(long));
18:      printf("\nSize of float = %d bytes", sizeof(float));
19:      printf("\nSize of double = %d bytes", sizeof(double));
20:
21:      /* Display the sizes of the three arrays */
22:
23:      printf("\nSize of intarray = %d bytes", sizeof(intarray));
24:      printf("\nSize of floatarray = %d bytes",
```

```
25              sizeof(floatarray));
26:      printf("\nSize of doublearray = %d bytes",
27              sizeof(doublearray));
28:
29:  }
```

```
Size of int = 2 bytes
Size of short = 2 bytes
Size of long = 4 bytes
Size of float = 4 bytes
Size of double = 8 bytes
Size of intarray = 200 bytes
Size of floatarray = 400 bytes
Size of doublearray = 800 bytes
```

 Enter and compile the program in this listing by using the procedures you learned on Day 1, "Getting Started." When the program runs, it displays the sizes—in bytes—of the three arrays and five numeric data types.

On Day 3 you ran a similar program; however, this listing uses sizeof() to determine the storage size of arrays. Lines 7, 8, and 9 declare three arrays, each of different types. Lines 23 through 27 print the size of each array. The size should equal the size of the array's variable type times the number of elements. For example, if an int is 2 bytes, intarray should be 2 times 100, or 200 bytes. Run the program and check the values.

Summary

This chapter introduced numeric arrays, a powerful data storage method that enables you to group a number of same-type data items under the same group name. Individual items, or elements, in an array are identified by using a subscript after the array name. Computer programming tasks that involve repetitive data processing lend themselves to array storage.

Like nonarray variables, arrays must be declared before they can be used. Optionally, array elements can be initialized when the array is declared.

Q&A

Q What happens if I use a subscript on an array that is larger than the number of elements in the array?

A If you use a subscript that is out of bounds from the array declaration, the program will probably compile and even run. However, the results from such a mistake can be unpredictable. This can be a difficult error to find once it starts causing problems, so make sure you're careful when initializing and accessing array elements.

Q What happens if I use an array without initializing it?

A This mistake doesn't produce a compiler error. If you don't initialize an array, there can be any value in the array elements. You may get unpredictable results. You should always initialize variables and arrays so that you know exactly what is in them. On Day 12, "Variable Scope," you are introduced to one exception to the need to initialize. For now, play it safe.

Q How many dimensions can an array have?

A As stated in the chapter, you can have as many dimensions as you want. As you add more dimensions, you use more data storage space. You should declare an array only as large as you need to avoid wasting storage space.

Q Is there an easy way I can initialize an entire array at once?

A Each element of an array must be initialized. The safest way for a beginning C programmer to initialize an array is either with a declaration as shown in this chapter or with a for statement. There are other ways to initialize an array, but they are beyond the scope of this book.

Q Can I add two arrays together (or multiply, divide, or subtract them)?

A If you declare two arrays, you cannot add the two together. Each element must be added individually. Exercise 10 illustrates this point.

Q Why is it better to use an array instead of individual variables?

A With arrays, you can group like values with a single name. In Listing 8.3, 1,000 values were stored. Creating 1,000 variable names and initializing each to a random number would have taken a tremendous amount of typing. By using an array, you made the task easy.

Workshop

The Workshop provides quiz questions to help you solidify your understanding of the material covered, and exercises to provide you with experience in using what you've learned.

Quiz

1. Which of C's data types can be used in an array?
2. If an array is declared with 10 elements, what is the subscript of the first element?
3. In a one-dimensional array declared with *n* elements, what is the subscript of the last element?
4. What happens if your program tries to access an array element with an out-of-range subscript?

8

5. How do you declare a multidimensional array?

6. An array is declared with the following statement. How many total elements does the array have?

```
int array[2][3][5][8];
```

7. What would be the name of the tenth element in the array from question 6?

Exercises

1. Write a C program line that would declare three one-dimensional integer arrays, named one, two, and three, with 1,000 elements each.

2. Write the statement that would declare a 10-element integer array and initialize all its elements to 1.

3. Given the following array, write the code to initialize all the array elements to 88:

```
int eightyeight[88];
```

4. Given the following array, write the code to initialize all the array elements to 0:

```
int stuff[12][10];
```

5. **BUG BUSTER:** What is wrong with the following code fragment?

```
int x, y;
int array[10][3];
main()
{
    for ( x = 0; x < 3; x++ )
        for ( y = 0; y < 10; y++ )
            array[x][y] = 0;
}
```

6. **BUG BUSTER:** What is wrong with the following?

```
int array[10];
int x = 1;

main()
{
    for ( x = 1; x <= 10; x++ )
        array[x] = 99;
}
```

7. Write a program that puts random numbers into a two-dimensional array that is 5 by 4. Print the values in columns on the screen. (Hint: use the rand() function from Listing 8.3.)

8. Rewrite Listing 8.3 to use a single-dimensional array. Print the average of the 1,000 variables before printing the individual values. Note: Don't forget to pause after every 10 values are printed.

9. Write a program that initializes an array of 10 elements. Each element should be equal to its subscript. The program should then print each of the 10 elements.

10. Modify the program from exercise nine. After printing the initialized values, the program should copy the values to a new array and add 10 to each value. Then the new array values should be printed.

Pointers

This chapter introduces you to pointers, an important part of the C language. Pointers provide a powerful and flexible method for manipulating data in your programs. Today, you learn

- The definition of a pointer
- The uses of pointers
- How to declare and initialize pointers
- How to use pointers with simple variables and arrays
- How to use pointers to pass arrays to functions

As you read through this chapter, the advantages of using pointers may not be clear immediately. The advantages fall into two categories: things that can be done better with pointers than without, and things that can be done only with pointers. The specifics should become clear as you read this and subsequent chapters. At present, just know that you must understand pointers if you want to be a proficient C programmer.

What Is a Pointer?

To understand pointers, you need a basic knowledge of how your computer stores information in memory. The following is a somewhat simplified account of PC memory storage.

Your Computer's Memory

A PC's RAM consists of many thousands of sequential storage locations, and each location is identified by a unique address. The memory addresses in a given computer range from 0 to a maximum value that depends on the amount of memory installed.

When you are using your computer, the operating system uses some of the system's memory. When you're running a program, the program's code and data (the machine language instructions for the program's various tasks and the information the program is using, respectively) also use some of the system's memory. This section examines the memory storage for program data.

When you declare a variable in a C program, the compiler sets aside a memory location with a unique address to store that variable. The compiler associates that address with the variable's name. When your program uses the variable name, it automatically accesses the proper memory location. The location's address is used, but it is hidden from you, and you need not be concerned with it.

Figure 9.1 shows this schematically. A variable named rate has been declared and initialized to 100. The compiler has set aside storage at address 1004 for the variable and has associated the name rate with the address 1004.

Figure 9.1.
A program variable is stored at a specific memory address.

1000	1001	1002	1003	1004	1005
				100	

↑
rate

Creating a Pointer

You should note that the address of the variable rate (or any other variable) is a number and can be treated like any other number in C. If you know a variable's address, you can create a second variable in which to store the address of the first. The first step is to declare a variable to hold the address of rate. Give it the name p_rate, for example. At first, p_rate is uninitialized. Storage has been allocated for p_rate, but its value is undetermined. This is shown in Figure 9.2.

Figure 9.2.
Memory storage space has been allocated for the variable p_rate.

1000	1001	1002	1003	1004	1005
	?			100	

↑   ↑
p_rate   rate

The next step is to store the address of the variable rate in the variable p_rate. Because p_rate now contains the address of rate, it indicates its storage location in memory. In C parlance, p_rate points to rate or is a pointer to rate. This is diagrammed in Figure 9.3.

Figure 9.3.
The variable p_rate contains the address of the variable rate and is therefore a pointer to rate.

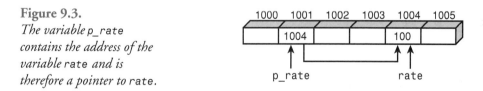

1000	1001	1002	1003	1004	1005
	1004			100	

↑   ↑ ↑
p_rate   rate

To summarize, a pointer is a variable that contains the address of another variable. Now you can get down to the details of using pointers in your C programs.

Pointers and Simple Variables

In the example just given, a pointer variable pointed to a simple (that is, nonarray) variable. This section shows you how to create and use pointers to simple variables.

Declaring Pointers

A pointer is a numeric variable and, like all variables, must be declared before it can be used. Pointer variable names follow the same rules as other variables and must be unique. This chapter uses the convention that a pointer to the variable `name` is called `p_name`. This is not necessary; you can name pointers anything you want (within C's naming rules).

A pointer declaration takes the following form:

```
typename *ptrname;
```

`typename` is any one of C's variable types and indicates the type of the variable that the pointer points to. The asterisk (*) is the *indirection operator,* and it indicates that `ptrname` is a pointer to type `typename` and not a variable of type `typename`. Pointers can be declared along with non-pointer variables. Here are some more examples:

```
char *ch1, *ch2;        /* ch1 and ch2 both are pointers to */
                        /* type char. */
float *value, percent;  /* value is a pointer to type float, and */
                        /* percent is an ordinary float */
                        /* variable */
```

> **Note:** The * symbol is used as both the indirection operator and the multiplication operator. Don't worry about the compiler becoming confused. The context in which * is used always provides enough information so that the compiler can figure out whether you mean indirection or multiplication.

Initializing Pointers

Now that you've declared a pointer, what can you do with it? You can't do anything with it until you make it point to something. Like regular variables, uninitialized pointers can be used, but the results are unpredictable and potentially disastrous. Until a pointer holds the address of a variable, it isn't useful. The address doesn't get stored in the pointer by magic; your program must put it there by using the address-of operator, the ampersand (&). When placed before the name of a variable, the address-of operator returns the address of the variable. Therefore, you initialize a pointer with a statement of the form

```
pointer = &variable;
```

Look back at the example in Figure 9.3. The program statement to initialize the variable `p_rate` to point at the variable `rate` would be

```
p_rate = &rate;     /* assign the address of rate to p_rate */
```

Before the initialization, `p_rate` didn't point to anything in particular. After the initialization, `p_rate` is a pointer to `rate`.

Using Pointers

Now that you know how to declare and initialize pointers, you are probably wondering how to use them. The indirection operator (*) comes into play again. When the * precedes the name of a pointer, it refers to the variable pointed to.

Continue now with the previous example, where the pointer p_rate has been initialized to point to the variable rate. If you write *p_rate, it refers to the variable rate. If you want to print the value of rate (which is 100 in the example), you could write

```
printf("%d", rate);
```

or you could write this statement:

```
printf("%d", *p_rate);
```

In C, the two statements are equivalent. Accessing the contents of a variable by using the variable name is called *direct access*. Accessing the contents of a variable by using a pointer to the variable is called *indirect access* or *indirection*. Figure 9.4 illustrates that a pointer name preceded by the indirection operator refers to the value of the pointed to variable.

Figure 9.4.
Use of the indirection operator with pointers.

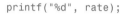

Pause a minute and think about this material. Pointers are an integral part of the C language, and it is essential that you understand them. Pointers have confused many people, so don't worry if you're feeling a bit puzzled. If you need to review, that's fine. Maybe the following summary can help. If you have a pointer named ptr that has been initialized to point to the variable var, the following are true:

- *ptr and var both refer to the contents of var (that is, whatever value the program has stored there).
- ptr and &var refer to the address of var.

As you can see, a pointer name without the indirection operator accesses the pointer value itself, which is, of course, the address of the variable pointed to.

The program in Listing 9.1 demonstrates basic pointer use. You should enter, compile, and run this program.

Type Listing 9.1. Illustration of basic pointer use.

```
1: /* Demonstrates basic pointer use. */
2:
3: #include <stdio.h>
4:
5: /* Declare and initialize an int variable */
6:
7: int var = 1;
8:
9: /* Declare a pointer to int */
10:
11: int *ptr;
12:
13: main()
14: {
15:     /* Initialize ptr to point to var */
16:
17:     ptr = &var;
18:
19:     /* Access var directly and indirectly */
20:
21:     printf("\nDirect access, var = %d", var);
22:     printf("\nIndirect access, var = %d", *ptr);
23:
24:     /* Display the address of var two ways */
25:
26:     printf("\n\nThe address of var = %d", &var);
27:     printf("\nThe address of var = %d", ptr);
28:
29:     return 0;
30: }
```

Output The address reported for var may not be 96 on your system.

```
Direct access, var = 1
Indirect access, var = 1

The address of var = 96
The address of var = 96
```

Analysis In this listing, two variables are declared. In line 7, var is declared as an int and initialized to 1. In line 11, a pointer to a variable of type int is declared and named ptr. In line 17, the pointer ptr is assigned the address of var using the address-of operator (&). The rest of the program prints the values from these two variables to the screen. Line 21 prints the value of var, whereas line 22 prints the value stored in the location pointed to by ptr. In this program, this value is 1. Line 26 prints the address of var using the address-of operator. This is the same value printed by line 27 using the pointer variable, ptr.

This listing is good to study. It shows the relationship between a variable, its address, a pointer, and the dereferencing of a pointer.

DO understand what pointers are and how they work. The mastering of C requires mastering pointers.

DON'T use an uninitialized pointer. Results can be disastrous if you do.

Pointers and Variable Types

The previous discussion ignores the fact that different variable types occupy different amounts of memory. For the more common PC operating systems, an int takes two bytes, a float takes four bytes, and so on. Each individual byte of memory has its own address, so a multibyte variable actually occupies several addresses.

How, then, do pointers handle the addresses of multibyte variables? This is how it works: The address of a variable is actually the address of the lowest byte it occupies. This can be illustrated with an example that declares and initializes three variables:

```
int vint = 12252;
char vchar = 90;
float vfloat = 1200.156004;
```

These variables are stored in memory as shown in Figure 9.5. In this figure, the int variable occupies two bytes, the char variable occupies one byte, and the float variable occupies four bytes.

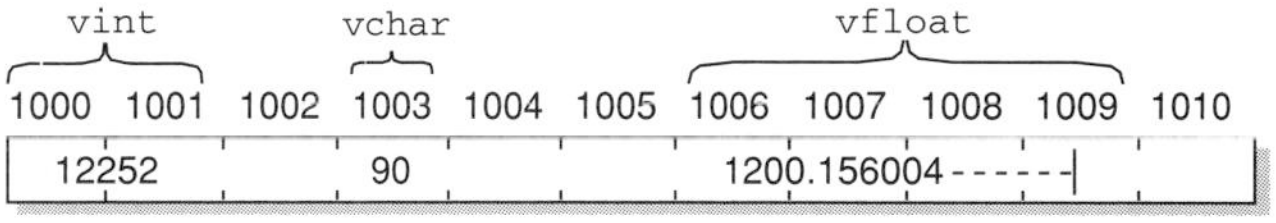

Figure 9.5.

Different types of numeric variables occupy different amounts of storage space in memory.

Now declare and initialize pointers to these three variables.

```
int *p_vint;
char *p_vchar;
float *p_vfloat;
/* additional code goes here */
p_vint = &vint;
p_vchar = &vchar;
p_vfloat = &vfloat;
```

Each pointer is equal to the address of the first byte of the pointed-to variable. Thus, p_vint equals `1000`, `p_vchar` equals `1003`, and `p_vfloat` equals `1006`. Remember, however, that each pointer was declared to point to a certain type of variable. The compiler "knows" that a pointer to type `int` points to the first of two bytes, a pointer to type `float` points to the first of four bytes, and so on. This is diagrammed in Figure 9.6.

Figure 9.6.

The compiler "knows" the size of the variable that a pointer points to.

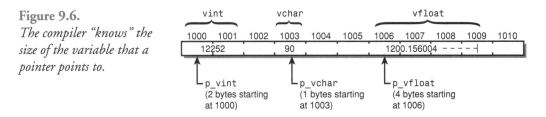

Figures 9.5 and 9.6 show some empty memory storage locations among the three variables. This is for the sake of visual clarity. In actual practice, the C compiler stores the three variables in adjacent memory locations with no unused bytes between them.

Pointers and Arrays

Pointers can be useful when you are working with simple variables, but they are more helpful with arrays. There is a special relationship between pointers and arrays in C. In fact, when you use the array subscript notation that you learned on Day 8, "Numeric Arrays," you really are using pointers without knowing it. The following sections explain how this works.

The Array Name as a Pointer

An array name without brackets is a pointer to the array's first element. Thus, if you have declared an array `data[]`, `data` is the address of the first array element.

"Wait a minute," you might be thinking, "don't you need the address-of operator to get an address?" Yes, you also can use the expression `&data[0]` to obtain the address of the array's first element. In C, the relationship (`data == &data[0]`) is true.

You've seen that the name of an array is a pointer to the array. Remember that this is a *pointer constant*; it can't be changed and remains fixed for the duration of program execution. This makes sense; if you changed its value, it would point elsewhere and not to the array (which remains at a fixed location in memory).

You can, however, declare a pointer variable and initialize it to point at the array. For example, the following code initializes the pointer variable `p_array` with the address of the first element of `array[]`:

```
int array[100], *p_array;
/* additional code goes here */
p_array = array;
```

Because p_array is a pointer variable, it can be modified to point elsewhere. Unlike array, p_array is not locked to pointing at the first element of array[]. It could, for example, be pointed at other elements of array[]. How would you do this? First, you need to look at how array elements are stored in memory.

Array Element Storage

As you might remember from Day 8, the elements of an array are stored in sequential memory locations with the first element in the lowest address. Subsequent array elements (those with an index greater than 0) are stored in higher addresses. How much higher depends on the array's data type (char, int, float, and so forth).

Take an array of type int. As you learned on Day 3, "Numeric Variables and Constants," a single int variable can occupy two bytes of memory. Each array element is therefore located two bytes above the preceding element, and the address of each array element is two higher than the address of the preceding element. A type float, on the other hand, can occupy four bytes. In an array of type float, each array element is located four bytes above the preceding element, and the address of each array element is four higher than the address of the preceding element.

Figure 9.7 illustrates the relationship between array storage and addresses for a six-element int array and a three-element float array.

Figure 9.7.
Array storage for different array types.

```
int x[6];

1000 1001 1002 1003 1004 1005 1006 1007 1008 1009 1010 1011
  x[0]      x[1]      x[2]      x[3]      x[4]      x[5]


float expenses[3];

1250 1251 1252 1253 1254 1255 1256 1257 1258 1259 1260 1261
    expenses[0]        expenses[1]        expenses[2]
```

By looking at Figure 9.7, you should be able to see why the following relationships are true:

```
1: x == 1000
2: &x[0] == 1000
3: &x[1] = 1002
4: expenses == 1250
5: &expenses[0] == 1250
6: &expenses[1] == 1254
```

x without the array brackets is the address of the first element (x[0]). You also can see that x[0] is at the address of 1000. Line 2 shows this also. It can be read as the address of the first element of the array x is equal to 1000. Line 3 shows that the address of the second element (subscripted as 1 in an array) is 1002. Again the figure can confirm this. Lines 4, 5, and 6 are virtually identical to 1, 2, and 3, respectively. They vary in the difference between the addresses of the two array elements. In the type int array x, the difference is two bytes, and in the type float array, expenses, the difference is four bytes.

How do you access these successive array elements using a pointer? You can see from these examples that a pointer must be increased by 2 to access successive elements of a type int array, and by 4 to access successive elements of a type float array. You can generalize and say that to access successive elements of an array of a particular data type, a pointer must be increased by sizeof(datatype). Remember from Day 3 that the sizeof() operator returns the size in bytes of a C data type.

The program in Listing 9.2 illustrates the relationship between addresses and the elements of different type arrays by declaring arrays of type int, float, and double, and by displaying the addresses of successive elements.

Listing 9.2. Displaying the addresses of successive array elements.

```
1: /* Demonstrates the relationship between addresses and */
2: /* elements of arrays of different data types. */
3:
4: #include <stdio.h>
5:
6: /* Declare three arrays and a counter variable. */
7:
8: int i[10], x;
9: float f[10];
10: double d[10];
11:
12: main()
13: {
14:     /* Print the table heading */
15:
16:     printf("\t\tInteger\t\tFloat\t\tDouble");
17:
18:     printf("\n=================================");
19:     printf("======================");
20:
21:     /* Print the addresses of each array element. */
22:
23:     for (x = 0; x < 10; x++)
24:         printf("\nElement %d:\t%d\t\t%d\t\t%d", x, &i[x],
25:             &f[x], &d[x]);
26:
27:     printf("\n=================================");
28:     printf("======================");
29:
30:     return 0;
31: }
```

	Integer	Float	Double
Element 0:	1392	1414	1454
Element 1:	1394	1418	1462
Element 2:	1396	1422	1470
Element 3:	1398	1426	1478
Element 4:	1400	1430	1486
Element 5:	1402	1434	1494
Element 6:	1404	1438	1502
Element 7:	1406	1442	1510
Element 8:	1408	1446	1518
Element 9:	1410	1450	1526

The exact addresses that your system displays may be different from these, but the relationships are the same. In the output above, there are two bytes between int elements, four bytes between float elements, and eight bytes between double elements. (Note: Some machines use different sizes for variable types. If your machine differs, the following output might have different size gaps; however, they will be consistent gaps.)

Analysis This listing takes advantage of the escape characters learned on Day 7, "Basic Input/ Output." The printf() calls in lines 16 and 24 use the tab escape character (\t) to help format the table by aligning the columns.

Looking more closely at the listing, you can see that three arrays are created in lines 8, 9, and 10. Line 8 declares array i of type int, line 9 declares array f of type float, and line 10 declares array d of type double. Line 16 prints the column headers for the table that will be displayed. Lines 18 and 19 along with lines 27 and 28 print dashed lines across the top and bottom of the table data. This is a nice touch to a report. Lines 23, 24, and 25 are a for loop that prints each of the table's rows. The number of the element, x, is printed first. This is followed by the address of the element in each of the three arrays.

Pointer Arithmetic

You have a pointer to the first array element; the pointer must increment by an amount equal to the size of the data type stored in the array. How do you access array elements using pointer notation? You use *pointer arithmetic.*

"Just what I don't need," you might think, "another kind of arithmetic to learn!" Don't worry. Pointer arithmetic is simple, and it makes using pointers in your programs much easier. You have to be concerned with only two pointer operations: incrementing and decrementing.

Incrementing Pointers

When you increment a pointer, you are increasing its value. For example, when you increment a pointer by 1, pointer arithmetic automatically increases the pointer's value so that it points to the next array element. In other words, C "knows" the data type that the pointer points to (from the pointer declaration), and increases the address stored in the pointer by the size of the data type.

Suppose that `ptr_to_int` is a pointer variable to some element of an `int` array. If you execute the statement

```
ptr_to_int++;
```

the value of `ptr_to_int` is increased by the size of type `int` (usually two bytes), and `ptr_to_int` now points to the next array element. Likewise, if `ptr_to_float` points to an element of a type `float` array, then

```
ptr_to_float++;
```

increases the value of `ptr_to_float` by the size of type `float` (usually four bytes).

The same holds true for increments greater than 1. If you add the value[] to a pointer, C increments the pointer by *n* array elements of the associated data type. Therefore,

```
ptr_to_int += 4;
```

increases the value stored in `ptr_to_int` by 8, so it points 4 array elements ahead. Likewise,

```
ptr_to_float += 10;
```

increases the value stored in `ptr_to_float` by 40, so it points 10 array elements ahead.

Decrementing Pointers

The same concepts hold true for decrementing a pointer that apply to incrementing pointers. Decrementing a pointer is actually a special case of incrementing by adding a *negative* value. If you decrement a pointer with the `--` or `-=` operators, pointer arithmetic automatically adjusts for the size of the array elements.

Listing 9.3 presents an example of how pointer arithmetic can be used to access array elements. By incrementing pointers, the program can step through all elements of the arrays efficiently.

Listing 9.3. Using pointer arithmetic and pointer notation to access array elements.

```
1: /* Demonstrates using pointer arithmetic to access */
2: /* array elements with pointer notation. */
3:
4: #include <stdio.h>
5: #define MAX 10
6:
7: /* Declare and initialize an integer array. */
8:
```

```
9: int i_array[MAX] = { 0,1,2,3,4,5,6,7,8,9 };
10:
11: /* Declare a pointer to int and an int variable. */
12:
13: int *i_ptr, count;
14:
15: /* Declare and initialize a float array. */
16:
17: float f_array[MAX] = { .0, .1, .2, .3, .4, .5, .6, .7, .8, .9 };
18:
19: /* Declare a pointer to float. */
20:
21: float *f_ptr;
22:
23: main()
24: {
25:     /* Initialize the pointers. */
26:
27:     i_ptr = i_array;
28:     f_ptr = f_array;
29:
30:     /* Print the array elements. */
31:
32:     for (count = 0; count < MAX; count++)
33:         printf("\n%d\t%f", *i_ptr++, *f_ptr++);
34:
35:     return 0;
36: }
```

Output

```
0       0.000000
1       0.100000
2       0.200000
3       0.300000
4       0.400000
5       0.500000
6       0.600000
7       0.700000
8       0.800000
9       0.900000
```

Analysis In this program, a defined constant named MAX is set to 10 on line 5; it is used throughout the listing. On line 9, MAX is used to set the number of elements in an array of ints named i_array. The elements in this array are initialized at the same time that the array is declared. Line 13 declares two additional int variables. The first is a pointer named i_ptr. You know this is a pointer because an indirection operator (*) is used. The other variable is a simple type int variable named count. In line 17, a second array is defined and initialized. This array is of type float, contains MAX values, and is initialized with float values. Line 21 declares a pointer to a float named f_ptr.

The main() function is on lines 23–36. The program assigns the beginning address of the two arrays to the pointers of their respective types on lines 27 and 28. Remember, an array name without the subscript is the same as the address of the array's beginning. A for statement in lines 32 and 33 uses the int variable count to count from 0 to the value of MAX. For each count, line 33 dereferences the two pointers and prints their values in a printf() function call. The increment operator then increments each of the pointers so that each points to the next element in the array before continuing with the next iteration of the for loop.

You might be thinking that the program in Listing 9.3 could just as well have used array subscript notation and dispensed with pointers altogether. This is true, and in simple programming tasks like this, the use of pointer notation doesn't offer any major advantages. As you start to write more complex programs, however, you should find the use of pointers advantageous.

Please remember that you cannot perform incrementing and decrementing operations on pointer constants. (An array name without brackets is a *pointer constant*.) Also remember that when you're manipulating pointers to array elements, the C compiler does not keep track of the start and finish of the array. If you're not careful, you can increment or decrement the pointer so it points somewhere in memory before or after the array. There is something stored there, but it isn't an array element. You should keep track of pointers and where they're pointing.

Other Pointer Manipulations

The only other pointer arithmetic operation is called *differencing,* which refers to subtracting two pointers. If you have two pointers to different elements of the same array, you can subtract them and find out how far apart they are. Again, pointer arithmetic automatically scales the answer so that it refers to array elements. Thus, if ptr1 and ptr2 point to elements of an array (of any type), the following expression tells you how far apart the elements are:

```
ptr1 - ptr2
```

Pointer comparisons are valid only between pointers that point to the same array. Under these circumstances, the relational operators ==, !=, >, <, >=, and <= work properly. Lower array elements (that is, those having a lower subscript) always have a lower address than higher array elements. Thus, if ptr1 and ptr2 point to elements of the same array, the comparison

```
ptr1 < ptr2
```

is true if ptr1 points to an earlier member of the array than ptr2 does.

This covers all allowed pointer operations. Many arithmetic operations that can be performed with regular variables, such as multiplication and division, do not make sense with pointers. The C compiler does not allow them. For example, if ptr is a pointer, the statement

```
ptr *= 2;
```

generates an error message. As Table 9.1 indicates, you can do a total of six operations with a pointer, all of which have been covered in this chapter.

Table 9.1. Pointer operations.

Operation	Description
Assignment	You can assign a value to a pointer. The value should be an address, obtained with the address-of operator (&) or from a pointer constant (array name).
Indirection	The indirection operator (*) gives the value stored in the pointed-to location.
Address of	You can use the address-of operator to find the address of a pointer, so you can have pointers to pointers. This is an advanced topic and is covered on Day 15, "More on Pointers."
Incrementing	You can add an integer to a pointer in order to point to a different memory location.
Differencing	You can subtract an integer from a pointer in order to point to a different memory location.
Comparisons	Valid only with two pointers that point to the same array.

Pointer Cautions

When you are writing a program that uses pointers, you must avoid one serious error: using an uninitialized pointer on the left side of an assignment statement. For example, the following statement declares a pointer to type int:

```
int *ptr;
```

This pointer is not yet initialized, so it doesn't point to anything. To be more exact, it doesn't point to anything *known*. An uninitialized pointer has some value; you just don't know what it is. In many cases it is zero. If you use an uninitialized pointer in an assignment statement, therefore, this is what happens:

```
*ptr = 12;
```

The value 12 is assigned to whatever address ptr points to. That address can be almost anywhere in memory—where the operating system is stored or somewhere in the program's code. The 12 that is stored there may overwrite some important information, and the result can be anything from strange program errors to a full system crash.

The left side of an assignment statement is the most dangerous place to use an uninitialized pointer. Other errors, although less serious, can also result from using an uninitialized pointer anywhere in your program, so be sure your program's pointers are properly initialized before you use them. You must do this yourself. The compiler doesn't watch out for you!

DO	**DON'T**

DON'T try to do mathematical operations such as division, multiplication, and modulus on pointers. Adding (incrementing) and subtracting (differencing) pointers are acceptable.

DON'T forget that subtracting or adding to a pointer changes the pointer based on the size of the data type it points to, not by 1 or the number being added (unless it is a pointer to a one-byte character).

DO understand the size of variable types on your computer. As you can begin to see, you need to know variable sizes when working with pointers and memory.

DON'T try to increment or decrement an array variable. Assign a pointer to the beginning address of the array and increment it (see Listing 9.3).

Array Subscript Notation and Pointers

An array name without brackets is a pointer to the array's first element. You can, therefore, access the first array element using the indirection operator. If array[] is a declared array, the expression *array is the array's first element, *(array + 1) is the array's second element, and so on. If you generalize for the entire array, the following relationships hold true:

```
*(array) == array[0]
*(array + 1) == array[1]
*(array + 2) == array[2]
...
*(array + n) == array[n]
```

This illustrates the equivalence of array subscript notation and array pointer notation. You can use either in your program; the C compiler sees them as two different ways of accessing array data using pointers.

Passing Arrays to Functions

This chapter already has discussed the special relationship that exists in C between pointers and arrays. This relationship comes into play when you need to pass an array as an argument to a function. The only way you can pass an array to a function is by means of a pointer.

As you learned on Day 5, "Functions: The Basics," an argument is a value that the calling program passes to a function. It can be an int, a float, or any other simple data type, but it has to be a single numerical value. It can be a single array element, but it cannot be an entire array. What if you need to pass an entire array to a function? Well, you can have a pointer to an array, and that pointer is a single numeric value (the address of the array's first element). If you pass that value to a function, the function "knows" the address of the array and can access the array elements using pointer notation.

Consider another problem, however. If you write a function that takes an array as an argument, you want a function able to handle arrays of different sizes. For example, you could write a function that finds the largest element in an integer array. The function wouldn't be much use if it were limited to dealing with arrays of one fixed size (number of elements).

How does the function know the size of the array whose address it was passed? Remember, the value passed to a function is a pointer to the first array element. It could be the first of 10 elements or the first of 10,000. There are two methods for letting a function "know" an array's size.

You can identify the last array element by storing some special value there. As the function processes the array, it looks for that value in each element. When the value is found, the end of the array has been reached. The disadvantage of this method is that it forces you to reserve some value as the end-of-array indicator, reducing the flexibility you have for storing real data in the array.

The other method is more flexible and straightforward: pass the function the array size as an argument. This can be a simple type int argument. Thus, the function is passed two arguments: a pointer to the first array element and an integer specifying the number of elements in the array. This second method is used in this book.

Listing 9.4 accepts a list of values from the user and stores them in an array. It then calls a function named largest(), passing the array (both pointer and size). The function finds the largest value in the array and returns it to the calling program.

Type   **Listing 9.4. Demonstration of passing an array to a function.**

```
1: /* Passing an array to a function. */
2:
3: #include <stdio.h>
4:
5: #define MAX 10
6:
7: int array[MAX], count;
8:
9: int largest(int x[], int y);
10:
11: main()
12: {
13:     /* Input MAX values from the keyboard. */
14:
15:     for (count = 0; count < MAX; count++)
16:     {
```

continues

Listing 9.4. continued

```
17:            printf("Enter an integer value: ");
18:            scanf("%d", &array[count]);
19:      }
20:
21:      /* Call the function and display the return value. */
22:      printf("\n\nLargest value = %d", largest(array, MAX));
23:
24:      return 0;
25: }
26: /* Function largest() returns the largest value */
27: /* in an integer array */
28:
29: int largest(int x[], int y)
30: {
31:      int count, biggest = -12000;
32:
33:      for ( count = 0; count < y; count++)
34:      {
35:          if (x[count] > biggest)
36:              biggest = x[count];
37:      }
38:
39:      return biggest;
40: }
```

Input Output

```
Enter an integer value: 1
Enter an integer value: 2
Enter an integer value: 3
Enter an integer value: 4
Enter an integer value: 5
Enter an integer value: 10
Enter an integer value: 9
Enter an integer value: 8
Enter an integer value: 7
Enter an integer value: 6

Largest value = 10
```

 Analysis There is a function prototype in line 9 and a function header in line 29 that are nearly identical except for a semicolon:

```
int largest(int x[], int y)
```

Most of this line should make sense to you: largest() is a function that returns an int to the calling program; its second argument is an int represented by the parameter y. The only thing new is the first parameter int x[], which indicates that the first argument is a pointer to type int, represented by the parameter x. You also could write the function declaration and header as follows:

```
int largest(int *x, int y);
```

This is equivalent to the first form; both int x[] and int *x mean "pointer to int." The first form may be preferable because it reminds you that the parameter represents a pointer to an array. Of course, the pointer doesn't know that it points to an array, but the function uses it that way.

Now look at the function largest(). When it is called, the parameter x holds the value of the first argument and is therefore a pointer to the first element of the array. You can use x anywhere an array pointer could be used. In largest(), the array elements are accessed using subscript notation on lines 35 and 36. You also have used pointer notation, rewriting the if loop to be

```
for (count = 0; count < y; count++)
{
    if (*(x+count) > biggest)
        biggest = *(x+count);
}
```

Listing 9.5 shows the other way of passing arrays to functions.

Listing 9.5. An alternative way for passing an array to a function.

```
1: /* Passing an array to a function. Alternative way. */
2:
3: #include <stdio.h>
4:
5: #define MAX 10
6:
7: int array[MAX+1], count;
8:
9: int largest(int x[]);
10:
11: main()
12: {
13:     /* Input MAX values from the keyboard. */
14:
15:     for (count = 0; count < MAX; count++)
16:     {
17:         printf("Enter an integer value: ");
18:         scanf("%d", &array[count]);
19:
20:         if ( array[count] == 0 )
21:             count = MAX;                     /* will exit for loop */
22:     }
23:     array[MAX] = 0;
24:
25:     /* Call the function and display the return value. */
26:     printf("\n\nLargest value = %d", largest(array));
27:
28:     return 0;
29: }
30: /* Function largest() returns the largest value */
31: /* in an integer array */
```

continues

189

Listing 9.5. continued

```
32:
33: int largest(int x[])
34: {
35:     int count, biggest = -12000;
36:
37:     for ( count = 0; x[count] != 0; count++)
38:     {
39:         if (x[count] > biggest)
40:             biggest = x[count];
41:     }
42:
43:     return biggest;
44: }
```

Input Output

```
Enter an integer value: 1
Enter an integer value: 2
Enter an integer value: 3
Enter an integer value: 4
Enter an integer value: 5
Enter an integer value: 10
Enter an integer value: 9
Enter an integer value: 8
Enter an integer value: 7
Enter an integer value: 6

Largest value = 10
```

This program uses a `largest()` function that has the same functionality as the previous listing. The difference is that only the array tag is needed. The `for` loop in line 37 continues looking for the largest value until it encounters a 0, at which point it knows it is done.

Looking at the early parts of the listing, you can see the differences between Listing 9.4 and Listing 9.5. First, in line 7 you need to add an extra element to the array to store the value that flags the end. In lines 20 and 21 an `if` statement is added to see whether the users entered a zero, thus signaling that they are done entering values. If zero is entered, `count` is set to its maximum value so that the `for` loop can be cleanly exited. Line 23 ensures that the last element is a zero in case users entered the maximum number of values (`MAX`).

By adding the extra commands when entering the data, you can make the `largest()` function work with any size of array; however, there is one catch. What happens if you forget to put a zero at the end of the array? Then `largest()` continues past the end of the array, comparing values in memory until it finds a zero.

As you can see, passing an array to a function is not particularly difficult. You simply pass a pointer to the array's first element. In most situations, you also need to pass the number of elements in the array. In the function, the pointer value can be used to access the array elements with either subscript or pointer notation.

9

> **Caution:** Recall from Day 5 that when a simple variable is passed to a function, only a copy of the variable's value is passed. The function can use the value but cannot change the original variable because it doesn't have access to the variable itself. When you pass an array to a function, things are different. A function is passed the array's address, not just a copy of the values in the array. The code in the function is working with the actual array elements and can modify the values stored in the array.

Summary

This chapter introduced you to pointers, a central part of C programming. A pointer is a variable that holds the address of another variable; a pointer is said to "point to" the variable whose address it holds. The two operators needed with pointers are the address-of operator (&) and the indirection operator (*). When placed before a variable name, the address-of operator returns the variable's address. When placed before a pointer name, the indirection operator returns the contents of the pointed-to variable.

Pointers and arrays have a special relationship. An array name without brackets is a pointer to the array's first element. The special features of pointer arithmetic make it easy to access array elements using pointers. Array subscript notation is in fact a special form of pointer notation.

You also learned to pass arrays as arguments to functions by passing a pointer to the array. Once the function "knows" the array's address and length, it can access the array elements using either pointer notation or subscript notation.

Q&A

Q Why are pointers so important in C?

A Pointers give you more control of the computer and your data. When used with functions, pointers enable you to change the values of variables that were passed, regardless of where they have originated. On Day 15, "More on Pointers," you will learn additional uses for pointers.

Q How does the compiler know the difference among * for multiplication, for dereferencing, and for declaring a pointer?

A The compiler interprets the different uses of the asterisk based on the context in which it is used. If the statement being evaluated starts with a variable type, it can be assumed that the asterisk is for declaring a pointer. If the asterisk is used with a variable that has been declared as a pointer, but not in a variable declaration, the asterisk is assumed to dereference. If it is used in a mathematical expression, but not with a pointer variable, the asterisk can be assumed to be the multiplication operator.

Q **What happens if I use the address-of operator on a pointer?**

A You get the address of the pointer variable. Remember, a pointer is just another variable that holds the address of the variable to which it points.

Q **Are variables always stored in the same location?**

A No. Each time a program runs, its variables can be stored at different addresses. You should never assign a constant address value to a pointer.

Workshop

The Workshop provides quiz questions to help you solidify your understanding of the material covered and exercises to provide you with experience in using what you've learned.

Quiz

1. What operator is used to determine the address of a variable?
2. What operator is used to determine the value at the location pointed to by a pointer?
3. What is a pointer?
4. What is indirection?
5. How are the elements of an array stored in memory?
6. Show two ways to obtain the address of the first element of the array `data[]`.
7. If an array is passed to a function, what are two ways to know where the end of that array is?
8. What are the six operations covered in this chapter that can be done with a pointer?
9. Assume you have two pointers. If the first points to the third element in an array of `ints` and the second points to the fourth element, what value is obtained if you subtract the first pointer from the second?
10. Assume the array in the previous question is of `float` values. What value is obtained if the two pointers are subtracted?

Exercises

1. Show a declaration for a pointer to a type `char` variable. Name the pointer `char_ptr`.
2. If you have a type `int` variable named `cost`, how would you declare and initialize a pointer named `p_cost` that points to that variable?

3. Continuing with exercise 2, how would you assign the value `100` to the variable `cost` using both direct access and indirect access?

4. Continuing with exercise 3, how would you print the value of the pointer, plus the value being pointed to?

5. Show how to assign the address of a `float` value called `radius` to a pointer.

6. Show two ways to assign the value `100` to the third element of `data[]`.

7. Write a function named `sumarrays()` that accepts two arrays as arguments, totals all values in both arrays, and returns the total to the calling program.

8. Use the function created in exercise 7 in a simple program.

9. Write a function named `addarrays()` that accepts two arrays which are the same size. The function should add each element in the arrays together and place the values in a third array.

10. Modify the function in exercise 9 to return a pointer to the array containing the totals. Place this function in a program that also prints the values in all three arrays.

Characters and Strings

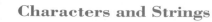
A *character* is a single letter, numeral, punctuation mark, or other such symbol. A *string* is any sequence of characters. Strings are used to hold text data—comprised of letters, numerals, punctuation marks, and other symbols. Clearly, characters and strings are extremely useful in many programming applications. Today, you learn

- How to use C's char data type to hold single characters
- How to create arrays of type char to hold multiple-character strings
- How to initialize characters and strings
- How to use pointers with strings
- How to print and input characters and strings

The *char* Data Type

C uses the char data type to hold characters. You saw on Day 3, "Numeric Variables and Constants," that char is one of C's numeric integer data types. If char is a numeric type, how can it be used to hold characters?

The answer lies in how C stores characters. Your computer's memory stores all data in numeric form. There is no direct way to store characters. A numeric code exists for each character, however. This is called the *ASCII code* or the ASCII character set. (ASCII stands for American Standard Code for Information Interchange.) The code assigns values between 0 and 255 for upper- and lowercase letters, numeric digits, punctuation marks, and other symbols. The ASCII character set is listed in Appendix A, "ASCII Character Chart."

For example, 97 is the ASCII code for the letter a. When you store the character a in a type char variable, you're really storing the value 97. Because the allowable numeric range for type char matches the standard ASCII character set, char is ideally suited for storing characters.

At this point, you might be a bit puzzled. If C stores characters as numbers, how does your program know whether a given type char variable is a character or a number? As you learn later, declaring a variable as type char is not enough; you must do something else with the variable:

- If a char variable is used somewhere in a C program where a character is expected, it is interpreted as a character.
- If a char variable is used somewhere in a C program where a number is expected, it is interpreted as a number.

This gives you some understanding of how C uses a numeric data type to store character data. Now you can go on to the details.

Using Character Variables

Like other variables, you must declare chars before using them, and you can initialize them at the time of declaration. Here are some examples:

```
char a, b, c;          /* Declare three uninitialized char variables */
char code = 'x';       /* Declare the char variable named code */
                       /* and store the character x there */
code = '!';            /* Store ! in the variable named code */
```

To create literal character constants, enclose a single character in single quotation marks. The compiler automatically translates literal character constants into the corresponding ASCII codes, and the numeric code value is assigned to the variable.

You can create symbolic character constants by using either the #define directive or the const keyword.

```
#define EX 'x'
char code = EX;        /* Sets code equal to 'x' */
const char A = 'Z';
```

Now that you know how to declare and initialize character variables, it's time for a demonstration. The program in Listing 10.1 illustrates the numeric nature of character storage using the printf() function you learned on Day 7, "Basic Input/Output." The function printf() can be used to print both characters and numbers. The format string %c instructs printf() to print a character, whereas %d instructs it to print a decimal integer. Listing 10.1 initializes two type char variables and prints each one, first as a character and then as a number.

Type

Listing 10.1. Demonstration of the numeric nature of type char variables.

```
 1:  /* Demonstrates the numeric nature of char variables */
 2:
 3:  #include <stdio.h>
 4:
 5:  /* Declare and initialize two char variables */
 6:
 7:  char c1 = 'a';
 8:  char c2 = 90;
 9:
10:  main()
11:  {
12:      /* Print variable c1 as a character then as a number */
13:
14:      printf("\nAs a character, variable c1 is %c", c1);
15:      printf("\nAs a number, variable c1 is %d", c1);
16:
17:      /* Do the same for variable c2 */
18:
```

continues

Listing 10.1. continued

```
19:      printf("\nAs a character, variable c2 is %c", c2);
20:      printf("\nAs a number, variable c2 is %d", c2);
21:
22:      return 0;
23: }
```

```
As a character, variable c1 is a
As a number, variable c1 is 97
As a character, variable c2 is Z
As a number, variable c2 is 90
```

You learned on Day 3 that the allowable range for a variable of type char goes only to 127, whereas the ASCII codes go to 255. The ASCII codes are actually divided into two parts. The standard ASCII codes go only to 127; this range includes all letters, numbers, punctuation marks, and other keyboard symbols. The codes 128–255 are the extended ASCII codes and represent special characters such as foreign letters and graphics symbols (see Appendix A for a complete list). Thus, for standard text data, you can use type char variables; if you want to print the extended ASCII characters, you must use unsigned char.

The program in Listing 10.2 demonstrates printing some of the extended ASCII characters.

Type   ## Listing 10.2. Printing extended ASCII characters.

```
1:  /* Demonstrates printing extended ASCII characters */
2:
3:  #include <stdio.h>
4:
5:  unsigned char x;    /* Must be unsigned for extended ASCII */
6:
7:  main()
8:  {
9:      /* Print extended ASCII characters 180 through 203 */
10:
11:     for (x = 180; x < 204; x++)
12:     {
13:         printf("\nASCII code %d is character %c", x, x);
14:     }
15:
16:         return 0;
17: }
```

Output

```
ASCII code 180 is character ┤
ASCII code 181 is character ╡
ASCII code 182 is character ╢
ASCII code 183 is character ╖
ASCII code 184 is character ╕
ASCII code 185 is character ╣
ASCII code 186 is character ║
ASCII code 187 is character ╗
```

```
ASCII code 188 is character ╝
ASCII code 189 is character ╜
ASCII code 190 is character ╛
ASCII code 191 is character ┐
ASCII code 192 is character └
ASCII code 193 is character ┴
ASCII code 194 is character ┬
ASCII code 195 is character ├
ASCII code 196 is character ─
ASCII code 197 is character ┼
ASCII code 198 is character ╞
ASCII code 199 is character ╟
ASCII code 200 is character ╚
ASCII code 201 is character ╔
ASCII code 202 is character ╩
ASCII code 203 is character ╦
```

 Looking at this program, you see that line 5 declares an unsigned character variable, x. This gives a range of 0 to 255. As with other numeric data types, you must not initialize a char variable to a value outside of the allowed range or you may get unexpected results. In line 11, x is not initialized outside the range; instead, it is initialized to 180. In the for statement, x is incremented by 1 until it reaches 204. Each time x is incremented, line 13 prints the value of x and the character value of x. Remember that %c prints the character, or ASCII, value of x.

10

DO	DON'T

DO use %c to print the character value of a number.

DON'T use double quotations when initializing a character variable.

DO use single quotations when initializing a variable.

DON'T try to put extended ASCII character values into a type signed char variable.

DO look at the ASCII chart in Appendix A to see the interesting characters that can be printed.

 Note: Some computer systems may use a different character set; however, most use the same values for 0 to 127.

Using Strings

Variables of type char can hold only a single character, so they have limited usefulness. You also need a way to store *strings*, which are sequences of characters. An individual's name or address are examples of strings. Although there is no special data type for strings, C handles this type of information with arrays of characters.

Arrays of Characters

To hold a string of six characters, for example, you need to declare an array of type char with *seven* elements. Arrays of type char are declared like arrays of other data types. For example, the statement

```
char string[10];
```

declares a ten-element array of type char. This array could be used to hold a string of nine or fewer characters.

"But wait," you may be thinking, "it's a 10-element array, so why can it hold only nine characters? In C, a string is defined as a sequence of characters ending with the null character, a special character represented by \0. Although it's represented by two characters (backslash and zero), the null character is interpreted as a single character and has the ASCII value of 0. It's one of C's escape sequences, covered on Day 7.

When a C program stores the string Alabama, for example, it actually stores the seven characters A, l, a, b, a, m, and a, followed by the null character \0, for a total of eight characters. Thus, a character array can hold a string of characters numbering one less than the total number of elements in the array.

A type char variable is one byte in size, so the number of bytes in an array of type char variables is the same as the number of elements in the array.

Initializing Character Arrays

Like other C data types, character arrays can be initialized when they are declared. Character arrays can be assigned values element by element, as shown here:

```
char string[10] = { 'A', 'l', 'a', 'b', 'a', 'm', 'a', '\0' };
```

It's more convenient, however, to use a *literal string,* which is a sequence of characters enclosed in double quotes:

```
char string[10] = "Alabama";
```

When you use a literal string in your program, the compiler automatically adds the terminating null character at the end of the string. If you do not specify the number of subscripts when you declare an array, the compiler calculates the size of the array for you. Thus, the following line creates and initializes an eight-element array:

```
char string[] = "Alabama";
```

Remember that strings require a terminating null character. The C functions that manipulate strings (covered on Day 17, "Manipulating Strings") determine string length by looking for the null character. The functions have no other way of recognizing the end of the string. If the null character is missing, your program thinks that the string extends until the next null character in memory. Pesky program bugs can result from this sort of error.

Strings and Pointers

You've seen that strings are stored in arrays of type char, with the end of the string (which may not occupy the entire array) marked by the null character. Because the end of the string is marked, all you need to define a given string is something that points to its beginning. (Is *points* the right word? Indeed it is!)

With that hint, you might be leaping ahead of the game. From Day 9, "Pointers," you know that the name of an array is a pointer to the first element of the array. Therefore, for a string that's stored in an array, you need only the array name in order to access it. In fact, using the array's name is C's standard method for accessing strings.

To be more precise, using the array's name for accessing strings is the method the C library functions expect. The C standard library includes a number of functions that manipulate strings. (These functions are covered on Day 17.) To pass a string to one of these functions, you pass the array name. The same is true for the string display functions printf() and puts(), discussed later in this chapter.

You may have noticed that the phrase, "strings stored in an array," is used. Does this imply that some strings are not stored in arrays? Indeed it does, and the next section explains how.

Strings Without Arrays

From the last section, you know that a string is defined by the character array's name and by a null character. The array's name is a type char pointer to the beginning of the string. The null marks the string's end. The actual space occupied by the string in an array is incidental. In fact, the only purpose the array serves is to provide allocated space for the string.

What if you could find some memory storage space without allocating an array? You could then store a string with its terminating null character there instead. A pointer to the first character could serve to specify the string's beginning just as if the string were in an allocated array. How do you go about finding memory storage space? There are two methods: one allocates space for a literal string when the program is compiled and the other uses the malloc() function to allocate space while the program is executing, a process known as *dynamic allocation*.

Allocating String Space at Compilation

The start of a string, as mentioned earlier, is indicated by a pointer to a variable of type char. You might recall how to declare such a pointer:

```
char *message;
```

This statement declares a pointer to a variable of type char named message. It doesn't point to anything now, but what if you change the pointer declaration to read:

```
char *message = "Great Caesar's Ghost!";
```

When this statement executes, the string Great Caesar's Ghost! (with terminating null character) is stored somewhere in memory, and the pointer message is initialized to point at the first character of the string. Don't worry where in memory the string is stored; it's handled automatically by the compiler. Once defined, message is a pointer to the string and can be used as such.

The preceding declaration/initialization is equivalent to the following, and the two notations *message and message[] also are equivalent; they both mean "a pointer to."

```
char message[] = "Great Caesar's Ghost!";
```

This method of allocating space for string storage is fine when you know what you need while writing the program. What if the program has varying string storage needs, depending on user input or other factors that are unknown when you are writing the program? You use the malloc() function, which enables you to allocate storage space "on the fly."

The *malloc()* Function

The malloc() function is one of C's *memory allocation* functions. When you call malloc(), you pass it the number of bytes of memory needed. malloc() finds and reserves a block of memory of the required size and returns the address of the first byte in the block. You don't need to worry about where the memory is found; it's handled automatically.

The malloc() function returns an address, and its return type is a pointer to type void. Why void? A pointer to type void is compatible with all data types. Because the memory allocated by malloc() can be used to store any of C's data types, the void return type is appropriate.

The *malloc()* Function

```
#include <stdlib.h>
void *malloc(size_t size);
```

malloc() allocates a block of memory that is the number of bytes stated in *size*. By allocating memory as needed with malloc() instead of all at once when a program starts, you can use a computer's memory more efficiently. When using malloc(), you need to include the STDLIB.H header file. Some compilers have other header files that can be included; for portability, however, it is best to include STDLIB.H.

malloc() returns a pointer to the allocated block of memory. If malloc() was unable to allocate the required amount of memory, it returns null. Whenever you try to allocate memory, you should always check the return value, even if the amount of memory to be allocated is small.

Example 1

```
#include <stdlib.h>

main()
{
    /* allocate memory for a 100 character string */
    char *str;
    if (( str = (char *) malloc(100)) == NULL)
    {
        printf( "Not enough memory to allocate buffer\n");
        exit(1);
    }
    printf( "String was allocated!" );
    return 0;
}
```

Example 2

```
/* allocate memory for an array of 50 integers */
int *numbers;
numbers = (int *) malloc(50 * sizeof(int));
```

Example 3

```
/* allocate memory for an array of 10 float values */
float *numbers;
numbers = (float *) malloc(10 * sizeof(float));
```

Using the *malloc()* Function

You can use malloc() to allocate memory to store a single type char. First, declare a pointer to type char:

```
char *ptr;
```

Next, call `malloc()` and pass the size of the desired memory block. Because a type `char` usually occupies one byte, you need a block of one byte. The value returned by `malloc()` is assigned to the pointer:

```
ptr = malloc(1);
```

This statement allocates a memory block of one byte and assigns its address to `ptr`. Unlike variables that are declared in the program, this byte of memory has no name. Only the pointer can reference the variable. For example, to store the character `'x'` there, you would write

```
*ptr = 'x';
```

Allocating storage for a string with `malloc()` is almost identical to using `malloc()` to allocate space for a single variable of type `char`. The main difference is that you need to know the amount of space to allocate—the maximum number of characters in the string. This maximum depends on the needs of your program. For this example, say you want to allocate space for a string of 99 characters, plus one for the terminating null character, for a total of 100. First, you declare a pointer to type `char`, and then call `malloc()`:

```
char *ptr;
ptr = malloc(100);
```

Now, `ptr` points to a reserved block of 100 bytes that can be used for string storage and manipulation. You can use `ptr` just as though your program had explicitly allocated that space with the following array declaration:

```
char ptr[100];
```

Using `malloc()` enables your program to allocate storage space as needed in response to demand. Of course, available space is not unlimited; it depends on the amount of memory installed in your computer and on the program's other storage requirements. If not enough memory is available, `malloc()` returns `0` (null). Your program should test the return value of `malloc()`, so you are sure the memory requested was allocated successfully. You always should test `malloc()`'s return value against the symbolic constant `NULL`, which is defined in STDLIB.H. Listing 10.3 illustrates the use of `malloc()`. Any program using `malloc()` must `#include` the header file STDLIB.H.

 Listing 10.3. Using the `malloc()` function to allocate storage space for string data.

```
1:  /* Demonstrates the use of malloc() to allocate storage */
2:  /* space for string data. */
3:
4:  #include <stdio.h>
5:  #include <stdlib.h>
6:
7:  char count, *ptr, *p;
8:
```

```
 9:  main()
10:  {
11:      /* Allocate a block of 35 bytes. Test for success. */
12:      /* The exit() library function terminates the program. */
13:
14:      ptr = malloc(35 * sizeof(char));
15:
16:      if (ptr == NULL)
17:      {
18:          puts("Memory allocation error.");
19:          exit(1);
20:      }
21:
22:      /* Fill the string with values 65 through 90, */
23:      /* which are the ASCII codes for A-Z. */
24:
25:      /* p is a pointer used to step through the string. */
26:      /* You want ptr to remain pointed at the start */
27:      /* of the string. */
28:
29:      p = ptr;
30:
31:      for (count = 65; count < 91 ; count++)
32:          *p++ = count;
33:
34:      /* Add the terminating null character. */
35:
36:      *p = '\0';
37:
38:      /* Display the string on the screen. */
39:
40:      puts(ptr);
41:
42:      return 0;
43:  }
```

ABCDEFGHIJKLMNOPQRSTUVWXYZ

This program uses malloc() in a simple way. Although this program seems long, it is filled with comments. Lines 1, 2, 11, 12, 22–27, 34, and 38 are all comments that detail everything that the program does. Line 5 includes the STDLIB.H header file needed for malloc(), and line 4 includes the STDIO.H header file for the puts() functions. Line 7 declares two pointers and a character variable used later in the listing. None of these variables are initialized, so they should not be used—yet!

The malloc() function is called in line 14 with a parameter of 35 multiplied by *the size of* a char. Could you have just put 35? Yes, but you are making an assumption that everyone running this program will be using a computer that stores char type variables as one byte in size. Remember from Day 3 that different compilers can use different size variables. Using the sizeof operator is an easy way to create portable code.

205

Never assume that `malloc()` gets the memory you tell it to get. In fact, you are not telling it to get memory, you are asking it. Line 16 shows the easiest way to check to see whether `malloc()` provided the memory. If the memory was allocated, `ptr` points to it; otherwise, `ptr` is null. If the program failed to get the memory, lines 18 and 19 display an error message and gracefully exit the program.

Line 29 initializes the other pointer declared in line 7, `p`. It is assigned the same address value as `ptr`. A `for` loop uses this new pointer to place values into the allocated memory. Looking at line 31, you see that `count` is initialized to 65 and incremented by 1 until it reaches 91. For each loop of the `for` statement, the value of `count` is assigned to the address pointed to by `p`. Notice that each time `count` is incremented, the address pointed to by `p` is also incremented. This means that each value is placed one after the other in memory.

You should have noticed that numbers are being assigned to `count`, which is a type `char` variable. Don't forget the discussion about the ASCII characters and their numeric equivalents. The number 65 is equivalent to A, 66 = B, 67 = C, and so on. The `for` loop ends after the alphabet is assigned to the memory locations pointed to. Line 36 caps off the character values pointed to by putting a null at the final address pointed to by `p`. By appending the null, you now can use these values as a string. Remember that `ptr` still points to the first value, A, so if you use it as a string, it prints every character until it reaches the null. Line 40 uses `puts()` to prove this point and to show the results of what has been done.

DO	DON'T

DON'T allocate more memory than you need. Not everyone has a lot of memory, so you should try to use it sparingly.

DON'T try to assign a new string to a character array that was previously allocated only enough memory to hold a smaller string. For example,

```
char a_string[] = "NO";
```

In this declaration, `a_string` points to `"NO"`. If you try to assign `"YES"` to this array, you could have serious problems. The array initially could hold only three characters, `'N'`, `'O'`, and a null. `"YES"` is four characters, `'Y'`, `'E'`, `'S'` and a null. You have no idea what the fourth character, null, overwrites.

Displaying Strings and Characters

If your program uses string data, it probably needs to display the data on the screen at some time. String display is usually done with either the `puts()` function or the `printf()` function.

The *puts()* Function

You've seen the puts() library function used in some of the programs given in this book. The puts() function puts a string on the screen—hence its name. A pointer to the string to be displayed is the only argument puts() takes. Because a literal string evaluates as a pointer to a string, puts() can be used to display literal strings as well as string variables. The puts() function automatically inserts a newline character at the end of each string that it displays, so each subsequent string displayed with puts() is on its own line.

The program in Listing 10.4 illustrates the use of puts().

Listing 10.4. Using the puts() function to display text on the screen.

```
1: /* Demonstrates displaying strings with puts(). */
2:
3: #include <stdio.h>
4:
5: char *message1 = "C";
6: char *message2 - "is the";
7: char *message3 = "best";
8: char *message4 = "programming";
9: char *message5 = "language!!";
10:
11: main()
12: {
13:    puts(message1);
14:    puts(message2);
15:    puts(message3);
16:    puts(message4);
17:    puts(message5);
18:
19:    return 0;
20: }
```

```
C
is the
best
programming
language!!
```

This is a fairly simple listing to follow. Because puts() is a standard input/output function, the STDIO.H header file "needs" to be included as done on line 3. Lines 5–9 declare and initialize five different message variables. Each of these variables is a character pointer, or string variable. Lines 13–17 use the puts() function to print each string.

The *printf()* Function

You also can display strings with the `printf()` library function. Recall from Day 7 that `printf()` uses a format string and conversion specifiers to shape its output. To display a string, use the conversion specifier `%s`.

When `printf()` encounters a `%s` in its format string, the function matches the `%s` with the corresponding argument in its argument list. For a string, this argument must be a pointer to the string that you want displayed. The `printf()` function displays the string on-screen, stopping when it reaches the string's terminating null character. For example,

```
char *str = "A message to display";
printf("%s", str);
```

You also can display multiple strings and mix them with literal text and/or numeric variables.

```
char *bank = "First Federal";
char *name = "John Doe";
int balance = 1000;
printf("The balance at %s for %s is %d.", bank, name, balance);
```

The resulting output is

```
The balance at First Federal for John Doe is 1000.
```

For now, this information should be sufficient for you to be able to display string data in your programs. Complete details on using `printf()` are given on Day 14, "Working with the Screen, Printer, and Keyboard."

Reading Strings from the Keyboard

In addition to displaying strings, programs often need to accept inputted string data from the user, via the keyboard. The C library has two functions that can be used for this purpose, `gets()` and `scanf()`. Before you can read in a string from the keyboard, however, you must have somewhere to put it. Space for string storage can be created with either of the methods discussed earlier today, an array declaration or the `malloc()` function.

Inputting Strings with the *gets()* Function

The `gets()` function gets a string from the keyboard. When `gets()` is called, it reads all characters typed at the keyboard up to the first newline character (which you generate by pressing Enter). The function discards the newline, adds a null character, and gives the string to the calling program. The string is stored at the location indicated by a pointer to type `char` passed to `gets()`. A program that uses `gets()` must `#include` the file STDIO.H. Listing 10.5 presents an example.

Listing 10.5. Using `gets()` to input string data from the keyboard.

```
1:  /* Demonstrates using the gets() library function. */
2:
3:  #include <stdio.h>
4:
5:  /* Allocate a character array to hold input. */
6:
7:  char input[81];
8:
9:  main()
10: {
11:     puts("Enter some text, then press Enter ");
12:     gets(input);
13:     printf("You entered %s", input);
14:
15:     return 0;
16: }
```

10

```
Enter some text, then press Enter This is a test
You entered This is a test
```

In this example, the argument to `gets()` is the expression `input`, which is the name of a type `char` array and therefore a pointer to the first array element. The array was declared with 81 elements in line 7. Because the maximum line length possible on most computer screens is 80 characters, this array size provides space for the longest possible input line (plus the null character that `gets()` adds at the end).

The `gets()` function has a return value, which was ignored in the previous example. `gets()` returns a pointer to type `char` with the address where the input string is stored. Yes, this is the same value that is passed to `gets()`, but having the value returned to the program in this way enables your program to test for a blank line. Listing 10.6 shows how to do this.

Listing 10.6. Using the `gets()` return value to test for input of a blank line.

```
1:  /* Demonstrates using the gets() return value. */
2:
3:  #include <stdio.h>
4:
5:  /* Declare a character array to hold input, and a pointer. */
6:
7:  char input[81], *ptr;
8:
9:  main()
10: {
11:     /* Display instructions. */
12:
```

continues

Listing 10.6. continued

```
13:     puts("Enter text a line at a time, then press Enter.");
14:     puts("Enter a blank line when done.");
15:
16:     /* Loop as long as input is not a blank line. */
17:
18:     while ( *(ptr = gets(input)) != NULL)
19:         printf("You entered %s\n", input);
20:
21:     puts("Thank you and good-bye");
22:
23:     return 0;
24: }
```

Input
Output

```
Enter text a line at a time, then press Enter.
Enter a blank line when done.
First string
You entered First string
Two
You entered Two
Bradley L. Jones
You entered Bradley L. Jones

Thank you and good-bye
```

Analysis

Now you can see how the program works. If you enter a blank line (that is, if you simply press Enter) in response to line 18, the string (which contains 0 characters) is still stored with a null character at the end. Because the string has a length of 0, the null character is stored in the first position. This is the position pointed to by the return value of gets(), so if you test that position and find a null character, you know that a blank line was entered.

Listing 10.6 performs this test in the while statement in line 18. This statement is a bit complicated, so look carefully at the details in order.

Figure 10.1 labels the components of the statement for easy reference.

Figure 10.1.

The components of a while statement that test for input of a blank line.

```
        4   3     1     2      6  5
        ↓   ↓     ↓     ↓      ↓  ↓
while ( *( ptr = gets(input)) != NULL)
```

1. The gets() function accepts input from the keyboard until it reaches a newline character.

2. The input string, minus the newline and with a trailing null character, is stored in the memory location pointed to by input.

3. The address of the string (the same value as input) is returned to the pointer ptr.

4. An assignment statement is an expression that evaluates to the value of the variable on the left side of the assignment operator. Therefore, the entire expression

210

`ptr = gets(input)` evaluates to the value of `ptr`. By enclosing this expression in parentheses and preceding it with the indirection operator (`*`), the value stored at the pointed-to address is obtained. This is, of course, the first character of the input string.

5. `NULL` is a symbolic constant defined in the header file STDIO.H. It has the value of the null character (zero).

6. If the first character of the input string is not the null character (if a blank line has not been entered), the comparison operator returns True and the `while` loop executes. If the first character is the null character (if a blank line has been entered), the comparison operator returns False and the `while` loop terminates.

When you use `gets()` or any other function that stores data using a pointer, be sure that the pointer points to allocated space. It's easy to make a mistake such as the following:

```
char *ptr;
gets(ptr);
```

The pointer `ptr` has been declared but not initialized. It points somewhere, but you don't know where. The `gets()` function can't know this, so it simply goes ahead and stores the input string at the address contained in `ptr`. The string may overwrite something important, such as program code or the operating system. The compiler doesn't catch these kinds of mistakes, so you, the programmer, must be vigilant.

The *gets()* Function

```
#include <stdio.h>
char *gets(char *str);
```

The `gets()` function gets a string, `str`, from the standard input device, usually the keyboard. The string consists of any characters entered until a newline character is read. At that point, a null is appended to the end of the string.

Then the `gets()` function also returns a pointer to the string just read. If there is a problem getting the string, `gets()` returns null.

Example

```
/* gets() example */
#include <stdio.h>

char line[256];

void main()
{
    printf( "Enter a string:\n");
    gets( line );
    printf( "\nYou entered the following string:\n" );
    printf( "%s", line );
}
```

Inputting Strings with the *scanf()* Function

You saw on Day 7 that the `scanf()` library function accepts numeric data input from the keyboard. This function also can input strings. Remember that `scanf()` uses a *format string* that tells it how to read the input. To read a string, include the specifier `%s` in `scanf()`'s format string. Like `gets()`, `scanf()` is passed a pointer to the string's storage location.

How does `scanf()` decide where the string begins and ends? The beginning is the first non-whitespace character encountered. The end can be specified in one of two ways. If you use `%s` in the format string, the string runs up to (but not including) the next whitespace character (space, tab, or newline). If you use `%ns` (where *n* is an integer constant that specifies field width), `scanf()` inputs the next *n* characters or up to the next whitespace character, whichever comes first.

You can read in multiple strings with `scanf()` by including more than one `%s` in the format string. For each `%s` in the format string, `scanf()` uses the preceding rules to find the requested number of strings in the input. For example,

```
scanf("%s%s%s", s1, s2, s3);
```

If in response to this statement, you enter January February March, January is assigned to the string s1, February is assigned to s2, and March to s3.

What about using the field width specifier? If you execute the statement

```
scanf("%3s%3s%3s", s1, s2, s3);
```

and in response, you enter the following, Sep is assigned to s1, tem is assigned to s2, and ber is assigned to s3:

```
September
```

What if you enter fewer or more strings than the `scanf()` function expects? If you enter fewer strings, `scanf()` continues to "look" for the missing strings, and the program does not continue until they are entered. For example, if in response to the statement

```
scanf("%s%s%s", s1, s2, s3);
```

you enter the following:

```
January February
```

the program sits and waits for the third string specified in the `scanf()` format string. If you enter more strings than requested, the unmatched strings remain pending (waiting in the keyboard buffer) and are read by any subsequent `scanf()` or other input statements. For example, if in response to the statements

```
scanf("%s%s", s1, s2);
scanf("%s", s3);
```

you enter the following, the result is that January is assigned to the string s1, February is assigned to s2, and March to s3:

January February March

The scanf() function has a return value, an integer value equaling the number of items successfully inputted. The return value is often ignored. When you are reading text only, the gets() function is usually preferable to scanf(). The scanf() function is best used when you are reading in a combination of text and numeric data. This is illustrated by the program in Listing 10.7. Remember from Day 7 that you must use the address-of operator (&) when inputting numeric variables with scanf().

Type **Listing 10.7. Inputting numeric and text data with scanf().**

```
1:  /* Demonstrates using scanf() to input numeric and text data. */
2:
3:  #include <stdio.h>
4:
5:  char lname[81], fname[81];
6:  int count, id_num;
7:
8:  main()
9:  {
10:     /* Prompt the user. */
11:
12:     puts("Enter last name, first name, ID number separated");
13:     puts("by spaces, then press Enter.");
14:
15:     /* Input the three data items. */
16:
17:     count = scanf("%s%s%d", lname, fname, &id_num);
18:
19:     /* Display the data. */
20:
21:     printf("%d items entered: %s %s %d", count, fname, lname, id_num);
22:
23:     return 0;
24: }
```

Enter last name, first name, ID number separated by spaces, then press Enter.
Jones Bradley 12345
3 items entered: Bradley Jones 12345

Remember that scanf() requires the addresses of variables for parameters. In Listing 10.7, lname and fname are pointers (that is, addresses), so they do not need the preceding address-of operator (&). In contrast, id_num is a regular variable name, so it requires the & when passed to scanf() on line 17.

Some programmers feel that data entry with scanf() is prone to errors. They prefer to input all data, numeric and string, using gets(), and then have the program separate the numbers and

213

convert them to numeric variables. Such techniques are beyond the scope of this book, but they would make a good programming exercise. For that task, you need the string manipulation functions covered on Day 17.

Summary

This chapter covered C's char data type. One use for type char variables is storing individual characters. You saw that characters are actually stored as numbers: the ASCII code has assigned a numerical code to each character. Therefore, you can use type char to store small integer values as well. Both signed and unsigned char types are available.

A string is a sequence of characters terminated by the null character. Strings can be used for text data. C stores strings in arrays of type char. To store a string of length *n*, you need an array of type char with *n*+1 elements.

You can use memory allocation functions such as malloc() to make your programs more dynamic. By using malloc(), you can allocate the right amount of memory for your program. Without such functions, you would have to guess at the amount of memory storage the program needs. Your estimate is usually high, so you allocate more memory than needed.

Q&A

Q **What is the difference between a string and an array of characters?**

A A string is defined as a sequence of characters ending with the null character. An array is a sequence of characters. A string, therefore, is a null-terminated array of characters.

If you define an array of type char, the actual storage space allocated for the array is the specified size, not the size −1. You are limited to that size; you cannot store a larger string. Here's an example:

```
char state[10]="Minneapolis"; /* Wrong! String longer than array.*/
char state2[10]="MN";         /* OK, but wastes space because */
                              /* string shorter than array. */
```

If, on the other hand, you define a pointer to type char, these restrictions do not apply. The variable is a storage space only for the pointer. The actual strings are stored elsewhere in memory (but you need not worry about where in memory). There's no length restriction or wasted space. The actual string is stored elsewhere. A pointer can be pointed to a string of any length.

Q Why shouldn't I just declare big arrays to hold values instead of using a memory allocation function such as `malloc()`?

A Although it may seem easier to declare large arrays, it is not an effective use of memory. When writing small programs, such as those in this chapter, it may seem trivial to use a function such as `malloc()` instead of arrays, but as your programs get bigger, you will want to be able to allocate memory only as needed. When you are done with memory, you can put it back by *freeing* it. When you free memory, some other variable or array in a different part of the program can use the memory. (Day 20, "Working with Memory," covers freeing allocated memory.)

Q Do all computers support the extended ASCII character set?

A No. Most PCs support the extended ASCII set. Some older PCs don't, but the number of older PCs lacking this support is diminishing. Most programmers use the line and block characters of the extended set.

Q What happens if I put a string into a character array that is bigger than the array?

A This can cause a hard-to-find error. You can do this in C, but anything stored in the memory directly after the character array is overwritten. This could be an area of memory not used, some other data, or some vital system information. Your results are going to depend on what you overwrite. Many times nothing happens for a while. You don't want to do this.

Workshop

The Workshop provides quiz questions to help you solidify your understanding of the material covered and exercises to provide you with experience in using what you've learned.

Quiz

1. What is the range of numeric values in the ASCII character set?
2. When the C compiler encounters a single character enclosed in single quotation marks, how is it interpreted?
3. What is C's definition of a string?
4. What is a literal string?
5. To store a string of n characters, you need a character array of n+1 elements. Why is the extra element needed?
6. When the C compiler encounters a literal string, how is it interpreted?
7. Using the ASCII chart in Appendix A, "ASCII Character Chart," state the numeric value stored for each of the following:

a. a

    b. A

    c. 9

    d. a space

    e. ╬

    f. ♠

8. Using the ASCII chart in Appendix A, translate the following numeric values to their equivalent characters:

    a. 73

    b. 32

    c. 99

    d. 97

    e. 110

    f. 0

    g. 2

9. How many bytes of storage are allocated for each of the following variables?

    a. `char *str1 = { "String 1" };`

    b. `char str2[] = { "String 2" };`

    c. `char string3;`

    d. `char str4[20] = { "This is String 4" };`

    e. `char str5[20];`

10. Using the following declaration:

```
char *string = "A string!";
```

What are the values of the following?

    a. `string[0]`

    b. `*string`

    c. `string[9]`

    d. `string[33]`

    e. `*string+8`

    f. `string`

Exercises

1. Write a line of code that declares a type `char` variable named `letter` and initialize it to the character `$`.

2. Write a line of code that declares an array of type `char` and initialize it to the string `"Pointers are fun!"` Make the array just large enough to hold the string.

3. Write a line of code that allocates storage for the string `"Pointers are fun!"` as in exercise 2, but without using an array.

4. Write code that allocates space for an 80-character string, and then inputs a string from the keyboard and stores it in the allocated space.

5. Write a function that copies one array of characters into another. (Hint: Do this just like the programs you did on Day 9, "Pointers.")

6. Write a function that accepts two strings. Count the number of characters in each and return a pointer to the longer string.

7. Write a function that accepts two strings. Use the `malloc()` function to allocate enough memory to hold the two strings after they have been concatenated (linked together). Return a pointer to this new string.

   For example, if I pass `"Hello "` and `"World!"`, the function returns a pointer to `"Hello World!"`. Having the concatenated value be the third string is easiest. (You may be able to use your answers from exercises 5 and 6.)

8. **BUG BUSTER:** Is anything wrong with the following?

   ```
   char a_string[10] = "This is a string";
   ```

9. **BUG BUSTER:** Is anything wrong with the following?

   ```
   char *quote[100] = { "Smile, Friday is almost here!" };
   ```

10. **BUG BUSTER:** Is anything wrong with the following?

    ```
    char *string1;
    char *string2 = "Second";
    string1 = string2;
    ```

11. **BUG BUSTER:** Is anything wrong with the following?

    ```
    char string1[];
    char string2[] = "Second";
    string1 = string2;
    ```

12. Using the ASCII chart, write a program that prints a box on the screen using the double-line characters.

Structures

Many programming tasks are simplified by the C data constructs called *structures*. A structure is a data storage method designed by you, the programmer, to suit your program needs exactly. Today, you learn

- What simple and complex structures are
- How to define and declare structures
- How to access data in structures
- How to create structures that contain arrays and arrays of structures
- How to declare pointers in structures and pointers to structures
- How to pass structures as arguments to functions
- How to define, declare, and use unions
- How to use type definitions with structures

Simple Structures

A structure is a collection of one or more variables grouped under a single name for easy manipulation. The variables in a structure, unlike those in an array, can be of different variable types. A structure can contain any of C's data types, including arrays and other structures. Each variable within a structure is called a *member* of the structure. The next section shows a simple example.

You should start with simple structures. Note that the C language makes no distinction between simple and complex structures, but it is easier to explain structures in this way.

Defining and Declaring Structures

If you are writing a graphics program, your code needs to deal with the coordinates of points on the screen. Screen coordinates are written as an x value, giving horizontal position, and a y value, giving vertical position. You can define a structure named coord that contains both the x and y values of a screen location as follows:

```
struct coord {
    int x;
    int y;
};
```

The struct keyword, which identifies the beginning of a structure definition, must be followed immediately by the structure name, or *tag* (which follows the same rules as other C variable names). Within the braces following the structure name is a list of the structure's member variables. You must give a variable type and name for each member.

The previous statements define a structure type named coord that contains two integer variables, x and y. They do not, however, actually create any instances of the structure coord. That is, they do not declare (set aside storage for) any structures. There are two ways to declare structures. One is to follow the structure definition with a list of one or more variable names, as is done here:

```
struct coord {
    int x;
    int y;
} first, second;
```

These statements define the structure type coord and declare two structures, named first and second, of type coord. first and second are each *instances* of type coord; first contains two integer members named x and y, as does second.

The previous method of declaring structures combines the declaration with the definition. The second method is to declare structure variables at a different location in your source code from the definition. The following statements also declare two instances of type coord:

```
struct coord {
    int x;
    int y;
};
/* Additional code may go here */
struct coord first, second;
```

Accessing Structure Members

Individual structure members can be used like other variables of the same type. Structure members are accessed using the *structure member operator* (.), also called the *dot operator*, between the structure name and the member name. Thus, to have the structure named first refer to a screen location with coordinates x=50, y=100, you could write

```
first.x = 50;
first.y = 100;
```

To display the screen locations stored in the structure second, you could write

```
printf("%d,%d", second.x, second.y);
```

At this point, you might be wondering what the advantage is of using structures rather than individual variables. One major advantage is the ability to copy information between structures of the same type with a simple equation statement. Continuing with the previous example, the statement

```
first = second;
```

is the equivalent of this statement:

```
first.x = second.x;
first.y = second.y;
```

When your program uses complex structures with many members, this notation can be a great time-saver. Other advantages of structures will become apparent as you learn some advanced capabilities. In general, you'll find structures to be useful any time information of different variable types needs to be treated as a group. For example, in a mailing list database, each entry could be a structure, and each piece of information (name, address, city, and so on) could be a structure member.

The *struct* Keyword

```
struct tag {
structure_member(s)
/* additional statements may go here */
} instance;
```

The struct keyword is used for declaring structures. A structure is a collection of one or more variables *(structure_members)* that have been grouped under a single name for easy manipulation. The variables do not have to be of the same variable types, nor do they have to be simple variables. Structures also can hold arrays, pointers, and other structures.

The keyword struct identifies the beginning of a structure definition. It is followed by a tag that is the name given to the structure. Following the tag are the structure members enclosed in braces. An *instance*, the actual declaration of a structure, also can be defined. If you define the structure without the instance, it is just a template that can be used later in a program to declare structures. Here is a template's format:

```
struct tag {
    structure_member(s)
    /* additional statements may go here */
};
```

To use the template, you use the following format:

```
struct tag instance;
```

To use this format, you must have previously declared a structure with the given tag.

Example 1

```
/* Declare a structure template called SSN */

struct SSN {
    int first_three;
    char dash1;
    int second_two;
    char dash2;
    int last_four;
}
/* Use the structure template */
struct SSN customer_ssn;
```

Example 2

```
/* Declare a structure and instance together */
struct date {
    char month[2];
    char day[2];
    char year[4];
} current_date;
```

Example 3

```
/* Declare and initialize a structure */
struct time {
    int hours;
    int minutes;
    int seconds;
} time_of_birth = { 8, 45, 0 };
```

More Complex Structures

Now that you have been introduced to simple structures, you can get to the more interesting and complex types of structures. These are structures that contain other structures as members and structures that contain arrays as members.

Structures that Contain Structures

As mentioned earlier, a C structure can contain any of C's data types. For example, a structure can contain other structures. The previous example can be extended to illustrate this.

Assume that your graphics program now needs to deal with rectangles. A *rectangle* can be defined by the coordinates of two diagonally opposite corners. You have already seen how to define a structure that can hold the two coordinates required for a single point. You need two such structures to define a rectangle. You can define a structure as follows (assuming, of course, that you have already defined the type coord structure):

```
struct rectangle {
    struct coord topleft;
    struct coord bottomrt;
};
```

This statement defines a structure of type rectangle that contains two structures of type coord. These two type coord structures are named topleft and bottomrt.

The previous statement defines only the type rectangle structure. To declare a structure, you must then include a statement such as

```
struct rectangle mybox;
```

You could have combined the definition and declaration, as you did before for the type `coord`:

```
struct rectangle {
    struct coord topleft;
    struct coord bottomrt;
} mybox;
```

To access the actual data locations (the type `int` members), you must apply the member operator (.) twice. Thus, the expression

```
mybox.topleft.x
```

refers to the `x` member of the `topleft` member of the type `rectangle` structure named `mybox`. To define a rectangle with coordinates (0,10),(100,200), you would write

```
mybox.topleft.x = 0;
mybox.topleft.y = 10;
mybox.bottomrt.x = 100;
mybox.bottomrt.y = 200;
```

Maybe this is getting a bit confusing. You might understand better if you look at Figure 11.1, which shows the relationship between the type `rectangle` structure, the two type `coord` structures it contains, and the two type `int` variables each type `coord` structure contains. The structures are named as in the previous example.

Figure 11.1.
A diagram of the relationship between a structure, structures within a structure, and the structure members.

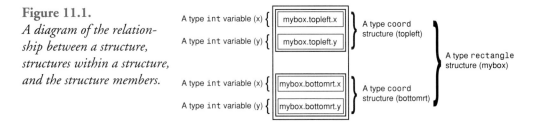

It's time to look at an example of using structures that contain other structures. The program in Listing 11.1 takes input from the user for the coordinates of a rectangle, and then calculates and displays the rectangle's area. Note the program's assumptions, given in comments near the start of the code (lines 3–8).

Listing 11.1. A demonstration of structures that contain other structures.

```
1: /* Demonstrates structures that contain other structures. */
2:
3: /* Receives input for corner coordinates of a rectangle and
4:    calculates the area. Assumes that the y coordinate of the
5:    upper-left corner is greater than the y coordinate of the
6:    lower-right corner, that the x coordinate of the lower-
7:    right corner is greater than the x coordinate of the upper-
```

```
 8:    left corner, and that all coordinates are positive. */
 9:
10: #include <stdio.h>
11:
12: int length, width;
13: long area;
14:
15: struct coord{
16:     int x;
17:     int y;
18: };
19:
20: struct rectangle{
21:     struct coord topleft;
22:     struct coord bottomrt;
23: } mybox;
24:
25: main()
26: {
27:     /* Input the coordinates */
28:
29:     printf("\nEnter the top left x coordinate: ");
30:     scanf("%d", &mybox.topleft.x);
31:
32:     printf("\nEnter the top left y coordinate: ");
33:     scanf("%d", &mybox.topleft.y);
34:
35:     printf("\nEnter the bottom right x coordinate: ");
36:     scanf("%d", &mybox.bottomrt.x);
37:
38:     printf("\nEnter the bottom right y coordinate: ");
39:     scanf("%d", &mybox.bottomrt.y);
40:
41:     /* Calculate the length and width */
42:
43:     width = mybox.bottomrt.x - mybox.topleft.x;
44:     length = mybox.bottomrt.y - mybox.topleft.y;
45:
46:     /* Calculate and display the area */
47:
48:     area = width * length;
49:     printf("The area is %ld units.", area);
50:
51:     return 0;
52: }
```

**Input
Output**

```
Enter the top left x coordinate: 1

Enter the top left y coordinate: 1

Enter the bottom right x coordinate: 10

Enter the bottom right y coordinate: 10
The area is 81 units.
```

The coord structure is defined in lines 15–18 with its two members, x and y. Lines 20–23 declare and define an instance, called mybox, of the rectangle structure. The two members of the rectangle structure are topleft and bottomrt, both structures of type coord.

Lines 29–39 fill in the values in the mybox structure. At first, it might seem that there are only two values to fill because mybox has only two members. Each of mybox's members, however, has its own members. topleft and bottomrt have two members each, x and y from the coord structure. This gives a total of four members to be filled. After the members are filled with values, the area is calculated using the structure and member names. When using the x and y values, you must include the structure instance name. Because x and y are in a structure within a structure, you must use the instance names of both structures—mybox.bottomrt.x, mybox.bottomrt.y, mybox.topleft.x, and mybox.topleft.y—in the calculations.

C places no limits on the nesting of structures. While memory allows, you can define structures that contain structures that contain structures that contain structures—well, you get the idea! Of course, there's a limit beyond which nesting becomes unproductive. Rarely are more than three levels of nesting used in any C program.

Structures that Contain Arrays

You can define a structure that contains one array or more as members. The array can be of any C data type (integer, character, and so on). For example, the statements

```
struct data{
    int x[4];
    char y[10];
};
```

define a structure of type data that contains a 4-element integer array member named x, and a 10-element character array member named y. You can then declare a structure named record of type data as follows:

```
struct data record;
```

The organization of this structure is shown in Figure 11.2. Note that in this figure the elements of array x take up twice as much space as the elements of array y. This is because (as you learned on Day 3, "Numeric Variables and Constants") a type int typically requires two bytes of storage, whereas a type char usually requires only one byte.

Accessing individual elements of arrays that are structure members is done with a combination of the member operator and array subscripts:

```
record.x[2] = 100;
record.y[1] = 'x';
```

Figure 11.2.
*The organization of a
structure that contains
arrays as members.*

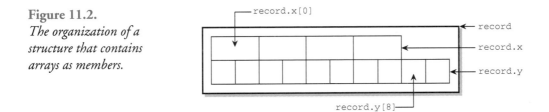

You probably remember that character arrays are most frequently used to store strings. You also should remember (from Day 9, "Pointers") that the name of an array, without brackets, is a pointer to the array. Because this holds true for arrays that are structure members, the expression

`record.y`

is a pointer to the first element of array y[ ] in the structure record. You could, therefore, print the contents of y[ ] on the screen with the statement

`puts(record.y);`

Now look at another example. The program in Listing 11.2 uses a structure that contains a type float variable and two type char arrays.

Listing 11.2. A demonstration of a structure that contains array members.

```
1:  /* Demonstrates a structure that has array members. */
2:
3:  #include <stdio.h>
4:
5:  /* Define and declare a structure to hold the data. */
6:  /* It contains one float variable and two char arrays. */
7:
8:  struct data{
9:      float amount;
10:     char fname[30];
11:     char lname[30];
12: } rec;
13:
14: main()
15: {
16:     /* Input the data from the keyboard. */
17:
18:     printf("Enter the donor's first and last names,\n");
19:     printf("separated by a space: ");
20:     scanf("%s %s", rec.fname, rec.lname);
21:
22:     printf("\nEnter the donation amount: ");
23:     scanf("%f", &rec.amount);
24:
```

continues

Listing 11.2 continued

```
25:     /* Display the information. */
26:     /* Note: %.2f specifies a floating point value */
27:     /* to be displayed with two digits to the right */
28:     /* of the decimal point. */
29:
30:     /* Display the data on the screen. */
31:
32:     printf("\nDonor %s %s gave $%.2f.", rec.fname, rec.lname,
33:             rec.amount);
34:
35:     return 0;
36: }
```

```
Enter the donor's first and last names,
separated by a space: Bradley Jones

Enter the donation amount: 1000.00
Donor Bradley Jones gave $1000.00.
```

This program includes a structure that contains array members named `fname[30]` and `lname[30]`. Both are arrays of characters that hold a person's first name and last name, respectively. The structure declared in lines 8–12 is called `data`. It contains the `fname` and `lname` character arrays with a type `float` variable called `amount`. This structure is ideal for holding a person's name (in two parts, first name and last name) and a value, such as the amount the person donated to a charitable organization.

An instance of the array, called `rec`, has also been declared in line 12. The rest of the program uses `rec` to get values from the user (lines 18–23), and then print them (lines 32–33).

Arrays of Structures

If you can have structures that contain arrays, can you also have arrays of structures? You bet you can! In fact, arrays of structures are very powerful programming tools. Here's how it's done.

You've seen how a structure definition can be tailored to fit the data your program needs to work with. Usually a program needs to work with more than one instance of the data. For example, in a program to maintain a list of phone numbers, you can define a structure to hold each person's name and number:

```
struct entry{
    char fname[10];
    char lname[12];
    char phone[8];
};
```

A phone list has to hold many entries, however, so a single instance of the entry structure isn't of much use. What you need is an array of structures of type `entry`. After the structure has been defined, you can declare an array as follows:

```
struct entry list[1000];
```

This statement declares an array named list that contains 1,000 elements. Every element is a structure of type entry and is identified by subscript like other array element types. Each of these structures has three elements, each of which is an array of type char. This entire complex creation is diagrammed in Figure 11.3.

Figure 11.3.
The organization of the array of structures defined in the text.

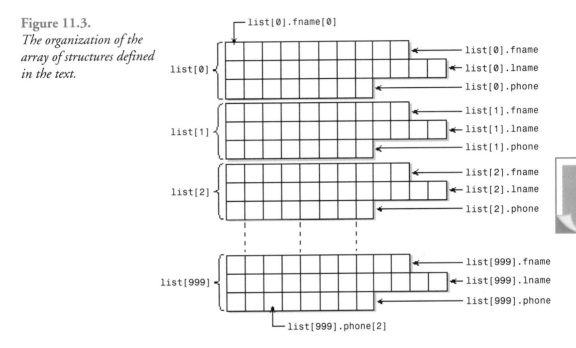

When you have declared the array of structures, you can manipulate the data in many ways. For example, to assign the data in one array element to another array element, you write

```
list[1] = list[5];
```

This statement assigns to each member of the structure list[1] the values contained in the corresponding members of list[5]. You also can move data between individual structure members. The statement

```
strcpy(list[1].phone, list[5].phone);
```

copies the string in list[5].phone to list[1].phone. (The strcpy() library function copies one string to another string. You learn the details of this on Day 17, "Manipulating Strings.") You also can, if you desire, move data between individual elements of the structure member arrays:

```
list[5].phone[1] = list[2].phone[3];
```

This statement moves the second character of list[5]'s phone number to the fourth position in list[2]'s phone number. (Don't forget that subscripts start at offset 0.)

The program in Listing 11.3 demonstrates the use of arrays of structures. Moreover, it demonstrates arrays of structures that contain arrays as members.

Listing 11.3. Demonstration of arrays of structures.

```
1:  /* Demonstrates using arrays of structures. */
2:
3:  #include <stdio.h>
4:
5:  /* Define a structure to hold entries. */
6:
7:  struct entry {
8:      char fname[20];
9:      char lname[20];
10:     char phone[10];
11: };
12:
13: /* Declare an array of structures. */
14:
15: struct entry list[4];
16:
17: int i;
18:
19: main()
20: {
21:
22:     /* Loop to input data for four people. */
23:
24:     for (i = 0; i < 4; i++)
25:     {
26:         printf("\nEnter first name: ");
27:         scanf("%s", list[i].fname);
28:         printf("Enter last name: ");
29:         scanf("%s", list[i].lname);
30:         printf("Enter phone in 123-4567 format: ");
31:         scanf("%s", list[i].phone);
32:     }
33:
34:     /* Print two blank lines. */
35:
36:     printf("\n\n");
37:
38:     /* Loop to display data. */
39:
40:     for (i = 0; i < 4; i++)
41:     {
42:         printf("Name: %s %s", list[i].fname, list[i].lname);
43:         printf("\t\tPhone: %s\n", list[i].phone);
44:     }
45:
46:     return 0;
47: }
```

```
Enter first name: Bradley
Enter last name: Jones
Enter phone in 123-4567 format: 555-1212

Enter first name: Peter
Enter last name: Aitken
Enter phone in 123-4567 format: 555-3434

Enter first name: Melissa
Enter last name: Jones
Enter phone in 123-4567 format: 555-1212

Enter first name: John
Enter last name: Smith
Enter phone in 123-4567 format: 555-1234


Name: Bradley Jones          Phone: 555-1212
Name: Peter Aitken          Phone: 555-3434
Name: Melissa Jones          Phone: 555-1212
Name: John Smith          Phone: 555-1234
```

This listing follows the same general format as most of the other listings. It starts with the comment in line 1 and, for the input/output functions, the #include file STDIO.H in line 3. Lines 7–11 define a template structure called entry that contains three character arrays: fname, lname, and phone. Line 15 uses the template to define an array of four entry structure variables called list. Line 17 defines a variable of type int to be used as a counter throughout the program. main() starts in line 19. The first function of main() is to perform a loop four times with a for statement. This loop is used to get information for the array of structures. This can be seen in lines 24–32. Notice that list is being used with a subscript in the same way as the array variables on Day 8, "Numeric Arrays," were subscripted.

Line 36 provides a break from the input before starting with the output. It prints two blank lines in a manner that should not be new to you. Lines 40–44 display the data that the user entered in the preceding step. The values in the array of structures are printed with the subscripted array name followed by the member operator (.) and the structure member name.

Familiarize yourself with the techniques used in Listing 11.3. Many real-world programming tasks are best accomplished by using arrays of structures containing arrays as members.

DO	DON'T

DON'T forget the structure instance name and member operator (.) when using a structure's members.

DON'T confuse a structure's tag with its instances! The tag is to declare the structure's template, or format. The instance is a variable declared using the tag.

DON'T forget the struct keyword when declaring an instance from a previously defined structure.

DO declare structure instances with the same scope rules as other variables. (Day 12, "Variable Scope," will cover this topic fully.)

Initializing Structures

Like other C variable types, structures can be initialized when they are declared. The procedure is similar to that for initializing arrays. The structure declaration is followed by an equal sign and a list of initialization values separated by commas and enclosed in braces. For example, look at the following statements:

```
1: struct sale {
2:     char customer[20];
3:     char item[20];
4:     float amount;
5: } mysale = { "Acme Industries",
6:               "Left-handed widget",
7:                1000.00
8:             };
```

When these statements are executed, they perform the following actions:

1. Define a structure type named sale (lines 1–5).

2. Declare an instance of structure type sale named mysale (line 5).

3. Initialize the structure member mysale.customer to the string "Acme Industries" (line 5).

4. Initialize the structure member mysale.item to the string "Left-handed widget" (line 6).

5. Initialize the structure member mysale.amount to the value 1000.00 (line 7).

For a structure that contains structures as members, list the initialization values in order. They are placed in the structure members in the order in which the members are listed in the structure definition. Here's an example that expands slightly on the previous one:

```
1: struct customer {
2:     char firm[20];
3:     char contact[25];
4: }
5:
6: struct sale {
7:     struct customer buyer;
8:     char item[20];
9:     float amount;
```

```
10: } mysale = { { "Acme Industries", "George Adams"},
11:                "Left-handed widget",
12:                1000.00
13:            };
```

These statements perform the following initializations:

1. The structure member `mysale.buyer.firm` is initialized to the string `"Acme Industries"` (line 10).

2. The structure member `mysale.buyer.contact` is initialized to the string `"George Adams"` (line 10).

3. The structure member `mysale.item` is initialized to the string `"Left-handed widget"` (line 11).

4. The structure member `mysale.amount` is initialized to the amount `1000.00` (line 12).

You also can initialize arrays of structures. The initialization data that you supply is applied, in order, to the structures in the array. For example, to declare an array of structures of type `sale` and initialize the first two array elements (that is, the first two structures), you could write

```
1: struct customer {
2:     char firm[20];
3:     char contact[25];
4: };
5:
6: struct sale {
7:     struct customer buyer;
8:     char item[20];
9:     float amount;
10: };
11:
12:
13: struct sale y1990[100] = {
14:     { { "Acme Industries", "George Adams"},
15:         "Left-handed widget",
16:         1000.00
17:     }
18:     { { "Wilson & Co.", "Ed Wilson"},
19:         "Type 12 gizmo",
20:         290.00
21:     }
22: };
```

This is what occurs in the preceding code:

1. The structure member `y1990[0].buyer.firm` is initialized to the string `"Acme Industries"` (line 14).

2. The structure member `y1990[0].buyer.contact` is initialized to the string `"George Adams"` (line 14).

3. The structure member `y1990[0].item` is initialized to the string `"Left-handed widget"` (line 15).

4. The structure member y1990[0].amount is initialized to the amount 1000.00 (line 16).

5. The structure member y1990[1].buyer.firm is initialized to the string "Wilson & Co." (line 18).

6. The structure member y1990[1].buyer.contact is initialized to the string "Ed Wilson" (line 18).

7. The structure member y1990[1].item is initialized to the string "Type 12 gizmo" (line 19).

8. The structure member y1990[1].amount is initialized to the amount 290.00 (line 20).

Structures and Pointers

Given that pointers are such an important part of C, you shouldn't be surprised to find that they can be used with structures. You can use pointers as structure members, and you also can declare pointers to structures. These are covered, in turn, in the following paragraphs.

Pointers as Structure Members

You have complete flexibility in using pointers as structure members. Pointer members are declared in the same manner as pointers that are not members of structures—that is, by using the indirection operator (*). Here's an example:

```
struct data {
    int *value;
    int *rate;
} first;
```

These statements define and declare a structure whose two members are both pointers to type int. As with all pointers, declaring them is not enough; you must, by assigning them the address of a variable, initialize them to point to something. If cost and interest have been declared to be type int variables, you could write

```
first.value = &cost;
first.rate = &interest;
```

Now that the pointers have been initialized, you can use the indirection operator (*), as explained on Day 9. The expression *first.value evaluates to the value of cost, and the expression *first.rate evaluates to the value of interest.

Perhaps the type of pointer most frequently used as a structure member is a pointer to type char. Recall from Day 10, "Characters and Strings," that a string is a sequence of characters delineated by a pointer that points to the string's first character and a null character that indicates the end of the string. To refresh your memory, you can declare a pointer to type char and initialize it to point at a string as follows:

```
char *p_message;
p_message = "Teach Yourself C In 21 Days";
```

You can do the same thing with pointers to type char that are structure members:

```
struct msg {
    char *p1;
    char *p2;
} myptrs;

myptrs.p1 = "Teach Yourself C In 21 Days";
myptrs.p2 = "By SAMS Publishing";
```

Figure 11.4 illustrates the result of executing the previous statements. Each pointer member of the structure points to the first byte of a string, stored elsewhere in memory. Contrast this with Figure 11.3, which shows how data is stored in a structure that contains arrays of type char.

Figure 11.4.

A structure that contains pointers to type char.

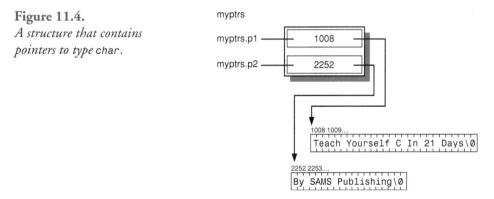

You can use pointer structure members anywhere a pointer can be used. For example, to print the pointed-to strings, you would write

```
printf("%s %s", myptrs.p1, myptrs.p2);
```

What is the difference between using an array of type char as a structure member and using a pointer to type char? These are both methods for "storing" a string in a structure, as shown here in the structure msg that uses both methods:

```
struct msg {
    char p1[30];
    char *p2;
} myptrs;
```

Recall that an array name without brackets is a pointer to the first array element. You can, therefore, use these two structure members in similar fashion:

```
strcpy(myptrs.p1, "Teach Yourself C In 21 Days");
strcpy(myptrs.p2, "By SAMS Publishing");
/* additional code goes here */
puts(myptrs.p1);
puts(myptrs.p2);
```

What is the difference between these methods? It is this: If you define a structure that contains an array of type char, every instance of that structure type contains storage space for an array of the specified size. Furthermore, you are limited to the specified size and cannot store a larger string in the structure. Here's an example:

```
struct msg {
    char p1[10];
    char p2[10];
} myptrs;
...
strcpy(p1, "Minneapolis"); /* Wrong! String longer than array.*/
strcpy(p2, "MN");          /* OK, but wastes space because    */
                           /* string shorter than array.      */
```

If, on the other hand, you define a structure that contains pointers to type char, these restrictions do not apply. Each instance of the structure contains storage space for only the pointer. The actual strings are stored elsewhere in memory (but you need not worry about *where* in memory). There's no length restriction or wasted space. The actual strings are not stored as part of the structure. Each pointer in the structure can be pointed to a string of any length. That string becomes part of the structure, even though it is not stored in the structure.

Pointers to Structures

A C program can declare and use pointers to structures, just as it can declare pointers to any other data storage type. As you will see later today, pointers to structures are often used when passing a structure as an argument to a function. Pointers to structures are also used in a very powerful data storage method known as *linked lists*. Linked lists are explored on Bonus Day 5, "Advanced Structures: Linked Lists."

For now, take a look at how your program can create and use pointers to structures. First, define a structure:

```
struct part {
    int number;
    char name[10];
};
```

Now, declare a pointer to type part:

```
struct part *p_part;
```

Remember, the indirection operator (*) in the declaration says that p_part is a pointer to type part and not an instance of type part.

Can the pointer be initialized now? No, because the structure part has been defined but no instances of it have been declared. Remember that it's a declaration, not a definition, that sets aside storage space in memory for a data object. Because a pointer needs a memory address to point to, you must declare an instance of type part before anything can point at it. So here's the declaration:

```
struct part gizmo;
```

Now you can perform the pointer initialization:

```
p_part = &gizmo;
```

The preceding statement assigns the address of gizmo to p_part. (Recall the address-of operator, &, from Day 9.) The relationship between a structure and a pointer to the structure is shown in Figure 11.5.

Figure 11.5.

A pointer to a structure points to the structure's first byte.

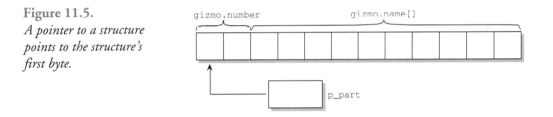

Now that you have a pointer to the structure gizmo, how do you make use of it? One method uses the indirection operator (*). Recall from Day 9 that if

```
ptr
```

is a pointer to a data object, the following expression refers to the object pointed to:

```
*ptr
```

Applying this to the current example, you know that p_part is a pointer to the structure gizmo and therefore *p_part refers to gizmo. You then apply the structure member operator (.) to access individual members of gizmo. To assign the value 100 to gizmo.number, you could write

```
(*p_part).number = 100;
```

The *p_part must be enclosed in parentheses because the (.) operator has a higher precedence than the (*) operator.

A second method to access structure members using a pointer to the structure is to use the *indirect membership operator,* which consists of the symbols ->, (a hyphen followed by the greater than symbol). (Note that when they are used together in this way, C treats them as a single operator, not two.) The symbol is placed between the pointer name and the member name. To access the number member of gizmo with the p_part pointer, you write

```
p_part->number
```

Looking at another example, if str is a structure, p_str is a pointer to str, and memb is a member of str, you can access str.memb by writing

```
p_str->memb
```

There are three ways, therefore, to access a structure member:

- Using the structure name
- Using a pointer to the structure with the indirection operator (*)
- Using a pointer to the structure with the indirect membership operator (->)

If p_str is a pointer to the structure str, the following expressions are all equivalent:

```
str.memb
(*p_str).memb
p_str->memb
```

Pointers and Arrays of Structures

You've seen that arrays of structures can be a very powerful programming tool, as can pointers to structures. You can combine the two, using pointers to access structures that are array elements.

To illustrate, here is a structure definition from an earlier example:

```
struct part {
    int number;
    char name[10];
};
```

After the structure part is defined, you can declare an array of type part:

```
struct part data[100];
```

Next, you can declare a pointer to type part and initialize it to point at the first structure in the array data:

```
struct part *p_part;
p_part = &data[0];
```

Recall that the name of an array without brackets is a pointer to the first array element, so the second line could also have been written

```
p_part = data;
```

You now have an array of structures of type part, and a pointer to the first array element (that is, the first structure in the array). You could, for example, print the contents of the first element with the statement

```
printf("%d %s", p_part->number, p_part->name);
```

What if you want to print all the array elements? You would probably use a `for` loop, printing one array element with each iteration of the loop. To access the members using pointer notation, you must change the pointer `p_part` so that with each iteration of the loop it points at the next array element (that is, the next structure in the array). How do you do this?

C's pointer arithmetic comes to your aid. The unary increment operator (++) has a special meaning when applied to a pointer: it means "increment the pointer by the size of the object it points to." Put another way, if you have a pointer `ptr` that points to a data object of type `obj`, the statement

```
ptr++;
```

has the same effect as this statement:

```
ptr += sizeof(obj);
```

This aspect of pointer arithmetic is particularly relevant to arrays as follows: array elements are stored sequentially in memory. If a pointer points to array element n, incrementing the pointer with the (++) operator causes it to point to element n + 1. This is illustrated in Figure 11.6, which shows an array named `x[]` that consists of four-byte elements (for example, a structure containing two type `int` members, each two bytes long). The pointer `ptr` was initialized to point at `x[0]`; each time `ptr` is incremented, it points at the next array element.

Figure 11.6.
With each increment, a pointer "steps" to the next array element.

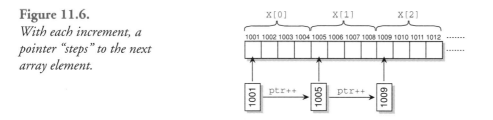

What this means is that your program can step though an array of structures (or an array of any other data type, for that matter) by incrementing a pointer. This sort of notation is usually easier to use and more concise than using array subscripts to perform the same task.

The program in Listing 11.4 demonstrates how you do this.

Type

Listing 11.4. Accessing successive array elements by incrementing a pointer.

```
1:  /* Demonstrates stepping through an array of structures */
2:  /* using pointer notation. */
3:
4:  #include <stdio.h>
5:
```

continues

Listing 11.4. continued

```
 6:  #define MAX 4
 7:
 8:  /* Define a structure, then declare and initialize */
 9:  /* an array of 4 structures. */
10:
11:  struct part {
12:       int number;
13:       char name[10];
14:  } data[MAX] = {1, "Smith",
15:                  2, "Jones",
16:                  3, "Adams",
17:                  4, "Wilson"
18:                  };
19:
20:  /* Declare a pointer to type part, and a counter variable. */
21:
22:  struct part *p_part;
23:  int count;
24:
25:  main()
26:  {
27:       /* Initialize the pointer to the first array element. */
28:
29:       p_part = data;
30:
31:       /* Loop through the array, incrementing the pointer */
32:       /* with each iteration. */
33:
34:       for (count = 0; count < MAX; count++)
35:       {
36:           printf("\nAt address %d: %d %s", p_part, p_part->number,
37:                    p_part->name);
38:           p_part++;
39:       }
40:
41:       return 0;
42:  }
```

```
At address 96: 1 Smith
At address 108: 2 Jones
At address 120: 3 Adams
At address 132: 4 Wilson
```

First, this program declares and initializes an array of structures in lines 11–18 called data. A pointer called p_part is then defined to be used to point to the data structure. The main() function's first task is to set the pointer, p_part, to point to the part structure that was declared. All the elements are then printed using a for loop that increments the pointer to the array with each iteration. The program displays the address of each element.

Look closely at the addresses displayed. The precise values might differ on your system, but they are in equal-sized increments—just the size of the structure part (most systems will have an increment of 12). This illustrates clearly that incrementing a pointer increases it by an amount equal to the size of the data object it points to.

Passing Structures as Arguments to Functions

Like other data types, a structure can be passed as an argument to a function. The program in Listing 11.5 shows how to do this. This program is a modification of the program in Listing 11.2, using a function to display data on the screen (whereas Listing 11.2 uses statements that are part of main()).

Listing 11.5. Passing a structure as a function argument.

```
1:  /* Demonstrates passing a structure to a function. */
2:
3:  #include <stdio.h>
4:
5:  /* Declare and define a structure to hold the data. */
6:
7:  struct data{
8:      float amount;
9:      char fname[30];
10:     char lname[30];
11: } rec;
12:
13: /* The function prototype. The function has no return value, */
14: /* and it takes a structure of type data as its one argument. */
15:
16: void print_rec(struct data x);
17:
18: main()
19: {
20:     /* Input the data from the keyboard. */
21:
22:     printf("Enter the donor's first and last names,\n");
23:     printf("separated by a space: ");
24:     scanf("%s %s", rec.fname, rec.lname);
25:
26:     printf("\nEnter the donation amount: ");
27:     scanf("%f", &rec.amount);
28:
29:     /* Call the display function. */
30:     print_rec( rec );
31:
32:     return 0;
33: }
34: void print_rec(struct data x)
35: {
36:     printf("\nDonor %s %s gave $%.2f.", x.fname, x.lname,
37:             x.amount);
38: }
```

```
Enter the donor's first and last names,
separated by a space: Bradley Jones

Enter the donation amount: 1000.00
Donor Bradley Jones gave $1000.00.
```

Analysis Looking at line 16, you see the function prototype for the function that is to receive the structure. As you would with any other data type that was going to be passed, you need to include the proper arguments. In this case, it is a structure of type data. This is repeated in the header for the function in line 34. When calling the function, you only need to pass the structure instance name, in this case rec (line 30). That's all there is to it. Passing a structure to a function is not very different from passing a simple variable.

You also can pass a structure to a function by passing the structure's address (that is, a pointer to the structure). In fact, in older versions of C, this was the only way to pass a structure as an argument. It's not necessary now, but you might see older programs that still use this method. If you pass a pointer to a structure as an argument, remember that you must use the indirect membership operator (->) to access structure members in the function.

DO	DON'T

DON'T confuse arrays with structures!

DO take advantage of declaring a pointer to a structure—especially when using arrays of structures.

DON'T forget that when you increment a pointer, it moves a distance equivalent to the size of the data to which it points. In the case of a pointer to a structure, this is the size of the structure.

DO use the indirect membership operator (->) when working with a pointer to a structure.

Unions

Unions are similar to structures. A union is declared and used in the same ways that a structure is. A union differs from a structure in that only one of its members can be used at a time. The reason for this is simple. All the members of a union occupy the same area of memory. They are laid on top of each other.

Defining, Declaring, and Initializing Unions

Unions are defined and declared in the same fashion as structures. The only difference in the declarations is that the keyword union is used instead of struct. To define a simple union of a char variable and an integer variable, you would do the following:

```
union shared {
    char c;
    int i;
};
```

This union, shared, can be used to create instances of a union that can hold either a character value c or an integer value i. This is an OR condition. Unlike a structure that would hold both values, the union can only hold one value at a time. Figure 11.7 illustrates how the shared union would appear in memory.

Figure 11.7
The union can hold only one value at a time.

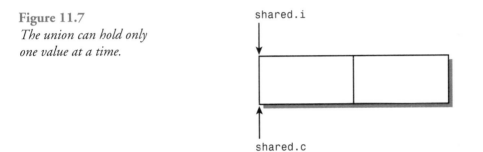

A union can be initialized on its declaration. Because only one member can be used at a time, only one can be initialized. To avoid confusion, only the first member of the union can be initialized. The following shows an instance of the shared union being declared and initialized:

```
union shared generic_variable = {'@'};
```

Notice that the generic_variable union was initialized just as the first member of a structure would be initialized.

Accessing Union Members

Individual union members can be used in the same way that structure members can be used—by using the member operator (.). There is an important difference in accessing union members. Only one union member should be accessed at a time. Because a union stores its members on top of each other, it is important to access only one member at a time. Listing 11.6 presents an example.

Listing 11.6. An example of the wrong use of unions.

```
 1:    /* Example of using more than one union member at a time */
 2:    #include <stdio.h>
 3:
 4:    main()
 5:    {
 6:        union shared_tag {
 7:            char   c;
 8:            int    i;
 9:            long   l;
10:            float  f;
11:            double d;
12:        } shared;
13:
14:        shared.c = '$';
15:
16:        printf("\nchar c   = %c",  shared.c);
17:        printf("\nint i    = %d",  shared.i);
18:        printf("\nlong l   = %ld", shared.l);
19:        printf("\nfloat f  = %f",  shared.f);
20:        printf("\ndouble d = %f",  shared.d);
21:
22:        shared.d = 123456789.8765;
23:
24:        printf("\n\nchar c   = %c",  shared.c);
25:        printf("\nint i    = %d",  shared.i);
26:        printf("\nlong l   = %ld", shared.l);
27:        printf("\nfloat f  = %f",  shared.f);
28:        printf("\ndouble d = %f",  shared.d);
29:
30:        return 0;
31:    }
```

```
char c   = $
int i    = 4900
long l   = 437785380
float f  = 0.000000
double d = 0.000000

char c   = 7
int i    = -30409
long l   = 1468107063
float f  = 284852666499072.000000
double d = 123456789.876500
```

Analysis In this listing, you can see that a union named shared was defined and declared in lines 6–12. shared contains five members, each of a different type. Lines 14 and 22 initialize individual members of shared. Lines 16–20 and 24–28 then present the values of each member using printf() statements.

Note that with the exceptions of char c = $ and double d = 123456789.876500, the output might not be the same on your computer. Because the character variable, c, was initialized in line 14, it is the only value that should be used until a different member is initialized. The results from printing the other union member variables (i, l, f, and d) can be unpredictable (lines 16–20). Line 22 puts a value into the double variable, d. Notice that the printing of the variables again is unpredictable for all but d. The value entered into c in line 14 has been lost because it was overwritten when the value of d in line 22 was entered. This is evidence that the members all occupy the same space.

The *union* Keyword

```
union tag {
union_member(s)
/* additional statements may go here */
}instance;
```

The union keyword is used for declaring unions. A union is a collection of one or more variables (*union_members*) that have been grouped under a single name. In addition, each of these union members occupy the same area of memory.

The keyword union identifies the beginning of a union definition. It is followed by a tag that is the name given to the union. Following the tag are the union members enclosed in braces. An *instance*, the actual declaration of a union, also can be defined. If you define the structure without the instance, it is just a template that can be used later in a program to declare structures. Following is a template's format:

```
union tag {
    union_member(s)
    /* additional statements may go here */
};
```

To use the template, you would use the following format:

```
union tag instance;
```

To use this format, you must have previously declared a union with the given tag.

Example 1

```
/* Declare a union template called tag */
union tag {
    int nbr;
    char character;
}
/* Use the union template */
union tag mixed_variable;
```

Example 2

```
/* Declare a union and instance together */
union generic_type_tag {
    char c;
    int i;
    float f;
    double d;
} generic;
```

11

Example 3

```
/* Initialize a union. */
union date_tag {
    char full_date[9];
    struct part_date_tag {
        char month[2];
        char break_value1;
        char day[2];
        char break_value2;
        char year[2];
    } part_date;
}date = {"01/01/97"};
```

Listing 11.7 shows a more practical use of a union. Although this use is simplistic, it is one of the more common uses of a union.

Type

Listing 11.7. A practical use of a union.

```
1:    /* Example of a typical use of a union */
2:
3:    #include <stdio.h>
4:
5:    #define CHARACTER    'C'
6:    #define INTEGER      'I'
7:    #define FLOAT        'F'
8:
9:    struct generic_tag{
10:       char type;
11:       union shared_tag {
12:           char    c;
13:           int     i;
14:           float   f;
15:       } shared;
16:    };
17:
18:    void print_function( struct generic_tag generic );
19:
20:    main()
21:    {
22:        struct generic_tag var;
23:
24:        var.type = CHARACTER;
25:        var.shared.c = '$';
26:        print_function( var );
27:
28:        var.type = FLOAT;
29:        var.shared.f = 12345.67890;
30:        print_function( var );
31:
32:        var.type = 'x';
33:        var.shared.i = 111;
34:        print_function( var );
35:        return 0;
36:    }
```

```
37:     void print_function( struct generic_tag generic )
38:     {
39:         printf("\n\nThe generic value is...");
40:         switch( generic.type )
41:         {
42:             case CHARACTER: printf("%c",  generic.shared.c);
43:                             break;
44:             case INTEGER:   printf("%d",  generic.shared.i);
45:                             break;
46:             case FLOAT:     printf("%f",  generic.shared.f);
47:                             break;
48:             default:        printf("an unknown type: %c",
49:                                    generic.type);
50:                             break;
51:         }
52:     }
```

```
The generic value is...$

The generic value is...12345.678711

The generic value is...an unknown type: x
```

This program is a very simplistic version of what could be done with a union. This program provides a way of storing multiple data types in a single storage space. The `generic_tag` structure enables you to store either a character, an integer or a floating point number within the same area. This area is a union called `shared` that operates just like the examples in Listing 11.6. Notice that the `generic_tag` structure also adds an additional field called `type`. This field is used to store information on the type of variable contained in `shared`. `type` helps prevent `shared` from being used in the wrong way—thus helping to avoid erroneous data such as that presented in Listing 11.6.

A formal look at the program shows that lines 5, 6, and 7 define constants CHARACTER, INTEGER, and FLOAT. These are used later in the program to make the listing more readable. Lines 9–16 define a `generic_tag` structure that will be used later. Line 18 presents a prototype for the `print_function()`. The structure var is declared in line 22 and is first initialized to hold a character value in lines 24 and 25. A call to `print_function()` in 26 lets the value be printed. Lines 28–30 and 32–34 repeat this process with other values.

The `print_function()` is the heart of this listing. Although this function is used to print the value from a `generic_tag` variable, a similar function could have been used to initialize it. `print_function()` will evaluate the `type` variable in order to print a statement with the appropriate variable type. This prevents getting erroneous data such as that in Listing 11.6.

DO	**DON'T**

DON'T try to initialize more than the first union member.

DO remember which union member is being used. If you fill in a member of one type and try to use a different type, you can get unpredictable results.

DON'T forget that the size of a union is equal to its largest member.

DO note that unions are an advanced C topic.

typedef and Structures

You can use the `typedef` keyword to create a synonym for a structure or union type. For example, the following statements define `coord` as a synonym for the indicated structure:

```
typedef struct {
    int x;
    int y;
} coord;
```

You can then declare instances of this structure using the `coord` identifier:

```
coord topleft, bottomright;
```

Note that a `typedef` is different from a structure tag, as described earlier in this chapter. If you write

```
struct coord {
    int x;
    int y;
};
```

the identifier `coord` is a tag for the structure. You can use the tag to declare instances of the structure, but unlike with a `typedef`, you must include the `struct` keyword:

```
structzcoord topleft, bottomright;
```

Whether you use `typedef` or a structure tag to declare structures makes little practical difference. Using `typedef` results in slightly more concise code because the `struct` keyword need not be used. On the other hand, using a tag and having the `struct` keyword explicit makes it clear that it is a structure being declared.

Summary

This chapter showed you how to use structures, a data type that you design to meet the needs of your program. A structure can contain any of C's data types, including other structures, pointers, and arrays. Each data item within a structure, called a member, is accessed using the structure member operator (.) between the structure name and the member name. Structures can be used individually, and they also can be used in arrays.

Unions were presented as being similar to structures. The main difference between a union and a structure is that the union stores all of its members in the same area. This means that only an individual member of a union can be used at a time.

Q&A

Q **Is there any purpose to declaring a structure without an instance?**

A Two ways were shown to declare a structure. The first was to declare a structure body, tag, and instance all at once. The second was to declare a structure body and tag without an instance. An instance can then be declared later by using the `struct` keyword, the tag, and a name for the instance. It is a common programming practice to use the second method. Many programmers will declare the structure body and tag without any instances. The instances will then be declared later in the program. In the next chapter, variable scope is described. Scope will apply to the instance, but not to the tag or structure body.

Q **Is it more common to use a `typedef` or a structure tag?**

A Many programmers use `typedef`s to make their code easier to read; it makes little practical difference, however. Many add-in libraries that contain functions can be purchased. These add-in products usually have a lot of `typedef`s to make the product unique. This is especially true of database add-in products.

Q **Can I simply assign one structure to another with the assignment operator?**

A Yes and No! Newer versions of C compilers will let you assign one structure to another; however, older versions might not. In older versions of C, you might need to assign each member of the structures individually! This is true of unions also.

Q **How big is a union?**

A Because each of the members in a union is stored in the same memory location, the amount of room required to store the union is equal to that of its largest member.

Workshop

The Workshop provides quiz questions to help you solidify your understanding of the material covered and exercises to provide you with experience in using what you've learned.

Quiz

1. How is a structure different from an array?

2. What is the structure member operator, and what purpose does it serve?

3. What keyword is used in C to create a structure?

4. What is the difference between a structure tag and a structure instance?

5. What is the following code fragment doing?

```
struct address {
    char name[31];
    char add1[31];
    char add2[31];
    char city[11];
    char state[3];
    char zip[11];
} myaddress = { "Bradley Jones",
                "RTSoftware",
                "P.O. Box 1213",
                "Carmel", "IN", "46032-1213"};
```

6. Assume you have declared an array of structures, and that `ptr` is a pointer to the first array element (that is, the first structure in the array). How would you change `ptr` to point at the second array element?

Exercises

1. Write the code that defines a structure named `time`, which contains three `int` members.

2. Write the code that does two tasks: defines a structure named `data` that contains one type `int` member and two type `float` members, and declares an instance of type `data` named `info`.

3. Continuing from exercise 2, how would you assign the value `100` to the integer member of the structure `info`?

4. Write the code that declares and initializes a pointer to `info`.

5. Continuing from exercise 4, show two ways to use pointer notation to assign the value `5.5` to the first `float` member of `info`.

6. Write the definition for a structure type named `data` that can hold a single string of up to 20 characters.

7. Create a structure containing five strings: `address1`, `address2`, `city`, `state`, and `zip`. Create a `typedef` called `RECORD` that can be used to create instances of this structure.

8. Using the `typedef` from exercise 7, allocate and initialize an element called `myaddress`.

9. **BUG BUSTER:** What is wrong with the following code fragment?

```c
struct {
    char zodiac_sign[21];
    int month;
} sign = "Leo", 8;
```

10. **BUG BUSTER:** What is wrong with the following code fragment?

```c
/* setting up a union */
union data{
    char a_word[4];
    long a_number;
}generic_variable = { "WOW", 1000 };
```

Variable Scope

On Day 5, "Functions: The Basics," you saw that a variable defined within a function is different from a variable defined outside a function. Without knowing it, you were being introduced to the concept of *variable scope,* an important aspect of C programming. Today, you learn

- About scope and why it's important
- What external variables are and why you should usually avoid them
- The ins and outs of local variables
- The difference between static and automatic variables
- About local variables and blocks
- How to select a storage class

What Is Scope?

The *scope* of a variable refers to the extent to which different parts of a program have access to the variable, or, in other words, where the variable is *visible*. When referring to C variables, the terms *accessibility* and *visibility* are used interchangeably. When speaking about scope, the term *variable* refers to all C data types: simple variables, arrays, structures, pointers, and so forth. It refers, too, to symbolic constants defined with the `const` keyword.

Scope also affects a variable's lifetime: how long the variable persists in memory, or when the variable's storage is allocated and deallocated. First, this chapter examines visibility.

A Demonstration of Scope

Look at the program in Listing 12.1. It defines the variable x in line 5, uses `printf()` to display the value of x in line 11, and then calls the function `print_value()` to display the value of x again. Note that the function `print_value()` is not passed the value of x as an argument; it simply uses x as an argument to `printf()` in line 17.

Listing 12.1. The variable x is accessible within the function `print_value()`.

```
1: /* Illustrates variable scope. */
2:
3: #include <stdio.h>
4:
5: int x = 999;
6:
7: void print_value(void);
8:
9: main()
10: {
11:     printf("%d\n", x);
```

```
12:     print_value();
13: }
14:
15: void print_value(void)
16: {
17:     printf("%d\n", x);
18: }
```

Output

```
999
999
```

Analysis

The program in Listing 12.1 compiles and runs with no problems. Now make a minor modification in the program, moving the definition of the variable x to a location within the main() function. The new source code is shown in Listing 12.2.

Type

Listing 12.2. The variable x is not accessible within the function print_value().

```
1: /* Illustrates variable scope. */
2:
3: #include <stdio.h>
4:
5: void print_value(void);
6:
7: main()
8: {
9:     int x = 999;
10:
11:     printf("%d\n", x);
12:     print_value();
13: }
14:
15: void print_value(void)
16: {
17:     printf("%d\n", x);
18: }
```

Analysis

If you try to compile Listing 12.2, the compiler generates an error message similar to the following:

```
list1202.c(17) : Error: undefined identifier 'x'.
```

Remember that in an error message, the number in parentheses refers to the program line where the error was found. Line 17 is the call to printf() within the print_value() function.

This error message tells you that within the print_value() function, the variable x is undefined or, in other words, not visible. Note, however, that the call to printf() in line 11 does not generate an error message; in this part of the program, the variable x is visible.

The only difference between Listings 12.1 and 12.2 is where variable x is defined. By moving the definition of x, you change its scope. In Listing 12.1, x is an *external* variable, and its scope is the entire program. It is accessible within both the main() function and the print_value() function. In Listing 12.2, x is a *local* variable, and its scope is limited to within the main() function. As far as print_value() is concerned, x doesn't exist. Later in this chapter, you learn more about local and external variables, but first, you need some understanding of the importance of scope.

Why Is Scope Important?

To understand the importance of variable scope, you need to recall the discussion of structured programming on Day 5. The structured approach, you may remember, divides the program into independent functions that perform a specific task. The key word here is *independent*. For true independence, it's necessary that each function's variables be isolated from interference caused by other functions. Only by isolating each function's data can you make sure the function goes about its job without some other part of the program throwing a monkey wrench into the works.

You may be thinking that complete data isolation between functions is not always desirable, and you are correct. You soon will realize that by specifying the scope of variables, a programmer has a great deal of control over the degree of data isolation.

External Variables

An *external* variable is one defined outside of any function. This means outside of main() as well, because main() is a function, too. Until now, most of the variable definitions in this book have been external, placed in the source code before the start of main(). External variables are sometimes referred to as *global* variables. If you do not explicitly initialize an external variable when it is defined, the compiler initializes it to 0.

External Variable Scope

The scope of an external variable is the entire program. This means that an external variable is visible throughout main() and every other function in the program. For example, the variable x in Listing 12.1 is an external variable. As you saw when you compiled and ran the program, x is visible within both functions, main() and print_value().

Strictly speaking, however, it's not accurate to say the scope of an external variable is the entire program. The scope is, rather, the entire source code file that contains the variable definition. If the entire program is contained in one source code file, the two scope definitions are equivalent. Most small-to-moderate sized C programs are contained in one file, and that's certainly true of the programs you're writing now.

It's possible, however, for a program's source code to be contained in two or more separate files. You learn how and why this is done on Day 21, "Taking Advantage of Preprocessor Directives and More," and what special handling is required for external variables in these situations.

When to Use External Variables

Although the sample programs to this point have used external variables, in actual practice, you should use them rarely. Why? Because when you use external variables, you are violating the principle of *modular independence* that is central to structured programming. Modular independence is the idea that each function, or module, in a program contains all the code and data it needs to do its job. With the relatively small programs you are writing now, this may not seem important, but as you progress to larger and more complex programs, over reliance on external variables can start to cause problems.

When should you use external variables? Make a variable external only when all or most of the program's functions need access to the variable. Symbolic constants defined with the const keyword are often good candidates for external status. If only some of your functions need access to a variable, pass it to the functions as an argument rather than making it external.

The *extern* Keyword

When a function uses an external variable, it is good programming practice to declare the variable within the function using the extern keyword. The declaration takes the form

```
extern type name;
```

in which *type* is the variable type and *name* is the variable name. For example, you would add the declaration of x to the functions main() and print_value() in Listing 12.1. The resulting program is shown in Listing 12.3.

Listing 12.3. The external variable x is declared as extern within the functions main() and print_value().

```
1: /* Illustrates declaring external variables. */
2:
3: #include <stdio.h>
4:
5: int x = 999;
6:
7: void print_value(void);
8:
9: main()
10: {
11:     extern int x;
12:
```

continues

Listing 12.3. continued

```
13:     printf("%d\n", x);
14:     print_value();
15: }
16:
17: void print_value(void)
18: {
19:
20:     extern int x;
21:     printf("%d", x);
22: }
```

Output

```
999
999
```

Analysis

This program prints the value of x twice, first in line 13 as a part of main(), and then in line 21 as a part of print_value(). Line 5 defines x as a type int variable equal to 999. Lines 11 and 20 declare x as an extern int. Note the distinction between a variable definition, which sets aside storage for the variable, and an extern declaration. The latter says: "This function uses an external variable with such and such a name and type that is defined elsewhere." In this case, the extern declaration is not needed, strictly speaking—the program will work the same without lines 11 and 20. If, however, the function print_value() were in a different code module than the global declaration of the variable x (in line 5), the extern declaration would be required.

Local Variables

A *local variable* is one that is defined within a function. The scope of a local variable is limited to the function in which it is defined. Day 5 describes local variables within functions, how to define them, and what their advantages are. Local variables are not automatically initialized to 0 by the compiler. If you do not initialize a local variable when it is defined, it has an undefined or *garbage* value. You must explicitly assign a value to local variables before they're used for the first time.

A variable can be local to the main() function as well. This is the case for x in Listing 12.2. It is defined within main(), and as compiling and executing that program illustrates, it's also visible only within `main()`.

Static Versus Automatic Variables

Local variables are *automatic* by default. This means that local variables are created anew each time the function is called, and they are destroyed when execution leaves the function. What this means, in practical terms, is that an automatic variable does not retain its value between calls to the function in which it is defined.

Suppose your program has a function that uses a local variable x. Also suppose that the first time it is called, the function assigns the value 100 to x. Execution returns to the calling program, and the function is called again later. Does the variable x still hold the value 100? No, it does not. The first instance of variable x was destroyed when execution left the function after the first call. When the function was called again, a new instance of x was created. The old x is gone forever.

What if the function needs to retain the value of a local variable between calls? For example, a printing function may need to remember the number of lines already sent to the printer to determine when a new page is needed. For a local variable to retain its value between calls, it must be defined as *static* with the `static` keyword. For example,

```
void func1(int x)
{
    static int a;
...
```

12

Listing 12.4. The difference between automatic and static local variables.

```
1: /* Demonstrates automatic and static local variables. */
2: #include <stdio.h>
3: void func1(void);
4: main()
5: {
6:     int count;
7:
8:     for (count = 0; count < 20; count++)
9:     {
10:         printf("At iteration %d: ", count);
11:         func1();
12:     }
13: }
14:
15: void func1(void)
16: {
17:     static int x = 0;
18:     int y = 0;
19:
20:     printf("x = %d, y = %d\n", x++, y++);
21: }
```

```
At iteration 0: x = 0, y = 0
At iteration 1: x = 1, y = 0
At iteration 2: x = 2, y = 0
At iteration 3: x = 3, y = 0
At iteration 4: x = 4, y = 0
At iteration 5: x = 5, y = 0
At iteration 6: x = 6, y = 0
At iteration 7: x = 7, y = 0
At iteration 8: x = 8, y = 0
At iteration 9: x = 9, y = 0
At iteration 10: x = 10, y = 0
At iteration 11: x = 11, y = 0
At iteration 12: x = 12, y = 0
At iteration 13: x = 13, y = 0
At iteration 14: x = 14, y = 0
At iteration 15: x = 15, y = 0
At iteration 16: x = 16, y = 0
At iteration 17: x = 17, y = 0
At iteration 18: x = 18, y = 0
At iteration 19: x = 19, y = 0
```

Analysis This program has a function that defines and initializes one variable of each type. This function is func1() in lines 15–21. Each time the function is called, both variables are displayed on the screen and incremented (line 20). The main() function in lines 4–13 contains a for loop (lines 8–12) that prints a message (line 10) and then calls func1() (line 11). The for loop iterates 20 times.

In the preceding output listing, note that x, the static variable, increases with each iteration because it retains its value between calls. The automatic variable y, on the other hand, is reinitialized to 0 with each call.

This program also illustrates a difference in the way explicit variable initialization is handled (that is, when a variable is initialized at the time of definition). A static variable is initialized only the first time the function is called. At later calls, the program "remembers" that the variable has already been initialized and does not reinitialize. Instead, the variable retains the value it had when execution last exited the function. In contrast, an automatic variable is initialized to the specified value every time the function is called.

If you do some experimenting with automatic variables, you may get results that disagree with what you've read here. For example, if you modify the program in Listing 12.4 so that the two local variables aren't initialized when they're defined, the function func1() in lines 15 to 21 reads

```
15: void func1(void)
16: {
17:     static int x;
18:     int y;
19:
20:     printf("x = %d, y = %d\n", x++, y++);
21: }
```

When you run the modified program, you may find that the value of y increases by one with each iteration. This means that y is keeping its value between calls to the function. Is what you've read here about automatic variables losing their value a bunch of malarkey?

No, what you read is true (Have faith!). If you get the results described previously, in which an automatic variable keeps its value on repeated calls to the function, it's only by chance. Here's what happens. Each time the function is called, a new y is created. The compiler may use the same memory location for the new y that was used for y the preceding time the function was called. If y is not explicitly initialized by the function, the storage location may contain the value that y had during the preceding call. The variable seems to have kept its old value, but it's just a chance occurrence; you definitely cannot count on it happening every time.

Because automatic is the default for local variables, it need not be specified in the variable definition. If you want, you can include the auto keyword in the definition before the type keyword, as shown here:

```
void func1(int y)
{
    auto int count;
    /* Additional code goes here */
}
```

12

The Scope of Function Parameters

A variable that is contained in a function heading's parameter list has *local* scope. For example, look at the following function:

```
void func1(int x)
{
    int y;
    /* Additional code goes here */
}
```

Both x and y are local variables with a scope that is the entire function func1(). Of course, x initially contains whatever value was passed to the function by the calling program. Once you've made use of that value, you can use x like any other local variable.

Because parameter variables always start with the value passed as the corresponding argument, it is meaningless to think of them as being either static or automatic.

External Static Variables

An external variable can be made static by including the static keyword in its definition:

```
static float rate;

main()
{
    /* Additional code goes here */
}
```

The difference between an ordinary external variable and a static external variable is one of scope. An ordinary external variable is visible to all functions in the file and can be used by functions in other files. A static external variable is visible only to functions in its own file and below the point of definition.

The previous distinctions obviously apply mostly to programs with source code that is contained in two or more files. This topic is covered on Day 21.

Register Variables

The register keyword is used to suggest to the compiler that an automatic local variable be stored in a processor register rather than in regular memory. What is a *processor register* and the advantage of using it?

The central processing unit, or CPU, of your computer contains a few data storage locations called *registers*. It is in the CPU registers that actual data operations, such as addition and division, take place. To manipulate data, the CPU must move the data from memory to its registers, perform the manipulations, and then move the data back to memory. Moving data to and from memory takes a finite amount of time. If a particular variable could be kept in a register to begin with, manipulations of the variable would proceed much faster.

By using the `register` keyword in the definition of an automatic variable, you ask the compiler to store that variable in a register. Take a look at the following example:

```
void func1(void)
{
    register int x;
    /* Additional code goes here */
}
```

Note that the term is "ask" and not "tell." Depending on the needs of the program, a register may not be available for the variable. In this case, the compiler treats it as an ordinary automatic variable. The `register` keyword is a suggestion—not an order. The benefits of the `register` storage class are largest for variables that are used frequently by the function, such as the counter variable for a loop.

The `register` keyword can be used only with simple numeric variables, not arrays or structures. Also, it cannot be used with either static or external storage classes. You cannot define a pointer to a register variable.

DO	DON'T

DO initialize local variables or you won't know what value they will contain.

DO initialize global variables even though they're initialized to 0 by default. If you always initialize your variables, you avoid problems such as forgetting to initialize local variables.

DO pass data items as function parameters instead of declaring them as global if they are needed in only a few functions.

DON'T use register variables for nonnumeric values, structures, or arrays.

Local Variables and the *main()* Function

Everything said so far about local variables applies to `main()`, as well as to all other functions. Strictly speaking, `main()` is a function like any other. The `main()` function is called when the program is started from the operating system you are using, and control is returned to the operating system from `main()` when the program terminates.

This means that local variables defined in `main()` are created when the program begins, and their lifetime is over when the program ends. The notion of a static local variable retaining its value between calls to `main()` really makes no sense: a variable cannot remain in existence between program executions. Within `main()`, therefore, there is no difference between automatic and static local variables. You can define a local variable in `main()` as being static, but it has no effect.

<table>
<tr><td>**DO**</td><td>**DON'T**</td></tr>
</table>

DO remember that main() is a function similar in most respects to any other function.

DON'T declare static variables in main() because doing so gains nothing.

Which Storage Class Should You Use?

When you're deciding which storage class to use for particular variables in your programs, it may be helpful to refer to Table 12.1, which summarizes the five storage classes available in C.

Table 12.1. C's five variable storage classes.

Storage Class	Keyword	Lifetime	Where Defined	Scope
Automatic	None[1]	Temporary	In a function	Local
Static	static	Temporary	In a function	Local
Register	register	Temporary	In a function	Local
External	None[2]	Permanent	Outside a function	Global (all files)
External Static	static	Permanent	Outside a function	Global (one file)

[1] The auto keyword is optional.

[2] The extern keyword is used in functions to declare a static external variable that is defined elsewhere.

When you're deciding on a storage class, you should use an automatic storage class whenever possible and use other classes only when needed. Here are some guidelines to follow:

- Give each variable automatic local storage class to begin with.
- If the variable is to be frequently manipulated, add the register keyword to its definition.
- In functions other than main(), make a variable static if its value must be retained between calls to the function.
- If a variable is used by most or all of the program's functions, define it with the external storage class.

Local Variables and Blocks

So far, this chapter has discussed only variables that are local to a function. This is the primary way local variables are used, but you can define variables that are local to any program block (any section enclosed in braces). When declaring variables within the block, you must remember that the declarations must be first. For an example, see Listing 12.5.

Type

Listing 12.5. Defining local variables within a program block.

```
1: /* Demonstrates local variables within blocks. */
2:
3: #include <stdio.h>
4:
5: main()
6: {
7:     /* Define a variable local to main(). */
8:
9:     int count = 0;
10:
11:     printf("\nOutside the block, count = %d", count);
12:
13:     /* Start a block. */
14:     {
15:     /* Define a variable local to the block. */
16:
17:     int count = 999;
18:     printf("\nWithin the block, count = %d", count);
19:     }
20:
21:     printf("\nOutside the block again, count = %d", count);
22: }
```

 Output

```
Outside the block, count = 0
Within the block, count = 999
Outside the block again, count = 0
```

 Analysis

From this program, you can see that the count defined within the block is independent of the count defined outside the block. Line 9 defines count as a type int variable equal to 0. Because it is declared at the beginning of main(), it can be used throughout the entire main() function. The code in line 11 shows that the variable count has been initialized to zero by printing its value. A block is declared in lines 14–19, and within the block, another count variable is defined as a type int variable. This count variable is initialized to 999 (line 17). Line 18 prints the block's count variable value of 999. Because the block ends in line 19, the print statement in line 21 uses the original count initially declared in line 9 of main().

The use of this type of local variable is not common in C programming, and you may never find a need for it. Its most common use is probably when a programmer tries to isolate a problem

within a program. You can temporarily isolate sections of code in braces and establish local variables to assist in tracking down the fault. Another advantage is that the variable declaration-initialization can be placed closer to the point where it's used, which can help in understanding the program.

DO	**DON'T**

DON'T try to put variable definitions at any place within a program other than at the beginning of a function or at the beginning of a block.

DON'T use variables at the beginning of a block unless it makes the program clearer.

DO use variables at the beginning of a block (temporarily) to help track down problems.

Summary

This chapter covered C's variable storage classes. Every C variable, whether a simple variable, an array, a structure, or whatever, has a specific storage class that determines two things: its scope or where in the program it's visible, and its lifetime or how long the variable persists in memory.

Proper use of storage classes is an important aspect of structured programming. By keeping most variables local to the function that uses them, you enhance the independence of functions from each other. A variable should be given automatic storage class unless there is a specific reason to make it external or static.

Q&A

Q If global variables can be used anywhere in the program, why not make all variables global?

A As your programs get bigger, you will begin to declare more and more variables. As stated in the chapter, there are limits on the amount of memory available. Variables declared as global take up memory for the entire time the program is running; however, local variables do not. For the most part, a local variable takes up memory only while the function to which it is local is active. (A static variable takes up memory from the time it is first used to the end of the program.) Additionally, global variables are subject to unintentional alteration by other functions. If this occurs, the variables may not contain the values you expect them to when they are used in the functions for which they were created.

Q Day 11, "Structures," stated that scope affects a structure instance but not a structure tag or body. Why doesn't scope affect the structure tag or body?

A When declaring a structure without instances, you are creating a template. You do not actually declare any variables. It is not until you create an instance of the structure that you declare a variable. For this reason, you can leave a structure body external to any functions with no real effect on external memory. Many programmers put commonly used structure bodies with tags into header files, and then include these header files when they need to create an instance of the structure. (Header files are covered on Day 21, "Taking Advantage of Preprocessor Directives and More.")

Q How does the computer know the difference between a global and a local variable with the same name?

A The answer to this question is beyond the scope of this chapter. The important thing to know is that when a local variable is declared with the same name as a global variable, the program temporarily ignores the global variable. It continues to ignore the global variable until the local variable goes out of scope.

Q Can I declare a local variable with a different variable type, yet use the same variable name as a global variable?

A Yes. When you declare a local variable with the same name as a global variable, it is a completely different variable. This means you can make it whatever type you want. You should be careful, however, when declaring global and local variables with the same name. In Bonus Day 1, "Coding Styles," you learn how to use Hungarian notation to create variable names that reflect the data type.

12

Workshop

The Workshop provides quiz questions to help you solidify your understanding of the material covered, and exercises to provide you with experience in using what you've learned.

Quiz

1. What does scope refer to?
2. What is the most important difference between local storage class and external storage class?
3. How does the location of a variable definition affect its storage class?
4. When defining a local variable, what are the two options for the variable's lifetime?
5. Your program can initialize both automatic and static local variables when they are defined. When do the initializations take place?

6. True or false: A register variable will always be placed in a register.

7. What value does an uninitialized global variable contain?

8. What value does an uninitialized local variable contain?

9. What will line 21 print in Listing 12.5 if lines 9 and 11 are removed? Think about this and then try the program to see what happens.

10. If a function "needs to remember" the value of a local type int variable between calls, how should the variable be declared?

11. What does the extern keyword do?

12. What does the static keyword do?

Exercises

1. Write a declaration for a variable to be placed in a CPU register.

2. Change Listing 12.2 to prevent the error. Do this without using any external variables.

3. Write a program that declares a global variable of type int called var. Initialize var to any value. The program should print the value of var in a function (not main()). Do you need to pass var as a parameter to the function?

4. Change the program in exercise 3. Instead of declaring var as a global variable, change it to a local variable in main(). The program should still print var in a separate function. Do you need to pass var as a parameter to the function?

5. Can a program have a global and a local variable with the same name? Write a program that uses a global and a local variable with the same name to prove your answer.

6. **BUG BUSTER:** Can you spot the problem with this code? Hint: It has to do with where a variable is declared.

```
void a_sample_function( void )
{
    int ctr1;

    for ( ctr1 = 0; ctr1 < 25; ctr1++ )
        printf( "*" );

    puts( "\nThis is a sample function" );
    {
        char star = '*';
        puts( "It has a problem" );
        for ( int ctr2 = 0; ctr2 < 25; ctr2++ )
        {
            printf( "%c", star);
        }
    }
}
```

7. **BUG BUSTER:** What is wrong with the following code?

```
/*Count the number of even numbers between
  0 and 100. */

#include <stdio.h>

main()
{
    int x = 1;
    static int tally = 0;

    for (x = 0; x < 101; x++)
    {
        if (x % 2 == 0)  /*if x is even...*/
            tally++;..  /*add 1 to tally.*/

    }

    printf("There are %d even numbers.", tally);
}
```

8. **BUG BUSTER:** Is anything wrong with the following program?

```
#include <stdio.h>

void print_function( char star );

int ctr;

main()
{
    char star;

    print_function( star );
    return 0;
}

void print_function( char star )
{
    char dash;

    for ( ctr = 0; ctr < 25; ctr++ )
    {
        printf( "%c%c", star, dash );
    }
}
```

9. What does the following program print? Don't run the program—try to figure it out by reading the code.

```
#include <stdio.h>
void print_letter2(void);              /* function prototype */

int ctr;
char letter1 = 'X';
```

```
char letter2 = '=';

main()
{
    for( ctr = 0; ctr < 10; ctr++ )
    {
        printf( "%c", letter1 )
        print_letter2();
    }
}

void print_letter2(void)
{
    for( ctr = 0; ctr < 2; ctr++ )
        printf( "%c", letter2 );
}
```

10. **BUG BUSTER:** Will the preceding program run? If not, what's the problem? Rewrite it so that it is correct.

13

WEEK
2

More Program Control

Day 6, "Basic Program Control," introduced some of C's program control statements that govern the execution of other statements in your program. This chapter covers more advanced aspects of program control, including the goto statement and some of the more interesting things you can do with loops in your programs. Today, you learn

- How to use the break and continue statements
- What infinite loops are and why you might use them
- What the goto statement is and why you should avoid it
- How to use the switch statement
- How to control program exits
- How to execute functions automatically on program completion
- How to execute system commands in your program

Ending Loops Early

On Day 6 you learned how the for loop, the while loop, and the do...while loop can control program execution. These loop constructions execute a block of C statements never, once, or more than one time, depending on conditions in the program. In all three cases, termination or exit of the loop occurs only when a certain condition occurs.

At times, however, you might want to exert more control over loop execution. The break and continue statements provide this control.

The *break* Statement

The break statement can be placed only in the body of a for loop, while loop, or do...while loop. (It's valid in a switch statement too, but that topic isn't covered until later in this chapter.) When a break statement is encountered, execution exits the loop. The following is an example:

```
for ( count = 0; count < 10; count++ )
{
    if ( count == 5 )
    break;
}
```

Left to itself, the for loop would execute 10 times. On the sixth iteration, however, count is equal to 5 and the break statement executes, causing the for loop to terminate. Execution then passes to the statement immediately following the for loop's closing brace. When a break statement is encountered inside a nested loop, it causes exit of the innermost loop only.

The program in Listing 13.1 demonstrates break usage.

Listing 13.1. Using the break statement.

```
1: /* Demonstrates the break statement. */
2:
3: #include <stdio.h>
4:
5: char s[] = "This is a test string. It contains two sentences.";
6:
7: main()
8: {
9:     int count;
10:
11:     printf("\nOriginal string: %s", s);
12:
13:     for (count = 0; s[count]!='\0'; count++)
14:         if (s[count] == '.')
15:         {
16:             s[count+1] = '\0';
17:             break;
18:         }
19:
20:     printf("\nModified string: %s", s);
21: }
```

Output

```
Original string: This is a test string. It contains two sentences.
Modified string: This is a test string.
```

Analysis The program extracts the first sentence from a string. It searches the string, character by character, for the first period (which should mark the end of a sentence). This is done in the for loop in lines 13–18. Line 13 starts the for loop, incrementing count to go from character to character in the string, s. Line 14 checks to see whether the current character in the string is equal to a period. If it is, a null character is inserted immediately after the period (line 16). This, in effect, trims the string. Once you trim the string, you no longer need to continue the loop, so a break statement (line 17) quickly terminates the loop and sends control to the first line after the loop (line 20). If no period is found, the string is not altered.

A loop can contain multiple break statements, but only the first break executed (if any) has any effect. If no break is executed, the loop terminates normally (according to its test condition). Figure 13.1 shows the operation of the break statement.

13

Figure 13.1.
Operation of the break *and*
continue *statements.*

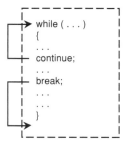

Syntax

The *break* Statement

```
break;
```

break is used inside a loop or switch statement. It causes the control of a program to skip past the end of the current loop (for, while, or do...while) or switch statement. No further iterations of the loop execute; the first command following the loop or switch statement executes.

Example

```
int x;
printf ( "Counting from 1 to 10\n" );
/* having no condition in the for loop will cause
    it to loop forever */
for( x = 1; ; x++ )
{
    if( x == 10 )    /* This checks for the value of 10 */
        break;       /* This ends the loop */
    printf( "\n%d", x );
}
```

The *continue* Statement

Like the break statement, the continue statement can be placed only in the body of a for loop, a while loop, or a do...while loop. When a continue statement executes, the next iteration of the enclosing loop begins immediately. The statements between the continue statement and the end of the loop are not executed. The operation of continue is shown in Figure 13.1. Notice how this differs from the operation of a break statement.

A program that uses continue is presented in Listing 13.2. The program accepts a line of input from the keyboard and then displays it with all lowercase vowels removed.

Type   **Listing 13.2. Using the continue statement.**

```
1: /* Demonstrates the continue statement. */
2:
3: #include <stdio.h>
4:
```

```
5: main()
6: {
7:      /* Declare a buffer for input and a counter variable. */
8:
9:      char buffer[81];
10:     int ctr;
11:
12:     /* Input a line of text. */
13:
14:     puts("Enter a line of text:");
15:     gets(buffer);
16:
17:     /* Go through the string, displaying only those */
18:     /* characters that are not lowercase vowels. */
19:
20:     for (ctr = 0; buffer[ctr] !='\0'; ctr++)
21:     {
22:
23:         /* If the character is a lowercase vowel, loop back */
24:         /* without displaying it. */
25:
26:         if (buffer[ctr] == 'a' || buffer[ctr] == 'e' ||
            buffer[ctr] == 'i'
27:             || buffer[ctr] == 'o' || buffer[ctr] == 'u')
28:             continue;
29:
30:         /* If not a vowel, display it. */
31:
32:         putchar(buffer[ctr]);
33:     }
34: }
```

Input
Output

```
Enter a line of text:
This is a line of text
Ths s  ln f txt
```

Analysis

Although this is not the most practical program, it does use a `continue` statement effectively. Lines 9 and 10 declare the program's variables. `buffer[]` holds the string the user enters on line 15. The other variable, `ctr`, increments through the elements of the array `buffer[]` while the `for` loop on lines 20–33 searches for vowels. For each letter in the loop, an `if` statement on lines 26 and 27 checks the letter against lowercase vowels. If there is a match, a `continue` statement executes, sending control back to line 20, the `for` statement. If the letter is not a vowel, control passes to the `if` statement and line 32 is executed. Line 32 contains a new library function, `putchar()`, which displays a single character on the screen.

The *continue* Statement

```
continue;
```

`continue` is used inside a loop. It causes the control of a program to skip the rest of the current iteration of a loop and start the next iteration.

Example

```
int x;
printf("Printing only the even numbers from 1 to 10\n");
for( x = 1; x <= 10; x++ )
{
    if( x % 2 != 0 )    /* See if the number is NOT even */
        continue;       /* Get next instance x */
    printf( "\n%d", x );
}
```

The *goto* Statement

The goto statement is one of C's *unconditional jump,* or *branching,* statements. When program execution reaches a goto statement, execution immediately jumps, or branches, to the location specified by the goto statement. The statement is unconditional because execution always branches when a goto statement is encountered; the branch does not depend on any program conditions (unlike if statements, for example).

A goto statement and its target label must be in the same function, although they can be in different blocks. Take a look at Listing 13.3, a simple program that uses a goto statement.

Type

Listing 13.3. Using the goto statement.

```
1: /* Demonstrates the goto statement */
2:
3: #include <stdio.h>
4:
5: main()
6: {
7:     int n;
8:
9: start: ;
10:
11:     puts("Enter a number between 0 and 10: ");
12:     scanf("%d", &n);
13:
14:     if (n < 0 ||n > 10 )
15:         goto start;
16:     else if (n == 0)
17:         goto location0;
18:     else if (n == 1)
19:         goto location1;
20:     else
21:         goto location2;
22:
23: location0: ;
24:     puts("You entered 0.");
25:     goto end;
26:
27: location1: ;
```

```
28:      puts("You entered 1.");
29:      goto end;
30:
31: location2: ;
32:      puts("You entered something between 2 and 10.");
33:
34: end: ;
35: }
```

```
C:\>list1303
Enter a number between 0 and 10:
1
You entered 1.

C:\>list1303
Enter a number between 0 and 10:
9
You entered something between 2 and 10.
```

 This is a simple program that accepts a number between 0 and 10. If the number is not between 0 and 10, the program uses a goto statement on line 15 to go to start, which is on line 9. Otherwise, the program checks on line 16 to see whether the number equals 0. If it does, a goto statement on line 17 sends control to location0 (line 23), which prints a statement on line 24 and executes another goto. The goto on line 25 sends control to end at the end of the program. The program executes the same logic for the value of 1 and all values between 2 and 10 as a whole.

The target of a goto statement can come either before or after that statement in the code. The only restriction, as mentioned previously, is that both the goto and the target must be in the same function. They can be in different blocks, however; you can use goto to transfer execution both into and out of loops, such as a for statement. You should never do this, however, and we strongly recommend that you never use the goto statement anywhere in your programs. There are two reasons:

- You don't need it. There are no programming tasks that require the goto statement. You always can write the needed code using C's other branching statements.

- It's dangerous. The goto statement may seem like an ideal solution for certain programming problems, but it is easy to abuse. When program execution branches with a goto statement, no record is kept of where the execution came from, so execution can weave willy-nilly in the program. This type of programming is known in the trade as *spaghetti code.*

Now, some careful programmers can write perfectly fine programs that use goto. There might be situations where a judicious use of goto is the simplest solution to a programming problem. It is never the only solution, however. If you're going to ignore this warning, at least be careful!

13

DO	**DON'T**

DO avoid using the goto statement if possible.

DON'T confuse break and continue. break ends a loop, whereas continue starts the next iteration.

The *goto* Statement

```
goto target;
```

target is a label statement that identifies the program location where execution is to branch. A *label statement* consists of an identifier followed by a colon and a C statement:

```
location1: a C statement;
```

If you want the label by itself on a line, you can follow it with the null statement (a semicolon by itself).

```
location1: ;
```

Infinite Loops

What is an infinite loop and why would you want one in your program? An infinite loop is one that, left to its own devices, would run forever. It can be a for loop, a while loop, or a do...while loop. For example, if you write

```
while (1)
{
    /* additional code goes here */
}
```

you create an infinite loop. The condition that the while tests is the constant 1, which is always true and cannot be changed by program execution. Therefore, on its own, the loop never terminates.

In the last section, however, you saw that the break statement can be used to exit a loop. Without the break statement, an infinite loop would be useless. With break, you can take advantage of infinite loops.

You also can create an infinite for loop or an infinite do...while loop, as follows:

```
for (;;)
{
    /* additional code goes here */
}
do
{
```

```
    /* additional code goes here */
} while (1);
```

The principle remains the same for all three loop types. This section's examples use the `while` loop.

An infinite loop can be used to test many conditions and determine whether the loop should terminate. It might be difficult to include all the test conditions in parentheses after the `while` statement. It might be easier to test the conditions individually in the body of the loop, and then exit by executing a `break` as needed.

An infinite loop also can create a menu system that directs your program's operation. You may remember from Day 5, "Functions: The Basics," that a program's `main()` function often serves as a sort of "traffic cop," directing execution among the various functions that do the real work of the program. This is often accomplished by a menu of some kind: the user is presented with a list of choices and makes an entry by selecting one of them. One of the available choices should be to terminate the program. Once a choice is made, one of C's decision statements is used to direct program execution accordingly.

Listing 13.4 demonstrates a menu system.

Listing 13.4. Using an infinite loop to implement a menu system.

```
1: /* Demonstrates using an infinite loop to implement */
2: /* a menu system. */
3: #include <stdio.h>
4: #define DELAY  1500000        /* Used in delay loop. */
5:
6: int menu(void);
7: void delay(void);
8:
9: main()
10: {
11:     int choice;
12:
13:     while (1)
14:     {
15:
16:     /* Get the user's selection. */
17;
18:     choice = menu();
19:
20:     /* Branch based on the input. */
21:
22;     if (choice == 1)
23:     {
24:         puts("\nExecuting choice 1.");
25:         delay();
26:     }
27:     else if (choice == 2)
28:         {
```

continues   279

Listing 13.4. continued

```
29:                        puts("\nExecuting choice 2.");
30:                        delay();
31:                }
32:        else if (choice == 3)
33:                {
34:                        puts("\nExecuting choice 3.");
35:                        delay();
36:                }
37:        else if (choice == 4)
38:                {
39:                        puts("\nExecuting choice 4.");
40:                        delay();
41:                }
42:        else if (choice == 5)       /* Exit program. */
43:                {
44:                        puts("Exiting program now...");
45:                        delay();
46:                        break;
47:                }
48:            else
49:                {
50:                        puts("Invalid choice, try again.");
51:                        delay();
52:                }
53:        }
54: }
55:
56: int menu(void)
57: /* Displays a menu and inputs user's selection. */
58: {
59:     int reply;
60:
61:     puts("\nEnter 1 for task A.");
62:     puts("Enter 2 for task B.");
63:     puts("Enter 3 for task C.");
64:     puts("Enter 4 for task D.");
65:     puts("Enter 5 to exit program.");
66:
67:     scanf("%d", &reply);
68:
69:     return reply;
70: }
71:
72: void delay( void )
73: {
74:     long x;
75:     for ( x = 0; x < DELAY; x++ )
76:             ;
77: }
```

```
Enter 1 for task A.
Enter 2 for task B.
Enter 3 for task C.
Enter 4 for task D.
```

```
Enter 5 to exit program.
1

Executing choice 1.

Enter 1 for task A.
Enter 2 for task B.
Enter 3 for task C.
Enter 4 for task D.
Enter 5 to exit program.
6
Invalid choice, try again.

Enter 1 for task A.
Enter 2 for task B.
Enter 3 for task C.
Enter 4 for task D.
Enter 5 to exit program.
5
Exiting program now...
```

In Listing 13.4, a function named menu() is called on line 18 and defined on lines 56–70. menu() displays a menu on the screen, accepts user input, and returns the input to the main program. In main(), a series of nested if statements tests the returned value and directs execution accordingly. The only thing this program does is display messages on the screen. In a real program, the code would call various functions to perform the selected task.

This program also uses a second function, named delay(). delay() is defined on lines 72–77 and really does not do much. Simply stated, the for statement on line 75 loops, doing nothing (line 76). The statement loops DELAY times. This is an effective method to pause the program momentarily. If the delay is too short or too long, the defined value of DELAY can be adjusted accordingly.

Both Borland and Symantec offer a function similar to delay(), called sleep(). This function pauses program execution for the number of seconds that is passed as its argument. To use sleep(), a program must include the header file TIME.H if you are using the Symantec compiler. You must use DOS.H if you are using a Borland compiler. If you are using either of these compilers or a compiler that supports sleep(), you could use it instead of delay().

The *switch* Statement

C's most flexible program control statement is the switch statement, which enables your program to execute different statements based on an expression that can have more than two values. Earlier control statements, such as if, were limited to evaluating an expression that could have only two values: true or false. To control program flow based on more than two values, you had to use multiple, nested if statements, as Listing 13.4 illustrates. The switch statement makes such nesting unnecessary.

The general form of the switch statement is as follows:

```
switch (expression)
{
    case  template_1: statement(s);
    case  template_2: statement(s);

    ...
    case  template_n: statement(s);
    default: statement(s);
}
```

In this statement, *expression* is any expression that evaluates to an integer value: type long, int, or char. The switch statement first evaluates *expression* and compares the value against the templates following each case label, and then

- If a match is found between *expression* and one of the templates, execution is transferred to the statement that follows the case label.

- If no match is found, execution is transferred to the statement following the optional default label.

- If no match is found and there is no default label, execution passes to the first statement following the switch statement's closing brace.

The switch statement is demonstrated by the simple program in Listing 13.5 that displays a message based on the user's input.

Type   **Listing 13.5. Using the switch statement.**

```
 1: /* Demonstrates the switch statement. */
 2:
 3: #include <stdio.h>
 4:
 5: main()
 6: {
 7:     int reply;
 8:
 9:     puts("Enter a number between 1 and 5:");
10:      scanf("%d", &reply);
11:
12:     switch (reply)
13:     {
14:         case 1:
15:             puts("You entered 1.");
16:         case 2:
17:             puts("You entered 2.");
18:         case 3:
19:             puts("You entered 3.");
20:         case 4:
21:             puts("You entered 4.");
22:         case 5:
23:             puts("You entered 5.");
24:         default:
25:             puts("Out of range, try again.");
26:     }
27: }
```

```
Enter a number between 1 and 5:
2
You entered 2.
You entered 3.
You entered 4.
You entered 5.
Out of range, try again.
```

Well, that's certainly not right, is it? It looks as though the switch statement finds the first matching template, and then executes everything that follows (not just the statements associated with the template). That's exactly what does happen, though. That's how switch is supposed to work. In effect, it performs a goto to the matching template. To ensure that only the statements associated with the matching template are executed, include a break statement where needed. Listing 13.6 shows the program rewritten with break statements. Now it functions properly.

Type

Listing 13.6. Correct use of switch, including break statements as needed.

```
1: /* Demonstrates the switch statement correctly. */
2:
3: #include <stdio.h>
4:
5: main()
6: {
7:     int reply;
8:
9:     puts("Enter a number between 1 and 5:");
10:    scanf("%d", &reply);
11:
12:    switch (reply)
13:    {
14:      case 0:
15:          break;
16:      case 1:
17:          {
18:          puts("You entered 1.");
19:          break;
20:          }
21:      case 2:
22:          {
23:          puts("You entered 2.");
24:          break;
25:          }
26:      case 3:
27:          {
28:          puts("You entered 3.");
29:          break;
30:          }
31:      case 4:
32:          {
33:          puts("You entered 4.");
34:          break;
```

continues

Listing 13.6. continued

```
35:          }
36:       case 5:
37:          {
38:          puts("You entered 5.");
39:          break;
40:          }
41:       default:
42:          puts("Out of range, try again.");
43:          }
44: }
```

```
C:\>list1306
Enter a number between 1 and 5:
1
You entered 1.

c:\>list1306
Enter a number between 1 and 5:
6
Out of range, try again.
```

Compile and run this version; it runs correctly.

One common use of the switch statement is to implement the sort of menu shown in Listing 13.4. Using switch is much better than using the nested if statements, as used in the earlier version of the menu program in Listing 13.4.

The program in Listing 13.7 uses switch instead of if.

Listing 13.7. Using the switch statement to execute a menu system.

```
1: /* Demonstrates using an infinite loop and the switch */
2: /* statement to implement a menu system. */
3: #include <stdio.h>
4: #include <stdlib.h>
5:
6: #define DELAY 150000
7:
8: int menu(void);
9: void delay(void);
10:
11: main()
12: {
13:
14:     while (1)
15:        {
16:     /* Get user's selection and branch based on the input.     */
17:
18:             switch(menu())
19:             {
```

```
20:            case 1:
21:                {
22:                puts("\nExecuting choice 1.");
23:                delay();
24:                break;
25:                }
26:            case 2:
27:                {
28:                puts("\nExecuting choice 2.");
29:                delay();
30:                break;
31:                }
32:            case 3:
33:                {
34:                puts("\nExecuting choice 3.");
35:                delay();
36:                break;
37:                }
38:            case 4:
39:                {
40:                puts("\nExecuting choice 4.");
41:                delay();
42:                break;
43:                }
44:            case 5:     /* Exit program. */
45:                {
46:                puts("Exiting program now...");
47:                delay();
48:                exit(0);
49:                }
50:            default:
51:                {
52:                puts("Invalid choice, try again.");
53:                delay();
54:                }
55:            }
56:        }
57: }
58:
59: int menu(void)
60: /* Displays a menu and inputs user's selection. */
61: {
62:     int reply;
63:
64:     puts("\nEnter 1 for task A.");
65:     puts("Enter 2 for task B.");
66:     puts("Enter 3 for task C.");
67:     puts("Enter 4 for task D.");
68:     puts("Enter 5 to exit program.");
69:
70:     scanf("%d", &reply);
71:
72:     return reply;
73: }
74:
75: void delay( void )
```

13

continues

Listing 13.7. continued

```
76: {
77:    long x;
78:    for( x = 0; x < DELAY; x++ )
79:        ;
80: }
```

```
Enter 1 for task A.
Enter 2 for task B.
Enter 3 for task C.
Enter 4 for task D.
Enter 5 to exit program.
1

Executing choice 1.

Enter 1 for task A.
Enter 2 for task B.
Enter 3 for task C.
Enter 4 for task D.
Enter 5 to exit program.
6
Invalid choice, try again.

Enter 1 for task A.
Enter 2 for task B.
Enter 3 for task C.
Enter 4 for task D.
Enter 5 to exit program.
5
Exiting program now...
```

Analysis
One other new statement is in this version: the exit() library function in the statements associated with case 5: on line 48. You cannot use break here, as you did in Listing 13.4's version. Executing a break would merely break out of the switch statement but would not break out of the infinite while loop. As you learn in the next section, the exit() function terminates the program.

Having execution "fall through" parts of a switch construction, however, can be useful at times. Say, for example, you want the same block of statements executed if one of several values is encountered. Simply omit the break statements and list all the case templates before the statements. If the test expression matches any of the case conditions, execution will "fall through" the following case statements until it reaches the block of code you want executed. This is illustrated by the program in Listing 13.8.

Type

Listing 13.8. Another way to use the switch statement.

```
1: /* Another use of the switch statement. */
2:
3: #include <stdio.h>
4: #include <stdlib.h>
```

SAMS
Sams
Learning
Center
SAMS
PUBLISHING

```
5:
6: main()
7: {
8:     int reply;
9:
10:    while (1)
11:    {
12:        puts("Enter a value between 1 and 10, 0 to exit: ");
13:        scanf("%d", &reply);
14:
15:        switch (reply)
16:        {
17:            case 0:
18:                exit(0);
19:            case 1:
20:            case 2:
21:            case 3:
22:            case 4:
23:            case 5:
24:                {
25:                puts("You entered 5 or below.");
26:                break;
27:                }
28:            case 6:
29:            case 7:
30:            case 8:
31:            case 9:
32:            case 10:
33:                {
34:                puts("You entered 6 or higher.");
35:                break;
36:                }
37:            default:
38:                puts("Between 1 and 10, please!");
39:        }
40:    }
41: }
```

**Input
Output**

```
Enter a value between 1 and 10, 0 to exit:
11
Between 1 and 10, please!
Enter a value between 1 and 10, 0 to exit:
1
You entered 5 or below.
Enter a value between 1 and 10, 0 to exit:
6
You entered 6 or higher.
Enter a value between 1 and 10, 0 to exit:
0
```

Analysis

This program accepts a value from the keyboard and then states whether the value is 5 or below, 6 or higher, or not between 1 and 10. If the value is 0, line 18 executes a call to the exit() function, thus ending the program.

Syntax

The *switch* Statement

```
switch  (expression)
{
    case  template_1: statement(s);
    case  template_2: statement(s);
    ...
    case  template_n: statement(s);
    default: statement(s);
}
```

The switch statement allows for multiple branches from a single expression. It is more efficient and easier to follow than a multileveled if statement. A switch statement evaluates an expression, and then branches to the case statement that contains the template matching the expression's result. If no template matches the expression's result, control goes to the default statement. If there is no default statement, control goes to the end of the switch statement.

Program flow continues from the case statement down unless a break statement is encountered. If a break statement is encountered, control goes to the end of the switch statement.

Example 1

```
switch( letter )
{
    case 'A':
    case 'a':
        printf( "You entered A" );
        break;
    case 'B':
    case 'b':
        printf( "You entered B");
        break;
    ...
    ...
    default:
        printf( "I don't have a case for %c", letter );
}
```

Example 2

```
switch( number )
{
    case 0:    puts( "Your number is 0 or less.");
    case 1:    puts( "Your number is 1 or less.");
    case 2:    puts( "Your number is 2 or less.");
    case 3:    puts( "Your number is 3 or less.");
    ...
    ...
    case 99:   puts( "Your number is 99 or less.");
               break;
    default:   puts( "Your number is greater than 99.");
}
```

Because there are no break statements for the first case statements, this example finds the case that matches the number and prints every case from that point down to the break in case 99.

If the number was 3, you would be told that your number is equal to or less than 3, equal to or less than 4, equal to or less than 5 ... equal to or less than 99. The program continues printing until it reaches the break statement in case 99.

Exiting the Program

A C program normally terminates when execution reaches the closing brace of the `main()` function. However, you can terminate a program at any time by calling the library function `exit()`. You also can specify one or more functions to be automatically executed at termination.

The *exit()* Function

The `exit()` function terminates program execution and returns control to the operating system. This function takes a single type `int` argument that is passed back to the operating system to indicate the success or failure of the program. The syntax of the `exit()` function is

```
exit(status);
```

If `status` has a value of 0, it indicates that the program terminated normally. A value of 1 indicates that the program terminated with some sort of error. The return value is usually ignored. In a DOS system, you can test the return value with a DOS batch file and the `if errorlevel` statement. This is not a book about DOS, however; you need to refer to your DOS documentation if you want to use a program's return value.

To use the `exit()` function, a program must include the header file STDLIB.H. This header file also defines two symbolic constants for use as arguments to the `exit()` function, as follows:

```
#define EXIT_SUCCESS   0
#define EXIT_FAILURE   1
```

Thus, to exit with a return value of 0, call `exit(EXIT_SUCCESS)`; for a return value of 1, call `exit(EXIT_FAILURE)`.

13

DO	DON'T

DON'T forget to use `break` statements if your `switch` statements need them.

DO use a `default` case in a `switch` statement even if you think you have covered all possible cases.

DO use a `switch` statement instead of an `if` statement if there are more than two conditions being evaluated for the same variable.

DO line up your `case` statements so that they are easy to read.

The *atexit()* Function

The atexit() function is used to specify, or register, one or more functions that are automatically executed when the program terminates. This function might not be available on non-DOS systems. You can register as many as 32 functions; at program termination, they are executed in reverse order. The last function registered is the first function executed. When all functions registered by atexit() have been executed, the program terminates and returns control to the operating system.

The prototype of the atexit() function is located in the header file STDLIB.H, which must be included in any program that uses atexit(). The prototype reads as follows:

```
int atexit(void (*)(void));
```

You may not recognize this format. It means that atexit() takes a function pointer as its argument. (Day 15, "More On Pointers," covers function pointers in more detail.) Functions registered with atexit() must have a return type of void. To execute the functions cleanup1() and cleanup2() in that order on termination, for instance, you could use Listing 13.9.

Listing 13.9. Executing functions automatically on program termination.

```
1: #include <stdlib.h>
2:
3: void cleanup1(void);
4: void cleanup2(void);
5:
6: main()
7: {
8:     atexit(cleanup2);
9:     atexit(cleanup1);
10:
11:
12: }        /* End of main() */
13:
14:
15: void cleanup1(void)
16: {
17: /* cleanup code goes here */
18: }
19:
20: void cleanup2(void)
21: {
22: /* cleanup code goes here */
23: }
```

When this program runs, line 8 registers cleanup2() with the atexit() function, and line 9 registers cleanup1(). When the program terminates, the registered functions are called in reverse order: cleanup1() is called, followed by cleanup2(), and the program then terminates. Functions registered with atexit() are executed whether program termination is caused by executing the exit() function or by reaching the end of main(). You could place printf() statements in the two cleanup functions for a visible demonstration of their being executed.

The program in Listing 13.10 shows you how the exit() and atexit() functions are used.

Listing 13.10. Using the exit() and atexit() functions.

```
1:  /* Demonstrates the exit() and atexit() functions. */
2:  #include <stdio.h>
3:  #include <stdlib.h>
4:  #include <time.h>
5:  #define DELAY 150000
6:
7:  void cleanup( void );
8:  void delay( void );
9:
10: main()
11: {
12:     int reply;
13:
14:     /* Register the function to be called at exit. */
15:
16:     atexit( cleanup );
17:
18:     puts("Enter 1 to exit, any other to continue.");
19:     scanf("%d", &reply);
20:
21:     if (reply == 1)
22:         exit( EXIT_SUCCESS );
23:
24:     /* Pretend to do some work. */
25:
26:     for (reply = 0; reply < 5; reply++)
27:     {
28:         puts("Working...");
29:         delay();
30:     }
31: }       /* End of main() */
32:
33: void cleanup( void )
34: {
35:     puts("\nPreparing for exit...");
36:     delay();
37: }
38:
39: void delay(void)
40: {
41:     long x;
42:     for( x = 0; x < DELAY; x++ )
43:         ;
44: }
```

```
C:\>list1310
Enter 1 to exit, any other to continue.
1

Preparing for exit...

C:\>list1310
Enter 1 to exit, any other to continue.
8
Working...
Working...
Working...
Working...
Working...

Preparing for exit...
```

This program registers the function cleanup() on line 16 with the atexit() function. When the program terminates, either with the exit() on line 22 or by reaching the end of main(), cleanup() executes.

Why would you need to use a "cleanup" function at program termination? Clearly, Listing 13.9 does nothing useful; it merely serves to demonstrate the function. In real-world programs, however, often there are tasks that need to be performed at termination: closing files and streams, for example, or releasing dynamically allocated memory. Files and streams are covered on Days 14 and 16, and working with memory is covered in Day 20. These may not mean anything to you now, but they are covered later in the book. Then you can see how to use atexit() in a real situation.

DO	DON'T

DON'T overuse the atexit() function. Limit it to those functions that must be executed if there is a problem when the program terminates, such as closing an opened file.

DO use the exit() command to get out of the program if there is a problem.

Executing Operating System Commands in a Program

The C standard library includes a function, system(), that enables you to execute operating system commands in a running C program. This can be useful, enabling you to read a disk's directory listing or format a disk without exiting the program. To use the system() function, a program must include the header file STDLIB.H. The format of system() is

```
system(command);
```

The argument *command* can be either a string constant or a pointer to a string. For example, to obtain a directory listing in DOS, you could write either

```
system("dir");
```

or

```
char *command = "dir";
system(command);
```

After the operating system command is executed, execution returns to the program at the location immediately following the call to `system()`. If the command you pass to `system()` is not a valid operating system command, you get a `Bad command or file name` error message before returning to the program. The use of `system()` is illustrated in Listing 13.11.

Type **Listing 13.11. Using the `system()` function to execute system commands.**

```
1: /* Demonstrates the system() function. */
2: #include <stdio.h>
3: #include <stdlib.h>
4:
5: main()
6: {
7:     /* Declare a buffer to hold input. */
8:
9:     char input[40];
10:
11:     while (1)
12:     {
13:         /* Get the user's command. */
14:
15:         puts("\nInput the desired DOS command, blank to exit");
16:         gets(input);
17:
18:         /* Exit if a blank line was entered. */
19:
20:         if (input[0] == '\0')
21:             exit(0);
22:
23:         /* Execute the command. */
24:
25:         system(input);
26:     }
27: }
```

```
Input the desired DOS command, blank to exit
dir *.bak

Volume in drive E is STACVOL_000
Directory of E:\BOOK\LISTINGS
LIST1414 BAK      1416 08-22-92    5:18p
1 file(s)       1416 bytes
```

```
24068096 bytes free

Input the desired DOS command, blank to exit
```

 Listing 13.11 illustrates the use of system(). Using a while loop in lines 11–26, this program enables operating system commands. Lines 15–16 prompt the user to enter the operating system command. If Enter was pressed without entering a command, lines 20–21 call exit() to end the program. Line 25 calls system() with the command entered by the user. If you run this program on your system, you'll get different output, of course.

The commands that you pass to system() are not limited to simple operating commands, such as listing directories or formatting disks. You also can pass the name of any executable file or batch file—yes, and that program is executed normally. For example, if you pass the argument LIST1309, you would execute the program called LIST1309. When you exit the program, execution passes back to where the system() call was made.

The only restrictions on using system() have to do with memory. When system() is executed, the original program remains loaded in your computer's RAM, and a new copy of the operating system command processor and any program you run are loaded as well. This works only if the computer has sufficient memory. If not, you get an error message.

Summary

This chapter covered a variety of topics related to program control. You learned about the goto statement and why you should avoid using it in your programs. You saw that the break and continue statements give additional control over the execution of loops and that these statements can be used in conjunction with infinite loops to perform useful programming tasks.

This chapter also explained how to use the exit() function to control program termination and how atexit() can be used to register functions to be executed automatically on program completion. Finally, you saw how to use the system() function to execute system commands from within your program.

Q&A

Q Is it better to use a switch statement or a nested loop?

A If you're checking a variable that can take on more than two values, the switch statement is almost always better. The resulting code is easier to read, too. If you're checking a true/false condition, go with an if statement.

Q Why should I avoid a goto statement?

A When you first see a goto statement, it is easy to believe that it could be useful. goto, however, can cause you more problems than it fixes. A goto statement is an unstructured command that takes you to another point in a program. Many debuggers (software that helps you to trace program problems) cannot interrogate a goto properly. goto statements also lead to spaghetti code—code that goes all over the place.

Q Why don't all compilers have the same functions?

A In this chapter, you saw that certain C functions are not available with all compilers or all computer systems. For example, atexit() is available on DOS systems but not on UNIX or Macintosh systems. Likewise, sleep() is available with the Borland C compiler but not with the Microsoft compiler.

Isn't C supposed to be a standardized language? C is, in fact, highly standardized. The American National Standards Institute (ANSI) has developed the ANSI C Standard, which specifies almost all details of the C language, including the functions that are provided. Some compiler vendors have added additional functions—ones not part of the ANSI standard—to their C compilers in an effort to one-up the competition. In addition, you sometimes come across a compiler that does not claim to meet the ANSI standard. If you limit yourself to ANSI standard compilers, however, you'll find that 99 percent of program syntax and functions are common between them.

Q Is it good to use the system() function to execute system functions?

A The system() function might appear to be an easy way to do such things as list the files in a directory; however, caution should be used. Most operating system commands are specific to a particular operating system. If you use a system() call, your code probably won't be portable. If you want to run another program (not an operating system command), you shouldn't have portability problems.

Workshop

The Workshop provides quiz questions to help you solidify your understanding of the material covered and exercises to provide you with experience in using what you've learned.

Quiz

1. When is it advisable to use the goto statement in your programs?
2. What is the difference between the break statement and the continue statement?
3. What is an infinite loop and how do you create one?
4. What two events cause program execution to terminate?

5. What variable types can a switch evaluate to?

6. What does the default statement do?

7. What does the atexit() function do?

8. What does the system() function do?

Exercises

1. Write a statement that causes control of the program to go to the next iteration in a loop.

2. Write the statement(s) that sends control of a program to the end of a loop.

3. Write code that causes the functions f1(), f2(), and f3() to execute, in that order, on program termination.

4. Write a line of code that displays a listing of all files in the current directory (for a DOS system).

5. **BUG BUSTER:** Is anything wrong with the following code? If so, what?

```
switch( answer )
{
    case 'Y': printf("You answered yes");
              break;
    case 'N': printf( "You answered no");
}
```

6. **BUG BUSTER:** Is anything wrong with the following code? If so, what?

```
switch( choice )
{
    default:
            printf("You did not choose 1 or 2");
    case 1:
            printf("You answered 1");
            break;
    case 2:
            printf( "You answered 2");
            break;
}
```

7. Rewrite exercise 6 using if statements.

8. Write an infinite do...while loop.

Because of the multitude of possible answers for the following two exercises, answers are not provided.

9. Write a program that works like a calculator. The program should allow for addition, subtraction, multiplication, and division.

10. Write a program that provides a menu with five different options. The fifth option should quit the program. Each of the other options should execute a system command using the system() function.

14

Working with the Screen, Printer, and Keyboard

Almost every program must perform input and output. How well a program handles input and output is often the best judge of a program's usefulness. You've already learned how to perform some basic input and output. Today, you learn

- How C uses streams for input and output
- Various ways of accepting input from the keyboard
- Methods of displaying text and numeric data on the screen
- How to send output to the printer
- How to redirect program input and output

Streams and C

Before you get to the details of program input/output, you need to learn about *streams*. All C input/output is done with streams, no matter where input is coming from or where output is going to. As you will see later, this standard way of handling all input and output has definite advantages for the programmer. Of course, this makes it essential that you understand what streams are and how they work. First, however, you need to know exactly what the term input/output means.

What Exactly Is Program Input/Output?

As you learned earlier in this book, a C program keeps data in random access memory (RAM) while executing. This data is in the form of variables, structures, and arrays that have been declared by the program. Where did this data come from, and what can the program do with it?

- Data can come from some location external to the program. Data moved from an external location into RAM, where the program can access it, is called *input*. The keyboard and disk files are the most common sources of program input.
- Data also can be sent to a location external to the program; this is called *output*. The most common destinations for output are the screen, a printer, and disk files.

Input sources and output destinations are collectively referred to as *devices*. The keyboard is a device, the screen is a device, and so on. Some devices (the keyboard) are for input only; others (the screen), for output only; and still others (disk files), for both input and output. This is illustrated in Figure 14.1.

Whatever the device, and whether it's performing input or output, C carries out all input and output operations by means of streams.

Figure 14.1.
Input and output can take place between your program and a variety of external devices.

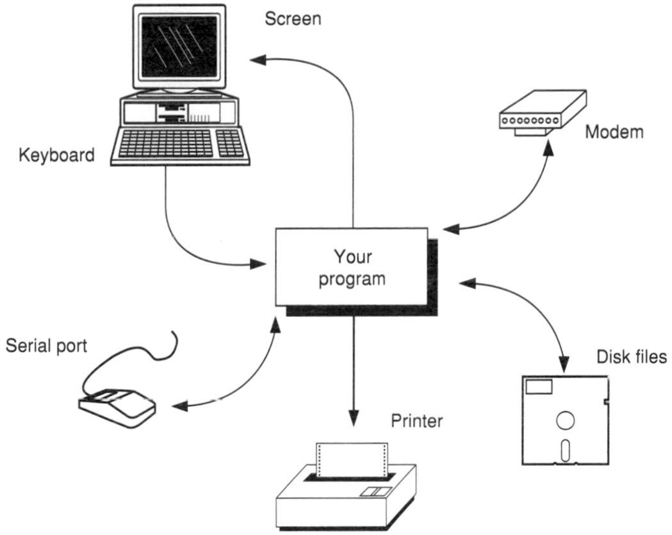

What Is a Stream?

A *stream* is a sequence of characters. More exactly, it is a sequence of bytes of data. A sequence of bytes flowing into a program is an input stream; a sequence of bytes flowing out of a program is an output stream. The major advantage of streams is that input/output programming is *device independent*. Programmers don't need to write special input/output functions for each device (keyboard, disk, and so on). The program "sees" input/output as a continuous stream of bytes no matter where the input is coming from or going to.

Every C stream is connected to a file. In this context, the term *file* does not refer to a disk file. Rather, it is an intermediate step between the stream that your program deals with and the actual physical device being used for input or output. For the most part, the beginning C programmer doesn't need to be concerned with these files because the details of interactions between streams, files, and devices are taken care of automatically by the C library functions and the operating system.

Text Versus Binary Streams

C streams fall into two modes: text and binary. A *text* stream consists only of characters, such as text data being sent to the screen. Text streams are organized into lines, which can be up to 255 characters long and are terminated by an end-of-line, or newline, character. Certain characters in a text stream are recognized as having special meaning, such as the newline character. This chapter deals with text streams.

A *binary* stream can handle any sort of data including, but not limited to, text data. Bytes of data in a binary stream are not translated or interpreted in any special way; they are read and written exactly as is. Binary streams are used primarily with disk files, which are covered on Day 16, "Using Disk Files."

The Predefined Streams

ANSI C has three predefined streams, also referred to as the *standard input/output files*. If you're programming for an IBM-compatible PC running DOS, two additional standard streams are available to you. These streams are automatically opened when a C program starts executing, and are closed when the program terminates. The programmer doesn't need to take any special action to make these streams available. The standard streams and the devices they normally are connected with are listed in Table 14.1. All five of the standard streams are text-mode streams.

Table 14.1. The five standard streams; the last two are supported only under DOS.

Name	Streams	Device
stdin	Standard input	Keyboard
stdout	Standard output	Screen
stderr	Standard error	Screen
stdprn*	Standard printer	Printer (LPT1:)
stdaux*	Standard auxiliary	Serial port (COM1:)
*Supported only under DOS.		

Whenever you have used the printf() or puts() functions to display text on the screen, you have used the stdout stream. Likewise, when you use gets() or scanf() to read keyboard input, you use the stdin stream. The standard streams are automatically opened, but other streams, such as those used to manipulate information stored on disk, must be opened explicitly. You learn how to do this on Day 16. The remainder of this chapter deals with the standard streams.

C's Stream Functions

The C standard library has a variety of functions that deal with stream input and output. Most of these functions come in two varieties: one that always uses one of the standard streams, and the other that requires the programmer to specify the stream. These functions are listed in Table 14.2. This table does not list all of C's input/output functions, nor are all of the functions in the table covered in this chapter.

Table 14.2. The standard library's stream input/output functions.

Uses One of the Standard Streams	Requires a Stream Name	Action
printf()	fprintf()	Formatted output
vprintf()	vfprintf()	Formatted output with variable argument list
puts()	fputs()	String output
putchar()	putc(), fputc()	Character output
scanf()	fscanf()	Formatted input
gets()	fgets()	String input
getchar()	getc(), fgetc()	Character input
perror()	_	String output to stderr only

The function perror() may require STDLIB.H. All other functions require STDIO.H; vprintf() and vfprintf() also require STDARGS.H. A few other functions require CONIO.H.

An Example

The short program in Listing 14.1 demonstrates the equivalence of streams. On line 10, the gets() function is used to input a line of text from the keyboard (stdin). Because gets() returns a pointer to the string, it can be used as the argument to puts(), which displays the string on the screen (stdout). When run, the program inputs a line of text from the user and then immediately displays the string on the screen.

Type **Listing 14.1. The equivalence of streams.**

```
1: /* Demonstrates the equivalence of stream input and output. */
2: #include <stdio.h>
3:
4: main()
5: {
6:     char buffer[81];
7:
8:     /* Input a line, then immediately output it. */
9:
10:     puts(gets(buffer));
11: }
```

DO	**DON'T**

DO take advantage of the standard input/output streams that C provides.

DON'T rename or change the standard streams unnecessarily.

DON'T try to use an input stream such as stdin for an output function such as fprintf().

Accepting Keyboard Input

Almost every C program requires some form of input from the keyboard (that is, from stdin). Input functions are divided into a hierarchy of three levels: character input, line input, and formatted input.

Character Input

The character input functions read input from a stream one character at a time. When called, each of these functions returns the next character in the stream, or EOF if the end of the file has been reached or an error has occurred. EOF is a symbolic constant defined in STDIO.H as –1. Character input functions differ in terms of buffering and echoing.

- Some character input functions are *buffered.* This means that the operating system holds all characters in a temporary storage space until you press Enter, and then the system sends the characters to the stdin stream. Others are *unbuffered,* and each character is sent to stdin as soon as the key is pressed.

- Some input functions automatically echo each character to stdout as it is received. Others do not echo; the character is sent to stdin and not stdout. Because stdout is assigned to the screen, that's where input is echoed.

The uses of buffered, unbuffered, echoing, and non-echoing character input are explained in sections to follow.

The *getchar( )* Function

The function getchar() obtains the next character from the stream stdin. It provides buffered character input with echo, and its prototype is

```
int getchar(void);
```

The use of getchar() is demonstrated in Listing 14.2. Notice that the putchar() function, explained in detail later in this chapter, simply displays a single character on the screen.

Listing 14.2. Demonstration of the `getchar()` function.

```
1: /* Demonstrates the getchar() function. */
2:
3: #include <stdio.h>
4:
5: main()
6: {
7:     int ch;
8:
9:     while ((ch = getchar()) != '\n')
10:         putchar(ch);
11: }
```

Input Output

This is what's typed in.
This is what's typed in.

Analysis

On line 9, the `getchar()` function is called and waits to receive a character from `stdin`. Because `getchar()` is a buffered input function, no characters are received until you press Enter. However, each key you press is echoed immediately on the screen.

When you press Enter, all of the characters you entered, including the newline, are sent to `stdin` by the operating system. The `getchar()` function returns the characters one at a time, assigning each in turn to `ch`.

Each character is compared with the newline character `'\n'` and, if not equal, displayed on the screen with `putchar()`. When a newline is returned by `getchar()`, the `while` loop terminates.

The `getchar()` function can be used to input entire lines of text, as shown in Listing 14.3. Other input functions are better suited for this task, however, as you learn later in the chapter.

Listing 14.3. Using the `getchar()` function to input an entire line of text.

```
1: /* Using getchar() to input strings. */
2:
3: #include <stdio.h>
4:
5: #define MAX 80
6:
7: main()
8: {
9:     char ch, buffer[MAX+1];
10:    int x = 0;
11:
12:    while ((ch = getchar()) != '\n' && x < MAX)
13:        buffer[x++] = ch;
14:
```

14

continues

Listing 14.3. continued

```
15:     buffer[x] = '\0';
16:
17:     printf("%s", buffer);
18: }
```

This is a string
This is a string

This program is similar to Listing 14.2 in the way that it uses getchar(). An extra condition has been added to the loop. This time the while loop accepts characters from getchar() until either a newline character is reached or 80 characters are read. Each character is assigned to an array called buffer. When the characters have been input, line 15 puts a null on the end of the array so the printf() function on line 17 can print the entered string.

On line 9, why was buffer declared with a size of MAX + 1 instead of just MAX? By declaring buffer with the size of MAX + 1, the string can be 80 characters plus a null terminator. Don't forget to include a place for the null terminator at the end of your strings.

The *getch()* Function

The getch() function obtains the next character from the stream stdin. It provides unbuffered character input without echo. The prototype for getch() is in the header file CONIO.H, as follows:

```
int getch(void);
```

Because it is unbuffered, getch() returns each character as soon as the key is pressed, without waiting for the user to press Enter. Because getch() does not echo its input, the characters are not displayed on-screen. The use of getch() is illustrated by the program in Listing 14.4.

Type

Listing 14.4. Using the getch() function.

```
1: /* Demonstrates the getch() function. */
2:
3: #include <stdio.h>
4: #include <conio.h>
5:
6: main()
7: {
8:     int ch;
9:
10:     while ((ch = getch()) != '\r')
11:         putchar(ch);
12:}
```

Input
Output

Testing the getch() function
Testing the getch() function

Analysis

When this program runs, getch() returns each character as soon as you press a key—it doesn't wait for you to press Enter. There's no echo, so the only reason that each character is displayed on-screen is the call to putchar(). But why does the program compare each character to \r instead of to \n?

The code \r is the escape sequence for the carriage return character. When you press Enter, the keyboard device sends a carriage return (CR) to stdin. The buffered character input functions automatically translate the carriage return to a newline, so the program must test for \n to determine whether Enter has been pressed. The unbuffered character input functions do not translate, so a carriage return is input as \r and that's what the program must test for.

Using getch() to input an entire line of text is illustrated in Listing 14.5. Running this program illustrates clearly that getch() does not echo its input. With the exception of substituting getch() for getchar(), this program is identical to Listing 14.3.

Type

Listing 14.5. Using the getch() function to input an entire line.

```
1: /* Using getch() to input strings. */
2:
3: #include <stdio.h>
4: #include <conio.h>
5:
6: #define MAX 80
7:
8: main()
9: {
10:     char ch, buffer[MAX+1];
11:     int x = 0;
12:
13:     while ((ch = getch()) != '\r' && x < MAX)
14:         buffer[x++] = ch;
15:
16:     buffer[x] = '\0';
17:
18:     printf("%s", buffer);
19:}
```

14

Input
Output

Here's a string
Here's a string

Warning: `getch()` is not an ANSI-standard command. This means that your compiler (and other compilers) might, or might not, support it. `getch()` is supported by Symantec and Borland. Microsoft supports `_getch()`. If you have problems using it, you should check your compiler and see whether it supports `getch()`. If you are concerned with portability, you should avoid non-ANSI functions.

The *getche()* Function

This is a short section because `getche()` is exactly like `getch()`, except that it echoes each character to `stdout`. Modify the program in Listing 14.4 to use `getche()` instead of `getch()`. When the program runs, each key you press is displayed twice on the screen: once as echoed by `getche()` and once by `putchar()`.

Warning: `getche()` is not an ANSI-standard command, although many C compilers support it.

The *getc()* and *fgetc()* Functions

These two character input functions do not automatically work with `stdin`. Rather, they let the program specify the input stream. They are used primarily to read characters from disk files, which Day 16 covers in detail.

DO	DON'T

DO understand the difference between echoed and non-echoed input.

DO understand the difference between buffered and unbuffered input.

DON'T use non-ANSI standard functions if portability is a concern.

Getting Special Keys on an IBM PC

So far, you've learned how to input all the regular characters of the keyboard: letters, numerals, and punctuation marks. The IBM-PC keyboard (and compatibles) also has a number of special keys, such as the function keys F1–F10 (or F12 on newer keyboards), as well as the arrow and other direction keys on the numeric keypad. You also can type key combinations, such as Ctrl and PgDn; Alt and 1; and Shift and F1. How do you accept input from these special keys in your C programs? Remember, we're talking only about PCs running DOS.

To do this, you first need to know how these keys and key combinations work. These keys differ from the regular character keys in that they send a pair of values to stdin rather than just one. In each pair, the first value is always the null character, with a numeric value of 0. The second has a numeric value that identifies the key pressed. For example, pressing F1 sends a pair consisting of 0 followed by 59, and pressing the Home key sends a pair consisting of 0 followed by 71. The keys that return a two-character code to stdin are called the *extended keys,* and their codes are called the *extended key codes.*

How does a program deal with extended key input? Specifically, how can a program accept only the press of a special key, ignoring other characters? It's simple:

1. Accept characters from stdin, discarding them until a 0, or \0 is received. (To the C compiler, the number 0 and the character \0 are the same.) This signals the first of two values sent by one of these keys.

2. Look at the next value that identifies the key that was pressed.

A function that performs this task, ext_key(), is presented in Listing 14.6. The program uses ext_key() to accept extended key presses, ignoring all other input. The second value of the key is displayed on-screen; pressing F1 exits the program. The second value sent by the F1 key is 59, so that's the value the program tests for in its if statement.

Type **Listing 14.6. Accepting extended key input.**

```
1: /* Demonstrates reading extended keys from the keyboard. */
2:
3: #include <stdio.h>
4: #include <conio.h>
5:
6: int ext_key(void);
7:
8: main()
9: {
10:     int ch;
11:
12:     puts("Press any extended key; press F1 to exit.");
13:
14:     while (1)
15:     {
16:         ch = ext_key();
17:         if (ch == 59)        /* F1? */
18:             break;
19:         else
20:             printf("\nThat key's code has a value of %d.", ch);
21:     }
22: }
23:
```

continues

Listing 14.6. continued

```
24: int ext_key(void)
25: {
26:     int ch;
27:
28:     /* Wait until a zero byte comes in. */
29:
30:     while ((ch = getch()) != 0)
31:         ;
32:
33:     /* Return the next character. */
34:
35:     return getch();
36: }
```

That key's code has a value of 61

That key's code has a value of 63

As long as characters are entered into the program, `main()` stays in an infinite `while` loop. In the loop, line 16 makes a call to `ext_key()`, which is defined on lines 24–36. `ext_key()` has its own `while` loop that does nothing but look for the character `\0`, the signal that an extended character has been pressed. Once it obtains the null character, `ext_key()` sends back the next character by calling `getch()` again.

Back in `main()`, line 17 evaluates the next value to see whether it equals 59 (equivalent to F1). If it does, a break exits the infinite loop and the program ends. If it was not F1, the program prints the value of the extended key and the loop continues.

Some compilers make dealing with extended key input easier by defining a set of symbolic constants in a header file. This file is usually CONIO.H. In the Symantec compiler, each of these constants starts with the characters `_KB_`, and identifies one of the extended keys mnemonically. Its value is equal to the value returned by the key. For example, the constant `_KB_F1` is defined as the value 59. These constants and their values are shown in Table 14.3.

Table 14.3. Symbolic constants for DOS extended keys defined in CONIO.H of the Symantec compiler.

Constant Definition	Value	Comments
`#define _KB_F1`	59	`/* Function Keys F1–F10 */`
`#define _KB_F2`	60	
`#define _KB_F3`	61	
`#define _KB_F4`	62	
`#define _KB_F5`	63	

Constant Definition	Value	Comments
#define _KB_F6	64	
#define _KB_F7	65	
#define _KB_F8	66	
#define _KB_F9	67	
#define _KB_F10	68	
#define _KB_HOME	71	/* Editing keys */
#define _KB_UP	72	
#define _KB_PGUP	73	
#define _KB_LEFT	75	
#define _KB_RIGHT	77	
#define _KB_END	79	
#define _KB_DOWN	80	
#define _KB_PGDN	81	
#define _KB_INS	82	
#define _KB_BACK_TAB	15	
#define _KB_SF1	84	/* Shift F1-F10 */
#define _KB_SF2	85	
#define _KB_SF3	86	
#define _KB_SF4	87	
#define _KB_SF5	88	
#define _KB_SF6	89	
#define _KB_SF7	90	
#define _KB_SF8	91	
#define _KB_SF9	92	
#define _KB_SF10	93	
#define _KB_CF1	94	/* Control F1-F10 */
#define _KB_CF2	95	
#define _KB_CF3	96	
#define _KB_CF4	97	
#define _KB_CF5	98	
#define _KB_CF6	99	

continues

Table 14.3. continued

Constant Definition	Value	Comments
#define _KB_CF7	100	
#define _KB_CF8	101	
#define _KB_CF9	102	
#define _KB_CF10	103	
#define _KB_AF1	104	/* Alt F1-F10 */
#define _KB_AF2	105	
#define _KB_AF3	106	
#define _KB_AF4	107	
#define _KB_AF5	108	
#define _KB_AF6	109	
#define _KB_AF7	110	
#define _KB_AF8	111	
#define _KB_AF9	112	
#define _KB_AF10	113	
#define _KB_DEL	83	
#define _KB_CPGUP	132	/* Control PgUp */
#define _KB_CLEFT	115	/* Control left cursor key */
#define _KB_CRIGHT	116	/* Control right cursor key */
#define _KB_CEND	117	/* Control End */
#define _KB_CPGDN	118	/* Control PgDn */
#define _KB_CHOME	119	/* Control Home */
#define _KB_A1	120	/* Alt 1 */
#define _KB_A2	121	
#define _KB_A3	122	
#define _KB_A4	123	
#define _KB_A5	124	
#define _KB_A6	125	
#define _KB_A7	126	
#define _KB_A8	127	
#define _KB_A9	128	

Constant Definition	Value	Comments
#define _KB_A0	129	/* Alt 0 */
#define _KB_AMINUS	130	/* Alt '-'. */
#define _KB_APLUS	131	/* Alt '+'. */

You should check your compiler manual to determine if it contains defined constants for the extended keys. If it does not, add the #define statement(s) to the beginning of your program for the specific keys that your program needs. If your compiler does not define the extended keys for you, you may want to create a header file with all of the above defined constants. This way, you can include the file in any program that needs the extended key codes. (On Day 21, "Taking Advantage of Preprocessor Directives and More," you learn specifics about header files.) Or, if you prefer, you can edit your compiler's CONIO.H file to add the constants.

The function ext_key() can be modified to accept a subset of the extended keys. You can use extended keys to create flexible and user-friendly interfaces, menus, and the like. The program in Listing 14.7 modifies ext_key() to accept function key presses only, and then implements a function-key-driven menu system. This listing defines constants for the extended keyboard codes following the naming conventions of the Symantec compiler. If you're using the Symantec compiler, you should delete the 10 #define lines from the program because they will conflict with the identical #define statements in Symantec's CONIO.H header file. If you're using another compiler that defines its own constants for the extended key codes, you can either leave the #define statements in, or you can remove them and then modify the case statements to reflect the constants your compiler uses.

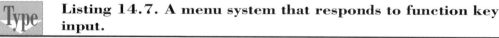

Listing 14.7. A menu system that responds to function key input.

```
1: /* Demonstrates a function key driven menu. */
2: #include <stdlib.h>
3: #include <stdio.h>
4: #include <conio.h>
5: #include <time.h>
6: #define _KB_F1 59
7: #define _KB_F2 60
8: #define _KB_F3 61
9: #define _KB_F4 62
10: #define _KB_F5 63
11: #define _KB_F6 64
12: #define _KB_F7 65
13: #define _KB_F8 66
14: #define _KB_F9 67
15: #define _KB_F10 68
16:
```

continues

Listing 14.7. continued

```
17: int fnc_key(void);
18: int menu(void);
19:
20: main()
21: {
22:     /* Set up infinite loop. */
23:
24:     while (1)
25:     {
26:         /* Switch based on return value of menu(). */
27:
28:         switch (menu())
29:         {
30:             case _KB_F1:
31:                 puts("Task 1");
32:                 break;
33:             case _KB_F2:
34:                 puts("Task 2");
35:                 break;
36:             case _KB_F3:
37:                 puts("Task 3");
38:                 break;
39:             case _KB_F4:
40:                 puts("Task 4");
41:                 break;
42:             case _KB_F5:
43:                 puts("Task 5");
44:                 break;
45:             case _KB_F6:
46:                 puts("Task 6");
47:                 break;
48:             case _KB_F7:
49:                 puts("Task 7");
50:                 break;
51:             case _KB_F8:
52:                 puts("Task 8");
53:                 break;
54:             case _KB_F9:
55:                 puts("Task 9");
56:                 break;
57:             case _KB_F10:
58:                 puts("Exiting program...");
59:                 exit(0);
60:         }
61:     }
62: }
63:
64: int menu(void)
65: {
66:     /* Display menu choices. */
67:
```

```
68:     puts("\nF1 -> task 1");
69:     puts("F2 -> task 2");
70:     puts("F3 -> task 3");
71:     puts("F4 -> task 4");
72:     puts("F5 -> task 5");
73:     puts("F6 -> task 6");
74:     puts("F7 -> task 7");
75:     puts("F8 -> task 8");
76:     puts("F9 -> task 9");
77:     puts("F10 -> exit\n");
78:
79:     /* Get a function key press. */
80:
81:     return (fnc_key());
82: }
83:
84: int fnc_key(void)
85: {
86:     int ch;
87:
88:     while (1)
89:     {
90:         /* Wait until a zero byte comes in. */
91:
92:         while ((ch = getch()) != 0)
93:             ;
94:         /* Get the next character. */
95:
96:         ch = getch();
97:
98:         /* Is it a function key? */
99:
100:         if ( ch >= _KB_F1 && ch <= _KB_F10 )
101:             return ch;
102:     }
103: }
```

Output

```
F1 -> task 1
F2 -> task 2
F3 -> task 3
F4 -> task 4
F5 -> task 5
F6 -> task 6
F7 -> task 7
F8 -> task 8
F9 -> task 9
F10 -> exit

Exiting program...
```

14

Ungetting a Character with *ungetc()*

What does "ungetting" a character mean? An example should explain. Say, for instance, your program is reading characters from an input stream and can detect the end of input only by reading one character too many. For example, you may be inputting digits only, so you know that input has ended when the first non-digit character is encountered. That first non-digit character may be an important part of subsequent data, but it has been removed from the input stream. Is it lost? No, it can be "ungotten" or returned to the input stream where it is then the first character read by the next input operation on that stream.

To "unget" a character, you use the `ungetc()` library function. Its prototype is

```
int ungetc(int ch, FILE *fp);
```

The argument `ch` is the character to be returned. The argument `*fp` specifies the stream that the character is to be returned to, which can be any input stream. For now, simply specify `stdin` as the second argument: `ungetc(ch, stdin);`. The notation `FILE *fp` is used with streams associated with disk files; you learn about this on Day 16.

You can unget only a single character to a stream between reads, and you cannot unget `EOF` at any time. The function `ungetc()` returns `ch` on success and `EOF` if the character cannot be returned to the stream. Listing 17.16 uses `ungetc()`.

Line Input

The line-input functions read a line from an input stream—they read all characters up to the next newline character. The standard library has two line input functions, `gets()` and `fgets()`.

The *gets()* Function

You were introduced to the `gets()` function on Day 10, "Characters and Strings." This is a straightforward function, reading a line from `stdin` and storing it in a string. The function prototype is

```
char *gets(char *str);
```

You probably can interpret this prototype by yourself. `gets()` takes a pointer to type `char` as its argument, and returns a pointer to type `char`. The `gets()` function reads characters from `stdin` until a newline (`\n`) or end-of-file is encountered; the newline is replaced with a null character, and the string is stored at the location indicated by `str`.

The return value is a pointer to the string (the same as `str`). If `gets()` encounters an error or reads end-of-file before any characters are input, a null pointer is returned.

Before calling `gets()`, you must allocate sufficient memory space to store the string, using the methods covered on Day 10. The function has no way of knowing whether space pointed to by ptr is allocated or not; the string is input and stored starting at ptr in either case. If the space has not been allocated, the string may overwrite other data and cause program errors.

Listings 10.5 and 10.6 use gets().

The *fgets()* Function

The fgets() library function is similar to gets() in that it reads a line of text from an input stream. It is more flexible because it allows the programmer to specify the specific input stream to use and the maximum number of characters to be input. The fgets() function is often used to input text from disk files, covered on Day 16. To use it for input from stdin, you specify stdin as the input stream. The prototype of fgets() is

```
char *fgets(char *str, int n, FILE *fp);
```

The last parameter FILE *fp is used to specify the input stream. For now, simply specify stdin as the stream argument.

The pointer str indicates where the input string is stored. The argument n specifies the maximum number of characters to be input. The fgets() function reads characters from the input stream until a newline or end-of-line is encountered, or n - 1 characters have been read. The newline is included in the string, terminated with a \0 before it is stored. The return values of fgets() are the same as described earlier for gets().

Strictly speaking, fgets() does not input a single line of text (if you define a line as a sequence of characters ending with a newline). It can read less than a full line if the line contains more than n - 1 characters. When used with stdin, execution does not return from fgets() until you press Enter, but only the first n - 1 characters are stored in the string. The newline is included in the string only if it falls within the first n - 1 characters.

The program in Listing 14.8 demonstrates fgets(). When running the program, enter lines of length less than and greater than MAXLEN to see what happens. If a line greater than MAXLEN is entered, the first MAXLEN - 1 characters are read by the first call to fgets(); the remaining characters remain in the keyboard buffer and are read by the next call to fgets() or any other function that reads from stdin.

Type **Listing 14.8. Using the fgets() function for keyboard input.**

```
1: /* Demonstrates the fgets() function. */
2:
3: #include <stdio.h>
4:
5: #define MAXLEN 10
6:
7: main()
8: {
9:     char buffer[MAXLEN];
```

continues

Listing 14.8. continued

```
10:
11:     puts("Enter text a line at a time; enter a blank to exit.");
12:
13:     while (1)
14:     {
15:         fgets(buffer, MAXLEN, stdin);
16:
17:         if (buffer[0] == '\n')
18:             break;
19:
20:         puts(buffer);
21:     }
22: }
```

```
Enter text a line at a time; enter a blank to exit.
Roses are red
Roses are
 red
Violets are blue
Violets a
re blue

Programming in C
Programmi
ng in C

Is for people like you!
Is for pe
ople like
you!
```

Formatted Input

The input functions covered until now have simply taken one or more characters from an input stream and put them somewhere in memory. No interpretation or formatting of the input has been done, and you still have no method of inputting numeric variables. How, for example, would you input the value 12.86 from the keyboard and assign it to a type `float` variable? Enter the `scanf()` and `fscanf()` functions. You were introduced to `scanf()` on Day 7, "Basic Input/Output." This section explains its use in more detail.

These two functions are identical except that `scanf()` always uses `stdin`, whereas the user can specify the input stream in `fscanf()`. This section covers `scanf()`; `fscanf()` generally is used with disk file input and is covered on Day 16.

The *scanf()* Function's Arguments

The `scanf()` function takes a variable number of arguments; it requires a minimum of two. The first argument is a format string that uses special characters to tell `scanf()` how to interpret the input. The second and additional arguments are the addresses of the variable(s) to which the input data is assigned. Here's an example:

```
scanf("%d", &x);
```

The first argument "%d" is the format string. In this case, %d tells scanf() to look for one signed integer value. The second argument uses the *address-of* operator (&) to tell scanf() to assign the input value to the variable x. Now you can look at the format string details.

The scanf() format string can contain

- Spaces and tabs, which are ignored (they can be used to make the format string more readable).
- Characters (but not %), which are matched against non-white characters in the input.
- One or more *conversion specifications,* which consist of the % character followed by special characters. Generally, the format string contains one conversion specification for each variable.

The only required part of the format string is the conversion specifications. Each conversion specification begins with the % character and contains optional and required components in a certain order. The scanf() function applies the conversion specifications in the format string, in order, to the input fields. An *input field* is a sequence of non-whitespace characters that ends when the next white space is encountered or when the field width, if specified, is reached. The conversion specification components are

- The optional assignment suppression flag (*) that immediately follows the %. If present, this character tells scanf() to perform the conversion corresponding to the current conversion specifier, but to ignore the result (not assign it to any variable).
- The next component, the field width, which is also optional. The field width is a decimal number specifying the width, in characters, of the input field. In other words, the field width specifies how many characters from stdin that scanf() should examine for the current conversion. If a field width is not specified, the input field extends to the next white space.
- The next component is the optional precision modifier, a single character that can be h, l, or L. If present, the precision modifier changes the meaning of the type specifier that follows it. Details are given later in the chapter.
- The only required component of the conversion specifier (besides the %) is the type specifier. The type specifier is one or more characters that tell scanf() how to interpret the input. The characters are listed and explained in Table 14.4. The Argument column lists the required type of the corresponding variable; for example, the type specifier d requires int * (a pointer to type int).

Table 14.4. The type specifier characters used in `scanf()` conversion specifiers.

Type	Meaning	Argument
d	A decimal integer.	int *
i	An integer in decimal, octal (with leading 0), or hexadecimal (with leading 0X or 0x) notation.	int *
o	An integer in octal notation with or without the leading 0.	int *
u	An unsigned decimal integer.	unsigned int *
x	A hexadecimal integer with or without the leading 0X or 0x.	int *
c	One or more characters are read and assigned sequentially to the memory location indicated by the argument. No terminating \0 is added. If a field width argument is not given, one character is read. If a field width argument is given, that number of characters, including whitespace (if any), is read.	char *
s	A string of non-whitespace characters is read into the specified memory location, and a terminating \0 is added.	char *
e,f,g	A floating point number. Numbers can be input in decimal or scientific notation.	float *
[...]	A string. Only the characters listed between the brackets are accepted. Input ends as soon as a non-matching character is encountered, the specified field width is reached, or Enter is pressed. To accept the] character, list it first: []...]. A \0 is added at the end of the string.	char *
[^...]	The same as [...] except that only characters not listed between the brackets are accepted.	char *
%	Literal %: reads the % character. No assignment is made.	none

Before seeing some examples of scanf(), you need to understand the precision modifiers:

Precision Modifier	Meaning
h	When placed before the type specifier d, i, o, u, or x, the modifier h specifies that the argument is a pointer to type short instead of type int. On a PC, the type short is the same as type int, so the h precision modifier is never needed.
l	When placed before the type specifier d, i, o, u, or x, the modifier l specifies that the argument is a pointer to type long. When placed before the type specifier e, f, or g, the modifier l specifies that the argument is a pointer to type double.
L	When placed before the type specifier e, f, or g, the modifier L specifies that the argument is a pointer to type long double.

Handling Extra Characters

Input from scanf() is buffered; no characters are actually received from stdin until the user presses Enter. The entire line of characters then "arrives" from stdin, and is processed, in order, by scanf(). Execution returns from scanf() only when enough input has been received to match the specifications in the format string. Also, scanf() processes only enough characters from stdin to satisfy its format string. Extra, unneeded characters, if any, remain "waiting" in stdin. These characters can cause problems. Take a closer look at the operation of scanf() to see how.

When a call to scanf() is executed and the user has entered a single line, you can have three situations. For these examples, assume that scanf("%d %d", &x, &y); is being executed; in other words, scanf() is expecting two decimal integers. The possibilities are

- The line the user inputs matches the format string. For example, the user enters 12 14 followed by Enter. In this case, there are no problems; scanf() is satisfied, and there are no characters left over in stdin.

- The line that the user inputs has too few elements to match the format string. For example, the user enters 12 followed by Enter. In this case, scanf() continues to wait for the missing input. Once the input is received, execution continues and there are no characters left over in stdin.

- The line that the user enters has more elements than required by the format string. For example, the user enters 12 14 16 followed by Enter. In this case, scanf() reads the 12 and the 14, and then returns. The extra characters, the 1 and the 6, are left "waiting" in stdin.

14

It is this third situation (specifically, those leftover characters) that can cause problems. They remain waiting for as long as your program is running, until the next time the program reads input from stdin. Then the leftover characters are the first ones read, ahead of any input the user makes at the time. It's clear how this could cause errors. For example, the following code asks the user to input an integer and then to input a string:

```
puts("Enter your age.");
scanf("%d", &age);
puts("Enter your first name.");
scanf("%s", name);
```

Say, for example, that in response to the first prompt, the user decides to be precise and enters 29.00, and then presses Enter. The first call to scanf() is looking for an integer, so it reads the characters 29 from stdin and assigns the value 29 to the variable age. The characters .00 are left waiting in stdin. The next call to scanf() is looking for a string. It goes to stdin for input and finds .00 waiting there. The result is that the string .00 is assigned to name.

How can you avoid this problem? If the people who use your programs never make mistakes, that's one solution—but it's rather impractical.

A better solution is to make sure there are no extra characters waiting in stdin before prompting the user for input. You can do this by calling gets(), which reads any remaining characters from stdin, up to and including the end of the line. Rather than calling gets() directly from the program, you can put it in a separate function with the descriptive name clear_kb(). This function is shown in Listing 14.9.

Listing 14.9. Clearing stdin of extra characters to avoid errors.

```
1: /* Clearing stdin of extra characters. */
2:
3: #include <stdio.h>
4:
5: void clear_kb(void);
6:
7: main()
8: {
9:     int age;
10:     char name[20];
11:
12:     /* Prompt for user's age. */
13:
14:     puts("Enter your age.");
15:     scanf("%d", &age);
16:
17:     /* Clear stdin of any extra characters. */
18:
19:     clear_kb();
20:
21:     /* Now prompt for user's name. */
```

```
22:
23:     puts("Enter your first name.");
24:     scanf("%s", name);
25:     /* Display the data. */
26:
27:     printf("Your age is %d.\n", age);
28:     printf("Your name is %s.\n", name);
29: }
30:
31: void clear_kb(void)
32:
33: /* Clears stdin of any waiting characters. */
34: {
35:     char junk[80];
36:     gets(junk);
37: }
```

```
Enter your age.
29
Enter your first name.
Bradley
Your age is 29.
Your name is Bradley.
```

When you run the program in Listing 14.9, enter some extra characters after your age, before pressing Enter. Make sure the program ignores them and correctly prompts you for your name. Then modify the program by removing the call to clear_kb(), and run it again. Any extra characters entered on the same line as your age are assigned to name.

scanf() Examples

The best way to become familiar with the operation of the scanf() function is to use it. It's a powerful function but can be a bit confusing at times. Try it and see what happens. The program in Listing 14.10 demonstrates some of the unusual ways to use scanf(). You should compile and run the program, and then do some experimentation by making changes in the scanf() format strings.

Listing 14.10. Some ways to use scanf() for keyboard input.

```
1: /* Demonstrates some uses of scanf(). */
2:
3: #include <stdio.h>
4:
5: void clear_kb(void);
6:
7: main()
8: {
9:     int i1, i2;
10:     long l1;
11:     float f1;
12:     double d1;
```

continues

321

Listing 14.10. continued

```
13:     char buf1[80], buf2[80];
14:
15:     /* Using the l modifier to enter long integers and doubles.*/
16:
17:     puts("Enter an integer and a floating point number.");
18:     scanf("%ld %lf", &l1, &d1);
19:     printf("You entered %ld and %lf.\n",l1, d1);
20:     puts("The scanf() format string used the l modifier to store");
21:     puts("your input in a type long and a type double.\n");
22:
23:     clear_kb();
24:
25:     /* Use field width to split input. */
26:
27:     puts("Enter a 5 digit integer (for example, 54321).");
28:     scanf("%2d%3d", &i1, &i2);
29:
30:     printf("You entered %d and %d.\n", i1, i2);
31:     puts("Note how the field width specifier in the scanf() format");
32:     puts("string split your input into two values.\n");
33:
34:     clear_kb();
35:
36:     /* Using an excluded space to split a line of input into */
37:     /* two strings at the space. */
38:
39:     puts("Enter your first and last names separated by a space.");
40:     scanf("%[^ ]%s", buf1, buf2);
41:     printf("Your first name is %s\n", buf1);
42:     printf("Your last name is %s\n", buf2);
43:     puts("Note how [^ ] in the scanf() format string, by excluding");
44:     puts("the space character, caused the input to be split.");
45: }
46:
47: void clear_kb(void)
48:
49: /* Clears stdin of any waiting characters. */
50: {
51:     char junk[80];
52:     gets(junk);
53: }
```

Input/Output

```
Enter an integer and a floating point number.
123 45.6789
You entered 123 and 45.678900.
The scanf() format string used the l modifier to store
your input in a type long and a type double.

Enter a 5 digit integer (for example, 54321).
54321
You entered 54 and 321.
Note how the field width specifier in the scanf() format
string split your input into two values.
```

```
Enter your first and last names separated by a space.
Peter Aitken
Your first name is Peter
Your last name is Aitken
Note how [^ ] in the scanf() format string, by excluding
the space character, caused the input to be split.
```

This listing starts by defining several variables on lines 9–13 for data input. The program then walks you through the steps of entering various types of data. Lines 17–21 have you enter and print long integers and a double. Line 23 calls the clear_kb() function to clear any unwanted characters from the input stream. Lines 27–28 get the next value, a five-character integer. Because there are width specifiers, the five-digit integer is split into two integers, one that is two characters and one that is three characters. Line 34 calls clear_kb() to clear the keyboard again. The final example, lines 36–44, use the exclude character. Line 40 uses "%[^]", which tells scanf() to get a string but to stop at any spaces. This effectively splits the input.

Take the time to modify this listing and enter additional values to see what the results are.

The scanf() function can be used for most of your input needs, particularly those involving numbers (strings are input more easily with gets()). It is often worthwhile, however, to write your own specialized input functions. You can see some examples of user-defined functions on Day 18, "Getting More from Functions."

DO	DON'T
DO take advantage of extended characters in your programs. When using extended characters, you should try to be consistent with other programs.	
DON'T forget to check the input stream for extra characters.	
DO use the gets() and scanf() functions instead of the fgets() and fscanf() functions if you are using the standard input file (stdin) only.	

Screen Output

Screen output functions are divided into three general categories along the same lines as the input functions: character output, line output, and formatted output. You've been introduced to some of these functions in earlier chapters. This section covers them all in detail.

14

Character Output with *putchar()*, *putc()*, and *fputc()*

The C library's character output functions send a single character to a stream. The function putchar() sends its output to stdout (normally the screen). The functions fputc() and putc() send their output to a stream specified in the argument list.

Using the *putchar()* Function

The prototype for putchar is located in STDIO.H and reads

```
int putchar(int c);
```

The function writes the character stored in c to stdout. Although the prototype specifies a type int argument, you pass putchar() a type char. You also can pass it a type int as long as its value is appropriate for a character (that is, in the range 0–255). The function returns the character that was just written, or EOF if an error has occurred.

You saw putchar() demonstrated in Listing 14.2. The program in Listing 14.11 displays the characters with ASCII values between 14 and 127.

Type **Listing 14.11. The putchar() function.**

```
1: /* Demonstrates putchar(). */
2:
3: #include <stdio.h>
4: main()
5: {
6:     int count;
7:
8:     for (count = 14; count < 128; )
9:         putchar(count++);
10: }
```

You also can display strings with the putchar() function (as in Listing 14.12), although other functions are better suited for this purpose.

Type **Listing 14.12. Displaying a string with putchar().**

```
1: /* Using putchar() to display strings. */
2:
3: #include <stdio.h>
4:
5: #define MAXSTRING 80
6:
7: char message[] = "Displayed with putchar().";
8: main()
9: {
```

```
10:     int count;
11:
12:     for (count = 0; count < MAXSTRING; count++)
13:     {
14:
15:         /* Look for the end of the string. When it's found, */
16:         /* write a newline character and exit the loop. */
17:
18:         if (message[count] == '\0')
19:         {
20:             putchar('\n');
21:             break;
22:         }
23:         else
24:
25:         /* If end of string not found, write the next character. */
26:
27:             putchar(message[count]);
28:     }
29: }
```

Displayed with putchar().

Using the *putc()* and *fputc()* Functions

These two functions perform the same action, sending a single character to a specified stream. putc() is a macro implementation of fputc(). You learn about macros on Day 21; for now, just stick to fputc(). Its prototype is

```
int fputc(int c, FILE *fp);
```

The FILE *fp part of the prototype might puzzle you. You pass fputc() the output stream in this argument. You learn more about this on Day 16. If you specify stdout as the stream, fputc() behaves exactly the same as putchar(). Thus, the following two statements are equivalent:

```
putchar('x');
fputc('x', stdout);
```

Using *puts()* and *fputs()* for String Output

Your programs display strings on the screen more often than they display single characters. The library function puts() displays strings. The function fputs() sends a string to a specified stream; otherwise, it is identical to puts(). The prototype for puts() is

```
int puts(char *cp);
```

*cp is a pointer to the first character of the string that you want displayed. The puts() function displays the entire string up to but not including the terminating null character, adding a newline

at the end. Then `puts()` returns a positive value if successful, EOF on error (remember, EOF is a symbolic constant with the value –1; it is defined in STDIO.H).

The `puts()` function can be used to display any type of string, as is demonstrated in Listing 14.13.

Type

Listing 14.13. Using the `puts()` function to display strings.

```
1: /* Demonstrates puts(). */
2:
3: #include <stdio.h>
4:
5: /* Declare and initialize an array of pointers. */
6:
7: char *messages[5] = { "This", "is", "a", "short", "message." };
8:
9: main()
10: {
11:     int x;
12:
13:     for (x=0; x<5; x++)
14:         puts(messages[x]);
15:
16:     puts("And this is the end!");
17: }
```

Output

```
This
is
a
short
message.
And this is the end!
```

Analysis

This listing declares an array of pointers, a subject not covered yet (but is covered tomorrow, Day 15, "More on Pointers"). Lines 13 and 14 print each of the strings stored in the message array.

Using *printf()* and *fprintf()* for Formatted Output

So far, the output functions have displayed characters and strings only. What about numbers? To display numbers, you must use the C library's formatted output functions `printf()` and `fprintf()`. These functions also can display strings and characters. You were officially introduced to `printf()` on Day 7, and have used it in almost every chapter; this section provides the remainder of the details.

The two functions `printf()` and `fprintf()` are identical except that `printf()` always sends output to `stdout`, whereas `fprintf()` specifies the output stream. `fprintf()` is used generally for output to disk files and is covered on Day 16.

The `printf()` function takes a variable number of arguments, with a minimum of one. The first and only required argument is the format string that tells `printf()` how to format the output. The optional arguments are variables and expressions whose values you want to display. Take a look at these few simple examples, giving you a feel for `printf()`, before you really get into the nitty-gritty:

- The statement `printf("Hello, world.");` displays the message `Hello, world.` on-screen. This is an example of using `printf()` with only one argument, the format string. In this case, the format string contains only a literal string to be displayed on the screen.

- The statement `printf("%d", i);` displays the value of the integer variable `i` on the screen. The format string contains only the format specifier `%d`, which tells `printf()` to display a single decimal integer. The second argument `i` is the name of the variable whose value is to be displayed.

- The statement `printf("%d plus %d equals %d.", a, b, a+b);` displays `2 plus 3 equals 5` on-screen (assuming `a` and `b` are integer variables with the values of 2 and 3, respectively). This use of `printf()` has four arguments: a format string that contains literal text as well as format specifiers, and two variables and an expression whose values are to be displayed.

Now look at the `printf()` format string in more detail. It can contain

- One or more conversion commands that tell `printf()` how to display a value in its argument list. A conversion command consists of `%` followed by one or more characters.

- Characters that are not part of a conversion command and are displayed as is.

The third example's format string is `%d plus %d equals %d`. In this case, the three `%d`s are conversion commands and the remainder of the string, including the spaces, is literal characters that are displayed directly.

Now you can dissect the conversion command. The components of the command are given here and explained next; components in brackets are optional.

`%[flag][field_width][.[precision]][l]conversion_char`

The `conversion_char` is the only required part of a conversion command (other than the `%`). The conversion characters and their meanings are listed in Table 14.5.

Table 14.5. The `printf()` and `fprintf()` conversion characters.

Conversion Character	Meaning
d, i	Display a signed integer in decimal notation.
u	Display an unsigned integer in decimal notation.
o	Display an integer in unsigned octal notation.
x, X	Display an integer in unsigned hexadecimal notation. Use x for lower case output, X for uppercase output.
c	Display a single character (the argument gives the character's ASCII code).
e, E	Display a `float` or `double` in scientific notation (for example, `123.45` is displayed as `1.234500e+002`). Six digits are displayed to the right of the decimal point unless another precision is specified with the f specifier. Use e or E to control the case of output.
f	Display a `float` or `double` in decimal notation (for example, `123.45` is displayed as `123.450000`). Six digits are displayed to the right of the decimal point unless another precision is specified.
g, G	Use e, E, or f format. The e or E format is used if the exponent is less than `-3` or greater than the precision (which defaults to `6`). f format is used otherwise. Trailing zeros are truncated.
n	Nothing is displayed. The argument corresponding to an n conversion command is a pointer to type `int`. The `printf()` function assigns to this variable the number of characters output so far.
s	Display a string. The argument is a pointer to `char`. Characters are displayed until a null character is encountered or the number of characters specified by precision (which defaults to `32767`) is displayed. The terminating null character is not output.
%	Display the % character.

You can place the l modifier just before the conversion character. This modifier applies only to the conversion characters o, u, x, X, i, d, b. When applied, this modifier specifies that the argument is a type `long` rather than a type `int`. If the l modifier is applied to the conversion characters e, E, f, g, G, it specifies that the argument is a type `double`. If an l is placed before any other conversion characters, it is ignored.

The precision specifier consists of a decimal point (.) by itself or followed by a number. A precision specifier applies only to the conversion characters e E f g G s. It specifies the number of digits to display to the right of the decimal point or, when used with s, the number of characters to output. If the decimal point is used alone, it specifies a precision of 0.

The field-width specifier determines the minimum number of characters output. The field-width specifier can be

- A decimal integer not starting with 0. The output is padded on the left with spaces to fill the designated field width.
- A decimal integer starting with 0. The output is padded on the left with zeros to fill the designated field width.
- The * character. The value of the next argument (which must be an int) is used as the field width. For example, if w is a type int with a value of 10, the statement `printf("%*d", w, a);` prints the value of a with a field width of 10.

If no field width is specified, or if the specified field width is narrower than the output, the output field is just as wide as needed.

The last optional part of the `printf()` format string is the flag, which immediately follows the % character. There are four available flags:

-    -   This means the output is left-justified in its field rather than right-justified, which is the default.
-    +   This means that signed numbers always are displayed with a leading + or -.
-    ' '   A space means that positive numbers are preceded by a space.
-    #   This applies only to x, X, and o conversion characters. It specifies that non-zero numbers are displayed with a leading 0X or 0x (for x and X) or a leading 0 (for o).

When you use `printf()`, the format string can be a string literal enclosed in double quotes in the `printf()` argument list. It also can be a null-terminated string stored in memory, in which case you pass a pointer to the string to `printf()`. For example,

```
char *fmt = "The answer is %f.";
printf(fmt, x);
```

is equivalent to this statement:

```
printf("The answer is %f.", x);
```

As explained on Day 7, the `printf()` format string can contain escape sequences that provide special control over the output. Table 14.6 lists the most frequently used escape sequences. For example, including the newline sequence (\n) in a format string causes subsequent output to appear starting on the next screen line.

Table 14.6. The most frequently used escape sequences.

Sequence	Meaning
\a	Bell (alert)
\b	Backspace
\n	Newline
\t	Horizontal tab
\\	Backslash
\?	Question mark
\'	Single quote
\"	Double quote

printf() is somewhat complicated. The best way to learn how to use it is to look at examples and then experiment on your own. The program in Listing 14.14 demonstrates many of the ways you can use printf().

Type

Listing 14.14. Some ways to use the printf() function.

```
1: /* Demonstration of printf(). */
2:
3: #include <stdio.h>
4: #include <conio.h>
5: char *m1 = "Binary";
6: char *m2 = "Decimal";
7: char *m3 = "Octal";
8: char *m4 = "Hexadecimal";
9:
10: main()
11: {
12:     float d1 = 10000.123;
13:     int n, f;
14:
15:
16:     puts("Outputting a number with different field widths.\n");
17:
18:     printf("%5f\n", d1);
19:     printf("%10f\n", d1);
20:     printf("%15f\n", d1);
21:     printf("%20f\n", d1);
22:     printf("%25f\n", d1);
23:
24:     getch();
25:
26:     puts("\nUse the * field width specifier to obtain field width");
27:     puts("from a variable in the argument list.\n");
28:
29:     for (n=5;n<=25; n+=5)
```

```
30:        printf("%*f\n", n, d1);
31:
32:    getch();
33:
34:    puts("\nInclude leading zeros.\n");
35:
36:    printf("%05f\n", d1);
37:    printf("%010f\n", d1);
38:    printf("%015f\n", d1);
39:    printf("%020f\n", d1);
40:    printf("%025f\n", d1);
41:
42:    getch();
43:
44:    puts("Display in octal, decimal, and hexadecimal.");
45:    puts("Use # to precede octal and hex output with 0 and 0X.");
46:    puts("Use - to left-justify each value in its field.");
47:    puts("First display column labels.\n");
48:
49:    printf("%-15s%-15s%-15s", m2, m3, m4);
50:
51:    for (n = 1;n< 20; n++)
52:        printf("\n%-15d%-#15o%-#15X", n, n, n);
53:
54:    getch();
55:
56:    puts("\n\nUse the %n conversion command to count characters.\n");
57:
58:    printf("%s%s%s%s%n", m1, m2, m3, m4, &n);
59:
60:    printf("\n\nThe last printf() output %d characters.", n);
61:
62:    getch();
63: }
```

Output

Outputting a number with different field widths.

```
10000.123047
10000.123047
    10000.123047
        10000.123047
            10000.123047
```

Use the * field width specifier to obtain field width
from a variable in the argument list.

```
10000.123047
10000.123047
    10000.123047
        10000.123047
            10000.123047
```

Include leading zeros.

```
10000.123047
10000.123047
00010000.123047
```

```
0000000010000.123047
000000000000010000.123047
Display in octal, decimal, and hexadecimal.
Use # to precede octal and hex output with 0 and 0X.
Use - to left-justify each value in its field.
First display column labels.


Decimal      Octal       Hexadecimal
1            01          0X1
2            02          0X2
3            03          0X3
4            04          0X4
5            05          0X5
6            06          0X6
7            07          0X7
8            010         0X8
9            011         0X9
10           012         0XA
11           013         0XB
12           014         0XC
13           015         0XD
14           016         0XE
15           017         0XF
16           020         0X10
17           021         0X11
18           022         0X12
19           023         0X13

Use the %n conversion command to count characters.
BinaryDecimalOctalHexadecimal
The last printf() output 29 characters.
```

Redirection of Input and Output

A program that uses stdin and stdout can utilize an operating-system feature called *redirection*. Redirection enables you to do the following:

- Output sent to stdout can be sent to a disk file or the printer rather than to the screen.
- Program input from stdin can come from a disk file rather than from the keyboard.

You don't code redirection into your programs; you specify it on the command line when you run the program. In DOS, as in UNIX, the symbols for redirection are < and >. Redirection of output is covered first.

Remember your first C program, HELLO.C? It used the printf() library function to display the message Hello, world on-screen. As you now know, printf() sends output to stdout, so it can be redirected. When you enter the program name at the DOS prompt, follow it with the > symbol and the name of the new destination, as in this example:

```
hello > destination
```

Thus, if you enter `hello >prn`, the program output goes to the printer instead of to the screen (prn is the DOS name for the printer attached to port LPT1:). If you enter `hello >hello.txt`, the output is placed in a disk file with the name `hello.txt`.

When you redirect output to a disk file, be careful. If the file already exists, the old copy is deleted and replaced with the new file. If the file does not exist, it is created. When redirecting output to a file, you also can use the `>>` symbol. If the specified destination file already exists, the program output is appended at the end of the file.

The program in Listing 14.15 demonstrates redirection. This program accepts a line of input from `stdin` and then sends the line to `stdout`, preceding it by `The input was:`. After compiling and linking the program, run it without redirection (assuming the program is named LIST1415) by entering `LIST1415` at the DOS prompt. If you then enter `I am teaching myself C`, the program displays the following onscreen:

```
The input was: I am teaching myself C
```

If you run the program by entering `LIST1415 >test.txt` and make the same entry, there is nothing displayed on-screen. Instead, a file named `test.txt` is created on the disk. Use the DOS `TYPE` (or an equivalent) command to display the contents of the file:

```
type test.txt
```

and you see the file contains the one line `The input was: I am teaching myself C`. Similarly, if you had run the program by entering the following line, the output line would have been printed on your printer:

```
LIST1415 >prn
```

Run the program again, this time redirecting output to TEST.TXT with the >> symbol. Instead of replacing the file, the new output is appended to the end of TEST.TXT.

Listing 14.15. Program to demonstrate redirection of input and output.

```
1: /* Can be used to demonstrate redirection of stdin and stdout. */
2:
3: #include <stdio.h>
4:
5: main()
6: {
7:     char buf[80];
8:
9:     gets(buf);
10:     printf("The input was: %s", buf);
11: }
```

14

Now take a look at redirecting input. First, you need a source file. Use your editor to create a file named INPUT.TXT that contains the single line William Shakespeare. Now, run the previous program by entering the following at the DOS prompt:

```
list1415 <input.txt
```

The program does not wait for you to make an entry at the keyboard. Rather, it immediately displays the following message on-screen:

```
The input was: William Shakespeare
```

The stream stdin was redirected to the disk file input.txt, so the program's call to gets() reads one line of text from the file rather than the keyboard.

You can redirect input and output at the same time. Try running the program with the following command to redirect stdin to the file input.txt and redirect stdout to junk.txt:

```
list1415 <input.txt >junk.txt
```

Redirection of stdin and stdout can be useful in certain situations. A sorting program, for example, could sort either keyboard input or the contents of a disk file. Likewise, a mailing list program could display addresses on-screen, send them to the printer for mailing labels, or place them in a file for some other use.

Remember that redirection of stdin and stdout is a feature of the operating system and not of the C language itself. It does provide, however, another example of the flexibility of streams.

When to Use *fprintf()*

As mentioned earlier, the library function fprintf() is identical to printf() except that you can specify the stream to which output is sent. The main use for fprintf() is with disk files, covered on Day 16. There are two other uses, as explained here.

Using *stderr*

One of C's predefined streams is stderr, standard error. A program's error messages traditionally are sent to the stream stderr and not stdout. Why is this?

As you just learned, output to stdout can be redirected to a destination other than the display screen. If stdout is redirected, the user may not be aware of any error messages the program sends to stdout. Unlike stdout, stderr cannot be redirected and is always connected to the screen (at least in DOS—UNIX systems may allow redirection of stderr). By directing error messages to stderr, you can be sure the user always sees them. You do this with fprintf():

```
fprintf(stderr, "An error has occurred.");
```

You can write a function to handle error messages, and then call the function when an error occurs rather than calling `fprintf()`.

```
error_message("An error has occurred.");

void error_message(char *msg)
{
fprintf(stderr, msg);
}
```

By using your own function instead of directly calling `fprintf()`, you provide additional flexibility (one of the advantages of structured programming). For example, in special circumstances you might want a program's error messages to go to the printer or a disk file. All you need to do is modify the `error_message()` function so that output is sent to the desired destination.

Printer Output Under DOS

On a DOS system, you send output to your printer by accessing the predefined stream `stdprn`. On IBM PCs and compatibles, the stream `stdprn` is connected to the device LPT1: (the first parallel printer port). Listing 14.16 presents a simple example.

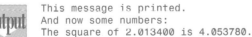

Listing 14.16. Sending output to the printer.

```
1: /* Demonstrates printer output. */
2:
3: #include <stdio.h>
4:
5: main()
6: {
7:     float f = 2.0134;
8:
9:     fprintf(stdprn, "\nnThis message is printed.\r\n");
10:     fprintf(stdprn, "And now some numbers:\r\n");
11:     fprintf(stdprn, "The square of %f is %f.", f, f*f);
12:
13:     /* Send a form feed. */
14:
15:     fprintf(stdprn, "\f");
16: }
```

```
This message is printed.
And now some numbers:
The square of 2.013400 is 4.053780.
```

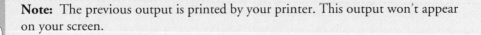

Note: The previous output is printed by your printer. This output won't appear on your screen.

If your DOS system has a printer connected to port LPT1:, you can compile and run the program in Listing 14.16. It prints three lines on the page. Line 15 sends a "\f" to the printer. \f is the escape sequence for a form feed, the command that causes the printer to advance a page (or, in the case of a laser printer, to eject the current page).

DO	DON'T

DON'T ever try to redirect `stderr`.

DO use `fprintf()` to create programs that can send output to `stdout`, `stderr`, `stdprn`, or any other stream.

DO use `fprintf()` with `stderr` to print error messages to the screen.

DON'T use `stderr` for purposes other than printing error messages or warnings.

DO create functions such as `error_message` to make your code more structured and more maintainable.

Summary

This was a long day, full of important information on program input and output. You learned how C uses streams, treating all input and output as a sequence of bytes. You also learned that C has five predefined streams, `stdin` (the keyboard), `stdout` (the screen), `stderr` (the screen), `stdprn` (the printer), and `stdaux` (the communications port).

Input from the keyboard arrives from the stream `stdin`. Using C's standard library functions, you can accept keyboard input character by character, a line at a time, or as formatted numbers and strings. Character input can be buffered or unbuffered, echoed or unechoed.

Output to the display screen is normally done with the `stdout` stream. Like input, program output can be by character, by line, or as formatted numbers and strings. For output to the printer, you use `fprintf()` to send data to the stream `stdprn`.

When you use `stdin` and `stdout`, you can redirect program input and output. Input can come from a disk file rather than the keyboard, and output can go to a disk file or to the printer rather than the display screen.

Finally, you learned why error messages should be sent to the stream `stderr` instead of `stdout`. Because `stderr` is usually connected to the display screen, you are assured of seeing error messages even when the program output is redirected.

8. Write a program that prints your C source files. Use redirection to enter the source file, and use `fprintf()` to do the printing.

9. Write a "typing" program that accepts keyboard input, echoing it on the screen, and then reproduces this input on the printer. The program should count lines and advance the paper in the printer to a new page when necessary. Use a function key to terminate the program.

10. Modify the program from exercise eight to put line numbers at the beginning of the listing when it prints it. (A hint is provided in Appendix F, "Answers.")

2

You have finished your second week of learning how to program in C. By now you should feel comfortable with the C language. You have covered almost all of the basic C commands. The following program pulls together many of the topics from the previous week.

Note that this program uses the library function getch(). This is not an ANSI C function, and it might not be supported by your compiler if you are not using DOS. If it is not supported, you can replace it with getchar().

Note: The numbers to the left of the line numbers indicate the chapter that covers the concept presented on that line. If you are confused by the line, refer to the referenced chapter for more information.

Type **Listing R2.1. Week two's review listing.**

```
1: /* Program Name:  week2.c                              */
2: /* program to enter information for up to 100      */
3: /* people.  The program prints a report            */
4: /* based on the numbers entered.                   */
5: /*------------------------------------------------*/
6: /*--------------------*/
7: /* included files      */
8: /*--------------------*/
9: #include <stdio.h>
10:#include <conio.h>
11: /*--------------------*/
12: /* defined constants   */
13: /*--------------------*/
14:
15: #define MAX    100
16: #define YES    1
17: #define NO     0
18:
19: /*--------------------*/
20: /* variables           */
21: /*--------------------*/
22:
23: struct record {
24:     char fname[15+1];              /* first name + NULL   */
25:     char lname[20+1];              /* last name + NULL    */
26:     char phone[9+1];               /* phone number + NULL */
27:     long income;                   /* incomes             */
28:     int  month;                    /* birthday month      */
29:     int  day;                      /* birthday day        */
30:     int  year;                     /* birthday year       */
31: };
32:
33: struct record list[MAX];       /* declare structure      */
34:
35: int last_entry = 0;            /* total number of entries */
36:
37: /*--------------------*/
38: /* function prototypes */
39: /*--------------------*/
40:
41: void main(void);
42: void get_data(void);
43: void display_report(void);
44: int  continue_function(void);
45: void clear_kb(void);
46:
47: /*--------------------*/
48: /* start of program    */
49: /*--------------------*/
50:
51: void main()
52: {
```

Left margin labels:
CH11 (line 23)
CH10 (line 24)
CH11 (line 33)
CH12 (line 35)
CH14 (line 45)

```
CH12     53:     int cont = YES;
         54:     int ch;
         55:
         56:     while( cont == YES )
         57:     {
         58:         printf( "\n");
         59:         printf( "\n     MENU");
         60:         printf( "\n   =======\n");
         61:         printf( "\n1.  Enter names");
         62:         printf( "\n2.  Print report");
         63:         printf( "\n3.  Quit");
         64:         printf( "\n\nEnter Selection ==> ");
         65:
CH14     66:         ch = getch();
         67:
CH13     68:         switch( ch )
         69:         {
         70:             case '1': get_data();
         71:                     break;
         72:             case '2': display_report();
         73:                     break;
         74:             case '3': printf("\n\nThank you for using this program!");
         75:                     cont = NO;
         76:                     break;
         77:             default:  printf("\n\nInvalid choice, Please select 1 to 3!");
         78:                     break;
         79:         }
         80:     }
         81: }
         82:
         83: /*----------------------------------------------------------*
         84:  *   Function:  get_data()                                  *
         85:  *   Purpose: This function gets the data from the user. It  *
         86:  *            continues to get data until either 100 people are *
         87:  *            entered, or the user chooses not to continue.  *
         88:  *   Returns: nothing                                       *
         89:  *   Notes: This allows 0/0/0 to be entered for birthdates in *
         90:  *         case the user is unsure.  It also allows for 31 days *
         91:  *         in each month.                                   *
         92:  *----------------------------------------------------------*/
         93:
         94: void get_data(void)
         95: {
         96:     int cont;
         97:     int ctr;
         98:
         99:     for ( cont = YES; last_entry < MAX && cont == YES;last_entry++ )
        100:     {
        101:         printf("\n\nEnter information for Person %d.",last_entry+1 );
        102:
CH14    103:         printf("\n\nEnter first name: ");
        104:         gets(list[last_entry].fname);
        105:
CH14    106:         printf("\nEnter last name: ");
        107:         gets(list[last_entry].lname);
        108:
```

continues

343

Listing R2.1. continued

```
CH14    109:        printf("\nEnter phone in 123-4567 format: ");
        110:        gets(list[last_entry].phone);
        111:
CH11    112:        printf("\nEnter Yearly Income (whole dollars): ");
        113:        scanf("%ld", &list[last_entry].income);
        114:
        115:        printf("\nEnter Birthday:");
        116:
        117:        do
        118:        {
        119:            printf("\n\tMonth (0 - 12): ");
        120:            scanf("%d", &list[last_entry].month);
        121:        }while ( list[last_entry].month < 0 ||
        122:                list[last_entry].month > 12 );
        123:
        124:        do
        125:        {
        126:            printf("\n\tDay (0 - 31): ");
        127:            scanf("%d", &list[last_entry].day);
        128:        }while ( list[last_entry].day <  0 ||
        129:                list[last_entry].day > 31 );
        130:
        131:        do
        132:        {
        133:            printf("\n\tYear (1800 - 1996): ");
        134:            scanf("%d", &list[last_entry].year);
        135:        }while (list[last_entry].year != 0 &&
        136:                (list[last_entry].year < 1800 ||
        137:                list[last_entry].year > 1996 ));
        138:
        139:        cont = continue_function();
        140:    }
        141:
        142:    if( last_entry == MAX)
        143:        printf("\n\nMaximum Number of Names has been entered!\n");
        144: }
        145: /*------------------------------------------------------------*
        146:  *  Function:   display_report()                              *
        147:  *  Purpose:    This function displays a report to the screen *
        148:  *  Returns:    nothing                                       *
        149:  *  Notes:      More information could be displayed.          *
        150:  *             Change stdout to stdprn to Print report        *
        151:  *------------------------------------------------------------*/
        152:
        153: void display_report()
        154: {
        155:    long   month_total = 0,
        156:           grand_total = 0;        /* For totals */
        157:    int    x, y;
        158:
CH14    159:    fprintf(stdout, "\n\n");        /* skip a few lines */
        160:    fprintf(stdout, "\n            REPORT");
        161:    fprintf(stdout, "\n            ========");
        162:
```

SAMS

Sams
Learning
Center

SAMS
PUBLISHING

```
163:        for( x = 0; x <= 12; x++ )    /* for each month, including 0 */
164:        {
165:            month_total = 0;
166:            for( y = 0; y < last_entry; y++ )
167:            {
168:                if( list[y].month == x )
169:                {
170:                    fprintf(stdout,"\n\t%s %s %s %ld",list[y].fname,
171:                        list[y].lname, list[y].phone,list[y].income);
172:                    month_total += list[y].income;
173:                }
174:            }
175:            fprintf(stdout, "\nTotal for month %d is %ld",x,month_total);
176:            grand_total += month_total;
177:        }
178:        fprintf(stdout, "\n\nReport totals:");
179:        fprintf(stdout, "\nTotal Income is %ld", grand_total);
180:        fprintf(stdout, "\nAverage Income is %ld", grand_total/last_entry );
181:
182:        fprintf(stdout, "\n\n* * * End of Report * * *");
183: }
184: /*---------------------------------------------------------------*
185:  *  Function:   continue_function()                              *
186:  *  Purpose:    This function asks the user if they wish to continue. *
187:  *  Returns:    YES - if user wishes to continue                 *
188:  *             NO  - if user wishes to quit                      *
189:  *---------------------------------------------------------------*/
190:
191: int continue_function( void )
192: {
193:     char ch;
194:
195:     printf("\n\nDo you wish to continue? (Y)es/(N)o: ");
196:     ch = getch();
197:
198:     while( ch != 'n' && ch != 'N' && ch != 'y' && ch != 'Y' )
199:     {
200:         printf("\n%c is invalid!", ch);
201:         printf("\n\nPlease enter \'N\' to Quit or \'Y\' to Continue: ");
202:         ch = getch();
203:     }
204:
205:     clear_kb();
206:
207:     if(ch == 'n' || ch == 'N')
208:         return(NO);
209:     else
210:         return(YES);
211: }
212:
213: /*---------------------------------------------------------------*
214:  *  Function:   clear_kb()                                       *
215:  *  Purpose:    This function clears the keyboard of extra characters. *
216:  *  Returns:    Nothing                                          *
217:  *---------------------------------------------------------------*/
```

CH14
CH11

CH14

CH14

CH14

continues

345

Listing R2.1. continued

```
218: void clear_kb(void)
219: {
220:     char junk[80];
221:     gets(junk);
222: }
```

It appears that as you learn about C, your programs grow larger. Although this program resembles the one presented after your first week of programming in C, it changes a few of the tasks and adds a few more. Like week one's review, you can enter up to 100 sets of information. The data entered is information about people. You should notice that this program can display the report while you enter information. With the other program, you could not print the report until you had finished entering the data.

You also should notice the addition of a structure used to save the data. The structure is defined on lines 23–31 of this program. Structures often are used to group similar data (Day 11, "Structures"). This program groups all the data for each person into a structure named record. Much of this data should look familiar; however, there are a few new items being tracked. Lines 24–26 contain three arrays, or strings, of characters to hold the first name, last name, and phone number. Notice that each of these strings is declared with a +1 in their array size. You should remember from Day 10, "Characters and Strings," that this extra spot holds the NULL character that signifies the end of a string.

This program demonstrates proper use of variable scope (Day 12, "Variable Scope"). Lines 33 and 35 contain two global variables. Line 35 uses an int called last_entry to hold the number of people that have been entered. This is similar to the variable ctr used in the review at the end of week one. The other global variable is list[MAX], an array of record structures. Local variables are used in each of the functions throughout the program. Of special note are the variables month_total, grand_total, x, and y on lines 155–157 in display_report(). In the week one review, these were global variables. Because these variables only apply to the display_report(), they are better placed as local variables.

An additional program control statement, the switch statement (Day 13, "More Program Control") is used on lines 68–79. Using a switch statement instead of several if...else statements makes the code easier to follow. Lines 70–77 execute various tasks based on a menu choice. Notice that the default statement is also included in case you enter a value that is not a valid menu option.

Looking at the get_data() function, you should notice that there are some additional changes from the week one review. Lines 103–104 prompt for a string. Line 104 uses the gets() function (Day 14, "Working with the Screen, Printer, and Keyboard") to accept a person's first name. The gets() function gets a string and places the value in list[last_entry].fname. You should remember from Day 11 that this places the first name into fname, a member of the structure list.

`display_report()` has been modified, using `fprintf()` instead of `printf()` to display the information. The reason for this change is simple. If you want the report to go to the printer instead of the screen, on each `fprintf()` statement, change `stdout` to `stdprn`. Day 14 covered `fprintf()`, `stdout`, and `stdprn`. Remember that `stdout` and `stdprn` are streams that output to the screen and the printer respectively.

`continue_function()` on lines 191–211 also has been modified. You now respond to the question with Y or N instead of 0 or 1. This is more friendly. Also notice that the `clear_kb()` function from Listing 13.9 has been added on line 205 to remove any extra characters that the user entered.

This program uses what you learned in your first two weeks of teaching yourself C. As you can see, many of the concepts from the second week make your C programs more functional and coding in C easier. Week three continues to build on these concepts.

3

You have finished your second week of learning how to program in C. You should feel comfortable with the C language now, having touched on most areas of the language.

Where You're Going

In the third week, you'll learn what we call "Getting the Most Out of C." Using many of the topics from the first and second weeks, you'll explore what they can do for you.

This next week wraps up your learning of C in 21 days; you should know C when you complete this week (although you'll find some advanced material in the Bonus Week that follows). Day 15, "More on Pointers," tackles one of the hardest parts of C—advanced pointers. As with Day 9, "Pointers," you should dedicate a little extra time to the topics covered. Day 16, "Using Disk Files," covers one of the most useful subjects for creating applications—disk files. You will learn how to use disk files for data storage and retrieval. Days 17, "Manipulating Strings;" 18, "Getting More from Functions;" and 19, "Exploring the Function Library," bombard you with a multitude of library functions. Day 20 covers memory management in greater detail. The last day covers the odds and ends of C, explaining such issues as command-line arguments and preprocessor directives.

More on Pointers

On Day 9, "Pointers," you were introduced to the basics of pointers, which are an important part of the C programming language. Today, you go further, exploring some advanced pointer topics that can add flexibility to your programming. Today, you learn

- How to declare a pointer to a pointer
- How to use pointers with multidimensional arrays
- How to declare arrays of pointers
- How to declare pointers to functions

Pointers-to-Pointers

As you learned on Day 9, a pointer is a numeric variable with a value that is the address of another variable. You declare a pointer using the indirection operator (*). For example, the declaration

```
int *ptr;
```

declares a pointer named ptr that can point to a type int variable. You then use the address-of operator (&) to make the pointer point to a specific variable of the corresponding type. Assuming x has been declared as a type int variable, the statement

```
ptr = &x;
```

assigns the address-of x to ptr and makes ptr point to x. Again using the indirection operator, you can access the pointed-to variable by using its pointer. Both of the following statements assign the value 12 to x:

```
x = 12;
*ptr = 12;
```

Because a pointer is itself a numeric variable, it is stored in your computer's memory at a particular address. Therefore, you can create a pointer to a pointer, a variable whose value is the address of a pointer. Here's how:

```
int x = 12;               /* x is a type int variable. */
int *ptr = &x;            /* ptr is a pointer to x. */
int **ptr_to_ptr = &ptr;  /* ptr_to_ptr is a pointer to a */
/* pointer to type int. */
```

Note the use of a double indirection operator (**) when declaring the pointer-to-pointer. You also use the double indirection operator when accessing the pointed-to variable with a pointer-to-pointer. Thus, the statement

```
**ptr_to_ptr = 12;
```

assigns the value 12 to the variable x, and the statement

```
printf("%d", **ptr_to_ptr);
```

displays the value of x on the screen. If you mistakenly use a single indirection operator, you get errors. The statement

```
*ptr_to_ptr = 12;
```

assigns the value 12 to ptr, which results in ptr pointing to whatever happens to be stored at address 12. This clearly is a mistake.

When you declare and use a pointer-to-pointer, it is called *multiple indirection.* The relationships between a variable, a pointer, and a pointer-to-pointer are illustrated in Figure 15.1. There's really no limit to the level of multiple indirection possible—you can have a pointer-to-pointer-to-pointer *ad infinitum,* but there's rarely any advantage to going beyond two levels.

Figure 15.1.
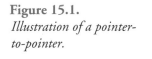
Illustration of a pointer-to-pointer.

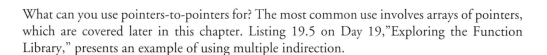

What can you use pointers-to-pointers for? The most common use involves arrays of pointers, which are covered later in this chapter. Listing 19.5 on Day 19,"Exploring the Function Library," presents an example of using multiple indirection.

Pointers and Multidimensional Arrays

Day 8, "Numeric Arrays," covers the special relationship between pointers and arrays. Specifically, the name of an array without its following brackets is a pointer to the first element of the array. As a result, it is easier to use pointer notation when accessing certain types of arrays. These earlier examples, however, were limited to single-dimensional arrays. What about multidimensional arrays?

Remember that a multidimensional array is declared with one set of brackets for each dimension. For example, the following statement declares a two-dimensional array that contains eight type int variables:

```
int multi[2][4];
```

You can visualize the array as having a row and column structure—two rows and four columns in this case. There's another way to visualize a multidimensional array, however, and one that is closer to the way C actually handles the arrays. You can consider `multi` to be a two-element array; each of those two elements is an array of four integers.

This might not be clear to you. Figure 15.2 dissects the array declaration statement into its component parts.

Figure 15.2.

The components of a multidimensional array declaration.

```
 4   1   2 3
 ↓   ↓   ↓ ↓
int multi[2][4];
```

You interpret the components of the declaration as follows:

1. Declare an array named `multi`.
2. The array `multi` contains two elements.
3. Each of those two elements contains four elements.
4. Each of the four elements is a type `int`.

A multidimensional array declaration is read starting with the array name and moving to the right, one set of brackets at a time. When the last set of brackets (the last dimension) is read, the array's basic data type, to the left of the name, is considered.

Under the array-of-arrays scheme, you visualize a multidimensional array as shown in Figure 15.3.

Figure 15.3.

A two-dimensional array is visualized as an array of arrays.

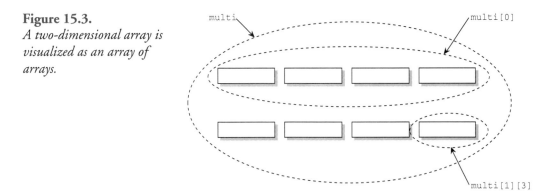

Now, back to the topic of array names as pointers. (This is a chapter about pointers, after all!) As with a one-dimensional array, the name of a multidimensional array is a pointer to the first array element. Continuing with the example, multi is a pointer to the first element of the two-dimensional array that was declared as int multi[2][4]. What exactly is the first element of multi? It is not the type int variable multi[0][0], as you might think. Remember that multi is an array of arrays, so its first element is multi[0], which is an array of four type int variables (one of the two such arrays contained in multi).

Now, if multi[0] is also an array, does it point to anything? Yes, indeed! multi[0] points to its first element, multi[0][0]. You might wonder why multi[0] is a pointer. Remember that the name of an array without brackets is a pointer to the first array element. The term multi[0] is the name of the array multi[0][0] with the last pair of brackets missing, so it qualifies as a pointer.

If you're a bit confused at this point, don't worry. This material is difficult to grasp. It might help if you remember the following rules for any array of *n* dimensions:

- The array name followed by *n* pairs of brackets (each pair containing an appropriate index, of course) evaluates as array data (that is, the data stored in the specified array element).

- The array name followed by fewer than *n* pairs of brackets evaluates as a pointer to an array element.

In the example, therefore, multi evaluates as a pointer, multi[0] evaluates as a pointer, and multi[0][0] evaluates as array data.

Now look at what all these pointers actually point to. The program in Listing 15.1 declares a two-dimensional array—similar to those you've been using in the examples, prints the pointers that you've been learning, and also prints the address of the first array element.

Listing 15.1. The relationship between a multidimensional array and pointers.

```
1:   /* Demonstrates pointers and multidimensional arrays. */
2:
3:   #include <stdio.h>
4:
5:   int multi[2][4];
6:
7:   main()
8:   {
9:       printf("\nmulti = %u", multi);
10:      printf("\nmulti[0] = %u", multi[0]);
11:      printf("\n&multi[0][0] = %u", &multi[0][0]);
12:  }
```

 Output
```
multi = 1328
multi[0] = 1328
&multi[0][0] = 1328
```

 Analysis

The actual value may not be 1328 on your system, but all three values are the same. The address of the array `multi` is the same as the address of the array `multi[0]`, and both are equal to the address of the first integer in the array, `multi[0][0]`.

If these pointers have the same value, what is the practical difference between them in terms of your program? Remember from Day 9 that the C compiler "knows" what a pointer is pointing to. To be more exact, the compiler knows the size of the item a pointer is pointing to.

What are the sizes of the elements you have been using? Listing 15.2 uses the operator `sizeof()` to display the sizes, in bytes, of these elements.

 Type

Listing 15.2. Determining the sizes of the elements.

```
1: /* Demonstrates the sizes of multidimensional array elements. */
2:
3: #include <stdio.h>
4:
5: int multi[2][4];
6:
7: main()
8: {
9:     printf("\nThe size of multi = %u", sizeof(multi));
10:     printf("\nThe size of multi[0] = %u", sizeof(multi[0]));
11:     printf("\nThe size of multi[0][0] = %u",
                sizeof(multi[0][0]));
12: }
```

 Output

The output of this program (assuming your compiler uses two-byte integers) is as follows:

```
The size of multi = 16
The size of multi[0] = 8
The size of multi[0][0] = 2
```

If you are running a 32-bit operating system, such as IBM's OS/2, your output will be 32, 16, and 4. This is because a type `int` contains four bytes on these systems.

 Analysis

Think about these size values. The array `multi` contains two arrays, each of which contains four integers. Each integer requires two bytes of storage. With a total of eight integers, the size of 16 bytes makes sense.

Next, `multi[0]` is an array containing four integers. Each integer takes two bytes, so the size of eight bytes for `multi[0]` also makes sense.

Finally, `multi[0][0]` is an integer; so its size is, of course, two bytes.

Now, keeping these sizes in mind, recall the discussion on Day 9 about pointer arithmetic. The C compiler "knows" the size of the object being pointed to, and pointer arithmetic takes this size into account. When you increment a pointer, its value is increased by the amount needed to make it point to the "next" of whatever it is pointing to. In other words, it is incremented by the size of the object to which it points.

When you apply this to the example, `multi` is a pointer to a four-element integer array with a size of 8. If you increment `multi`, its value should increase by 8 (the size of a four-element integer array). If `multi` points to `multi[0]`, therefore, `(multi + 1)` should point to `multi[1]`. The program in Listing 15.3 tests this theory.

Listing 15.3. This program demonstrates pointer arithmetic with multidimensional arrays.

```
1: /*  Demonstrates pointer arithmetic with pointers */
2: /*  to multidimensional arrays. */
3:
4: #include <stdio.h>
5:
6:  int multi[2][4];
7:
8: main()
9: {
10:     printf("\nThe value of (multi) = %u", multi);
11:     printf("\nThe value of (multi + 1) = %u", (multi+1));
12:     printf("\nThe address of multi[1] = %u", &multi[1]);
13: }
```

```
The value of (multi) = 1376
The value of (multi + 1) = 1384
The address of multi[1] = 1384
```

The precise values might be different on your system, but the relationships are the same. Incrementing `multi` by 1 increases its value by 8 and makes it point to the next element of the array, `multi[1]`.

In this example, you've seen that `multi` is a pointer to `multi[0]`. You've also seen that `multi[0]` is itself a pointer (to `multi[0][0]`). Therefore, `multi` is a pointer to a pointer. To use the expression `multi` to access array data, you must use double indirection. To print the value stored in `multi[0][0]`, you could use any of the following three statements:

```
printf("%d", multi[0][0]);
printf("%d", *multi[0]);
printf("%d", **multi);
```

These concepts apply equally to arrays with three or more dimensions. Thus, a three-dimensional array is an array with elements that are each a two-dimensional array; each of these elements is itself an array of one-dimensional arrays.

This material on multidimensional arrays and pointers might seem a bit confusing. When you work with multidimensional arrays, keep this point in mind: an array with *n* dimensions has elements that are arrays with *n-1* dimensions. When *n* becomes 1, that array's elements are variables of the data type specified at the beginning of the array declaration line.

So far, you have been using array names that are pointer constants and cannot be changed. How would you declare a pointer variable that points to an element of a multidimensional array? Now let's continue with the previous example, which has declared a two-dimensional array as

```
int multi[2][4];
```

To declare a pointer variable `ptr` that can point to an element of `multi` (that is, can point to a four-element integer array), you would write

```
int (*ptr)[4];
```

You could then make `ptr` point to the first element of `multi` by writing

```
ptr = multi;
```

You might wonder why the parentheses are necessary in the pointer declaration. Brackets [ ] have a higher precedence than *. If you wrote

```
int *ptr[4];
```

you would be declaring an array of four pointers to type `int`. Indeed, you can declare and use arrays of pointers. This is not what you want to do now, however.

How can you use pointers to elements of multidimensional arrays? As with single-dimensional arrays, pointers must be used to pass an array to a function. This is illustrated for a multi-dimensional array in Listing 15.4, which uses two methods of passing a multidimensional array to a function.

Listing 15.4. Passing a multidimensional array to a function using a pointer.

```
1: /* Demonstrates passing a pointer to a multidimensional */
2: /* array to a function. */
3: #include <conio.h>
4: #include <stdio.h>
5:
6: void printarray_1(int (*ptr)[4]);
7: void printarray_2(int (*ptr)[4], int n);
8:
9: main()
10:{
11:    int  multi[3][4] = { { 1, 2, 3, 4 },
12:                         { 5, 6, 7, 8 },
13:                         { 9, 10, 11, 12 } };
14:    /* ptr is a pointer to an array of 4 ints. */
15:
16:    int (*ptr)[4], count;
17:
18:    /* Set ptr to point to the first element of multi. */
19:
20:    ptr = multi;
21:
22:    /* With each loop, ptr is incremented to point at the next*/
```

```
23:     /* element (that is, next 4-element integer array) of multi.*/
24:
25:     for (count = 0; count < 3; count++)
26:         printarray_1(ptr++);
27:
28:     puts("\n\nPress a key...");
29:     getch();
30:
31:     printarray_2(multi, 3);
32:
33: }
34:
35:  void printarray_1(int (*ptr)[4])
36: {
37:     /* Prints the elements of a single 4-element integer array. */
38:     /* p is a pointer to type int. You must use a type cast */
39:     /* to make p equal to the address in ptr. */
40:
41:     int *p, count;
42:     p = (int *)ptr;
43:
44:     for (count = 0; count < 4; count++)
45:         printf("\n%d", *p++);
46: }
47:
48: void printarray_2(int (*ptr)[4], int n)
49: {
50:     /* Prints the elements of an[]by four-element integer array. */
51:
52:     int *p, count;
53:     p = (int *)ptr;
54:
55:     for (count = 0; count < (4 * n); count++)
56:         printf("\n%d", *p++);
57: }
```

Output

```
1
2
3
4
5
6
7
8
9
10
11
12

Press a key...

1
2
3
4
5
6
```

```
7
8
9
10
11
12
```

The program declares and initializes an array of integers, `multi[3][4]` on lines 11–13. It has two functions, `printarray_1()` and `printarray_2()`, that print the contents of the array.

The function `printarray_1()` (lines 35–46) is passed only one argument, a pointer to an array of four integers. The function prints all four elements of the array. The first time `main()` calls `printarray_1()` on line 26, it passes a pointer to the first element (the first four-element integer array) in `multi`. It then calls the function two more times, incrementing the pointer each time to point to the second, and then the third, element of `multi`. After all three calls are made, the 12 integers in `multi` are displayed.

The second function, `printarray_2()`, takes a different approach. It too is passed a pointer to an array of four integers, but it also is passed an integer variable giving the number of elements (the number of arrays of four integers) that the multidimensional array contains. With a single call from line 31, `printarray_2()` displays the entire contents of `multi`.

Both functions use pointer notation to step through the individual integers in the array. The notation `(int *)ptr` in both functions (lines 42 and 53) might not be clear. The `(int *)` is a type cast, which temporarily changes the variable's data type from its declared data type to a new one. The type cast is required when assigning the value of `ptr` to `p` because they are pointers to different types (`p` is a pointer to type `int`, whereas `ptr` is a pointer to an array of four integers). C doesn't allow you to assign the value of one pointer to a pointer of a different type. The type cast tells the compiler "for this statement only, treat `ptr` as a pointer to type `int`." Day 20, "Working with Memory," covers type casts in more detail.

DO	**DON'T**

DON'T forget to use the double indirection operator (`**`) when declaring a pointer to a pointer.

DON'T forget that a pointer increments by the size of the pointer's type (usually what is being pointed to).

DON'T forget to use parentheses when declaring pointers to arrays.

To declare a pointer to an array of characters, use this format:

```
char (*letters)[26];
```

To declare an array of pointers to characters, use this format:

```
char *letters[26];
```

Arrays of Pointers

Recall from Day 8, "Numeric Arrays," that an array is a collection of data storage locations that have the same data type and are referred to by the same name. Because pointers are one of C's data types, you can declare and use arrays of pointers. This type of program construct can be very powerful in certain situations.

Perhaps the most common use for an array of pointers is with strings. A string, as you learned on Day 10, "Characters and Strings," is a sequence of characters stored in memory. The start of the string is indicated by a pointer to the first character (a pointer to type char); the end of the string is marked by a null character. By declaring and initializing an array of pointers to type char, you can access and manipulate a large number of strings using the pointer array.

Strings and Pointers—A Review

This is a good time to review some material from Day 10 regarding string allocation and initialization. If you want to allocate and initialize a string, you declare an array of type char as follows:

```
char message[] = "This is the message.";
```

You could also declare a pointer to type char:

```
char *message = "This is the message.";
```

Both declarations are equivalent. In each case, the compiler allocates enough space to hold the string with its terminating null character, and the expression message is a pointer to the start of the string. What about these two declarations?

```
char message1[20];
char *message2;
```

The first line declares an array of type char that is 20 characters long, and message1 is a pointer to the first array position. Although the array space is allocated, it has not been initialized. The second line declares message2, a pointer to type char. No storage space for a string is allocated by this statement. If you want to create a string and then point message2 at it, you must allocate space for the string first. On Day 10 you learned how to use the malloc() memory allocation function for this purpose. Remember that any string must have space allocated for it, whether at compilation in a declaration or at runtime with malloc().

Array of Pointers to *char*

Now that you're done with the review, how do you declare an array of pointers? The following statement declares an array of 10 pointers to type `char`:

```
char *message[10];
```

Each element of the array `message[]` is an individual pointer to type `char`. As you might have guessed, you can combine the declaration with initialization and allocation of storage space for the strings.

```
char *message[10] = { "one", "two", "three" };
```

This declaration does the following:

- It allocates a 10-element array named `message`; each element of `message` is a pointer to type `char`.

- It allocates space somewhere in memory (where exactly doesn't concern you) and stores the three initialization strings, each with a terminating null character.

- It initializes `message[0]` to point at the first character of the string `one`, `message[1]` to point at the first character of the string `two`, and `message[2]` to point at the first character of the string `three`.

This is illustrated in Figure 15.4, which shows the relationship between the array of pointers and the strings. Note that in this example, array elements `message[3]` through `message[9]` are not initialized to point at anything.

Figure 15.4.

An array of pointers to type char.

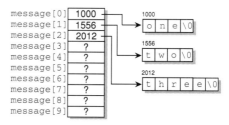

Now look at Listing 15.5, which is an example of using an array of pointers.

 Listing 15.5. Initializing and using an array of pointers to type `char`**.**

```
1: /* Initializing an array of pointers to type char. */
2:
3: #include <stdio.h>
4:
5: main()
6: {
```

```
 7:     char *message[8] = { "Four", "score", "and", "seven",
 8:                     "years", "ago,", "our", "forefathers" };
 9:   int count;
10:
11:     for (count = 0; count < 8; count++)
12:         printf("%s ", message[count]);
13: }
```

Four score and seven years ago, our forefathers

The program in Listing 15.5 declares an array of 8 pointers to type char and initializes them to point to 8 strings (lines 7–8). It then uses a for loop on lines 11 and 12 to display each element of the array on the screen.

You probably can see how manipulating the array of pointers is easier than manipulating the strings themselves. This advantage is obvious in more complicated programs, such as the one presented later in this chapter. As you will see in that program, the advantage is greatest when you are using functions. It's much easier to pass an array of pointers to a function than to pass several strings, which can be illustrated by rewriting the program in Listing 15.5 so that it uses a function to display the strings. This modified program is given in Listing 15.6.

Listing 15.6. Passing an array of pointers to a function.

```
 1: /* Passing an array of pointers to a function. */
 2:
 3: #include <stdio.h>
 4:
 5: void print_strings(char *p[], int n);
 6:
 7: main()
 8: {
 9:     char *message[8] = { "Four", "score", "and", "seven",
10:                     "years", "ago,", "our", "forefathers" };
11:
12:     print_strings(message, 8);
13: }
14:
15: void print_strings(char *p[], int n)
16: {
17:     int count;
18:
19:     for (count = 0; count < n; count++)
20:         printf("%s ", p[count]);
21: }
```

Four score and seven years ago, our forefathers

Analysis — Looking at line 15, you see that the function `print_strings()` takes two arguments. One is an array of pointers to type `char`, the other is the number of elements in the array. Thus, `print_strings()` could be used to print the strings pointed to by any array of pointers.

You may remember that in the section on pointers-to-pointers, you were told that you would see a demonstration later. Well, you've just seen it. Listing 15.6 declared an array of pointers, and the name of the array is a pointer to its first element. When you pass that array to a function, you are passing a pointer (the array name) to a pointer (the first array element).

An Example

Now it's time for a more complicated example. The program in Listing 15.7 uses many of the programming skills that you have learned, including arrays of pointers. The program accepts lines of input from the keyboard, allocating space for each line as it is entered and keeping track of the lines by means of an array of pointers to type `char`. When you signal the end of an entry by entering a blank line, the program sorts the strings alphabetically and displays them on-screen.

You should approach the design of this program from a structured programming perspective. First, make a list of the things the program must do:

1. Accept lines of input from the keyboard one at a time until a blank line is entered.
2. Sort the lines into alphabetical order.
3. Display the sorted lines on the screen.

This list suggests that the program should have at least three functions: one to accept input, one to sort the lines, and one to display the lines. Now you can design each function independently. What do you need the input function—called `get_lines()`—to do? Again, make a list:

1. Keep track of the number of lines entered and return that value to the calling program once all lines are entered.
2. Do not allow input of more than a preset maximum number of lines.
3. Allocate storage space for each line.
4. Keep track of all lines by storing pointers to strings in an array.
5. Return to the calling program when a blank line is entered.

Now think about the second function, the one that sorts the lines. It could be called `sort()`. (Really original, right?) The sort technique used is a simple, brute-force method that compares adjacent strings and swaps them if the second string is less than the first string. More exactly, the function compares the two strings whose pointers are adjacent in the array of pointers and swaps the two pointers if necessary.

To be sure that the sorting is complete, you must go through the array from start to finish, comparing each pair of strings and swapping if necessary. For an array of n elements you must go through the array n-1 times. Why is this necessary?

Each time you go through the array, a given element can be shifted by, at most, one position. For example, if the string that should be first is actually in the last position, the first pass through the array moves it to the next-to-last position, the second pass through the array moves it up one more position, and so on. It requires n-1 passes to move it to the first position, where it belongs.

Please note that this is a very inefficient and inelegant sorting method. It is, however, easy to implement and easy to understand, and it is more than adequate for the short lists that the example program sorts.

The final function displays the sorted lines on the screen. It is, in effect, already written in Listing 15.6, and requires only minor modification.

Listing 15.7. A program that reads lines of text from the keyboard, sorts them alphabetically, and displays the sorted list.

```
1: /* Inputs a list of strings from the keyboard, sorts them, */
2: /* then displays them on the screen. */
3: #include <stdlib.h>
4: #include <stdio.h>
5: #include <string.h>
6:
7: #define MAXLINES 25
8:
9: int get_lines(char *lines[]);
10: void sort(char *p[], int n);
11: void print_strings(char *p[], int n);
12:
13: char *lines[MAXLINES];
14:
15: main()
16: {
17:     int number_of_lines;
18:
19:     /* Read in the lines from the keyboard. */
20:
21:     number_of_lines = get_lines(lines);
22:
23:     if ( number_of_lines < 0 )
24:     {
25:         puts(" Memory allocation error");
26:         exit(-1);
27:     }
28:
29:     sort(lines, number_of_lines);
30:      print_strings(lines, number_of_lines);
31:
32: }
33:
```

Listing 15.7. continued

```
34: int get_lines(char *lines[])
35: {
36:     int n = 0;
37:     char buffer[80];   /* Temporary storage for each line. */
38:
39:     puts("Enter one line at time; enter a blank when done.");
40:
41:     while ((n < MAXLINES) && (gets(buffer) != 0) &&
42:             (buffer[0] != '\0'))
43:     {
44:         if ((lines[n] = (char *)malloc(strlen(buffer)+1)) == NULL)
45:             return -1;
46:         strcpy( lines[n++], buffer );
47:     }
48:     return n;
49:
50: } /* End of get_lines() */
51:
52: void sort(char *p[], int n)
53: {
54:     int a, b;
55:     char *x;
56:
57:     for (a = 1; a < n; a++)
58:     {
59:         for (b = 0; b < n-1; b++)
60:         {
61:             if (strcmp(p[b], p[b+1]) > 0)
62:             {
63:                 x = p[b];
64:                 p[b] = p[b+1];
65:                 p[b+1] = x;
66:             }
67:         }
68:     }
69: }
70:
71: void print_strings(char *p[], int n)
72: {
73:     int count;
74:
75:     for (count = 0; count < n; count++)
76:         printf("\n%s ", p[count]);
77: }
```

```
Enter one line at time; enter a blank when done.
dog
apple
zoo
program
merry
```

```
apple
dog
merry
program
zoo
```

Analysis Examine some of the details of the program. Several new library functions are used for various types of string manipulation. They are explained briefly here, and in more detail on Day 17, "Manipulating Strings." The header file STRING.H must be included in a program that uses these functions.

In the get_lines() function, input is controlled by the while statement on lines 41–42, which read as follows:

```
while ((n < MAXLINES) && (gets(buffer) != 0) &&
       (buffer[0] != '\0'))
```

The condition tested by the while has three parts. The first part, n < MAXLINES, ensures that the maximum number of lines has not been input already. The second part, gets(buffer) != 0, calls the gets() library function to read a line from the keyboard into buffer, and verifies that end-of-file or some other error has not occurred. The third part, buffer[0] != '\0', verifies that the first character of the line just input is not the null character, which would signal that a blank line was entered.

If any of the three conditions is not satisfied, the while loop terminates and execution returns to the calling program, with the number of lines entered as the return value. If all three conditions are satisfied, the following if statement on line 44 is executed:

```
if ((lines[n] = (char *)malloc(strlen(buffer)+1)) == NULL)
```

The first part of the condition calls malloc() to allocate space for the string just input. The strlen() function returns the length of the string passed as an argument; the value is incremented by 1 so that malloc() allocates space for the string plus its terminating null character.

The library function malloc(), you might remember, returns a pointer. The statement assigns the value of the pointer returned by malloc() to the corresponding element of the array of pointers. If malloc() returns NULL, the if loop returns execution to the calling program with a return value of –1. The code in main() tests the return value of get_lines() and whether a value less than 0 is returned; lines 23–27 report a memory allocation error and terminate the program.

If the memory allocation was successful, the program uses the strcpy() function on line 46 to copy the string from the temporary storage location buffer to the storage space just allocated by malloc(). The while loop then repeats, getting another line of input.

Once execution returns to main() from get_lines(), the following has been accomplished (assuming a memory allocation error did not occur):

- A number of lines of text have been read from the keyboard and stored in memory as null-terminated strings.
- The array lines[] contains a pointer to each string. The order of pointers in the array is the order in which the strings were input.
- The variable number_of_lines holds the number of lines that were input.

Now it's time to sort. Remember, you're not actually going to move the strings around, only the order of the pointers in the array lines[]. Look at the code in the function sort(). It contains one for loop nested in another (lines 57–68). The outer loop executes number_of_lines - 1 times. Each time the outer loop executes, the inner loop steps through the array of pointers, comparing (string n) with (string n+1) for n = 0 to n = number_of_lines - 1. The comparison is performed by line 61's library function strcmp(), which receives pointers to two strings. The function strcmp() returns one of the following:

- A value greater than zero if the first string is greater than the second string.
- Zero if the two strings are identical.
- A value less than zero if the second string is greater than the first string.

In the program, a return value from strcmp() of greater than zero means the first string is "greater than" the second string, and they must be swapped (that is, their pointers in lines[] must be swapped). This is done using a temporary variable x. Lines 63–65 perform the swap.

When program execution returns from sort(), the pointers in lines[] are ordered properly: a pointer to the "lowest" string is in lines[0], a pointer to the next "lowest" is in lines[1], and so on. Say, for example, you entered the following five lines, in this order:

```
dog
apple
zoo
program
merry
```

The situation before calling sort() is illustrated in Figure 15.5, and the situation after the return from sort() is illustrated in Figure 15.6.

Figure 15.5.

Before sorting, the pointers are in the same order in which the strings were entered.

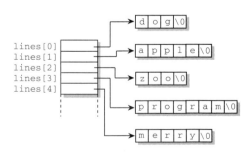

Figure 15.6.

After sorting, the pointers are ordered according to the alphabetical order of the strings.

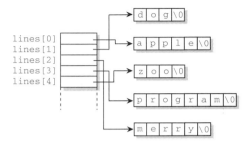

Finally, the program calls the function `print_strings()` to display the sorted list of strings on the screen. This function should be familiar from previous examples in this chapter.

The program in Listing 15.7 is the most complex you have encountered in this book. It uses many of the C programming techniques that have been covered in previous chapters. With the aid of the preceding explanation, you should be able to follow the operation of the program and understand each step. If you find areas that are not clear to you, review the related sections of the book until you do understand, before going on to the next section.

Pointers to Functions

Pointers to functions provide another way of calling functions. "Hold on," you might be saying, "how can you have a pointer to a function? A pointer holds the address where a variable is stored, doesn't it?"

Well, yes and no. It's true that a pointer holds an address, but it doesn't have to be the address where a variable is stored. When your program runs, the code for each function is loaded into memory starting at a specific address. A pointer to a function holds the starting address of a function, its entry point.

Why use a pointer to a function? As mentioned earlier, it provides a more flexible way of calling a function. It enables the program to "pick" among several functions, selecting the one that is appropriate for the current circumstances.

Declaring a Pointer to a Function

Like other pointers, you must declare a pointer to a function. The general form of the declaration is as follows:

```
type (*ptr_to_func)(parameter_list);
```

This statement declares `ptr_to_func` as a pointer to a function that returns `type` and is passed the parameters in `parameter_list`. Here are some more concrete examples:

```
int (*func1)(int x);
void (*func2)(double y, double z);
char (*func3)(char *p[]);
void (*func4)();
```

The first line declares `func1` as a pointer to a function that takes one type `int` argument and returns a type `int`. The second line declares `func2` as a pointer to a function that takes two type `double` arguments and has a `void` return type (no return value). The third line declares `func3` as a pointer to a function that takes an array of pointers to type `char` as its argument and returns a type `char`. The final line declares `func4` as a pointer to a function that does not take any arguments and has a `void` return type.

Why do you need the parentheses around the pointer name? Why can't you write, for the first example,

```
int *func1(int x);
```

The reason has to do with the precedence of the indirection operator, `*`. It has a relatively low precedence, lower than the parentheses surrounding the parameter list. The declaration just given, without the first set of parentheses, declares `func1` as a function that returns a pointer to type `int`. (Functions that return pointers are covered on Day 18.) When you declare a pointer to a function, always remember to include a set of parentheses around the pointer name and indirection operator, or you will get into trouble for sure.

Initializing and Using a Pointer to a Function

A pointer to a function must not only be declared, but initialized to point to something. That "something" is, of course, a function. There's nothing special about a function that gets pointed to. The only requirement is that its return type and parameter list match the return type and parameter list of the pointer declaration. For example, the following code declares and defines a function and a pointer to that function:

```
float square(float x);      /* The function prototype.  */
float (*p)(float x);        /* The pointer declaration. */

float square(float x)       /* The function definition. */
{
return x * x;
}
```

Because the function `square()` and the pointer `p` have the same parameter and return types, you can initialize `p` to point to `square` as follows:

```
p = square;
```

Then you can call the function using the pointer as follows:

```
answer = p(x);
```

It's that simple. For a real example, compile and run the program in Listing 15.8, which declares and initializes a pointer to a function, and then calls the function twice, using the function name the first time and the pointer the second time. Both calls produce the same result.

Listing 15.8. Using a pointer to a function to call the function.

```
1: /* Demonstration of declaring and using a pointer to a function.*/
2:
3: #include <stdio.h>
4:
5: /* The function prototype. */
6:
7: float square(float x);
8:
9: /* The pointer declaration. */
10:
11: float (*p)(float x);
12:
13: main()
14: {
15:     /* Initialize p to point to square(). */
16:
17:      p = square;
18:
19:     /* Call square() two ways. */
20:
21:     printf("%f  %f", square(6.6), p(6.6));
22: }
23:
24: float square(float x)
25: {
26:     return x * x;
27: }
```

```
43.559999   43.559999
```

Note: Precision of the values may cause some numbers to not display as the exact values entered. For example, the correct answer, 43.56, may appear as 43.559999.

Line 7 declares square(), and line 11 declares the pointer, p, to a function containing a float argument and returning a float value, matching the declaration of square(). Line 17 sets the pointer, p, equal to square. Notice that parentheses are not used with square or p. Line 21 prints the return values from calls to square() and p().

A function name without the parentheses is a pointer to the function (sounds similar to the situation with arrays, doesn't it?). What's the point of declaring and using a separate pointer to

371

the function? Well, the function name itself is a pointer constant and cannot be changed (again, a parallel to arrays). A pointer variable, in contrast, can be changed. Specifically, it can be made to point to different functions as the need arises.

The program in Listing 15.9 calls a function, passing it an integer argument. Depending on the value of the argument, the function initializes a pointer to point to one of three other functions, and then uses the pointer to call the corresponding function. Each of these three functions displays a specific message on the screen.

 Listing 15.9. Using a pointer to a function to call different functions depending on program circumstances.

```
1: /* Using a pointer to call different functions. */
2:
3: #include <stdio.h>
4:
5: /* The function prototypes. */
6:
7: void func1(int x);
8: void one(void);
9:  void two(void);
10: void other(void);
11:
12:  main()
13: {
14:      int a;
15:
16:     for (;;)
17:     {
18:         puts("\nEnter an integer between 1 and 10, 0 to exit: ");
19:          scanf("%d", &a);
20:
21:         if (a == 0)
22:             break;
23:
24:         func1(a);
25:     }
26: }
27:
28: void func1(int x)
29: {
30:     /* The pointer to function. */
31:
32:     void (*ptr)(void);
33:
34:     if (x == 1)
35:         ptr = one;
36:     else if (x == 2)
37:         ptr = two;
38:     else
39:         ptr = other;
40:
41:     ptr();
42: }
```

```
43:
44: void one(void)
45: {
46:     puts("You entered 1.");
47: }
48:
49: void two(void)
50: {
51:     puts("You entered 2.");
52: }
53:
54: void other(void)
55: {
56:     puts("You entered something other than 1 or 2.");
57: }
```

```
Enter an integer between 1 and 10, 0 to exit:
2
You entered 2.

Enter an integer between 1 and 10, 0 to exit:
11
You entered something other than 1 or 2.

Enter an integer between 1 and 10, 0 to exit:
0
```

This program employs an infinite loop on line 16 to continue the program until a value of zero is entered. When a non-zero value is entered, it's passed to func1(). Note that line 32, in func1(), contains a declaration for a pointer to a function (ptr). This makes it local to func1(), appropriate because no other part of the program needs access to it. func1() then uses this value to set ptr equal to the appropriate function (lines 34–39). Line 41 then makes a single call to ptr(), which calls the appropriate function.

Of course, the program in Listing 15.9 is for illustration purposes only. You easily could have accomplished the same result without using a pointer to a function.

Now you can learn another way to use pointers to call different functions: passing the pointer as an argument to a function. The program in Listing 15.10 is a revision of Listing 15.9.

Listing 15.10. Passing a pointer to a function as an argument.

```
1: /* Passing a pointer to a function as an argument. */
2:
3: #include <stdio.h>
4:
5: /* The function prototypes. The function func1() takes as */
6: /* its one argument a pointer to a function that takes no */
7: /* arguments and has no return value. */
8:
9: void func1(void (*p)(void));
10: void one(void);
```

Listing 15.10. continued

```
11: void two(void);
12: void other(void);
13:
14: main()
15: {
16:     /* The pointer to a function. */
18:     void (*ptr)(void);
19:     int  a;
20:
21:     for (;;)
22:     {
23:         puts("\nEnter an integer between 1 and 10, 0 to exit: ");
24:         scanf("%d", &a);
25:
26:         if (a == 0)
27:             break;
28:         else if (a == 1)
29:             ptr = one;
30:         else if (a == 2)
31:             ptr = two;
32:         else
33:             ptr = other;
34:
35:         func1(ptr);
36:     }
37: }
38:
39: void func1(void (*p)(void))
40: {
41:     p();
42: }
43:
44: void one(void)
45: {
46:     puts("You entered 1.");
47: }
48:
49: void two(void)
50: {
51:     puts("You entered 2.");
52: }
53:
54: void other(void)
55: {
56:     puts("You entered something other than 1 or 2.");
57: }
```

```
Enter an integer between 1 and 10, 0 to exit:
2
You entered 2.

Enter an integer between 1 and 10, 0 to exit:
11
You entered something other than 1 or 2.
```

```
Enter an integer between 1 and 10, 0 to exit:
0
```

Analysis Notice the differences between Listing 15.9 and Listing 15.10. The declaration of the pointer to a function has been moved to line 18 in main(), where it is needed. Code in main() now initializes the pointer to point to the correct function (lines 26–33), and then passes the initialized pointer to func1(). This function, func1() really serves no purpose in Listing 15.10; all it does is call the function pointed to by ptr. Again, this program is for illustration. The same principles can be used in real-world programs, such as the example in the next section.

One programming situation in which you might use pointers to functions is when sorting is required. At times, you may want different sorting rules used. For example, you might want to sort in alphabetical order one time and in reverse alphabetical order another time. By using pointers to functions, your program can call the correct sorting function. More precisely, it's usually a different comparison function that's called.

Look back at the program in Listing 15.7. In the sort() function, the actual sort order is determined by the value returned by the strcmp() library function, which tells the program whether a given string is "less than" another string. What if you wrote two comparison functions, one that sorts alphabetically (saying that A is less than Z, for example), and another that sorts in reverse alphabetical order (saying that Z is less than A). The program can ask the user what order is desired and, by using pointers, the sorting function can call the proper comparison function. Listing 15.11 modifies the program in Listing 15.7 and incorporates this feature.

Type **Listing 15.11. Using pointers to functions to control sort order.**

```
1:  /* Inputs a list of strings from the keyboard, sorts them */
2:  /* in ascending or descending order, then displays them */
3:  /* on the screen. */
4:  #include <stdlib.h>
5:  #include <stdio.h>
6:  #include <string.h>
7:
8:  #define MAXLINES 25
9:
10:  int get_lines(char *lines[]);
11:  void sort(char *p[], int n, int sort_type);
12:  void print_strings(char *p[], int n);
13:  int alpha(char *p1, char *p2);
14:  int reverse(char *p1, char *p2);
15:
16:  char *lines[MAXLINES];
17:
18:   main()
19:  {
20:     int number_of_lines, sort_type;
21:
```

Listing 15.11. continued

```
22:     /* Read in the lines from the keyboard. */
23:
24:     number_of_lines = get_lines(lines);
25:
26:     if ( number_of_lines < 0 )
27:     {
28:        puts("Memory allocation error");
29:        exit(-1);
30:     }
31:
32:     puts("Enter 0 for reverse order sort, 1 for alphabetical:" );
33:     scanf("%d", &sort_type);
34:
35:     sort(lines, number_of_lines, sort_type);
36:     print_strings(lines, number_of_lines);
37:
38:  }
39:
40:  int get_lines(char *lines[])
41:  {
42:     int n = 0;
43:     char buffer[80];   /* Temporary storage for each line. */
44:
45:     puts("Enter one line at time; enter a blank when done.");
46:
47:     while (n < MAXLINES && gets(buffer) != 0 && buffer[0] != '\0')
48:     {
49:         if ((lines[n] = (char *)malloc(strlen(buffer)+1)) == NULL)
50:         return -1;
51:         strcpy( lines[n++], buffer );
52:     }
53:     return n;
54:
55:  } /* End of get_lines() */
56:
57:  void sort(char *p[], int n, int sort_type)
58:  {
59:     int a, b;
60:      char *x;
61:
62:     /* The pointer to function.   */
63:
64:     int (*compare)(char *s1, char *s2);
65:
66:     /* Initialize the pointer to point at the proper comparison */
67:     /* function depending on the argument sort_type. */
68:
69:     compare = (sort_type) ? reverse : alpha;
70:
71:     for (a = 1; a < n; a++)
72:     {
73:         for (b = 0; b < n-1; b++)
74:         {
75:             if (compare(p[b], p[b+1]) > 0)
```

```
76:                {
77:                    x = p[b];
78:                    p[b] = p[b+1];
79:                    p[b+1] = x;
80:                }
81:            }
82:        }
83:  } /* end of sort() */
84:
85:  void print_strings(char *p[], int n)
86:  {
87:      int count;
88:
89:      for (count = 0; count < n; count++)
90:          printf("\n%s ", p[count]);
91:  }
92:
93:  int alpha(char *p1, char *p2)
94:  /* Alphabetical comparison. */
95:  {
96:      return(strcmp(p2, p1));
97:  }
98:
99:  int reverse(char *p1, char *p2)
100: /* Reverse alphabetical comparison. */
101: {
102:     return(strcmp(p1, p2));
103: }
```

Input
Output

```
Enter one line at time; enter a blank when done.
Roses are red
Violets are blue
C has been around,
But it is new to you!

Enter 0 for reverse order sort, 1 for alphabetical:
0

Violets are blue
Roses are red
C has been around,
But it is new to you!
```

Analysis

Lines 32 and 33 in main() prompt the user for the desired sort order. The order selected is placed in sort_type. This value is passed to the sort() function along with the other information described for Listing 15.7. The sort() function contains a couple of changes. Line 64 declares a pointer to a function called compare() that takes two character pointers (strings) as arguments. Line 69 sets compare() equal to one of the two new functions added to the listing based on the value of sort_type. The two new functions are alpha() and reverse(). alpha() uses the strcmp() library function just as it was used in Listing 15.7; reverse() does not. reverse() switches the parameters passed so that a reverse order sort is done.

DO	**DON'T**

DO use structured programming.

DON'T forget to use parentheses when declaring pointers to functions.

Declaring a pointer to a function that takes no arguments and returns a character looks like this:

```
char (*func)();
```

Declaring a function that returns a pointer to a character looks like this:

```
char *func();
```

DO initialize a pointer before using it.

DON'T use a function pointer that has been declared with a different return type or different arguments than what you need.

Summary

This chapter has covered some of the advanced uses of pointers. As you might realize, pointers are central to the C language; C programs that don't use pointers are rare. You've seen how to use pointers-to-pointers and how arrays of pointers can be very useful when dealing with strings. You've also learned how C treats multidimensional arrays as being arrays of arrays, and you've seen how to use pointers with such arrays. Finally, you've learned how to declare and use pointers to functions, an important and flexible programming tool.

This has been a long and involved chapter. Although some of its topics are a bit complicated, they're exciting as well. With this chapter, you're really getting into some of the sophisticated capabilities of the C language. Power and flexibility are among the main reasons C is such a popular language.

Q&A

Q How many levels can I go with pointers-to-pointers?

A You need to check your compiler manuals to determine whether there are any limitations. It is usually impractical to go more than three levels deep with pointers (pointers-to-pointers-to-pointers). Most programs rarely go over two levels.

Q Is there a difference between a pointer to a string and a pointer to an array of characters?

A No. A string can be looked at as an array of characters.

Q Is it necessary to use the concepts presented in this chapter to take advantage of C?

A You can use C without ever using any advanced pointer concepts; however, you won't take advantage of the power that C offers. By doing pointer manipulations such as those shown in this chapter, you should be able to do virtually any programming task in a quick, efficient manner.

Q Are there other times when function pointers are useful?

A Yes. Pointers to functions also are used with menus. Based on a value returned from a menu, a pointer is set to an appropriate function.

Workshop

The Workshop provides quiz questions to help you solidify your understanding of the material covered and exercises to provide you with experience in using what you've learned.

Quiz

1. Write code that declares a type float variable, declares and initializes a pointer to the variable, and declares and initializes a pointer to the pointer.

2. Continuing with the example in question one, say that you want to use the pointer-to-pointer to assign the value 100 to the variable x. What, if anything, is wrong with the following assignment statement? If it is not correct, how should it be written?

```
*ppx = 100;
```

3. Assume that you have declared an array as follows:

```
int array[2][3][4];
```

What is the structure of this array, as seen by the C compiler?

4. Continuing with the array declared in question three, what does the expression array[0][0] mean?

5. Again using the array from question three, which of the following comparisons is true?

```
array[0][0] == &array[0][0][0];
array[0][1] == array[0][0][1];
array[0][1] == &array[0][1][0];
```

6. Write the prototype for a function that takes an array of pointers to type char as its one argument and returns void.

7. How would the function that you wrote a prototype for in question 6 "know" how many elements are in the array of pointers passed to it?

8. What is a pointer to a function?

9. Write a declaration of a pointer to a function that returns a type char and takes an array of pointers to type char as an argument.

10. You might have answered question nine with

    ```
    char *ptr(char *x[]);.
    ```

    What is wrong with this declaration?

Exercises

1. What do the following declare?

    a. `int *var1;`

    b. `int var2;`

    c. `int **var3;`

2. What do the following declare?

    a. `int a[3][12];`

    b. `int (*b)[12];`

    c. `int *c[12];`

3. What do the following declare?

    a. `char *z[10];`

    b. `char *y(int field);`

    c. `char (*x)(int field);`

4. Write a declaration for a pointer to a function that takes an integer as an argument and returns a type `float` variable.

5. Write a declaration for an array of pointers to functions. The functions should all take a character string as a parameter and return an integer. What could such an array be used for?

6. Write a statement to declare an array of ten pointers to type `char`.

7. **BUG BUSTER:** Is anything wrong with the following code?

    ```
    int x[3][12];
    int *ptr[12];
    ptr = x;
    ```

    Because of the many possible solutions, answers are not provided for the following exercises.

8. Write a program that declares a 12×12 array of characters. Place X's in every other element. Use a pointer to the array to print the values to the screen in a grid format.

9. Write a program that stores ten pointers to `double` variables. The program should accept the ten numbers from the user, sort them, and then print them to the screen. (See Listing 15.10.)

10. Modify the program in exercise nine to allow the user to determine whether the sort order is low-to-high or high-to-low.

Using Disk Files

Many of the programs you write use disk files for one purpose or another: data storage, configuration information, and so on. Today, you learn about

- Relating streams to disk files
- C's two disk file types
- Opening a file
- Writing data to a file
- Reading data from a file
- Closing a file
- Disk file management
- Using temporary files

Streams and Disk Files

As you learned on Day 14, "Working with the Screen, Printer, and Keyboard," C performs all input and output by means of streams. You saw how to use C's predefined streams that are connected to specific devices such as the keyboard, screen, and (on DOS systems) the printer. Disk file streams essentially work the same way—one of the advantages of stream input/output. The major difference with disk file streams is that your program must explicitly create a stream associated with a specific disk file.

Types of Disk Files

On Day 14, you saw that C streams come in two flavors: *text* and *binary*. You can associate either type of stream with a file, and it's important that you understand the distinction in order to use the proper mode for your files.

A *text stream* (or text-mode file) is a sequence of lines; each line contains zero or more characters and ends with one or more characters that signal *end-of-line*. Maximum line length is 255 characters. A "line" is not a string; there is no terminating \0. When you use a text-mode stream, translation occurs between C's newline character \n and whatever character(s) the operating system uses to mark end-of-line on disk files. On DOS systems, it's a carriage-return linefeed (CR-LF) combination. When data is written to a text-mode file, each \n is translated to a CR-LF; when data is read from a disk file, each CR-LF is translated to a \n. On UNIX systems, no translation is done—newline characters remain unchanged.

A *binary stream* (or binary mode file) is anything else. Any and all data is written and read unchanged. The null and end-of-line characters have no special significance.

Some file input/output functions are restricted to one file mode, whereas other functions can use either mode. This chapter teaches you which mode to use with which functions.

Filenames

You must use filenames when dealing with disk files. Filenames are stored in strings just as is other text data. The names are the same as those used by the operating system, and they must follow the same rules. In DOS, a complete filename consists of a 1- to 8-character name, optionally followed by a period and a 1- to 3-character extension. Note, however, that filename restrictions are system specific. For example, the new Windows 95 operating system, as well as most UNIX systems, permit filenames up to 256 characters long.

The characters allowed in a filename are the letters a–z, numerals 0–9, and certain other characters such as _, !, and $. A filename in a C program also can contain drive and directory information or both. Remember, DOS uses the backslash character to separate directory names. For example, to DOS, the name

```
c:\data\list.txt
```

refers to a file named LIST.TXT in the directory \DATA on drive C. You also know that the backslash character has a special meaning to C when it is in a string. To represent the backslash character itself, you must precede it by a backslash. Thus, in a C program, you represent the filename as follows:

```
char *filename = "c:\\data\\list.txt";
```

If you are entering a filename from the keyboard, however, enter only a single backslash.

Not all systems use the backslash as the directory separator. For example, UNIX uses the forward slash (/).

Opening a File for Use

The process of creating a stream linked to a disk file is called *opening* the file. When you open a file, it becomes available for reading (meaning that data is input from the file to the program), writing (meaning that data from the program is saved in the file), or both. When you're done using the file, you must close it. Closing a file is covered later in the chapter.

To open a file, you use the fopen() library function. The prototype of fopen() is located in STDIO.H and reads as follows:

```
FILE *fopen(const char *filename, const char *mode);
```

This prototype tells you that fopen() returns a pointer to type FILE, which is a structure declared in STDIO.H. The members of the FILE structure are used by the program in the various file access operations, but you don't need to be concerned about them. However, for each file that you want to open, you must declare a pointer to type FILE. When you call fopen(), that function creates an instance of the FILE structure and returns a pointer to that structure. You use this pointer in all subsequent operations on the file. If fopen() fails, it returns NULL.

The argument filename is the name of the file to be opened. As noted earlier, filename can contain drive and directory specifications. The filename argument can be a literal string enclosed in double quotation marks or a pointer to a string stored elsewhere in memory.

The argument mode specifies the mode in which to open the file. In this context, mode controls whether the file is binary or text and whether it is for reading, writing, or both. Possible values for mode are given in Table 16.1.

Table 16.1. Values of mode.

mode	Meaning
r	Open the file for reading. If the file does not exist, fopen() returns NULL.
w	Open the file for writing. If a file of the specified name does not exist, it is created. If the file already exists, existing data in the file is erased.
a	Open the file for appending. If a file of the specified name does not exist, it is created. If the file already exists, new data is appended at the end of the file.
r+	Open the file for reading and writing. If a file of the specified name does not exist, it is created. If the file already exists, new data is added at the start of the file, overwriting existing data.
w+	Open the file for reading and writing. If a file of the specified name does not exist, it is created. If the file already exists, it is overwritten.
a+	Open a file for reading and appending. If a file of the specified name does not exist, it is created. If the file already exists, new data is appended to the end of the file.

The default file mode is text. To open a file in binary mode, you append a b to the mode argument. Thus, a mode argument of a would open a text-mode file for appending, whereas ab would open a binary-mode file for appending.

Remember that fopen() returns NULL if an error occurs. Error conditions that can cause a return value of NULL include the following:

- Using an invalid filename.
- Trying to open a file on a disk that isn't ready (the drive door is not closed or the disk is not formatted, for example).
- Trying to open a file in a nonexistent directory or on a nonexistent disk drive.
- Trying to open a nonexistent file in mode r.

Whenever you use fopen(), you need to test for the occurrence of an error. There's no way to tell exactly which error occurred, but you can display a message to the user and try to open the file again; or you can end the program.

The program in Listing 16.1 demonstrates fopen().

Listing 16.1. Using fopen() to open disk files in various modes.

```
1: /* Demonstrates the fopen() function. */
2: #include <conio.h>
3: #include <stdio.h>
4:
5: main()
6: {
7:     FILE *fp;
8:     char ch, filename[40], mode[4];
9:
10:     while (1)
11:     {
12:
13:         /* Input filename and mode. */
14:
15:         printf("\nEnter a filename: ");
16:         gets(filename);
17:         printf("\nEnter a mode (max 3 characters): ");
18:         gets(mode);
19:
20:         /* Try to open the file. */
21:
22:         if ( (fp = fopen( filename, mode )) != NULL )
23:         {
24:             printf("\nSuccessful opening %s in mode %s.\n",
25:                     filename, mode);
26:             fclose(fp);
27:             puts("Enter x to exit, any other to continue.");
28:             if ( (ch = getch()) == 'x' )
29:                 break;
30:             else
31:                 continue;
32:         }
33:         else
34:         {
35:             fprintf(stderr, "\nError opening file %s in mode %s.\n",
36:                     filename, mode);
37:             puts("Enter x to exit, any other to try again.");
38:             if ( (ch = getch()) == 'x' )
39:                 break;
40:             else
41:                 continue;
42:         }
43:     }
44: }
```

```
Enter a filename: list1601.c

Enter a mode (max 3 characters): r

Successful opening list1601.c in mode r.
Enter x to exit, any other to continue.

Enter a filename: list1601.c

Enter a mode (max 3 characters): w

Successful opening list1601.c in mode w.
Enter x to exit, any other to continue.
```

The program prompts you for both the filename and the mode specifier on lines 15–18. After getting the names, line 22 attempts to open the file and assign its file pointer to fp. As an example of good programming practice, the if statement on line 22 checks to see that the opened file's pointer is not equal to NULL. If fp is not equal to NULL, a message stating that the open was successful and that the user can continue is printed. If the file pointer is NULL, the else condition of the if loop executes. The else condition on lines 33–42 prints a message stating there was a problem. It then prompts the user to determine whether the program should continue.

You can experiment with different names and modes to see which ones give you an error. If an error occurs, you are given the choice of entering the information again or quitting the program. To force an error, enter an invalid filename such as [ ].

Writing and Reading File Data

A program that uses a disk file can write data to a file, read data from a file, or do a combination of both. You can write data to a disk file in three ways:

- You can use formatted output to save formatted data to a file. You should use formatted output only with text-mode files. The primary use of formatted output is to create files containing text and numeric data to be read by other programs such as spreadsheets or databases. You rarely, if ever, use formatted output to create a file to be read again by a C program.

- You can use character output to save single characters or lines of characters to a file. Although technically it is possible to use character output with binary-mode files, it can be tricky. You should restrict character-mode output to text files. The main use for character output is to save text (but not numeric) data in a form that can be read by C, as well as other programs such as word processors.

- You can use direct output to save the contents of a section of memory directly to a disk file. This method is for binary files only. Direct output is the best way to save data for later use by a C program.

When you want to read data from a file, you have the same three options: formatted input, character input, or direct input. The type of input you use in a particular case depends almost entirely on the nature of the file being read.

The previous descriptions of the three types of file input and output suggest tasks best suited for each type of output. This is by no means a set of strict rules. The C language is very flexible (one of its advantages!), so a clever programmer can make any type of file output suit almost any need. As a beginning programmer, you might find things easier if you follow these guidelines, at least initially.

Formatted File Input and Output

Formatted file input/output deals with text and numeric data that is formatted in a specific way. It is directly analogous to formatted keyboard input and screen output done with the printf() and scanf() functions, as described on Day 14. Formatted output is discussed first, followed by input.

Formatted File Output

Formatted file output is done with the library function fprintf(). The prototype of fprintf() is in the header file STDIO.H and reads as follows:

```
int fprintf(FILE *fp, char *fmt, ...);
```

The first argument is a pointer to type FILE. To write data to a particular disk file, you pass the pointer that was returned when you opened the file with fopen().

The second argument is the format string. You've learned about format strings before, in the discussion of printf() on Day 14. The format string used by fprintf() follows exactly the same rules as for printf(). Please refer to Day 14 for details.

The final argument is ... What does that mean? In a function prototype, ellipses represent a variable number of arguments. In other words, in addition to the file pointer and the format string arguments, fprintf() takes zero, one, or more additional arguments. This is just like printf(). These arguments are the names of the variables to be output to the specified stream.

Remember, fprintf() works just like printf(), except it sends its output to the stream specified in the argument list. In fact, if you specify a stream argument of stdout, fprintf() is identical to printf().

The program in Listing 16.2 uses fprintf().

Listing 16.2. Demonstrating the equivalence of `fprintf()` formatted output both to a file and to `stdout`.

```
1: /* Demonstrates the fprintf() function. */
2: #include <stdlib.h>
3: #include <stdio.h>
4:
5: void clear_kb(void);
6:
7: main()
8: {
9:     FILE *fp;
10:    float data[5];
11:    int count;
12:    char filename[20];
13:
14:    puts("Enter 5 floating-point numerical values.");
15:
16:    for (count = 0; count < 5; count++)
17:        scanf("%f", &data[count]);
18:
19:    /* Get the filename and open the file. First clear stdin */
20:    /* of any extra characters. */
21:
22:    clear_kb();
23:
24:    puts("Enter a name for the file.");
25:    gets(filename);
26:
27:    if ( (fp = fopen(filename, "w")) == NULL)
28:    {
29:        fprintf(stderr, "Error opening file %s.", filename);
30:        exit(1);
31:    }
32:
33:    /* Write the numerical data to the file and to stdout. */
34:
35:    for (count = 0; count < 5; count++)
36:    {
37:        fprintf(fp, "\ndata[%d] = %f", count, data[count]);
38:        fprintf(stdout, "\ndata[%d] = %f", count, data[count]);
39:    }
40:
41:    fclose(fp);
42: }
43:
44: void clear_kb(void)
45: /* Clears stdin of any waiting characters. */
46: {
47:     char junk[80];
48:     gets(junk);
49: }
```

Input
Output

```
Enter 5 floating-point numerical values.
3.14159
9.99
1.50
3.
1000.0001
Enter a name for the file.
numbers.txt

data[0] = 3.141590
data[1] = 9.990000
data[2] = 1.500000
data[3] = 3.000000
data[4] = 1000.000122
```

You might wonder why the program displays 1000.000122 when the value you entered was 1000.0001. This is not an error in the program, but rather a normal consequence of the way that C stores numbers internally. Some floating-point values can not be stored exactly, so minor inaccuracies such as this one sometimes result.

This program uses fprintf() on lines 37 and 38 to send some formatted text and numeric data to stdout and a disk file. The only difference between the two lines is the first argument. After running the program, use your editor to look at the contents of the file. They should be an exact duplicate of the screen output.

Note that Listing 16.2 uses the clear_kb() function developed on Day 14. This is necessary to remove from stdin any extra characters that might be left over from the call to scanf(). If you don't clear stdin, these extra characters (specifically the newline) are read by the gets() that inputs the filename, and the result is a file creation error.

Formatted File Input

For formatted file input, use the fscanf() library function, which is used like scanf() (see Day 14) except that input comes from a specified stream instead of from stdin. The prototype for fscanf() is

```
int fscanf(FILE *fp, const char *fmt, ...);
```

The argument fp is the pointer to type FILE returned by fopen(), and fmt is a pointer to the format string that specifies how fscanf() is to read the input. The components of the format string are the same as for scanf(). Finally, the ellipses ... indicate one or more additional arguments, the addresses of the variables where fscanf() is to assign the input.

To use fscanf(), you might want to review the section on scanf() on Day 14. The function fscanf() works exactly the same as scanf(), except that characters are taken from the specified stream rather than from stdin.

To demonstrate fscanf(), you need a text file containing some numbers or strings in a format readable by the function. Use your editor to create a file named INPUT.TXT and enter five floating-point numbers with some spacing between them (spaces or newlines). For example, your file might look like this:

```
123.45     87.001
100.02
0.00456    1.0005
```

Now, compile and run the program in Listing 16.3.

Listing 16.3. Using `fscanf()` to read formatted data from a disk file.

```
1: /* Reading formatted file data with fscanf(). */
2: #include <stdlib.h>
3: #include <stdio.h>
4:
5: main()
6: {
7:     float f1, f2, f3, f4, f5;
8:     FILE *fp;
9:
10:    if ( (fp = fopen("INPUT.TXT", "r")) == NULL)
11:    {
12:        fprintf(stderr, "Error opening file.");
13:        exit(1);
14:    }
15:
16:    fscanf(fp, "%f %f %f %f %f", &f1, &f2, &f3, &f4, &f5);
17:    printf("The values are %f, %f, %f, %f, and %f.",
18:           f1, f2, f3, f4, f5);
19:
20:    fclose(fp);
21: }
```

```
The values are 123.45, 87.0001, 100.02, 0.00456, and 1.0005.
```

Note: Precision of the values might cause some numbers to not display as the exact values entered. For example, `100.02` might appear as `100.01999`.

This program reads the five values from the file you created and then displays them on the screen. The `fopen()` call on line 10 opens the file for read mode. It also checks to see that the file opened correctly. If the file was not opened, an error message is displayed on line 12, and the program exits (line 13). Line 16 demonstrates the use of the `fscanf()` function. With the exception of the first parameter, this is identical to `scanf()`, which you have been using throughout the book. The first parameter points to the file that you want the program to read.

You can do further experiments with fscanf(), creating input files with your programming editor and seeing how fscanf() reads the data.

Character Input and Output

When used with disk files, the term *character I/O* refers to single characters as well as lines of characters. Remember, a line is a sequence of zero or more characters terminated by the newline character. Use character I/O with text mode files. The sections that follow describe character input/output functions, and they are followed by a demonstration program.

Character Input

There are three character input functions: getc() and fgetc() for single characters, and fgets() for lines.

The *getc()* and *fgetc()* Functions

The functions getc() and fgetc() are identical and can be used interchangeably. They input a single character from the specified stream. The prototype of getc() is in STDIO.H.

```
int getc(FILE *fp);
```

The argument fp is the pointer returned by fopen() when the file was opened. The function returns the character input or EOF on error.

The *fgets()* Function

To read a line of characters from a file, use the fgets() library function. The prototype is

```
char *fgets(char *str, int n, FILE *fp);
```

The argument str is a pointer to a buffer in which the input is to be stored, n is the maximum number of characters to be input, and fp is the pointer to type FILE that was returned by fopen() when the file was opened.

When called, fgets() reads characters from fp into memory, starting at the location pointed to by str. Characters are read until a newline is encountered or n-1 characters have been read. By setting n equal to the number of bytes allocated for the buffer str, you prevent input from overwriting memory beyond allocated space. (The n-1 is to allow space for the terminating \0 that fgets() adds on.) If successful, fgets() returns str. Two types of errors can occur.

- If a read error or EOF is encountered before any characters have been assigned to str, NULL is returned and the memory pointed to by str is unchanged.

- If a read error or EOF is encountered after one or more characters have been assigned to str, NULL is returned, and the memory pointed to by str contains garbage.

You can see that fgets() does not necessarily input an entire line (that is, up to the next newline character). If n-1 characters are read before a newline is encountered, fgets() stops. The next read operation from the file starts where the last one leaves off. To be sure that fgets() reads in entire strings, stopping only at newlines, be sure that the size of your input buffer and the corresponding value of n passed to fgets() are large enough.

Character Output

You need to know about two character output functions, putc() and fputs().

The *putc()* Function

The library function putc() writes a single character to a specified stream. Its prototype, in STDIO.H, reads

```
int putc(int ch, FILE *fp);
```

The argument ch is the character to output. As with other character functions, it is formally called a type int, but only the lower-order byte is used. The argument fp is the pointer associated with the file (the pointer returned by fopen() when the file was opened). The function putc() returns the character just written if successful or EOF if an error occurs. The symbolic constant EOF is defined in STDIO.H, and it has the value −1. Because no "real" character has that numeric value, EOF can be used as an error indicator (with text-mode files only).

The *fputs()* Function

To write a line of characters to a stream, use the library function fputs(). This function works just like puts(), covered on Day 14. The only difference is that with fputs(), you can specify the output stream. Also, fputs() does not add a newline at the end of the string; you must explicitly include it, if desired. Its prototype in STDIO.H is

```
char fputs(char *str, FILE *fp);
```

The argument str is a pointer to the null-terminated string to be written, and fp is the pointer to type FILE returned by fopen() when the file was opened. The string pointed to by str is written to the file, minus its terminating \0. The function fputs() returns a non-negative value if successful, EOF on error.

Direct File Input and Output

You use direct file I/O most often when you save data to be read later by the same or a different C program. Direct I/O is used only with binary-mode files. With direct output, blocks of data are written from memory to disk. Direct input reverses the process: a block of data is read from a disk file into memory. For example, a single direct-output function call can write an entire array of type double to disk, and a single direct-input function call can read the entire array from disk back into memory. The direct I/O functions are fread() and fwrite().

The *fwrite()* Function

The fwrite() library function writes a block of data from memory to a binary-mode file. Its prototype, in STDIO.H, is

```
int fwrite(void *buf, int size, int count, FILE *fp);
```

The argument buf is a pointer to the region of memory holding the data to be written to the file. The pointer type is void; it can be a pointer to anything.

The argument size specifies the size, in bytes, of the individual data items, and count specifies the number of items to be written. For example, if you want to save a 100-element integer array, size would be 2 (because each int occupies 2 bytes), and count would be 100 (because the array contains 100 elements). To obtain the size argument, you can use the sizeof() operator.

The argument fp is, of course, the pointer to type FILE, returned by fopen() when the file was opened. The fwrite() function returns the number of items written on success; if the value returned is less than count, it means some error has occurred. To check for errors, you usually program fwrite() as follows:

```
if( (fwrite(buf, size, count, fp)) != count)
fprintf(stderr, "Error writing to file.");
```

Here are some examples of using fwrite(). To write a single type double variable x to a file, use the following:

```
fwrite(&x, sizeof(double), 1, fp);
```

To write an array data[] of 50 structures of type address to a file, you have two choices:

```
fwrite(data, sizeof(address), 50, fp);
```

```
fwrite(data, sizeof(data), 1, fp);
```

The first method writes the array as 50 elements, with each element having the size of a single type address structure. The second method treats the array as a single element. The two methods accomplish exactly the same thing.

The following section explains fread() and then presents a program demonstrating both commands.

The *fread()* Function

The fread() library function reads a block of data from a binary-mode file into memory. Its prototype in STDIO.H is

```
int fread(void *buf, int size, int count, FILE *fp);
```

The argument buf is a pointer to the region of memory that receives the data read from the file. As with fwrite(), the pointer type is void.

The argument size specifies the size, in bytes, of the individual data items being read, and count specifies the number of items to read, paralleling the arguments used by fwrite(). Again, the sizeof() operator is often used to provide the size argument. The argument fp is (as always) the pointer to type FILE that was returned by fopen() when the file was opened. The fread() function returns the number of items read; this can be less than count if end-of-file was reached or an error occurred.

The program in Listing 16.4 demonstrates the use of fwrite() and fread().

Listing 16.4. Using `fwrite()` and `fread()` for direct file access.

```
1: /* Direct file I/O with fwrite() and fread(). */
2: #include <stdlib.h>
3: #include <stdio.h>
4:
5: #define SIZE 20
6:
7: main()
8: {
9:     int count, array1[SIZE], array2[SIZE];
10:     FILE *fp;
11:
12:     /* Initialize array1[]. */
13:
14:     for (count = 0; count < SIZE; count++)
15:         array1[count] = 2 * count;
16:
17:     /* Open a binary mode file. */
18:
19:     if ( (fp = fopen("direct.txt", "wb")) == NULL)
20:     {
21:         fprintf(stderr, "Error opening file.");
22:         exit(1);
23:     }
24:     /* Save array1[] to the file. */
25:
26:     if (fwrite(array1, sizeof(int), SIZE, fp) != SIZE)
27:     {
28:         fprintf(stderr, "Error writing to file.");
29:         exit(1);
30:     }
31:
32:     fclose(fp);
33:
34:     /* Now open the same file for reading in binary mode. */
35:
36:     if ( (fp = fopen("direct.txt", "rb")) == NULL)
37:     {
```

```
38:            fprintf(stderr, "Error opening file.");
39:            exit(1);
40:        }
41:
42:        /* Read the data into array2[]. */
43:
44:        if (fread(array2, sizeof(int), SIZE, fp) != SIZE)
45:        {
46:            fprintf(stderr, "Error reading file.");
47:            exit(1);
48:        }
49:
50:        fclose(fp);
51:
52:        /* Now display both arrays to show they're the same. */
53:
54:        for (count = 0; count < SIZE; count++)
55:            printf("%d\t%d\n", array1[count], array2[count]);
56:
57:  }
```

```
0       0
2       2
4       4
6       6
8       8
10      10
12      12
14      14
16      16
18      18
20      20
22      22
24      24
26      26
28      28
30      30
32      32
34      34
36      36
38      38
```

Listing 16.4 demonstrates the use of the fwrite() and fread() functions. The program initializes an array on lines 14 and 15. It then uses fwrite() on line 26 to save the array to disk. The program uses fread() on line 44 to read the data into a different array. Finally, the program displays both arrays on the screen to show that they now hold the same data (lines 54 and 55).

When you save data with fwrite(), there's not much that can go wrong besides some type of disk error. With fread(), you need to be careful, however. As far as fread() is concerned, the data on the disk is just a sequence of bytes. The function has no way of knowing what it represents. For example, a block of 100 bytes could be 100 char variables, 50 int variables, 25 `long` variables, or 25 `float` variables. If you ask `fread()` to read that block into memory, it obediently does so. However, if the block was saved from an array of type `int` and you retrieve it into an array of type `float`, no error occurs but you get strange results. When writing programs, you must be sure that `fread()` is used properly, reading data into the appropriate types of variables and arrays. Notice that in Listing 16.4, all calls to `fopen()`, `fwrite()`, and `fread()` are checked to ensure that they worked correctly.

File Buffering Closing and Flushing Files

When you're done using a file, you should close it with the `fclose()` function. You saw `fclose()` used in programs presented earlier in the chapter. Its prototype is

```
int fclose(FILE *fp);
```

The argument `fp` is the `FILE` pointer associated with the stream; `fclose()` returns `0` on success or `-1` on error. When you close a file, the file's buffer is flushed (written to the file). You also can close all open streams except the standard ones (`stdin`, `stdout`, `stdprn`, `stderr`, and `stdaux`). Its prototype is

```
int fcloseall(void);
```

The function `fcloseall()` also flushes any stream buffers and returns the number of streams closed.

When a program terminates (either by reaching the end of `main()` or executing the `exit()` function), all streams are automatically flushed and closed. However, it's a good idea to close streams explicitly—particularly those linked to disk files—as soon as you are finished using them. The reason has to do with stream buffers.

When you create a stream linked to a disk file, a buffer is automatically created and associated with the stream. A *buffer* is a block of memory used for temporary storage of data being written to and read from the file.

Buffers are needed because disk drives are block-oriented devices, which means that they operate most efficiently when data is read and written in blocks of a certain size. The size of the ideal block differs depending on the specific hardware in use and is typically on the order of a few hundred to a thousand bytes. You don't need to be concerned about the exact block size, however.

The buffer associated with a file stream serves as an interface between the stream (which is character oriented) and the disk hardware (which is block oriented). As your program writes data to the stream, the data is saved in the buffer until the buffer is full, and then the entire contents of the buffer are written, as a block, to the disk. An analogous process occurs when reading data from a disk file. The creation and operation of the buffer is entirely automatic; you don't have to be concerned with it. (C does offer some functions for buffer manipulation, but they are beyond the scope of this book.)

In practical terms, this buffer operation means that during program execution, data that your program wrote to the disk might still be in the buffer, not on the disk. If your program hangs up, if there's a power failure, or if some other problem occurs, the data that's still in the buffer might be lost, and you won't know what is contained in the disk file.

You can flush a stream's buffers without closing it by using the `fflush()` or `flushall()` library functions. Use `fflush()` when you want a file's buffer written to disk while still using the file. Use `flushall()` to flush the buffers of all open streams. The prototypes of these two functions are as follows:

```
int fflush(FILE *fp);
```

```
int flushall(void);
```

The argument `fp` is the `FILE` pointer returned by `fopen()` when the file was opened. If a file was opened for writing, `fflush()` writes its buffer to disk. If the file was opened for reading, the buffer is cleared. The function `fflush()` returns 0 on success or `EOF` if an error occurred. The function `flushall()` returns the number of open streams.

DO	DON'T

DO open a file before trying to read or write to it.

DON'T assume that a file access is okay. Always check after doing a read, write, or open to ensure that the function worked.

DO use the `sizeof()` operator with the `fwrite()` and `fread()` functions.

DO close all files that you have opened.

DON'T use `fcloseall()` unless you have a reason to close all the streams.

Sequential Versus Random File Access

Every open file has a file position indicator associated with it. The position indicator specifies where read and write operations take place in the file. The position is always given in terms of bytes from the beginning of the file. When a new file is opened, the position indicator is always at the beginning of the file, position 0. (Because the file is new with a length of 0, there's no other location to indicate.) When an existing file is opened, the position indicator is at the end of the file if the file was opened in append mode, or at the beginning of the file if the file was opened in any other mode.

The file input/output functions covered earlier in this chapter make use of the position indicator. Writing and reading operations occur at the location of the position indicator and update the position indicator as well. For example, if you open a file for reading and read in 10 bytes, you input the first 10 bytes in the file (the bytes at positions 0 through 9). After the read operation, the position indicator is at position 10, and the next read operation begins there. Thus, if you want to read all the data in a file *sequentially* or sequentially write data to a file, you don't need to be concerned about the position indicator, because the stream I/O functions take care of it automatically.

When you need more control, use the C library functions that enable you to determine and change the value of the position indicator. By controlling the position indicator, you can perform *random* file access. Here, random means you can read data from, or write data to, any position in a file without reading or writing all the preceding data.

The *ftell()* and *rewind()* Functions

To set the position indicator to the beginning of the file, use the library function `rewind()`. Its prototype, in STDIO.H, is

```
void rewind(FILE *fp);
```

The argument `fp` is the `FILE` pointer associated with the stream. After calling `rewind()`, the position indicator for the file is set at the beginning of the file (byte 0). Use `rewind()` if you've read some data from a file and want to start reading from the beginning of the file again without closing and reopening the file.

To determine the value of a file's position indicator, use `ftell()`. This function's prototype, located in STDIO.H, reads

```
long ftell(FILE *fp);
```

The argument `fp` is the `FILE` pointer returned by `fopen()` when the file was opened. The function `ftell()` returns a `long` that gives the current file position in bytes from the start of the file (the first byte is at position 0). If an error occurs, `ftell()` returns `-1L` (a type `long` `-1`).

To get a feel for the operation of `rewind()` and `ftell()`, look at the program in Listing 16.5.

Type **Listing 16.5. Using `ftell()` and `rewind()`.**

```
1: /* Demonstrates ftell() and rewind(). */
2: #include <stdlib.h>
3: #include <stdio.h>
4:
5: #define BUFLEN 6
6:
7: char msg[] = "abcdefghijklmnopqrstuvwxyz";
8:
```

```
9: main()
10: {
11:     FILE *fp;
12:     char buf[BUFLEN];
13:
14:     if ( (fp = fopen("TEXT.TXT", "w")) == NULL)
15:     {
16:         fprintf(stderr, "Error opening file.");
17:         exit(1);
18:     }
19:
20:     if (fputs(msg, fp) == EOF)
21:     {
22:         fprintf(stderr, "Error writing to file.");
23:         exit(1);
24:     }
25:
26:     fclose(fp);
27:
28:     /* Now open the file for reading. */
29:
30:     if ( (fp = fopen("TEXT.TXT", "r")) == NULL)
31:     {
32:         fprintf(stderr, "Error opening file.");
33:         exit(1);
34:     }
35:     printf("\nImmediately after opening, position = %ld", ftell(fp));
36:
37:     /* Read in 5 characters. */
38:
39:     fgets(buf, BUFLEN, fp);
40:     printf("\nAfter reading in %s, position = %ld", buf, ftell(fp));
41:
42:     /* Read in the next 5 characters. */
43:
44:     fgets(buf, BUFLEN, fp);
45:     printf("\n\nThe next 5 characters are %s, and position now = %ld",
46:             buf, ftell(fp));
47:
48:     /* Rewind the stream. */
49:
50:     rewind(fp);
51:
52:     printf("\n\nAfter rewinding, the position is back at %ld",
53:             ftell(fp));
54:
55:     /* Read in 5 characters. */
56:
57:     fgets(buf, BUFLEN, fp);
58:     printf("\nand reading starts at the beginning again: %s", buf);
59:     fclose(fp);
60: }
```

399

```
Immediately after opening, position = 0
After reading in abcde, position = 5

The next 5 characters are fghij, and position now = 10

After rewinding, the position is back at 0
and reading starts at the beginning again: abcde
```

Analysis
This program writes a string, msg, to a file called TEXT.TXT. Lines 14–18 open TEXT.TXT for writing and test to ensure that the open was successful. Lines 20–24 write msg to the file using fputs() and again check to ensure that the write was successful. Line 26 closes the file with fclose(), completing the process of creating a file for the rest of the program to use.

Lines 30–34 open the file again, only this time for reading. Line 35 prints the return value of ftell(). Notice that this position is at the beginning of the file. Line 39 performs a gets() to read five characters. The five characters and the new file position are printed on line 40. Notice that ftell() returns the correct offset. Line 50 calls rewind() to put the pointer back to the beginning of the file, before line 52 prints the file position again. This should confirm for you that rewind() resets the position. An additional read on line 57 further confirms that the program is indeed back at the beginning of the file. Line 59 closes the file before ending the program.

The *fseek()* Function

More precise control over a stream's position indicator is possible with the fseek() library function. By using fseek(), you can set the position indicator anywhere in the file. The function prototype, in STDIO.H, is

```
int fseek(FILE *fp, long offset, int origin);
```

The argument fp is the FILE pointer associated with the file. The distance that the position indicator is to be moved is given by offset in bytes. The argument origin specifies the move's relative starting point. There can be three values for origin, with symbolic constants defined in IO.H, as shown in Table 16.2.

Table 16.2. Possible origin values for fseek().

Constant	Value	Meaning
SEEK_SET	0	Move the indicator offset bytes from the beginning of the file.
SEEK_CUR	1	Move the indicator offset bytes from its current position.
SEEK_END	2	Move the indicator offset bytes from the end of the file.

The function `fseek()` returns 0 if the indicator was successfully moved or nonzero if an error occurred. The program in Listing 16.6 uses `fseek()` for random file access.

Listing 16.6. Random file access with `fseek()`.

```
1: /* Random access with fseek(). */
2: #include <stdlib.h>
3: #include <stdio.h>
4: #include <io.h>
5:
6: #define MAX 50
7:
8: main()
9: {
10:     FILE *fp;
11:     int data, count, array[MAX];
12:     long offset;
13:
14:     /* Initialize the array. */
15:
16:     for (count = 0; count < MAX; count++)
17:         array[count] = count * 10;
18:
19:     /* Open a binary file for writing. */
20:
21:     if ( (fp = fopen("RANDOM.DAT", "wb")) == NULL)
22:     {
23:         fprintf(stderr, "\nError opening file.");
24:         exit(1);
25:     }
26:
27:     /* Write the array to the file, then close it. */
28:
29:     if ( (fwrite(array, sizeof(int), MAX, fp)) != MAX)
30:     {
31:         fprintf(stderr, "\nError writing data to file.");
32:         exit(1);
33:     }
34:
35:     fclose(fp);
36:
37:     /* Open the file for reading. */
38:
39:     if ( (fp = fopen("RANDOM.DAT", "rb")) == NULL)
40:     {
41:         fprintf(stderr, "\nError opening file.");
42:         exit(1);
43:     }
44:
45:     /* Ask user which element to read. Input the element */
46:     /* and display it, quitting when -1 is entered. */
47:
48:     while (1)
```

continues

Listing 16.6. continued

```
49:     {
50:         printf("\nEnter element to read, 0-%d, -1 to quit: ",MAX-1);
51:         scanf("%ld", &offset);
52:
53:         if (offset < 0)
54:             break;
55:         else if (offset > MAX-1)
56:             continue;
57:
58:         /* Move the position indicator to the specified element. */
59:
60:         if ( (fseek(fp, (offset*sizeof(int)), SEEK_SET)) != 0)
61:         {
62:             fprintf(stderr, "\nError using fseek().");
63:             exit(1);
64:         }
65:
66:         /* Read in a single integer. */
67:
68:         fread(&data, sizeof(int), 1, fp);
69:
70:         printf("\nElement %ld has value %d.", offset, data);
71:     }
72:
73:     fclose(fp);
74: }
```

Enter element to read, 0-49, -1 to quit: **5**

Element 5 has value 50.
Enter element to read, 0-49, -1 to quit: **6**

Element 6 has value 60.
Enter element to read, 0-49, -1 to quit: **49**

Element 49 has value 490.
Enter element to read, 0-49, -1 to quit: **1**

Element 1 has value 10.
Enter element to read, 0-49, -1 to quit: **0**

Element 0 has value 0.
Enter element to read, 0-49, -1 to quit: **-1**

Lines 14–35 are similar to the previous program. Lines 16 and 17 initialize an array called data with 50 type int values. Then the array is written to a binary file called RANDOM.DAT. You know it is binary because the file was opened with mode "wb" on line 21.

Line 39 reopens the file in binary read mode before going into an infinite while loop. The while loop prompts users to enter the number of the array element that they wish to read. Notice that lines 53–56 check to see that the entered element is within the range of the file. Does C let you read an element that was beyond the end of the file? Yes. Like going beyond the end of an array with values, C also lets you read beyond the end of a file. If you do read beyond the end (or before the beginning), your results are unpredictable. It is always best to check what you are doing (as lines 53–56 do in this listing).

After receiving the element to find, line 60 jumps to the appropriate offset with a call to `fseek()`. Because `SEEK_SET` is being used, the seek is done from the beginning of the file. Notice that the distance into the file is not just `offset`, but `offset` multiplied by the size of the elements being read. Line 68 then reads the value, and line 70 prints it.

Detecting the End of a File

At times you know exactly how long a file is, so there's no need to be able to detect the file's end. For example, if you used `fwrite()` to save a 100-element integer array, you know the file is 200 bytes long (assuming z-bite integers). At other times, however, you don't know how long the file is, but you still want to read data from the file, starting at the beginning and proceeding to the end. There are two ways to detect end-of-file.

When reading from a text-mode file character-by-character, you can look for the end-of-file character. The symbolic constant `EOF` is defined in STDIO.H as –1, a value never used by a "real" character. When a character input function reads `EOF` from a text-mode stream, you can be sure that you have reached the end of the file. For example, you could write the following:

```
while ( (c = fgetc( fp )) != EOF )
```

With a binary-mode stream, you cannot detect the end-of-file by looking for –1 because a byte of data from a binary stream could have that value, which would result in premature end of input. Instead, you can use the library function `feof()` (which can be used for both binary- and text-mode files):

```
int feof(FILE *fp);
```

The argument `fp` is the FILE pointer returned by `fopen()` when the file was opened. The function `feof()` returns 0 if the end of file `fp` has not been reached, or nonzero if end-of-file has been reached. If a call to `feof()` detects end-of-file, no further read operations are permitted until a `rewind()` has been done, `fseek()` is called, or the file is closed and reopened.

The program in Listing 16.7 demonstrates the use of `feof()`. When you are prompted for a filename, enter the name of any text file—one of your C source files, for example, or a header file such as STDIO.H. The program reads the file one line at a time, displaying each line on `stdout`, until `feof()` detects end-of-file.

Type Listing 16.7. Using `feof()` to detect the end of a file.

```c
1: /* Detecting end-of-file. */
2: #include <stdlib.h>
3: #include <stdio.h>
4:
5: #define BUFSIZE 100
6:
7: main()
8: {
9:      char buf[BUFSIZE];
10:     char filename[20];
11:     FILE *fp;
12:
13:     puts("Enter name of text file to display: ");
14:     gets(filename);
15:
16:     /* Open the file for reading. */
17:     if ( (fp = fopen(filename, "r")) == NULL)
18:     {
19:         fprintf(stderr, "Error opening file.");
20:         exit(1);
21:     }
22:
23:     /* If end of file not reached, read a line and display it. */
24:
25:     while ( !feof(fp) )
26:     {
27:         fgets(buf, BUFSIZE, fp);
28:         printf("%s",buf);
29:     }
30:
31:     fclose(fp);
32: }
```

Input/Output

```
Enter name of text file to display:
list1607.c
/* Detecting end-of-file. */
#include <stdlib.h>
#include <stdio.h>

#define BUFSIZE 100

main()
{
char buf[BUFSIZE];
char filename[20];
FILE *fp;

puts("Enter name of text file to display: ");
gets(filename);

/* Open the file for reading. */
if ( (fp = fopen(filename, "r")) == NULL)
{
```

16

```
fprintf(stderr, "Error opening file.");
exit(1);
}

/* If end of file not reached, read a line and display it. */

while ( !feof(fp) )
{
fgets(buf, BUFSIZE, fp);
printf("%s",buf);
}

fclose(fp);
}
```

The `while` loop in this program (lines 25–29) is typical of a `while` used in more complex programs that do sequential processing. As long as you are not at the end of the file, you execute the lines within the `while` statement (lines 27 and 28). When the `feof()` returns a nonzero value, the loop ends, the file is closed, and the program ends.

DO	DON'T

DO check your position within a file so that you do not read beyond the end or before the beginning of a file.

DO use either `rewind()` or `fseek( fp, SEEK_SET, 0 )` to reset the file position to the beginning of the file.

DO use `feof()` to check for the end of the file when working with binary files.

DON'T use `EOF` with binary files.

File-Management Functions

The term *file management* refers to dealing with existing files—not reading from or writing to them, but erasing, renaming, and copying them. The C standard library contains functions for erasing and renaming files, and you also can write your own file-copying function.

Erasing a File

To erase a file, you use the library function `remove()`. Its prototype is in STDIO.H, as follows:

```
int remove( const char *filename );
```

The variable `*filename` is a pointer to the name of the file to be erased. (See the section on filenames earlier in this chapter.) The specified file must not be open. If the file exists, it is erased (just as if you used the DEL command from the DOS prompt or the rm command in UNIX) and remove() returns 0. If the file does not exist, is read-only, or some other error occurs, remove() returns -1.

The short program in Listing 16.8 demonstrates the use of remove(). Be careful—if you remove a file, it's gone forever.

Type

Listing 16.8. Using the function `remove()` to delete a disk file.

```
 1: /* Demonstrates the remove() function. */
 2:
 3: #include <stdio.h>
 4:
 5: main()
 6: {
 7:     char filename[80];
 8:
 9:     printf("Enter the filename to delete: ");
10:      gets(filename);
11:
12:     if ( remove(filename) == 0)
13:         printf("The file %s has been deleted.", filename);
14:     else
15:         fprintf(stderr, "Error deleting the file %s.", filename);
16: }
```

```
C:>list1608
Enter the filename to delete: *.bak
Error deleting the file *.bak.

C:>list1608
Enter the filename to delete: list1414.bak
The file list1414.bak has been deleted.
```

This program prompts the user on line 9 for the name of the file to be deleted. Line 12 then calls remove() to erase the entered file. If the return value is 0, the file was removed, and a message is displayed stating this. If the return value is not zero, an error occurred and the file was not removed.

Renaming a File

The rename() function changes the name of an existing disk file. The function prototype is in STDIO.H as follows:

```
int rename( const char *oldname, const char *newname );
```

The filenames pointed to by oldname and newname follow the rules given earlier in this chapter. The only restriction is that both names must refer to the same disk drive; you cannot rename a file to a different disk drive. The function rename() returns 0 on success, or -1 if an error occurs.

Errors can be caused by the following conditions (among others):

- The file oldname does not exist.
- A file with the name newname already exists.
- You try to rename to another disk.

The program in Listing 16.9 demonstrates the use of rename().

Listing 16.9. Using rename() to change the name of a disk file.

```
1: /* Using rename() to change a filename. */
2:
3: #include <stdio.h>
4:
5: main()
6: {
7:     char oldname[80], newname[80];
8:
9:     printf("Enter current filename: ");
10:     gets(oldname);
11:     printf("Enter new name for file: ");
12:     gets(newname);
13:
14:     if ( rename( oldname, newname ) == 0 )
15:         printf("%s has been renamed %s.", oldname, newname);
16:     else
17:         fprintf(stderr, "An error has occurred renaming %s.",
18:                     oldname);
18: }
```

```
Enter current filename: list1609.c
Enter new name for file: rename.c
list1609.exe has been renamed rname.exe.
```

Listing 16.9 shows how powerful C can be. With only 18 lines of code, this program replaces a DOS command, and it's a much more friendly function. Line 9 prompts for the name of the file to be renamed. Line 11 prompts for the new filename. The call to the rename() function is wrapped in an if statement on line 14. The if statement checks to ensure that the renaming of the file occurred correctly. If so, line 15 prints an affirmative message; otherwise line 17 prints a message stating that there was an error.

Copying a File

It's frequently necessary to make a copy of a file—an exact duplicate with a different name (or with the same name but in a different drive or directory). In DOS, this is done with the COPY command. How do you copy a file in C? There's no library function available, so you need to write your own.

This might sound a bit complicated to you, but it's really quite simple thanks to C's use of streams for input and output. Here's the approach you take:

1. Open the source file for reading in binary mode (using binary mode ensures that the function can copy all sorts of files, not just text files).

2. Open the destination file for writing in binary mode.

3. Read a character from the source file. Remember, when a file is first opened, the pointer is at the start of the file, so there's no need to position the file pointer explicitly.

4. Does the function feof() indicate that you've reached the end of the source file? If so, you're done and can close both files and return to the calling program.

5. If you haven't reached end-of-file, write the character to the destination file, and then loop back to step three.

The program in Listing 16.10 contains a function, copy_file(), which is passed the names of the source and destination files, and then performs the copy operation as the previous scheme outlined. If there's an error opening either file, the function does not attempt the copy and returns -1 to the calling program. When the copy operation is complete, the program closes both files and returns 0.

Type   **Listing 16.10. A function that copies a file.**

```
1: /* Copying a file. */
2:
3: #include <stdio.h>
4:
5: int file_copy( char *oldname, char *newname );
6:
7: main()
8: {
9:     char source[80], destination[80];
10:
11:     /* Get the source and destination names. */
12:
13:     printf("\nEnter source file: ");
14:     gets(source);
15:     printf("\nEnter destination file: ");
16:     gets(destination);
17:
18:     if ( file_copy( source, destination ) == 0 )
19:         puts("Copy operation successful");
20:     else
21:         fprintf(stderr, "Error during copy operation");
22: }
23:
24: int file_copy( char *oldname, char *newname )
25: {
26:     FILE *fold, *fnew;
27:     int c;
```

```
28:
29:     /* Open the source file for reading in binary mode. */
30:
31:     if ( ( fold = fopen( oldname, "rb" ) ) == NULL )
32:         return -1;
33:
34:     /* Open the destination file for writing in binary mode. */
35:
36:     if ( ( fnew = fopen( newname, "wb" ) ) == NULL  )
37:     {
38:         fclose ( fold );
39:         return -1;
40:     }
41:
42:     /* Read one byte at a time from the source; if end of file */
43:     /* has not been reached, write the byte to the */
44:     /* destination. */
45:
46:     while (1)
47:     {
48:         c = fgetc( fold );
49:
50:         if ( !feof( fold ) )
51:             fputc( c, fnew );
52:         else
53:             break;
54:     }
55:
56:     fclose ( fnew );
57:     fclose ( fold );
58:
59:     return 0;
60: }
```

Enter source file: **list1610.c**

Enter destination file: **tmpfile.c**
Copy operation successful

Analysis The function copy_file() works perfectly well, permitting you to copy anything from a small text file to a huge program file. It does have limitations, however. If the destination file already exists, the function erases it without asking. A good programming exercise for you would be to modify copy_file() to check whether the destination file already exists, and then query the user whether the old file should be overwritten.

main() in Listing 16.10 should look very familiar. It is nearly identical to main() in Listing 16.9 with the exception of line 14. Instead of rename(), this function uses copy(). Because C does not have a copy function, lines 24–60 create a copy function. Lines 31–32 open the source file, fold, in binary read mode. Lines 36–40 open the destination file, fnew, in binary write mode. Notice line 38 closes the source file if there is an error opening the destination file. The while loop in lines 46–54 does the actual copying of the file. Line 48 gets a character from the source file, fold. Line 50 checks to see whether the end-of-file marker was read. If the end of the file has been reached, a `break` statement is executed in order to get out of the `while` loop. If the end of the file has not been reached, the character is written to the destination file, `fnew`. Lines 56 and 57 close the two files before returning to `main()`.

Using Temporary Files

Some programs make use of one or more temporary files during execution. A *temporary file* is a file that is created by the program, used for some purpose during program execution, and then deleted before the program terminates. When you create a temporary file, you don't really care what its name is because it gets deleted. All that is necessary is that you use a name that is not already in use for another file. The C standard library includes a function `tmpnam()` that creates a valid filename that does not conflict with any existing file. Its prototype in STDIO.H reads as follows:

```
char *tmpnam(char *s);
```

The argument `s` must be a pointer to a buffer large enough to hold the filename. You also can pass a null pointer (`NULL`), in which case the temporary name is stored in a buffer internal to `tmpnam()`, and the function returns a pointer to that buffer. The program in Listing 16.11 demonstrates both methods of using `tmpnam()` to create temporary filenames.

Type

Listing 16.11. Using `tmpnam()` to create temporary filenames.

```
 1: /* Demonstration of temporary filenames. */
 2:
 3: #include <stdio.h>
 4:
 5: main()
 6: {
 7:     char buffer[10], *c;
 8:
 9:     /* Get a temporary name in the defined buffer. */
10:
11:     tmpnam(buffer);
12:
13:     /* Get another name, this time in the function's */
14:     /* internal buffer. */
15:
16:     c = tmpnam(NULL);
17:
18:     /* Display the names. */
19:
20:     printf("Temporary name 1: %s", buffer);
21:     printf("\nTemporary name 2: %s", c);
22: }
```

Output

```
Temporary name 1: TMP1.$$$
Temporary name 2: TMP2.$$$
```

410

Analysis The temporary names generated on your system will likely be different from these. This program only generates and prints the temporary names. Line 11 stores a temporary name in the character array, buffer. Line 16 assigns the character pointer to the name returned by tmpnam() to c. Your program would have to use the generated name to open the temporary file, and then delete the file before program execution terminates.

```
char tempname[80];
FILE *tmpfile;
tmpnam(tempname);
tmpfile = fopen(tempname, "w");   /* Use appropriate mode */

fclose(tmpfile);
remove(tempname);
```

DO	DON'T

DON'T remove a file that you might need again.

DON'T try to rename files across drives.

DON'T forget to remove temporary files that you create. They are not automatically deleted.

Summary

In this chapter, you learned how C programs can use disk files. C treats a disk file like a stream, a sequence of characters, just like the predefined streams you learned about on Day 14. A stream associated with a disk file must be opened before it can be used, and it must be closed after use. A disk file stream can be opened in either text or binary mode.

After a disk file has been opened, you can read data from the file into your program, write data from the program to the file, or both. There are three general types of file I/O: formatted, character, and direct. Each type of I/O is best used for certain types of data storage and retrieval tasks.

Each open disk file has a file position indicator associated with it. This indicator specifies the position in the file, measured as the number of bytes from the start of the file, where subsequent read and write operations occur. With some types of file access, the position indicator is updated automatically, and you don't have to be concerned with it. For random file access, the C standard library provides functions for manipulating the position indicator.

Finally, C provides some rudimentary file management functions, enabling you to delete and rename disk files. In this chapter, you developed your own function for copying a file.

Q&A

Q Can I use drives and paths with filenames when using erase(), rename(), fopen(), and the other file functions?

A Yes. You can use full filenames with paths and drives or just the filename by itself. If you use the filename by itself, the function looks for the file in the current directory. Remember, when using backslashes, you need to use the escape sequences. Remember also that UNIX uses the forward slash (/) as a directory separator.

Q Can I read beyond the end of a file?

A Yes. You also can read before the beginning of a file. Results from such reads can be disastrous. Reading files is just like working with arrays. You are looking at offsets within memory. If you are using fseek(), you should check to make sure that you do not go beyond the end of the file.

Q What happens if I don't close a file?

A It is good programming practice to close any files that you open. By default, the file should be closed when the program exits; however, you should never count on this. If the file isn't closed, you might not be able to access it later because the operating system will think that the file is already in use.

Q How many files can I open at once?

A This question cannot be answered with a simple number. The limitation on the number of files that can be opened is based on variables set within your operating system. On DOS systems, an environment variable called FILES determines the number of files that can be opened (this variable includes programs that are running, too). Consult your operating system manuals for more information.

Q Can I read a file sequentially with random access functions?

A When reading a file sequentially, there is no need to use such functions as fseek(). Because the file pointer is left at the last position it occupied, it is always where you want it for sequential reads. You can use fseek() to read a file sequentially; however, you gain nothing.

Workshop

The Workshop provides quiz questions to help you solidify your understanding of the material covered and exercises to provide you with experience in using what you've learned.

Quiz

1. What is the difference between a text-mode stream and a binary stream?

2. What must your program do before it can access a disk file?

3. When you open a file with fopen(), what information must you specify and what does the function return?

4. What are the three general methods of file access?

5. What are the two general methods of reading a file's information?

6. What is the value of EOF?

7. When is EOF used?

8. How do you detect the end of a file in text and binary modes?

9. What is the file position indicator, and how can you modify it?

10. When a file is first opened, where is the file position indicator pointing to? (If unsure, see Listing 16.5.)

Exercises

1. Write the code to close all file streams.

2. Show two different ways to reset the file position pointer to the beginning of the file.

3. **BUG BUSTER:** Is anything wrong with the following?

```
FILE *fp;
int c;

if ( ( fp = fopen( oldname, "rb" ) ) == NULL )
    return -1;

while (( c = fgetc( fp)) != EOF )
    fprintf( stdout, "%c", c );

fclose ( fp );
```

Because of the many possible solutions, answers are not provided for exercises 4–10 .

4. Write a program that displays a file to the screen.

5. Write a program that opens a file and prints it to the printer (stdprn). The program should print only 55 lines per page.

6. Modify the program in exercise five to print headings on each page. The headings should contain the filename and the page number.

7. Write a program that opens a file and counts the number of characters. The program should print the number of characters when finished.

8. Write a program that opens an existing text file and copies it to a new text file with all lowercase letters changed to uppercase, and all other characters unchanged.

9. Write a program that opens any disk file, reads it in 128-byte blocks, and displays the contents of each block on the screen in both hexadecimal and ASCII formats.

10. Write a function that opens a new temporary file with a specified mode. All temporary files created by this function should automatically be closed and deleted when the program terminates. (Hint: Use the `atexit()` library function.)

Manipulating
Strings

Text data, which C stores in strings, is an important part of many programs. So far, you have learned how to input and output strings and how your program stores them. C offers a variety of functions for other types of string manipulations as well. Today, you learn

- How to determine the length of a string
- How to copy and join strings
- Functions that compare strings
- How to search strings
- How to convert strings
- How to test characters

String Length and Storage

You should remember from earlier chapters that in C programs, a string is a sequence of characters, with its beginning indicated by a pointer and its end marked by the null character \0. At times, you need to know the length of a string (the number of characters between the start and the end of the string). This is done with the library function strlen(). Its prototype, in STRING.H, is

```
size_t strlen(char *str);
```

You might be puzzling over the size_t return type. This is defined in STRING.H as unsigned, so the function strlen() returns an unsigned integer. The size_t type is used with many of the string functions. Just remember that it means unsigned.

The argument passed to strlen is a pointer to the string the length of which you want to know. The function strlen() returns the number of characters between str and the next null character, not counting the null character. The program in Listing 17.1 demonstrates strlen().

 Listing 17.1. Using the strlen() function to determine the length of a string.

```
1: /* Using the strlen() function. */
2:
3: #include <stdio.h>
4: #include <string.h>
5:
6: main()
7: {
8:     size_t length;
9:     char buf[80];
10:
11:     while (1)
12:     {
13:         puts("\nEnter a line of text; a blank line terminates.");
```

```
14:        gets(buf);
15:
16:        length = strlen(buf);
17:
18:        if (length != 0)
19:            printf("\nThat line is %u characters long.",
length);
20:        else
21:            break;
22:    }
23: }
```

Enter a line of text; a blank line terminates.
Just do it!

That line is 11 characters long.
Enter a line of text; a blank line terminates.

This program does little more than demonstrate the use of strlen(). Lines 13 and 14 display a message and get a string called buf. Line 16 uses strlen() to assign the length of buf to the variable length. Line 18 checks whether the string was blank by checking for a length of zero. If the string wasn't blank, line 19 prints the string's size.

Copying Strings

The C library has three functions for copying strings. Because of the way C handles strings, you cannot simply assign one string to another, as you can in other computer languages. You must copy the source string from its location in memory to the memory location of the destination string. The string-copying functions are strcpy(), strncpy(), and strdup(). All of the string-copying functions require the header file STRING.H.

The *strcpy()* Function

The library function strcpy() copies an entire string to another memory location. Its prototype is as follows:

```
char *strcpy( char *destination, char *source );
```

The function strcpy() copies the string (including the terminating null character \0) pointed to by source to the location pointed to by destination. The return value is a pointer to the new string, destination.

When using strcpy(), you must allocate storage space for the destination string first. The function has no way of knowing whether destination points to allocated space; if space has not been allocated, the function overwrites strlen(source) bytes of memory, starting at destination. The use of strcpy() is illustrated in Listing 17.2.

Note: When a program uses `malloc()` to allocate memory, as Listing 17.2 does, good programming practice requires the use of the `free()` function to free up the memory once the program is finished with it. You'll learn about `free()` on Day 20, "Working with Memory."

 Listing 17.2. Before using `strcpy()`, you must allocate storage space for the destination string.

```
1: /* Demonstrates strcpy(). */
2: #include <stdlib.h>
3: #include <stdio.h>
4: #include <string.h>
5:
6: char source[] = "The source string.";
7:
8: main()
9: {
10:     char dest1[80];
11:     char *dest2, *dest3;
12:
13:     printf("\nsource: %s", source );
14:
15:     /* Copy to dest1 is okay because dest1 points to */
16:     /* 80 bytes of allocated space. */
17:
18:     strcpy(dest1, source);
19:     printf("\ndest1:  %s", dest1);
20:
21:     /* To copy to dest2 you must allocate space. */
22:
23:     dest2 = (char *)malloc(strlen(source) +1);
24:     strcpy(dest2, source);
25:     printf("\ndest2:  %s", dest2);
26:
27:     /* Copying without allocating destination space is a no-no. */
28:     /* The following could cause serious problems. */
29:
30:     /* strcpy(dest3, source); */
31: }
```

```
source: The source string.
dest1:  The source string.
dest2:  The source string.
```

 This program demonstrates copying strings to both character arrays such as `dest1` (declared on line 10) and character pointers such as `dest2` (declared along with `dest3` on line 11). Line 13 prints the original source string. This string is then copied to `dest1` with `strcpy()` on line 18. Line 24 copies source to `dest2`. Both `dest1` and `dest2` are printed to show that the function was successful. Notice that line 23 allocates the appropriate amount of space for dest2 with the malloc() function. If you copy a string to a character pointer that has not been allocated memory, you get unpredictable results.

The *strncpy()* Function

The strncpy() function is similar to strcpy(), except that strncpy() enables you to specify how many characters to copy. Its prototype is

```
char *strncpy(char *destination, char *source, size_t n);
```

The arguments destination and source are pointers to the destination and source strings. The function copies, at most, the first n characters of source to destination. If source is shorter than n characters, enough null characters are added at the end of source to make a total of n characters copied to destination. If source is longer than n characters, no terminating \0 is added to destination. The function's return value is destination.

The program in Listing 17.3 demonstrates the use of strncpy().

Type   **Listing 17.3. The strncpy function.**

```
1: /* Using the strncpy() function. */
2:
3: #include <stdio.h>
4: #include <string.h>
5:
6: char dest[] = ".........................";
7: char source[] = "abcdefghijklmnopqrstuvwxyz";
8:
9: main()
10: {
11:     size_t n;
12:
13:     while (1)
14:     {
15:         puts("Enter the number of characters to copy (1-26)");
16:         scanf("%d", &n);
17:
18:         if (n > 0 && n< 27)
19:             break;
20:     }
21:
22:     printf("\nBefore strncpy destination = %s", dest);
23:
24:     strncpy(dest, source, n);
25:
26:     printf("\nAfter strncpy destination = %s", dest);
27: }
```

```
Enter the number of characters to copy (1-26)
15

Before strncpy destination = ........................
After strncpy destination = abcdefghijklmno..........
```

This program demonstrates the `strncpy()` function and an effective way to ensure that only correct information is entered. Lines 13–20 contain a `while` loop that prompts the user for a number from 1–26. The loop continues until a valid value is entered. When a number from 1–26 is entered, line 22 prints the value of `dest`, line 24 copies the number of characters decided by the user, and line 26 prints the result.

The *strdup()* Function

The library function `strdup()` is similar to `strcpy()`, except that `strdup()` performs its own memory allocation for the destination string with a call to `malloc()`. In effect, it does what you did in Listing 17.2, allocating space with `malloc()` and then calling `strcpy()`. The prototype for `strdup()` is

```
char *strdup( char *source );
```

The argument source is a pointer to the source string. The function returns a pointer to the destination string—the space allocated by `malloc()`—or `NULL` if the needed memory could not be allocated. Listing 17.4 demonstrates the use of `strdup()`. Note that `strdup()` is not an ANSI-standard function. It is included in the Microsoft, Borland, and Symantec C libraries, but might not be present (or might be different) in other C compilers.

Listing 17.4. Using `strdup()` to copy a string with automatic memory allocation.

```
1: /* The strdup() function. */
2: #include <stdlib.h>
3: #include <stdio.h>
4: #include <string.h>
5:
6: char source[] = "The source string.";
7:
8: main()
9: {
10:     char *dest;
11:
12:     if ( (dest = strdup(source)) == NULL)
13:     {
14:         fprintf(stderr, "Error allocating memory.");
15:         exit(1);
16:     }
17:
18:     printf("The destination = %s", dest);
19: }
```

Output

```
The destination = The source string.
```

Analysis

In this listing, strdup() allocates the appropriate memory for dest. It then makes a copy of the passed string, source. Line 18 prints the duplicated string.

Concatenating Strings

If you're not familiar with the term *concatenation,* you might be asking yourself, "What is it?" and "Is it legal?" Well, it means to join two strings—to tack one string onto the end of another—and in most states, it is legal. The C standard library contains two string concatenation functions, strcat() and strncat(), both of which require the header file STRING.H.

The *strcat()* Function

The prototype of strcat() is

```
char *strcat(char *str1, char *str2);
```

The function appends a copy of str2 onto the end of str1, moving the terminating null character to the end of the new string. You must allocate enough space for str1 to hold the resulting string. The return value of strcat() is a pointer to str1. The program in Listing 17.5 demonstrates strcat().

Type

Listing 17.5. Using strcat() to concatenate strings.

```
1: /* The strcat() function. */
2:
3: #include <stdio.h>
4: #include <string.h>
5:
6: char str1[27] = "a";
7: char str2[2];
8:
9: main()
10: {
11:     int n;
12:
13:     /* Put a null character at the end of str2[]. */
14:
15:     str2[1] = '\0';
16:
17:     for (n = 98; n< 123; n++)
18:     {
19:         str2[0] = n;
20:         strcat(str1, str2);
21:         puts(str1);
22:     }
23: }
```

Output

```
ab
abc
abcd
abcde
abcdef
abcdefg
abcdefgh
abcdefghi
abcdefghij
abcdefghijk
abcdefghijkl
abcdefghijklm
abcdefghijklmn
abcdefghijklmno
abcdefghijklmnop
abcdefghijklmnopq
abcdefghijklmnopqr
abcdefghijklmnopqrs
abcdefghijklmnopqrst
abcdefghijklmnopqrstu
abcdefghijklmnopqrstuv
abcdefghijklmnopqrstuvw
abcdefghijklmnopqrstuvwx
abcdefghijklmnopqrstuvwxy
abcdefghijklmnopqrstuvwxyz
```

Analysis

The ASCII codes for the letters *b–z* are 98–122. This program uses these ASCII codes in its demonstration of `strcat()`. The `for` loop on lines 17–22 assigns these values in turn to `str2[0]`. Because `str2[1]` is already the null character (line 15), the effect is to assign the strings `"b"`, `"c"`, and so on to `str2`. Each of these strings is concatenated with `str1` (line 20) and `str1` displayed on the screen (line 21).

The *strncat()* Function

The library function `strncat()` also performs string concatenation, but it enables you to specify how many characters of the source string are appended to the end of the destination string. The prototype is

```
char *strncat(char *str1, char *str2, size_t n);
```

If `str2` contains more than `n` characters, the first `n` characters are appended to the end of `str1`. If `str2` contains fewer than `n` characters, all of `str2` is appended to the end of `str1`. In either case, a terminating null character is added. You must allocate enough space for `str1` to hold the resulting string. The function returns a pointer to `str1`. The program in Listing 17.6 uses `strncat()` to produce the same output as Listing 17.5.

Listing 17.6. Using the `strncat()` function to concatenate strings.

```c
1: /* The strncat() function. */
2:
3: #include <stdio.h>
4: #include <string.h>
5:
6: char str2[] = "abcdefghijklmnopqrstuvwxyz";
7:
8: main()
9: {
10:     char str1[27];
11:     int n;
12:
13:     for (n=1; n< 27; n++)
14:     {
15:         strcpy(str1, "");
16:         strncat(str1, str2, n);
17:         puts(str1);
18:     }
19: }
```

```
a
ab
abc
abcd
abcde
abcdef
abcdefg
abcdefgh
abcdefghi
abcdefghij
abcdefghijk
abcdefghijkl
abcdefghijklm
abcdefghijklmn
abcdefghijklmno
abcdefghijklmnop
abcdefghijklmnopq
abcdefghijklmnopqr
abcdefghijklmnopqrs
abcdefghijklmnopqrst
abcdefghijklmnopqrstu
abcdefghijklmnopqrstuv
abcdefghijklmnopqrstuvw
abcdefghijklmnopqrstuvwx
abcdefghijklmnopqrstuvwxy
abcdefghijklmnopqrstuvwxyz
```

17

Analysis You might wonder about the purpose of line 15, `strcpy(str1, "");`. This line copies an empty string consisting of only a single null character to `str1`. The result is that the first character in `str1`, `str1[0]`, is set equal to 0 (the null character). The same thing could have been accomplished with the statement `str1[0] = 0;` or `str1[0] = '\0';`.

Comparing Strings

Strings are compared to determine whether they are equal or unequal. If they are unequal, one string is "greater than" or "less than" the other. Determinations of "greater" and "less" are made with the ASCII codes of the characters. In the case of letters, this is equivalent to alphabetical order. The C library contains functions for three types of string comparisons: comparing two entire strings, comparing two strings without regard to the case of the characters, and comparing a certain number of characters in two strings. Because these three functions are not ANSI standard, not all compilers treat them the same way.

Comparing Two Strings

The function `strcmp()` compares two strings, character by character. Its prototype is

```
int strcmp(char *str1, char *str2);
```

The arguments `str1` and `str2` are pointers to the strings being compared. The function's return values are given in Table 17.1. The program in Listing 17.7 demonstrates `strcmp()`.

Table 17.1. The values returned by `strcmp()`.

Return Value	Meaning
< 0	str1 is less than str2.
0	str1 is equal to str2.
> 0	str1 is greater than str2.

Type **Listing 17.7. Using `strcmp()` to compare strings.**

```
 1: /* The strcmp() function. */
 2:
 3: #include <stdio.h>
 4: #include <string.h>
 5:
 6: main()
 7: {
 8:     char str1[80], str2[80];
 9:     int x;
10:
```

```
11:     while (1)
12:     {
13:
14:         /* Input two strings. */
15:
16:         printf("\n\nInput the first string, a blank to exit: ");
17:         gets(str1);
18:
19:         if ( strlen(str1) == 0 )
20:             break;
21:
22:         printf("\nInput the second string: ");
23:         gets(str2);
24:
25:         /* Compare them and display the result. */
26:
27:         x = strcmp(str1, str2);
28:
29:         printf("\nstrcmp(%s,%s) returns %d", str1, str2, x);
30:     }
31:}
```

**Input
Output**

```
Input the first string, a blank to exit: First string

Input the second string: Second string

strcmp(First string,Second string) returns -13

Input the first string, a blank to exit: test string

Input the second string: test string

strcmp(test string,test string) returns 0

Input the first string, a blank to exit: zebra

Input the second string: aardvark

strcmp(zebra,aardvark) returns 25

Input the first string, a blank to exit:
```

Analysis
The program in Listing 17.7 demonstrates strcmp(), prompting the user for two strings (lines 16, 17, 22, and 23) and displaying the result returned by strcmp() on line 29. Experiment with this program to get a feel for how strcmp() compares strings. Try entering two strings that are identical except for case, such as Smith and SMITH. You learn that strcmp() is case-sensitive, meaning that the program considers upper- and lowercase letters different.

Comparing Two Strings—Ignoring Case

String comparison functions that are not case-sensitive operate in the same format as the case-sensitive function strcmp(). Most compilers have their own non-case-sensitive comparison function. Symantec uses the library function strcmpl(). Microsoft uses a function called _stricmp(). Borland has two functions, strcmpi() and stricmp(). You need to check your library reference manual to determine which function is appropriate for your compiler. When you use a function that is not case-sensitive, the strings Smith and SMITH compare as equal. Modify line 27 in Listing 17.7 to use the appropriate compare function for your compiler.

Comparing Partial Strings

The library function strncmp() compares a specified number of characters of one string to another string. Its prototype is

```
int strncmp(char *str1, char *str2, size_t n);
```

The function strncmp() compares n characters of str2 to str1. The comparison proceeds until n characters have been compared or the end of str1 has been reached. The method of comparison and return values are the same as for strcmp(). The comparison is case-sensitive. Listing 17.8 demonstrates strncmp().

Type **Listing 17.8. Comparing parts of strings with strncmp().**

```
1: /* The strncmp() function. */
2:
3: #include <stdio.h>
4: #include <string.h>
5:
6: char str1[] = "The first string.";
7: char str2[] = "The second string.";
8:
9: main()
10: {
11:     size_t n, x;
12:
13:     puts(str1);
14:     puts(str2);
15:
16:     while (1)
17:     {
18:         puts("\n\nEnter number of characters to compare, 0 to exit.");
19:         scanf("%d", &n);
20:
21:         if (n <= 0)
22:             break;
23:
24:         x = strncmp(str1, str2, n);
```

```
25:
26:            printf("\nComparing %d characters, strncmp() returns \%d.", n, x);
27:    }
28: }
```

Input Output

```
The first string.
The second string.

Enter number of characters to compare, 0 to exit.
3

Comparing 3 characters, strncmp() returns 0.

Enter number of characters to compare, 0 to exit.
6

Comparing 6 characters, strncmp() returns -13.

Enter number of characters to compare, 0 to exit.
0
```

Analysis This program compares two strings defined on lines 6 and 7. Lines 13 and 14 print the strings to the screen so that the user can see what they are. The program executes a while loop on lines 16–28 so that multiple compares can be done. If the user asks to compare zero characters on lines 18 and 19, the program breaks on line 22; otherwise, a strncmp() executes on line 24 and the result is printed on line 26.

Searching Strings

The C library contains a number of functions that search strings. Searches determine whether one string occurs within another string and, if so, where. There are six string searching functions, all of which require the header file STRING.H.

The *strchr()* Function

The strchr() function finds the first occurrence of a specified character in a string. The prototype is

```
char *strchr(char *str, int ch);
```

The function strchr() searches str from left to right until the character ch is found or the terminating null character is found. If ch is found, a pointer to it is returned. If not, NULL is returned.

17

427

When strchr() finds the character, it returns a pointer to that character. Knowing that str is a pointer to the first character in the string, you can obtain the position of the found character by subtracting str from the pointer value returned by strchr(). The program in Listing 17.9 illustrates this. Remember that the first character in a string is at position 0.

Listing 17.9. Using `strchr()` to search a string for a single character.

```
1: /* Searching for a single character with strchr(). */
2:
3: #include <stdio.h>
4: #include <string.h>
5:
6: main()
7: {
8:     char *loc, buf[80];
9:     int ch;
10:
11:     /* Input the string and the character. */
12:
13:     printf("Enter the string to be searched: ");
14:     gets(buf);
15:     printf("Enter the character to search for: ");
16:     ch = getchar();
17:
18:     /* Perform the search. */
19:
20:     loc = strchr(buf, ch);
21:
22:     if ( loc == NULL )
23:         printf("The character %c was not found.", ch);
24:     else
25:         printf("The character %c was found at position %d.",
26:                 ch, loc-buf);
27: }
```

Input/Output

```
Enter the string to be searched: How now Brown Cow?
Enter the character to search for: C
The character C was found at position 14.
```

Analysis

This program uses strchr() on line 20 to search for a character within a string. strchr() returns a pointer to the location where the character is first found, or NULL if the character is not found. Line 22 checks whether the value of loc is NULL and prints an appropriate message.

The *strrchr()* Function

The library function strrchr() is identical to strchr(), except that it searches a string for the last occurrence of a specified character. Its prototype is

```
char *strrchr(char *str, int ch);
```

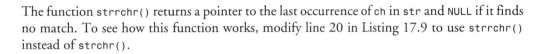

The function `strrchr()` returns a pointer to the last occurrence of `ch` in `str` and `NULL` if it finds no match. To see how this function works, modify line 20 in Listing 17.9 to use `strrchr()` instead of `strchr()`.

The *strcspn()* Function

The library function `strcspn()` searches one string for the first occurrence of any of the characters in a second string. Its prototype is

```
size_t strcspn(char *str1, char *str2);
```

The function `strcspn()` starts searching at the first character of `str1`, looking for any of the characters contained in `str2`. If it finds a match, it returns the offset from the beginning of `str1` where the matching character is located. If it finds no match, `strcspn()` returns the value of `strlen(str1)`. This indicates that the first match was the null character terminating the string. The program in Listing 17.10 shows you how to use `strcspn()`.

Type

Listing 17.10. Searching for a set of characters with strcspn().

```
1: /* Searching with strcspn(). */
2:
3: #include <stdio.h>
4: #include <string.h>
5:
6: main()
7: {
8:     char  buf1[80], buf2[80];
9:     size_t loc;
10:
11:     /* Input the strings. */
12:
13:     printf("Enter the string to be searched: ");
14:     gets(buf1);
15:     printf("Enter the string containing target characters: ");
16:     gets(buf2);
17:
18:     /* Perform the search. */
19:
20:     loc = strcspn(buf1, buf2);
21:
22:     if ( loc ==  strlen(buf1) )
23:         printf("No match was found.");
24:     else
25:         printf("The first match was found at position %d.",
loc);
26: }
```

Input/Output

```
Enter the string to be searched: How now Brown Cow?
Enter the string containing target characters: Cat
The first match was found at position 14.
```

This listing is similar to Listing 17.10. Instead of searching for the first occurrence of a single character, it searches for the first occurrence of any of the characters entered in the second string. The program calls strcspn() on line 20 with buf1 and buf2. If any of the characters in buf2 are in buf1, strcspn() returns the offset from the beginning of buf1 to the location of the first occurrence. Line 22 checks the return value to determine whether it is NULL. If the value is NULL, no characters were found and an appropriate message is displayed on line 23. If a value was found, a message is displayed stating the character's position in the string.

The *strspn()* Function

This function is related to the previous one, strcspn(), as the following paragraph explains. Its prototype is

```
size_t strspn(char *str1, char *str2);
```

The function strspn() searches str1, comparing it character by character with the characters contained in str2. It returns the position of the first character in str1 that doesn't match a character in str2. In other words, strspn() returns the length of the initial segment of str1 that consists entirely of characters found in str2. The return is 0 if no characters match. The program in Listing 17.11 demonstrates strspn().

Type
Listing 17.11. Searching for the first nonmatching character with strspn().

```
1: /* Searching with strspn(). */
2:
3: #include <stdio.h>
4: #include <string.h>
5:
6: main()
7: {
8:     char  buf1[80], buf2[80];
9:     size_t loc;
10:
11:     /* Input the strings. */
12:
13:     printf("Enter the string to be searched: ");
14:     gets(buf1);
15:     printf("Enter the string containing target characters: ");
16:     gets(buf2);
17:
18:     /* Perform the search. */
19:
20:     loc = strspn(buf1, buf2);
21:
22:     if ( loc ==  0 )
23:         printf("No match was found.");
24:     else
```

```
25:        printf("Characters match up to position %d.", loc-1);
26:
27: }
```

Enter the string to be searched: **How now Brown Cow?**
Enter the string containing target characters: **How now what?**
Characters match up to position 7.

This program is re/identical to the previous example, except it calls strspn() instead of strcspn() on line 20. The function returns the offset into buf1 where the first character not in buf2 is found. Lines 22–25 evaluate the return value and print an appropriate message.

The *strpbrk()* Function

The library function strpbrk() is similar to strcspn(), searching one string for the first occurrence of any character contained in another string. It differs in that it doesn't include the terminating null characters in the search. The function prototype is

```
char *strpbrk(char *str1, char *str2);
```

The function strpbrk() returns a pointer to the first character in str1 that matches any of the characters in str2. If it doesn't find a match, the function returns NULL. As previously explained for the function strchr(), you can obtain the offset of the first match in str1 by subtracting the pointer str1 from the pointer returned by strpbrk() (if it isn't NULL, of course). For example, replace strcspn() on line 20 of Listing 17.10 with strpbrk().

The *strstr()* Function

The final, and perhaps most useful, C string searching function is strstr(). This function searches for the first occurrence of one string within another. Its prototype is

```
char *strstr(char *str1, char *str2);
```

The function strstr() returns a pointer to the first occurrence of str2 within str1. If it finds no match, the function returns NULL. If the length of str2 is zero, the function returns str1. When strstr() finds a match, you can obtain the offset of str2 within str1 by pointer subtraction, as explained earlier for strchr(). The matching procedure that strstr() uses is case-sensitive. The program in Listing 17.12 demonstrates how to use strstr().

17

Listing 17.12. Using `strstr()` to search for one string within another.

```
1: /* Searching with strstr(). */
2:
3: #include <stdio.h>
4: #include <string.h>
5:
6: main()
7: {
8:     char *loc, buf1[80], buf2[80];
9:
10:     /* Input the strings. */
11:
12:     printf("Enter the string to be searched: ");
13:     gets(buf1);
14:     printf("Enter the target string: ");
15:     gets(buf2);
16:
17:     /* Perform the search. */
18:
19:     loc = strstr(buf1, buf2);
20:
21:     if ( loc ==  NULL )
22:         printf("No match was found.");
23:     else
24:         printf("%s was found at position %d.", buf2, loc-buf1);
25: }
```

Input Output

```
Enter the string to be searched: How now brown cow?
Enter the target string: cow
Cow was found at position 14.
```

 Analysis Here you are presented with an alternative way to search a string. This time you can search for a string within a string. Lines 12–15 prompt for two strings. Line 19 uses `strstr()` to search for the second string, `buf2`, within the first string, `buf1`. A pointer to the first occurrence is returned, or NULL if the string is not found. Lines 21–24 evaluate the returned value, `loc`, and print an appropriate message.

DO	DON'T

DO remember that for many of the string functions, there are equivalent functions that enable you to specify a number of characters to manipulate. The functions that allow specification of the number of characters are usually named `strnxxx()`, where *xxx* is specific to the function.

DON'T forget that C is case-sensitive. A and a are different.

String Conversions

Many C libraries contain two functions that change the case of characters within a string. These functions are not ANSI standard and, therefore, might differ or not even exist in your compiler. Their prototypes, in STRING.H, should be similar to

```
char *strlwr(char *str);
char *strupr(char *str);
```

The function `strlwr()` converts all the letter characters in `str` from upper- to lowercase; `strupr()` does the reverse, converting all the characters in `str` to uppercase. Nonletter characters are not affected. Both functions return `str`. Note that neither function actually creates a new string but modifies the existing string in place. The program in Listing 17.13 demonstrates these functions.

Listing 17.13. Converting the case of characters in a string with `strlwr()` and `strupr()`.

```
1: /* The character conversion functions strlwr() and strupr(). */
2:
3: #include <stdio.h>
4: #include <string.h>
5:
6: main()
7: {
8:     char buf[80];
9:
10:    while (1)
11:    {
12:        puts("Enter a line of text, a blank to exit.");
13:        gets(buf);
14:
15:        if ( strlen(buf) == 0 )
16:            break;
17:
18:        puts(strlwr(buf));
19:        puts(strupr(buf));
20:    }
21: }
```

```
Enter a line of text, a blank to exit.
Bradley L. Jones

bradley l. jones
BRADLEY L. JONES
Enter a line of text, a blank to exit.
```

This listing prompts for a string on line 12. It then checks to ensure that the string is not blank (line 15). Line 18 prints the string after converting it to lowercase. Line 19 prints the string in all uppercase.

These functions are a part of the Symantec C and Borland C libraries. In Microsoft C, the functions are preceded by an underscore (_strlwr() and _strupr()). You need to check the Library Reference for your compiler before using these functions. If portability is a concern, you should avoid using non-ANSI functions such as these.

Miscellaneous String Functions

This section covers a few string functions that don't fall into any other category. They all require the header file STRING.H.

The *strrev()* Function

The function strrev() reverses the order of all the characters in a string. Its prototype is

```
char *strrev(char *str);
```

The order of all characters in str is reversed, with the terminating null character remaining at the end. The function returns str. After strset() and strnset() are defined in the next section, strrev() is demonstrated in Listing 17.14.

The *strset()* and *strnset()* Functions

Like the previous function, strrev(), strset(), and strnset() are not part of the ANSI C standard library. These functions change all characters (strset()) or a specified number of characters (strnset()) in a string to a specified character. The prototypes are

```
char *strset(char *str, int ch);
char *strnset(char *str, int ch, size_t n);
```

The function strset() changes all the characters in str to ch except the terminating null character. The function strnset() changes the first n characters of str to ch. If n >= strlen(str), strnset() changes all the characters in str. Listing 17.14 demonstrates both functions.

 Listing 17.14. A demonstration of strrev(), strnset(), and strset().

```
1: /* Demonstrates strrev(), strset(), and strnset(). */
2: #include <stdio.h>
3: #include <string.h>
4:
5: char str[] = "This is the test string.";
6:
7: main()
8: {
9:     printf("\nThe original string: %s", str);
10:     printf("\nCalling strrev(): %s", strrev(str));
```

```
11:        printf("\nCalling strrev() again: %s", strrev(str));
12:        printf("\nCalling strnset(): %s", strnset(str, '!', 5));
13:        printf("\nCalling strset(): %s", strset(str, '!'));
14: }
```

```
The original string: This is the test string.
Calling strrev(): .gnirts tset eht si sihT
Calling strrev() again: This is the test string.
Calling strnset(): !!!!!is the test string.
Calling strset(): !!!!!!!!!!!!!!!!!!!!!!!!!
```

This program demonstrates the three different string functions. The demonstrations are done by printing the value of a string, str. Line 9 prints the string normally. Line 10 prints the string after it has been reversed with strrev(). Line 11 reverses it back to its original state. Line 12 uses the strnset() function to set the first five characters of str to exclamation marks. To finish the program, line 13 changes the entire string to exclamation marks.

Although these functions are not ANSI standard, they are included in the Symantec, Microsoft, and Borland C compiler function libraries. You should check your compiler's Library Reference manual to determine whether your compiler supports these functions.

String-to-Number Conversions

There are times when you need to convert the string representation of a number to an actual numeric variable. For example, the string "123" can be converted to a type int variable with the value 123. There are three functions that convert a string to a number, explained in the following paragraphs, and their prototypes are in STDLIB.H.

The *atoi()* Function

The library function atoi() converts a string to an integer. The prototype is

```
int atoi(char *ptr);
```

The function atoi() converts the string pointed to by ptr to an integer. Besides digits, the string can contain leading whitespace and a + or − sign. Conversion starts at the beginning of the string and proceeds until a nonconvertible character (for example, a letter or punctuation mark) is encountered. The resulting integer is returned to the calling program. If it finds no convertible characters, atoi() returns zero. Table 17.2 lists some examples.

Table 17.2. String-to-number conversions with `atoi()`.

String	Value Returned by `atoi()`
`"157"`	157
`"-1.6"`	-1
`"+50x"`	50
`"twelve"`	0
`"x506"`	0

The first example is straightforward. In the second example, you might be confused as to why the `".6"` did not translate. Remember, this is a string-to-integer conversion. The third example is also straightforward; the function "understands" the plus sign and considers it a part of the number. The fourth example uses `"twelve"`. The `atoi()` function cannot translate words; all it sees are characters. Because the string did not start with a number, `atoi()` returns 0. This is true of the last example also.

The *atoi()* Function

The library function `atol()` works exactly like `atoi()`, except that it returns a type `long`. The function prototype is

```
long atol(char *ptr);
```

The values returned by `atol()` would be the same as shown for `atoi()` in Table 17.2, except that each return value would be a type `long` instead of a type `int`.

The *atof()* Function

The function `atof()` converts a string to a type `double`. The prototype is

```
double atof(char *str);
```

The argument `str` points to the string to be converted. This string can contain leading whitespace and a + or – character. The number can contain the digits 0–9, the decimal point, and the exponent indicator E or e. If there are no convertible characters, `atof()` returns zero. Table 17.3 lists some examples of using `atof()`.

The program in Listing 17.15 enables you to enter your own strings for conversion.

Table 17.3. String-to-number conversions with atof().

String	Value Returned by atof()
"12"	12.000000
"-0.123"	-0.123000
"123E+3"	123000.000000
"123.1e-5"	0.001231

Listing 17.15. Using atof() to convert strings to type double numeric variables.

 Type

```
1: /* Demonstration of atof(). */
2:
3: #include <string.h>
4: #include <stdio.h>
5: #include <stdlib.h>
6:
7: main()
8: {
9:     char buf[80];
10:     double d;
11:
12:     while (1)
13:     {
14:         printf("\nEnter the string to convert (blank to exit):    ");
15:         gets(buf);
16:
17:         if ( strlen(buf) == 0 )
18:             break;
19:
20:         d = atof( buf );
21:
22:         printf("The converted value is %f.", d);
23:     }
24:}
```

 Input Output

```
Enter the string to convert (blank to exit):    1009.12
The converted value is 1009.120000.
Enter the string to convert (blank to exit):    abc
The converted value is 0.000000.
Enter the string to convert (blank to exit):    3
The converted value is 3.000000.
Enter the string to convert (blank to exit):
```

 Analysis

The while loop on lines 12–23 enables you to keep running the program until you enter a blank line. Lines 14–15 prompt for the value. Line 17 checks whether a blank line was entered. If it was, the program breaks out of the while loop and ends. Line 20 calls atof(), converting the value entered, buf, to a type double, d. Line 22 prints the final result.

Character Test Functions

The header file CTYPE.H contains the prototypes for a number of functions that test characters, returning TRUE or FALSE depending on whether the character meets a certain condition. For example, is it a letter or is it a numeral? The is*xxxx*() functions are actually macros, defined in CTYPE.H. You learn about macros on Day 21, "Taking Advantage of Preprocessor Directives and More," at which time you might want to look at the definitions in CTYPE.H to see how they work. For now, you only need to see how they're used.

The is*xxxx*() macros all have the same prototype.

```
int isxxxx(int ch);
```

In the preceding line, ch is the character being tested. The return value is TRUE (nonzero) if the condition is met or FALSE (zero) if it is not. Table 17.4 lists the complete set of is*xxxx*() macros.

Table 17.4. The is*xxxx*() macros.

Macro	Action
isalnum()	Returns TRUE if ch is a letter or a digit.
isalpha()	Returns TRUE if ch is a letter.
isascii()	Returns TRUE if ch is a standard ASCII character (between 0 and 127).
iscntrl()	Returns TRUE if ch is a control character.
isdigit()	Returns TRUE if ch is a digit.
isgraph()	Returns TRUE if ch is a printing character (other than a space).
islower()	Returns TRUE if ch is a lowercase letter.
isprint()	Returns TRUE if ch is a printing character (including a space).
ispunct()	Returns TRUE if ch is a punctuation character.
isspace()	Returns TRUE if ch is a whitespace character (space, tab, vertical tab, line feed, form feed, or carriage return).
isupper()	Returns TRUE if ch is an uppercase letter.
isxdigit()	Returns TRUE if ch is a hexadecimal digit (0–9, a–f, A–F).

You can do many interesting things with the character-test macros. One example is the function get_int() in Listing 17.16. This function inputs an integer from stdin and returns it as a type int variable. The function skips over leading whitespace and returns 0 if the first nonspace character is not a numeric character.

Listing 17.16. Using the is*xxxx*() macros to implement a function that inputs an integer.

```
1:  /* Using character test macros to create an integer */
2:  /* input function. */
3:
4:  #include <stdio.h>
5:  #include <ctype.h>
6:
7:  int get_int(void);
8:
9:  main()
10: {
11:     int x;
12:     x =  get_int();
13:
14:     printf("You entered %d.", x);
15: }
16:
17: int get_int(void)
18: {
19:     int ch, i, sign = 1;
20:
21:     /* Skip over any leading whitespace. */
22:
23:     while ( isspace(ch = getchar()) )
24:         ;
25:
26:     /* If the first character is non-numeric, unget */
27:     /* the character and return 0. */
28:
29:     if (ch != '-' && ch != '+' && !isdigit(ch) && ch != EOF)
30:     {
31:         ungetc(ch, stdin);
32:         return 0;
33:     }
34:
35:     /* If the first character is a minus sign, set */
36:     /* sign accordingly. */
37:
38:     if (ch == '-')
39:         sign = -1;
40:
41:     /* If the first character was a plus or minus sign, */
42:     /* get the next character. */
43:
44:     if (ch == '+' || ch == '-')
45:         ch = getchar();
46:
47:     /* Read characters until a nondigit is input. Assign */
48:     /* values, multiplied by proper power of 10, to i. */
49:
50:     for (i = 0; isdigit(ch); ch = getchar() )
51:         i - 10 * i + (ch - '0');
52:
53:     /* Make result negative if sign is negative. */
```

continues

Listing 17.16. continued

```
54:
55:      i *= sign;
56:
57:      /* If EOF was not encountered, a nondigit character */
58:      /* must have been read in, so unget it. */
59:
60:      if (ch != EOF)
61:          ungetc(ch, stdin);
62:
63:      /* Return the input value. */
64:
65:      return i;
66: }
```

```
C:\>list1716
-100
You entered -100.
C:\>list1716
abc3.145
You entered 0.
C:\>list1716
9 9 9
You entered 9.
C:\>list1716
2.5
You entered 2.
```

This program uses the library function ungetc() on lines 31 and 61, which you learned about on Day 14, "Working with the Screen, Printer, and Keyboard." Remember that this function "ungets," or returns, a character to the specified stream. This returned character is the first one input the next time the program reads a character from that stream. This is necessary in case the function get_int() reads a nonnumeric character from stdin because you want to put that character back in case the program needs it later.

In this program, main() is simple. An integer variable, x, is declared (line 11), assigned the value of the get_int() function (line 12), and printed to the screen (line 14). The get_int() function makes up the rest of the program.

The get_int() function is not so simple. To remove leading whitespace that might be entered, line 23 loops with a while command. The isspace() macro tests a character, ch, obtained with the getchar() function. If ch is a space, another character is retrieved, until a nonwhitespace character is received. Line 29 checks whether the character is one that can be used. Line 29 could be read, "If the character input is not a negative sign, a plus sign, a digit, or the end of the file(s)." If this is true, ungetc() is used on line 31 to put the character back, and the function returns to main(). If the character is usable, execution continues.

440

Lines 38–45 handle the sign of the number. Line 38 checks to see whether the character entered was a negative sign. If it was, a variable, sign, is set to -1. sign is used to make the final number either positive or negative (line 55). Because positive numbers are the default, once you have taken care of the negative sign, you are almost ready to continue. If a sign was entered, the program needs to get another character. Lines 44 and 45 take care of this.

The heart of the function is the for loop on lines 50–51, which continues to get characters as long as the characters gotten are digits. Line 51 might be a little confusing at first. This line takes the individual character entered and turns it into a number. Subtracting the character '0' from your number changes a character number to a real number. (Remember the ASCII values.) When the correct numerical value is obtained, the numbers are multiplied by the proper power of 10. The for loop continues until a nondigit number is entered. At that point, line 55 applies the sign to the number, making it complete.

Before returning, the program needs to do a little cleanup. If the last number was not the end of file, it needs to be put back in case it is needed elsewhere. Line 61 does this before line 65 returns.

DO	DON'T

DON'T use non-ANSI functions if you plan on porting your application to other platforms.

DO take advantage of the string functions that are available.

DON'T confuse characters with numbers. It is easy to forget that '1' is not the same thing as 1.

Summary

This chapter showed various ways you can manipulate strings. Using C standard library functions (and possibly compiler-specific functions as well), you can copy, concatenate, compare, and search strings. These are all needed tasks in most programming projects. The standard library also contains functions for converting the case of characters in strings and for converting strings to numbers. Finally, C provides a variety of character-test functions or, more accurately, macros that perform a variety of tests on individual characters. By using these macros to test characters, you can create your own custom input functions.

Q&A

Q How do I know whether a function is ANSI compatible?

**A Most compilers have a Library Function Reference manual or section. This manual or
section of a manual lists all the compiler's library functions and how to use them.
Usually, the manual includes information on the compatibility of the function.
Sometimes the descriptions state not only whether the function is ANSI compatible,
but also whether it is compatible with DOS, UNIX, Windows, C++, or OS/2. (Most
compilers only tell you what is relevant to their compiler.)**

Q Are all of the available string functions presented in this chapter?

**A No. However, the string functions presented in this chapter should cover virtually all
of your needs. Consult your compiler's Library Reference to see what other functions
are available.**

Q Does `strcat()` ignore trailing spaces when doing a concatenation?

A No. `strcat()` looks at a space as just another character.

Q Can I convert numbers to strings?

**A Yes. You can write a function similar to the one in Listing 17.16, or you can check
your Library Reference for available functions. Some functions available include
`itoa()`, `ltoa()`, and `ultoa()`. `sprint(f)` can also be used.**

Workshop

The Workshop provides quiz questions to help you solidify your understanding of the material
covered and exercises to provide you with experience in using what you've learned.

Quiz

1. What is the length of a string, and how can the length be determined?

2. Before copying a string, what must you be sure to do?

3. What does the term *concatenate* mean?

4. When comparing strings, what is meant by "One string is greater than another
    string?"

5. What is the difference between `strcmp()` and `strncmp()`?

6. What is the difference between `strcmp()` and `strcmpi()`?

7. What values does `isascii()` test for?

8. Using Table 17.4, which macros would return TRUE for var?

```
int var = 1;
```

9. Using Table 17.4, which macros would return TRUE for x?

```
char x = 65;
```

10. What are the character-test functions used for?

Exercises

1. What values do the test functions return?

2. What would the atoi() function return if passed the following values?

    a. "65"

    b. "81.23"

    c. "-34.2"

    d. "ten"

    e. "+12hundred"

    f. "negative100"

3. What would the atof() function return if passed the following?

    a. "65"

    b. "81.23"

    c. "-34.2"

    d. "ten"

    e. "+12hundred"

    f. "1e+3"

4. **BUG BUSTER:** Is anything wrong with the following?

```
char *string1, string2;
string1 = "Hello World";
strcpy( string2, string1);
printf( "%s %s", string1, string2 );
```

Because of the many possible solutions, answers are not provided for the following exercises.

5. Write a program that prompts for the user's last name, first name, and middle name individually. Then store the name in a new string as first initial, period, space, middle initial, period, space, last name. For example, if "Bradley," "Lee," and "Jones" were entered, store "B. L. Jones." Display the new name to the screen.

6. Write a program to prove your answers to quiz questions 8 and 9.

7. The function `strstr()` finds the first occurrence of one string within another, and it is case-sensitive. Write a function that performs the same task without case-sensitivity.

8. Write a function that determines the number of times one string occurs within another.

9. Write a program that searches a text file for occurrences of a user-specified target string, and then reports the line numbers where the target is found. For example, if you search one of your C source code files for the string `"printf("`, the program should list all the lines where the `printf()` function is called by the program.

10. Listing 17.16 demonstrates a function that inputs an integer from `stdin`. Write a function `get_float()` that inputs a floating-point value from `stdin`.

Getting More from Functions

As you should know by now, functions are central to C programming. Today, you learn about

- Using pointers as arguments to functions
- Passing type `void` pointers as arguments
- Using functions with a variable number of arguments
- Returning a pointer from a function

Some of these topics have been discussed earlier in the book, but this chapter gives you more detailed information.

Passing Pointers to Functions

The default method of passing an argument to a function is *by value*. Passing by value means the function is passed a copy of the argument's value. This method has three steps:

1. The argument expression is evaluated.
2. The result is copied onto the *stack,* a temporary storage area in memory.
3. The function retrieves the argument's value from the stack.

The procedure of passing an argument by value is illustrated in Figure 18.1. In this case, the argument is a simple type `int` variable, but the principle is the same for other variable types and more complex expressions.

When a variable is passed to a function by value, the function has access to the variable's value but not to the original copy of the variable. As a result, the code in the function cannot modify the original variable. This is the main reason *by value* is the default method of passing arguments. Data outside a function is protected from inadvertent modification.

Passing by value is possible with the basic data types (`char`, `int`, `long`, `float`, and `double`) and structures. There is another way to pass an argument to a function, however; pass a pointer to the argument variable rather than the value of the variable itself. This method of passing an argument is called *passing by reference.*

As you learned on Day 9, "Pointers," passing by reference is the only way to pass an array to a function; passing by value is not possible with arrays. With other data types, however, you can use either method. If your program uses large structures, passing them by value might cause your program to run out of stack space. Aside from this consideration, passing an argument by reference instead of by value offers an advantage as well as a disadvantage:

- The advantage of passing by reference is that the function can modify the value of the argument variable.
- The disadvantage of passing by reference is that the function can modify the value of the argument variable.

Figure 18.1.

Passing an argument by value. The function cannot modify the original argument variable.

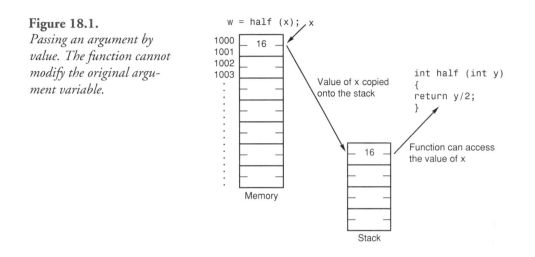

"Help!" you might be hollering. "An advantage that's also a disadvantage?" Yes, it all depends on the specific situation. If your program requires a function to modify an argument variable, passing by reference is an advantage. If there is no such need, it is a disadvantage because of the possibility of inadvertent modifications.

You might be wondering why you don't use the function's return value to modify the argument variable. You can do this, of course, as shown in the following example:

```
x = half(x);

int half(int y)
{
return y/2;
}
```

Remember, however, that a function can return only a single value. By passing one or more arguments by reference, you allow a function to "return" more than one value to the calling program. Figure 18.2 illustrates passing by reference for a single argument.

The function used in Figure 18.2 is not a good example of something you would use *passing by reference* for in a real program, but it does illustrate the concept. When you pass by reference, you must ensure that the function definition and prototype reflect the fact that the argument passed to the function is a pointer. Within the body of the function, you must also use the *indirection* operator to access the variable(s) passed by reference.

The program in Listing 18.1 demonstrates passing by reference and the default passing by value. Its output clearly shows that a variable passed by value cannot be changed by the function, whereas a variable passed by reference can be changed. Of course, a function does not need to modify a variable passed by reference, but if the function doesn't need to, there is no reason to pass by reference.

Figure 18.2.

Passing by reference allows the function to modify the original argument's variable.

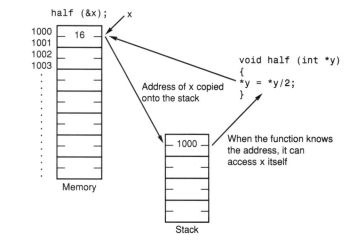

Type

Listing 18.1. Passing by value and passing by reference.

```
1: /* Passing arguments by value and by reference. */
2:
3: #include <stdio.h>
4:
5: void by_value(int a, int b, int c);
6: void by_ref(int *a, int *b, int *c);
7:
8: main()
9: {
10:     int x = 2, y = 4, z = 6;
11:
12:     printf("\nBefore calling by_value(), x = %d, y = %d, z =%d.",
13:         x, y, z);
14:
15:     by_value(x, y, z);
16:
17:     printf("\nAfter calling by_value(), x = %d, y = %d, z = %d.",
18:         x, y, z);
19:
20:     by_ref(&x, &y, &z);
21:
22:     printf("\nAfter calling by_ref(), x = %d, y = %d, z = %d.",
23:         x, y, z);
24: }
25:
26: void by_value(int a, int b, int c)
27: {
28:     a = 0;
29:     b = 0;
30:     c = 0;
31: }
```

```
32:
33: void by_ref(int *a, int *b, int *c)
34: {
35:     *a = 0;
36:     *b = 0;
37:     *c = 0;
38: }
```

Output

Before calling by_value(), x = 2, y = 4, z = 6.
After calling by_value(), x = 2, y = 4, z = 6.
After calling by_ref(), x = 0, y = 0, z = 0.

Analysis
This program demonstrates the difference between passing variables by value and passing them by reference. Lines 5 and 6 contain prototypes for the two functions called in the program. Notice that line 5 describes three arguments of type int for the by_value() function, but by_ref() differs on line 6 because it requires three pointers to type int variables as arguments. The function headers for these two functions on lines 26 and 33 follow the same format as the prototypes. The bodies of the two functions are similar, but not the same. Both functions assign 0 to the three variables passed to them. In the by_value() function, 0 is assigned directly to the variables. In the by_ref() function, pointers are used, so the variables must be dereferenced.

Each function is called once by main(). First, the three variables to be passed are assigned values other than zero on line 10. Line 12 prints these values to the screen. Line 15 calls the first of the two functions, by_value(). Line 17 prints the three variables once again. Notice that they are not changed. The by_value() function received the variables by value and therefore could not change their original content. Line 20 calls by_ref(), and line 22 prints the values again. This time the values have all changed to 0. Passing the variables by reference gave by_ref() access to the actual contents of the variables.

You can write a function that receives some arguments by reference and others by value. Just remember to keep them straight inside the function, using the indirection operator (*) to dereference arguments passed by reference.

DO	DON'T

DON'T pass large amounts of data by value if it is not necessary. You could run out of stack space.

DO pass variables by value if you don't want the original value altered.

DON'T forget that a variable passed by reference should be a pointer. Also, use the indirection operator to dereference the variable in the function.

18

Type *void* Pointers

You've seen the void keyword used to specify that a function either doesn't take arguments or doesn't return a value. The void keyword also can be used to create a *generic* pointer, a pointer that can point to any type of data object. For example, the statement

```
void *x;
```

declares x as a generic pointer. x points to something; you just haven't yet specified *what*.

The most common use for type void pointers is in declaring function parameters. You might want to create a function that can handle different types of arguments: you can pass it a type int one time, a type float the next time, and so on. By declaring that the function takes a void pointer as an argument, you don't restrict it to accepting only a single data type. If you declare the function to take a void pointer as an argument, you can pass the function a pointer to anything.

Here's a simple example: you want a function that accepts a numeric variable as an argument and divides it by 2, returning the answer in the argument variable. Thus, if the variable x holds the value 4, after a call to half(x) the variable x is equal to 2. Because you want to modify the argument, you pass it by reference. Because you want to use the function with any of C's numeric data types, you declare the function to take a void pointer:

```
void half(void *x);
```

Now you can call the function, passing it any pointer as an argument. There's one more thing necessary, however. Although you can pass a void pointer without knowing what data type it points to, you cannot dereference the pointer. Before the code in the function can do anything with the pointer, the data type must be known. This is done with a *type cast*, which is nothing more than a way of telling the program to treat this void pointer as a pointer to type. If x is a void pointer, you type cast it as follows:

```
(type *)x
```

where type is the appropriate data type. To tell the program that x is a pointer to type int, write

```
(int *)x
```

To dereference the pointer—that is, to access the int that x points to—write

```
*(int *)x
```

Type casts are covered in more detail in Day 20, "Working with Memory." Getting back to the original topic (passing a void pointer to a function), you can see that to use the pointer, the function must know the data type to which it points. In the case of the function you're writing to halve its argument, there are four possibilities for type: int, long, float, and double. In addition to the void pointer to the variable to be halved, you must tell the function the type of variable to which the void pointer points. You can modify the function definition as follows:

```
void half(void *x, char type);
```

Based on the argument type, the function casts the void pointer x to the appropriate type. Then the pointer can be dereferenced and the value of the pointed-to variable can be used. The final version of the function half() is shown in Listing 18.2.

Listing 18.2. Using a void pointer to pass different data types to a function.

```
1:  /* Using type void pointers. */
2:
3:  #include <stdio.h>
4:
5:  void half(void *x, char type);
6:
7:  main()
8:  {
9:      /* Initialize one variable of each type. */
10:
11:     int i = 20;
12:     long l = 100000;
13:     float f - 12.456;
14:     double d = 123.044444;
15:
16:     /* Display their initial values. */
17:
18:     printf("\n%d", i);
19:     printf("\n%ld", l);
20:     printf("\n%f", f);
21:     printf("\n%lf\n\n", d);
22:
23:     /* Call half() for each variable. */
24:
25:     half(&i, 'i');
26:     half(&l, 'l');
27:     half(&d, 'd');
28:     half(&f, 'f');
29:
30:     /* Display their new values. */
31:
32:     printf("\n%d", i);
33:     printf("\n%ld", l);
34:     printf("\n%f", f);
35:     printf("\n%lf", d);
36: }
37:
38: void half(void *x, char type)
39: {
```

continues

Listing 18.2. continued

```
40:        /* Depending on the value of type, cast the */
41:        /* pointer x appropriately and divide by 2. */
42:
43:        switch (type)
44:        {
45:            case 'i':
46:                {
47:                *((int *)x) /= 2;
48:                break;
49:                }
50:            case 'l':
51:                {
52:                *((long *)x) /= 2;
53:                break;
54:                }
55:            case 'f':
56:                {
57:                *((float *)x) /= 2;
58:                break;
59:                }
60:            case 'd':
61:                {
62:                *((double *)x) /= 2;
63:                break;
64:                }
65:        }
66: }
```

```
20
100000
12.456000
123.044444
```

```
10
50000
6.228000
61.522222
```

As implemented, the function `half()` on lines 38–66 includes no error checking (for example, if an invalid type argument is passed). However, in a real program you would not use a function to perform a task as simple as dividing a value by 2. This is an illustrative example only.

You might think that the need to pass the type of the pointed-to variable makes the function less flexible. The function would be more general if it didn't need to know the type of the pointed-to data object, but that's not the way C works. You must always cast a `void` pointer to a specific type before you dereference it. By taking the preceding approach, you write only one function. If you do not make use of a `void` pointer, you need to write four separate functions, one for each data type.

When you need a function that can deal with different data types, you often can write a *macro* to take the place of the function. The example just presented—in which the task performed by the function is relatively simple—would be a good candidate for a macro. (Day 21, "Taking Advantage of Preprocessor Directives and More," covers macros.)

Note that type void pointers cannot be incremented or decremented.

DO	DON'T

DO cast a void pointer when you use the value it points to.

DON'T try to increment or decrement a void pointer.

Functions with Variable Numbers of Arguments

You have used several library functions, such as printf() and scanf(), that take a variable number of arguments. You can write your own functions that take a variable argument list. Programs that have functions with variable argument lists must include the header file STDARG.H.

When you declare a function that takes a variable argument list, you first list the fixed parameters, those that are always present (there must be at least one fixed parameter). You then include an *ellipsis* (...) at the end of the parameter list to indicate that zero or more additional arguments are passed to the function. During this discussion, please remember the distinction between a parameter and an argument, as explained on Day 5, "Functions: The Basics."

How does the function know how many arguments have been passed to it on a specific call? You tell it. One of the fixed parameters informs the function of the total number of arguments. For example, when using the printf() function, the number of conversion specifiers in the format string tells the function how many additional arguments to expect. More directly, one of the function's fixed arguments can be the number of additional arguments. The example that follows uses this approach, but first you need to look at the tools that C provides for dealing with a variable argument list.

The function must also know the type of each argument in the variable list. In the case of printf(), the conversion specifiers indicate the type of each argument. In other cases—such as the following example—all arguments in the variable list are of the same type, so there's no problem. To create a function that accepts different types in the variable argument list, you must devise a method of passing information about the argument types.

The tools for using a variable argument list are defined in STDARG.H. These tools are used within the function to retrieve the arguments in the variable list. They are as follows:

`va_list`	A pointer data type.
`va_start()`	A macro used to initialize the argument list.
`va_arg()`	A macro used to retrieve each argument, in turn, from the variable list.
`va_end()`	A macro used to "clean up" when all arguments have been retrieved.

The way these macros are used in a function is outlined here, followed by an example. When the function is called, the code in the function must perform the following steps to access its arguments:

1. Declare a pointer variable of type `va_list`. This pointer is used to access the individual arguments. It is common practice, although certainly not required, to call this variable `arg_ptr`.

2. Call the macro `va_start()`, passing it the pointer `arg_ptr` as well as the name of the last fixed argument. The macro `va_start()` has no return value; it initializes the pointer `arg_ptr` to point at the first argument in the variable list.

3. To retrieve each argument, call `va_arg()`, passing it the pointer `arg_ptr` and the data type of the next argument. The return value of `va_arg()` is the value of the next argument. If the function has received n arguments in the variable list, call `va_arg()` n times to retrieve the arguments in the order listed in the function call.

4. When all of the arguments in the variable list have been retrieved, call `va_end()`, passing it the pointer `arg_ptr`. In some implementations, this macro performs no action; but in others, it performs necessary cleanup actions. You should get in the habit of calling `va_end()` in case you use a C implementation that requires it.

Now for that example. The function `average()` in Listing 18.3 calculates the arithmetic average of a list of integers.

Type

Listing 18.3. Using a variable argument list.

```
1: /* Functions with a variable argument list. */
2:
3: #include <stdio.h>
4: #include <stdarg.h>
5:
6: float average(int num, ...);
7:
8: main()
9: {
10:     float x;
11:
12:     x = average(10, 1, 2, 3, 4, 5, 6, 7, 8, 9, 10);
13:     printf("\nThe first average is %f.", x);
```

```
14:
15:     x = average(5, 121, 206, 76, 31, 5);
16:     printf("\nThe second average is %f.", x);
17: }
18:
19: float average(int num, ...)
20: {
21:     /* Declare a variable of type va_list. */
22:
23:     va_list arg_ptr;
24:     int count, total = 0;
25:
26:     /* Initialize the argument pointer. */
27:
28:     va_start(arg_ptr, num);
29:
30:     /* Retrieve each argument in the variable list. */
31:
32:     for (count = 0; count < num; count++)
33:         total += va_arg( arg_ptr, int );
34:
35:     /* Perform clean up. */
36:
37:     va_end(arg_ptr);
38:
39:     /* Divide the total by the number of values to get the */
40:     /* average. Cast the total to type float so the value */
41:     /* returned is type float. */
42:
43:     return ((float)total/num);
44: }
```

Output

```
The first average is 5.500000.
The second average is 87.800000.
```

Analysis

The function average() is first called on line 19. The first argument passed, the only fixed argument, specifies the number of values in the variable argument list. As an argument in the variable list is retrieved on lines 32–33, it is added to the variable total. After all arguments have been retrieved, line 43 casts total as type float and then divides total by num to obtain the average.

Two other things should be pointed out in this listing. Line 28 calls va_start() to initialize the argument list. This must be done before the values are retrieved. Line 37 calls va_end() to "clean up" because the function is done with the values. Both of these functions should be used in your programs.

Strictly speaking, a function that accepts a variable number of arguments does not need to have a fixed parameter informing it of the number of arguments being passed. You could, for example, mark the end of the argument list with a special value not used elsewhere. This method places limitations on the arguments that can be passed, however, and is best avoided.

Functions that Return a Pointer

You have seen several functions from the C standard library that return a pointer to the calling program. You can write your own functions that return a pointer as well. As you might expect, the indirection operator (*) is used in both the function declaration and the function definition. The general form is

```
type *func(parameter_list);
```

This statement declares a function `func()` that returns a pointer to `type`. Here are two concrete examples:

```
double *func1(parameter_list);
struct address *func2(parameter_list);
```

The first line declares a function that returns a pointer to type `double`. The second line declares a function that returns a pointer to type `address` (which you assume is a user-defined structure).

Don't confuse a *function that returns a pointer* and a *pointer to a function*. If you include an additional pair of parentheses in the declaration, you declare the latter, as illustrated in these two examples:

```
double (*func)(...);    /* Pointer to a function that returns a double. */

double *func(...);      /* Function that returns a pointer to a double. */
```

Now that you have the declaration format straight, how do you use a function that returns a pointer? There's nothing special about such functions—you use them like any other function, assigning their return value to a variable of the appropriate type (in this case, a pointer). Because the function call is a C expression, you can use it anywhere a pointer of that type would be used.

Listing 18.4 presents a simple example, a function that is passed two arguments and determines which is larger. In the listing, two different functions accomplish this task: one returning an `int` and the other returning a pointer to `int`.

Type
Listing 18.4. Returning a pointer from a function.

```
1: /* Function that returns a pointer. */
2:
3: #include <stdio.h>
4:
5: int larger1(int x, int y);
6: int *larger2(int *x, int *y);
7:
8: main()
9: {
10:     int a, b, bigger1, *bigger2;
11:
12:     printf("Enter two integer values: ");
13:     scanf("%d %d", &a, &b);
```

```
14:
15:     bigger1 = larger1(a, b);
16:     printf("\nThe larger value is %d.", bigger1);
17:
18:     bigger2 = larger2(&a, &b);
19:     printf("\nThe larger value is %d.", *bigger2);
20: }
21:
22: int larger1(int x, int y)
23: {
24:     if (y > x)
25:         return y;
26:     return x;
27: }
28:
29: int *larger2(int *x, int *y)
30: {
31:     if (*y > *x)
32:         return y;
33:
34:     return x;
35: }
```

Enter two integer values: **1111 3000**

The larger value is 3000.
The larger value is 3000.

18

This is a relatively easy program to follow. Lines 5 and 6 contain the prototypes for the two functions. The first, larger1(), receives two int variables and returns an int. The second, larger2(), receives two pointers to int variables and returns a pointer to an int. The main() function on lines 8–20 is straightforward. Line 10 declares four variables. a and b hold the two variables to be compared. bigger1 and bigger2 hold the return values from the larger1() and larger2() functions respectively. Notice that bigger2 is a pointer to an int and bigger1 is just an int.

Line 15 calls larger1() with the two ints, a and b. The value returned from the function is assigned to bigger1, which is printed on line 16. Line 18 calls larger2() with the address of the two ints. The value returned from larger2(), a pointer, is assigned to bigger2, also a pointer. This value is dereferenced and printed on the following line.

The two comparison functions are very similar. They both compare the two values. The larger value is returned. The difference between the functions is in larger2(). In this function, the values pointed to are compared on line 31. Then the pointer for the larger value's variable is returned. Notice that the dereference operator is used in the comparisons, but not in the return statements on lines 32 or 34.

In many cases, as in the previous example, it is equally feasible to write a function to return a value or a pointer. Which you select depends on the specifics of your program—mainly on how you intend to use the return value.

DO	**DON'T**

DO use all the elements described previously when writing functions with variable arguments. This is true even if your compiler does not require all the elements. The parts are va_list, va_start(), va_arg(), and va_end().

DON'T confuse pointers to functions with functions that return pointers.

Summary

In this chapter, you learned some additional things your C programs can do with functions. You learned the difference between passing arguments by value and by reference, and how the latter technique allows a function to "return" more than one value to the calling program. You also saw how the void type can be used to create a generic pointer that can point to any type of C data object. Type void pointers are most commonly used with functions that can be passed arguments not restricted to a single data type. Remember that a type void pointer must be cast to a specific type before you can dereference it.

This chapter also showed you how to use the macros defined in STDARG.H to write a function that accepts a variable number of arguments. Such functions provide considerable programming flexibility. Finally, you saw how to write a function that returns a pointer.

Q&A

Q Is passing pointers a common practice in C programming?

A Definitely! In many instances a function needs to change multiple variables; there are two ways this can be accomplished. The first is to declare and use global variables. The second is to pass pointers so that the function can modify the data directly. The first option is good only if nearly every function is going to use the variable. (See Day 12, "Variable Scope.")

Q Is it better to modify a value by returning it or by passing a pointer to the actual data?

A When you need to modify only one value with a function, usually it is best to return the value from the function rather than pass a pointer to the function. The logic behind this is simple. By not passing a pointer, you don't run the risk of changing any data that you did not intend to change, and you keep the function independent of the rest of the code.

Workshop

The Workshop provides quiz questions to help you solidify your understanding of the material covered and exercises to provide you with experience in using what you've learned.

Quiz

1. When passing arguments to a function, what's the difference between passing by value and passing by reference?

2. What is a type void pointer?

3. What is a reason to use a void pointer?

4. When using a void pointer, what is meant by a type cast and when must you use it?

5. Can you write a function that takes a variable argument list only, with no fixed arguments?

6. What macros should be used when you write functions with variable argument lists?

7. What value is added to a void pointer when it is incremented?

8. Can a function return a pointer?

Exercises

1. Write the prototype for a function that returns an integer. It should take a pointer to a character array as its argument.

2. Write a prototype for a function called numbers that takes three integer arguments. The integers should be passed by reference.

3. Show how you would call the numbers function in exercise two with the three integers, int1, int2, and int3.

4. **BUG BUSTER:** Is anything wrong with the following?

```
void squared(void *nbr)
{
    *nbr *= *nbr;
}
```

5. **BUG BUSTER:** Is anything wrong with the following?

```
float total( int num, ...)
{
    int count, total = 0;
    for ( count = 0; count < num; count++ )
            total += va_arg( arg_ptr, int );
    return ( total );
}
```

Because of the many possible solutions, answers are not provided for the following exercises.

6. Write a function that (a) is passed a variable number of strings as arguments,(b) concatenates the strings, in order, into one longer string, and (c) returns a pointer to the new string to the calling program.

7. Write a function that (a) is passed an array of any numeric data type as an argument, (b) finds the largest and smallest values in the array, and (c) returns pointers to these values to the calling program. (Hint: You need some way to tell the function how many elements are in the array.)

8. Write a function that accepts a string and a character. The function should look for the first occurrence of the character in the string and return a pointer to that location.

WEEK
3

Exploring the
Function Library

As you see throughout this book, much of C's power comes from the standard library functions. In this chapter, you explore some of the functions that do not fit into the subject matter of other chapters. Today, you learn

- Mathematical functions
- Functions that deal with time
- Error-handling functions
- Functions for searching and sorting data

Mathematical Functions

The C standard library contains a variety of functions that perform mathematical operations. Prototypes for the mathematical functions are in the header file MATH.H. The math functions all return a type `double`. For the trigonometric functions, angles are expressed in *radians*. Remember, one radian equals 57.296 degrees, and a full circle (360 degrees) contains 2 radians.

Trigonometric Functions

The trigonometric function perform calculations that are used in some graphical and geometrical applications.

`double acos(double x)`	The function `acos()` returns the arccosine of its argument. The argument must be in the range `-1 <= x <= 1`, and the return value is in the range `0 <= acos <= `.
`double asin(double x)`	The function `asin()` returns the arcsine of its argument. The argument must be in the range `-1 <= x <= 1`, and the return value is in the range `- /2 <= asin <= /2`
`double atan(double x)`	The function `atan()` returns the arctangent of its argument. The return value is in the range `- /2 <= atan <= /2`.
`double atan2` `(double x, double y)`	The function `atan2()` returns the arctangent of `x/y`. The value returned is in the range `- <= atan2 <= `.
`double cos(double x)`	The function `cos()` returns the cosine of its argument.
`double sin(double x)`	The function `sin()` returns the sine of its argument.
`double tan(double x)`	The function `tan()` returns the tangent of its argument.

Exponential and Logarithmic Functions

The exponential and logarithmic functions are needed for certain types of mathematical calculations.

`double exp(double x)`	The function `exp()` returns the natural exponent of its argument, that is, e^x where e == `2.7182818284590452354`.
`double log(double x)`	The function `log()` returns the natural logarithm of its argument. The argument must be greater than 0.
`double log10(double x)`	The function `log10()` returns the base 10 logarithm of its argument. The argument must be greater than 0.
`double frexp` `(double x, int *y)`	The function `frexp()` calculates the normalized fraction representing the value x. The function's return value r is a fraction in the range `0.5 <= r <= 1.0`. The function assigns to y an integer exponent such that $x = r * 2^y$. If the value passed to the function is 0, both r and y are 0.
`double ldexp` `(double x, int y)`	The function `ldexp()` returns $x * 2^y$.

Hyperbolic Functions

The hyperbolic functions perform hyperbolic trigonometric calculations.

`double cosh(double x)`	The function `cosh()` returns the hyperbolic cosine of its argument.
`double sinh(double x)`	The function `sinh()` returns the hyperbolic sine of its argument.
`double tanh(double x)`	The function `tanh()` returns the hyperbolic tangent of its argument.

Other Mathematical Functions

This section lists some miscellaneous mathematical functions.

`double sqrt(double x)`	The function `sqrt()` returns the square root of its argument. The argument must be zero or greater.
`double ceil(double x)`	The function `ceil()` returns the smallest integer not less than its argument. For example, `ceil(4.5)` returns `5.0`, and `ceil(-4.5)` returns `-4.0`. Although `ceil()` returns an integer value, it is returned as a type `double`.

`int abs(int x)` and `long labs(long x)`	The functions `abs()` and `labs()` return the absolute value of their arguments.
`double floor(double x)`	The function `floor()` returns the largest integer not greater than its argument. For example, `floor(4.5)` returns `4.0` and `floor(-4.5)` returns `-5.0`.
`double modf` `(double x, double *y)`	The function `modf()` splits x into integral and fractional parts, each with the same sign as x. The fractional part is returned by the function, and the integral part is assigned to *y.
`double pow` `(double x, double y)`	The function `pow()` returns xʸ. An error occurs if x == 0 and y <= 0, or if x < 0 and y is not an integer.
`double fmod` `(double x, double y)`	The function `fmod()` returns the floating point remainder of x/y, with the same sign as x. The function returns 0 if x == 0.

A Demonstration

An entire book could be filled with programs demonstrating all of the math functions. Listing 19.1 contains a single program that demonstrates a couple of the functions.

 Listing 19.1. Using the C library math functions.

```
1: /* Demonstrate some math functions */
2:
3: #include <stdio.h>
4: #include <math.h>
5:
6: main()
7: {
8:
9:     double x;
10:
11:     printf("Enter a number: ");
12:     scanf( "%lf", &x);
13:
14:     printf("\n\nOriginal value: %lf", x);
15:
16:     printf("\nCeil: %lf", ceil(x));
17:     printf("\nFloor: %lf", floor(x));
18:     if( x >= 0 )
19:         printf("\nSquare root: %lf", sqrt(x) );
20:     else
21:         printf("\nNegative number" );
22:
23:     printf("\nCosine: %lf", cos(x));
24: }
```

```
Enter a number: 100.95

Original value: 100.950000
Ceil: 101.000000
Floor: 100.000000
Square root: 10.047388
Cosine: 0.913482
```

This listing uses just a few of the math functions. A value accepted on line 12 is printed after it is sent to four of the math functions: `ceil()`, `floor()`, `sqrt()`, and `cos()`. Notice that `sqrt()` is called only if the number is not negative. You cannot get the square root of a negative number. Any of the other math functions could be added to a program such as this to test their functionality.

Dealing with Time

The C library contains several functions that allow your program to work with times. The function prototypes and the definition of the structure used by many of the time functions are in the header file TIME.H.

Representation of Time

The C time functions represent time in two ways. The more basic method is the number of seconds elapsed since midnight on January 1, 1970. Negative values are used to represent times before that date.

These time values are stored as type `long` integers. In TIME.H, the symbols `time_t` and `clock_t` are both defined with a `typedef` statement as `long`. These symbols are used in the time function prototypes rather than `long`.

The second method represents a time broken down into its components: year, month, day, and so on. For this kind of time representation, the time functions use a structure `tm`, defined in TIME.H as follows:

```
struct tm {
    int tm_sec; /* seconds after the minute - [0,59]  */
    int tm_min; /* minutes after the hour - [0,59]    */
    int tm_hour;    /* hours since midnight - [0,23]  */
    int tm_mday;    /* day of the month - [1,31]      */
    int tm_mon; /* months since January - [0,11]      */
    int tm_year;    /* years since 1900               */
    int tm_wday;    /* days since Sunday - [0,6]       */
    int tm_yday;    /* days since January 1 - [0,365] */
    int tm_isdst;   /* daylight savings time flag      */
    };
```

The Time Functions

This section describes the various C library functions that deal with time. The term *time* refers to the date as well as hours, minutes, and seconds. A demonstration program follows the descriptions.

Obtaining the Current Time

To obtain the current time as set on your system's internal clock, use the `time()` function. The prototype is

```
time_t time(time_t *timeptr);
```

Remember, `time_t` is defined in TIME.H as a synonym for `long`. The function `time()` returns the number of seconds elapsed since midnight, January 1, 1970. If it is passed a non-`NULL` pointer, `time()` also stores this value in the type `time_t` variable pointed to by `timeptr`. Thus, to store the current time in the type `time_t` variable `now`, you could write

```
time_t now;

now = time(0);
```

You also could write

```
time_t now;
time_t *ptr_now = &now;
time(ptr_now);
```

Converting Between Time Representations

Because knowing the number of seconds since January 1, 1970, is not very useful, time represented as a `time_t` value can be converted to a `tm` structure by the `localtime()` function. A `tm` structure contains day, month, year, and other time information in a format more appropriate for display and printing. The prototype of this function is

```
struct tm *localtime(time_t *ptr);
```

This function returns a pointer to a static type `tm` structure, so you do not need to declare a type `tm` structure to use, but only a pointer to type `tm`. This static structure is reused and overwritten each time `localtime()` is called; if you want to save the value returned, your program must declare a separate type `tm` structure and copy the values from the static structure.

The reverse conversion—from a type `tm` structure to a type `time_t` value—is performed by the function `mktime()`. The prototype is

```
time_t mktime(struct tm *ntime);
```

The function returns the number of seconds between midnight, January 1, 1970, and the time represented by the type `tm` structure pointed to by `ntime`.

Displaying Times

To convert times into formatted strings appropriate for display, use the functions `ctime()` and `asctime()`. Both of these functions return the time as a string with a specific format. They differ because `ctime()` is passed the time as a type `time_t` value, whereas `asctime()` is passed the time as a type `tm` structure. Their prototypes are

```
char *asctime(struct tm *ptr);
char *ctime(time_t *ptr);
```

Both functions return a pointer to a static, null-terminated, 26-character string that gives the time of the function's argument in the following format:

```
Thu Jun 13 10:22:23 1991
```

The time is formatted in 24-hour "military" time. Both functions use a static string, overwriting it each time they are called.

For more control over the format of the time, use the `strftime()` function. This function is passed a time as a type `tm` structure. It formats the time according to a format string. The function prototype is

```
size_t strftime(char *s, size_t max, char *fmt, struct tm *ptr);
```

The function takes the time in the type `tm` structure pointed to by `ptr`, formats it according to the format string `fmt`, and writes the result as a null-terminated string to the memory location pointed to by `s`. The argument `max` should specify the amount of space allocated at `s`. If the resulting string (including the terminating null character) has more than `max` characters, the function returns `0` and the string `s` is invalid. Otherwise, the function returns the number of characters written—`strlen(s)`.

The format string consists of one or more conversion specifiers from Table 19.1.

Table 19.1. Conversion specifiers that can be used with `strftime()`.

Specifier	Is Replaced By
%a	Abbreviated weekday name.
%A	Full weekday name.
%b	Abbreviated month name.
%B	Full month name.
%c	Date and time representation (for example, 10:41:50. 30-Jun-91).
%d	Day of month as a decimal number 01–31.
%H	The hour (24-hour clock) as a decimal number 00–23.
%I	The hour (12-hour clock) as a decimal number 00–11.

continues

Table 19.1. continued

Specifier	Is Replaced By
%j	The day of the year as a decimal number 001–366.
%m	The month as a decimal number 01–12.
%M	The minute as a decimal number 00–59.
%p	AM or PM.
%S	The second as a decimal number 00–59.
%U	The week of the year as a decimal number 00–53; Sunday is considered the first day of the week.
%w	The weekday as a decimal number 0–6 (Sunday = 0).
%W	The week of the year as a decimal number 00–53; Monday is considered the first day of the week.
%x	The date representation (for example, 30-Jun-91).
%X	The time representation (for example, 10:41:50).
%y	The year, without century, as a decimal number 00–99.
%Y	The year, with century, as a decimal number.
%Z	The time zone name if the information is available or blank if not.
%%	A single percent sign %.

Calculating Time Differences

You can calculate the difference, in seconds, between two times with the difftime() macro, which subtracts two time_t values and returns the difference. The prototype is

```
double difftime(time_t later, time_t earlier);
```

The function subtracts earlier from later and returns the difference, the number of seconds between the two times. A common use for difftime() is to calculate elapsed time, as is demonstrated (along with other time operations) in Listing 19.2.

You can determine duration of a different sort with the clock() function, which returns the amount of time that has passed since the program started execution, in 1/100-second units. The prototype is

```
clock_t clock(void);
```

To determine the duration of some portion of a program, call clock() twice—before and after the process occurs—and subtract the two return values.

Using the Time Functions

The program in Listing 19.2 demonstrates how to use the C library time functions.

Type Listing 19.2. Using the C library time functions.

```
1: /* Demonstrates the time functions. */
2: #include <conio.h>
3: #include <stdio.h>
4: #include <time.h>
5:
6: main()
7: {
8:     time_t start, finish, now;
9:     struct tm *ptr;
10:     char *c, buf1[80];
11:     double duration;
12:
13:     /* Record the time the program starts execution. */
14:
15:     start = time(0);
16:
17:     /* Record the current time, using the alternate method of */
18:     /* calling time(). */
19:
20:     time(&now);
21:
22:     /* Convert the time_t value into a type tm structure. */
23:
24:     ptr = localtime(&now);
25:
26:     /* Create and display a formatted string containing */
27:     /* the current time. */
28:
29:     c = asctime(ptr);
30:     puts(c);
31:     getch();
32:
33:     /* Now use the strftime() function to create several different */
34:     /* formatted versions of the time. */
35:
36:     strftime(buf1, 80, "This is week %U of the year %Y", ptr);
37:     puts(buf1);
38:     getch();
39:
40:     strftime(buf1, 80, "Today is %A, %x", ptr);
41:     puts(buf1);
42:     getch();
43:
44:     strftime(buf1, 80, "It is %M minutes past hour %I.", ptr);
45:     puts(buf1);
46:     getch();
47:
48:     /* Now get the current time and calculate program duration. */
49:
```

19

continues

Listing 19.2. continued

```
50:      finish = time(0);
51:      duration = difftime(finish, start);
52:      printf("\nProgram execution time = %f seconds.", duration);
53:
54:      /* Also display program duration in hundredths of seconds */
55:      /* using clock(). */
56:
57:      printf("\nProgram execution time = %ld hundredths of sec.",
58:          clock());
59: }
```

```
Sat Feb 11 16:35:35 1995

This is week 06 of the year 1995
Today is Saturday, 02/11/95
It is 35 minutes past hour 04.

Program execution time = 4.000000 seconds.
Program execution time = 3240 hundredths of sec.
```

This program has numerous comment lines, so it should be easy to follow. Because the time functions are being used, the TIME.H header file is included on line 4. Line 8 declares three variables of type `time_t` called `start`, `finish`, and `now`. These variables can hold the time as an offset from January 1, 1970, in seconds. Line 9 declares a pointer to a tm structure. The tm structure was described previously. The rest of the variables have types that should be familiar to you.

The program records its starting time on line 15. This is done with a call to `time()`. The program then does virtually the same thing in a different way. Instead of using the value returned by the `time()` function, line 20 passes `time()` a pointer to the variable now. Line 24 does exactly what the comment on line 22 states. It converts the `time_t` value of now to a type tm structure. The next few sections of the program print the value of the current time to the screen in various formats. Line 29 uses the `asctime()` function to assign the information to a character pointer, c. Line 30 prints the formatted information. The program then waits for a character to be pressed.

Lines 36–46 use the `strftime()` function to print the date in three different formats. Using Table 19.1, you should be able to determine what these lines print.

The program then determines the time once again on line 50. This is the program-ending time. Line 51 uses this ending time along with the starting time to calculate the program's duration. This value is printed on line 52. The program concludes by printing the program execution time from the `clock()` function.

Error-Handling Functions

The C standard library contains a variety of functions and macros that assist you in dealing with program errors.

The *assert()* Function

The macro assert() can diagnose program bugs. It is defined in ASSERT.H, and its prototype is

```
void assert(int expression);
```

The argument *expression* can be anything you want to test—a variable or any C expression. If *expression* evaluates as TRUE, assert() does nothing. If *expression* evaluates as FALSE, assert() displays an error message on stderr and aborts program execution.

How do you use assert()? It is most frequently used to track down program bugs (which are distinct from compilation errors). For example, a financial-analysis program you are writing might give incorrect answers occasionally. You suspect that the problem is caused by the variable interest_rate taking on a negative value, which should never happen. To check this, place the statement

```
assert(interest_rate >= 0);
```

at locations in the program where interest_rate is used. If the variable ever does become negative, the assert() macro alerts you.

To see the workings of assert(), run the program in Listing 19.3. If you enter a nonzero value, the program displays the value and terminates normally. If you enter zero, the assert() macro forces abnormal program termination. The error message you see displayed is

```
Assertion failed: x, file list1903.c, line 13
```

Type

Listing 19.3. Using the assert() macro.

```
1: /* The assert() macro. */
2:
3: #include <stdio.h>
4: #include <assert.h>
5:
6: main()
7: {
8:     int x;
9:
10:     printf("\nEnter an integer value: ");
11:     scanf("%d", &x);
12:
13:     assert(x);
```

continues

Listing 19.3. continued

```
14:
15:     printf("You entered %d.", x);
16: }
```

```
C:\>list1903
Enter an integer value: 10
You entered 10.
C:\>list1903
Enter an integer value: 0

Assertion failed: x, file list1903.c, line 13

Abnormal program termination
```

Run this program to see that the error message displayed by assert() on line 13 includes the expression whose test failed, the name of the file, and the line number where the assert() is located.

The action of assert() depends on another macro named NDEBUG (for "no debugging"). If the macro NDEBUG is not defined (the default), assert() is active. If NDEBUG is defined, assert() is turned off and has no effect. If you placed assert() in various program locations to help with debugging and then solved the problem, you can define NDEBUG to turn assert() off. This is much easier than going through the program and removing the assert() statements (only to discover later that you want to use them again). To define the macro NDEBUG, use the #define directive. You can demonstrate this by adding the line

```
#define NDEBUG
```

to listing 19.3, on line 2. Now, the program prints the value entered and terminates normally, even if you enter 0.

Note that NDEBUG does not need to be defined as anything in particular, as long as it is included in a #define directive. You learn more about the #define directive on Day 21, "Taking Advantage of Preprocessor Directives and More."

The ERRNO.H Header File

The header file ERRNO.H defines several macros used to define and document runtime errors. These macros are used in conjunction with the perror() function, described in the following paragraphs.

The ERRNO.H definitions include an external integer named errno. Many of the C library functions assign a value to this variable if an error occurs during function execution. The file ERRNO.H also defines a group of symbolic constants for these errors, listed in Table 19.2.

Table 19.2. The symbolic error constants defined in ERRNO.H.

Name	Value	Message and Meaning
E2BIG	1000	Argument list too long (list length exceeds 128 bytes).
EACCES	5	Permission denied (for example, trying to write to a file opened for read only).
EBADF	6	Bad file descriptor.
EDOM	1002	Math argument out of domain (an argument passed to a math function was outside the allowable range).
EEXIST	80	File exists.
EMFILE	4	Too many open files.
ENOENT	2	No such file or directory.
ENOEXEC	1001	Exec format error.
ENOMEM	8	Not enough core (for example, not enough memory to execute the exec() function).
ENOPATH	3	Path not found.
ERANGE	1003	Result out of range (for example, result returned by a math function is too large or small for the return data type).

You can use errno two ways. Some functions signal, by means of their return value, that an error has occurred. If this happens, you can test the value of errno to determine the nature of the error and take appropriate action. Otherwise, when you have no specific indication that an error occurred, you can test errno. If it is nonzero, an error has occurred, and the specific value of errno indicates the nature of the error. Be sure to reset errno to zero after handling the error. After perror() is explained, use of errno is illustrated in Listing 19.4.

19

The *perror()* Function

The perror() function is another of C's error-handling tools. When called, perror() displays a message on stderr describing the most recent error that occurred during a library function call or system call. The prototype, in STDIO.H, is

```
void perror(char *msg);
```

The argument msg points to an optional user-defined message. This message is printed first, followed by a colon and the implementation-defined message that describes the most recent error. If you call perror() when no error has occurred, the message displayed is no error.

A call to perror() does nothing to deal with the error condition. It's up to the program to take action, which might consist of prompting the user to do something such as terminate the program. The action the program takes can be determined by testing the value of errno and the nature of the error. Note that a program need not include the header file ERRNO.H to use the external variable errno. That header file is required only if your program uses the symbolic error constants listed in Table 19.2. Listing 19.4 illustrates the use of perror() and errno for handling runtime errors.

Listing 19.4. Using perror() and errno to deal with runtime errors.

```
1: /* Demonstration of error handling with perror() and errno. */
2:
3: #include <stdio.h>
4: #include <stdlib.h>
5: #include <errno.h>
6:
7: main()
8: {
9:     FILE *fp;
10:     char filename[80];
11:
12:     printf("Enter filename: ");
13:     gets(filename);
14:
15:     if (( fp = fopen(filename, "r")) == NULL)
16:     {
17:         perror("You goofed!");
18:         printf("errno = %d.", errno);
19:         exit(1);
20:     }
21:     else
22:     {
23:         puts("File opened for reading.");
24:         fclose(fp);
25:     }
26: }
```

```
C:\>list1904
Enter file name: list1904.c
File opened for reading.

C:\>list1904
Enter file name: notafile.xxx
You goofed!: No such file or directory
errno = 2.
```

This program prints one of two messages based on whether a file can be opened for reading. Line 15 tries to open a file. If the file opens, the else part of the if loop executes, printing the following message:

```
File opened for reading.
```

474

If there is an error when the file is opened, such as the file not existing, lines 17–19 of the if loop execute. Line 17 calls the perror() function with the string "You goofed!". This is followed by printing out the error number. The result of entering a file that does not exist is

```
You goofed!: No such file or directory.
errno = 2
```

DO	DON'T

DO include the ERRNO.H header file if you are going to use the symbolic errors in Table 19.2.

DON'T include the ERRNO.H header file if you are not going to use the symbolic error constants described in Table 19.2.

DO check for possible errors in your programs. Never assume that everything is okay.

Searching and Sorting

Among the most common tasks that programs perform are searching and sorting data. The C standard library contains general-purpose functions that you can use for each task.

Searching with *bsearch()*

The library function bsearch() performs a binary search of a data array, looking for an array element that matches a key. To use bsearch(), the array must be sorted into ascending order. Also, the program must provide the comparison function used by bsearch() to determine whether one data item is greater than, less than, or equal to another item. The prototype of bsearch() is in STDLIB.H:

```
void *bsearch(void *key, void *base, size_t num, size_t width,
int (*cmp)(void *element1, void *element2));
```

This is a fairly complex prototype, so go through it carefully. The argument key is a pointer to the data item being searched for, and base is a pointer to the first element of the array being searched. Both are declared as type void pointers, so they can point to any of C's data objects.

The argument num is the number of elements in the array, and width is the size (in bytes) of each element. The type specifier size_t refers to the data type returned by the sizeof() operator, which is unsigned. The sizeof() operator is usually used to obtain the values for num and width.

The final argument, cmp, is a pointer to the comparison function. This can be a user-written function or, when searching string data, it can be the library function strcmp(). The comparison function must meet the following two criteria:

- It is passed pointers to two data items; and
- It returns a type int as follows:

< 0	element 1 is less than element 2.
0	element 1 == element 2.
> 0	element 1 is greater than element 2.

The return value of bsearch() is a type void pointer. The function returns a pointer to the first array element it finds that matches the key, or NULL if no match is found. You must cast the returned pointer to the proper type before using it.

The sizeof() operator can provide the num and width arguments as follows. If array[] is the array to be searched, the statement

```
sizeof(array[0]);
```

returns the value for width—the size (in bytes) of one array element. Because the expression sizeof(array) returns the size, in bytes, of the entire array, the following statement obtains the value of num, the number of elements in the array:

```
sizeof(array)/sizeof(array[0])
```

The binary search algorithm is very efficient; it can search a large array quickly. Its operation is dependent on the array being in ascending order. Here's how the algorithm works:

1. The key is compared to the element at the middle of the array. If there's a match, the search is done. Otherwise, the key must be either less than or greater than the array element.

2. If the key is less than the array element, the matching element, if any, must be located in the first half of the array. Likewise, if the key is greater than the array element, the matching element must be located in the second half of the array.

3. Restrict the search to the appropriate half of the array, and return to step one.

You can see that each comparison performed by a binary search eliminates half of the array being searched. For example, a 1,000-element array can be searched with only 10 comparisons, and a 16,000-element array with only 14 comparisons. In general, a binary search requires n comparisons to search an array of $2n$ elements.

Sorting with *qsort()*

The library function qsort() is an implementation of the *quicksort algorithm,* invented by C.A.R. Hoare. The function sorts an array into order. Usually the result is in ascending order, but qsort() can be used for descending order as well. The function prototype, defined in STDLIB.H, is

```
void qsort(void *base, size_t num, size_t size,
int (*cmp)(void *element1, void *element2));
```

The argument base points at the first element in the array, num is the number of elements in the array, and size is the size (in bytes) of one array element. The argument cmp is a pointer to a comparison function. The rules for the comparison function are the same as for the comparison function used by bsearch(), described in the last section: you often use the same comparison function for both bsearch() and qsort(). The function qsort() has no return value.

Searching and Sorting—Two Demonstrations

The program in Listing 19.5 demonstrates the use of qsort() and bsearch(). The program sorts and searches an array of values. Note that the non-ANSI function getch() is used here. If your compiler does not support it, you should replace it with the ANSI standard function getchar().

Listing 19.5. Using the qsort() and bsearch() functions with values.

```
1: /* Using qsort() and bsearch() with values.*/
2: #include <conio.h>
3: #include <stdio.h>
4: #include <stdlib.h>
5:
6: #define MAX 20
7:
8: int intcmp(const void *v1, const void *v2);
9:
10: main()
11: {
12:     int arr[MAX], count, key, *ptr;
13:
14:     /* Enter some integers from the user. */
15:
16:     printf("Enter %d integer values; press Enter after each.\n", MAX);
17:
18:     for (count = 0; count < MAX; count++)
19:         scanf("%d", &arr[count]);
20:
21:     puts("Press a key to sort the values.");
22:     getch();
23:
24:     /* Sort the array into ascending order. */
25:
26:     qsort(arr, MAX, sizeof(arr[0]), intcmp);
27:
28:     /* Display the sorted array. */
29:
30:     for (count = 0; count < MAX; count++)
31:         printf("\narr[%d] = %d.", count, arr[count]);
32:
33:     puts("\nPress a key to continue.");
```

continues

Listing 19.5. continued

```
34:    getch();
35:
36:    /* Enter a search key. */
37:
38:    printf("Enter a value to search for: ");
39:    scanf("%d", &key);
40:
41:    /* Perform the search. */
42:
43:    ptr = (int *)bsearch(&key, arr, MAX, sizeof(arr[0]), intcmp);
44:
45:    if ( ptr != NULL )
46:        printf("%d found at arr[%d].", key, (ptr - arr));
47:    else
48:        printf("%d not found.", key);
49: }
50:
51: int intcmp(const void *v1, const void *v2)
52: {
53:    return (*(int *)v1 - *(int *)v2);
54: }
```

Input Output

```
Enter 20 integer values; press Enter after each.
45
12
999
1000
321
123
2300
954
1968
12
2
1999
1776
1812
1456
1
9999
3
76
200
Press a key to sort the values.

arr[0] = 1.
arr[1] = 2.
arr[2] = 3.
arr[3] = 12.
```

```
arr[4] = 12.
arr[5] = 45.
arr[6] = 76.
arr[7] = 123.
arr[8] = 200.
arr[9] = 321.
arr[10] = 954.
arr[11] = 999.
arr[12] = 1000.
arr[13] = 1456.
arr[14] = 1776.
arr[15] = 1812.
arr[16] = 1968.
arr[17] = 1999.
arr[18] = 2300.
arr[19] = 9999.
Press a key to continue.
Enter a value to search for: 1776
1776 found at arr[14]
```

Listing 19.5 incorporates everything previously described about sorting and searching. The program lets you enter up to MAX values (20 in this case). It sorts the values and prints them in order. Then it enables you to enter a value to search for in the array. A printed message states the status of the search.

Obtaining the values for the array on lines 18 and 19 is familiar code. Line 26 contains the call to qsort() to sort the array. The first argument is a pointer to the array's first element. This is followed by MAX, the number of elements in the array. The size of the first element is then provided so that qsort() knows the width of each item. The call is finished with the argument for the sort function, intcmp.

The function intcmp() is defined on lines 51–54. It returns the difference of the two values passed to it. This might seem too simple at first, but remember what values the comparison function is supposed to return. If the elements are equal, 0 should be returned; if element one is greater than element two, a positive number should be returned; if element one is less than element two, a negative number should be returned. This is exactly what intcmp() does.

The searching is done with bsearch(). Notice that its arguments are virtually the same as those of qsort(). The difference is that the first argument of bsearch() is the key to be searched for. bsearch() returns a pointer to the location of the found key or NULL if the key is not found. On line 43, ptr is assigned the returned value of bsearch(). ptr is used in the if loop on lines 45–48 to print the status of the search.

Listing 19.6 has the same functionality as Listing 19.5; however, Listing 19.6 sorts and searches strings.

19

Type

Listing 19.6. Using `qsort()` and `bsearch()` with strings.

```
1: /* Using qsort() and bsearch() with strings. */
2:
3: #include <stdio.h>
4: #include <stdlib.h>
5: #include <string.h>
6:
7: #define MAX 20
8:
9: int comp(const void *s1, const void *s2);
10:
11: main()
12: {
13:     char *data[MAX], buf[80], *ptr, *key, **key1;
14:     int count;
15:
16:     /* Input a list of words. */
17:
18:     printf("Enter %d words, pressing Enter after each.\n",MAX);
19:
20:     for (count = 0; count < MAX; count++)
21:     {
22:         printf("Word %d: ", count+1);
23:         gets(buf);
24:         data[count] = malloc(strlen(buf)+1);
25:         strcpy(data[count], buf);
26:     }
27:
28:     /* Sort the words (actually, sort the pointers). */
29:
30:     qsort(data, MAX, sizeof(data[0]), comp);
31:
32:     /* Display the sorted words. */
33:
34:     for (count = 0; count < MAX; count++)
35:         printf("\n%d: %s", count+1, data[count]);
36:
37:     /* Get a search key. */
38:
39:     printf("\n\nEnter a search key: ");
40:     gets(buf);
41:
42:     /* Perform the search. First, make key1 a pointer */
43:     /* to the pointer to the search key.*/
44:
45:     key = buf;
46:     key1 = &key;
47:     ptr = bsearch(key1, data, MAX, sizeof(data[0]), comp);
48:
49:     if (ptr != NULL)
50:         printf("%s found.", buf);
51:     else
52:         printf("%s not found", buf);
53: }
```

```
54:
55: int comp(const void *s1, const void *s2)
56: {
57:     return (strcmp(*(char **)s1, *(char **)s2));
58: }
```

```
Enter 20 words, pressing Enter after each
Word 1: apple
Word 2: orange
Word 3: grapefruit
Word 4: peach
Word 5: plum
Word 6: pear
Word 7: cherries
Word 8: banana
Word 9: lime
Word 10: lemon
Word 11: tangerine
Word 12: star
Word 13: watermelon
Word 14: cantaloupe
Word 15: musk melon
Word 16: strawberry
Word 17: blackberry
Word 18: blueberry
Word 19: grape
Word 20: cranberry

1: apple
2: banana
3: blackberry
4: blueberry
5: cantaloupe
6: cherries
7: cranberry
8: grape
9: grapefruit
10: lemon
11: lime
12: musk melon
13: orange
14: peach
15: pear
16: plum
17: star
18: strawberry
19: tangerine
20: watermelon

Enter a search key: orange
orange found.
```

19

A couple of points about Listing 19.6 bear mentioning. This program makes use of an array of pointers to strings, a technique you were introduced to on Day 15, "More on Pointers." As you saw in that chapter, you can "sort" the strings by sorting the array of pointers. This method requires a modification in the comparison function, however. This function is passed pointers to the two items in the array that are compared. However, you want the array of pointers sorted based not on the values of the pointers themselves but based on the values of the strings they point to.

Because of this, you must use a comparison function that is passed pointers to pointers. Each argument to comp() is a pointer to an array element, and because each element is itself a pointer (to a string), the argument is therefore a pointer to a pointer. Within the function itself, you dereference the pointers so that the return value of comp() depends on the values of the strings pointed to.

The fact that the arguments passed to comp() are pointers to pointers creates another problem. You store the search key in buf[], and you also know that the name of an array (in this case buf) is a pointer to the array. However, you need to pass not buf itself, but a pointer to buf. The problem is that buf is a pointer constant, not a pointer variable; buf itself has no address in memory but is a symbol that evaluates to the address of the array. Because of this, you cannot create a pointer that points to buf by using the address-of operator in front of buf, as in &buf.

What to do? First, create a pointer variable and assign the value of buf to it. In the program, this pointer variable has the name key. Because key is a pointer variable, it has an address, and you can create a pointer that contains that address—in this case, key1. When you finally call bsearch(), the first argument is key1, a pointer to a pointer to the key string. The function bsearch() passes that argument on to comp(), and everything works properly.

DO	**DON'T**
DON'T forget to put your search array into ascending order before using bsearch().	

Summary

This chapter explored some of the more useful functions supplied in the C function library. There are functions that perform mathematical calculations, deal with time, and assist your program with error handling. The functions for sorting and searching data are particularly useful; they can save you considerable time when you're writing your programs.

Q&A

Q Why do nearly all of the math functions return `doubles`?

A The answer to this question is precision, not consistency. A `double` is more precise than the other variable types; therefore, your answers are more accurate. On Day 20, "Working with Memory," you learn specifics on casting variables and variable promotion. These topics are also applicable to the precision obtained.

Q Are `bsearch()` and `qsort()` the only ways in C to sort and search?

A These two functions are provided in the standard library; however, you do not have to use them. Many computer programming textbooks teach how to write your own searching and sorting programs. C contains all the commands you need to write your own. You can purchase specially written searching and sorting routines. The biggest benefits of `bsearch()` and `qsort()` are that they are already written and they are provided with any ANSI-compatible compiler.

Q Do the math functions validate bad data?

A Never assume that data entered is correct. Always validate data entered by a user. For example, if you pass a negative value to `sqrt()`, the function generates an error. If you are formatting the output, you probably don't want this error displayed as it is. Remove the `if` statement in Listing 19.1 and enter a negative number to see what we mean.

Workshop

The Workshop provides quiz questions to help you solidify your understanding of the material covered and exercises to provide you with experience in using what you've learned.

Quiz

1. What is the return data type for all of C's mathematical functions?
2. What C variable type is `time_t` equivalent to?
3. What are the differences between the `time()` function and the `clock()` function?
4. When you call the `perror()` function, what does it do to correct an existing error condition?
5. Before you search an array with `bsearch()`, what must you do?
6. Using `bsearch()`, how many comparisons would be required to find an element if the array had 16,000 items? (This answer is given in the chapter.)
7. Using `bsearch()`, how many comparisons would be required to find an element if an array had only 10 items?

8. Using bsearch(), how many comparisons would be required to find an element if an array had 2,000,000 items?

9. What values must a comparison function for bsearch() and qsort() return?

10. What does bsearch() return if it cannot find an element in an array?

Exercises

1. Write a call to bsearch(). The array to be searched is called names, the values are characters. The comparison function is called comp_names(). Assume all of the names are the same size.

2. **BUG BUSTER:** What is wrong with the following program?

```
#include <stdio.h>
#include <stdlib.h>
main()
{
    int values[10], count, key, *ptr;

    printf("Enter values");
    for( ctr = 0; ctr < 10; ctr++ )
        scanf( "%d", &values[ctr] );

    qsort(values, 10, compare_function());
}
```

3. **BUG BUSTER:** Is anything wrong with the following compare function?

```
int intcmp( int element1, int element2)
{
    if ( element 1 > element 2 )
        return -1;
    else if ( element 1 < element2 )
        return 1;
    else
        return 0;
}
```

Answers are not provided for the following exercises:

4. Modify Listing 19.1 so that the sqrt() function works with negative numbers. Do this by taking the absolute value of x.

5. Write a program that consists of a menu that does various math functions. Use as many of the math functions as you can.

6. Write a function that causes the program to pause for approximately five seconds using the time functions learned in this chapter.

7. Add the assert() function to the program from exercise four. The program should print a message if a negative value is entered.

SAMS
Sams
Learning
Center
SAMS
PUBLISHING

8. Write a program that accepts 30 names and sorts them using `qsort()`. The program should print the sorted names.

9. Modify the program in exercise 8 so that if the user enters `"QUIT"`, the program stops accepting input and sorts the entered values.

10. Refer to Day 15 for a "brute-force" method of sorting an array of pointers to strings based on the string values. Write a program that measures the time required to sort a large array of pointers with that method, and then compares that time with the time required to perform the same sort with the library function `qsort()`.

19

20

Working with
Memory

This chapter covers, in greater detail than earlier lessons, some important aspects about managing memory within your C programs. Today, you learn

- About type conversions
- How to allocate and free memory storage
- How to manipulate memory blocks

Type Conversions

All of C's data objects have a specific type. A numeric variable can be an int or a float, a pointer can be a pointer to double or char, and so on. Programs often require that different types be combined in expressions and statements. What happens in such cases? Sometimes C automatically handles the different types, and you need not be concerned. At other times, you must make an explicit conversion of one data type to another to avoid erroneous results. You've seen this in earlier chapters when you had to convert or *cast* a type void pointer to a specific type before using it. In this and other situations, you need a clear understanding of when explicit type conversions are necessary and what types of errors can result when the proper conversion is not applied. The following sections cover C's automatic and explicit type conversions.

Automatic Type Conversions

As the name implies, automatic type conversions are performed automatically by the C compiler without any need for you to do anything. However, you should be aware of what is going on so that you can understand how C evaluates expressions.

Type Promotion in Expressions

When a C expression is evaluated, the resulting value has a particular data type. If all components of the expression have the same type, the resulting type is that type as well. For example, if x and y are both type int, the following expression is type int also:

x + y

What if the components of an expression have different types? In that case, the expression has the same type as its most comprehensive component. From least comprehensive to most comprehensive, the numerical data types are char, int, long, float, and double. Thus, an expression containing an int and a char is type int, an expression containing a long and a float is type float, and so on.

Within expressions, individual operands are *promoted* as necessary to match the associated operands in the expression. Operands are promoted, in pairs, for each binary operator in the expression. Promotion is not needed, of course, if both operands are the same type. If they're not, promotion follows these rules:

- If either operand is a `double`, the other operand is promoted to type `double`.
- If either operand is a `float`, the other operand is promoted to type `float`.
- If either operand is a `long`, the other operand is converted to type `long`.

For example, if x is an int and y is a `float`, evaluating the expression x/y causes x to be promoted to type `float` before the expression is evaluated. This does not mean that the type of the variable x is changed. It means that a type `float` copy of x is created and used in the expression evaluation. The value of the expression is, as you just learned, type `float`.

Conversion by Assignment

Promotions also occur with the assignment operator. The expression on the right side of an assignment statement always is promoted to the type of the data object on the left side of the assignment operator. Note that this might cause a "demotion" rather than a promotion. If f is a type `float` and i is a type `int`, i is promoted to type `float` in this assignment statement:

```
f = i;
```

In contrast, the assignment statement

```
i = f;
```

causes f to be demoted to type `int`. Its fractional part is lost on assignment to i. Remember that f itself is not changed at all; promotion affects only a copy of the value. Thus, after the following statements are executed:

```
float f = 1.23;
int i;
i = f;
```

the variable i has the value 1, and f still has the value 1.23. As this example illustrates, the fractional part is lost when a floating point number is converted to an integer type.

You should be aware that when an integer type is converted to a floating-point type, the resulting floating-point value might not exactly match the integer value. This is because the floating-point format used internally by the computer cannot accurately represent every possible integer number. For example, the following code could result in display of 2.999995 instead of 3:

```
float f;
int i = 3;
f = i;
printf("%f", f);
```

In most cases, any loss of accuracy caused by this would be insignificant. To be sure, however, keep integer values in type `int` or type `long` variables.

Explicit Conversions Using Typecasts

A *typecast* uses the cast operator explicitly to control type conversions in your program. A typecast consists of a type name, in parentheses, before an expression. Casts can be performed on arithmetic expressions and on pointers. The result is that the expression is converted to the type specified by the cast. In this manner, you can control the type of expressions in your program rather than relying on C's automatic conversions.

Casting Arithmetic Expressions

Casting an arithmetic expression tells the compiler to represent the value of the expression in a certain way. In effect, a cast is similar to a promotion, which was discussed earlier. However, a cast is under your control and not the compiler's. For example, if i is a type int, the expression

```
(float)i
```

casts i to type float. In other words, the program makes an internal copy of the value of i in floating point format.

When would you use a typecast with an arithmetic expression? The most common use is to avoid losing the fractional part of the answer in an integer division. The program in Listing 20.1 illustrates this. You should compile and run the program.

Listing 20.1. When one integer is divided by another, any fractional part of the answer is lost.

```
1: #include <stdio.h>
2:
3: main()
4: {
5:     int i1 = 100, i2 = 40;
6:     float f1;
7:
8:     f1 = i1/i2;
9:
10:     printf("%lf", f1);
11: }
```

```
2.000000
```

The answer displayed by the program is `2.000000`, but 100/40 evaluates to 2.5. What happened? The expression i1/i2 on line 8 contains two type int variables. By the rules explained earlier in this chapter, the value of the expression is therefore type int itself. As such, it can represent only whole numbers, and so the fractional part of the answer is lost.

You might think that assigning the result of i1/i2 to a type float variable promotes it to type float. This is correct, but now it's too late; the fractional part of the answer is already gone.

To avoid this sort of inaccuracy, you must cast one of the type int variables to type float. If one of the variables is cast to type float, the previous rules tell you the other variable is promoted automatically to type float, and the value of the expression is also type float. The fractional part of the answer is thus preserved. To demonstrate this, change line 8 in the source code so the assignment statement reads as follows, and the program will display the correct answer:

```
f1 = (float)i1/i2;
```

Casting Pointers

You already have been introduced to the casting of pointers. As you saw on Day 18, "Getting More from Functions," a type void pointer is a generic pointer; it can point to anything. Before you can use a void pointer, you must cast it to the proper type. Note that you do not need to cast a pointer to assign a value to it or to compare it with NULL. However, you must cast it before dereferencing it or performing pointer arithmetic with it. For more details on casting void pointers, review Day 18.

DO	DON'T

DO use a cast to promote or demote variable values when necessary.

DON'T use a cast just to prevent a compiler warning. You might find that using a cast gets rid of a warning, but, before removing the warning this way, be sure you understand why you are getting the warning.

Allocating Memory Storage Space

20

The C library contains functions for allocating memory storage space at runtime, a process called *dynamic memory allocation*. This technique can have significant advantages over explicitly allocating memory in the program source code, such as declaring variables, structures, and arrays. This latter method, called *static memory allocation*, requires you to know when you are writing the program exactly how much memory is needed. Dynamic memory allocation allows the program to react, while it is executing, to demands for memory, such as user input. All the functions for handling dynamic memory allocation require the header file STDLIB.H; with some compilers, MALLOC.H is required as well. Note that all allocation functions return a type void pointer. As you learned on Day 18, a type void pointer must be cast to the appropriate type before being used.

Before moving on to the details, a few words are in order about memory allocation. What exactly does it mean? Each computer has a certain amount of memory installed. This amount varies from system to system. When you run a program, whether it be a word processor, a graphics program, or a C program you wrote yourself, the program is loaded from disk into the computer's memory. The memory space the program occupies includes the program code as well as space for all the program's static data—that is, data items that are declared in the source code. The memory left over is what's available for allocation using the functions in this section.

How much memory is available for allocation? It all depends. If you're running a large program on a system with only a modest amount of memory installed, the amount of available memory will be small. Conversely, when a small program is running on a multi-megabyte system, plenty of memory will be available. This means that your programs cannot make any assumptions about memory availability. When a memory-allocation function is called, you must check its return value to ensure that the memory was allocated successfully. In addition, your programs must be able to gracefully handle the situation when a memory-allocation request fails. Later in the chapter, you'll learn a technique for determining exactly how much memory is available.

Note also that the operating system you are running may have an effect on memory availability. Some operating systems make only a portion of physical RAM available. DOS 6.*x* and earlier falls into this category—even if your system has multiple megabytes of RAM, a DOS program will have direct access to only the first 640KB (special techniques can be used to access the other memory, but these are beyond the scope of this book). In contrast, UNIX usually will make all physical RAM available to a program. To complicate matters further, some operating systems, such as Windows and OS/2, provide *virtual memory* that permits storage space on the hard disk to be allocated as if it were RAM. In this situation, the amount of memory available to a program includes not only the RAM installed but also the virtual-memory space on the hard disk.

For the most part, these operating system differences in memory allocation should be transparent to the C programmer. If you use one of the C functions to allocate memory, the call either succeeds or fails, and you need not worry about the details of what's happening.

The *malloc()* Function

In earlier chapters, you learned how to use the `malloc()` library function to allocate storage space for strings. The `malloc()` function is not limited to strings, of course; it can allocate space for any storage need. This function allocates memory by the byte. Recall that `malloc()`'s prototype is

```
void *malloc(size_t num);
```

The argument `size_t` is defined in STDLIB.H as `unsigned`. The `malloc()` function allocates `num` bytes of storage space and returns a pointer to the first byte. The function returns `NULL` if the requested storage space could not be allocated or if `num == 0`. Review the section on `malloc()`

on Day 10, "Characters and Strings," if you're still a bit rusty on its operation. Listing 20.2 shows you how to use malloc() to determine the amount of free memory available in your system.

This program works fine under DOS, but you should not run it if you are using an operating system that has virtual memory, such as OS/2 (as explained earlier in this chapter). It will run under OS/2, but because there is so much memory "available" (essentially limited only by hard-disk space), the program will take a very long time to exhaust available memory. In any event, it's only with DOS, with its limited memory resources, that a program would need to know how much memory is available.

Type

Listing 20.2. Using `malloc()` to determine how much memory is free.

```
1: /* Using malloc() to determine free memory.*/
2:
3: #include <stdio.h>
4: #include <stdlib.h>
5:
6: /* Definition of a structure that is
7:    1024 bytes (1 kilobyte) in size.) */
8:
9: struct kilo {
10:    struct kilo *next;
11:    char dummy[1022];
12: };
13:
14: int FreeMem(void);
15:
16: main()
17: {
18:
19:    printf("\nYou have %d kilobytes free.", FreeMem());
20:
21: }
22:
23: int FreeMem(void)
24: {
25:    /*Returns the number of kilobytes (1024 bytes)
26:    of free memory. */
27:
28:    int counter;
29:    struct kilo *head, *current, *nextone;
30:
31:    current = head = (struct kilo*) malloc(sizeof(struct kilo));
32:
33:    if (head == NULL)
34:       return 0;      //No memory available.
35:
36:    counter = 0;
37:    do
38:    {
39:       counter++;
40:       current->next = (struct kilo*) malloc(sizeof(struct kilo));
```

20

Listing 20.2. continued

```
41:        current = current->next;
42:    } while (current != NULL);
43:
44:    /* Now counter holds the number of type kilo
45:       structures we were able to allocate. We
46:       must free them all before returning. */
47:
48:    current = head;
49:
50:    do
51:    {
52:       nextone = current->next;
53:       free(current);
54:       current = nextone;
55:    } while (nextone != NULL);
56:
57:    return counter;
58: }
```

```
C:\>LIST20_2

You have 60 kilobytes free.
```

Listing 20.2 operates in a brute-force manner. It simply loops, allocating blocks of memory, until the `malloc()` function returns `NULL`, indicating that there is no more memory available. The amount of available memory is then equal to the number of blocks allocated multiplied by the block size. The function then frees all the allocated blocks and returns the number of blocks allocated to the calling program. By making each block one kilobyte, the returned value indicates directly the number of kilobytes of free memory. As you may know, a kilobyte is not exactly one thousand bytes, but rather is 1024 bytes (2 to the 10th power). We obtain a 1024-byte item by defining a structure, which we cleverly named `kilo`, that contains a 1022-byte array plus a two-byte pointer.

The function `FreeMem()` uses the technique of linked lists that are covered in more detail on Bonus Day 5, "Advanced Structures: Linked Lists." In brief, a linked list consists of structures that contain a pointer to their own type (in addition to other data members). There is also a *head pointer* that points to the first item in the list (the variable `head`, a pointer to type `kilo`). The first item in the list points to the second, the second points to the third, and so on. The last item in the list is identified by a `NULL` pointer member. See Bonus Day 5 for more information.

The *calloc()* Function

The `calloc()` function also allocates memory. Rather than allocating a group of bytes as `malloc()` does, `calloc()` allocates a group of objects. The function prototype is

```
void *calloc(size_t num, size_t size);
```

Remember that size_t is a synonym for unsigned on most compilers. The argument num is the number of objects to allocate, and size is the size (in bytes) of each object. If allocation is successful, all the allocated memory is cleared (set to 0), and the function returns a pointer to the first byte. If allocation fails or if either num or size is 0, the function returns NULL.

The program in Listing 20.3 illustrates the use of calloc().

Listing 20.3. Using the `calloc()` function to allocate memory storage space dynamically.

```
1: /* Demonstrates calloc(). */
2:
3: #include <stdlib.h>
4: #include <stdio.h>
5:
6: main()
7: {
8:     unsigned num;
9:     int *ptr;
10:
11:     printf("Enter the number of type int to allocate: ");
12:     scanf("%d", &num);
13:
14:     ptr = (int*)calloc(num, sizeof(int));
15:
16:     if (ptr != NULL)
17:         puts("Memory allocation was successful.");
18:     else
19:         puts("Memory allocation failed.");
20: }
```

```
C:\>list20_3
Enter the number of type int to allocate: 100
Memory allocation was successful.

C:\>list20_3
Enter the number of type int to allocate: 99999999
Memory allocation failed.
```

Analysis

This program prompts for a value on lines 11 and 12. This number determines how much space is allocated. The program attempts to allocate enough memory (line 14) to hold the specified number of int variables. If the allocation fails, the return value from calloc() is NULL; otherwise, it's a pointer to the allocated memory. In the case of this program, the return value from calloc() is placed in the int pointer, ptr. An if statement on lines 16–19, checks the status of the allocation based on ptr's value and prints an appropriate message.

Enter different values and see how much memory can be successfully allocated. The maximum amount depends, to some extent, on your system configuration. On some systems allocating space for 25,000 occurrences of type int is successful, whereas 30,000 fails.

The *realloc()* Function

The `realloc()` function changes the size of a block of memory previously allocated with `malloc()` or `calloc()`. The function prototype is

```
void *realloc(void *ptr, size_t size);
```

The `ptr` argument points to the original block of memory. The new desired size, in bytes, is specified by `size`. There are several possible outcomes with `realloc()`:

- If sufficient space exists to expand the memory block pointed to by `ptr`, the additional memory is allocated and the function returns `ptr`.
- If sufficient space does not exist to expand the current block in its current location, a new block of the size for `size` is allocated and existing data is copied from the old block to the beginning of the new block. The old block is freed, and the function returns a pointer to the new block.
- If the `ptr` argument is `NULL`, the function acts like `malloc()`, allocating a block of `size` bytes and returning a pointer to it.
- If the argument size is 0, the memory that `ptr` points to is freed and the function returns `NULL`.
- If memory is insufficient for the reallocation (either expanding the old block or allocating a new one), the function returns `NULL` and the original block is unchanged.

The use of `realloc()` is demonstrated by the program in Listing 20.4.

Listing 20.4. Using `realloc()` to increase the size of a block of dynamically allocated memory.

```
 1: /* Using realloc() to change memory allocation. */
 2:
 3: #include <stdio.h>
 4: #include <stdlib.h>
 5: #include <string.h>
 6:
 7: main()
 8: {
 9:     char buf[80], *message;
10:
11:     /* Input a string. */
12:
13:     puts("Enter a line of text.");
14:     gets(buf);
15:
16:     /* Allocate the initial block and copy the string to it. */
17:
18:     message = realloc(NULL, strlen(buf)+1);
19:     strcpy(message, buf);
20:
```

```
21:      /* Display the message. */
22:
23:      puts(message);
24:
25:      /* Get another string from the user. */
26:
27:      puts("Enter another line of text.");
28:      gets(buf);
29:
30:      /* Increase the allocation, then concatenate the string to it. */
31:
32:      message = realloc(message,(strlen(message) + strlen(buf)+1));
33:      strcat(message, buf);
34:
35:      /* Display the new message. */
36:
37:      puts(message);
38: }
```

```
Enter a line of text.
This is the first line of text.
This is the first line of text.
Enter another line of text.
This is the second line of text.
This is the first line of text.This is the second line of text.
```

This program gets an input string on line 14. This string is read into an array of characters called buf. This value is then copied into a memory location pointed to by message (line 19). message was allocated using realloc() on line 18. realloc() was called even though there had not been a previous allocation. By passing NULL as the first parameter, realloc() knows that this is a first allocation.

Line 28 gets a second string in the buf buffer. This string is concatenated to the string already held in message. Because message is just big enough to hold the first string, it needs to be reallocated to make room to hold both the first and second strings. This is exactly what line 32 does. The program concludes by printing out the final concatenated string.

The *free()* Function

When you allocate memory with either malloc() or calloc(), it is taken from the dynamic memory pool available to your program. This pool is sometimes called the *heap*, and it is finite. When your program finishes using a particular block of allocated memory, you should deallocate, or free, the memory to make it available for future allocations. To free memory that was allocated dynamically, use free(). Its prototype is

```
void free(void *ptr);
```

The free() function releases the memory pointed to by ptr. This memory must have been allocated with malloc(), calloc(), or realloc(). If ptr is NULL, free() does nothing. Listing 20.5 demonstrates the free() function; it also was used in Listing 20.2.

20

Listing 20.5. Using `free()` to release previously allocated dynamic memory.

```
1: /* Using free() to release allocated dynamic memory. */
2:
3: #include <stdio.h>
4: #include <stdlib.h>
5: #include <string.h>
6:
7: #define BLOCKSIZE 30000
8:
9: main()
10: {
11:     void *ptr1, *ptr2;
12:
13:     /* Allocate one block. */
14:
15:     ptr1 = malloc(BLOCKSIZE);
16:
17:     if (ptr1 != NULL)
18:         printf("\nFirst allocation of %d bytes successful.",BLOCKSIZE);
19:     else
20:     {
21:         printf("\nAttempt to allocate %d bytes failed.",BLOCKSIZE);
22:         exit(1);
23:     }
24:
25:     /* Try to allocate another block. */
26:
27:     ptr2 = malloc(BLOCKSIZE);
28:
29:     if (ptr2 != NULL)
30:     {
31:         /* If allocation successful, print message and exit. */
32:
33:         printf("\nSecond allocation of %d bytes successful.",
34:                 BLOCKSIZE);
35:         exit(0);
36:     }
37:
38:     /* If not successful, free the first block and try again.*/
39:
40:     printf("\nSecond attempt to allocate %d bytes failed.",BLOCKSIZE);
41:     free(ptr1);
42:     printf("\nFreeing first block.");
43:
44:     ptr2 = malloc(BLOCKSIZE);
45:
46:     if (ptr2 != NULL)
47:         printf("\nAfter free(), allocation of %d bytes successful.",
48:                 BLOCKSIZE);
49: }
```

Output

First allocation of 30000 bytes successful.

Second allocation of 30000 bytes successful.

This program tries to dynamically allocate two blocks of memory. It uses the defined constant BLOCKSIZE to determine how much to allocate. Line 15 does the first allocation using malloc(). Lines 17–23 check the status of the allocation by checking to see whether the return value was equal to NULL. A message is displayed stating the status of the allocation. If the allocation failed, the program exits. Line 27 tries to allocate a second block of memory, again checking to see whether the allocation was successful (lines 29–36). If the second allocation was successful, a call to exit() ends the program. If it was not successful, a message states that the attempt to allocate memory failed. The first block is then freed with free() (line 41), and a new attempt is made to allocate the second block.

You might need to modify the value of the symbolic constant BLOCKSIZE. On some systems the value of 30000 produces the following program output:

```
First allocation of 30000 bytes successful.
Second attempt to allocate 30000 bytes failed.
Freeing first block.
After free(), allocation of 30000 bytes successful.
```

On systems with virtual memory, of course, allocation always will succeed.

DO	DON'T

DO free allocated memory when you are done with it.

DON'T assume that a call to malloc(), calloc(), or realloc() was successful. In other words, always check to see that the memory was indeed allocated.

Manipulating Memory Blocks

So far today, you've seen how to allocate and free blocks of memory. The C library also contains functions that can be used to manipulate blocks of memory—setting all bytes in a block to a specified value, and copying and moving information from one location to another.

The *memset()* function

To set all the bytes in a block of memory to a particular value, use memset(). The function prototype is

```
void * memset(void *dest, int c, size_t count);
```

The argument dest points to the block of memory. c is the value to set, and count is the number of bytes, starting at dest, to be set. Note that while c is a type int, it is treated as a type char. In other words, only the low-order byte is used, and you can specify values of c only in the range 0–255.

Use `memset()` to initialize a block of memory to a specified value. Because the function can use only a type `char` as the initialization value, it is not useful for working with blocks of data types other than type `char`, except when you want to initialize to 0. In other words, you could not use `memset()` to initialize an array of type `int` to the value 99, but you could initialize all array elements to the value 0. `memset()` will be demonstrated in Listing 20.6.

The *memcpy()* function

`memcpy()` copies bytes of data between memory blocks, or buffers. The function does not care about the type of data being copied—it simply makes an exact byte-for-byte copy. The function prototype is

```
void *memcpy(void *dest, void *src, size_t count);
```

The arguments `dest` and `src` point to the destination and source memory blocks, respectively. `count` specifies the number of bytes to be copied. The return value is `dest`. If the two blocks of memory overlap, the function might not operate properly—some of the data in `src` might be overwritten before being copied. Use the `memmove()` function, presented next, to handle overlapping memory blocks. `memcpy()` will be demonstrated in Listing 20.6.

The *memmove()* function

`memmove()` is very much like `memcpy()`, copying a specified number of bytes from one memory block to another. It's more flexible, however, in that it can handle overlapping memory blocks properly. Because `memmove()` can do everything `memcpy()` can do with the added flexibility of dealing with overlapping blocks, you rarely, if ever, should have a reason to use `memcpy()`. The prototype is

```
void *memmove(void *dest, void *src, size_t count);
```

`dest` and `src` point to the destination and source memory blocks, and `count` specifies the number of bytes to be copied. The return value is `dest`. If the blocks overlap, the function ensures that the source data in the overlapped region are copied before being overwritten. Listing 20.6 demonstrates `memset()`, `memcpy()`, and `memmove()`.

Listing 20.6. Demonstration of `memset()`, `memcpy()`, and `memmove()`.

```
1: /* Demonstrating memset(), memcpy(), and memmove(). */
2:
3: #include <stdio.h>
4: #include <string.h>
5: 
5: char message1[60] = "Four score and seven years ago ...";
6: char message2[60] = "abcdefghijklmnopqrstuvwxyz";
```

```
 7: char temp[60];
 8:
 9: main()
10: {
11:     printf("\nmessage1[] before memset():\t%s", message1);
12:     memset(message1 + 5, '@', 10);
13:     printf("\nmessage1[] after memset():\t%s", message1);
14:
15:     strcpy(temp, message2);
16:     printf("\n\nOriginal message: %s", temp);
17:     memcpy(temp + 4, temp + 16, 10);
18:     printf("\nAfter memcpy() without overlap:\t%s", temp);
19:     strcpy(temp, message2);
20:     memcpy(temp + 6, temp + 4, 10);
21:     printf("\nAfter memcpy() with overlap:\t%s", temp);
22:
23:     strcpy(temp, message2);
24:     printf("\n\nOriginal message: %s", temp);
25:     memmove(temp + 4, temp + 16, 10);
26:     printf("\nAfter memmove() without overlap:\t%s", temp);
27:     strcpy(temp, message2);
28:     memmove(temp + 6, temp + 4, 10);
29:     printf("\nAfter memmove() with overlap:\t%s", temp);
30:
31: }
```

```
message1[] before memset():    Four score and seven years ago ...
message1[] after memset():     Four @@@@@@@@@@seven years ago ...

Original message: abcdefghijklmnopqrstuvwxyz
After memcpy() without overlap: abcdqrstuvwxyzopqrstuvwxyz
After memcpy() with overlap:    abcdefefefefefqrstuvwxyz

Original message: abcdefghijklmnopqrstuvwxyz
After memmove() without overlap:       abcdqrstuvwxyzopqrstuvwxyz
After memmove() with overlap:   abcdefefghijklmnqrstuvwxyz
```

The operation of `memset()` is straightforward. Note how the pointer notation `message1 + 5` was used to specify that `memset()` was to start setting characters at the sixth character in `message1[]` (remember, arrays are 0-based). As a result, the sixth through fifteenth characters in `message1[]` have been changed to @.

Without overlapping source and destination, `memcpy()` works fine. The 10 characters of `temp[]` starting at position 17 (the letters *q* through *z*) have been copied to positions 5 though 14, where the letters *e* though *n* were originally located. If, however, the source and destination overlap, things are different. By trying to copy 10 characters starting at position 4 to position 6, an overlap of 8 positions occurs. You might expect the letters *e* through *n* to be copied over letters *g* through *p*. Instead, the letters *e* and *f* are repeated five times.

If there's no overlap, `memmove()` works just like `memcpy()`. With overlap, however, it makes all the difference—it copies the original source characters to the destination.

| **DO** | **DON'T** |

DO use `memmove()` in preference to `memcpy()` in case you are dealing with overlapping memory regions.

DON'T try to use `memset()` to initialize type `int`, `float`, or `double` arrays to any value other than 0.

Summary

This chapter covered a variety of C programming topics. You learned how to allocate, reallocate, and free memory at runtime, commands that give you flexibility in allocating storage space for program data. You also saw how and when to use typecasts with variables and pointers. Forgetting about typecasts, or using them improperly, is a common cause of hard-to-find program bugs, so this is a topic worth reviewing! You also learned how to use the `mem...()` functions to manipulate blocks of memory.

Q&A

Q What's the advantage of dynamic memory allocation? What can't I just declare the storage space I need in my source code?

A If you declare all your data storage in your source code, the amount of memory available to your program is fixed. You have to know ahead of time, when you write the program, how much memory will be needed. Dynamic memory allocation enables your program control the amount of memory used to suit the current conditions and user input. The program can use as much memory as it needs, up to the limit of what's available in the computer.

Q Why would I ever need to free memory?

A When you are first learning to use C, your programs are not very big. As your programs grow, their use of memory also grows. You should try to write your programs to use memory as efficiently as possible. When you are done with memory, you should release it. If you write programs that work in a multitasking environment, other applications might need memory that you aren't using.

Q What happens if I reuse a string without calling `realloc()`?

A You don't need to call `realloc()` if the string you are using was allocated enough room. Call `realloc()` when your current string is not big enough. Remember, the C compiler enables you to do almost anything, even things you shouldn't do! You can overwrite one string with a bigger string as long as the new string's length is equal or smaller than the original string's allocated space. If, however, the new string is bigger, you also will overwrite whatever was after the string in memory. This could be nothing, or it could be vital data. If you need a bigger allocated section of memory, call `realloc()`.

Q **What's the advantage of the** `mem...()` **memory block manipulation functions? Why can't I just use a loop with an assignment statement to initialize or copy memory?**

A You can use a loop with an assignment statement to initialize memory in some cases. In fact, sometimes this is the only way to do it—for example, setting all elements of a type `float` array to the value 1.23. In other situations, however, the memory will not have been assigned to an array or list, and the `mem...()` functions are your only choice. There also are times when a loop and assignment statement would work, but the `mem...` functions are simpler and faster.

Workshop

The Workshop provides quiz questions to help you solidify your understanding of the material covered and exercises to provide you with experience in using what you've learned.

Quiz

1. What is the difference between the `malloc()` and `calloc()` memory-allocation functions?

2. What is the most common reason for using a typecast with a numeric variable?

3. What variable type do the following expressions evaluate to? Assume that c is a type `char` variable, i is a type `int` variable, l is a type `long` variable, and f is a type `float` variable.

   a. `( c + i + l )`

   b. `( i + 32 )`

   c. `( c + 'A' )`

   d. `( i + 32.0 )`

   e. `( 100 + 1.0 )`

4. What is meant by *dynamically allocating* memory?

5. What is the difference between the `memcpy()` function and the `memmove()` function?

Exercises

1. Write a `malloc()` command that allocates memory for 1,000 `long`s.

2. Write a `calloc()` command that allocates memory for 1,000 `long`s.

3. Assume you have declared an array as follows:

   ```
   float data[1000];
   ```

   Show two ways to initialize all elements of the array to 0. Use a loop and an assignment statement for one method, and the `memset()` function for the other.

4. **BUG BUSTER:** Is anything wrong with the following code?

   ```
   void func()
   {
       int number1 = 100, number2 = 3;
       float answer;

       answer = number1 / number2;

       printf("%d/%d = %lf", number1, number2, answer)
   }
   ```

5. **BUG BUSTER:** What, if anything, is wrong with this code?

   ```
   void *p;
   p = (float*) malloc(sizeof(float));
   *p = 1.23;
   ```

Taking Advantage of Preprocessor Directives and More

This chapter, the last of your 21 days, covers some additional features of the C compiler. Today, you learn

- Programming with multiple source-code files
- Using the C preprocessor
- Using command-line arguments

Programming with Multiple Source Files

Until now, all your C programs have consisted of a single source-code file, exclusive of header files. A single source-code file is often all you need, particularly for small programs, but you can also divide the source code for a single program among two or more files, a practice called *modular programming*. Why would you want to do this? The following sections explain.

Advantages of Modular Programming

The primary reason to use modular programming is closely related to structured programming and its reliance on functions. As you become a more experienced programmer, you develop more general-purpose functions that you can use, not only in the program for which they were originally written, but in other programs as well. For example, you might write a collection of general-purpose functions for displaying information on the screen. By keeping these functions in a separate file, you can use them again in different programs that also display information on the screen. When you write a program that consists of multiple source-code files, each source file is called a *module*.

Modular Programming Techniques

A C program can have only one `main()` function. The module that contains the `main()` function is called the *main module*, and other modules are called *secondary modules*. A separate header file is usually associated with each secondary module (you learn why later in the chapter). For now, look at a few simple examples illustrating the basics of multiple module programming. Listings 21.1 through 21.3 show the main module, the secondary module, and the header file, respectively, for a program that inputs a number from the user and displays its square.

Listing 21.1. SQUARE.C, the main module.

```
1: /* Inputs a number and displays its square. */
2:
3: #include <stdio.h>
4: #include "calc.h"
5:
6: main()
7: {
8:    int x;
9:
10:    printf("Enter an integer value: ");
11:    scanf("%d", &x);
12:
13:    printf("\nThe square of %d is %ld.", x, sqr(x));
14: }
```

Listing 21.2. CALC.C, the secondary module.

```
1: /* Module containing calculation functions. */
2:
3: #include "calc.h"
4:
5: long sqr(int x)
6: {
7:    return ((long)x * x);
8: }
```

Listing 21.3. CALC.H, the header file for CALC.C.

```
1: /* CALC.H, header file for CALC.C. */
2:
3: long sqr(int x);
4:
5: /* end of CALC.H */
```

```
Enter an integer value: 100
The square of 100 is 10000.
```

Now look at the components of these three files in greater detail. The header file, CALC.H, contains the prototype for the sqr() function in CALC.C. Because any module that uses sqr() needs to know sqr()'s prototype, the module must include CALC.H.

The secondary module file, CALC.C, contains the definition of the sqr() function. The #include directive is used to include the header file CALC.H. Note that the header filename is enclosed in quotation marks rather than angle brackets. (You learn the reason for this later in the chapter.)

The main module SQUARE.C contains the `main()` function. This module also includes the header file CALC.H.

After you use your editor to create these three files, how do you compile and link the final executable program? Your compiler controls this for you. At the command line, enter

```
tcc square.c calc.c
```

where `tcc` is your compiler's command. This directs the compiler's components to perform the following tasks:

1. Compile SQUARE.C, creating SQUARE.OBJ (or SQUARE.O on a UNIX system). If it encounters any errors, the compiler displays descriptive error messages.

2. Compile CALC.C, creating CALC.OBJ (or CALC.O on a UNIX system). Again, error messages appear if they are needed.

3. Link SQUARE.OBJ, CALC.OBJ, and any needed functions from the standard library to create the final executable program SQUARE.EXE.

Module Components

As you can see, the mechanics of compiling and linking a multiple-module program are quite simple. The only real question is what to put in each file. The following paragraphs give you some general guidelines.

The secondary module should contain general utility functions, that is, functions that you might want to use in other programs. A common practice is to create one secondary module for each type of function; for example, KEYBOARD.C for your keyboard functions, SCREEN.C for your screen display functions, and so on. To compile and link more than two modules, list all source files on the command line.

```
tcc mainmod.c screen.c keyboard.c
```

The main module should contain `main()`, of course, and any other functions that are program-specific (meaning they have no general utility).

There is usually one header file for each secondary module. Each file has the same name as the associated module, with the .H extension. In the header file, put

- Prototypes for functions in the secondary module.
- `#define` directives for any symbolic constants and macros used in the module.
- Definitions of any structures or external variables used in the module.

Because this header file might be included in more than one source file, you want to prevent portions of it from compiling more than once. You can do this by using the *preprocessor* directives for conditional compilation (discussed later in the chapter).

External Variables and Modular Programming

In many cases, the only data communication between the main module and the secondary module is through arguments passed to and returned from the functions. In this case, you don't need to take special steps regarding data visibility, but what about an external variable that needs to be visible in both modules?

Recall from Day 12, "Variable Scope," that an external variable is one declared outside of any function. An external variable is visible throughout the entire source code file in which it is declared. It is not, however, automatically visible in other modules. To make it visible, you must declare the variable in each module, using the `extern` keyword. For example, if you have an external variable declared in the main module as

```
float interest_rate;
```

you make `interest_rate` visible in a secondary module by including the following declaration in that module (outside of any function):

```
extern float interest_rate;
```

The `extern` keyword tells the compiler that the original declaration of `interest_rate` (the one that set aside storage space for it) is located elsewhere, but that the variable should be made visible in this module. All `extern` variables have static duration and are visible to all functions in the module. Figure 21.1 illustrates the use of the `extern` keyword in a multiple-module program.

Figure 21.1.
Using the `extern` keyword to make an external variable visible across modules.

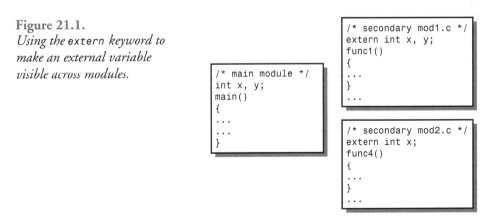

In Figure 21.1, the variable x is visible throughout all three modules. In contrast, y is visible only in the main module and secondary module 1.

Using .OBJ Files

After you've written and thoroughly debugged a secondary module, you don't need to recompile it every time you use it in a program. Once you have the object file for the module code, all you need to do is link it with each program that uses the functions in the module.

When you compile a program, the compiler creates an object file that has the same name as the C source code file along with the .OBJ extension. Say, for example, you are developing a module called KEYBOARD.C and compiling it, along with the main module DATABASE.C, with the following command:

```
tcc database.c keyboard.c
```

The KEYBOARD.OBJ file is also on your disk. Once you know the functions in KEYBOARD.C work properly, you can stop compiling it every time you recompile DATABASE.C (or any other program that uses it), instead linking the existing object file. To do this, use this command

```
tcc database.c keyboard.obj
```

The compiler then compiles DATABASE.C and links the resulting object file DATABASE.OBJ with KEYBOARD.OBJ to create the final executable file DATABASE.EXE. This saves time because the compiler doesn't have to recompile the code in KEYBOARD.C. However, if you modify the code in KEYBOARD.C, you must recompile it. In addition, if you modify a header file, you must recompile all the modules that use it.

DO	DON'T

DON'T try to compile multiple source files together if more than one module contains a `main()` function. You can have only one `main()`.

DO create generic functions in their own source files. This way they can be linked into any other programs that need them.

DON'T always use the C source files when compiling multiple files together. If you compile a source file into an object file, recompile only when the file changes. This saves a great deal of time.

Using the *make* Utility

Almost all C compilers come with a *make* utility that can simplify and speed the task of working with multiple source-code files. This utility, which is usually called NMAKE.EXE, enables you to write a so-called *make file* that defines the dependencies between your various program components. What does *dependency* mean?

Imagine a project that has a main module named PROGRAM.C and a secondary module named SECOND.C. There are also two header files, PROGRAM.H and SECOND.H. PROGRAM.C includes both of the header files, whereas SECOND.C includes only SECOND.H. Code in PROGRAM.C calls functions in SECOND.C.

PROGRAM.C is *dependent* on the two header files because it includes them both. If you make a change to either header file you must recompile PROGRAM.C so that it will include those changes. In contrast, SECOND.C is dependent on SECOND.H but not on PROGRAM.H. If you change PROGRAM.H, there is no need to recompile SECOND.C—you can just link the existing object file SECOND.OBJ that was created when SECOND.C was last compiled.

A make file describes the various dependencies in your project. Each time you edit one or more of your source code files, you use the NMAKE utility to "run" the make file. This utility examines the time and date stamps on the source code and object files and, based on the dependencies you have defined, instructs the compiler to recompile only those files that are dependent on the modified file(s). The result is that no unnecessary compilation is done, and you can work at the maximum efficiency.

For projects that involve one or two source code files, it usually is not worth the trouble of defining a make file. For larger projects, however, it is a real benefit. Please refer to your compiler documentation for information on how to use its NMAKE utility.

The C Preprocessor

The *preprocessor* is a part of all C compiler packages. When you compile a C program, the preprocessor is the first compiler component that processes your program. In most C compilers, the preprocessor is part of the compiler program. When you run the compiler, it automatically runs the preprocessor.

The preprocessor changes your source code based on instructions, or *preprocessor directives*, in the source code. The output of the preprocessor is a modified source-code file that is then used as the input for the next compilation step. Normally, you never see this file because it is deleted automatically by the compiler after it is used. However, later in the chapter you learn how to look at this intermediate file. First, you need to look at the preprocessor directives, all of which begin with the # symbol.

The #*define* Preprocessor Directive

The #define preprocessor directive has two uses: creating symbolic constants and creating macros.

Simple Substitution Macros Using *#define*

You learned about substitution macros on Day 3, "Numeric Variables and Constants," although the term used to describe them was *symbolic constants*. You create a *substitution macro* by using #define to replace text with other text. For example, to replace *text1* with *text2*, you write

```
#define text1 text2
```

This directive causes the preprocessor to go through the entire source code file, replacing every occurrence of *text1* with *text2*. The only exception occurs if *text1* is found within double quotation marks, in which case no change is made.

The most frequent use for substitution macros is to create symbolic constants, explained on Day 3. If your program contains the following lines:

```
#define MAX 1000

x = y * MAX;
z = MAX - 12;
```

the source code is changed to read as follows after preprocessing:

```
x = y * 1000;
z = 1000 - 12;
```

The effect is the same as using your editor's search-and-replace feature in order to change every occurrence of MAX to 1000. Your original source code file is not changed, of course. Rather, a temporary copy is created with the changes. Note that #define is not limited to creating symbolic numeric constants. You could write, for example,

```
#define ZINGBOFFLE printf

ZINGBOFFLE("Hello, world.");
```

although there is little reason to do so. You should also be aware that some authors refer to symbolic constants defined with #define as being macros themselves. (Symbolic constants are also called manifest constants.) However, in this book the word *macro* is reserved for the type of construction described next.

Creating Function Macros with *#define*

You can use the #define directive also to create function macros. A *function macro* is a type of shorthand, using something simple to represent something more complicated. The reason for the "function" name is that this type of macro can accept arguments, just like a real C function does. One advantage of function macros is that their arguments are not type-sensitive. Therefore, you can pass any numeric variable type to a function macro that expects a numeric argument.

Take a look at an example. The preprocessor directive

```
#define HALFOF(value) ((value)/2)
```

defines a macro named HALFOF that takes a parameter named value. Whenever the preprocessor encounters the text HALFOF(value) in the source code, it replaces it with the definition text and inserts the argument as needed. Thus, the source code line

```
result = HALFOF(10);
```

is replaced by this line:

```
result = ((10)/2);
```

Likewise, the program line

```
printf("%f", HALFOF(x[1]+y[2]));
```

is replaced by this line:

```
printf("%f", ((x[1]+y[2])/2));
```

A macro can have more than one parameter, and each parameter can be used more than once in the replacement text. For example, the following macro, which calculates the average of five values, has five parameters:

```
#define AVG5(v, w, x, y, z) (((v)+(w)+(x)+(y)+(z))/5)
```

This macro, in which the conditional operator determines the larger of two values, also uses each of its parameters twice. (You learned about the conditional operator on Day 4.)

```
#define LARGER(x, y) ((x) > (y) ? (x) : (y))
```

A macro can have as many parameters as needed, but all of the parameters in the list must be used in the substitution string. For example, the macro definition

```
#define ADD(x, y, z) ((x) + (y))
```

is invalid because the parameter z is not used in the substitution string. Also, when you invoke the macro, you must pass the correct number of arguments to the macro.

When you write a macro definition, the opening parenthesis must immediately follow the macro name; there can be no whitespace. The opening parenthesis tells the preprocessor that a function macro is being defined, and not a simple symbolic constant type substitution. Look at the following definition:

```
#define SUM (x, y, z) ((x)+(y)+(z))
```

Because of the space between SUM and (, the preprocessor treats this like a simple substitution macro. Every occurrence of SUM in the source code is replaced with (x, y, z) ((x)+(y)+(z)), clearly not what you wanted.

21

Also note that in the substitution string each parameter is enclosed in parentheses. This is necessary to avoid unwanted side effects when passing expressions as arguments to the macro. Look at the following example of a macro defined without parentheses:

```
#define SQUARE(x) x*x
```

If you invoke the macro with a simple variable as an argument, there's no problem. What if you pass an expression as an argument?

```
result = SQUARE(x + y);
```

The resulting macro expansion is as follows, which does not give the proper result:

```
result = x + y * x + y;
```

If you use parentheses, you can avoid the problem, as shown in this example:

```
#define SQUARE(x) (x)*(x)
```

This definition expands to the following line, which does give the proper result:

```
result = (x + y) * (x + y);
```

You can obtain additional flexibility in macro definitions by using the *string-izing* operator (#) (sometimes called the *string-literal* operator). When a macro parameter is preceded by # in the substitution string, the argument is converted into a quoted string when the macro is expanded. Thus, if you define a macro as

```
#define OUT(x) printf(#x)
```

and you invoke it with the statement

```
OUT(Hello Mom);
```

it expands to this statement:

```
printf("Hello Mom");
```

The conversion performed by the stringizing operator takes special characters into account. Thus, if a character in the argument normally requires an escape character, the # operator inserts a backslash before the character. Continuing now with the previous example, the invocation

```
OUT("Hello Mom");
```

expands to

```
printf("\"Hello Mom\"");
```

You can see a demonstration of the # operator in Listing 21.4. First, you need to look at one other operator used in macros, the *concatenation* operator (##). This operator concatenates, or joins, two strings in the macro expansion. It does not include quotation marks or special treatment of escape characters. Its main use is to create sequences of C source code. For example, if you define and invoke a macro as

```
#define CHOP(x) func ## x
salad = CHOP(3)(q, w);
```

the macro invoked in the second line is expanded to

```
salad = func3 (q, w);
```

You can see that by using the ## operator, you determine which function is called. You have actually modified the C source code.

The program in Listing 21.4 shows an example of one way to use the # operator.

Listing 21.4. Using the # operator in macro expansion.

```
1: /* Demonstrates the # operator in macro expansion. */
2:
3: #include <stdio.h>
4:
5: #define OUT(x) printf(#x " is equal to %d.", x)
6:
7: main()
8: {
9:    int value = 123;
10:
11:   OUT(value);
12: }
```

```
value is equal to 123.
```

By using the # operator on line 5, the call to the macro expands with the variable name value as a quoted string passed to the printf() function. After expansion on line 9, the macro OUT looks like this:

```
printf("value" " is equal to %d.",  value );
```

Macros Versus Functions

You have seen that function macros can be used in place of real functions, at least in situations where the resulting code is relatively short. Function macros can extend beyond one line but usually become impractical beyond a few lines. When you can use either a function or a macro, which should you use? It's a trade-off between program speed and program size.

A macro's definition is expanded into the code each time the macro is encountered in the source code. If your program invokes a macro 100 times, 100 copies of the expanded macro code are in the final program. In contrast, a function's code exists only as a single copy. Therefore, in terms of program size, the advantage goes to a true function.

When a program calls a function, a certain amount of processing overhead is required to pass execution to the function code and then return execution to the calling program. There is no processing overhead in "calling" a macro because the code is right there in the program. In terms of speed, a function macro has the advantage.

These size/speed considerations are not usually of much concern to the beginning programmer. Only with large, time-critical applications do they become important.

Viewing Macro Expansion

At times, you may want to see what your expanded macros look like, particularly when they are not working properly. To see the expanded macros, you instruct the compiler to create a listing file that includes macro expansion after the compiler's first pass of the code. You might not be able to do this if your C compiler uses an Integrated Development Environment (IDE); you might have to work from the command prompt. Most compilers have a flag that should be set during compilation. This flag is passed to the compiler as a command-line parameter.

For example, to precompile a program named PROGRAM.C with the Microsoft compiler, you would enter

```
cl /E program.c
```

On a UNIX compiler, you would enter

```
cc -E program.c
```

The preprocessor makes the first pass on your source code. All header files are included, `#define` macros are expanded, and other preprocessor directives are carried out. Depending on your compiler, the output goes either to `stdout` (that is, the screen) or to a disk file with the program name and a special extension. The Microsoft compiler sends the preprocessed output to `stdout`. It is not at all useful to have the processed code whip by on your screen! You can use the redirection command to send this output to a file, as in this example:

```
cl /E program.c > program.pre
```

You can then load the file into your editor for printing or viewing.

DO	**DON'T**

DO use #defines, especially for symbolic constants. Symbolic constants make your code much easier to read. Examples of things to put into defined constants are colors, TRUE/FALSE, YES/NO, the keyboard keys, and maximum values. Symbolic constants are used throughout this book.

DON'T overuse macro functions. Use them where needed, but be sure they are a better choice than a normal function.

The *#include* Directive

You have already learned how to use the #include preprocessor directive to include header files in your program. When it encounters an #include directive, the preprocessor reads the specified file and inserts it at the location of the directive. You cannot use the * or ? wildcards to read in a group of files with one #include directive. However, you can nest #include directives. That is, an included file can contain #include directives, which can contain #include directives. Most compilers limit the number of levels deep that you can nest, but you usually can nest up to 10 levels.

There are two ways to specify the filename for an #include directive. If the filename is enclosed in angle brackets, such as #include <stdio.h> (as you have seen throughout this book), the preprocessor first looks for the file in the standard directory. If the file is not found, or there is no standard directory specified, the preprocessor looks for the file in the current directory.

"What is the standard directory?" you might be asking. In DOS, it's the directory or directories specified by the DOS INCLUDE environment variable. Your DOS documentation contains complete information on the DOS environment. In brief, however, you set an environment variable with a SET command (usually, but not necessarily, in your AUTOEXEC.BAT file). Most compilers automatically set the INCLUDE variable in the AUTOEXEC.BAT file when the compiler is installed.

The second method of specifying the file to be included is enclosing the filename in double quotation marks: #include "myfile.h". In this case, the preprocessor does not search the standard directories, but looks instead in the directory containing the source code file being compiled. Generally speaking, header files that you write should be kept in the same directory as the C source code files, and they are included by using double quotation marks. The standard directory is reserved for header files supplied with your compiler.

21

Using *#if*, *#elif*, *#else*, and *#endif*

These four preprocessor directives control conditional compilation. The term *conditional compilation* means that blocks of C source code are compiled only if certain conditions are met. In many ways, the `#if` family of preprocessor directives operate like the C language's `if` statement. The difference is that `if` controls whether certain statements are executed, whereas `#if` controls whether they are compiled.

The structure of an `#if` block is as follows:

```
#if condition_1
statement_block_1
#elif condition_2
statement_block_2
...
#elif condition_n
statement_block_n
#else
default_statement_block
#endif
```

The test expression `#if` uses can be almost any expression that evaluates to a constant. You can't use the `sizeof()` operator, type casts, or the `float` type. For the most part, you use `#if` to test symbolic constants created with the `#define` directive.

Each `statement_block` consists of one or more C statements of any type, including preprocessor directives. They do not need to be enclosed in braces, although they can be.

The `#if` and `#endif` directives are required, but `#elif` and `#else` are optional. You can have as many `#elif` directives as you want, but only one `#else`. When the compiler reaches an `#if` directive, it tests the associated condition. If it evaluates as TRUE (non-zero), the statements following the `#if` are compiled. If it evaluates as FALSE (zero), the compiler tests, in order, the conditions associated with each `#elif` directive. The statements associated with the first TRUE `#elif` are compiled. If none of the conditions evaluates as TRUE, the statements following the `#else` directive are compiled.

Note that, at most, a single block of statements within the `#if...#endif` construction is compiled. If the compiler finds no `#else` directive, it might not compile any statements.

The possible uses for these conditional compilation directives are limited only by your imagination. Here's one example. Suppose you're writing a program that uses a great deal of country-specific information. This information is contained in a header file for each country. When you compile the program for use in different countries, you can use an `#if...#endif` construction as follows:

```
#if ENGLAND == 1
#include "england.h"
```

```
#elif FRANCE == 1
#include "france.h"
#elif ITALY == 1
#include "italy.h"
#else
#include "usa.h"
#endif
```

Then, by using #define to define the appropriate symbolic constant, you can control which header file is included during compilation.

Using *#if...#endif* to Help Debug

Another common use for #if...#endif is to include conditional debugging code in the program. You could define a DEBUG symbolic constant set to either 1 or 0. Throughout the program you can insert debugging code as follows:

```
#if DEBUG == 1

debugging code here

#endif
```

During program development, if you define DEBUG as 1, the debugging code is included to help track down any bugs. After the program is working properly, you can redefine DEBUG as 0 and recompile the program without the debugging code.

The defined() operator is useful when you write conditional compilation directives. This operator tests to see whether a particular name is defined. Thus, the expression

```
defined( NAME )
```

evaluates as TRUE or FALSE depending on whether or not NAME is defined. By using defined() you can control compilation, based on previous definitions, without regard to the specific value of a name. Referring to the previous debugging code example, you could rewrite the #if...#endif section as follows:

```
#if defined( DEBUG )

debugging code here

#endif
```

You also can use defined() to assign a definition to a name only if it has not been previously defined. Use the NOT operator (!) as follows:

```
#if !defined( TRUE )     /* if TRUE is not defined. */
#define TRUE 1
#endif
```

Notice the defined() operator does not require that a name be defined as anything in particular. For example, after the following program line, the name RED is defined, but not as anything in particular:

```
#define RED
```

Even so, the expression defined(RED) still evaluates as TRUE. Of course, occurrences of RED in the source code are removed and not replaced with anything, so you must use caution.

Avoiding Multiple Inclusions of Header Files

As programs grow, or as you use header files more often, you run a risk of accidentally including a header file more than once. This can cause the compiler to balk in confusion. Using the directives that you've learned, you can easily avoid this problem. Look at the example in Listing 21.5.

Type

Listing 21.5. Using preprocessor directives with header files.

```
1: /* PROG.H - A header file with a check to prevent multiple includes! */
2:
3. #if defined( PROG_H )
4: /* the file has been included already */
5: #else
6: #define PROG_H
7:
8: /* Header file information goes here... */
9:
10:
11:
12: #endif
```

Analysis

Examine what this header file does. On line 3, it checks whether PROG_H is defined. Notice that PROG_H is similar to the name of the header file. If PROG_H is defined, a comment is included on line 4, and the program looks for the #endif at the end of the header file. This means that nothing more is done.

How does PROG_H get defined? It is defined on line 6. The first time this header is included, the preprocessor checks whether PROG_H is defined. It won't be, so control goes to the #else statement. The first thing done after the #else is to define PROG_H so that any other inclusions of this file skip the body of the file. Lines 7–11 could contain any number of commands or declarations.

The *#undef* Directive

The #undef directive is the opposite of #define—it removes the definition from a name. Here's an example:

```
#define DEBUG 1

/* In this section of the program occurrences of DEBUG    */
/* are replaced with 1 and the expression defined( DEBUG ) */
/* evaluates to TRUE. *.

#undef DEBUG

/* In this section of the program occurrences of DEBUG  */
/* are not replaced and the expression defined( DEBUG ) */
/* evaluates to FALSE. */
```

You can use #undef and #define to create a name that is defined only in parts of your source code. You can use this in combination with the #if directive, as previously explained, for more control over conditional compilations.

Predefined Macros

Most compilers have a number of predefined macros. The most useful of these are __DATE__, __TIME__, __LINE__, and __FILE__. Notice that each of these are preceded and followed by double underscores. This is done to prevent you from redefining them, on the theory that programmers are unlikely to create their own definitions with leading and trailing underscores.

These macros work just like the macros described earlier in this chapter. When the precompiler comes across one of these macros, it replaces the macro with the macro's code. __DATE__ and __TIME__ are replaced with the current date and time. This is the date on and time at which the source file is precompiled. This can be useful information as you are working with different versions of a program. By having a program display its compilation date and time, you can tell whether you are running the latest version of the program or an earlier one.

The other two macros are even more valuable. __LINE__ is replaced by the current source-file line number. __FILE__ is replaced with the current sourcecode filename. These two macros are best used when trying to debug a program or deal with errors. Consider the following printf() statement:

```
31:
32: printf( "Program %s: (%d) Error opening file ", __FILE__, __LINE__ );
33:
```

If these lines were part of a program called MYPROG.C, this would print

```
Program MYPROG.C: (32) Error opening file
```

21

521

This might not seem important at this point, but as your programs grow and spread across multiple source files, finding errors becomes more difficult. Using __LINE__ and __FILE__ makes debugging a great deal easier.

DO	DON'T

DO use the __LINE__ and __FILE__ macros to make your error messages more helpful.

DON'T forget the #endif when using the #if statement.

DO put parentheses around the value to be passed to a macro. This prevents errors. For example:

```
#define CUBE(x)    (x)*(x)*(x)
instead of:
#define CUBE(x)    x*x*x
```

Using Command-Line Arguments

Your C program can access arguments passed to the program on the command line. This refers to information entered after the program name when you start the program. If you start a program named PROGNAME from the C:\> prompt, for example, you could enter

```
C:\>progname smith jones
```

The two command-line arguments smith and jones can be retrieved by the program during execution. You can consider this information to be arguments passed to the program's main() function. Such command-line arguments permit information to be passed to the program at startup rather than during execution, which can be convenient at times. You can pass as many command-line arguments as you like. Note that command-line arguments can be retrieved only within main(). To do so, declare main() as follows:

```
main(int argc, char *argv[])
{
/* Statements go here */
}
```

The first parameter, argc, is an integer giving the number of command-line arguments available. This value is always at least 1 because the program name is counted as the first argument. The parameter argv[] is an array of pointers to strings. The valid subscripts for this array are 0 through argc - 1. The pointer argv[0] points to the program name (including path information), argv[1] points to the first argument that follows the program name, and so on. Note that the names argc and argv[] are not required—you can use any valid C variable names you like to receive the command-line arguments. However, these two names are traditionally used for this purpose, so you should probably stick with them.

The command line is divided into discrete arguments by any white space. If you need to pass an argument that includes a space, enclose the entire argument in double quotation marks. For example, if you enter

```
C:>progname smith "and jones"
```

smith is the first argument (pointed to by argv[1]) and and jones is the second (pointed to by argv[2]). The program in Listing 21.6 demonstrates how to access command-line arguments.

Listing 21.6. Passing command-line arguments to main().

```
1: /* Accessing command-line arguments. */
2:
3: #include <stdio.h>
4:
5: main(int argc, char *argv[])
6: {
7:     int count;
8:
9:     printf("Program name: %s\n", argv[0]);
10:
11:     if (argc > 1)
12:     {
13:         for (count = 1; count < argc; count++)
14:             printf("Argument %d: %s\n", count, argv[count]);
15:     }
16:     else
17:         puts("No command line arguments entered.");
18: }
```

```
C:\>list21_6
Program name: C:\LIST21_6.EXE
No command line arguments entered.

C:\>list21_6 first second "3 4"
Program name: C:\LIST21_6.EXE
Argument 1: first
Argument 2: second
Argument 3: 3 4
```

This program does no more than print the command-line parameters entered by the user. Notice that line 5 uses the argc and argv parameters shown previously. Line 9 prints the one command-line parameter that you always have, the program name. Notice this is argv[0]. Line 11 checks to see whether there is more than one command-line parameter. Why more than one and not more than zero? Because there is always at least one—the program name. If there are additional arguments, a for loop prints each to the screen (lines 13–14). Otherwise, an appropriate message is printed (line 17).

Command-line arguments generally fall into two categories: those that are required because the program can't operate without them, and those that are optional, such as flags that instruct the program to act in a certain way. For example, imagine a program that sorts the data in a file. If you write the program to receive the input filename from the command line, the name is required information. If the user forgets to enter the input filename on the command line, the program must somehow deal with the situation. The program could also look for the argument /r, which signals a reverse-order sort. This argument is not required; the program looks for it and behaves one way if it is found, another way if not.

DO	DON'T

DO use argc and argv as the variable names for the command-line arguments for main(). Most C programmers are familiar with these names.

DON'T assume that program users have entered the correct number of command-line parameters. Check to be sure they did, and if not, display a message explaining the arguments they should enter.

Summary

This chapter covered some of the more advanced programming tools available with C compilers. You've learned to write a program that has source code divided among multiple files or modules. This practice, called modular programming, makes it easy to reuse general-purpose functions in more than one program. You saw how you can use preprocessor directives to create function macros, for conditional compilation, and other tasks. Finally, you saw that the compiler provides some function macros for you.

Q&A

Q When compiling multiple files, how does the compiler know which filename to use for the executable file?

A You might think the compiler uses the name of the file containing the main() function; however, this is not usually the case. When compiling from the command line, the first file listed is used to determine the name. For example, if you compiled the following with Borland's Turbo C, the executable would be called FILE1.EXE:

```
tcc file1.c main.c prog.c
```

Q Do header files need to have a .H extension?

A No. You can give a header file any name you want. It is standard practice to use the .H extension.

Q When including header files, can I use an explicit path?

A Yes. If you want to state the path where a file to be included is, you can. In such a case, you put the name of the include file between quotation marks.

Q Are all the predefined macros and preprocessor directives presented in this chapter?

A No. The predefined macros and directives presented in this chapter are ones common to most compilers. However, most compilers also have additional macros and constants.

Q Is the following header also acceptable when using `main()` with command-line parameters?

```
main( int argc, char **argv);
```

A You can probably answer this one on your own. This declaration uses a pointer to a character pointer instead of a pointer to a character array. Because an array is a pointer, this definition is virtually the same as the one presented in this chapter. This declaration is also commonly used. (See Day 8, "Numeric Arrays," and Day 10, "Characters and Strings," for more details.)

Workshop

The Workshop provides quiz questions to help you solidify your understanding of the material covered and exercises to provide you with experience in using what you've learned.

Quiz

1. What does the term *modular programming* refer to?
2. In modular programming, what is the main module?
3. When defining a macro, why should each argument be enclosed in parentheses?
4. What are the pros and cons of using a macro in place of a regular function?
5. What does the `defined()` operator do?
6. What must always be used if `#if` is used?
7. What extension do compiled C files have? (Assume that they have not been linked.)
8. What does `#include` do?
9. What is the difference between this line of code:

```
#include <myfile.h>
```

and the following line of code:

```
#include "myfile.h"
```

Taking Advantage of Preprocessor Directives and More

10. What is `__DATE__` used for?

11. What does `argv[0]` point to?

Exercises

Because many solutions are possible for the following exercises, answers are not provided.

1. Use your compiler to compile multiple source files into a single executable file. (You can use Listings 21.1 through 21.3 or your own listings.)

2. Write an error routine that receives an error number, line number, and module name. The routine should print a formatted error message and then exit the program. Use the predefined macros for the line number and module name (pass the line number and module name from the location where the error occurs). A possible example for a formatted error could be

```
module.c (Line ##): Error number ##
```

3. Modify the previous exercise to make the error more descriptive. Create a text file with your editor that contains an error number and message. Call this file ERRORS.TXT. It could contain information such as the following:

```
1    Error number 1
2    Error number 2
90   Error opening file
100  Error reading file
```

Have your error routine search this file and display the appropriate error message based on a number passed to it.

4. Some header files might be included more than once when you are writing a modular program. Use preprocessor directives to write the skeleton of a header file that compiles only the first time it is encountered during compilation.

5. Write a program that takes two filenames as command-line parameters. The program should copy the first file into the second file. (See Day 16, "Using Disk Files," if you need help working with files.)

6. This is the last exercise of the book, and its content is up to you. Select a programming task of interest to you that also meets a real need you have. For example, you could write programs to catalog your compact disk collection, keep track of your checkbook, or calculate financial figures related to a planned house purchase. There's no substitute for tackling a real-world programming problem in order to sharpen your programming skills and help you remember all the things you learned in this book.

You have finished your third and final week of learning how to program in C. You started the week covering such advanced topics as pointers and disk files. In the middle of the week, you saw just a few of the many functions contained in most C compilers' libraries of functions. You ended your week by discovering the odds and ends needed to get the most from your compiler and the C language. The following program should pull together many of these topics.

> **Note:** The numbers to the left of the line numbers indicate the chapter that covers the concept presented on that line. If you are confused by the line, refer to the referenced chapter for more information.

Listing R3.1. Week three's review listing.

```
1:  /* Program Name:  week3.c                                     */
2:  /*              Program to enter names and phone numbers. This */
3:  /*              information is written to a disk file          */
4:  /*              specified with a command-line parameter.       */
5:
6:  #include <conio.h>
7:  #include <stdlib.h>
8:  #include <stdio.h>
9:  #include <time.h>
10: #include <string.h>
11:
12: /*** defined constants ***/
13: #define YES    1
14: #define NO     0
15: #define REC_LENGTH  54
16:
17: /*** variables ***/
18:
19: struct record {
20:    char fname[15+1];                /* first name + NULL   */
21:    char lname[20+1];                /* last name + NULL    */
22:    char mname[10+1];                /* middle name         */
23:    char phone[9+1];                 /* phone number + NULL */
24: } rec;
25:
26: /*** function prototypes ***/
27:
28: int  main(int argc, char *argv[]);
29: void display_usage(char *filename);
30: int  display_menu(void);
31: void get_data(FILE *fp, char *progname, char *filename);
32: void display_report(FILE *fp);
33: int  continue_function(void);
34: int  look_up( FILE *fp );
35:
36: /* start of program    *
37:  *--------------------*/
38:
39: int main(int argc, char *argv[])
40: {
41:     FILE *fp;
42:     int  cont = YES;
```

Line references in left margin:
- Line 9: CH19
- Line 10: CH18
- Line 28: CH21
- Line 39: CH21
- Line 41: CH16

```
43:       int  ch;
44:
45:       if( argc < 2 )
46:       {
47:          display_usage("WEEK3");
48:          exit(1);
49:       }
50:
51:       if ((fp = fopen( argv[1], "a+")) == NULL)  /* open file */
52:       {
53:           fprintf( stderr, "%s(%d)--Error opening file %s",
54:                                     argv[0],__LINE__, argv[1]);
55:           exit(1);
56:       }
57:
58:       while( cont == YES )
59:       {
60:          switch( display_menu() )
61:          {
62:            case '1': get_data(fp, argv[0], argv[1]); /* Day 18*/
63:                      break;
64:             case '2': display_report(fp);
65:                      break;
66:             case '3': look_up(fp);
67:                      break;
68:             case '4': printf("\n\nThank you for using this program!");
69:                      cont = NO;
70:                      break;
71:             default:  printf("\n\nInvalid choice, Please select 1 to 4!");
72:                      break;
73:          }
74:       }
75:
76:       fclose(fp);        /* close file */
77:       return(0);
78: }
79:
80: /*-------------------------------------------------------------*
81:  *    display_menu()                                           *
82:  *-------------------------------------------------------------*/
83:
84: int display_menu(void)
85: {
86:      int ch;
87:
88:      printf( "\n");
89:      printf( "\n      MENU");
90:      printf( "\n   ========\n");
91:      printf( "\n1.  Enter names");
92:      printf( "\n2.  Print report");
93:      printf( "\n3.  Look up number");
94:      printf( "\n4.  Quit");
```

The margin labels (left of code): CH21 (line 45), CH16 (line 51), CH18 (line 62), CH16 (line 76).

continues

Listing R3.1. continued

```
95:     printf( "\n\nEnter Selection ==> ");
96:
97:     return(getch());
98: }
99:
100: /*-----------------------------------------------------------*
101:  *  Function:  get_data()                                    *
102:  *-----------------------------------------------------------*/
103:
104: void get_data(FILE *fp, char *progname, char *filename)
105: {
106:     int cont = YES;
107:
108:     while( cont == YES )
109:     {
110:         printf("\n\nPlease enter information:" );
111:
112:         printf("\n\nEnter first name: ");
113:         gets(rec.fname);
114:
115:         printf("\nEnter middle name: ");
116:         gets(rec.mname);
117:
118:         printf("\nEnter last name: ");
119:         gets(rec.lname);
120:
121:         printf("\nEnter phone in 123-4567 format: ");
122:         gets(rec.phone);
123:
124:         if (fseek( fp, 0, SEEK_END ) == 0)
125:             if( fwrite(&rec, 1, sizeof(rec), fp) != sizeof(rec))
126:             {
127:               fprintf( stderr, "%s(%d)--Error writing to file %s",
128:                                 progname,__LINE__, filename);
129:                 exit(2);
130:             }
131:         cont = continue_function();
132:     }
133: }
134: /*-----------------------------------------------------------*
135:  *  Function:  display_report()                              *
136:  *  Purpose:   To print out the formatted names of people    *
137:  *             in the file.                                   *
138:  *-----------------------------------------------------------*/
139:
140: void display_report(FILE *fp)
141: {
142:     time_t rtime;
143:     int num_of_recs = 0;
144:
145:     time(&rtime);
```

CH16 (line 123)

CH21 (line 127)

```
146:
147:        fprintf(stdout, "\n\nRun Time: %s", ctime( &rtime));
148:        fprintf(stdout, "\nPhone number report\n");
149:
150:        if(fseek( fp, 0, SEEK_SET ) == 0)
151:        {
152:           fread(&rec, 1, sizeof(rec), fp);
153:           while(!feof(fp))
154:           {
155:              fprintf(stdout,"\n\t%s, %s %c %s", rec.lname,
                            rec.fname, rec.mname[0],rec.phone);
156:              num_of_recs++;
157:              fread(&rec, 1, sizeof(rec), fp);
158:           }
159:           fprintf(stdout, "\n\nTotal number of records: %d",num_of_recs);
160:           fprintf(stdout, "\n\n* * * End of Report * * *");
161:        }
162:        else
163:           fprintf( stderr, "\n\n*** ERROR WITH REPORT ***\n");
164: }
165: /*-----------------------------------------------------------*
166:  *  Function:  continue_function()                          *
167:  *-----------------------------------------------------------*/
168:
169: int continue_function( void )
170: {
171:     char ch;
172:
173:     do
174:     {
175:       printf("\n\nDo you wish to enter another? (Y)es/(N)o ");
176:         ch = getch();
177:     } while( strchr( "NnYy", ch) == NULL );
178:
179:     if(ch == 'n' || ch == 'N')
180:         return(NO);
181:     else
182:         return(YES);
183: }
184:
185: /*-----------------------------------------------------------*
186:  *  Function:  display_usage()                              *
187:  *-----------------------------------------------------------*/
188:
189: void display_usage( char *filename )
190: {
191:     printf("\n\nUSAGE: %s filename", filename );
192:     printf("\n\n      where filename is a file to store people\'s names");
193:     printf("\n      and phone numbers.\n\n");
194: }
195:
196: /*-----------------------------------------------------------*
197:  *  Function:  look_up()                                    *
198:  *  Returns:   Number of names matched                      *
199:  *-----------------------------------------------------------*/
200:
```

continues

Listing R3.1. continued

```
201: int look_up( FILE *fp )
202: {
203:     char tmp_lname[20+1];
204:     int  ctr = 0;
205:
206:     fprintf(stdout, "\n\nPlease enter last name to be found: ");
207:     gets(tmp_lname);
208:
209:     if( strlen(tmp_lname) != 0 )
210:     {
211:         if (fseek( fp, 0, SEEK_SET ) == 0)
212:         {
213:             fread(&rec, 1, sizeof(rec), fp);
214:             while( !feof(fp))
215:             {
216:                 if( strcmp(rec.lname, tmp_lname) == 0 ) /* if matched */
217:                 {
218:                     fprintf(stdout, "\n%s %s %s - %s", rec.fname,rec.mname,
                                rec.lname,rec.phone);
219:                     ctr++;
220:                 }
221:                 fread(&rec, 1, sizeof(rec), fp);
222:             }
223:         }
224:         fprintf( stdout, "\n\n%d names matched.", ctr );
225:     }
226:     else
227:     {
228:         fprintf( stdout, "\nNo name entered." );
229:     }
230:     return(ctr);
231: }
```

CH16 (line 210)
CH16 (line 212)
CH17 (line 216)

You might consider this an extremely long program; however, it barely does what it needs to do. This program is similar to the programs presented in the reviews of week one and week two. A few of the data items tracked in the week two review program have been dropped. This program enables the user to enter information for people. The information to be tracked is a first name, last name, middle name and phone number. The major difference you should notice in this program is that there is no limit to the number of people that can be entered into the program. This is because a disk file is used.

This program enables the user to specify the name of a file to be used with the program. `main()` starts on line 39 with the `argc` and `argv` arguments required to get the command-line parameters. You saw this on Day 21, "Taking Advantage of Preprocessor Directives and More." Line 45 checks the value of `argc` to see how many parameters were entered on the command line. If `argc` is less than 2, only one parameter was entered (the command to run the program). Because a filename was not provided, `display_usage()` is called with `argv[0]` as an argument. `argv[0]`, the first parameter entered on the command line, is the name of the program.

The `display_usage()` function is on lines 189–194. Whenever you write a program that takes command-line arguments, it is a good idea to include a function similar to `display_usage()` that shows how to use the program. Why doesn't the function just write the name of the program instead of using the variable `filename`? The answer is simple. By using a variable, you don't have to worry if the user renames the program; the usage description is always accurate.

Be aware that a majority of the new concepts in this program come from Day 16, "Using Disk Files." Line 41 declares a file pointer called `fp` that is used throughout the program to access the file provided on the command line. Line 51 tries to open this file with a mode of `"a+"` (`argv[1]` is the second item listed on the command line). The `"a+"` mode is used because you want to be able to add to the file and read any records that already exist. If the open fails, lines 53–54 display an error message before line 55 exits the program. Notice that the error message contains descriptive information. Also notice that `__LINE__`, covered on Day 21, "Taking Advantage of Preprocessor Directives and More," indicates the line number where the error occurred. Once the file is opened, a menu is presented. When the user selects the option to exit the program, line 76 closes the file with `fclose()` before the program returns control to the operating system.

In the `get_data()` function, there are a few significant changes. Line 104 contains the function header. The function now accepts three pointers. The first pointer is the most important; it is the handle for the file to be written to. Lines 108–132 contain a `while` loop that continues to get data until the user wants to quit. Lines 110–122 prompt for the data in the same format that the review program from week two did. Line 124 calls `fseek()` to set the pointer in the disk file to the end to write the new information. Notice that this program does not do anything if the seek fails. A good program would handle such a failure. Line 125 writes the data to the disk file with a call to `fwrite()`.

The report presented in this program also has changed. One change typical of most "real world" reports is the addition of the current date and time to the top of the report. On line 142, the variable `rtime` is declared. This variable is passed to `time()` and then displayed using the `ctime()` function. These time functions were presented on Day 19, "Exploring the Function Library."

Before the program can start printing the records in the file, it needs to reposition the file pointer back to the beginning of the file. This is done on line 150 with another call to `fseek()`. Once the file pointer is positioned, records can be read. Line 152 does the first read. If the read is successful, the program begins a `while` loop that continues until the end of the file is reached (when `feof()` returns a nonzero value). If the end of the file hasn't been reached, line 155 prints the information, line 156 counts the record, and line 157 tries to read the next record. You should notice that functions are used without checking their return values. To protect the program against errors, the function calls should contain checks to ensure that no errors occurred.

The `continue_function()` contains one small modification. Line 177 has been changed to use the `strchr()` function. This function makes the line of code easier to understand.

The last function in the program is new. Lines 201–231 contain the function `look_up()`, which searches the disk file for all records with a given last name. Lines 206–207 prompt for the name to be found and store it in a local variable called `tmp_lname`. If `tmp_lname` is not blank (line 209), the file pointer is set to the beginning of the file. Each record is then read. Using `strcmp()` (line 216), the record's last name is compared to `tmp_lname`. If the names match, the record is printed (lines 218–219). This continues until the end of the file is reached. Again, you should notice that not all the functions had their return values checked. You always should check return values.

You should be able to modify this program to create your own files that can store any information. Using the functions you learned in the third week along with the other functions that your library has should enable you to create nearly any program you want.

Bonus Week

WEEK

AT A GLANCE

BD1

BD2

BD3

BD4

BD5

BD6

BD7

At this point you've learned all there is about the basics of C. You have, in fact, taught yourself C in 21 Days! This last, bonus week covers topics that either supplement or build on what you already know. Although these bonus days are not essential to your becoming a proficient C programmer, they are full of valuable information that you should find useful in your programming endeavors.

On Bonus Day 1, "Coding Styles," you learn some recommended coding styles. By following a style, you build consistency and readability into your programs. On Bonus Day 2, "Portability," you learn about writing programs that will work on multiple platforms. On Bonus Day 3, "Working with Bits," you learn what bits are and how you can exploit them.

Bonus Day 4, "Working with Different Number Systems," presents an overview of working with different number systems, including Hungarian notation. This day also explains the importance of numbers to programming. Bonus Days 5 and 6, "Advanced Structures: Linking Lists" and "Variable-Length Structures," respectively, discuss new advanced ways of using structures.

The week ends with the topic of C++. Bonus Day 7, "What Is C++?," provides an overview of what C++ is and how it differs from C.

Bonus Day

1+

Coding Styles

This first bonus day presents *coding style*—techniques you can use when writing a program to make your source code clear and easy to understand. These techniques have no effect on the final operation of your program, but they can make your life a lot easier. Today, you learn

- General rules for naming variables, constants, and functions
- How to use Hungarian Notation
- How to apply indentation logically

Naming Variables and Functions

The value of assigning descriptive names to variables and functions cannot be overemphasized. Although we've tried to "teach by example" throughout this book, we admit to being lazy sometimes and using a short, non-descriptive name where a longer descriptive name would be better! This topic was covered briefly on Day 3, "Numeric Variables and Constants," but this chapter provides more detail.

Variable Names

As you have already learned, variable names can contain letters, numerals, and the underscore character. The first character must be a letter, and the length of the name is essentially unlimited. By *essentially* we mean that although compilers generally will not report an error for a too-long name, they will use only the first *n* characters of the name internally. The value of *n* is 31 for most compilers, and so you can see that you have plenty of characters to use.

A variable name should describe the data it contains. The most direct, and sometimes the best, method of devising a variable name is simply to state what it is. If you have a variable that keeps track of the number of names in a database, for example, you could call it `NumberOfNames`. Or, if you have a variable that holds the maximum prime interest rate for last year, you could call it `max_prime_rate_last_year`. Note the use of two methods for separating words in a multi-word name: capitalizing each word, which is referred to as *camel* notation, and separating the words with an underscore. Although either method is perfectly acceptable, you should select one of them and use it consistently throughout your programs.

Short, cryptic variable names are sometimes okay, but you should use them only when there is no possibility for confusion. Such a variable should be used in only a few lines of code that are located near each other. One place where short variable names often are appropriate is in `for` loops as the counter variable. Someone who is very conscientious about using descriptive variable names might write a loop as follows:

```
for (array_index_counter = 0; array_index_counter <
    MAX_ARRAY_ELEMENTS; array_index_counter++)
    data[array_index_counter] = 0;
```

However, the following is just as clear and a lot easier to type:

```
for (i = 0; i < MAX_ARRAY_ELEMENTS; i++)
    data[i] = 0;
```

Constant Names

The rules for the names of defined constants are the same as for variable names. By tradition, however, the names of defined constants always are written in all uppercase, as in the following example:

```
#define MAX_DATA_POINTS 100
...
for (index = 0; index < MAX_DATA_POINTS; index++)
...
```

By using uppercase characters, it is always obvious when you're dealing with a defined constant instead of a variable. This is important because someone reading the program immediately knows two things: the value does not change, and the definition can be found (usually) in a header file. Obviously, you can't use camel notation in this case, and so underscores are used to separate words.

Hungarian Notation

In addition to a wonderful cuisine, lots of beautiful music, and a fascinating history, Hungary has given us Mr. Charles Simonyi, who works (or at least used to work) at Microsoft. Mr. Simonyi developed Hungarian notation, and the name derives from his background. Hungarian notation has nothing to do with the Hungarian language; rather, it is a system in which variable names begin with a prefix that indicates the nature of the variable. In some cases, a suffix also is used. Many programming tools, such as Microsoft Visual C++, use Hungarian notation for their built-in and generated variable names. You don't have to use Hungarian notation—there is no C or C++ compiler that requires it—but doing so can make programming a lot simpler, particularly when you start to tackle larger, more complex projects.

So, how does Hungarian notation work? As already mentioned, each variable name is given a prefix that indicates something about it. For example, when you see the variable iCount, you know it is a type int (integer)—the i prefix is Hungarian notation for *integer*. If you see lCount, however, you know it is a type long. Here's a look at the details.

The Hungarian prefix consists of up to three parts. You might use only one or two of these parts for a given variable, or you might use all three. The first part is the *type prefix*, which indicates the data type of the variable. For example, i means *integer*, a means *array*, and so on. Table B1.1 lists the most commonly used type prefixes.

Table B1.1. Type prefixes in Hungarian notation.

Prefix	Meaning
a	Array
b	BOOL
by	Byte
c	char or count
dw	Double word (DWORD)
fn	Function
fp	Far pointer
g	Global variable
h	Handle
i	Integer or index into an array
m_	Data member of a class (used in C++)
n	int
np	Near pointer
p	Pointer
l	Long
lp	Long pointer
s	String
sz	Zero-terminated string

Some entries in this table may be unfamiliar to you. You'll encounter data items such as long pointers and DWORDs if you continue your exploration of C to more advanced topics. Don't worry about them for now. However, as with many good habits, Hungarian notation can take some effort to get used to, and there's nothing like practice to develop a good habit! Note that Hungarian notation is not completely standardized, so you may see prefixes different from those in the table from time to time.

Tip: If you think that Hungarian notation will be useful to you, start using it now and use it consistently. Print a copy of the prefix table and post it next to your computer so that it's always available. Hungarian notation will soon become second nature.

The type letters can be combined, and this is what you'll usually see. Because p means *pointer*, piIndex indicates a pointer to an integer. Likewise, because sz indicates a zero-terminated string, pszLabel would indicate a pointer to a zero-terminated string. Note that the first letter of the variable name after the Hungarian prefix usually is uppercase to clearly mark where the prefix ends.

The next part of the prefix is the *base type*. There are no standard base types; rather, you define base types that are important to the current program. For example, if you're writing a word processing program, you might find the following base types useful:

Base Type	Meaning
scr	Screen region
pa	Paragraph of text
wd	Word of text
ln	Line of text

Base types can be used alone or with a type prefix. For example, you might give an array of screen regions the ascr prefix. When using base type prefixes, it is the usual practice to define data types using those same abbreviations. For example, if you designed a data structure for the information comprising a screen region, you could define the data structure and the data type identifier as follows:

```
typedef struct {
    /*Data members here.*/
} screen_region;

#define SCR screen_region
```

and then declare variables as shown here:

```
SCR scrMainEditingWindow;
```

The third part of a Hungarian notation prefix is the *qualifier*. A qualifier really is just the descriptive variable name you would use if you weren't using Hungarian notation. For example, in the variable name ascrScreenRegions, the ScreenRegions portion is the qualifier. There are, however, a few standard abbreviations that are used in qualifiers, as shown in Table B1.2.

Table B1.2. Standard Hungarian notation qualifiers.

Qualifier	Description
min	The absolute first element in an array or list.
max	The absolute last element in an array or list.
first	The first element in an array or list that needs to be dealt with in the current operation.
last	The last element in an array or list that needs to be dealt with in the current operation.

Qualifiers should be combined with base types and prefixes. If, for example, `paToPrint` is a paragraph to be printed, you can derive the following:

`apaToPrint`	Array of paragraphs to print.
`paFirstToPrint`	Array index of the first paragraph to print.
`paLastToPrint`	Array index of the last paragraph to print.

You've undoubtedly noticed that we did not use Hungarian notation for the programs in this book. It's not that we don't practice what we preach. It's that Hungarian notation is most useful for large and complex programs, whereas the programs in this book are all relatively short and simple. Using Hungarian notation in programs like these would offer no advantage. In large programs, where the variable's declaration is likely to be far removed from the location where you are using it, Hungarian notation really comes into its own. You don't need to scroll around looking for a variable's declaration to find out its type because the variable's name tells you.

It's important to note that using Hungarian notation does *not* free you from the necessity of declaring all variables in the usual way. Naming a variable `iCount`, for example, tells *you* that it's an integer but does not tell the compiler. You still must include the following declaration at the proper location in the code:

```
int iCount;
```

Indentation

Indentation refers to how far each line of code is set off from the left margin. Your compiler doesn't care one whit about indentation, but using it properly can be a big help in creating clear and readable source code. The point is to use indentation in a manner that relates to the structure of the program. That way the visual appearance of your source code will provide the reader with clues as to the program's logical structure. Generally speaking, you do that by indenting subordinate lines of code.

For instance, in an `if` construction, the lines of code within the block are subsidiary to the `if` statement itself (and to the `else` statement if one is present). Here's an example of proper indentation:

```
if ( input == "y")
    {
    x = 0;
    y = 1;
    }
else
    {
    x = 1;
    y = 0;
    }
```

The relationship between the if and else statements and the other lines of code is clear because of the indentation. You could have written the code this way, and it would compile and run just fine:

```
if ( input == "y")
{x = 0;
y = 1;}
else {x = 1;
y = 0;}
```

However, it's not nearly as easy to read by humans. The following are the elements of C code in which indentation should be used to indicate the subsidiary statements:

```
if...else
do...while
for
switch...case
```

You should use indentation in structure definitions and in function definitions as well. The following style for structure definitions—which does not place the braces on their own lines—is used often:

```
struct point {
    int x;
    int y; };
```

You also can write a structure definition like this:

```
struct point
 {
    int x;
    int y;
 };
```

As for indentation in function definitions, we simply mean that the function statements are indented with respect to the function header:

```
int foo ()
{
    long x;
    .
    .
    return;
}
```

Indentation often needs to be multilevel because most programs have several logical levels. For example, a do...while loop within an if block would be indented twice:

```
if (input == "y")
{
    do
    {
        array[i++] = 0;
        count++;
    } while (array[i] != 0);
}
```

Braces and Indentation

In most cases, lines of code that are indented will be enclosed in braces. There are two approaches to handling the braces. One approach does not indent them—they remain at the same level as the "parent" code:

```
if (input == "y")
{
    x = 0;
    y = 1;
}
```

The other approach is to indent them to the same level as the lines of code they enclose:

```
if (input == "y")
    {
    x = 0;
    y = 1;
    }
```

Both methods are equally valid; the point is that you should use them consistently. It's a good idea to keep matching braces at the same level of indent. Thus, the following is perfectly legal:

```
if (input == "y")
{
    x = 0;
    y = 1;}
```

However, it's less clear than the previous example—if paired braces are at the same indent level, it is easier to match them up.

> **Note:** Many programming editors have a "brace-matching" feature that can be very useful. When you place the cursor on one brace and issue the command, the editor automatically moves the cursor to the matching brace. In some cases, this feature works for parentheses and brackets as well.

Some programming editors have an automatic indentation feature. When you press Enter to start a new line, the new line is indented to the same level as the preceding line. Some editors go even further and automatically detect program statements that typically mark the start of a section of increased indentation, such as an `if` statement or a `do` statement, then indent the next line one extra tab stop. These features can be very useful, and you can turn them on or off as desired.

Controlling Indentation in Your Editor

Most programming editors permit you to control certain aspects of indentation. There are two things you may want to modify. One aspect is the amount of indentation you get each time you press the Tab key. Larger indents, such as eight spaces, may seem to make the code easier to read. However, when you have multiple levels of indentation—an `if` within a `do...while` within another `if` within a function, for example—you'll find that the lines of code indented the most extend off the right side of the screen. Thus, it's more practical to use smaller indents, such as four spaces.

The second aspect is whether indents are entered in your source code as tabs or as spaces. Many editors do not offer the choice of spaces, but if your editor does, you may want to consider using this option.

When indents are entered as tabs, pressing the Tab key enters a single Tab character in your code. You don't see this character, of course, but it instructs the editor to move to the next tab stop. The size of the indent is controlled by the editor's tab stop settings—change that setting, and all indents will change accordingly.

With indents entered as spaces, pressing Tab inserts a certain number of spaces in the document, just as if you had pressed the spacebar that number of times. The editor's tab stop settings have no effect on the size of the indents. You can, however, control the number of spaces that are inserted when you press the Tab key. Changing this setting, however, affects only the code you enter after you change the setting—existing indents are not affected.

How can you tell which method your editor uses for indents? Start a new line by pressing Enter, and then press Tab once. You should see the cursor move to the right by half an inch or so. Now, press Backspace once. If the cursor moves all the way back to the left margin, you are inserting indents as tabs. If it moves only one space to the left, you are inserting indents as spaces.

Is one indentation method superior to the other? Not really—as with many things, it depends on your personal preferences and the specific tasks you are doing. Tabs offer the advantage that you can modify all indents throughout an entire source code file by changing a single editor option. Spaces offer the advantage that your code's indents will remain the same even if you load it into another editor that has different tab stops set. It's your call. If you're unsure, use tabs.

Using Comments Effectively

We cannot overemphasize the importance of placing comments in your source code—and *useful* comments, too! What seems crystal clear to you as you are writing the code may not seem so clear next week or next month when you need to modify it. To be useful, comments need to explain the operation of the code at a level that is meaningful in the overall operation of the program. For example, consider this simple line of code:

```
ptr++;
```

Here's an example of a useless comment:

```
/*Increment ptr.*/
ptr++;
```

Anyone who knows C can see that you're incrementing the variable ptr. The comment is a waste of space. In contrast, here's a useful comment:

```
/*Increment ptr to point at the next element in data[].*/
ptr++;
```

Now you're talking! This comment tells you not only why you're incrementing ptr but how it relates to other program elements—in this case, the array data[]. If you use comments like this, you'll do yourself—and anyone else who reads your source code—a big favor.

Comments can be used also to explain and document larger sections of code, such as functions and entire programs. Many C programmers get in the habit of providing a "header" as part of every function, explaining what it does, what the arguments are, and so on. You can even be creative with formatting. Here's an example:

```
/************************************************************************/
/* FUNCTION                                                             */
/* float MonthlyPayment(float principle, float rate, int periods)       */
/*                                                                      */
/* Calculates the periodic payment on a loan.                          */
/* Arguments:                                                           */
/*    principle: amount of the loan.                                    */
/*    rate: periodic interest rate.                                     */
/*    periods: number of periods                                        */
/*                                                                      */
/*    NOTE: It is essential that the arguments rate and periods refer   */
/*          to the same period. If it is monthly payments you want to   */
/*          calculate, then you must pass the monthly interest rate     */
/*          and *NOT* the annual rate.                                  */
/*                                                                      */
/*    Return value: the periodic payment, rounded off to the           */
/*          nearest cent. Returns -1 on error.                          */
/************************************************************************/

float MonthlyPayment(float principle, float rate, int period)
{
/* code goes here.


}
```

When using comments to create a program header, you can include information such as the author's name, the compiler that was used, and a revision history. Here's an example:

```
/************************************************************************/
/* FRAMMIS.C                                                            */
/* Calculates the weight of a frammis.                                 */
/*                                                                      */
/* Author: Phyl Pots                                                    */
/* Compiler: Borland C++ version 4                                     */
```

```
/* Date: January 1994                                        */
/*                                                           */
/* Revisions:                                                */
/*          March 1994, to permit calculation of weight of   */
/*          Australian frammises.                            */
/*                                                           */
/*          July 1994, to handle really fat frammises.       */
/*                                                           */
/*          May 1995, to display weight in kilograms as      */
/*          well as pounds.                                  */
/*************************************************************/
```

Summary

This first bonus day covered several topics relevant to coding style. The names of the variables, constants, and functions in your program can have a significant effect on how readable your code is. Variable and constant names should describe the data or information stored there. Function names should reflect the action that the function performs or the value that it returns. Using Hungarian notation can be a big help by providing variable names that not only describe their data but also tell you what type they are as well as other useful information.

Source code indentation is another aspect of coding style that has an impact on the readability of your programs. The general rule is that indentation reflects the relationships between different sections of code—subsidiary code is indented with respect to higher-level code. This results in an indentation pattern that reflects the logical structure of your program.

Q&A

Q **I'm writing a short program in which there is little chance of confusing one variable with another. Why should I bother with the extra effort of creating and typing long, descriptive variable names?**

A It's true that in short, simple programs you may be able to get away with using cryptic variable names such as x and y. However, good programming practice should become a habit, not something you apply only when you think it's necessary. If you always assign descriptive names to variables, doing so will soon become second nature.

Q **The C compiler doesn't care about indentation—why should I?**

A If you ever had the experience of debugging or modifying a program that didn't use proper indentation, you wouldn't ask that question! Proper indentation makes it easy to see where loops begin and end, and how different sections of code relate to each other.

Q **I know that comments are an important part of source code, but I find it difficult to decide just how much detail is necessary. Are there any guidelines I can use?**

A This is a tough question, and unfortunately there are no official guidelines to help you. The real test occurs when you are looking at some source code you wrote six months or a year ago, or when another C programmer is examining your code. Do the comments make it clear what's going on in the program? If you find that you have to spend a lot of time looking at the C code itself to figure out what's happening, the comments are not detailed enough. On the other hand, if you are reading line after line of comments that explain trivial or unrelated aspects of program operation, the detail level is too high.

Workshop

The Workshop provides quiz questions to help you solidify your understanding of the material covered and exercises to provide you with experience in using what you've learned.

Quiz

1. You need a name for a type `int` variable that will hold the maximum number of lines that can be printed per page. How would you rate the following names?

   ```
   mlpp
   MaximumNumberOfPrintLinesPerPage
   MaxLinesPerPage
   ```

2. When creating multiword variable names, how can you make it easy to see when each word begins?

3. If you see the variable name `pachNames` in a program that uses Hungarian notation, what does it refer to?

4. Lines of code that are indented by two or three tab stops often extend past the right edge of your screen. What can you do to solve this problem?

Exercise

1. Create variable names using Hungarian notation for the following:

   a. A pointer to type `long`.

   b. A type `int`.

   c. An array of type `char`.

   d. An index into an array of zero-terminated strings.

Bonus Day 2+

Portability

When you write programs, it's easy to use everything the compiler provides. With a language such as C, it's also easy to write code that can be used on different computers, including PC compatibles, Macintoshes, minicomputers, and mainframes. Because of C's flexibility, you need to know in advance the direction your application is headed. Today, you learn

- The difference between portability, efficiency, and maintainability
- What types of applications are most likely to be non-portable
- How to ensure portability with the ANSI Standard

What Is Portability?

If you took a course in computer programming, you'd inevitably hear about three topics: efficiency, portability, and maintainability. These topics are especially important when programming in C.

Efficiency typically refers to writing the least amount of code to gain the most functionality. An efficient program is one that uses system resources only when needed. In addition, it contains as little redundant or unnecessary code as possible.

Maintainable code is code that is easy to update or change—by you as well as by other programmers. Just because code is intuitive to you doesn't mean it will be intuitive to other programmers. Unfortunately, writing maintainable code can have a negative impact on efficiency.

One of the major reasons people choose C as their programming language is its portability. C is one of the most portable languages. A program written in a portable language can be moved from one compiler to another, or from one computer system to another. When moved, the program can be recompiled without any coding modifications. These two areas—hardware portability and compiler portability—are what characterize a portable language. C programs can be written to be portable in both ways. A C program is truly portable if it can be recompiled on any type of machine with any C compiler.

The ANSI Standard

Portability doesn't happen by accident. It occurs when you adhere to a set of standards adhered to by other programmers and your compiler. If you use a compiler that doesn't adhere to the portability standards, you'll be unable to write portable code. For this reason, it is wise to choose a compiler that follows the standards for C programming set by the American National Standards Institute (ANSI). The ANSI committee sets standards for many areas including other programming languages. The ANSI standards are predominantly accepted and used by programmers and compilers.

> **Warning:** Standards aren't always good. Standards that are too specific or too detailed can limit your ability to create effective programs. Because C is a powerful language, it could be detrimental to implement too many standards. The ANSI standards leave a lot of undefined areas to prevent this power limitation. The downside to undefined areas is that each compiler can create its own implementations.

BD2

The ANSI Keywords

The C language contains relatively few keywords. A *keyword* is a word that is reserved for a program command. The ANSI C keywords are listed in Table B2.1.

Table B2.1. The ANSI C keywords.

asm	auto	break
case	char	const
continue	default	do
double	else	enum
extern	float	for
goto	if	int
long	register	return
short	signed	sizeof
static	struct	switch
typedef	union	unsigned
void	volatile	while

Most compilers provide other keywords as well. Examples of compiler-specific keywords are near and huge. Although several compilers might use the same compiler specific keywords, there is no guarantee that they will be portable to every ANSI standard compiler.

Case Sensitivity

Case sensitivity is an important issue in programming languages. Unlike some languages that ignore case, C is case-sensitive. This means that a variable named a is different than a variable named A. Listing B2.1 illustrates the difference.

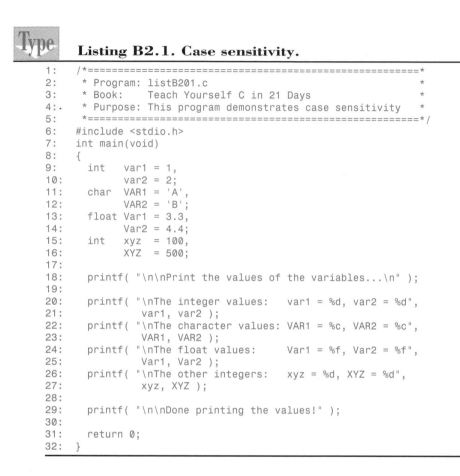

Listing B2.1. Case sensitivity.

```
1:  /*========================================================*
2:   * Program: listB201.c                                    *
3:   * Book:    Teach Yourself C in 21 Days                   *
4:.  * Purpose: This program demonstrates case sensitivity    *
5:   *========================================================*/
6:  #include <stdio.h>
7:  int main(void)
8:  {
9:    int   var1 = 1,
10:         var2 = 2;
11:   char  VAR1 = 'A',
12:         VAR2 = 'B';
13:   float Var1 = 3.3,
14:         Var2 = 4.4;
15:   int   xyz  = 100,
16:         XYZ  = 500;
17:
18:   printf( "\n\nPrint the values of the variables...\n" );
19:
20:   printf( "\nThe integer values:   var1 = %d, var2 = %d",
21:             var1, var2 );
22:   printf( "\nThe character values: VAR1 = %c, VAR2 = %c",
23:             VAR1, VAR2 );
24:   printf( "\nThe float values:     Var1 = %f, Var2 = %f",
25:             Var1, Var2 );
26:   printf( "\nThe other integers:   xyz = %d, XYZ = %d",
27:             xyz, XYZ );
28:
29:   printf( "\n\nDone printing the values!" );
30:
31:   return 0;
32: }
```

```
Print the values of the variables...

The integer values:   var1 = 1, var2 = 2
The character values: VAR1 = A, VAR2 = B
The float values:     Var1 = 3.300000, Var2 = 4.400000
The other integers:   xyz = 100, XYZ = 500

Done printing the values!
```

This program uses several variables with the same names. In lines 9 and 10, var1 and var2 are defined as integer values. In lines 11 and 12, the same variable names are used with different cases. This time VAR1 and VAR2 are all uppercase. In lines 13 and 14, a third set of declarations is made with the same names, but yet another different case. This time, Var1 and Var2 are declared as float values. In each of these three sets of declarations, values are placed in the variables so they can be printed later. The printing for these three sets of declarations occurs in lines 20–25. As you can see, the values placed in the variables are retained, and each is printed.

Lines 15 and 16 declare two variables of the same type—integers—and the same names. The only difference between these two variables is that one is uppercase and the other is not. Each of these variables has its own value, which is printed in lines 26 and 27.

Although it's possible to use only case to differentiate variables, this isn't a practice to enter into lightly. Not all computer systems that have C compilers available are case sensitive. Because of this, code may not be portable if only case is used to differentiate variables. For portable code, you always should ensure that variables are differentiated by something other than the case of the variable name.

Case sensitivity can cause problems in more than just the compiler. It also can cause problems with the linker. The compiler might be able to differentiate between variables with only case differences, but the linker might not.

Most compilers and linkers enable you to set a flag to cause case to be ignored. You should check your compiler to determine the flag that needs to be set. When you recompile a listing with variables differentiated by case only, you should get an error similar to the following. Of course, var1 would be whatever variable you are using.

```
listB201.c:
Error listB201.c 16: Multiple declaration for 'var1' in function main
*** 1 errors in Compile ***
```

Portable Characters

Characters within the computer are represented as numbers. On an IBM PC or compatible, the letter *A* is represented by the number 65, and the letter *a* is represented by the number 97. These numbers come from an ASCII table (see Appendix A).

If you're writing portable programs, you cannot assume that the ASCII table is the character translation table being used. A different table might be used on a different computer system. In other words, on a mainframe, character 65 might not be *A*.

Warning: You must be careful when using character numerics. Character numerics might not be portable.

There are two general rules about how a character set is to be defined. The first rule restricting the character set is that the size of a character's value can't be larger than the size of the char type. In an 8-bit system, 255 is the maximum value that can be stored in a single char variable. Because of this, you wouldn't have a character with a value greater than 255. If you are working on a machine with a 16-bit character, 65,535 is the maximum value for a character.

The second rule restricting the character set is that each character must be represented by a positive number. The portable characters within the ASCII character set are those from 1–127. The values from 128–255 are not guaranteed to be portable. These extended characters can't be guaranteed because a signed character has only 127 positive values.

Guaranteeing ANSI Compatibility

The predefined constant __STDC__ is used to help guarantee ANSI compatibility. When the listing is compiled with ANSI compatibility set on, this constant is defined—generally as 1. It is undefined when ANSI compatibility isn't on.

Virtually every compiler gives you the option to compile with ANSI enforced. This is usually done either by setting a switch within the IDE (Integrated Development Environment) or by passing an additional parameter on the command line when compiling. By setting the ANSI on, you help ensure that the program will be portable to other compilers and platforms.

To compile a program using Borland's Turbo C command line, you would enter the following on the command line:

```
TCC -A program.c
```

If you are compiling with a Microsoft compiler, you would enter

```
CL /Ze program.c
```

> **Note:** Most compilers with Integrated Development Environments (IDEs) provide an ANSI option. By selecting the ANSI option, you are virtually guaranteed ANSI compatibility.

The compiler then provides additional error checking to ensure that ANSI rules are met. In some cases, there are errors and warnings that are no longer checked. An example is prototype checking. Most compilers display warnings if a function isn't prototyped before it is used; however, the ANSI standards don't require this. Because ANSI doesn't require the prototypes, you might not receive the required prototype warnings.

Avoiding the ANSI Standard

There are several reasons why you wouldn't want to compile your program with ANSI compatibility on. The most common reason involves taking advantage of your compiler's added features. Many features, such as special screen-handling functions, either aren't covered within the ANSI standard or might be compiler-specific. If you decide to use these compiler-specific features, you won't want the ANSI flag set. In addition, if you use these features, you might eliminate the portability of your program. Later today, you'll see a way around this limitation.

DO	DON'T

DO use more than just case to differentiate variable names.

DON'T assume numeric values for characters.

Using Portable Numeric Variables

The numeric values that can be stored in a specific variable type might not be consistent across compilers. There are only a few rules that are defined within the ANSI standard regarding the numeric values that can be stored in each variable type. On Day 3, Table 3.2 presented the values typically stored in IBM-compatible PCs. These values, however, aren't guaranteed.

The following rules apply to variable types:

- A character (char) is the smallest data type. A character variable (type char) will be one byte.

- A short variable (type short) will be smaller than or equal to an integer variable (type int).

- An integer variable (type int) will be smaller than or equal to the size of a long variable (type long).

- An unsigned integer variable (type unsigned) is equal to the size of a signed integer variable (type int).

- A float variable (type float) will be less than or equal to the size of a double variable (type double).

Listing B2.2 presents a commonly used way to print the size of the variables based on the machine that the program is compiled on.

Listing B2.2. Printing the size of the data types.

```
 1:   /*=========================================================*
 2:    * Program: listB202.c                                     *
 3:    * Book:    Teach Yourself C in 21 Days                     *
 4:    * Purpose: This program prints the sizes of the variable  *
 5:    *          types of the machine the program is compiled on *
 6:    *=========================================================*/
 7:   #include <stdio.h>
 8:   int main(void)
 9:   {
10:     printf( "\nVariable Type Sizes" );
11:     printf( "\n=========================" );
12:     printf( "\nchar            %d", sizeof(char) );
13:     printf( "\nshort           %d", sizeof(short) );
14:     printf( "\nint             %d", sizeof(int) );
15:     printf( "\nfloat           %d", sizeof(float) );
16:     printf( "\ndouble          %d", sizeof(double) );
17:
18:     printf( "\n\nunsigned char   %d", sizeof(unsigned char) );
19:     printf( "\nunsigned short  %d", sizeof(unsigned short) );
20:     printf( "\nunsigned int    %d", sizeof(unsigned int) );
21:
22:     return 0;
23:   }
```

```
Variable Type Sizes
=========================
char            1
short           2
int             2
float           4
double          8

unsigned char   1
unsigned short  2
unsigned int    2
```

As you can see, the `sizeof()` operator is used to print the size in bytes of each variable type. The output shown is based on the program's being compiled on a 16-bit IBM-compatible PC with a 16-bit compiler. If compiled on a different machine or with a different compiler, the sizes might be different. For example, a 32-bit compiler on a 32-bit machine might yield four bytes for the size of an integer rather than two.

Maximum and Minimum Values

If different machines have variable types that are different sizes, how do you know what values can be stored? It depends on the number of bytes that make up the data type and whether the variable is signed or unsigned. Table 5.3 shows the different values you can store based on the number of bytes. The maximum and minimum values that can be stored for integral types, such as integers, are based on the bits. For floating values such as floats and doubles, larger values can be stored at the cost of precision. Table B2.2 shows both integral-variable and floating-decimal values.

Table B2.2. Possible values based on byte size.

Number of Bytes	Unsigned Maximum	Signed Minimum	Signed Maximum
Integral Types			
1	255	−128	127
2	65,535	−32,768	32,767
4	4,294,967,295	−2,147,483,648	2,147,438,647
8		$1.844674 \times E19$	
Floating Decimal Sizes			
4*		3.4 E–38	3.4 E38
8**		1.7 E–308	1.7 E308
10***		3.4 E–4932	1.1 E4932

*Precision taken to 7 digits.
**Precision taken to 15 digits.
***Precision taken to 19 digits.

Knowing the maximum value based on the number of bytes and variable type is good; however, as you saw earlier, you don't always know the number of bytes in a portable program. In addition, you can't be completely sure of the level of precision used in floating-point numbers. Because of this, you have to be careful about what numbers you assign to variables. For example, assigning the value of 3,000 to an integer variable is a safe assignment, but what about assigning 100,000? If it's an unsigned integer on a 16-bit machine, you'll get unusual results because the maximum value is 65,535. If a 4-byte integer is being used, then assigning 100,000 would be okay.

> **Warning:** You aren't guaranteed that the values in Table B2.2 are the same for every compiler. Each compiler might choose a slightly different number. This is especially true with the floating-point numbers, which may have different levels of precision. Tables B2.3 and B2.4 provide a compatible way of using these numbers.

ANSI has standardized a set of defined constants that are to be included in the header files LIMITS.H and FLOAT.H. These constants define the number of bits within a variable type. In addition, they define the minimum and maximum values. Table B2.3 lists the values defined in LIMITS.H. These values apply to the integral data types. The values in FLOAT.H contain the values for the floating-point types.

Table B2.3. The ANSI-defined constants within LIMITS.H.

Constant	Value
CHAR_BIT	Character variable's number of bits.
CHAR_MIN	Character variable's minimum value (signed).
CHAR_MAX	Character variable's maximum value (signed).
SCHAR_MIN	Signed character variable's minimum value.
SCHAR_MAX	Signed character variable's maximum value.
UCHAR_MAX	Unsigned character's maximum value.
INT_MIN	Integer variable's minimum value.
INT_MAX	Integer variable's maximum value.
UINT_MAX	Unsigned integer variable's maximum value.
SHRT_MIN	Short variable's minimum value.
SHRT_MAX	Short variable's maximum value.
USHRT_MAX	Unsigned short variable's maximum value.
LONG_MIN	Long variable's minimum value.
LONG_MAX	Long variable's maximum value.
ULONG_MAX	Unsigned long variable's maximum value.

Table B2.4. The ANSI-defined constants within FLOAT.H.

Constant	Value
FLT_DIG	Precision digits in a variable of type float.
DBL_DIG	Precision digits in a variable of type double.
LDBL_DIG	Precision digits in a variable of type long double.
FLT_MAX	Float variable's maximum value.
FLT_MAX_10_EXP	Float variable's exponent maximum value (base 10).
FLT_MAX_EXP	Float variable's exponent maximum value (base 2).
FLT_MIN	Float variable's minimum value.
FLT_MIN_10_EXP	Float variable's exponent minimum value (base 10).
FLT_MIN_EXP	Float variable's exponent minimum value (base 2).
DBL_MAX	Double variable's maximum value.
DBL_MAX_10_EXP	Double variable's exponent maximum value (base 10).
DBL_MAX_EXP	Double variable's exponent maximum value (base 2).
DBL_MIN	Double variable's minimum value.
DBL_MIN_10_EXP	Double variable's exponent minimum value (base 10).
DBL_MIN_EXP	Double variable's exponent minimum value (base 2).
LDBL_MAX	Long double variable's maximum value.
LDBL_MAX_10_DBL	Long double variable's exponent maximum value (base 10).
LDBL_MAX_EXP	Long double variable's exponent maximum value (base 2).
LDBL_MIN	Long double variable's minimum value.
LDBL_MIN_10_EXP	Long double variable's exponent minimum value (base 10).
LDBL_MIN_EXP	Long double variable's exponent minimum value (base 2).

The values in Tables B2.3 and B2.4 can be used when storing numbers. Ensuring that a number is above or equal to the minimum constant and less than or equal to the maximum constant will ensure that the listing will be portable. Listing B2.3 prints the values stored in the ANSI-defined constants and Listing B2.4 demonstrates the use of some of these constants. The output may be slightly different depending on the compiler used.

Listing B2.3. Printing the values stored in the ANSI-defined constants.

```
1:   /*=======================================================*
2:    * Program:   listB203.c                                 *
3:    * Book:      Teach Yourself C in 21 Days                *
4:    * Purpose:   Display of defined constants.              *
5:    *=======================================================*/
6:   #include <stdio.h>
7:   #include <float.h>
8:   #include <limits.h>
9:
10:  int main( void )
11:  {
12:      printf( "\n CHAR_BIT        %d ", CHAR_BIT );
13:      printf( "\n CHAR_MIN        %d ", CHAR_MIN );
14:      printf( "\n CHAR_MAX        %d ", CHAR_MAX );
15:      printf( "\n SCHAR_MIN       %d ", SCHAR_MIN );
16:      printf( "\n SCHAR_MAX       %d ", SCHAR_MAX );
17:      printf( "\n UCHAR_MAX       %d ", UCHAR_MAX );
18:      printf( "\n SHRT_MIN        %d ", SHRT_MIN );
19:      printf( "\n SHRT_MAX        %d ", SHRT_MAX );
20:      printf( "\n USHRT_MAX       %d ", USHRT_MAX );
21:      printf( "\n INT_MIN         %d ", INT_MIN );
22:      printf( "\n INT_MAX         %d ", INT_MAX );
23:      printf( "\n UINT_MAX        %ld ", UINT_MAX );
24:      printf( "\n LONG_MIN        %ld ", LONG_MIN );
25:      printf( "\n LONG_MAX        %ld ", LONG_MAX );
26:      printf( "\n ULONG_MAX       %e ", ULONG_MAX );
27:      printf( "\n FLT_DIG         %d ", FLT_DIG );
28:      printf( "\n DBL_DIG         %d ", DBL_DIG );
29:      printf( "\n LDBL_DIG        %d ", LDBL_DIG );
30:      printf( "\n FLT_MAX         %e ", FLT_MAX );
31:      printf( "\n FLT_MIN         %e ", FLT_MIN );
32:      printf( "\n DBL_MAX         %e ", DBL_MAX );
33:      printf( "\n DBL_MIN         %e ", DBL_MIN );
34:
35:      return(0);
36:  }
```

Output

```
CHAR_BIT        8
CHAR_MIN        -128
CHAR_MAX        127
SCHAR_MIN       -128
SCHAR_MAX       127
UCHAR_MAX       255
SHRT_MIN        -32768
SHRT_MAX        32767
USHRT_MAX       -1
INT_MIN         -32768
INT_MAX         32767
UINT_MAX        65535
LONG_MIN        -2147483648
LONG_MAX        2147483647
ULONG_MAX       3.937208e-302
```

```
FLT_DIG          6
DBL_DIG          15
LDBL_DIG         19
FLT_MAX          3.402823e+38
FLT_MIN          1.175494e-38
DBL_MAX          1.797693e+308
DBL_MIN          2.225074e-308
```

Note: Output values will vary from compiler to compiler; therefore, your output may differ from the output shown here for Listing B2.3.

BD2

Analysis Listing B2.3 is straightforward. The program consists of `printf()` function calls. Each function call prints a different defined constant. You'll notice the conversion character used (that is, `%d`) depends on the type of value being printed. This listing provides a synopsis of what values your compiler used. You could also have looked in the FLOAT.H and LIMITS.H header files to see if these values had been defined. This program should make determining the constant values easier.

Type

Listing B2.4. Using the ANSI-defined constants.

```
 1:   /*=========================================================*
 2:    * Program: listB204.c                                     *
 3:    * Book:    Teach Yourself C in 21 Days                    *
 4:    *                                                         *
 5:    * Purpose: To use maximum and minimum constants.          *
 6:    * Note:    Not all valid characters are displayable to the *
 7:    *          screen!                                        *
 8:    *=========================================================*/
 9:
10:   #include <float.h>
11:   #include <limits.h>
12:   #include <stdio.h>
13:
14:   int main( void )
15:   {
16:       unsigned char ch;
17:       int   i;
18:
19:       printf( "Enter a numeric value.");
20:       printf( "\nThis value will be translated to a character.");
21:       printf( "\n\n==> " );
22:
23:       scanf("%d", &i);
24:
25:       while( i < 0 || i > UCHAR_MAX )
26:       {
27:           printf("\n\nNot a valid value for a character.");
28:           printf("\nEnter a value from 0 to %d ==> ", UCHAR_MAX);
29:
```

continues

Listing B2.4. continued

```
30:        scanf("%d", &i);
31:      }
32:      ch = (char) i;
33:
34:      printf("\n\n%d is character %c", ch, ch );
35:
36:      return(0);
37:  }
```

Input
Output

```
Enter a numeric value.
This value will be translated to a character.

==> 5000


Not a valid value for a character.
Enter a value from 0 to 255 ==> 69


69 is character E
```

Analysis Listing B2.3 shows the UCHAR_MAX constant in action. The first new items you should notice is the includes in lines 10 and 11. As stated earlier, these two include files contain the defined constants. If you are questioning the need for FLOAT.H to be included in line 10, then you're doing well. Because none of the decimal point constants are being used, the FLOAT.H header file is not needed. Line 11, however, is needed. This is the header file that contains the definition of UCHAR_MAX that is used later in the listing.

Lines 16 and 17 declare the variables that will be used by the listing. An unsigned character, ch, is used along with an integer variable, i. When the variables are declared, several print statements are issued to prompt the user for a number. Notice that this number is entered into an integer. Because an integer is usually capable of holding a larger number, it is used for the input. If a character variable were used, a number that was too large would wrap to a number that fits a character variable. This can easily be seen by changing the i in line 23 to ch.

Line 25 uses the defined constant to see if the entered number is greater than the maximum for an unsigned character. We are comparing to the maximum for an unsigned character rather than an integer because the program's purpose is to print a character, not an integer. If the entered value isn't valid for a character (and that is an unsigned character), the user is told the proper values that can be entered (line 28) and is asked to enter a valid value.

Line 32 casts the integer to a character value. In a more complex program, you may find it's easier to switch to the character variable than to continue with the integer. This can help to prevent reallocating a value that isn't valid for a character into the integer variable. For this program, the line that prints the resulting character, line 34, could just as easily have used i rather than ch.

Classifying Numbers

There are several instances when you'll want to know information about a variable. For instance, you may want to know if the information is numeric, a control character, an uppercase character, or any of nearly a dozen different classifications. There are two different ways to check some of these classifications. Consider Listing B2.5, which demonstrates one way of determining if a value stored in a character is a letter of the alphabet.

Type

Listing B2.5. Is the character a letter of the alphabet?

```
1:   /*========================================================*
2:    * Program: listB205.c
3:    * Purpose: This program may not be portable due to the    *
4:    *          way it uses character values.                  *
5:    *========================================================*/
6:   #include <stdio.h>
7:   int main(void)
8:   {
9:     unsigned char x = 0;
10:    char trash[256];                /* used to remove extra keys */
11:    while( x != 'Q' && x != 'q' )
12:    {
13:       printf( "\n\nEnter a character (Q to quit) ==> " );
14:
15:       x = getchar();
16:
17:       if( x >= 'A' && x <= '7')
18:       {
19:          printf( "\n\n%c is a letter of the alphabet!", x );
20:          printf("\n%c is an uppercase letter!", x );
21:       }
22:       else
23:       {
24:          if( x >= 'a' && x <= 'z')
25:          {
26:             printf( "\n\n%c is a letter of the alphabet!", x );
27:             printf("\n%c is an lowercase letter!", x );
28:          }
29:          else
30:          {
31:             printf( "\n\n%c is not a letter of the alphabet!", x );
32:          }
33:       }
34:       gets(trash); /* eliminates enter key */
35:    }
36:    printf("\n\nThank you for playing!");
37:    return;
38: }
```

```
Enter a character (Q to quit) ==> A

A is a letter of the alphabet!
A is an uppercase letter!

Enter a character (Q to quit) ==> f

f is a letter of the alphabet!
f is an lowercase letter!

Enter a character (Q to quit) ==> 1

1 is not a letter of the alphabet!

Enter a character (Q to quit) ==> *

* is not a letter of the alphabet!

Enter a character (Q to quit) ==> q

q is a letter of the alphabet!
q is an lowercase letter!

Thank you for playing!
```

Analysis

This program checks to see if a letter is between the uppercase letter A and the uppercase letter Z. In addition, it checks to see if it is between the lowercase a and the lowercase z. If x is between one of these two ranges, you would think you could assume that the letter is alphabetic. This is a bad assumption! There is no standard for the order in which characters are stored. If you are using the ASCII character set, you can get away with using the character ranges; however, your program isn't guaranteed portability. To guarantee portability, you should use a character-classification function.

There are several character-classification functions. Each is listed in Table B2.5 with what it checks for. These functions will return a zero if the given character doesn't meet its check; otherwise it will return a value other than zero.

Table B2.5. Character-classification functions.

Function	Purpose
isalnum()	Checks to see if the character is alphanumeric.
isalpha()	Checks to see if the character is alphabetic.
iscntrl()	Checks to see if the character is a control character.
isdigit()	Checks to see if the character is a decimal digit.
isgraph()	Checks to see if the character is printable (space is an exception).
islower()	Checks to see if the character is lowercase.
isprint()	Checks to see if the character is printable.

Function	Purpose
ispunct()	Checks to see if the character is a punctuation character.
isspace()	Checks to see if the character is a whitespace character.
isupper()	Checks to see if the character is uppercase.
isxdigit()	Checks to see if the character is a hexadecimal digit.

BD2

With the exception of an equality check, you should never compare the values of two different characters. For example, you could check to see if the value of a character variable is equal to 'A', but you wouldn't want to check to see if the value of a character is greater than 'A'.

```
if( X > 'A' )      /* NOT PORTABLE!! */
...
if( X == 'A' )     /* PORTABLE */
...
```

Listing B2.6 is a rewrite of Listing 12.5. Instead of using range checks, the appropriate character classification values are used. Listing 12.6 is a much more portable program.

Type

Listing B2.6. Using character-classification functions.

```
 1:    /*=============================================================*
 2:     * Program: listB206.c                                        *
 3:     * Book:    Teach Yourself C in 21 Days                        *
 4:     * Purpose: This program is an alternative approach to         *
 5:     *          the same task accomplished in Listing B2.5.        *
 6:     *          This program has a higher degree of portability!   *
 7:     *=============================================================*/
 8:    #include <ctype.h>
 9:
10:    int main(void)
11:    {
12:      unsigned char x = 0;
13:      char trash[256];                  /* use to flush extra keys */
14:      while( x != 'Q' && x != 'q' )
15:      {
16:         printf( "\n\nEnter a character (Q to quit) ==> " );
17:
18:         x = getchar();
19:
20:         if( isalpha(x) )
21:         {
22:            printf( "\n\n%c is a letter of the alphabet!", x );
23:            if( isupper(x) )
24:            {
25:               printf("\n%c is an uppercase letter!", x );
26:            }
27:            else
28:            {
29:               printf("\n%c is an lowercase letter!", x );
```

continues

Listing B2.6 continued

```
30:          }
31:        }
32:        else
33:        {
34:            printf( "\n\n%c is not a letter of the alphabet!", x );
35:        }
36:        gets(trash);    /* get extra keys */
37:    }
38:    printf("\n\nThank you for playing!");
39:    return(0);
40: }
```

```
Enter a character (Q to quit) ==> z

z is a letter of the alphabet!
z is an lowercase letter!

Enter a character (Q to quit) ==> T

T is a letter of the alphabet!
T is an uppercase letter!

Enter a character (Q to quit) ==> #

# is not a letter of the alphabet!

Enter a character (Q to quit) ==> 7

7 is not a letter of the alphabet!

Enter a character (Q to quit) ==> Q

Q is a letter of the alphabet!
Q is an uppercase letter!

Thank you for playing!
```

The outcome should look virtually identical to that for Listing B2.5—assuming you ran the program with the same values. This time, instead of using range checks, the character-classification functions were used. Notice that line 8 includes the CTYPE.H header file. When this is included, the classification functions are ready to go. Line 20 uses the isalpha() function to ensure that the character entered is a letter of the alphabet. If it is, a message is printed in line 22 stating as much. Line 23 then checks to see if the character is uppercase with the isupper() function. If x is an uppercase character, a message is printed in line 25, otherwise the message in line 29 is printed. If the letter was not an alphabet letter, a message is printed in line 34. Because the while loop starts in line 14, the program continues until Q or q is pressed. You might think line 14 detracts from the portability of this program, but that is incorrect. Remember that equality checks for characters are portable, and non-equality checks aren't portable. "Not equal to" and "equal to" are both equality checks.

DO	DON'T

DON'T use numeric values when determining maximums for variables. Use the defined constants if you are writing a portable program.

DO use the character classification functions when possible.

DO remember that "!=" is considered an equality check.

Converting a Character's Case: A Portability Example

A common practice in programming is to convert the case of a character. Many people write a function similar to the following:

```
char conv_to_upper( char x )
{
    if( x >= 'a' && x <= 'z' )
    {
        x -= 32;
    }
    return( x )
}
```

As you saw earlier, the if statement might not be portable. The following is an update function with the if statement updated to the portable functions presented in the previous section:

```
char conv_to_upper( char x )
{
    if( isalpha( x ) && islower( x ) )
    {
        x -= 32;
    }
    return( x )
}
```

This example is better than the previous listing in terms of portability; however, it still isn't completely portable. This function makes the assumption that the uppercase letters are a numeric value that is 32 less than the lowercase letters. This is true if the ASCII character set is used. In the ASCII character set, 'A' + 32 equals 'a'; however, this is not necessarily true on every system. Particularly, it is untrue on non-ASCII character systems.

Two ANSI standard functions take care of switching the case of a character. The toupper() function converts a lowercase character to uppercase; the lowercase() function converts an uppercase character to lowercase. The previous function rewritten would look as follows:

```
toupper();
```

As you can see, this is a function that already exists. In addition, this function is defined by ANSI standards, so it should be portable.

Portable Structures and Unions

When using structures and unions, care must also be exercised if portability is a concern. Word alignment and the order in which members are stored are two areas of incompatibility that can occur when working with these constructs.

Word Alignment

Word alignment is an important factor in the portability of a structure. *Word alignment* is the aligning of data on a word boundary. A *word* is a set number of bytes. A word usually is equivalent to the size of the processor on the computer being used. For example, an IBM 16-bit PC generally will have a two-byte word. Two bytes equals 16 bits.

An example will make this easy to understand. Consider the following structure. Using two-byte integers and one-byte characters, determine how many bytes of storage are needed to store the structure.

```
struct struct_tag {
    int    x;    /* ints will be 2 bytes */
    char   a;    /* chars are 1 byte */
    int    y;
    char   b;
    int    z;
} sample = { 100, 'A', 200, 'B', 300);
```

Adding up the integers and the characters, you might come up with eight bytes for the amount of storage. This answer *could* be true. It could also be wrong! If word alignment is on, this structure will take 10 bytes of storage. Figures B2.1 and B2.2 illustrate how the structure would be stored in memory.

Figure B2.1.
Word alignment is off.

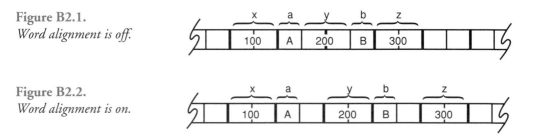

Figure B2.2.
Word alignment is on.

A program can't assume that the word alignment will be the same or that it will be on or off. The members could be aligned on every two bytes, four bytes, or eight bytes. You cannot assume that you know.

Reading and Writing Structures

When reading or writing structures, you must be cautious. It's best to never use a literal constant for the size of a structure or union. If you are reading or writing structures to a file, the file probably won't be portable. This means you only need to concentrate on making the program portable. The program would then need to read and write the data files specific to the machine compiled on. The following is an example of a read statement that would be portable:

```
fread( &the_struct, sizeof( the_struct ), 1, filepointer );
```

As you can see, the sizeof command is used instead of a literal. Regardless of whether byte alignment is on or off, the correct number of bytes should be read.

Structure Order

When you create a structure, you might assume that the members will be stored in the order in which they are listed. There isn't a standard that states that a certain order must be followed. Because of this, you can't make assumptions about the order of information within a structure.

Preprocessor Directives

On Day 21, "Taking Advantage of Preprocessor Directives and More," you learned that there are several preprocessor directives you can use. There are several preprocessor directives that have been defined in the ANSI standards. You use two of these all the time: #include and #define. Several other preprocessor directives are in the ANSI standards. The additional preprocessor directives available under the ANSI guidelines are listed in Table B2.6.

Table B2.6. ANSI standard preprocessor directives.

#define	#if
#elif	#ifdef
#else	#ifndef
#endif	#include
#error	#pragma

Using Predefined Constants

Every compiler comes with predefined constants. A majority of these are typically compiler-specific. This means that there is a good chance that they won't be portable from one compiler to the next. There are, however, several predefined constants that are defined in the ANSI standards. Some of these constants are:

Constant	Description
__DATE__	This is replaced by the date at the time the program is compiled. The date is in the form of a literal string (text enclosed in double quotes). The format is "Mmm DD, YYYY". For example, January 1, 1998 would be "Jan 1, 1998".
__FILE__	This is replaced with the name of the source file at the time of compilation. This will be in the form of a literal string.
__LINE__	This will be replaced with the number of the line on which __LINE__ appears in the source code. This will be a numeric decimal value.
__STDC__	This literal will be defined as 1 if the source file is compiled with the ANSI Standard. If the source file wasn't compiled with the ANSI flag set, this value will be undefined.
__TIME__	This is replaced by the time that the program is compiled. This time is in the form of a literal string (text enclosed in double quotes). The format is "HH:MM:SS". An example would be "12:15:03".

Using Non-ANSI Features in Portable Programs

A program can use non-ANSI-defined constants and other commands and still be portable. You accomplish this by ensuring that the constants are used only if compiled with a compiler that supports the features used. Most compilers provide defined constants that you can use to identify themselves. By setting up areas of the code that are supportive for each of the compilers, you can create a portable program. Listing B2.7 demonstrates how this can be done.

Type

Listing B2.7. A portable program with compiler specifics.

```
1:   /*=========================================================*
2:   * Program: listB207.c                                     *
3:   * Purpose: This program demonstrates using defined        *
4:   *          constants for creating a portable program.     *
5:   * Note:    This program gets different results with       *
6:   *          different compilers.                           *
7:   *=========================================================*/
8:   #include <stdio.h>
9:   #ifdef _WINDOWS
```

```
10:
11:   #define STRING "DOING A WINDOWS PROGRAM!"
12:
13:   #else
14:
15:   #define STRING "NOT DOING A WINDOWS PROGRAM"
16:
17:   #endif
18:
19:   int main(void)
20:   {
21:      printf( "\n\n") ;
22:      printf( STRING ) ;
23:
24:   #ifdef _MSC_VER
25:
26:      printf( "\n\nUsing a Microsoft compiler!" );
27:      printf( "\n   Your Compiler version is %s", _MSC_VER );
28:
29:   #endif
30:
31:   #ifdef __TURBOC__
32:
33:      printf( "\n\nUsing the Turbo C compiler!" );
34:      printf( "\n   Your compiler version is %x", __TURBOC__ );
35:
36:   #endif
37:
38:   #ifdef __BORLANDC__
39:
40:      printf( "\n\nUsing a Borland compiler!" );
41:
42:   #endif
43:
44:      return(0);
45:   }
```

Output

Output when running with Turbo C for DOS 3.0 compiler:

```
NOT DOING A WINDOWS PROGRAM

Using the Turbo C compiler!
   Your compiler version is 300
```

Output when running with Borland C++ compiler under DOS:

```
NOT DOING A WINDOWS PROGRAM

Using a Borland compiler!
```

Output when running with Microsoft compiler under DOS:

```
NOT DOING A WINDOWS PROGRAM

Using a Microsoft compiler!
   Your compiler version is >>
```

This listing takes advantage of defined constants to determine information about the compiler being used. In line 9, the #ifdef preprocessor directive is used. This directive checks to see if the following constant has been defined. If the constant has been defined, the statements following the #ifdef are executed until an #endif preprocessor directive is reached. In the case of line 9, a determination of whether _WINDOWS has been defined is made. An appropriate message is applied to the constant STRING. Line 22 then prints this string, which states whether this listing has been compiled as a Windows program or not.

Line 24 checks to see if _MSC_VER has been defined. _MSC_VER is a constant that contains the version number of a Microsoft compiler. If a compiler other than a Microsoft compiler is used, this constant won't be defined. If a Microsoft compiler is used, this will be defined with the version number of the compiler. Line 27 will print this compiler version number after line 26 prints a message stating that a Microsoft compiler was used.

Lines 31–36 and lines 38–42 operate in similar manners. They check to see if Borland's Turbo C or Borland's professional compiler were used. The appropriate message is printed based on these constants.

As you can see, this program determines what compiler is being used by checking the defined constants. The object of the program is the same regardless of which compiler is used—print a message stating which compiler is being used. If you are aware of the systems that you will be porting, you can put compiler-specific commands into the code. If you do use compiler-specific commands, you should ensure that the appropriate code is provided for each compiler.

ANSI Standard Header Files

Several header files that can be included are set by the ANSI standards. It's good to know which header files are ANSI standard since these can be used in creating portable programs. Appendix E, "Common C Functions Listed Alphabetically," contains the ANSI header files along with a list of their functions.

Summary

Today, you were exposed to a great deal of material. This information centered around portability. C is one of the most portable languages—if not the most portable language. Portability doesn't happen by accident. ANSI standards have been created to ensure that C programs can be ported from one compiler to another and from one computer system to another. There are several areas to consider when writing portable code. These areas include variable case, which character set to use, using portable numerics, ensuring variable sizes, comparing characters, using structures and unions, and using preprocessor directives and preprocessor constants. The day ended with a discussion of how to incorporate compiler specifics into a portable program.

Q&A

Q How do you write portable graphics programs?

A ANSI does not define any real standards for programming graphics. With graphics programming being more machine dependent than other programming areas, it can be somewhat difficult to write portable graphics programs.

Q Should you always worry about portability?

A No, it's not always necessary to consider portability. Some programs that you write will only be used by you on the system you are using. In addition, some programs won't be ported to a different computer system. Because of this, some nonportable functions, such as system(), can be used that wouldn't be used in portable programs.

Q Are comments done with // instead of /* and */ portable?

A No. The forward slash comments come from C++. Many C programmers now use these comments. Although they will most likely be a standard in the future, you may find that some current C compilers don't support them.

Workshop

The Workshop provides quiz questions to help you solidify your understanding of the material covered and exercises to provide you with experience in using what you've learned.

Quiz

1. Which is more important: efficiency or maintainability?
2. What is the numeric value of the letter *a*?
3. What is guaranteed to be the largest unsigned character value on your system?
4. What does ANSI stand for?
5. Are the following variable names valid in the same C program?

   ```
   int lastname,
   LASTNAME,
   LastName,
   Lastname;
   ```

6. What does isalpha() do?
7. What does isdigit() do?
8. Why would you want to use functions such as isalpha() and isdigit()?
9. Can structures be written to disk without worrying about portability?

10. Can `__TIME__` be used in a `printf()` statement to print the current time in a program? For example:

```
printf( "The Current Time is:  %s", __TIME__ );
```

Exercises

1. **BUG BUSTER:** What, if anything, is wrong with the following function?

```
void Print_error( char *msg )
{
    static int ctr = 0,
               CTR = 0;
    printf("\n" );
    for( ctr = 0; ctr < 60; ctr++ )
    {
        printf("*");
    }
    printf( "\nError %d, %s - %d: %s.\n", CTR,
            __FILE__, __LINE__, msg );
    for( ctr = 0; ctr < 60; ctr++ )
    {
        printf("*");
    }
}
```

2. Write a function that verifies that a character is a vowel.

3. Write a function that returns 0 if it receives a character that isn't a letter of the alphabet, 1 if it is an uppercase letter, and 2 if it is a lowercase letter. Keep the function as portable as possible.

4. **ON YOUR OWN:** Understand your compiler. Determine what flags must be set to ignore variable case, allow for byte alignment, and guarantee ANSI compatibility.

5. Is the following code portable?

```
void list_a_file( char *file_name )
{
    system("TYPE " file_name );
}
```

6. Is the following code portable?

```
int to_upper( int x )
{
    if( x >= 'a' && x <= 'z' )
    {
        toupper( x );
    }
    return( x );
}
```

Bonus Day

3+

Working with Bits

As you may know, the most basic unit of computer data storage is the *bit.* There are times when being able to manipulate individual bits in your C program's data is very useful. Today, you learn

- How to use the shift operators
- How to use the bitwise logical operators
- How to use bit fields in structures

Operating on Bits

The C *bitwise* operators enable you to manipulate the individual bits of integer variables. Remember, a bit is the smallest possible unit of data storage, and can have only the two values, 0 or 1. The bitwise operators can be used only with integer types: char, int, and long. Before continuing with this section, you should be familiar with *binary notation,* the way the computer internally stores integers. If you need to review binary notation, refer to Bonus Day 4, "Working with Different Number Systems."

The bitwise operators are most frequently used when your C program interacts directly with your system's hardware—a topic that is beyond the scope of this book. They do have other uses, however, which this chapter introduces you to.

The Shift Operators

Two *shift operators* shift the bits in an integer variable by a specified number of positions: the << operator shifts bits to the left, and the >> operator shifts bits to the right. The syntax for these binary operators is

```
x << n
x >> n
```

Each operator shifts the bits in x by n positions in the specified direction. For a right shift, zeros are placed in the n high-order bits of the variable; for a left shift, zeros are placed in the n low-order bits of the variable. Here are a few examples:

Binary 00001100 (decimal 12) right-shifted by 2 evaluates to binary 00000011 (decimal 3).

Binary 00001100 (decimal 12) left-shifted by 3 evaluates to binary 01100000 (decimal 96).

Binary 00001100 (decimal 12) right-shifted by 3 evaluates to binary 00000001 (decimal 1).

Binary 00110000 (decimal 48) left-shifted by 3 evaluates to binary 10000000 (decimal 128).

Under certain circumstances, the shift operators can be used to multiply and divide an integer variable by a power of 2. Left-shifting an integer by n places has the same effect as multiplying it by 2^n, and right-shifting an integer has the same effect as dividing it by 2^n. The results of a left-shift multiplication are accurate only if there is no overflow, that is, if no bits are "lost" by being shifted out of the high-order positions. A right-shift division is an integer division, with any fractional part of the result lost. For example, if you right-shift the value 5 (binary 00000101) by one place, intending to divide by 2, the result is 2 (binary 00000010) instead of the correct 2.5, as the fractional part (the .5) is lost. The program in Listing B3.1 demonstrates the shift operators.

Type

Listing B3.1. Using the shift operators.

```
1:  /* Demonstrating the shift operators. */
2:
3:  #include <stdio.h>
4:
5:  main()
6:  {
7:      unsigned char y, x = 255;
8:      int count;
9:
10:     printf("Decimal\t\tshift left by\tresult\n");
11:
12:     for (count = 1; count < 8; count++)
13:     {
14:         y = x << count;
15:         printf("%d\t\t%d\t\t%d\n", x, count, y);
16:     }
17:     printf("\n\nDecimal\t\tshift right by\tresull\n");
18:
19:     for (count = 1; count < 8; count++)
20:     {
21:         y = x >> count;
22:         printf("%d\t\t%d\t\t%d\n", x, count, y);
23:     }
24: }
```

Input Output

```
C:\bonus3_1
Decimal         shift left by    result
255             1                254
255             2                252
255             3                248
255             4                240
255             5                224
255             6                192
255             7                128


Decimal         shift right by   result
255             1                127
255             2                63
255             3                31
255             4                15
255             5                7
255             6                3
255             7                1
```

The Bitwise Logical Operators

Three *bitwise logical operators* are used to manipulate individual bits in an integer data type, as listed in Table B3.1. These operators have names similar to the TRUE/FALSE logical operators you learned about in earlier chapters, but their operations differ.

Table B3.1. The bitwise logical operators.

Operator	Action
&	AND
¦	Inclusive OR
^	Exclusive OR

These are all binary operators, setting bits in the result to 1 or 0 depending on the bits in the operands. They operate as follows:

- Bitwise AND sets a bit in the result to 1 only if the corresponding bits in both operands are 1; otherwise, the bit is set to 0. The AND operator is used to turn off, or *clear*, one or more bits in a value.

- Bitwise Inclusive OR sets a bit in the result to 0 only if the corresponding bits in both operands are 0; otherwise, the bit is set to 1. The OR operator is used to turn on, or *set*, one or more bits in a value.

- Bitwise Exclusive OR sets a bit in the result to 1 if the corresponding bits in the operands are different (one 1, the other 0); otherwise, the bit is set to 0.

Following are examples of how these operators work.

Operation	*Example*
AND	11110000
	& 01010101
	01010000
Inclusive OR	11110000
	¦ 01010101
	11110101
Exclusive OR	11110000
	^ 01010101
	10100101

You read earlier that bitwise AND and bitwise inclusive OR can be used to clear or set, respectively, specified bits in an integer value. Here's what that means. Suppose that you have a type char variable and you want to ensure that the bits in positions 0 and 4 are cleared (that is, equal to 0) while leaving the other bits at their original values. If you AND the variable with a second value that has the binary value 11101110, you'll obtain the desired result. Here's how this works.

In each position where the second value has a 1, the result will have the same value, 0 or 1, as was present in that position in the original variable:

```
0 & 1 == 0
1 & 1 == 1
```

In each position where the second value has a 0, the result will have a 0 regardless of the value that was present in that position in the original variable:

```
0 & 0 == 0
1 & 0 == 0
```

Settings bits with OR works in a similar way. In each position where the second value has a 1, the result will have a 1, and in each position where the second value has a 0, the result will be unchanged:

```
0 | 1 == 1
1 | 1 == 1
0 | 0 == 0
1 | 0 == 1
```

The Complement Operator

The final bitwise operator is the *complement operator, (~)*. This is a unary operator. Its action is to reverse every bit in its operand, changing all 0s to 1s and vice versa. For example, ~254 (binary 11111110) evaluates to 1 (binary 00000001).

All the examples in this bonus day use type char variables containing 8 bits. For type int, with 16 bits, and type long, with 32 bits, things work exactly the same.

Bit Fields in Structures

The final bit-related topic is the use of bit fields in structures. On Day 11, "Structures," you learned how to define your own data structures, customizing them to fit the data needs of your program. By using bit fields, you can accomplish even greater customization and save memory space as well.

A *bit field* is a structure member that contains a specified number of bits. You can declare a bit field to contain one bit, two bits, or whatever number of bits are required to hold the data stored in the field. What advantage does this provide?

Suppose that you are programming an employee database program that keeps records on your company's employees. Many of the items of information that the database stores are of the yes or no variety, such as, "Is the employee enrolled in the dental plan?" or "Did the employee graduate from college?" Each piece of yes/no information can be stored in a single bit, with 1 representing yes and 0 representing no.

Using C's standard data types, the smallest type you could use in a structure is a type char. You could indeed use a type char structure member to hold yes/no data, but seven of the char's eight bits would be wasted space. By using bit fields, you could store eight yes/no values in a single char.

Bit fields are not limited to yes/no values. Continuing with this database example, imagine that your firm has three different health insurance plans. Your database needs to store data about the plan, if any, in which each employee is enrolled. You could represent no health insurance by 0 and the three plans by values of 1–3. A bit field containing two bits is sufficient because two binary bits can represent values of 0–3. Likewise, a bit field containing three bits could hold values in the range 0–7, four bits could hold values in the range 0–15, and so on.

Bit fields are named and accessed like regular structure members. All bit fields have type unsigned int, and the size of the field (in bits) is specified by following the member name with a colon and the number of bits. To define a structure with a one-bit member named dental, another one-bit member named college, and a two-bit member named health, write the following:

```
struct emp_data {
    unsigned dental     : 1;
    unsigned college    : 1;
    unsigned health     : 2;
    ...
};
```

The ellipsis ... indicates space for other structure members. The members can be bit fields or fields made up of regular data types. Note that bit fields must be placed first in the structure definition, before any non-bit field structure members. To access the bit fields, use the structure member operator just as you do with any structure member. For the example, you can expand the structure definition to something more useful as in this example:

```
struct emp_data {
    unsigned dental     : 1;
    unsigned college    : 1;
    unsigned health     : 2;
    char fname[20];
    char lname[20];
    char ssnumber[10];
};
```

You then can declare an array of structures:

```
struct emp_data workers[100];
```

To assign values to the first array element, write something like the following:

```
workers[0].dental = 1;
workers[0].college = 0;
workers[0].health = 2;
strcpy(workers[0].fname, "Mildred");
```

Your code would be clearer, of course, if you use symbolic constants YES and NO with values of 1 and 0 when working with one-bit fields. In any case, you treat each bit field as a small, unsigned integer with the given number of bits. The range of values that can be assigned to a bit field with n bits is from 0 to 2^{n-1}. If you try to assign an out-of-range value to a bit field, the compiler does not report an error, but you do get unpredictable results.

DO	DON'T

DO use defined constants YES and NO, or TRUE and FALSE, when working with bits. These are much easier to read and understand than 1 and 0.

DON'T define a bit field that takes 8 or 16 bits. These are the same as other available variables such as type char or int.

Summary

This chapter covered the ways in which a C program can manipulate individual bits. The shift operators and the bitwise logical operators enable you to manipulate the individual bits in integer variables. Also, you can use bit fields in structures to maximize the efficiency of data storage.

Q&A

Q When would I use the shift operators and the bitwise logical operators?

A The most common use for these operators is when a program is interacting directly with the computer hardware—a task that often requires specific bit patterns to be generated and interpreted. This topic is beyond the scope of this book. Even if you never need to manipulate hardware directly, you can use the shift operators, in certain circumstances, to divide or multiply integer values by powers of 2.

Q Do I really gain that much by using bit fields?

A Yes, you can gain quite a bit with bit fields. (Pun intended!) Consider a circumstance similar to the example in this chapter in which a file contains information from a survey. People are asked to answer TRUE or FALSE to the questions asked. If you ask 100 questions of 10,000 people and store each answer as a type char as T or F, you will need 10,000 times 100 bytes of storage (because a character is 1 byte). This is 1,000,000 bytes of storage. If you use bit fields instead and allocate one bit for each answer, you will need 10,000 times 100 bits. Because 1 byte holds 8 bits, this amounts to 130,000 bytes of data, which is significantly less than 1 million bytes.

Workshop

The Workshop provides quiz questions to help you solidify your understanding of the material covered and exercises to provide you with experience in using what you've learned.

Quiz

1. Imagine that your program uses a structure that must (as one of its members) store the day of the week as a value between 1 and 7. What's the most memory-efficient way to do this?

2. What is the smallest amount of memory in which the current date can be stored? (Hint: *month/day/year*—think of *year* as an offset from 1900.)

3. What does `10010010 << 4` evaluate to?

4. What does `10010010 >> 4` evaluate to?

5. Describe the difference between the results of the following two expressions:

```
(01010101 ^ 11111111 )
( ~01010101 )
```

Exercises

1. **BUG BUSTER:** Is the following structure allowed?

```
struct quiz_answers {
    char student_name[15];
    unsigned answer1   : 1;
    unsigned answer2   : 1;
    unsigned answer3   : 1;
    unsigned answer4   : 1;
    unsigned answer5   : 1;
    }
```

2. Write a program that copies the time from the `tm` structure to the bit field structure described in quiz question 6.

3. Write a program that uses each of the bitwise logical operators. The program should apply the bitwise operator to a number and then reapply it to the result. You should observe the output to be sure you understand what is going on.

4. Write a program that displays the binary value of a number. For instance, if 3 is entered, the program should display `00000011`. (Hint: You will need to use the bitwise operators.)

> **Note:** Answers are not provided for exercises 2, 3, or 4.

BD3

Bonus Day

4

Working with Different Number Systems

Understanding numbers and number systems might seem like a strange topic; however, it is very important that you understand these in order to fully understanding the power of C. Today, you learn

- Why number systems are so important
- Which number systems are most important
- How to convert from one number system to another
- How to work with the number systems

The Importance of Number Systems

Numbers are the key to computer programming. This can become obvious within the C programming language. Numbers are very important for one simple reason: Every element of a computer program breaks down into a numeric value. As you probably already know, even what appears to be letters and symbols are actually just numbers to the computer.

You learned that each character can be stored as a numeric value. Using the ASCII chart, for example, you learned that the letter A is stored as the number 65. To go one step further, every numeric value within the computer—and hence every letter or symbol—can be represented with the numbers 0 and 1. To the computer, for example, the letter A is 01000001.

The computer uses 1s and 0s to represent the states on and off. A computer can store information in memory as magnetic charges that are positive or negative. If a charge is positive, it is on. This can be equated to 1. If a charge is negative, it is off. This negative charge can be equated to 0.

Note: The data stored on disks, CD-ROMs, tapes, RAM, and other storage mediums also are stored in a format using 1s and 0s. On a CD-ROM, there are holes or bumps that reflect light differences. For the most part, computers store information in a 1/0, on/off, or positive/negative format.

Deriving Letters

You might be wondering how the computer knows which number to use for each letter. Depending on the computer, the numbers used to represent various characters may be different. In the case of IBM-compatible computers, a set of number representations has been standardized. This set of numbers is represented within an ASCII character table. ASCII stands for *American Standard Code for Information Interchange*. The ASCII character table contains every standard character and its numeric equivalent. Appendix A contains a complete ASCII character table.

Warning: The ASCII table is viewed as being in two pieces. The values from 0 to 127 are the standard ASCII values. The values from 128 to 255 are the extended ASCII values. If you are concerned with cross-platform portability, you should use only the standard values—not the extended.

Listing B4.1 presents a program that displays the standard values available in the ASCII character table. You should be able to figure out what the code within this listing does because everything presented has been covered on previous days.

Type

Listing B4.1. The standard ASCII values.

```
1:   /* Program:   listb401.c
2:    * Book:      Teach Yourself C in 21 Days
3:    * Purpose:   Print the standard ASCII character values.
4:    *========================================================*/
5:
6:   #include <stdio.h>
7:
8:   int main(void)
9:   {
10:     unsigned char ch;
11:     char trash[256];
12:
13:     printf("\n\nThe ASCII VALUES:" );
14:
15:     for( ch = 0; ch < 128; ch++ )
16:     {
17:        printf("\n%3.3d:  %c", ch, ch );
18:
19:        if( ((ch % 20) == 0) && (ch != 0) )
20:        {
21:           printf("\nPress <Enter> to continue");
22:           gets(trash);
23:        }
24:     }
25:
26:     return 0;
27:   }
```

Output

```
The ASCII VALUES:
000:  null
001:  ☺
002:  ☻
003:  ♥
004:  ♦
005:  ♣
006:  ♠
007:  •
008:  ◘
009:  ○
010:  ◙
```

```
011:   ♂
012:   ♀
013:   ♪
014:   ♫
015:   ☼
016:   ▬
017:   ↕
018:   ‼
019:   ‼
020:   ¶
Press <Enter> to continue

021:   §
022:   ▬
023:   ↨
024:   ↑
025:   ↓
026:   →
027:   ←
028:   └
029:   ↔
030:   ▲
031:   ▼
032:   space
033:   !
034:   "
035:   #
036:   $
037:   %
038:   &
039:   '
040:   (
Press <Enter> to continue

041:   )
042:   *
043:   +
044:   ,
045:   -
046:   .
047:   /
048:   0
049:   1
050:   2
051:   3
052:   4
053:   5
054:   6
055:   7
056:   8
057:   9
058:   :
059:   ;
060:   <
Press <Enter> to continue
```

```
061:    =
062:    >
063:    ?
064:    @
065:    A
066:    B
067:    C
068:    D
069:    E
070:    F
071:    G
072:    H
073:    I
074:    J
075:    K
076:    L
077:    M
078:    N
079:    O
080:    P
Press <Enter> to continue

081:    Q
082:    R
083:    S
084:    T
085:    U
086:    V
087:    W
088:    X
089:    Y
090:    Z
091:    [
092:    \
093:    ]
094:    ^
095:
096:    ‾
097:    a
098:    b
099:    c
100:    d
Press <Enter> to continue

101:    e
102:    f
103:    g
104:    h
105:    i
106:    j
107:    k
108:    l
109:    m
110:    n
111:    o
112:    p
```

BD4

```
113:  q
114:  r
115:  s
116:  t
117:  u
118:  v
119:  w
120:  x
Press <Enter> to continue

121:  y
122:  z
123:  {
124:  |
125:  }
126:  ~
127:  Δ
```

Line 10 declares an unsigned character variable, ch, which is used to print the values in the table. As you can see in line 15, 128 values are printed, starting with 0 and ending with 127.

Line 17 does the actual printing. The numeric value is printed first, followed by the character value. Both the numeric and character values are of the same variable, ch. This line shows that the two values are, in essence, equivalent.

Line 19 contains an if statement that enables the program to pause after printing every 20 values. If your screen can display more lines, you can adjust this number. Line 22 uses the gets() function to get any information the user enters. In line 11, the variable trash is declared to be 256 bytes long, because this is the maximum number of characters the keyboard buffer allows before requiring the user to press Enter.

A few of the values might not print to the screen. Values such as a beep (ASCII value 7) cannot be seen, for example. If your computer has a speaker, when character 7 is printed in the output, you will hear a beep. In addition, you might notice that number 10 of the output precedes a blank line. This value is translated to a line feed. When the line feed is printed by the program, it causes a line to be skipped.

Note: You might want to adjust the listing to print the values from 32 to 127 rather than from 0 to 127. By starting at 32, you skip many of the unusual characters.

Determining Which Number Systems Are Important

A multitude of number systems are available. The number system you should be most familiar with is the decimal, or base 10, system. The decimal system is the number system that you learn in school and that you use every day. When you see a number such as the 21 in the title of this book, you know how many days it is going to cover. If you were asked to show a calendar with 21 days marked, you would present something like Figure B4.1.

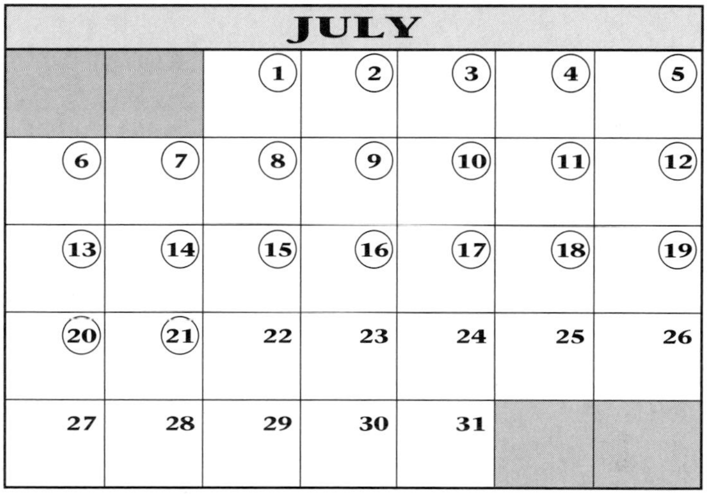

Figure B4.1.
A calendar with 21 (decimal) days marked.

BD4

In addition to the decimal system, three other number systems typically are referred to when programming. These systems are binary, octal, and hexadecimal; they are explained later in this section.

Listing B4.2 is a program that enables you to enter a decimal number. The program then translates the entered number into equivalent hexadecimal and octal values.

Type   Listing B4.2. A numeric translation program.

```
1:  /* Program:  listb402.c
2:   * Book:     Teach yourself C in 21 Days
3:   * Purpose:  Translate decimal to hexadecimal and octal.
4:   *=======================================================*/
5:
```

continues

Listing B4.2. continued

```
6:      #include <stdio.h>
7:      #include <stdlib.h>
8:
9:      int main(void)
10:     {
11:         int nbr;
12:
13:         printf("\n\nEnter a number ==> " );
14:         scanf( "%d", &nbr);
15:
16:         printf("\n\nYour Number:        %d", nbr );
17:         printf("\n Octal value:       %o", nbr);
18:         printf("\n Hexadecimal value: %x", nbr );
19:
20:         return 0;
21:     }
```

```
Enter a number ==> 21


Your Number:        21
 Octal value:       25
 Hexadecimal value: 15
```

This program uses the conversion parameter within the `printf()` function's string to display the decimal, octal, and hexadecimal values. Lines 13 and 14 prompt the user for a starting number. By default, this is a decimal value. Line 16 uses the `%d` conversion character in the `printf()` to directly print the decimal value. As you can see from the output, this is the same value you entered. Line 17 use the `%o` specifier to print the octal value. Line 18 uses the `%x` conversion value to print the hexadecimal value.

This program does not print the binary value. The binary value for a larger number can be quite complex. Additionally, although some compilers have conversion specifiers for binary, it is not standard. Later in this chapter, you will see a way to convert a character to its binary value.

DO	DON'T

DON'T be confused by all the number systems. Today, each number system is explained in detail.

DO read the rest of this chapter if you do not understand these number systems.

The Decimal Number System

As stated, the decimal system is the base 10 system that you started learning to count with in kindergarten. After you realize how the decimal system actually works, the other number systems will be easy to understand.

There are two keys to understanding a number system. First, you should know what number system you are using. Second, you should know the number system's *base*. In the case of the decimal number system, the base is 10. In fact, the name of the number system generally stands for the base number. Decimal stands for 10.

The base also states how many different numbers (or characters) are used when representing numbers. In addition, using the base, you can translate numbers from other number systems to the more familiar decimal system.

To aid in the understanding of the different number systems, consider the objects in Figure B4.2. How many objects are in the two pictures?

Figure B4.2.
Count the objects on each side.

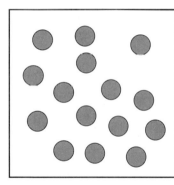 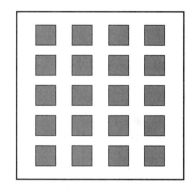

You should have answered 15 circles and 20 squares. These are decimal numbers. How did you determine that the answer for the left side was a 1 followed by a 5 (15)? You probably just counted, and the answer was obvious. However, the logic you may have used to determine this is slightly more complex.

From your elementary-school days, you should remember that the right-most digit—5, in the first case—is the "ones" value. The 1 is the "tens" value. Bigger numbers may have "hundreds," "thousands," or more.

As you already learned, the decimal number system is base 10. You also know that a base 10 system has only 10 digits to use: 0 through 9. The way a number is written is determined by its base. For each digit from right to left, the number is the base—10 in the case of decimal—to an exponential power. This starts at the right side with the base to the power of 0, and increases by an additional power for each digit to the left. Table B4.1 illustrates this concept for the decimal number system.

Table B4.1. Decimal digits.

Digit	Base Value	Decimal Equivalent	Digit Name
First	$10^0 =$	1	Ones
Second	$10^1 =$	10	Tens
Third	$10^2 =$	100	Hundreds
Fourth	$10^3 =$	1,000	Thousands
Fifth	$10^4 =$	10,000	Ten-thousands
Sixth	$10^5 =$	100,000	Hundred-thousands
Seventh	$10^6 =$	1,000,000	Millions

Data in Decimal

As you learned earlier, all computer information is represented as numbers. It is possible to view these numbers in their decimal formats. Listing B4.3 takes a file as a parameter and displays each line in its decimal format instead of characters.

Note: This listing and several of the following use a test file. This file or a similar test file can be created with your text editor. The test file contains the following:

```
1234567890
ABCDEFG
HIJKLMN
OPQRSTU
VWXYZ
abcdefg
hijklmn
opqrstu
vwxyz

!@#$%^&*()_+{}[];:'"<>?/.,'~
>                 <
Once upon a time there were three little pigs...
```

Listing B4.3. Program to type a file in decimal.

```
1:   /* Program:    decdump.c
2:    * Book:       Teach Yourself C in 21 Days
3:    * Purpose:    This program types out a file. It displays
4:    *             the decimal equivalent of each character.
5:    *====================================================*/
6:
7:   #include <stdio.h>
8:   #include <string.h>
9:   #include <stdlib.h>
10:
11:  int main(int argv, char *argc[])
12:  {
13:      int ch;
14:      unsigned int  line = 1;
15:
16:      FILE *fp;
17:
18:      if( argv != 2 )
19:      {
20:          printf("\n\nOops!  Proper usage is:");
21:          printf("\n\n%s in_file ", argc[0]);
22:          printf("\n\nOriginal file will be printed in decimal");
23:          return(1);
24:      }
25:
26:      /***  Open the file  ***/
27:      if (( fp = fopen( argc[1], "r" )) == NULL )
28:      {
29:          printf( "\n\nOops!  Error in opening file: %s\n\n", argc[1]);
30:          exit(99);
31:      }
32:
33:      printf("\n%5.5d:  ", line );
34:
35:      while( (ch = fgetc( fp )) != EOF )
36:      {
37:          printf("%d ", ch );
38:
39:          if(ch == '\n')
40:          {
41:              line++;
42:              printf("\n%5.5d:  ", line );
43:          }
44:      }
45:
46:      fclose( fp );
47:
48:      return(0);
49:  }
```

```
00001:   49 50 51 52 53 54 55 56 57 48 10
00002:   65 66 67 68 69 70 71 10
00003:   72 73 74 75 76 77 78 10
00004:   79 80 81 82 83 84 85 10
00005:   86 87 88 89 90 10
00006:   97 98 99 100 101 102 103 10
00007:   104 105 106 107 108 109 110 10
00008:   111 112 113 114 115 116 117 10
00009:   118 119 120 121 122 10
00010:   1 2 10
00011:   33 64 35 36 37 94 38 42 40 41 95 43 123 125 91 93 59 58 39
         34 60 62 63 47 46 44 96 126 10
00012:   62 32 32 32 32 32 32 32 32 32 32 32 32 32 32 32 60 10
00013:   10
00014:   79 110 99 101 32 117 112 111 110 32 97 32 116 105 109 101 32
         116 104 101 114 101 32 119 101 114 101 32 116 104 114 101
         101 32 108 105 116 108 101 32 112 105 103 115 46 46 46 10
00015:   10
00016:
```

This program uses a command-line argument. The preceding output was created by typing the following at the command line:

```
DECDUMP TEST
```

Line 11 uses the argv and argc variables to get the command-line parameter. Line 18 checks to see whether a single parameter was entered along with the program name at the time the user started the program. If not, error messages are printed and the program exits. Line 27 attempts to open the filename entered when the program was started. If the file cannot be opened for reading, an error message is printed and the program exits. The heart of this program is in lines 33 through 44. Line 33 does an initial print of the first line number. Line 35 then reads a character from the file. Line 37 prints the character as a decimal value using the %d within the printf() function. Line 39 then checks to see whether the character is a carriage return. If the character is a carriage return, a new line number is printed. When the end of the file is reached, the printing of the characters stops, and the file is closed before exiting the program.

This program prints line numbers followed by the data from the file. The output is from using the test file described earlier. You should notice that a few extra characters seem to get printed in the output. Most obvious should be the extra number 10 at the end of each line. This is the line feed or carriage return that you normally would not see in a text file. In addition, you should notice that in output line 00012, the spaces are printed as 32s. These values can be seen in the ASCII character table.

The Binary Number System

As you can see by the output in Listing B4.3, the decimal representations of characters are not very readable. In addition, these values really are not very helpful. One of the most descriptive number systems to use with computers is binary. Listing B4.4 is a rewrite of Listing B4.3, except that information is printed in binary.

Listing B4.4. Program to type a file in binary.

```
1:   /* Program:  bindump.c
2:    * Book:     Teach Yourself C in 21 Days
3:    * Purpose:  This program types a file to the screen.
4:    *           It displays the binary equivalent of each
5:    *           character
6:    *=======================================================*/
7:
8:   #include <stdio.h>
9:   #include <string.h>
10:  #include <stdlib.h>
11:
12:  char *char_to_binary( int );
13:
14:  int main(int argv, char *argc[])
15:  {
16:      int ch,
17:          letter = 0;
18:      char *tmp;
19:      unsigned int line = 1;
20:
21:      FILE *fp;
22:
23:      if( argv != 2 )
24:      {
25:         printf("\n\nOops!  Proper usage is:");
26:         printf("\n\n%s in_file ", argc[0]);
27:         printf("\n\nOriginal file will be printed in Binary.");
28:         exit(1);
29:      }
30:
31:      /***  Open the file  ***/
32:      if (( fp = fopen( argc[1], "r" )) == NULL )
33:      {
34:         printf( "\n\nOops!  Error opening file: %s\n\n", argc[1]);
35:         exit(99);
36:      }
37:
38:      printf("\n%5.5d: ", line );
39:
40:      while( (ch = fgetc( fp )) != EOF )
41:      {
42:         tmp = char_to_binary(ch);
43:         printf("%s ", tmp );
44:         free(tmp);
45:
46:         if(ch == '\n')
47:         {
48:           line++;
49:           letter = 0;
50:           printf("\n%5.5d: ", line );
51:         }
52:         else
53:         if( ++letter >= 7 )                  /* for formatting output */
```

Listing B4.4. continued

```
54:        {
55:            printf("\n        ");
56:            letter = 0;
57:        }
58:
59:      }
60:
61:    fclose( fp );
62:
63:    return(0);
64:  }
65:
66:
67:  char *char_to_binary( int ch )
68:  {
69:    int  ctr;
70:    char *binary_string;
71:    int  bitstatus;
72:
73:    binary_string = (char*) malloc( 9 * sizeof(char) );
74:
75:    for( ctr = 0; ctr < 8; ctr++)
76:    {
77:      switch( ctr )
78:      {
79:        case 0:  bitstatus = ch & 128;
80:                 break;
81:        case 1:  bitstatus = ch & 64;
82:                 break;
83:        case 2:  bitstatus = ch & 32;
84:                 break;
85:        case 3:  bitstatus = ch & 16;
86:                 break;
87:        case 4:  bitstatus = ch & 8;
88:                 break;
89:        case 5:  bitstatus = ch & 4;
90:                 break;
91:        case 6:  bitstatus = ch & 2;
92:                 break;
93:        case 7:  bitstatus = ch & 1;
94:                 break;
95:      }
96:
97:      binary_string[ctr] = (bitstatus) ? '1' : '0';
98:    }
99:
100:   binary_string[8] = 0;  /* Null Terminate */
101:
102:   return( binary_string );
103: }
```

```
00001: 00110001 00110010 00110011 00110100 00110101 00110110
       00110111 00111000 00111001 00110000 00001010
00002: 01000001 01000010 01000011 01000100 01000101 01000110
       01000111 00001010
00003: 01001000 01001001 01001010 01001011 01001100 01001101
       01001110 00001010
00004: 01001111 01010000 01010001 01010010 01010011 01010100
       01010101 00001010
00005: 01010110 01010111 01011000 01011001 01011010 00001010
00006: 01100001 01100010 01100011 01100100 01100101 01100110
       01100111 00001010
00007: 01101000 01101001 01101010 01101011 01101100 01101101
       01101110 00001010
00008: 01101111 01110000 01110001 01110010 01110011 01110100
       01110101 00001010
00009: 01110110 01110111 01111000 01111001 01111010 00001010
00010: 00000001 00000010 00001010
00011: 00100001 01000000 00100011 00100100 00100101 01011110
       00100110 00101010 00101000 00101001 01011111 00101011
       01111011 01111101 01011011 01011101 00111011 00111010
       00100111 00100010 00111100 00111110 00111111 00101111
       00101110 00101100 01100000 01111110 00001010
00012: 00111110 00100000 00100000 00100000 00100000 00100000
       00100000 00100000 00100000 00100000 00100000 00100000
       00100000 00100000 00100000 00100000 00111100 00001010
00013: 00001010
00014: 01001111 01101110 01100011 01100101 00100000 01110101
       01110000 01101111 01101110 00100000 01100001 00100000
       01110100 01101001 01101101 01100101 00100000 01110100
       01101000 01100101 01110010 01100101 00100000 01110111
       01100101 01110010 01100101 00100000 01110100 01101101
       01110010 01100101 01100101 00100000 01101100 01101001
       01110100 01101100 01100101 00100000 01110000 01101001
       01100111 01110011 00101110 00101110 00101110 00001010
00015: 00001010
00016:
```

This output also was obtained by running the program with the test file that was described earlier in the chapter. Note that there is much more data printed in the output. Because the information is in binary, it is the most accurate representation of what actually is stored.

Looking at the listing, you can see that it is very similar to Listing B4.3. The main() function enables a command-line argument to be received (line 14). Lines 23 through 29 verify that one, and only one, command-line parameter was entered. If there were more or less parameters, an error message is printed and the program exits. Line 32 attempts to open the file. If the open fails, line 35 prints an error message and exits.

The heart of the program is in lines 38 through 64. Line 38 prints the first line number before jumping into a while loop. Line 40 begins the loop. Each character is gotten from the file using the fgetc() function. The while loop continues until the end of the file is reached (EOF). Line

42 calls the `char_to_binary()` function. This function returns a pointer to a string containing the binary number. Line 43 prints the binary character using `printf()`. Notice that the string that is printed is the return value from the `char_to_binary()` function which is pointed to by `tmp`. Once the string is printed, you are done with the value pointed to by `tmp`, so the memory allocated by `char_to_binary()` can be freed.

Line 44 checks to see whether the character read—and just printed—was the newline character. If it is, line 48 increments the line number, line 49 resets the letter count, and line 49 prints the new line number on a new line. If the character read is not a newline character, then the `else` condition in lines 52 through 57 is executed. The `else` condition checks to see how many characters have been printed on the line. Because the binary representation of the file can get long, only seven characters from the file being used are printed on each line. Line 53 checks to see whether seven characters already have been printed. If seven characters have been printed, a new line is started that is indented over a few spaces (line 55). The letter count is reset to 0, and the next interaction of the `while` loop occurs.

The `char_to_binary()` function may not be as easy to follow as the rest of the program. Lines 69 through 71 declare three variables that will be used along with the `ch` integer that was passed in. `ch` contains the character that is to be converted. Each character will be translated into a single binary number. Because characters can be any number from 0 to 255, an eight-digit binary number will be needed.

Why eight digits? Consider Figure B4.2 again. This time, look at it in the context of binary numbers. How many items are there in the picture? Instead of the decimal 15 and 20 that you answered before, count the items using the binary system. The answers are 00001111 and 00010100.

Just as you had "ones," "tens," "hundreds," and so on in the decimal system, you have equivalent categories in the binary system. From the word *binary*, you can deduce that there are two different digits that can be used. These are 0 and 1. One object would be 1, two (decimal) objects would be 10 (read as one-zero, not ten). The categories for the binary system can be determined by using the base, just as you did for the decimal system earlier. Table B4.2 illustrates the digit groupings for the binary system.

Table B4.2. Binary digits.

Digit	Base Value	Decimal Equivalent	Digit Name
First	$2^0 =$	1	Ones
Second	$2^1 =$	2	Twos
Third	$2^2 =$	4	Fours
Fourth	$2^3 =$	8	Eights

Digit	Base Value	Decimal Equivalent	Digit Name
Fifth	$2^4 =$	16	Sixteens
Sixth	$2^5 =$	32	Thirty-twos
Seventh	$2^6 =$	64	Sixty-fours
Eighth	$2^7 =$	128	One-twenty-eights

Only the first eight digits are represented here. This typically is all you will need when converting characters. Eight bits make up a byte. A *byte* is the amount of space typically used to store a character. Consider the following binary numbers:

```
00000001 equals 1 in decimal
00000010 equals 2 in decimal
00000100 equals 4 in decimal
00000101 equals 4 + 1 or 5 in decimal
11111111 equals 128 + 64 + 32 + 16 + 8 + 4 + 2 + 1 or 255 in decimal
```

To translate the binary numbers to decimal, you simply add the decimal values from Table B4.2 for the corresponding digits that are not zero.

Now look back at the `char_to_binary()` function in Listing B4.4. You can see that lines 79 through 94 have the decimal equivalent values that are listed in Table B4.2. Instead of converting from binary to decimal as in the previous examples, the program converts the decimal value to binary. Following the flow of this function, you can see how to convert from decimal to binary. You know that there are only eight digits in the binary number, because a character can only be from 0 to 255. The program starts at the left of the eight-digit binary number and determines the value of each digit. Line 75 is a `for` statement that uses the `ctr` variable to keep track of which of the eight digits is being determined. Line 77 switches to a `case` statement that works with the individual digit. The first time through, the digit being worked on (`ctr`) will be 0. The `case`, in lines 79 and 81, does a binary math statement. The binary AND operator (`&`) is used to determine whether the character contains a bit value for 128. This is done by using the binary AND operator with the number for which you are testing—in this case, 128. If the character does contain the bit for 128, then `bitstatus` will be set to a nonzero number. After doing this, the `switch` statement is left, and the conditional operator is used in line 97. If the value in `bitstatus` does equals zero, then the number did not contain a bit value for 128. If `bitstatus` does not equal zero, you know that the character's decimal value did contain a bit for 128. Because the value of a character cannot be greater than 255, you know that 128 will be divisible at most one time into `ch`. Using the `for` loop, you then can cycle through each bit value for the character's numeric value. This continues through to the eight digits.

Line 100 null-terminates the binary number, which now is stored as a string. Line 102 returns this string. Notice that this string actually is a pointer to a character array. Line 73 used the `malloc()` function to allocate the nine characters needed to hold the binary number. This function allocates a string for holding the binary number. If this function were called often, the calling functions should free the binary strings. By not freeing the string, memory is being lost.

> **Tip:** You can test whether a bit is on or off by using the binary AND operator (&). If you AND a character with the value of 128, for example, then all the bits will be set to 0s (off) except for the bit in the 128 position. This bit will be left as it is. If it is on, it will remain on.

> **Note:** Two lines could be added to Listing B4.4 after line 97:
>
> ```
> printf( "\nbitstatus = %d, ch = %d, binary_string[%d] = %c",
>         bitstatus, ch, ctr, binary_string[ctr]);
> ```
>
> These lines print each step of the binary conversion.

The Hexadecimal Number System

As you saw in the preceding program, displaying a file in its binary values may be more helpful than looking at its decimal values. However, it also is easy to see that looking at the binary values provides much more information than is really needed. What is needed is a number system that can represent each of the 256 values of a character and still be converted easily to binary. Actually, using a base 256 number system would provide too many different characters to be useful. The number system that seems to provide the best representation is the hexadecimal, or base 16, system. It takes only two digits to represent all 256 character values. Table B4.3 presents the hexadecimal values.

Table B4.3. Hexadecimal digits.

Digit	Base Value	Decimal Equivalent	Digit Name
First	$16^0 =$	1	Ones
Second	$16^1 =$	16	Sixteens
Third	$16^2 =$	256	Two-hundred fifty-sixes

Looking at Table 6.3, you can see that by the time you get to the third digit of a hexadecimal number, you are already at a number equivalent to 256 in the decimal system. By including 0, you can represent all 256 characters with just two digits!

If hexadecimal is new to you, you might be wondering how you can represent 16 characters. Remember that the base determines the number of characters used in displaying the number. Table B4.4 illustrates the hexadecimal characters and the decimal equivalents.

Table B4.4. The hexadecimal digits.

Hexadecimal Digit	Decimal Equivalent	Binary Equivalent
0	0	0000
1	1	0001
2	2	0010
3	3	0011
4	4	0100
5	5	0101
6	6	0110
7	7	0111
8	8	1000
9	9	1001
A	10	1010
B	11	1011
C	12	1100
D	13	1101
E	14	1110
F	15	1111

The alpha characters in a hexadecimal number can be upper- or lowercase.

Note: Hexadecimal numbers generally are followed by a lowercase h to signify that they are hexadecimal. For example, 10h would be hexadecimal 10 (one-zero), not decimal 10 (ten). Its decimal equivalent would be 16 (sixteen).

There is a second reason why hexadecimal numbers are preferred by programmers. It is easy to convert a binary number to and from hexadecimal. Simply convert each of the two digits of the hexadecimal number individually and concatenate the result. Or, if converting from binary to hexadecimal, convert the left four digits to a single hexadecimal number and then convert the right four digits. Consider the following examples.

Converting from Hexadecimal to Binary

Hexadecimal value: F1h (or 241 decimal):

- Converting the first digit, F, to binary yields 1111.
- Converting the second digit, 1, to binary yields 0001.
- The total binary equivalent of F1 is 1111 0001 or 11110001.

Converting from Binary to Hexadecimal

Binary value: 10101001 (or 169 decimal):

- Converting the first four digits, 1010, yields A in hexadecimal.
- Converting the second four digits, 1001, yields 9 in hexadecimal.
- The total hexadecimal equivalent of 10101001 is A9h.

Listing B4.5, HEXDUMP.C, is a modification of the programs shown in Listings B4.3 and B4.4. This program simply prints the hexadecimal values of a file.

Listing B4.5. Program to type a file in hexadecimal.

```
 1:   /* Program:   hexdump.c
 2:    * Book:      Teach Yourself C in 21 Days
 3:    * Purpose:   This program types a file to the screen.
 4:    *            It displays the hexadecimal equivalent of
 5:    *            each character
 6:    *=====================================================*/
 7:
 8:   #include <stdio.h>
 9:   #include <string.h>
10:   #include <stdlib.h>
11:
12:   int main(int argv, char *argc[])
13:   {
14:       int ch;
15:       unsigned int line = 1;
16:
17:       FILE *fp;
18:
19:       if( argv != 2 )
20:       {
21:          printf("\n\nOops!  Proper usage is:");
22:          printf("\n\n%s in_file ", argc[0]);
23:          printf("\n\nOriginal file will be printed in HEX.");
24:          exit(1);
25:       }
26:
27:       /*** Open the file ***/
28:       if (( fp = fopen( argc[1], "r" )) == NULL )
29:       {
30:          printf( "\n\nOops!  Error in opening file: %s\n\n",
31:                      argc[1]);
```

```
32:        exit(99);
33:    }
34:
35:    printf("\n%5.5d:   ", line );
36:
37:    while( (ch = fgetc( fp )) != EOF )
38:    {
39:        printf("%X ", ch );
40:
41:        if(ch == '\n')
42:        {
43:          line++;
44:          printf("\n%5.5d:   ", line );
45:        }
46:    }
47:
48:    fclose( fp );
49:
50:    return(0);
51: }
```

```
00001:   31 32 33 34 35 36 37 38 39 30 A
00002:   41 42 43 44 45 46 47 A
00003:   48 49 4A 4B 4C 4D 4E A
00004:   4F 50 51 52 53 54 55 A
00005:   56 57 58 59 5A A
00006:   61 62 63 64 65 66 67 A
00007:   68 69 6A 6B 6C 6D 6E A
00008:   6F 70 71 72 73 74 75 A
00009:   76 77 78 79 7A A
00010:   1 2 A
00011:   21 40 23 24 25 5E 26 2A 28 29 5F 2B 7B 7D 5B 5D 3B 3A 27 22
         3C 3E 3F 2F 2E 2C 60 7E A
00012:   3E 20 20 20 20 20 20 20 20 20 20 20 20 20 20 20 3C A
00013:   A
00014:   4F 6E 63 65 20 75 70 6F 6E 20 61 20 74 69 6D 65 20 74 68 65
         72 65 20 77 65 72 65 20 74 68 72 65 65 20 6C 69 74 6C 65 20
         70 69 67 73 2E 2E 2E A
00015:   A
00016:
```

BD4

This program is similar to the binary and decimal dump programs that you saw in Listings B4.3 and B4.4. The big difference is in line 39. In order to print a hexadecimal value in C, you simply need to use the %X specifier. This automatically prints the hexadecimal value.

The Octal Number System

The octal number system rarely is used in C or by C programmers. It often is mentioned because it is easy to convert to using the printf() conversion character %o. The octal number system is the base 8 number system. As you should conclude from this, there are 8 digits: 0 through 7.

DO	**DON'T**

DO understand the number systems.

DON'T confuse different number systems. Generally, the following rules are used in using numeric constants:

- Octal numbers start with 0; 08 would be octal 8, for example.

- Hexadecimal numbers generally start with x; x8 is hexadecimal 8, for example. Warning: x08 would be octal!

- Decimal numbers do not start with 0 or x.

Summary

This chapter covered many of the number systems that commonly are referred to in programming. Although you use the decimal number system every day, it is not the most practical number system to use when dealing with computer data. The binary number system, which consists of only two digits, is the most accurate representative for showing the computer's view of data. The hexadecimal system easily can be converted to and from binary. This easy conversion, along with its capability to represent many numbers with just a few digits, makes the hexadecimal system the better number system for working with computer data. The octal system also is mentioned, because C provides ways of easily converting to it.

Q&A

Q Would you want to convert characters to decimal values?

A Once you are comfortable with the other number systems, you typically will not use the decimal system. If you are not comfortable with the other number systems, it is easier to add and subtract using decimal. To change an uppercase letter to lowercase, for example, you add 32 (decimal) to it. This makes more sense to most people. If you are looking at a file to determine what is there, the hexadecimal representation is the easiest to read.

Q Is the octal number system important?

A Typically, the octal number system is not used. Most programmers opt to use the hexadecimal system. The binary system is used mainly when doing bit manipulations or when working with binary data files (hence the name *binary*). Octal seldom is used.

Q **What is the difference between the lowercase x specifier and the uppercase X conversion specifier in the `printf()` function?**

A The **x**, or **X**, specifier prints out the hexadecimal value. If the lowercase **x** is used, the alpha digits of any hexadecimal numbers will be in lowercase. If the uppercase **X** is used, then the alpha digits of any hexadecimal numbers will be in uppercase. The difference is simply in the presentation of the hexadecimal numbers.

Workshop

The Workshop provides quiz questions to help you solidify your understanding of the material covered, and exercises to provide you with experience using what you have learned.

Quiz

1. Why are numbers important in computing?
2. What determines what numeric value a letter gets translated to?
3. What is meant by *decimal value*?
4. Why are binary numbers important?
5. Why would you want to use hexadecimal numbers?
6. Why would you want to look at the numeric values of your data?
7. What digits are used in the binary number system?
8. What digits are used in the decimal number system?
9. What digits are used in the octal number system?
10. What digits are used in the hexadecimal number system?

Exercises

1. What are the numeric equivalents of the letter C? Compute for binary, octal, decimal, and hexadecimal. (Don't use the programs from the chapter to answer this!)
2. What are the numeric equivalents of the following character: ♥
3. What are the decimal values of the following ASCII characters?
    a. space
    b. Y
    c. y
    d. 9
    e. +

4. What characters do the following numbers represent?

    a. 93

    b. 60

    c. 6

    d. 92

    e. 50

5. How many days are marked in the calendar in Figure 4.3? (Answer should include decimal, binary, hexadecimal, and octal values.)

Figure 4.3
This calendar has marked days.

JULY						
		1	2	3	4	5
6	7	8	9	10	11	12
13	14	15	16	17	18	19
20	21	22	23	24	25	26
27	28	29	30	31		

6. Rewrite Listing B4.2 to accept a character instead of a decimal number. Have the program print the decimal, hexadecimal, and octal representations.

7. Write a function that takes advantage of the information provided in the ASCII character table. This function should convert a lowercase letter to an uppercase letter, or an uppercase letter to a lowercase letter. Do not use library functions provided by the compiler! Name the function switch_case().

8. **BUG BUSTER:** What is wrong with the following code?

```
char x;
for ( x = 'a'; x < 'Z'; x++ )
{
    printf( "%c ", x);
}
```

9. Often, you will find that you want to see a program in more than one format. Write a program that prints both the hexadecimal and the character values from a file.

Bonus Day 5+

Advanced Structures: Linked Lists

Linked lists and their associated data types are considered advanced topics in C. Most beginning C books touch lightly on the topic of linked lists and leave it to the programmer to figure them out when they are needed. Today, you learn

- What linked lists are
- How to use single-linked lists
- What stacks and queues are
- How double-linked lists differ from single linked lists
- What binary trees are

Using Linked Lists

The term *linked list* refers to a general class of data storage methods in which each item of information is linked to one or more other items using pointers.

There are several kinds of linked lists, including single-linked lists, double-linked lists, and binary trees. Each type is suited for certain data-storage tasks. The one thing that these lists have in common is that the links between items are defined by information in the items themselves. This is a distinct difference from arrays, in which the links between data items result from the layout and storage of the array. This chapter explains the simplest kind of linked list: the single-linked list (which is referred to as a *linked list*).

Note: Linked lists are not used a great deal. There are instances where linked lists are a perfect solution, however.

Using a Single-Linked List

Linked lists use a structure that contains a pointer member. Following is a simplistic look at a linked list's structure. You should notice that the pointer member is special:

```
struct element {
   int data;
   struct element *next;
};
```

In this structure, there is a pointer that points to another structure of the same structure type. Note that this is a pointer to a structure of its own type. The pointer in the structure, called next in this case, points to another element structure. This means that each structure, or link, can point to another structure at the same time. Figure B5.1 illustrates a single link using the preceding element structure. Figure B5.2 illustrates using a linked list of such structures.

Figure B5.1.
An element link.

```
struct link_element {
  int data
  struct element*next;
};
```

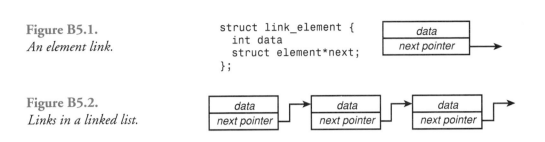

Figure B5.2.
Links in a linked list.

Notice that in Figure B5.2, each element structure points to the next element structure. The last element structure doesn't point to anything. To help show that the last element doesn't point to an additional link, the pointer is assigned the value of NULL. In C, NULL is equal to zero.

> **Note:** The structures that make up a link in a linked list can be referred to as *links*, *nodes*, or *elements* of a linked list.

Accessing the Links in a List

The last link in a single-linked list always points to NULL. You may wonder how you locate the other links, however. To prevent the loss of links, you must set up an additional pointer. This pointer commonly is referred to as a *head pointer*. The head pointer always points to the first element in the link. If you know where the first pointer is, you can access its pointer to the second element. The second element's pointer then can be accessed to get to the third pointer. This can continue until you reach a NULL pointer, which would signify the end of the list. It's possible that the head pointer could be NULL, which would mean that the list is empty. Figure B5.3 illustrates the head pointer along with a linked list.

BD5

Figure B5.3.
The head pointer.

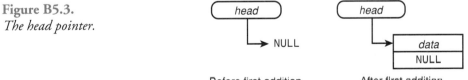
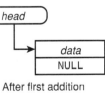

Note: The *head pointer* is a pointer to the first element in a linked list. The head pointer sometimes is referred to the *first element pointer* or *top pointer*.

An Example of Using Links

Listing B5.1 presents a program that isn't very practical. It creates a three-element linked list. Each of the elements is used by going through the original element. The purpose of this program is to illustrate the relationship between elements. In the following sections, you'll see more practical ways of creating and using linked lists.

Listing B5.1. A first look at a linked list.

```
 1:  /* Program:   listb501.c
 2:   * Book:      Teach Yourself C In 21 Days.
 3:   * Purpose:   Demonstrate the relations in a linked list
 4:   * Note:      Program assumes that malloc() is successful.
 5:   *            You should not make this assumption!
 6:   *=========================================================*/
 7:
 8:  #include <stdio.h>
 9:  #include <stdlib.h>
10:
11:  #define NULL 0
12:
13:  struct link                /* a structure to use in a link list */
14:  {
15:     char   ch;              /* link structure data element(s) */
16:     struct link *next;      /* pointer to next link structure */
17:  };
18:
19:  typedef struct link LINK;
20:
21:  typedef LINK *LINK_PTR;
22:
23:  int main( void )
24:  {
25:     LINK_PTR  first;              /* same as a head pointer */
26:
27:     /* Create first link */
28:     first = (LINK_PTR) malloc( sizeof(LINK) );
29:
30:     /* put data into first link */
31:     first->ch = 'a';
32:     /* create a new link: put pointer to it in the first link */
33:     first->next = (LINK_PTR) malloc( sizeof(LINK) );
34:
35:     /* repeat process */
36:     first->next->ch = 'b';
37:     first->next->next = (LINK_PTR) malloc( sizeof(LINK) );
```

```
38:
39:        first->next->next->ch = 'c';
40:        /* Don't want another link, so set next pointer to NULL */
41:        first->next->next->next = NULL;
42:
43:        /* Print data from links */
44:        printf("\n\nPrint the character values...");
45:
46:        printf("\n\nValues from the first link:");
47:        printf("\n   ch is %c", first->ch );
48:        printf("\n   next is %d", first->next );
49:
50:        printf("\n\nValues from the second link:");
51:        printf("\n   ch is %c", first->next->ch );
52:        printf("\n   next is %d", first->next->next );
53:
54:        printf("\n\nValues from the third link:");
55:        printf("\n   ch is %c", first->next->next->ch );
56:        printf("\n   next is %d", first->next->next->next );
57:
58:        free( first->next->next );
59:        free( first->next );
60:        free( first );
61:
62:        return(0);
63:   }
```

```
Print the character values...

Values from the first link:
   ch is a
   next is 3018

Values from the second link:
   ch is b
   next is 3006

Values from the third link:
   ch is c
   next is 0
```

Analysis
As stated before, Listing B5.1 isn't the most practical listing; however, it demonstrates many of the important aspects of linked lists. First, in reviewing the listing, you should notice that the linked list's structure is declared in lines 13 through 17. In addition, lines 19 and 21 use the typedef command to create two constants. The first is LINK, which will be a new data type for declaring a structure of type link. The second defined constant, in line 21, is a pointer to a LINK data type called LINK_PTR. This data type, LINK_PTR, will be used to create the links to the different LINK elements in the linked list.

The main part of the program actually starts in line 25, where a pointer to a list structure is declared using the LINK_PTR constant. This pointer, called first, will be used to indicate the beginning of the linked list that is being created. Line 28 allocates memory for the first element in the link. Using `malloc()`, enough space is allocated for one `LINK` element. A pointer is returned by `malloc()` and is stored in `first`.

> **Warning:** Notice that the program doesn't check to ensure that `malloc()` was successful. This is a poor assumption on the program's part. It's a good programming practice to always check the return value of a memory allocation function.

Line 31 assigns a value to the character variable, `ch`, in the `first` structure that was allocated. If you were using a more complex linked list, you could fill the other data at this point. Line 33 contains the pointer called `next`, which links this element with the next element in the list. If this were the only element in the list, the value of `NULL`, or zero, could be assigned to the `next` pointer as follows:

```
first->next = NULL;
```

Because an additional link is being added to the list, the `next` pointer is used. In this case, another `malloc()` statement is called to allocate memory for the following element of the list. Remember that `malloc()` returns a pointer to the allocated memory. Upon completion of the allocation, line 36 assigns a value of 'b' to the data item, `ch`. Line 37 repeats the process of allocating memory for a third element. Because the third element is the last being assigned, line 41 caps off the linked list by assigning the value of `NULL` to the `next` pointer.

Lines 46 through 56 print the values of the elements to the screen so that you can observe the output. The values printed for `next` may vary. Lines 58 through 60 release the memory allocated for the elements in the reverse order in which they were allocated.

> **Note:** This program accesses each element by starting with the first element in the list. As you can see, this could be impractical if you have a large number of links. This program is effective only for providing an example, but it isn't practical for actually using linked lists.

Using a Linked List

Using linked lists is similar to using disk files. Elements or links can be added, deleted, or modified. Modifying an element presents no real challenge; however, adding and deleting an element can be challenging. As stated earlier, elements in a list are connected with pointers. When a new element is added, the pointers must be adjusted. Where the new element is added affects how pointers are modified. Elements can be added to the beginning, middle, or end of a linked list.

Adding the First Link

You will know you are adding the first element to a linked list if the head pointer is NULL. The head pointer should be changed to point to the new element. In addition, because the element being added is the only element, the "next" pointer should be set to NULL. Figure B5.4 illustrates the final result.

Figure B5.4.
Adding the first element to a linked list.

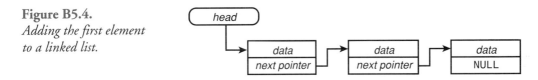

The following code fragment includes an element structure similar to the structures used before:

```
struct _element {
    int data;
    struct _element *next;
};
```

To make using this structure easier, two type definitions again are used:

```
typedef struct _element ELEMENT;
typedef ELEMENT *LINK;
```

The _element structure will be used by means of the two type definitions. When an instance of _element needs to be declared, ELEMENT will be used. Using ELEMENT is just like using struct _element. The second defined data type, LINK, is a pointer to an _element structure. These defined constants will be used in later examples. The following code fragment illustrates adding an initial element to a linked list:

```
LINK first = NULL;
LINK new = NULL;

/* enter a new item */
new = (LINK) malloc( sizeof(ELEMENT) );
scanf("%d", &(new->data));

if (first == NULL)
{
    new->next = NULL;
    first = new;
}
```

This fragment starts by including two declarations for pointers to an _element structure using the LINK typedef. Because these are pointer values, they are initialized to NULL. The first LINK

Advanced Structures: Linked Lists

pointer, called `first`, will be used as a head pointer. The second `LINK`, called `new`, will contain the link that will be added to the list. The link is created, and then data for the link is retrieved. The addition of the new element to the list occurs in the last five lines. If the `first` pointer—which is the head pointer—is equal to `NULL`, then you know the list is empty. You can set the pointer in the new element to `NULL` because there isn't another one to point to. You then can set the head pointer, `first`, to the new element. At this point, the initial element is linked in.

Notice that `malloc()` is used to allocate the memory for the new element. As each new element is added, only the memory needed for it is allocated. The `calloc()` function also could be used. You should be aware of the difference between these two functions. The main difference is that `calloc()` will clear out the new element; the `malloc()` function will not.

Warning: The `malloc()` in the preceding code fragment didn't ensure that the memory was allocated. You always should check the return value of a memory allocation function.

Tip: When possible, initialize pointers to `NULL` when you declare them. Never leave a pointer uninitialized.

Adding to the Beginning

Adding an element to the beginning of a linked list is similar to adding an element to a new list. When an element is added to the beginning, two steps are involved. First, the "next" pointer of the new element must be set to the original first element of the list. This can be done by setting the new element's "next" pointer equal to the head pointer. After this is done, the head pointer must be reset to point to the new element that now begins the list. Figure B5.5 illustrates this process.

Again using the `_element` structure, the following code fragment illustrates the process of adding an element to the beginning of a linked list:

```
LINK new = NULL;                        /* pointer for new link */

/* enter a new item */
new = (LINK) malloc( sizeof(ELEMENT) ); /* allocate memory */
scanf("%d", &(new->data));              /* get data */
```

```
/* add the new element to the beginning of a list */
{
   new->next = first;        /* first is the head pointer    */
   first = new;              /* set first to point to new link */
}
```

Figure B5.5.
Adding an element to the
beginning of a linked list.

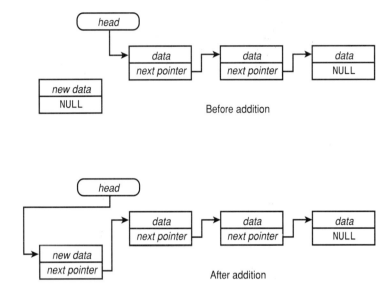

The first few lines of the preceding fragment set up the storage space and get the element's data. It is the last couple of lines that are important. The next pointer in the new element is set to point to the value of the head pointer, first. After this is set, the head pointer is reset to point to the new element.

Warning: It is important to take the two steps of switching the pointers in the correct order. If you reassign the head pointer first, you will lose the list!

Adding to the Middle

Adding an element to the middle of a list is a little more complicated, yet this process still is relatively easy. After the location for the new element is determined, you will adjust the pointers on a couple of elements. Figure B5.6 illustrates the process of adding an element to the middle of a linked list.

BD5

Figure B5.6.

Adding an element to the middle of a linked list.

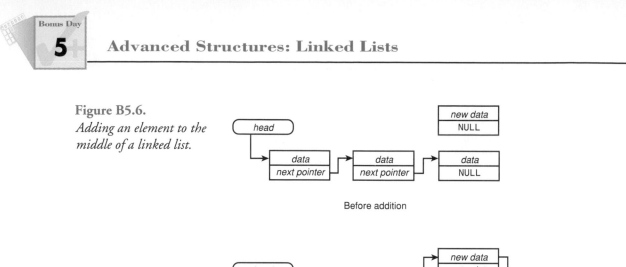

As you can see from Figure B5.6, when a new element is added to the middle, two pointers have to be adjusted. The "next" pointer of the previous element has to be adjusted to point to the new element. In addition, the "next" pointer of the new element needs to be set to the original value of the "next" pointer in the previous element. After these pointers are readjusted, the new element is a part of the list. The following code fragment illustrates this addition:

```
/* adding an element to the middle */
insert_link( LINK prev_link, LINK new_link )
{
    new_link->next = prev_link->next
    prev_link->next = new_link;
}
```

This fragment presents a function that moves the previous link's next pointer to the new link's next pointer. It then sets the previous link's next pointer to point to the new element.

Adding to the End

The final location to which you can add an element or link is the end of a list. Adding an element to the end is identical to adding a link to the middle. This case is mentioned separately because the value of the previous element's "next" pointer is NULL (or zero). Figure B5.7 illustrates adding an element to the end of a linked list.

Figure B5.7.
*Adding an element to the
end of a linked list.*

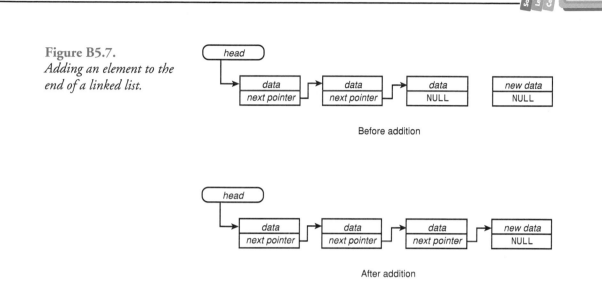

Before addition

After addition

Implementing a Linked List

Now that you have seen the ways to add links to a list, it's time to see them in action. Listing B5.2 presents a rather long program that uses a linked list to hold a list of five characters. The characters are stored in memory by using a linked list. These characters just as easily could have been names, addresses, or any other data. To keep the example as simple as possible, only a single character is stored in each link.

What makes this linked list program complicated is the fact that it sorts the links as they are added. Of course, this also is what makes this program so valuable. Each link is added to the beginning, middle, or end depending on its value. The link always is sorted. If you were to write a program to simply add the links to the end, then the logic would be much simpler. However, the program also would be less useful.

Type   **Listing B5.2. Adding to a linked list of characters.**

```
 1:   /*========================================================*
 2:    * Program:   linklist.c                                  *
 3:    * Copyright: Bradley L. Jones                            *
 4:    * Purpose:   Adding to a single link list                *
 5:    *========================================================*/
 6:   #include <stdio.h>
 7:   #include <stdlib.h>
 8:
 9:   #ifndef NULL
10:   #define NULL 0
11:   #endif
12:
13:   /*----- Link Structure -----*/
14:   struct list
15:   {
```

continues

Listing B5.2. continued

```
16:    int    ch;                       /* using an int to hold a char */
17:    struct list *next_rec;
18:  };
19:
20:  typedef struct list LIST;
21:  typedef LIST *LISTPTR;            /* Pointer to the structure list */
22:  /*-------------------------*/
23:
24:  LISTPTR add_to_list( int, LISTPTR );
25:  void show_list(LISTPTR);
26:  void free_memory_list(LISTPTR);
27:
28:  int main( void )
29:  {
30:     LISTPTR first = NULL;   /* head pointer */
31:     int i=0;
32:     int ch;
33:     char trash[256];        /* to clear stdin buffer. */
34:
35:     while ( i++ < 5 )       /* build a list based on 5 items given */
36:     {
37:        ch = 0;
38:        printf("\nEnter character %d, ", i);
39:
40:        do {
41:             printf("\nMust be a to z: ");
42:             ch = getc(stdin);  /* get next char in buffer  */
43:             gets(trash);       /* remove trash from buffer */
44:          } while( (ch < 'a' || ch > 'z') && (ch < 'A' || ch > 'Z'));
45:
46:        first = add_to_list( ch, first );
47:     }
48:
49:     show_list( first );               /* Dumps the entire list */
50:     free_memory_list( first );        /* Release all memory */
51:
52:     return(0);
53:  }
54:
55:  /*=========================================================*
56:   * Function: add_to_list()
57:   * Purpose : Inserts new link in the list
58:   * Entry   : int ch = character to store
59:   *             LISTPTR first = address of original head pointer
60:   * Returns : Address of head pointer (first)
61:   *=========================================================*/
62:
63:  LISTPTR add_to_list( int ch, LISTPTR first )
64:  {
65:     LISTPTR new_rec=NULL;                 /* Holds address of new rec */
66:     LISTPTR tmp_rec=NULL;                 /* Hold tmp pointer        */
67:     LISTPTR prev_rec=NULL;
68:
69:     new_rec = (LISTPTR)malloc(sizeof(LIST)); /* Get memory loc     */
```

```
70:     if (!new_rec)                              /* Unable to get mem */
71:     {
72:        printf("\nUnable to allocate memory!\n");
73:        exit(1);
74:     }
75:
76:     /* set new link's data */
77:     new_rec->ch = ch;
78:     new_rec->next_rec = NULL;
79:
80:     if (first == NULL)    /* adding first link to list */
81:     {
82:         first = new_rec;
83:         new_rec->next_rec = NULL;   /* redundant but safe */
84:     }
85:     else     /* not first record */
86:     {
87:        /* see if it goes before the first link */
88:        if ( new_rec->ch < first->ch)
89:        {
90:           new_rec->next_rec = first;
91:           first = new_rec;
92:        }
93:        else    /* it is being added to the middle or end */
94:        {
95:           tmp_rec = first->next_rec;
96:           prev_rec = first;
97:
98:           /* Check to see where link is added. */
99:
100:          if ( tmp_rec == NULL )
101:          {
102:              /* we are adding second record to end */
103:              prev_rec->next_rec = new_rec;
104:          }
105:          else
106:          {
107:              /* check to see if adding in middle */
108:              while (( tmp_rec->next_rec != NULL))
109:              {
110:                 if( new_rec->ch < tmp_rec->ch )
111:                 {
112:                    new_rec->next_rec = tmp_rec;
113:                    if (new_rec->next_rec != prev_rec->next_rec)
114:                    {
115:                       printf("ERROR");
116:                       getc(stdin);
117:                       exit(0);
118:                    }
119:                    prev_rec->next_rec = new_rec;
120:                    break;   /* link is added, exit while */
121:                 }
122:                 else
123:                 {
124:                    tmp_rec = tmp_rec->next_rec;
125:                    prev_rec = prev_rec->next_rec;
```

BD5

continues

Listing B5.2. continued

```
126:                 }
127:             }
128:
129:             /* check to see if adding to the end */
130:             if (tmp_rec->next_rec == NULL)
131:             {
132:                 if (new_rec->ch < tmp_rec->ch ) /* 1 b4 end */
133:                 {
134:                     new_rec->next_rec = tmp_rec;
135:                     prev_rec->next_rec = new_rec;
136:                 }
137:                 else  /* at the end */
138:                 {
139:                     tmp_rec->next_rec = new_rec;
140:                     new_rec->next_rec = NULL;  /* redundant */
141:                 }
142:             }
143:         }
144:     }
145:     }
146:     return(first);
147: }
148:
149: /*========================================================*
150:  * Function: show_list
151:  * Purpose : Displays the information current in the list
152:  *========================================================*/
153:
154: void show_list( LISTPTR first )
155: {
156:     LISTPTR cur_ptr;
157:     int counter = 1;
158:
159:     printf("\n\nRec addr  Position  Data  Next Rec addr\n");
160:     printf("========  ========  ====  =============\n");
161:
162:     cur_ptr = first;
163:     while (cur_ptr != NULL )
164:     {
165:         printf("  %X    ", cur_ptr );
166:         printf("     %2i       %c", counter++, cur_ptr->ch);
167:         printf("      %X  \n",cur_ptr->next_rec);
168:         cur_ptr = cur_ptr->next_rec;
169:     }
170: }
171:
172: /*========================================================*
173:  * Function: free_memory_list
174:  * Purpose : Frees up all the memory collected for list
175:  *========================================================*/
176:
177: void free_memory_list(LISTPTR first)
178: {
179:     LISTPTR cur_ptr, next_rec;
180:
```

```
181:    cur_ptr = first;                    /* Start at beginning */
182:
183:    while (cur_ptr != NULL)             /* Go while not end of list */
184:    {
185:        next_rec = cur_ptr->next_rec;   /* Get address of next record */
186:        free(cur_ptr);                  /* Free current record */
187:        cur_ptr = next_rec;             /* Adjust current */
188:    }
189: }
```

Enter character 1,
Must be a to z: **q**

Enter character 2,
Must be a to z: **b**

Enter character 3,
Must be a to z: **z**

Enter character 4,
Must be a to z: **c**

Enter character 5,
Must be a to z: **a**

Rec addr	Position	Data	Next Rec addr
C3A	1	a	C22
C22	2	b	C32
C32	3	c	C1A
C1A	4	q	C2A
C2A	5	z	0

Note: On different machines, the above output may result in slightly different presentations of the record addresses.

 This program demonstrates adding a link to a linked list. It is not the easiest listing to understand; however, if you walk through the listing, you will see that it is a combination of the three methods of adding links mentioned earlier. The listing can be used to add links to the beginning, middle, or end of a linked list. Additionally, the listing takes into consideration the special cases of adding the first link and adding the second link.

Tip: The easiest way to fully understand this listing is to step line by line through the listing in your compiler's debugger along with reading the following analysis. By seeing the logic executed, you will better understand the listing.

There are several items at the beginning of Listing B5.2 that should be familiar or easy to understand. Lines 9 to 11 check to see whether the value of NULL already is defined. If it is not, then 10 line defines it to be zero. Lines 14 to 21 set up the structure for the linked list. These lines also declare the type definitions to make working with the structure easier.

The main() function should be easy to follow. A head pointer called first is declared in line 30. Notice that this is set to NULL. Remember that you should never let a pointer go uninitialized. Lines 35 to 47 contain a while loop used to get five characters from the user. A do...while is used to ensure that each character entered is a letter. The isalpha() function just as easily could have been used. The purpose of the while and do...while is simply to get data to illustrate adding links. After a piece of data is obtained, add_to_list() is called. The pointer to the beginning of the list and the data being added to the list are passed to the function.

The main() function ends by calling show_list() and then free_memory_list(). show_list() displays all the data in the linked list. free_memory_list() releases all the allocated memory that was used to hold the links in the list. Both these functions operate in a similar manner. Each starts at the beginning of the linked list using the head pointer, first. A while loop is used to go from one link to the next using the next_ptr value. When the next_ptr is equal to NULL, the end of the linked list is reached and the functions return.

Adding Links

The important function in this listing is the add_to_list() function in lines 63 to 147. This also is the most complicated code in the listing! Lines 65 to 67 declare three pointers that will be used to point at three different links. The new_rec pointer will point at the new link that is to be added. The tmp_rec pointer will point at the current link in the list being evaluated. If there is more than one link in the list, then the prev_rec pointer will be used to point at the previous link that was evaluated.

Line 69 allocates memory for the new link that is being added. The new_rec pointer is set to this new memory. If the memory cannot be allocated, then lines 72 and 73 print an error message and exit the program. If the memory was allocated, then the program continues.

Line 77 sets the data in the structure to the data passed in to this function. Although this simply consists of assigning the new record's character field (new_rec->ch) to the character, ch, in a more complex program this could entail the assigning of several fields. Line 78 sets the next_rec in the new record to NULL so that it is not pointing to some random location.

Adding the First Link

Line 80 starts the "link adding" logic by checking to see whether there are any links in the list. If the link being added is the first link in the list, then the head pointer, first, simply is set equal to the new pointer, and you are done.

Adding to the Beginning of the List

If this link is not the first, then the function continues within the else at line 85. Line 88 checks to see whether the new link goes at the beginning of the list. As you should remember, this is one of the three cases for adding a link. If the link does go first, line 90 sets the next_rec pointer in the new link to point to the previous "first" link. Line 91 then sets the head pointer, first, to point to the new link. The new link then is added to the beginning of the list.

Adding to the Middle of the List

If the new link is not the first link to be added to a new list, and if it is not the first link to be added, then you know it has to be in the middle or at the end of the list. Lines 95 and 96 set up the tmp_rec and prev_rec pointers that were declared earlier. The tmp_rec is set to equal the address of the second link in the list. prev_rec is set to equal the first pointer in the list.

You should note that if there is only one link in the list, then tmp_rec will be equal to NULL. This is because tmp_rec is set to the next_ptr in the first link, which will be equal to NULL. Line 100 checks for this special case. If tmp_rec does equal NULL, then you know this is the second link being added to the list. Because you know the new link doesn't come before the first link, it can only go at the end. To accomplish this, you simply set the prev_rec->next_ptr to the new link, and then you are done.

If the tmp_rec pointer was not NULL, then you know that you have more than two links in your list. The while statement in lines 108 to 127 is used to loop through the rest of the links to determine where the new link fits. Line 110 checks to see whether the new link's data value is less than the link currently being pointed to. If it is, then you know this is where you want to add the link. If the new data is greater than the current link's data, then you need to look at the next link in the list. Lines 124 and 125 increment the tmp_rec and the next_rec to the next links.

BD5

If the character was less than the current link's character, then you would follow the logic presented earlier in the chapter for adding to the middle of a linked list. This process can be seen in lines 112 to 120. In line 112, the new link's next pointer is set to equal the current link's address (tmp_rec). Line 119 sets the previous link's next pointer to point to the new link. With this, you are done. In order to get out of the while statement, a break is needed.

> **Note:** Lines 113 to 118 contain debugging code that was left in the listing for you to see. These lines could be removed; however, as long as the program is running correctly, they will never be called. After the new link's next pointer is set to the current pointer, it should be equal to the previous link's next pointer, which also points to the current record. If they are not equal, then something went wrong!

Adding to the End of the List

The previously covered logic takes care of links being added to the middle of the list. If the end of the list is reached, then the `while` loop in lines 108 to 127 will end without adding the link. Lines 130 to 142 take care of adding the link to the end.

If the last link in the list was reached, then `tmp_rec->next_rec` will equal `NULL`. Line 130 checks for this condition. Line 132 checks to see whether the link goes before the last link or whether it goes after the last link. If it goes after the last link, then the last link's `next_rec` is set to the new link (line 130) and the new link's next pointer is set to `NULL` (line 140).

Expanding Listing B5.2

Linked lists are not the easiest thing to learn. As you can see by Listing B5.2, they are an excellent way of storing data in a sorted order. As each character was added, it was placed in sorted order. This listing easily could be converted to sort names, phone numbers, or any other data. Additionally, although this listing sorted in ascending order (a to z), it just as easily could have sorted in descending order (z to a).

Deleting from a Linked List

The capability to add information to a linked list is good; however, there are times when you will want to remove information too. Deleting links, or elements, is similar to adding them. You can delete links from the beginning, middle, and end of linked lists. In addition, you can delete the last link in the list. In each case, the appropriate pointers need to be adjusted. Also, the memory used by the deleted link needs to be freed.

> **Note:** Don't forget to free memory when deleting links!

DO	**DON'T**

DON'T forget to free any memory allocated for links when deleting them.

DO understand the difference between `calloc()` and `malloc()`. Most important, remember that `malloc()` doesn't initialize allocated memory—`calloc()` does.

Special Forms of Linked Lists

There are many special forms of linked lists. Most of these are special uses of the single-linked list described earlier, or expansions of the single-linked list. The main special linked lists that you should be aware of follow:

- Stacks
- Queues
- Double-linked lists
- Binary trees

Note: Using these special forms of linked lists is beyond the scope of a beginning-level C book. Exercises with answers have been provided for creating some of these advanced structures. For more information on working with these advanced forms of linked lists, consult a data structures book or an advanced programming book.

Stacks

A *stack* is a special linked list. A stack differs from the normal linked list because it always is accessed from its top. This means that new elements always are added at the top, and if an element is to be removed, it is taken from the top. This gives the stack a *Last In First Out*, or LIFO, order. It is this LIFO nature that makes a stack what it is. For comparison, consider dishes; you stack them on a shelf one at a time. To remove the first dish that you placed on the shelf—the one on the bottom—you must remove each of the dishes that you placed on top of it. The first dish placed on the shelf is the last dish you can remove. Figure B5.8 illustrates a stack.

BD5

Figure B5.8.
Two sketches of stacks: elements in a linked list and dishes on a shelf.

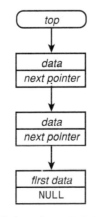

```
top
 │
 ▼
data
next pointer
 │
 ▼
data
next pointer
 │
 ▼
first data
NULL
```

A data-element stack

A stack of dishes

Queues

Queues, like stacks, are special forms of linked lists. A queue is similar to a stack because it is accessed in a specific way. However, a stack is LIFO (Last In First Out), and a queue is *First In First Out* (FIFO). That is, instead of being accessed only from the top like a stack, it is accessed from both the top and the bottom. A queue has new items added only to the top. When an element is removed, it always is taken from the bottom. A queue can be compared to a ticket line. The person who gets in line first is served first. In addition, people always must enter at the end of the line. Figure B5.9 illustrates a queue.

Figure B5.9.
Two sketches of queues: elements in a linked list and people in a line.

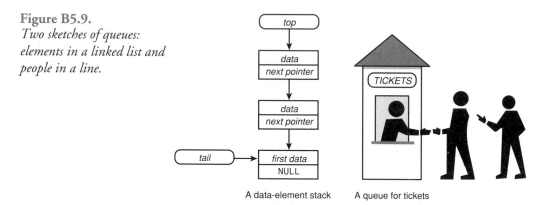

A data-element stack   A queue for tickets

A queue can be accomplished with a single-linked list; however, working with a queue becomes much easier with a double-linked list.

Double-Linked Lists

Single-linked lists enable the user to move between the elements starting at the top and working toward the bottom (or end). Sometimes it is advantageous to be able to work back toward the top. You can traverse a list from both ends by adding a second set of links (pointers) between the elements. The double set of pointers causes the list to be double linked. Figure B5.10 illustrates a double-linked list.

In Figure B5.10, you should notice that all the components of a single-linked list are present. In addition, a head pointer and a tail pointer are both present. As with a single-linked list, the head pointer always will point at the top or first element of the list. The tail pointer always will point to the last element. If there are no elements in the list, the head and the tail pointers both will point to NULL. If there is only one element, then the two pointers will be equal to the first—and only—element.

Figure B5.10.
A double-linked list.

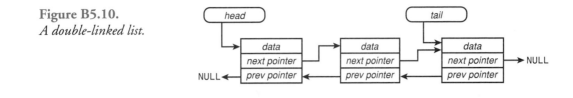

Note: A double-linked list must have a tail pointer in addition to its head pointer. With the exception of queues, single-linked lists don't have to have tail pointers; they are required only in double-linked lists.

Layout of a Double-Linked List

The structure for an element in a double-linked list is different from that of a single-linked list because it contains an additional pointer. The format of a structure for a double-linked list would be similar to the following:

```
struct element {
    <data>
    struct element *next;
    struct element *previous;
};
```

The `<data>` can be whatever data you are storing in your linked list. The `next` pointer points to the following element in the list. If the element is the last in the list, then `next` will contain the `NULL` value. The `previous` pointer contains the address of the previous element in the list. In the case of the first element, where there isn't a previous element, the value of `previous` will be `NULL`.

Binary Trees

A *binary tree* is a special double-linked list. It also is a special type of data tree. A *data tree* is a set of data elements that are linked together into a hierarchical structure. Each element in a tree is called a *node*. Like a linked list that starts at its head pointer, a tree starts with what is its *root*. The root then has *subnodes* that are connected to it. Subnodes can have even more subnodes below them. The bottom nodes—those that do not have any additional subnodes—are called *leaf nodes*. Figure B5.11 illustrates a tree structure.

BD5

Figure B5.11.
A tree structure.

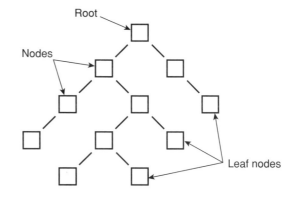

Each node in a binary tree can have a maximum of two subnodes. This includes the node that is the root. In a binary tree, the subnodes commonly are referred to as the *left node* and *right node*. Figure B5.11 could be considered a binary tree because none of the nodes have more than two subnodes.

Layout of a Binary Tree

As with linked lists, nodes in a tree are connected by using pointers to the element structures. For a binary tree, the structure contains two pointers: one for the left node and one for the right node. Following is a generic structure for a binary tree node:

```
struct node {
    <data>
    struct node *left;
    struct node *right;
};
```

The `<data>` can be any data that is to be joined in the binary tree. The node pointer `left` points to the subnode to the left. The node pointer `right` points to the subnode to the right.

Using a Binary Tree

A binary tree offers faster access time over a regular linked list. To find a single element in a linked list, you must access each element from one end of the list until you find the appropriate element. With a binary tree, a logarithmic number of checks can be made to determine where a specific link is located.

Consider the order in which a binary tree's nodes are accessed. There are three general orders for accessing the elements in a linked list. You can access them *in order*, starting with the left subnode, working toward the root, and then down the right subnode. *Pre-order* access is accessing the root first, then the left subnode, followed by the right subnode. The third way to access a binary tree is in *post order*. This is accessing the left subnode first, then the right subnode, followed by the root. Figure B5.12 illustrates the order in which the nodes would be accessed in each of these methods.

> **Tip:** Binary trees are used to sort information. You should use a binary tree instead of a single-linked list or double-linked list when you need to access a single element in the fewest steps.

Figure B5.12.
Binary tree access orders.

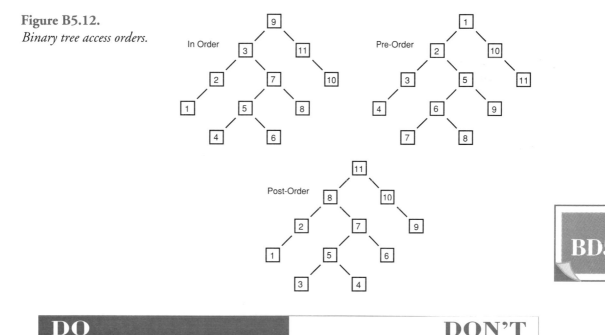

BD5

DO	DON'T

DO use a double-linked list when you must be able to go forward and backward in a linked list.

DO use a binary tree when access time is critical.

Summary

Today you were presented with several advanced structures that can be used in C. Most of the chapter concentrated on simple linked lists. Although you will not use linked lists a great deal, you will find that the concepts involved are used a great deal.

In addition to single-linked lists, several special linked lists were presented. Stacks and queues are among the most common special linked lists. Stacks use a LIFO, or Last In First Out, order of access. Queues use a FIFO, or First In First Out, order of access. Double-linked lists enable both the preceding and following elements to be accessed. This is different from a single-linked list that can be traversed only from beginning to end. Binary trees are another form of linked data. Binary trees have even quicker retrieval times, at the cost of storing additional linkage information.

Q&A

Q What is the difference between a single-linked list, a linear-linked list, and a singly-linked list?

A There is no difference. These are three terms for the same thing. In addition, a doubly-linked list is the same thing as a double-linked list. These are all different ways of saying the same thing.

Q Are any additional pointers, other than the tail pointer and head pointer, used with a linked list?

A A third pointer that is external to the elements in a linked list may be used. This is a "current" pointer. This additional pointer may be used if it is important to know where you currently are working in a list.

Q What is the advantage of a binary tree over a linked list?

A A binary tree enables quicker searching of the element saved. The cost of the quicker search is the need to store additional pointer information.

Q Are there other trees than just binary trees?

A Yes. Binary trees are a special form of tree. They are easier to understand than general trees. A general tree involves much more complex manipulations than were presented with the binary trees.

Workshop

The Workshop provides quiz questions to help you solidify your understanding of the material covered, and exercises to provide you with experience in using what you have learned.

Quiz

1. What does NULL equal?
2. What does it mean if the head pointer is equal to NULL?

3. How are single-linked lists connected?

4. How does a stack differ from a normal linked list?

5. How does a queue differ from a normal linked list?

6. What is a tail pointer? What is a top pointer?

7. Is a tail pointer needed in a single-linked list?

8. What is the advantage of a double-linked list over a single-linked list?

9. What is the benefit of using `calloc()` instead of `malloc()` when allocating memory for new list elements?

10. What is the advantage of using a binary tree instead of a single-linked list?

Exercises

1. Write a structure that is to be used in a single-linked list. The structure should hold the name and addresses of your friends.

2. Write a structure that is to be used in a double-linked list. The structure is to hold the name of a *Star Trek* character.

3. Write a structure that is to be used with a binary tree. The structure is to hold the name and phone number of everyone in your city or town.

4. **BUG BUSTER:** What is wrong with the following linked list structure?

```
struct client {
    char name[35+1];
    char ssn[11+1];
    int  age;
    struct client next;
};
```

5. When you add an element to a stack, you "push" it on. Write a function called `push_stack()` that passes in a pointer and a value to be added to a stack list. The function should allocate the memory needed for the new element.

6. When you remove an element from a stack, you "pop" it off. Write a function called `pop_stack()` that passes the link that is to be removed. The function should return the data from the link being removed. The data should be returned via a parameter.

7. If you are feeling adventurous, try writing a program that uses the `push_stack()` and `pop_stack()` functions.

Bonus Day

6+

Variable-Length Structures

Today's coverage of structures builds on the basics you learned about on Day 11, "Structures," and the few advanced uses of structures, primarily the linked list, you learned about on Bonus Day 5, "Advanced Structures: Linked Lists." Today, you learn

- Additional advanced uses of structures
- What dynamic or variable-length structures are
- How to store variable amounts of data without wasting storage space

Creating Complex Data Types by Grouping Data

By using the basic data types, you can create complex data types. For instance, you can create new ways of associating and accessing data by grouping basic data types such as integers and characters. There are three methods commonly used to group data types in C programs:

- Arrays
- Structures
- Unions

The basics of arrays were covered on Day 8, "Numeric Arrays," and structures and unions were covered on Day 11, "Structures."

It is easy to create new data types by grouping the data types that already exist. For example, you can create a new type of date by using a simple structure like this one:

```
typedef struct {
    int  month;
    char breaker1;
    int  day;
    char breaker2;
    int  year;
} date;
```

You then can use the new date type to declare a new variable. This single variable will contain a month, day, year, and two breakers. You can access each of the parts of the declared variable as well as the date as a whole. Listing B6.1 uses a date type created as a structure.

Type

Listing B6.1. Using the date structure.

```
1:  /* Program:   STRUCT.C
2:   * Book:      Teach Yourself C In 21 Days
3:   * Purpose:   Program to use a date structure
4:   *================================================*/
5:
```

```
6:    #include <stdio.h>
7:
8:    typedef struct {
9:       int   month;
10:      char breaker1;
11:       int   day;
12:      char breaker2;
13:       int   year;
14:   } date;
15:
16:   int main(void)
17:   {
18:     date date1;
19:     date date2 = { 1, '/', 1, '/', 1998 };
20:
21:     printf("\n\nEnter information for date 1: ");
22:     printf("\n\nEnter month: ");
23:     scanf("%d", &date1.month);
24:     printf("\nEnter day: ");
25:     scanf("%d", &date1.day);
26:     printf("\nEnter year: ");
27:     scanf("%d", &date1.year);
28:
29:     date1.breaker1 = '-';
30:     date1.breaker2 = '-';
31:
32:     printf("\n\n\nYour dates are:\n\n");
33:     printf("Date 1: %d%c%d%c%d\n\n", date1.month,
34:                                      date1.breaker1,
35:                                      date1.day,
36:                                      date1.breaker2,
37:                                      date1.year );
38:
39:     printf("Date 2: %d%c%d%c%d\n\n", date2.month,
40:                                      date2.breaker1,
41:                                      date2.day,
42:                                      date2.breaker2,
43:                                      date2.year );
44:
45:     printf("\n\n\nSize of date structure: %d",
46:     sizeof(date1));
47:
48:     return 0;
49:   }
```

BD6

Input Output

```
Enter information for date 1:

Enter month: 12

Enter day: 25

Enter year: 1996
```

```
Your dates are:

Date 1: 12-25-1996

Date 2: 1/1/1998


Size of date structure: 8
```

Note: The size of your structure may vary, depending on your compiler and machine.

This listing should provide a review of the basics of structures. You can see in lines 8–14 that a structure has been defined to hold a date. Because this structure was `typedefed`, you now can declare "date-type" variables—variables that hold dates. In lines 18 and 19, the variables `date1` and `date2` are declared using the `date` type. At the time of `date2`'s declaration, each of its elements is initialized.

Lines 21–27 enable the user to enter the information for `date1`. Using `printf()`, the listing prompts the user for each of the numeric elements of the structure. Lines 29 and 30 set the breaker values to dashes, but they could have been slashes or any other values. Lines 33–43 print the values from the individual dates.

Combining Data to Form Complex Data Types

Virtually all of the basic data types presented in this book can be combined. When you combine data types, you create what could be referred to as *complex data types*. These data types really aren't any more complex than the basic types. You just need to be aware of what combinations you've made. One of the more common combinations of data types is variable-length structures.

A "Structural" Problem with Structures

Structures are an excellent means of storing combinations of data. However, there is a structural problem with complex structures. In a normal structure, such as the following, you can find out the size:

```
struct rental_info_tag{
  char first_name[15+1];
```

```
    char last_name [19+1];
    char video1[19+1];
    char video2[19+1];
};
```

You should be able to determine from looking at the code that variables declared with the `rental_info_tag` will be 76 characters long. You calculate this by adding the sizes of the individual elements, plus any word alignment that may occur. The `rental_info_tag` structure would work well for all the people who take two videos or fewer, but what if John Smith wants to rent five videos for a weekend videorama? You wouldn't be able to store all his video titles in a single structure.

There are several solutions to get around this problem. The first is to modify the structure to declare five video records rather than two. The following code uses an array to do this instead of individual video variables:

```
struct rental_info_tag{
    char first_name[15+1];
    char last_name [19+1];
    char video[19+1][5];
};
```

This structure enables you to store the first and last name of the person along with up to five video names. As long as the array size is big enough to hold the maximum number of videos that any person would want, this structure works; however, it typically is not an optimal solution. Figure B6.1 shows what the memory usage of this structure would be when a variable is declared. Notice that a great deal of memory is allocated. If most people rent only one video, a majority of the allocated space will never be used.

Figure B6.1.

The `rental_info_tag` structure for five videos—potentially a lot of wasted space.

first_name
last_name
video1
video2
video3
video4
video5

BD6

Variable-Length Structures

Variable-length structures offer a solution to the storage problem by enabling you to change the number of elements in the array. If Lilian Lee wants to rent two videos, you declare the array with two elements. If Jerry Jones wants six videos, you declare the structure with six elements. Figure B6.2 shows how the memory usage should be.

Figure B6.2.

Variable-length struc-
tures—conserving memory
usage.

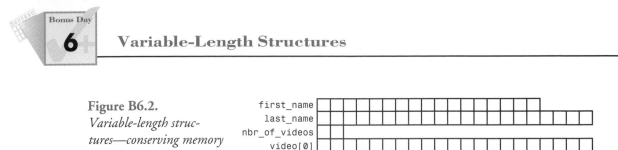

As you can see from the figure, memory isn't completely conserved. The spaces at the end of each name and video are wasted. However, space still is saved because only the necessary video names are stored.

The following example declares the structure so different numbers of children can be stored:

```
struct rental_info_tag{
    char first_name[15+1];
    char last_name [19+1];
    int  number_of_videos;
    char video[];
};
```

Notice that two things have changed. First, an additional integer, number_of_videos, states how many videos there are. Without this, you would have a much harder time knowing how many videos there are, and thus how big the structure is. Second, the video array is different—there isn't a number in the array! This signals that the array is a variable-length array. It will be up to you to determine how big it is (hence, the previously mentioned number_of_videos.)

Warning: Some compilers—such as most Macintosh compilers—won't allow you to declare an array without a value. For those compilers, you should leave the last member, video[], out of the structure or simply comment it out.

When to Use Variable-Length Structures

You might think that it would be easier to use a consistent number of array elements. As long as you selected a size that meets a majority of your needs, you could be happy. Although this would work, you may find many circumstances in which you need to use variable-length structures. Small or simple programs can afford the luxury of wasting space, but more complex programs cannot. Also, many programs that work with disk files require you to work with variable-length structures.

Several types of programs use variable-length structures: calendar programs, programs that modify executable (EXE) files, programs that work with bitmapped graphics files, and word processor programs, to name a few. The following section presents an example of using a variable-length structure.

A Variable-Length Structure Example

The best way to understand variable-length structures is to use them. The program in Listing B6.2 uses a variable-length structure to create a journal entry. The format of the journal entry is as follows:

```
struct journal_entry_tag {
   int text_size;
   char text_entry[];
}
```

As you can see, this is a relatively simple structure. The first member of the structure is an integer that tells the size of the following character array, text_entry. Listing B6.2 uses this structure.

Type

Listing B6.2. Program using variable-length structure.

```
 1:   /*   Program: List2702.c
 2:    *   Copyright: Bradley L. Jones
 3:    *   Purpose: Demonstrates a variable length file.
 4:    *=================================================*/
 5:
 6:   #include <stdio.h>
 7:   #include <stdlib.h>
 8:   #include <string.h>
 9:
10:   typedef struct {
11:      int text_size;
12:      char text_entry[];
13:   } JOURNAL_ENTRY;
14:
15:   int main( void )
16:   {
17:       JOURNAL_ENTRY entry[10];
18:
19:       char  buffer[256];
20:       int   ctr;
21:
22:       FILE *out_file;
23:
24:       out_file = fopen( "TMP_FILE.TXT", "w+" );
25:       if( out_file == NULL )
26:       {
27:          printf("\n\nError opening file.");
28:          exit(99);
29:       }
30:
31:       printf("\n\nYou will be prompted to enter 10 strings.\n");
32:
33:       for( ctr = 0; ctr < 10; ctr++ )
34:       {
35:          printf("\nEnter string %d:\n", ctr+1);
36:          gets(buffer);
37:          entry[ctr].text_size - strlen(buffer);
```

BD6

continues

```
38:          fwrite( &entry[ctr].text_size, 1, sizeof( int), out_file);
39:          fwrite( buffer, 1, entry[ctr].text_size, out_file);
40:      }
41:
42:      printf("\n\nTo view your file, type the following:");
43:      printf("\n\n    TYPE TMP_FILE.TXT");
44:
45:      fclose(out_file);
46:
47:      return 0;
48:  }
```

You will be prompted to enter 10 strings.

Enter string 1:
aaaa

Enter string 2:
BBBBBBBBBBB

Enter string 3:
CCCCCCCCCCCCCCCCCCCCCCCCCCCCCCCCCCCCCCCCCC

Enter string 4:
DDDDDDDDDDDDDDDDDDDDDDDDDDDDDDDDDDDDDDDDDDDDDDDDDDDDDDDDDDDDDDDDDDD

Enter string 5:
EEE

Enter string 6:
FFFFFFFFFFFFFFFFFFFFF

Enter string 7:
GGGGGGGGGGGGGGGGGGGGGGGGGGGGGGGGGGGGGGGGGGG

Enter string 8:
HHHHHHHH

Enter string 9:
IIIIIIIIIIIIIIIIIIIIIIIIIIIIIIIIIIIIIIIIIIIIIIIIIIIIIIIIIIIIIIIIIIIIIIIIII

Enter string 10:
JJJJJJJJJJJJJJJJJJJJJJJJJJJJJJJ

To view your file, type the following:

    TYPE TMP_FILE.TXT

Typing the TMP_FILE.TXT file displays the following:

```
_ _aaaa_ _BBBBBBBBBBB_ _CCCCCCCCCCCCCCCCCCCCCCCCCCCCCCCCCCCCCCCCCC_ _
DDDDDDDDDDDDDDDDDDDDDDDDDDDDDDDDDDDDDDDDDDDDDDDDDDDDDDDDDDDDDDDDDDD
_ _EEE_ _FFFFFFFFFFFFFFFFFFFFF_  GGGGGGGGGGGGGGGGGGGGGGGGGGGGGGGGGGGGGGGGGGG_ _
HHHHHHHH_ _IIIIIIIIIIIIIIIIIIIIIIIIIIIIIIIIIIIIIIIIIIIIIIIIIIIIIIIIIIIIIIIIIIIIIIIIII_
JJJJJJJJJJJJJJJJJJJJJJJJJJJJJJJ
```

You should note that the underscores in the output from typing TMP_FILE.TXT actually are numeric values. These will appear as unusual symbols on your screen.

This listing isn't exactly clear on using the variable-length structure. To accurately demonstrate variable-length structures will take several pages of code. The previous output demonstrates how a file can be created that applies to a simplistic variable-length structure. You could easily reverse this program so that it reads the file that was created. You could read each of these into the JOURNAL_ENTRY structures. You would need to dynamically allocate space for the character array within the structure.

This program presents some interesting code. In line 22, a file pointer is declared. This pointer is used in line 24 to point to the TMP_FILE.TXT file. This is the file for the variable-length journal entries. Lines 38 and 39 write the information out to the file. In line 38, the portions of the structure that are constant in size are written. In this case, it is a single field. In line 39, the variable length portion is written out. An exercise at the end of this chapter asks you to write a program that reads this file and prints out the information.

Creating A Page of Journal Entries

The journal-entry structure presented in Listing B6.2 easily could be expanded. The JOURNAL_ENTRY type can be grouped into journal pages, as shown in the following structure:

```
typedef struct {
    int journal_page;
    int nbr_of_lines;
    JOURNAL_ENTRY line[];
} JOURNAL_PAGE;
```

This is a variable-length structure that contains a variable-length structure. You might think that creating a program using the JOURNAL_PAGE structure presented here is more complex than you would see in most programs; however, it actually is very similar to what you would see.

Reading a Journal Entry

You have learned how to write a variable-length data structure, but to complete the circle, you also should learn how to read it. The program in Listing B6.3 reads the file written by Listing B6.2. Listing B6.3 illustrates some of the concepts involved in reading a variable-length structure. Because of the simplicity of this example, it operates a little easier than most programs that use variable-length structures.

BD6

Type   **Listing B6.3. Reading variable-length records.**

```
1:    /*  Program: read.c
2:     *  Copyright: Bradley L. Jones
3:     *  Purpose: Demonstrates a variable length file.
4:     *=================================================*/
5:
6:    #include <stdio.h>
7:    #include <stdlib.h>
8:    #include <string.h>
9:
10:   typedef struct
11:   {
12:       int    text_size;
13:   } JOURNAL_ENTRY;
14:
15:   int main( void )
16:   {
17:       JOURNAL_ENTRY entry;
18:       char *text_entry;
19:
20:       int   rv;
21:       FILE *in_file;
22:
23:       in_file = fopen( "TMP_FILE.TXT", "r+" );
24:       if( in_file == NULL )
25:       {
26:           printf("\n\nError opening file.");
27:           exit(99);
28:       }
29:
30:       printf("Reading file.....\n");
31:
32:       while((rv = fread( &(entry.text_size), sizeof(int), (int) 1,
➡            in_file)) != 0 )
33:       {
34:           text_entry = (char *) malloc( entry.text_size+1 );
35:           if( text_entry == NULL )
36:           {
37:               printf("\nError allocating memory....");
38:               exit(1);
39:           }
40:
41:           rv = fread( text_entry, entry.text_size, (int) 1, in_file);
42:           if( rv == 0 )
43:           {
44:               printf("\n\nRead Error, %d", __LINE__);
45:               exit(99);
46:           }
47:
48:           text_entry[entry.text_size] = 0;
49:
50:           printf( "\n(%3d) %s",entry.text_size, text_entry);
51:           free(text_entry );
```

```
52:      }
53:      printf("\n\nQuitting....");
54:
55:      fclose(in_file);
56:
57:      return 0;
58: }
```

```
Reading file.....

(  4) aaaa
( 12) BBBBBBBBBBBB
( 43) CCCCCCCCCCCCCCCCCCCCCCCCCCCCCCCCCCCCCCCCCCC
( 69) DDDDDDDDDDDDDDDDDDDDDDDDDDDDDDDDDDDDDDDDDDDDDDDDDDDDDDDDDDDDDDDDDDDDDDDDD
(  3) EEE
( 21) FFFFFFFFFFFFFFFFFFFFF
( 38) GGGGGGGGGGGGGGGGGGGGGGGGGGGGGGGGGGGGGG
(  8) HHHHHHHH
( 65) IIIIIIIIIIIIIIIIIIIIIIIIIIIIIIIIIIIIIIIIIIIIIIIIIIIIIIIIIIIIIIIIIII
( 32) JJJJJJJJJJJJJJJJJJJJJJJJJJJJJJJJ

Quitting....
```

This listing reads the variable-length JOURNAL_ENTRY structures one at a time. Notice that there is a difference between the JOURNAL_ENTRY structure in lines 10–13 in this listing and the one in lines 10–13 of Listing B6.2. The variable part of the structure in this listing has been removed, and, instead, the area needed for the variable part of the structure is declared separately (line 18). Until you read the initial part of the structure, you don't know how long the variable part is.

In the main() function, you start by declaring the entry and text_entry (lines 17 and 18). In line 23, the TMP_FILE.TXT file that was written in Listing B6.2 is opened for reading. If the file cannot be opened, an error is printed and the program exits. If the file is opened, you can start reading in the data.

Lines 32–52 contain the while loop that reads the variable-length data one record (or structure) at a time. Each is read in two steps. First, the entry structure is read in line 32. If the read is successful, space is allocated for the variable portion of the structure. Line 41 then reads the next set of characters from the file. The number of characters read is determined by entry.text_size, which was taken from the initial data read. Line 48 caps the read characters with a zero in order to NULL terminate it. This is necessary so that the text entry can be printed in line 50. Because there is nothing more to be done with the data read, line 51 frees the memory that was allocated with malloc(). The while then loops to see if there is more data in the structure.

Listing B6.3 presented a simplistic example in that it has only a single integer for the initial part of the structure, and it has only an array of characters for the variable portion. In a more complex example, you might have a dozen elements as a part of the initial structure. Instead of reading

BD6

645

just a single array of characters, the variable portion could consist of an array or even another structure with another variable section. You might even have a structure with multiple sections that are of a variable length. The key is to read each section one at a time in order to determine the size of the next section.

DO	DON'T

DO use variable-length structures to save storage space.

DON'T forget to free dynamically allocated memory.

Summary

There are several advanced data types (or advanced groupings of data types). These include arrays, structures, and unions. Today's material focused on an individual topic: variable-length structures. Variable-length structures are used to minimize storage requirements. Many real-world programs use variable-length structures. This includes applications such as relational databases, word processors, graphics file formats, and icon and cursor structures.

Q&A

Q Do all compilers support variable-length structures?

A Yes and no. Variable-length structures can be used within all compilers. Some compilers don't support array's with empty brackets; however, you don't need this support to use the structures.

Q What are some examples of when variable-length structures are used?

A On an IBM and Macintosh computers, there are several examples of programs that take advantage of variable-length structures. Graphics stored in BMP format are one example. Microsoft Word also uses such structures. If you are using Microsoft Windows, the icon files, font files, card files, and Microsoft Write files are all created with variable-length structures. These are just a few examples on just a few platforms.

Workshop

The Workshop provides quiz questions to help you solidify your understanding of the material covered and exercises to provide you with experience in using what you've learned.

Quiz

1. What are considered the basic data types?
2. What are three ways of grouping data?
3. What is a benefit of using variable-length structures?
4. What are some examples of files stored with variable-length structures?
5. Can you read a variable-length structure from a disk file using a single read statement?

Exercises

1. Write the code for the data type that is necessary to create a data type that will store a social security number of the format 999-99-9999. Don't use a simple character array—use a structure.
2. Write the structure to store the name of an employee and her two children.
3. Rewrite the structure in exercise 2 so that it can store a variable number of children.
4. **ON YOUR OWN:** Write a program that reads a page of journal entries. The page can have a variable number of entries.
5. **ON YOUR OWN:** Write a program that sorts the TMP_FILE.TXT text entries and writes them back out.
6. **ON YOUR OWN:** If you are using a Windows compiler, consult your documentation for information on the Microsoft Windows file formats. Most of the file formats used by Microsoft Windows employ variable-length structures similar to those presented today. Another good reference book would be Tom Swan's book, *Inside Windows File Formats*, from Sams Publishing.

BD6

Bonus Day

7+

What Is C++?

You may have heard about the new language called C++ (pronounced "C plus plus"). It's definitely true that C++ is becoming more and more popular with programmers. Should you worry that you've wasted the time spent learning to program in C? Not at all! In fact, if you ever decide to tackle C++, it's a good idea to know C first. But we're getting ahead of ourselves. We can't teach you C++ in a single chapter, but we can give you an introduction to what it is and when you might want to use it. Today, you learn

- The relationship between C and C++
- How to write a simple C++ program
- Object-oriented programming fundamentals
- What type of compiler to use

Procedural Versus Object-Oriented Programming

C is a *procedural* language, and so are BASIC, Pascal, FORTRAN, and most other programming languages. In a procedural language, functions (sometimes called *procedures*) take center stage, and the data plays second fiddle. If you think about what you've learned in this book, you probably will agree that this is true. The entire structure of your program is designed around functions, with data being shuffled around from one function to another. The emphasis is on what is *done* to the data—display it, sort it, save it to disk, and so on.

Procedural programming is a very powerful approach and has been used to create the majority of the commercial programs available today. Yet, as programs became more complex, certain shortcomings of the procedural approach started to become evident. The difficulty of writing, debugging, maintaining, and modifying procedural programs became unmanageable. Rather than trying to design a "better" procedural language, the necessary next step seemed to be to create a whole new approach to programming.

That approach was *object-oriented programming* (OOP). C++ is an object-oriented language, as is Smalltalk, the only other object-oriented language you're likely to have heard of. OOP places the emphasis on data, and functions play a subsidiary role. That's what an *object* is—a chunk of data. However, as you'll see, an object in C++ is nothing like the data you're accustomed to work with in C.

What's the Object?

An object is a chunk of data. Using OOP, you design your program around the data that it will handle. If you are using objects in your C++ program (and, as you'll soon see, you don't have to use objects), much of your programming time will be spent creating objects. What is different about a C++ object and a C data item? The difference is that a C++ object is smart—it knows what to do.

Confused? We can't blame you. Hang on, though, and we'll try to explain. A C++ object contains both data *and* code. To be more specific, an object contains data plus the code required to manipulate the data in the desired ways. An example should clarify this.

Suppose you need to maintain a long list of numbers, and manipulate it in various ways. For example, you need to be able to get the largest value in the list, the smallest value, the average value, and the median value. You also need to sort the list into both ascending and descending order. In C, you would write a variety of functions to perform the needed actions, and you would declare an array to hold the numbers. The array would be passed to the functions as an argument, and the result might be passed back as the return value.

In C++, you would design an object (also called a *class*) to hold and manipulate the data. The object would contain an array for storage of the data and would also contain the functions to manipulate the data. In effect, the data object would "know" how to find its minimum, its maximum, and so on. Most importantly, the data and the functions would be isolated from the rest of the program, removing the possibility of the sort of unintentional interaction that can cause problems in procedural programs.

There's more to OOP than this, but we hope this gives you some idea of what it's all about. There's more to C++ than its object-oriented capabilities, however. Now for a closer look at C++.

Good Old C, With a Plus

If you apply your deductive skills, you can tell something about C++ from its name alone. Remember what ++ means in the C language—it's the unary increment operator. So the expression "C++" evaluates to the value of C plus 1. And that's exactly the reasoning behind the choice of the name C++ for this new language—it's the C language plus something. Actually there are several new somethings in C++, but that's not the point. The point is that the entire C language is part of C++. With a few minor changes that are simple to learn, everything you've learned about C can be used in a C++ program. The relationship between C and C++ is illustrated in Figure B7.1.

You can see that there's a large region common to both languages. This means that if you know C, you are well on your way to learning C++. The large area representing things present in C++ but not in C shows how much as been added in the new language. Objects are a big part of this, but certainly not all of it. Objects aside, there are lots of neat new things in C++. We can't go into details here, but once you have a little C programming under your belt, you may want to give C++ a try—we think you'll like it!

BD7

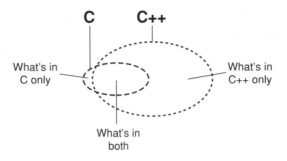

Figure B7.1.
The relationship between C and C++.

Your First (and Possibly Last) C++ Program

Although we can't teach you C++ in a single chapter, we can show you a simple C++ program that illustrates how C++ doesn't look all that different from C. It also demonstrates one of C++'s new features. We have created a variation on the traditional "Hello, world." program, as shown in Listing B7.1.

 Listing B7.1. A simple C++ program.

```
1: #include <iostream.h>
2:
3: main()
4: {
5:     float pi = 3.14;
6:     cout << "The value of pi is " << pi;
7:     return 0;
8: }
```

 The value of pi is 3.14

Much of this program should make sense to you. There's an `#include` statement on line 1, and although the name of the file may be strange, you should be able to understand what's being done here. The `main()` function with its enclosing brackets on lines 3, 4, and 8 is familiar, as is the declaration and initialization of a type `float` variable on line 5.

Line 6 is certainly strange, though. What does `cout` refer to, and why are there two left-shift operators in the line of code? `cout` is one of C++'s predefined streams. It actually is the same stream as `stdout`, but you use it differently. To send data to `cout`, you use the *insertor* operator `<<` (so called because it inserts data into the stream). But isn't `<<` the left-shift operator? Indeed it is, but here you're seeing one of C++'s new and most powerful features in action: *operator overloading*. An operator can have different meanings in different contexts. When placed after an integer variable, << is interpreted as the left-shift operator, but when placed after the name of an output stream, it is interpreted as the insertor operator. What line 6 is doing is to insert the string constant `"The value of pi is"` into the `cout` stream then insert the value of the variable `pi`. The `cout` stream is smart enough to apply default formatting to the numerical value.

Finally there's the `return` statement on line 7. Isn't `return` used to return a value from a function to the program that called the function? Yes indeed. Remember that `main()` itself is a function, and you can consider running a C++ program as calling the `main()` function from the operating system. The operating system may or may not make use of the return value. A C program could return a value from `main()`, but C++ requires it. This is an example of C++'s stricter rules that are designed to enforce consistently good programming practice.

What About Compilers?

If you've been shopping for a commercial C compiler, you may have noticed that it's difficult to find one. Everything seems to be for C++ these days. Remember, however, that C is part of C++, so go ahead and buy that C++ compiler that's on sale—you can use it for your C programs, and you'll be ready if and when you decide to take up C++.

A C++ compiler is actually three compilers in one. If your program's source code file has the C extension (such as PROGRAM.C), the compiler will treat it as a C program. All of C's rules apply, and all of its capabilities are available. This is what you should do if you are using a C++ compiler to work through this book. On the other hand, if your program has the CPP extension (or, with some compilers, CXX), it is treated as a C++ program, and C++'s rules and features are available. In other words, you control the rules and restrictions the compiler applies with the source-code file extension.

The math wizards among you no doubt will have noticed that this is only two compilers. Where's the third one we promised? This "third" compiler comes into play when you *write* a C program and then *compile* it as a C++ program (by giving it a CPP extension). Just because you use a C++ compiler doesn't mean you have to use all of C++'s object-oriented features in your program—or any of them, for that matter! This approach offers two advantages. Your program is subjected to C++'s stricter rules, which are designed in part to prevent certain programming practices that, although perfectly legal in C, sometimes create problems. Also, you can slowly start incorporating elements of C++ in your programs, which can be an excellent way to learn that language as you work.

Where to Go From Here

If you are seriously interested in learning C++, we strongly recommend getting a good introductory book. You can't do better than *Teach Yourself C++ Programming in 21 Days* by Jesse Liberty, which takes the same structured approach to C++ that was used in this book.

Summary

This bonus day provided a brief introduction to the C++ language. You learned that C++ is an object-oriented extension of the C language. It includes everything C does plus a host of additions and enhancements that provide significantly more programming power and convenience. The major addition is support for object-oriented programming, a technique that gives priority to a program's data in designing the program. C++ can be used for any size program, but its advantages are particularly evident when creating large, complex programs. You also saw a simple C++ program that illustrates two of the language's new features: operator overloading and improved standard streams.

Q&A

Q I'm pretty comfortable with the material presented in this book. How can I continue improving my skills as a programmer?

A One way is to start learning C++. You also can explore more advanced C programming topics. There are numerous good books on this topic, including *Teach Yourself Advanced C in 21 Days* by Brad Jones. The best way to improve your skills, however, is by programming. There's no substitute for writing real programs.

Q When are you most likely to see an advantage of C++ over C?

A The new features of C++ can be put to good use in almost any program, no matter how small. It's in large and complex programs, however, that these advantages can really make a difference.

Q I'm not sure whether I need to learn C++. I don't want to waste time learning something I won't ever use, but on the other hand I don't want to fall behind. Do you have any advice?

A This is a tough question to answer because we don't know the kind of programming you'll be doing. Generally speaking, the more serious you are about programming, the more strongly we suggest that you learn C++. In particular, if you plan to use programming to put food on the table, you need to know this language.

Workshop

There are no workshop questions for this day. Because this is the last lesson of the book, you will now be entering the big workshop of the real world. We hope you've found this book useful, and maybe even enjoyable, in your quest to learn C programming. You might program only occasionally as a hobby, or you might become an ace programmer working for Microsoft, Borland, or Lotus. In any event, we think the lessons you've learned here will serve you well.

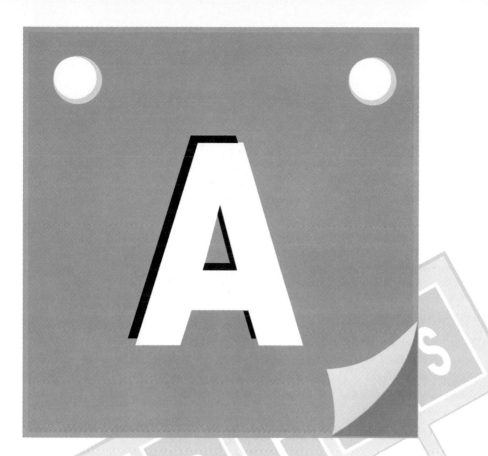

ASCII Character Chart

ASCII Character Chart

Dec	Hex	ASCII	Dec	Hex	ASCII
000	00	null	027	1B	←
001	01	☺	028	1C	∟
002	02	☻	029	1D	↔
003	03	♥	030	1E	▲
004	04	◆	031	1F	▼
005	05	♣	032	20	space
006	06	♠	033	21	!
007	07	•	034	22	"
008	08	◘	035	23	#
009	09	○	036	24	$
010	0A	◙	037	25	%
011	0B	♂	038	26	&
012	0C	♀	039	27	'
013	0D	♪	040	28	(
014	0E	♫	041	29	)
015	0F	☼	042	2A	*
016	10	►	043	2B	+
017	11	◄	044	2C	,
018	12	↕	045	2D	-
019	13	‼	046	2E	.
020	14	¶	047	2F	/
021	15	§	048	30	0
022	16	▬	049	31	1
023	17	↨	050	32	2
024	18	↑	051	33	3
025	19	↓	052	34	4
026	1A	→	053	35	5

Dec	Hex	ASCII	Dec	Hex	ASCII
054	36	6	081	51	Q
055	37	7	082	52	R
056	38	8	083	53	S
057	39	9	084	54	T
058	3A	:	085	55	U
059	3B	;	086	56	V
060	3C	<	087	57	W
061	3D	=	088	58	X
062	3E	>	089	59	Y
063	3F	?	090	5A	Z
064	40	@	091	5B	[
065	41	A	092	5C	\
066	42	B	093	5D	]
067	43	C	094	5E	^
068	44	D	095	5F	–
069	45	E	096	60	`
070	46	F	097	61	a
071	47	G	098	62	b
072	48	H	099	63	c
073	49	I	100	64	d
074	4A	J	101	65	e
075	4B	K	102	66	f
076	4C	L	103	67	g
077	4D	M	104	68	h
078	4E	N	105	69	i
079	4F	O	106	6A	j
080	50	P	107	6B	k

Dec	Hex	ASCII	Dec	Hex	ASCII
108	6C	l	135	87	ç
109	6D	m	136	88	ê
110	6E	n	137	89	ë
111	6F	o	138	8A	è
112	70	p	139	8B	ï
113	71	q	140	8C	î
114	72	r	141	8D	ì
115	73	s	142	8E	Ä
116	74	t	143	8F	Å
117	75	u	144	90	É
118	76	v	145	91	æ
119	77	w	146	92	Æ
120	78	x	147	93	ô
121	79	y	148	94	ö
122	7A	z	149	95	ò
123	7B	{	150	96	û
124	7C	¦	151	97	ù
125	7D	}	152	98	ÿ
126	7E	~	153	99	Ö
127	7F	Δ	154	9A	Ü
128	80	Ç	155	9B	¢
129	81	ü	156	9C	£
130	82	é	157	9D	¥
131	83	â	158	9E	₧
132	84	ä	159	9F	ƒ
133	85	à	160	A0	á
134	86	å	161	A1	í

Dec	Hex	ASCII	Dec	Hex	ASCII
162	A2	ó	189	BD	┛
163	A3	ú	190	BE	┙
164	A4	ñ	191	BF	┐
165	A5	Ñ	192	C0	└
166	A6	ª	193	C1	┴
167	A7	º	194	C2	┬
168	A8	¿	195	C3	├
169	A9	⌐	196	C4	─
170	AA	¬	197	C5	┼
171	AB	½	198	C6	╞
172	AC	¼	199	C7	╟
173	AD	¡	200	C8	╚
174	AE	«	201	C9	╔
175	AF	»	202	CA	╩
176	B0	░	203	CB	╦
177	B1	▒	204	CC	╠
178	B2	▓	205	CD	═
179	B3	│	206	CE	╬
180	B4	┤	207	CF	╧
181	B5	╡	208	D0	╨
182	B6	╢	209	D1	╤
183	B7	╖	210	D2	╥
184	B8	╕	211	D3	╙
185	B9	╣	212	D4	╘
186	BA	║	213	D5	╒
187	BB	╗	214	D6	╓
188	BC	╝	215	D7	╫

ASCII Character Chart

Dec	Hex	ASCII	Dec	Hex	ASCII
216	D8	╤	241	F1	±
217	D9	╛	242	F2	≥
218	DA	╭	243	F3	≤
219	DB	■	244	F4	⌠
220	DC	▄	245	F5	⌡
221	DD	▌	246	F6	÷
222	DE	▐	247	F7	≈
223	DF	▀	248	F8	°
224	E0	α	249	F9	•
225	E1	β	250	FA	·
226	E2	Γ	251	FB	$\sqrt{}$
227	E3	π	252	FC	^{n}
228	E4	Σ	253	FD	^{2}
229	E5	σ	254	FE	■
230	E6	μ	255	FF	
231	E7	γ			
232	E8	Φ			
233	E9	θ			
234	EA	Ω			
235	EB	δ			
236	EC	∞			
237	ED	$\varnothing$			
238	EE	$\in$			
239	EF	$\cap$			
240	F0	$\equiv$			

Reserved Words

The following identifiers are reserved C keywords. They should not be used for any other purpose in a C program. They are allowed, of course, within double quotation marks. Also included is a list of words that aren't reserved in C but are C++ reserved words. The C++ reserved words are not described here, but if there's a chance your C program may eventually be ported to C++, you need to avoid these words as well.

Keyword	Description
asm	C keyword that denotes inline assembly language code.
auto	The default storage class.
break	C command that exits for, while, switch, and do...while statements unconditionally.
case	C command used within the switch statement.
char	The simplest C data type.
const	C data modifier that prevents a variable from being changed. See volatile.
continue	C command that resets a for, while, or do...while statement to the next iteration.
default	C command used within the switch statement to catch any instances not specified with a case statement.
do	C looping command used in conjunction with the while statement. The loop will always execute at least once.
double	C data type that can hold double-precision floating-point values.
else	statement signaling alternative statements to be executed when an if statement evaluates to FALSE.
enum	C data type that allows variables to be declared that accept only certain values.
extern	C data modifier indicating that a variable will be declared in another area of the program.
float	C data type used for floating-point numbers.
for	C looping command that contains *initialization, incrementation,* and *conditional* sections.
goto	C command that causes a jump to a predefined label.
if	C command used to change program flow based on a TRUE/FALSE decision.
int	C data type used to hold integer values.
long	C data type used to hold larger integer values than int.

Keyword	Description
register	storage modifier that specifies that a variable should be stored in a register, if possible.
return	C command that causes program flow to exit from the current function and return to the calling function. It also can be used to return a single value.
short	C data type that is used to hold integers. It is not commonly used, and is the same size as an int on most computers.
signed	C modifier that is used to signify that a variable can have both positive and negative values.
sizeof	C operator that returns the size (number of bytes) of the item.
static	C modifier that is used to signify that the compiler should retain the variable's value.
struct	C keyword used to combine C variables of any data type into a group.
switch	C command used to change program flow into a multitude of directions. Used in conjunction with the case statement.
typedef	C modifier used to create new names for existing variable and function types.
union	C keyword used to allow multiple variables to share the same memory space.
unsigned	C modifier that is used to signify that a variable will only contain positive values. See signed.
void	C keyword used to signify either that a function does not return anything or that a pointer being used is considered generic or able to point to any data type.
volatile	C modifier that signifies that a variable can be changed. See const.
while	C looping statement that executes a section of code as long as a condition remains TRUE.

In addition to the above keywords, the following are C++ reserved words:

catch	inline	template
class	new	this
delete	operator	throw
except	private	try
finally	protected	virtual
friend	public	

Operator
Precedence

The following are all the C operators in order of decreasing precedence. Operators on the same line have the same precedence.

```
Level  1:  ()  []  ->  .
Level  2:  !  ~  ++  --  *(indirection)  &(address of)  (type)
           sizeof +(unary)  -(unary)
Level  3:  *(multiplication)  /  %
Level  4:  +  -
Level  5:  <<  >>
Level  6:  <  <=  >  >=
Level  7:  ==  !=
Level  8:  &(bitwise AND)
Level  9:  ^
Level 10:  |
Level 11:  &&
Level 12:  ||
Level 13:  ?:
Level 14:  =  +=  -=  *=  /=  %=  &=  ^=  |=  <<=  >>=
Level 15:  ,
```

Note: () is the function operator; [] is the array operator.

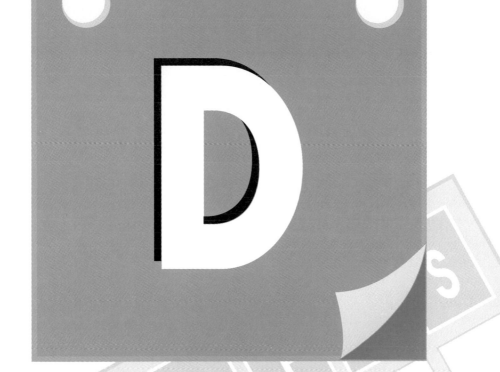

Function
Prototypes and
Header Files

This appendix lists the function prototypes contained in each of the header files supplied with most C compilers. Those functions marked with an asterisk in the left column are covered in this book.

The functions are listed alphabetically by name within the header file in which they are declared. Following each name is the complete prototype. Notice that the header file prototypes use different notation than used elsewhere in the book. For each parameter that a function takes, only the type is given in the prototype; no parameter name is included. Here are two examples:

```
int func1(int, int *);
int func1(int x, int *y);
```

Both declarations specify two parameters: the first a type int, and the second a pointer to type int. As far as the compiler is concerned, these two declarations are equivalent.

Table D.1. STDLIB.H: Standard library of general functions.

Covered in This Book	Function	Function Prototype
*	abort:	void abort(void);
	abs:	int abs(int);
*	atexit:	int atexit(void (*)(void));
*	atof:	double atof(const char *);
*	atoi:	int atoi(const char *);
*	atol:	long atol(const char *);
*	bsearch:	void *bsearch(const void*,const void *, size_t,size_t, int (*) (const void *,const void *));
*	calloc:	void *calloc(size_t,size_t);
	div:	div_t div(int, int);
*	exit:	void exit(int);
*	free:	void free(void *);
	getenv:	char *getenv(const char *);
	labs:	long int labs(long int);
	ldiv:	ldiv_t div(long int, long int);
*	malloc:	void *malloc(size_t);
	mblen:	int mblen(const char *, size_t);
	mbstowcs:	size_t mbstowcs(wchar_t *, const char *, size_t);
	mbtowc:	int mbtowc(wchar_t *, const char *, size_t);

Covered in This Book	Function	Function Prototype
*	qsort:	void qsort(void *,size_t,size_t,int (*) (const void*, const void *));
	rand:	int rand(void);
*	realloc:	void *realloc(void *,size_t);
	srand:	void srand(unsigned);
	strtod:	double strtod(const char *,char **);
	strtol:	long strtol(const char *, char **, int);
	strtoul:	unsigned long strtoul(const char *, char **, int);
*	system:	int system(const char *);
	wcstombs:	size_t wcstombs(char *, const wchar_t *, size_t);
	wctomb:	int wctomb(char *, wchar_t);

Table D.2. STDIO.H: Standard input/output functions.

Covered in This Book	Function	Function Prototype
	clearerr:	void clearerr(FILE *);
*	fclose:	int fclose(FILE *);
*	fcloseall:	int fcloseall(void);
*	feof:	int feof(FILE *);
*	fflush:	int fflush(FILE *);
*	fgetc:	int fgetc(FILE *);
	fgetpos:	int fgetpos(FILE *, fpos_t *);
*	fgets:	char *fgets(char *,int,FILE *);
*	flushall:	int flushall(void);
*	fopen:	FILE *fopen(const char *,const char *);
*	fprintf:	int fprintf(FILE *,const char *,...);
*	fputc:	int fputc(int,FILE *);
*	fputs:	int fputs(const char *,FILE *);
*	fread:	size_t fread(void *, size_t,size_t,FILE *);

continues

Table D.2. continued

Covered in This Book	Function	Function Prototype
	freopen:	FILE *freopen(const char *, const char *, FILE *);
*	fscanf:	int fscanf(FILE *,const char *,...);
*	fseek:	int fseek(FILE *,long,int);
	fsetpos:	int fsetpos(FILE *, const fpos_t *);
*	ftell:	long ftell(FILE *);
*	fwrite:	size_t fwrite(const void*,size_t, size_t,FILE *);
*	getc:	int getc(FILE *);
*	getch:	int getch(void);
*	getchar:	int getchar(void);
*	getche:	int getche(void);
*	gets:	char *gets(char *);
*	perror:	void perror(const char *);
*	printf:	int printf(const char *,...);
*	putc:	int putc(int,FILE *);
*	putchar:	int putchar(int);
*	puts:	int puts(const char *);
*	remove:	int remove(const char *);
*	rename:	int rename(const char *, const char *);
*	rewind:	void rewind(FILE *);
*	scanf:	int scanf(const char *,...);
	setbuf:	void setbuf(FILE *, char *);
	setvbuf:	int setvbuf(FILE *, char *, int, size_t);
	sprintf:	int sprintf(char *, const char *,...);
	sscanf:	int sscanf(const char *, const char *,...);
	tmpfile:	FILE *tmpfile(void);
*	tmpnam:	char *tmpnam(char *);
*	ungetc:	int ungetc(int,FILE *);
	vfprintf:	int vfprintf(FILE *, const char *,...);
	vprintf:	int vprintf(FILE *, const char *,...);
	vsprintf:	int vsprintf(char *, const char *,...);

Table D.3. TIME.H: Time and date functions.

Covered in This Book	Function	Function Prototype
*	asctime:	char *asctime(const struct tm *);
*	clock:	clock_t clock(void);
*	ctime:	char *ctime(const time_t *);
	difftime:	double diff_time(time_t, time_t);
	gmtime:	struct tm *gmtime(const time_t*);
*	localtime:	struct tm *localtime(const time_t *);
*	mktime:	time_t mktime(struct tm *);
*	sleep:	void sleep(time_t);
*	strftime:	size_t strftime(char *,size_t,const char *, const struct tm *);
*	time:	time_t time(time_t *);

Table D.4. STRING.H: String and character functions.

Covered in This Book	Function	Function Prototype
	memchr:	void *memchr(const void *, int, size_t);
	memcmp:	int memcmp(const void *, const void *, size_t);
	memcpy:	void *memcpy(void *, const void*, size_t);
	memmove:	void *memmove(void *, const void *, size_t);
	memset:	void *memset(void *, int, size_t);
*	strcat:	char *strcat(char *,const char *);
*	strchr:	char *strchr(const char *,int);
*	strcmp:	int strcmp(const char *,const char *);
*	strcmpi:	int strcmpi(const char *,const char *);
*	strcpy:	char *strcpy(char *,const char *);
*	strcspn:	size_t strcspn(const char *,const char *);
*	strdup:	char *strdup(const char *);
	strerror:	char *strerror(int);
*	strlen:	size_t strlen(const char *);

continues

Table D.4. continued

Covered in This Book	Function	Function Prototype
*	strlwr:	char *strlwr(char *);
*	strncat:	char *strncat(char *,const char *,size_t);
*	strncmp:	int strncmp(const char *,const char *,size_t);
*	strncpy:	char *strncpy(char *,const char *,size_t);
*	strnset:	char *strnset(char *,int,size_t);
*	strpbrk:	char *strpbrk(const char *,const char *);
*	strrchr:	char *strrchr(const char *,int);
*	strspn:	size_t strspn(const char *,const char *);
*	strstr:	char *strstr(const char *,const char *);
	strtok:	char *strtok(char *,const char *);
*	strupr:	char *strupr(char *);

Table D.5. CTYPE.H: Character classification and conversion macros.

Covered in This Book	Function	Function Prototype
*	isalnum:	int isalnum(int);
*	isalpha:	int isalpha(int);
*	isascii:	int isascii(int);
*	iscntrl:	int iscntrl(int);
*	isdigit:	int isdigit(int);
*	isgraph:	int isgraph(int);
*	islower:	int islower(int);
*	isprint:	int isprint(int);
*	ispunct:	int ispunct(int);
*	isspace:	int isspace(int);
*	isupper:	int isupper(int);
*	isxdigit:	int isxdigit(int);
	tolower:	int tolower(int);
	toupper:	int toupper(int);

Table D.6. MATH.H: Mathematical functions.

Covered in This Book	Function	Function Prototype
*	acos:	double acos(double);
*	asin:	double asin(double);
*	atan:	double atan(double);
*	atan2:	double atan2(double,double);
*	atof:	double atof(const char *);
*	ceil:	double ceil(double);
*	cos:	double cos(double);
*	cosh:	double cosh(double);
*	exp:	double exp(double);
*	fabs:	double fabs(double);
*	floor:	double floor(double);
*	fmod:	double fmod(double,double);
*	frexp:	double frexp(double,int *);
	ldexp:	double ldexp(double, int);
*	log:	double log(double);
*	log10:	double log10(double);
	modf:	double modf(double, double *);
*	pow:	double pow(double,double);
*	sin:	double sin(double);
*	sinh:	double sinh(double);
*	sqrt:	double sqrt(double);
*	tan:	double tan(double);
*	tanh:	double tanh(double);

Table D.7. ASSERT.H: Diagnostic functions.

Covered in This Book	Function	Function Prototype
*	assert:	void assert(int);

Table D.8. STDARG.H: Variable argument control macros.

Covered in This Book	Function	Function Prototype
*	va_arg:	`(type) va_arg(va_list, (type));`
*	va_end:	`void va_end(va_list);`
*	va_start:	`void va_start(va_list, lastfix);`

Common
C Functions

Common C Functions

This appendix lists the function prototypes contained in each of the header files supplied with most C compilers. Those functions marked with an asterisk in the left column are covered in the text of *Teach Yourself C Programming In 21 Days.*

The functions are listed alphabetically by name. Following each name is the complete prototype. Notice that the header file prototypes use a notation different from that used throughout the book. For each parameter that a function takes, only the type is given in the prototype; no parameter name is included. Here are two examples:

```
int func1(int, int *);
int func1(int x, int *y);
```

Both declarations specify two parameters: the first a type `int`, and the second a pointer to type `int`. As far as the compiler is concerned, these two declarations are equivalent.

Table E.1. Common C functions listed in alphabetical order.

Function	Header File	Function Prototype
abort:*	STDLIB.H	`void abort(void);`
abs:	STDLIB.H	`int abs(int);`
acos:*	MATH.H	`double acos(double);`
asctime:*	TIME.H	`char *asctime(const struct tm *);`
asin:*	MATH.H	`double asin(double);`
assert:*	ASSERT.H	`void assert(int);`
atan:*	MATH.H	`double atan(double);`
atan2:*	MATH.H	`double atan2(double,double);`
atexit:*	STDLIB.H	`int atexit(void (*)(void));`
atof:*	STDLIB.H	`double atof(const char *);`
atof:*	MATH.H	`double atof(const char *);`
atoi:*	STDLIB.H	`int atoi(const char *);`
atol:*	STDLIB.H	`long atol(const char *);`
bsearch:*	STDLIB.H	`void *bsearch(const void *, const void *, size_t,size_t, int(*) (const void*, const void *));`
calloc:*	STDLIB.H	`void *calloc(size_t,size_t);`
ceil:*	MATH.H	`double ceil(double);`
clearerr:	STDIO.H	`void clearerr(FILE *);`
clock:*	TIME.H	`clock_t clock(void);`

Function	Header File	Function Prototype
cos:*	MATH.H	`double cos(double);`
cosh:*	MATH.H	`double cosh(double);`
ctime:*	TIME.H	`char *ctime(const time_t *);`
difftime:	TIME.H	`double diff_time(time_t, time_t);`
div:	STDLIB.H	`div_t div(int, int);`
exit:*	STDLIB.H	`void exit(int);`
exp:*	MATH.H	`double exp(double);`
fabs:*	MATH.H	`double fabs(double);`
fclose:*	STDIO.H	`int fclose(FILE *);`
fcloseall:*	STDIO.H	`int fcloseall(void);`
feof:*	STDIO.H	`int feof(FILE *);`
fflush:*	STDIO.H	`int fflush(FILE *);`
fgetc:*	STDIO.H	`int fgetc(FILE *);`
fgetpos:	STDIO.H	`int fgetpos(FILE *, fpos_t *);`
fgets:*	STDIO.H	`char *fgets(char *,int,FILE *);`
floor:*	MATH.H	`double floor(double);`
flushall:*	STDIO.H	`int flushall(void);`
fmod:*	MATH.H	`double fmod(double,double);`
fopen:*	STDIO.H	`FILE *fopen(const char *,const char *);`
fprintf:*	STDIO.H	`int fprintf(FILE *,const char *, ...);`
fputc:*	STDIO.H	`int fputc(int,FILE *);`
fputs:*	STDIO.H	`int fputs(const char *,FILE *);`
fread:*	STDIO.H	`size_t fread(void *,size_t,size_t, FILE *);`
free:*	STDLIB.H	`void free(void *);`
freopen:	STDIO.H	`FILE *freopen(const char *, const char *, FILE *);`
frexp:*	MATH.H	`double frexp(double,int *);`
fscanf:*	STDIO.H	`int fscanf(FILE *,const char *,...);`
fseek:*	STDIO.H	`int fseek(FILE *,long,int);`
fsetpos:	STDIO.H	`int fsetpos(FILE *,const fpos_t *`
ftell:*	STDIO.H	`long ftell(FILE *);`
fwrite:*	STDIO.H	`size_t fwrite(const void *,size_t, size_t,FILE *);`

continues

Table E.1. continued

Function	Header File	Function Prototype
getc:*	STDIO.H	int getc(FILE *);
getch:*	STDIO.H	int getch(void);
getchar:*	STDIO.H	int getchar(void);
getche:*	STDIO.H	int getche(void);
getenv:	STDLIB.H	char *getenv(const char *);
gets:*	STDIO.H	char *gets(char *);
gmtime:	TIME.H	struct tm *gmtime(const time_t *);
isalnum:*	CTYPE.H	int isalnum(int);
isalpha:*	CTYPE.H	int isalpha(int);
isascii:*	CTYPE.H	int isascii(int);
iscntrl:*	CTYPE.H	int iscntrl(int);
isdigit:*	CTYPE.H	int isdigit(int);
isgraph:*	CTYPE.H	int isgraph(int);
islower:*	CTYPE.H	int islower(int);
isprint:*	CTYPE.H	int isprint(int);
ispunct:*	CTYPE.H	int ispunct(int);
isspace:*	CTYPE.H	int isspace(int);
isupper:*	CTYPE.H	int isupper(int);
isxdigit:*	CTYPE.H	int isxdigit(int);
labs:	STDLIB.H	long int labs(long int);
ldexp:	MATH.H	double ldexp(double, int);
ldiv:	STDLIB.H	ldiv_t div(long int, long int);
localtime:*	TIME.H	struct tm *localtime(const time_t *);
log:*	MATH.H	double log(double);
log10:*	MATH.H	double log10(double);
malloc:*	STDLIB.H	void *malloc(size_t);
mblen:	STDLIB.H	int mblen(const char *, size_t);
mbstowcs:	STDLIB.H	size_t mbstowcs(wchar_t *, const char *, size_t);
mbtowc:	STDLIB.H	int mbtowc(wchar_t *, const char *, size_t);
memchr:	STRING.H	void *memchr(const void *, int, size_t);

Function	Header File	Function Prototype
memcmp:	STRING.H	`int memcmp(const void *,` `                const void *, size_t);`
memcpy:	STRING.H	`void *memcpy(void *, const void *, size_t);`
memmove:	STRING.H	`void *memmove(void *, const void*, size_t);`
memset:	STRING.H	`void *memset(void *, int, size_t);`
mktime:*	TIME.H	`time_t mktime(struct tm *);`
modf:	MATH.H	`double modf(double, double *);`
perror:*	STDIO.H	`void perror(const char *);`
pow:*	MATH.H	`double pow(double,double);`
printf:*	STDIO.H	`int printf(const char *,...);`
putc:*	STDIO.H	`int putc(int,FILE *);`
putchar:*	STDIO.H	`int putchar(int);`
puts:*	STDIO.H	`int puts(const char *);`
qsort:*	STDLIB.H	`void qsort(void*,size_t,size_t,` `                int (*)(const void*, const void *));`
rand:	STDLIB.H	`int rand(void);`
realloc:*	STDLIB.H	`void *realloc(void *,size_t);`
remove:*	STDIO.H	`int remove(const char *);`
rename:*	STDIO.H	`int rename(const char *,const char *);`
rewind:*	STDIO.H	`void rewind(FILE *);`
scanf:*	STDIO.H	`int scanf(const char *,...);`
setbuf:	STDIO.H	`void setbuf(FILE *, char *);`
setvbuf:	STDIO.H	`int setvbuf(FILE *, char *, int, size_t);`
sin:*	MATH.H	`double sin(double);`
sinh:*	MATH.H	`double sinh(double);`
sleep:*	TIME.H	`void sleep(time_t);`
sprintf:	STDIO.H	`int sprintf(char *, const char *,...);`
sqrt:*	MATH.H	`double sqrt(double);`
srand:	STDLIB.H	`void srand(unsigned);`
sscanf:	STDIO.H	`int sscanf(const char *, const  char *,...);`
strcat:*	STRING.H	`char *strcat(char *,const char *);`
strchr:*	STRING.H	`char *strchr(const char *,int);`

E

continues

Table E.1. continued

Function	Header File	Function Prototype
strcmp:*	STRING.H	int strcmp(const char *,const char *);
strcmpl:*	STRING.H	int strcmpl(const char *,const char *);
strcpy:*	STRING.H	char *strcpy(char *,const char *);
strcspn:*	STRING.H	size_t strcspn(const char *, const char *);
strdup:*	STRING.H	char *strdup(const char *);
strerror:	STRING.H	char *strerror(int);
strftime:*	TIME.H	size_t strftime(char *,size_t, const char *, const struct tm *);
strlen:*	STRING.H	size_t strlen(const char *);
strlwr:*	STRING.H	char *strlwr(char *);
strncat:*	STRING.H	char *strncat(char *,const char *, size_t);
strncmp:*	STRING.H	int strncmp(const char *, const char *,size_t);
strncpy:*	STRING.H	char *strncpy(char *,const char *, size_t);
strnset:*	STRING.H	char *strnset(char *,int,size_t);
strpbrk:*	STRING.H	char *strpbrk(const char *, const char *);
strrchr:*	STRING.H	char *strrchr(const char *,int);
strspn:*	STRING.H	size_t strspn(const char *, const char *);
strstr:*	STRING.H	char *strstr(const char *,const char *);
strtod:	STDLIB.H	double strtod(const char *, char **);
strtok:	STRING.H	char *strtok(char *, const char*);
strtol:	STDLIB.H	long strtol(const char *, char **, int);
strtoul:	STDLIB.H	unsigned long strtoul(const char*, char **, int);
strupr:*	STRING.H	char *strupr(char *);
system:*	STDLIB.H	int system(const char *);
tan:*	MATH.H	double tan(double);
tanh:*	MATH.H	double tanh(double);
time:*	TIME.H	time_t time(time_t *);
tmpfile:	STDIO.H	FILE *tmpfile(void);
tmpnam:*	STDIO.H	char *tmpnam(char *);

Function	Header File	Function Prototype
tolower:	CTYPE.H	`int tolower(int);`
toupper:	CTYPE.H	`int toupper(int);`
ungetc:*	STDIO.H	`int ungetc(int,FILE *);`
va_arg:*	STDARG.H	`(type) va_arg(va_list, (type));`
va_end:*	STDARG.H	`void va_end(va_list);`
va_start:*	STDARG.H	`void va_start(va_list, lastfix)`
vfprintf:	STDIO.H	`int vfprintf(FILE *, constchar *,...);`
vprintf:	STDIO.H	`int vprintf(FILE*, constchar *,...`
vsprintf:	STDIO.H	`int vsprintf(char *, constchar *,...);`
wcstombs:	STDLIB.H	`size_t wcstombs(char *, const wchar_t *,` `                  size_t);`
wctomb:	STDLIB.H	`int wctomb(char *, wchar_t);`

E

F

Answers

This appendix lists the answers for the quizzes and the exercise sections at the end of each chapter. Notice that for the exercises, more than one solution is possible for each problem. In most cases, there is only one of the many possible answers. In other cases, there is additional information to help you solve the exercise.

Answers for Day 1, "Getting Started"

Quiz

1. C is powerful, popular, and portable.

2. The compiler translates C source code into machine-language instructions your computer can understand.

3. Editing, compiling, linking, and testing.

4. The answer to this question is going to depend on your compiler. Consult your manuals.

5. The answer to this question is going to depend on your compiler. Consult your manuals.

6. The appropriate extension to use for C source files is .C (or .c—the case doesn't matter).

7. FILENAME.TXT would compile. It is more appropriate, however, to use a .C extension rather than .TXT.

8. You should make changes to the source code to correct the problems. You should then recompile and relink. After relinking, you should run the program again to see whether your corrections fixed the program.

9. Machine language is digital, or binary, instructions that the computer can understand. Because the computer cannot understand C source code, a compiler translates the source code to machine code, also called object code.

10. The linker combines the object code from your program to the object code from the function library and creates an executable file.

Exercises

1. When you look at the object file, you see a lot of control characters and other gibberish. Throughout the gibberish you also see pieces of the source file.

2. The program calculates the area of a circle. It prompts the user for the radius and then displays the area. This is the program referenced in the chapter.

3. This program prints a 10×10 block made of the character X. A similar program is used and explained on Day 6, "Basic Program Control."

4. This program generates a compiler error. You should get a message similar to the following:

```
Error: ch1ex4.c: Declaration terminated incorrectly
```

This error is caused by the semicolon at the end of line 3. If you remove the semicolon, this program should compile and link correctly.

5. This program compiles okay, but it generates a linker error. You should get a message similar to the following:

```
Error: Undefined symbol _do_it in module...
```

This error occurs because the linker cannot find a function called do_it. To fix this program, change do_it to printf.

6. Rather than a 10×10 block filled with the character X, the program now prints a 10×10 block of smiley faces.

7. This exercise had you enter a program that can be used to print listings. There is no applicable answer.

Answers for Day 2, "The Components of a C Program"

Quiz

1. A block.

2. The main() function.

3. Any text between /* and */ is a program comment and is ignored by the compiler. Use program comments to make notations about the program's structure and operation.

4. A function is an independent section of program code that performs a certain task and has been assigned a name. By using a function's name, a program can execute the code in the function.

5. A user-defined function is created by the programmer. A library function is supplied with the C compiler.

6. An #include directive instructs the compiler to add the code from another disk file into your source code during the compilation process.

7. Comments should not be nested. Although some compilers let you to do this, others do not. To keep your code portable, you should not nest them.

8. Yes. Comments can be as long as needed. A comment starts with /* and does not end until a */ is encountered.

F

9. An include file is also known as a header file.

10. An include file is a separate disk file that contains information needed by the compiler to use various functions.

Exercises

1. Remember, only the main() function is required in C programs. The following is the smallest possible program, but it doesn't do anything:

```
void main()
{
}
```

This also could be written

```
void main(){}
```

2. For an explanation of these answers, refer back to the chapter.

   a. Statements are on lines 8, 9, 10, 12, 20, and 21.

   b. The only variable definition is on line 18.

   c. The only function prototype (for display_line()) is on line 4.

   d. The function definition for display_line() is on lines 16–22.

   e. Comments are on lines 1, 15, and 23.

3. A comment is any text included between /* and */. Examples include the following:

```
/* This is a comment */
/*???*/
/*
This is a
        third comment */
```

4. Exercise 4 is a program that prints the alphabet in all capital letters. You should understand this program better when you finish Day 10, "Characters and Strings."

   The output is

```
ABCDEFGHIJKLMNOPQRSTUVWXYZ
```

5. This program counts and prints the number of characters and spaces that you enter. This program also will be clearer after you finish Day 10.

Answers for Day 3, "Numeric Variables and Constants"

Quiz

1. An integer variable can hold a whole number (a number without a fractional part), and a floating-point variable can hold a real number (a number with a fractional part).

2. A type `double` variable has a greater range than type `float` (it can hold larger and smaller values). A type `double` variable also is more precise than type `float`.

3. The file criteria that ANSI provides are the following:

    a. The size of a `char` is one byte.

    b. The size of a `short` is less than or equal to the size of an `int`.

    c. The size of an `int` is less than or equal to the size of a `long`.

    d. The size of an `unsigned` is equal to the size of an `int`.

    e. The size of a `float` is less than or equal to the size of a `double`.

4. The names of symbolic constants make your source code easier to read. They also make it much easier to change the constant's value.

5. Either of the following:

    ```
    #define MAXIMUM 100

    const int MAXIMUM = 100;
    ```

6. Letters, numerals, and the underscore.

7. Names of variables and constants should be descriptive of the data being stored. Variable names should be in lowercase, constant names in uppercase.

8. Symbolic constants are symbols that represent literal constants.

9. If it is an `unsigned int` that is two bytes long, the minimum value it can hold is 0. If it is signed, –32,768 is the minimum.

Exercises

1. Here are the answers:

    a. Because a person's age can be considered a whole number, and a person cannot be a negative age, an `unsigned int` is suggested.

    b. `unsigned int`

    c. `float`

F

d. If your expectations on yearly salary are not very high, a simple `unsigned int` variable would work. If you feel you have potential to go above $65,535, you probably should use a `long`. (Have faith in yourself; use a `long`.)

e. `float` (Don't forget the decimal places for the cents.)

f. Because the highest grade is always going to be 100, it is a constant. Use either `const int` or a `#define` statement.

g. `float` (If you are going to use only whole numbers, use either `int` or `long`.)

h. Definitely a signed field. Either `int`, `long`, or `float`. See answer 1.d.

i. `double`

2. Answers for 2 and 3 are combined here.

   Remember, a variable name should be representative of the value it holds. A variable declaration is the statement that initially creates the variable. The declaration may or may not initialize the variable to a value. You can use any name for a variable, except the C keywords.

   a. `unsigned int age;`

   b. `unsigned int weight;`

   c. `float radius = 3;`

   d. `long annual_salary;`

   e. `float cost = 29.95;`

   f. `const int max_grade = 100;` or
      `#define MAX_GRADE 100`

   g. `float temperature;`

   h. `long net_worth = -30000;`

   i. `double star_distance;`

3. See answer 2.

4. The valid variable names are b, c, e, g, h, i, and j.

   Notice that j is correct; however, it is not wise to use variable names that are this long. (Besides, who would want to type it?) Most compilers don't look at the entire name provided by j; instead, they only look at the first few characters. Most compilers differentiate only the first 31 characters.

   The following were invalid:

   a. You cannot start a variable name with a number.

   d. You cannot use a pound sign (#) in a variable name.

   f. You cannot use a hyphen (-) in a variable name!

Answers for Day 4, "Statements, Expressions, and Operators"

Quiz

1. It is an assignment statement that instructs the computer to add 5 and 8, assigning the result to the variable x.

2. An expression is anything that evaluates to a numerical value.

3. The relative precedence of the operators.

4. After the first statement, the value of a is 10 and the value of x is 11. After the second statement, both a and x have the value 11. (The statements must be executed separately.)

5. 1

6. 19

7. (5 + 3) * 8 / (2 + 2)

8. 0

9. Appendix C, "Operator Precedence," shows the C operators and their precedence.

   a. < has higher precedence than ==

   b. * has higher precedence than +

   c. != and == have the same precedence, therefore they are evaluated left to right.

   d. >= has the same precedence as >. Use parentheses if you need to use more than one relational operator in a single statement or expression.

10. The compound assignment operators enable you to combine a binary mathematical operation with an assignment operation, thus providing a shorthand notation. The compound operators presented on Day 4, "Statements, Expressions, and Operators," are +=, -=, /=, *=, and %=.

F

Exercises

1. The listing should have worked even though it was poorly structured. The purpose of the listing was to demonstrate that whitespace is irrelevant to how the program runs. You should use whitespace to make your programs readable.

2. The following is a better way to structure the exercise 1 listing:

```
#include <stdio.h>

int x, y;
```

```
main()
{
    printf("\nEnter two numbers ");
    scanf( "%d %d",&x,&y);
    printf("\n\n%d is bigger",(x>y)?x:y);
    return 0;
}
```

The listing asks for two numbers, x and y, and then prints which is bigger.

3. The only changes needed in Listing 4.1 are the following:

```
16:        printf("\n%d    %d", a++, ++b);
17:        printf("\n%d    %d", a++, ++b);
18:        printf("\n%d    %d", a++, ++b);
19:        printf("\n%d    %d", a++, ++b);
20:        printf("\n%d    %d", a++, ++b);
```

4. The following code fragment is just one of many possible examples. It checks to see if x is greater than or equal to 1 and if x is less than or equal to 20. If these two conditions are met, x is assigned to y. If these conditions are not met, x is not assigned to y; therefore, y remains the same.

```
if ((x >= 1) && (x <= 20))
    y = x;
```

5. The code is as follows:

```
y = ((x >= 1) && (x <= 20)) ? x : y;
```

Again, if the statement is true, x is assigned to y; otherwise, y is assigned to itself, thus having no effect.

6. The code is as follows:

```
if (x < 1 && x > 10 )
    statement;
```

7. The answers are as follows:

   a. (1 + 2 * 3) = 7

   b. 10 * 3 * 3 - (1 + 2) = 0

   c. ((1 + 2) * 3) = 9

   d. (5 == 5) = 1 (true)

   e. (x = 5) = 5

8. The answers are as follows:

   a. True

   b. False

   c. True. Notice that there is a single equal sign, making the `if` an assignment instead of a relation.

   d. True

9. We did not do what this exercise asked; however, you can get the answer to the question from this nested `if`. (You also could have indented this differently.)

```
if( age < 21 )
    printf( "You are not an adult" );
else if( age >= 65 )
        printf( "You are a senior citizen!");
    else
        printf( "You are an adult" );
```

10. This program had four problems. The first is on line 4. The assignment statement should end with a semicolon, not a colon. The second problem is the semicolon at the end of the `if` statement on line 8. The third problem is common; the assignment operator (`=`) was used rather than the relational operator (`==`) in the `if` statement. The final problem is the word `otherwise` on line 10. This should be `else`.

```
1: /* a program with problems... */
2: #include <stdio.h>
3:
4: int x = 1;
5:
6: main()
7: {
8:     if( x == 1)
9:         printf(" x equals 1" );
10:    else
11:        printf(" x does not equal 1");
12:
13:    return
14: }
```

Answers for Day 5, "Functions: The Basics"

Quiz

1. Yes! (Well, OK, this is a trick question, but you had better answer "yes" if you want to become a good C programmer.)

2. Structured programming takes a complex programming problem and breaks it down into a number of simpler tasks that are easier to handle one at a time.

3. After you've broken your program into a number of simpler tasks, you can write a function to perform each task.

4. The first line of a function definition must be the function header. It contains the function's name, its return type, and its parameter list.

5. A function can return either one value or no values. The value can be of any of the C variable types. On Day 18, "Getting More from Functions," you see how to get more values back from a function.

6. A function that returns nothing should be type `void`.

7. A function definition is the complete function, including the header and all the function's statements. The definition determines what actions take place when the function executes. The prototype is a single line, identical to the function header, but it ends with a semicolon. The prototype informs the compiler of the function's name, return type, and parameter list.

8. A local variable is declared within a function.

9. Local variables are independent from other variables in the program.

Exercises

1. `float do_it(char a, char b, char c)`

   Add a semicolon to the end, and you have the function prototype. As a function header, it should be followed by the function's statements enclosed by braces.

2. This is a `void` function. As in exercise one, to create the prototype, add a semicolon to the end. In an actual program, the header is followed by the function's statements.

   `void print_a_number( int a_number )`

3. The answers are as follows:

   a. `int`

   b. `long`

4. There are two problems with this listing. First, the function is declared as a `void`; however, it returns a value. The `return` statement should be removed. The second problem is on line 5. The call to `print_msg()` passes a parameter (a string). The prototype states that this function has a `void` parameter list and therefore should not be passed anything. The following is the corrected listing:

   ```
    include <studio.h>
   void print_msg (void)
   main
   {
       print_msg();
   }
   void print_msg(void)
   { return 0
   puts( "This is a message to print" );
   }
   ```

5. There should not be a semicolon at the end of the function header.

6. Only the `larger_of()` function needs to be changed:

   ```
   19: int larger_of( int a, int b)
   20: {
   21:     int save;
   22:
   23:     if (a > b)
   24:         save = a;
   ```

```
25:      else
26:          save = b;
27:
28:      return save;
29: }
```

7. The following assumes the two values are integers, and an integer is returned:

```
int product( int x, int y )
{
    return (x * y);
}
```

8. This listing asks you to check the values passed. You should never assume that the values passed are correct.

```
int divide_em( int a, int b )
{
    int answer = 0;

    if( b == 0 )
        answer = 0;
    else
        answer = a/b;

    return answer;
}
```

9. Although the following uses main(), it could be any function. Lines 7, 8, and 9 show the calls to the two functions. Lines 11–14 print the values.

```
 1: main()
 2: {
 3:      int number1 = 10,
 4:          number2 = 5;
 5:      int x, y, z;
 6:
 7:      x = product( number1, number2 );
 8:      y = divide_em( number1, number2 );
 9:      z = divide_em( number1, 0 );
10:
11:      printf( "\nnumber1 is %d and number2 is %d", number1, number2 );
12:      printf( "\nnumber1 * number2 is %d", x );
13:      printf( "\nnumber1 / number2 is %d", y );
14:      printf( "\nnumber1 / 0 is %d", z );
15:
16:      return 0;
17: }
```

10. The code is as follows:

```
/* Averages five float values entered by the user. */

#include <stdio.h>

float v, w, x, y, z, answer;

float average(float a, float b, float c, float d, float e);
```

```
main()
{
    puts("Enter five numbers:");
    scanf("%f%f%f%f%f", &v, &w, &x, &y, &z);

    answer = average(v, w, x, y, z);

    printf("The average is %f.", answer);
}

float average( float a, float b, float c, float d, float e)
{
    return ((a+b+c+d+e)/5);
}
```

11. The following is the answer using type int variables. It can only run with values less than or equal to 9. To use values larger than 9, you need to change the values to type long.

```
/* this is a program with a recursive function */

#include <stdio.h>

int three_powered( int power );

main()
{
    int a = 4;
    int b = 9;

    printf( "\n3 to the power of %d is %d", a,
            three_powered(a) );
    printf( "\n3 to the power of %d is %d", b,
            three_powered(b) );

}

int three_powered( int power )
{

    if ( power < 1 )
        return( 1 );
    else
        return( 3 * three_powered( power - 1 ));
}
```

Answers for Day 6, "Basic Program Control"

Quiz

1. The first index value of an array in C is 0.

2. A `for` statement contains initializing and increment expressions as parts of the command.

3. A `do...while` contains the `while` statement at the end and always executes the loop at least one time.

4. Yes, a `while` statement can accomplish the same task as a `for` statement; however, you need to do two additional things. You must initialize any variables before starting the `while` command, and you need to increment any variables as a part of the `while` loop.

5. You cannot overlap the loops. The nested loop must be entirely inside the outer loop.

6. Yes, a `while` statement can be nested in a `do...while` loop. You can nest any command within any other command.

Exercises

1. `long array[50];`

2. Notice that in the following answer, the 50th element is indexed to 49. Remember that arrays start at 0.

   ```
   array[49] = 123.456;
   ```

3. When the statement is completed, x equals 100.

4. When the statement is completed, `ctr` equals 11. (`ctr` starts at 2 and is incremented by 3 while it is less than 10.)

5. The inner loop prints 5 Xs. The outer loop prints the inner loop 10 times. This totals to 50 Xs.

6. The code is as follows:

   ```
   int x;
   for( x = 1; x <= 100; x += 3) ;
   ```

7. The code is as follows:

   ```
   int x - 1;
   while( x <= 100 )
       x += 3;
   ```

8. The code is as follows:

```
int ctr = 1;
do
{
    ctr += 3;
} while( ctr < 100 );
```

9. This program never ends. `record` is initialized to 0. The `while` loop then checks to see whether `record` is less than 100. 0 is less than 100, so the loop executes, thus printing the two statements. The loop then checks the condition again. 0 is still, and always will be, less than 100, so the loop continues. Within the brackets, `record` needs to be incremented. The following line should be added after the second `printf()` function call:

```
record++;
```

10. Using a defined constant is common in looping; you see examples similar to this code fragment in weeks two and three. The problem with this fragment is simple. The semicolon does not belong at the end of the `for` statement. This is a common bug.

Answers for Day 7, "Basic Input/Output"

Quiz

1. There are two differences between `puts()` and `printf()`:
   - `printf()` can print variable parameters.
   - `puts()` automatically adds a newline character to the end of the string it prints.

2. The STDIO.H header file should be included when using `printf()`.

3. The following is what the escape sequences do:
   a. `\\` prints a backslash
   b. `\b` prints a backspace
   c. `\n` prints a newline
   d. `\t` prints a tab
   e. `\a` beeps the bell (alert)

4. The following conversion specifiers should be used:
   a. `%s` for a character string
   b. `%d` for a signed decimal integer
   c. `%f` for a decimal floating point number

5. The following is what is printed in the literal text of `puts()`:

   a. b prints the literal character b

   b. \b prints a backspace character

   c. \ looks at the next character to determine an escape character (See Table 7.1).

   d. \\ prints a single backslash

Exercises

1. The code is as follows:

```
puts( ) automatically adds the newline, printf( ) does not.
printf( "\n" );
puts( " " );
```

2. The code is as follows:

```
char c1, c2;
int d1;
scanf( "%c %ud %c", &c1, &d1, &c2 );
```

3. Your answer may vary from this code:

```
#include <stdio.h>
int x;

main()
{
    puts( "Enter an integer value" );
    scanf( "%d", &x );

    printf( "\nThe value entered is %d", x );
}
```

4. It's typical to add edits that allow only specific values to be accepted. The following is one way to accomplish this exercise.

```
#include <stdio.h>
int x;

main()
{
    puts( "Enter an even integer value" );
    scanf( "%d", &x );
    while( x % 2 != 0)
    {
        printf( "\n%d is not even, Please enter an even \
                number: ", x );
        scanf( "%d", &x );
    }
    printf( "\nThe value entered is %d", x );
}
```

F

5. The code is as follows:

```
#include <stdio.h>
int array[6], x, number;

main()
{
    /* loop 6 times or until the last entered element is 99 */
    for( x = 0; x < 6 && number != 99; x++ )
    {
        puts( "Enter an even integer value, or 99 to quit" );
        scanf( "%d", &number );
        while( number % 2 == 1 && number != 99)
        {
            printf( "\n%d is not even, Please enter an even \
                    number: ", number);
            scanf( "%d", &number );
        }
        array[x] = number;
    }
    /* now print them out... */
    for( x = 0; x < 6 && array[x] != 99; x++ )
    {
        printf( "\nThe value entered is %d", array[x] );
    }
}
```

6. The previous answers already are executable programs. The only change that needs to be made is in the final `printf()`. To print each value separated by a tab, change the `printf()` statement to the following:

```
printf( "%d\t", array[x]);
```

7. You cannot include quotes within quotes. To print quotes within quotes, you must use the escape character `\"`. The following is the corrected version:

```
printf( "Jack said, \"Peter Piper picked a peck of pickled \
        peppers.\"");
```

8. This listing has three errors. The first is the lack of quotes in the `printf()` statement. The second is the missing address of operator on the `answer` variable in the `scanf()`. The final error is also in the `scanf()` statement. Instead of `"%f"`, it should have `"%d"` because `answer` is a type `int` variable, not a type `float`. The following is corrected:

```
int get_1_or_2( void )
{
    int answer = 0;

    while( answer < 1 || answer > 2 )
    {
        printf("Enter 1 for Yes, 2 for No ");      /* corrected */

        scanf( "%d", &answer );                     /* corrected */
    }
    return answer;
}
```

9. The following is the completed `print_report` function for Listing 7.1:

```c
void print_report( void )
{
    printf( "\nSAMPLE REPORT" );
    printf( "\n\nSequence\tMeaning" );
    printf( "\n========\t=======" );
    printf( "\n\\a\t\tbell (alert)" );
    printf( "\n\\b\t\tbackspace" );
    printf( "\n\\n\t\tnew line" );
    printf( "\n\\t\t\thorizontal tab" );
    printf( "\n\\\\\t\tbackslash" );
    printf( "\n\\?\t\tquestion mark" );
    printf( "\n\\'\t\tsingle quote" );
    printf( "\n\\\"\t\tdouble quote" );
    printf( "\n...\t\t...");
}
```

10. The code is as follows:

```c
/* Inputs two floating point values and */
/* displays their product. */

#include <stdio.h>

float x, y;

main()
{
    puts("Enter two values: ");
    scanf("%f %f", &x, &y);
    printf("\nThe product is %f", x * y);
}
```

11. The following program prompts for 10 integers and displays their sum:

```c
/* Input 10 integers and display their sum. */

#include <stdio.h>

int count, temp;
long total = 0;      /* Use type long to ensure we don't */
                     /* exceed the maximum for type int. */

main()
{
    for (count = 1; count <=10; count++)
        {
            printf("Enter integer # %d: ", count);
            scanf("%d", &temp);
            total += temp;
        }

    printf("\n\nThe total is %d", total);
}
```

12. The code is as follows:

```
/* Inputs integers and stores them in an array, stopping */
/* when a zero is entered. Finds and displays the array's */
/* largest and smallest values */
#include <stdio.h>

#define MAX 100

int array[MAX];
int count = -1, maximum, minimum, num_entered, temp;

main()
{
    puts("Enter integer values one per line.");
    puts("Enter 0 when finished.");

    /* Input the values */

    do
    {
        scanf("%d", &temp);
        array[++count] = temp;
    } while ( count < (MAX-1) && temp != 0 );

    num_entered = count;

    /* Find the largest and smallest */
    /* First set maximum to a very small value, */
    /* and minimum to a very large value. */

    maximum = -32000;
    minimum = 32000;

    for (count = 0; count <= num_entered && array[count]! = 0; count++)
    {
        if (array[count] > maximum)
            maximum = array[count];

        if (array[count] < minimum )
            minimum = array[count];
    }

    printf("\nThe maximum value is %d", maximum);
    printf("\nThe minimum value is %d", minimum);
}
```

Answers for Day 8, "Numeric Arrays"

Quiz

1. All of them, but one at a time. A given array can contain only a single data type.

2. 0. Regardless of the size of an array, in C all arrays start with subscript 0.

3. n-1.

4. The program compiles and runs but produces unpredictable results.

5. In the declaration statement, follow the array name with one set of brackets for each dimension. Each set of brackets contains the number of elements in the corresponding dimension.

6. 240. This is determined by multiplying 2 by 3 by 5 by 8.

7. array [0] [0] [1] [1]

Exercises

1. `int one[1000], two[1000], three[1000];`

2. `int array[10] = { 1, 1, 1, 1, 1, 1, 1, 1, 1, 1 };`

3. This exercise can be solved in numerous ways. The first way is to initialize the array when it is declared:

```
int eightyeight[88] = {88,88,88,88,88,88,88,...,88};
```

This would require that 88 88s be placed between the braces instead of using ... as I did. This method is not recommended for initializing such a big array. The following is a better method:

```
int eightyeight[88];
int x;

for ( x = 0; x < 88; x++ )
    eightyeight[x] = 88;
```

4. The code is as follows:

```
int stuff[12][10];
int sub1, sub2;

for( sub1 = 0; sub1 < 12; sub1++ )
    for( sub2 = 0; sub2 < 10; sub2++ )
        stuff[sub1][sub2] = 0;
```

5. Be careful with this fragment. The bug presented here is easy to create. Notice that the array is 10×3, but is initialized as a 3×10 array.

To describe this differently, the left subscript is declared as 10; however, the for loop uses x as the left subscript. x is incremented with 3 values. The right subscript is declared as 3; however, the second for loop uses y as the right subscript. y is incremented with 10 values. This can cause unpredictable results. You can fix this program in one of two ways. The first is to switch x and y in the line that does the initialization.

```
int x, y;
int array[10][3];
main()
{
```

```
        for ( x = 0; x < 3; x++ )
            for ( y = 0; y < 10; y++ )
                array[y][x] = 0;            /* changed */
    }
```

The second way (which is recommended) is to switch the values in the for loops.

```
int x, y;
int array[10][3];
main()
{
    for ( x = 0; x < 10; x++ )       /* changed */
        for ( y = 0; y < 3; y++ )    /* changed */
            array[x][y] = 0;
}
```

6. This, we hope, was an easy bug to bust. This program initializes an element in the array that is out of bounds. If you have an array with 10 elements, their subscripts are 0 to 9. This program initializes elements with subscripts 1 through 10. You cannot initialize array[10] because it does not exist. The for statement should be changed to one of the following two examples:

```
for( x = 1; x <=9; x++ )   /* initializes 9 of the 10 elements */
```

```
for( x = 0; x <= 9; x++ )
```

Notice that x <= 9 is the same as x < 10. Either is appropriate; x < 10 is more common.

7. The following is one of many possible answers:

```
/* Exercise 8.7 - Using 2 dimensional arrays and rand() */

#include <stdio.h>
#include <stdlib.h>

/* Declare the array */

int array[5][4];
int a, b;

main()
{
    for ( a = 0; a < 5; a++ )
    {
        for ( b = 0; b < 4; b++ )
        {
            array[a][b] = rand();
        }
    }

    /* Now print the array elements */

    for ( a = 0; a < 5; a++ )
    {
        for ( b = 0; b < 4; b++ )
```

```
        {
            printf( "%d\t", array[a][b] );
        }
        printf( "\n" );     /* go to a new line */
    }

    return 0;
}
```

8. The following is one of many possible answers:

```
/* EX8-8.C - RANDOM.C using a single-dimensional array */

#include <stdio.h>
#include <stdlib.h>
/* Declare a single-dimensional array with 1000 elements */

int random[1000];
int a, b, c;
long total = 0;

main()
{
    /* Fill the array with random numbers. The C library */
    /* function rand() returns a random number. Use one */
    /* for loop for each array subscript. */

    for (a = 0; a < 1000; a++)
    {
        random[a] = rand();
        total += random[a];
    }
    printf("\n\nAverage is: %ld\n",total/1000);
    /* Now display the array elements 10 at a time */

    for (a = 0; a < 1000; a++)
    {
        printf("\nrandom[%d] = ", a);
        printf("%d", random[a]);

        if ( a % 10 == 0 && a > 0 )
        {
            printf("\nPress a key to continue, CTRL-C to quit.");
                getch();
        }
    }
}           /* end of main() */
```

9. Following are two solutions. The first initializes the array at the time it is declared, the second initializes it in a for loop:

Answer 1:

```
/* EX8-9.c */

#include <stdio.h>
```

```
/* Declare a single-dimensional array */

int elements[10] = { 0, 1, 2, 3, 4, 5, 6, 7, 8, 9 };
int idx;

main()
{
    for (idx = 0; idx < 10; idx++)
    {
        printf( "\nelements[%d] = %d ", idx, elements[idx] );
    }
}           /* end of main() */
```

Answer 2:

```
/* EX8-9b.c */

#include <stdio.h>

/* Declare a single-dimensional array */

int elements[10];
int idx;

main()
{
    for (idx = 0; idx < 10; idx++)
        elements[idx] = idx ;

    for (idx = 0; idx < 10; idx++)
        printf( "\nelements[%d] = %d ", idx, elements[idx] );
}
```

10. The following is one of many possible answers:

```
/* EX8-10.c */

#include <stdio.h>

/* Declare a single-dimensional array */

int elements[10] = { 0, 1, 2, 3, 4, 5, 6, 7, 8, 9 };
int new_array[10];
int idx;

main()
{
    for (idx = 0; idx < 10; idx++)
    {
        new_array[idx] = elements[idx] + 10 ;
    }

    for (idx = 0; idx < 10; idx++)
    {
        printf( "\nelements[%d] = %d \tnew_array[%d] = %d",
                idx, elements[idx], idx, new_array[idx] );
    }
}
```

Answers for Day 9, "Pointers"

Quiz

1. The address-of operator is the & sign.
2. The indirection operator * is used. When you precede the name of a pointer by *, it refers to the variable pointed to.
3. A pointer is a variable that contains the address of another variable.
4. Indirection is the act of accessing the contents of a variable by using a pointer to the variable.
5. They are stored in sequential memory locations, with lower array elements at lower addresses.
6. `&data[0]`

   `data`
7. One way is to pass the length of the array as a parameter to the function. The second way is to have a special value in the array, such as `NULL`, signify the array's end.
8. Assignment, indirection, address of, incrementing, differencing, and comparison.
9. Differencing two pointers returns the number of elements in between. In this case, the answer is 1.
10. The answer is also 1.

Exercises

Answers are not provided for exercises 9 and 10 because of the many possibilities.

1. To declare a pointer to a character, do the following:

   ```
   char *char_ptr;
   ```
2. The following declares a pointer to `cost`, and then assigns the address of `cost`, (`&cost`), to it:

   ```
   int *p_cost;
   p_cost = &cost;
   ```
3. Direct access: `cost = 100;`

   Indirect access: `*p_cost = 100;`
4. The code is as follows:

   ```
   printf( "Pointer value: %d, points at value: %d", p_cost,
           *p_cost);
   ```

F

5. `float *variable = &radius;`

6. The code is as follows:
```
data[2] = 100;
*(data + 2) = 100;
```

7. This code also includes the answer for exercise 8:
```
#include <stdio.h>

#define MAX1 5
#define MAX2 8

int array1[MAX1] = { 1, 2, 3, 4, 5 };
int array2[MAX2] = { 1, 2, 3, 4, 5, 6, 7, 8 };
int total;

int sumarrays(int x1[], int len_x1, int x2[], int len_x2);

main()
{
    total = sumarrays(array1, MAX1, array2, MAX2);
    printf("The total is %d", total);
}

int sumarrays(int x1[], int len_x1, int x2[], int len_x2)
{

    int total = 0, count = 0;

    for (count = 0; count < len_x1; count++)
        total += x1[count];

    for (count = 0; count < len_x2; count++)
        total += x2[count];

    return total;
}
```

Answers for Day 10, "Characters and Strings"

Quiz

1. The values in the ASCII character set range from 0–255. From 0–127 is the standard ASCII character set, and 128–255 is the extended ASCII character set.

2. As the ASCII code of the character.

3. A string is a sequence of characters terminated by the null character.

4. A sequence of one or more characters enclosed in double quotation marks.

5. To hold the string's terminating null character.

6. As a sequence of ASCII values corresponding to the quoted characters, followed by 0 (the ASCII code for the null character).

7. The answers are as follows:

   a. 97

   b. 65

   c. 57 (This is a character nine, not a numeric nine.)

   d. 32

   e. 206

   f. 6

8. The answers are as follows:

   a. I

   b. a space

   c. c

   d. a

   e. n

   f. NUL

   g. ☻

9. The answers are as follows:

   a. 9 bytes. (Actually, the variable is a pointer to a string, and the string requires 9 bytes of memory—8 for the string and 1 for the null terminator.)

   b. 9 bytes

   c. 1 byte

   d. 20 bytes

   e. 20 bytes

10. The answers are as follows:

    a. A

    b. A

    c. 0 (NUL)

    d. This is beyond the end of the string, so it could have any value.

    e. !

    f. This contains the address of the first element of the string.

Exercises

Because of the number of different possible answers, exercises 5, 6, 7, and 12 are not answered.

1. `char letter = '$';`

2. `char array[18] = "Pointers are fun!";`

3. `char *array = "Pointers are fun!";`

4. The code is as follows:
   ```
   char *ptr;
   ptr = malloc(81);
   gets(ptr);
   ```

8. `a_string` is declared as an array of 10 characters; however, it is initialized with a string larger than 10 characters. `a_string` needs to be bigger.

9. If the intent of this line of code is to initialize a string, this is wrong. You should use either `char *quote`, or `char quote[100]`.

10. No.

11. Yes. Although you can assign one pointer to another, you cannot assign one array to another. You should change the assignment to a string-copying command such as `strcpy()`.

Answers for Day 11, "Structures"

Quiz

1. The data items in an array must all be of the same type. A structure can contain data items of different types.

2. The structure member operator is a period. It is used to access members of a structure.

3. `struct`

4. A structure tag is tied to a template of a structure and is not an actual variable. A structure instance is an allocated structure that can hold data.

5. The statements define a structure and declare an instance called `myaddress`. This instance is then initialized. The structure member `myaddress.name` is initialized to the string `"Bradley Jones"`, `yaddress.add1` is initialized to `"RTSoftware"`, `myaddress.add2` is initialized to `"P.O. Box 1213"`, `myaddress.city` is initialized to `"Carmel"`, `myaddress.state` is initialized to `"IN"`, and finally, `myaddress.zip` is initialized to `"46032-1213"`.

6. `ptr++;`

7. One member must be a pointer to the structure's own type.

8. The first advantage has to do with inserting and deleting elements in a sorted list. In an array, you would have to shift all the elements already in the array to insert a new element. In a linked list, you only need to change the pointer of the element before the one being inserted or deleted.

   The second advantage has to do with size. An array must have its size declared in advance, potentially causing a lot of unused space. A linked list allocates space as needed. You are more likely to run out of memory if you are using an array.

9. The argument for `malloc()` is the number of bytes of storage needed. Its return value is a pointer to the first byte of allocated storage or, if the call failed, `NULL`.

10. For this, refer to Figure 11.9. If you start with the "After" picture, you see that `Adams` points to `Baker`, which in turn points to `Clark`. If you want to delete `Baker`, all you need to do is get the element that points to it (`Adams`) and make its (`Adams`'s) pointer point to the element that `Baker` points to (`Clark`).

Exercises

1. The code is as follows:

```
struct time {
    int hours;
    int minutes;
    int seconds;
} ;
```

2. The code is as follows:

```
struct data {
    int value1;
    float value2;
    float value3;

} info ;
```

3. `info.value1 = 100;`

4. The code is as follows:

```
struct data *ptr;
ptr = &info;
```

5. The code is as follows:

```
ptr->value2 = 5.5;
(*ptr).value2 = 5.5;
```

6. The code is as follows:

```
struct data {
    char name[21];
    struct data *ptr;
};
```

7. The code is as follows:

```
typedef struct {
    char address1[31];
    char address2[31];
    char city[11];
    char state[3];
    char zip[11];
} RECORD;
```

8. The following uses the values from quiz question five for the initialization:

```
RECORD myaddress = {"RTSoftware",
                    "P.O. Box 1213",
                    "Carmel", "IN", "46032-1213" };
```

9. This code fragment has two problems. The first is that the structure should contain a tag. The second problem is the way that sign is initialized. The initialization values should be in braces. The corrected code is

```
struct zodiac {
    char zodiac_sign[21];
    int month;
} sign = {"Leo", 8};
```

10. The `union` declaration has only one problem. Only one variable in a union can be used at a time. This is true of initializing the union also. Only the first member of the union can be initialized. The correct initialization is

```
/* setting up a union */
union data{
    char a_word[4];
    long a_number;
}generic_variable = { "WOW" };
```

11. If the structure is intended to be used in a linked list, it should contain a pointer to the next name of the structure type. The following is the corrected code.

```
/* a structure to be used in a linked list */
struct data{
    char firstname[10];
    char lastname[10];
    char middlename[10];
    struct data *next_name;
};
```

Answers for Day 12, "Variable Scope"

Quiz

1. The scope of a variable refers to the extent to which different parts of a program have access to the variable, or where the variable is visible.

2. A variable with local storage class is visible only in the function where it is defined. A variable with external storage class is visible throughout the entire program.

3. Defining a variable in a function makes it local; defining a variable outside of any function makes it external.

4. Automatic (the default) or static. An automatic variable is created each time the function is called and destroyed when the function ends. A static local variable persists and retains its value between calls to the function.

5. An automatic variable is initialized every time the function is called. A static variable is initialized only the first time that the function is called.

6. False. When declaring register variables, you are making a request. There is no guarantee that the compiler will honor the request.

7. An uninitialized global variable is automatically initialized to 0; however, it is best to initialize variables explicitly.

8. An uninitialized local variable is not automatically initialized; it could contain anything. You should never use an uninitialized local variable.

9. Because the variable count is now local to the block, the printf() no longer has access to a variable called count. The compiler gives you an error.

10. If the value needs to be remembered, it should be declared as static. If the variable were called vari, the declaration would be

```
static int vari;
```

11. The extern keyword is used as a storage-class modifier. It indicates that the variable has been declared somewhere else in the program.

12. The static keyword is used as a storage-class modifier. It tells the compiler to retain the value of a variable or function for the duration of a program. Within a function, the variable keeps its value between function calls.

Exercises

1. `register int x = 0;`

2. The code is as follows:
```
/* Illustrates variable scope. */
#include <stdio.h>

void print_value(int x);

main()
{
    int x = 999;

    printf("%d", x);
```

```
        print_value( x );
    }

    void print_value( int x)
    {
        printf("%d", x);
    }
```

3. Because you are declaring var as a global, you do not need to pass it as a parameter.

```
    /* Exercise 12.3 - Using a global variable */
    #include <stdio.h>

    int var = 99;

    void print_value(void);

    main()
    {
        print_value();
    }

    void print_value(void)
    {
        printf( "The value is %d", var );
    }
```

4. Yes, you need to pass the variable var in order to print it in a different function.

```
    /* Exercise 12.4 _ Using a local variable*/
    #include <stdio.h>

    void print_value(int var);

    main( )
    {
        int var = 99;
        print_value(  var );
    }

    void print_value(int var)
    {
        printf( "The value is %d", var );
    }
```

5. Yes, a program can have a local and global variable with the same name. In such cases, active local variables take precedence.

```
    /* Exercise 12.5 _ Using a global *\
    #include <stdio.h>

    int var = 99;

    void print_func(void);

    main( )
    {
        int var = 77;
```

```
    printf( "Printing in function with local and global:");
    printf( "\nThe Value of var is %d", var );
    print_func( );
}
void print_func( void )
{
    printf( "\nPrinting in function  only global:");
    printf( "\nThe value of var is %d", var );
}
```

6. There is only one problem with a_sample_function(). Variables can be declared at the beginning of any block; therefore, the declarations of crt1 and star are fine. The other variable, ctr2, is not declared at the beginning of a block; it needs to be declared. The following is the corrected function within a complete program.

```
/* Exercise 12,6 */
#include <stdio.h>

void a_sample_function( );
main()
{
    a_sample_function();
    return 0;
}

void a_sample_function( void )
{
    int ctr1;

    for ( ctr1 = 0; ctr1 < 25; ctr1++ )
        printf( "*" );

    puts( "\nThis is a sample function" );
    {
        char star = '*';
        int ctr2;      /* fix */
        puts( "It has a problem" );
        for ( ctr2 = 0; ctr2 < 25; ctr2++ )
        {
            printf( "%c", star);
        }
    }
}
```

7. The program actually works properly, but it could be better. First of all, there is no need to initialize the variable x to 1 because it is initialized to 0 in the for statement. Also, declaring the variable tally to be static is pointless because within the main() function the static keyword has no effect.

8. What is the value of star? What is the value of dash? These two variables were never initialized. Because they are both local variables, each could contain any value. Notice that this program compiles with no errors or warnings, but there is a problem.

There is a second issue that should be brought up about this program. The variable ctr is declared as a global, but it is only used in print_function(). This is not a good assignment. The program would be better if ctr was a local variable in print_function().

9. This program prints the following pattern forever. See exercise 10.

   ```
   X==X==X==X==X==X==X==X==X==X==X==X==X==X==X==X==X==X==...
   ```

10. This program poses a problem because of the global scope of ctr. Both the main() function and print_letter2() function use ctr in loops at the same time. Because print_letter2() changes the value, the for loop in main() never completes. This could be fixed in a number of ways. One way is to use two different counter variables. A second way is to change the scope of the counter variable, ctr. It could be declared in both main() and print_letter2() as local variables.

    An additional comment on letter1 and letter2. Because each of these is only used in one function, they should be declared as locals. Following is the corrected listing:

    ```c
    #include <stdio.h>
    void print_letter2(void);              /* function prototype */

    main()
    {
        char letter1 = 'X';
        int ctr;

        for( ctr = 0; ctr < 10; ctr++ )
        {
            printf( "%c", letter1 );
            print_letter2();
        }
    }

    void print_letter2(void)
    {
        char letter2 = '=';
        int ctr;                           /* this is a local
                                              variable */
                                           /* it is different from
                                              ctr in main() */

        for( ctr = 0; ctr < 2; ctr++ )
            printf( "%c", letter2 );
    }
    ```

Answers for Day 13, "More Program Control"

Quiz

1. Never. (Unless you are very careful.)

2. When a `break` statement is encountered, execution immediately exits the `for`, `do...while`, or `while` loop that contains the `break`. When a `continue` statement is encountered, the next iteration of the enclosing loop begins immediately.

3. An infinite loop is a loop that executes forever. It is created by writing a `for`, `do...while`, or `while` loop with a test condition that is always true.

4. Execution terminates when the program reaches the end of `main()` or the `exit()` function is called.

5. The expression in a `switch` statement can evaluate to a `long`, `int`, or `char` value.

6. The `default` statement is a case in a `switch` statement. When the expression in the `switch` statement evaluates to a value that does not have a matching case, control goes to the default case.

7. The `atexit()` function registers functions to be executed when the program ends.

8. The `system()` function executes a command at the operating-system level.

Exercises

1. `continue;`

2. `break;`

3. The code is as follows:
   ```
   atexit(f3);
   atexit(f2);
   atexit(f1);
   ```

4. `system("dir");`

5. This code fragment is correct. You do not need a `break` statement after the `printf()` for `'N'`, because the `switch` statement ends anyway.

6. You might think the `default` needs to go at the bottom of the `switch` statement; that is not true. The `default` can go anywhere. There is a problem, however. There should be a `break` statement at the end of the `default` case.

F

7. The code is as follows:

```
if( choice == 1 )
    printf("You answered 1");
else if( choice == 2 )
        printf( "You answered 2");
    else
        printf( "You did not choose 1 or 2");
```

8. The code is as follows:

```
do {
/* any C statements */
} while ( 1 );
```

9. No answer is provided for this exercise question because there are numerous ways a program could be written to perform this task. The point is not for you to get the "right" answer but rather to gain valuable experience by tackling the project.

10. See the answer to exercise 9.

Answers for Day 14, "Working with the Screen, Printer, and Keyboard"

Quiz

1. A stream is a sequence of bytes. A C program uses streams for all input and output.

2. The answers are as follows:

   a. A printer is an output device.

   b. A keyboard is an input device.

   c. A modem is both an input and an output device.

   d. A monitor is an output device. (Although a touch screen would be an input device and an output device.)

   e. A disk drive can be both an input and an output device.

3. All C compilers support the three predefined streams: stdin (the keyboard), stdout (the screen), and stderr (the screen). Some compilers, including DOS, also support stdprn (the printer), and stdaux (the serial port COM1). Note that the Macintosh does not support the stdprn function.

4. The answers are as follows:

   a. printf() and puts() use the stdout stream.

   b. scanf() and gets() use the stdin stream.

   c. fprintf() can use any output stream. Of the five standard streams, it can use stdout, stderr, stdprn, and stdaux.

5. Buffered input is sent to the program only when the user presses Enter. Unbuffered input is sent one character at a time, as soon as each key is pressed.

6. Echoed input automatically sends each character to stdout as it is received; unechoed input does not.

7. You can "unget" only one character between reads. The EOF character cannot be put back into the input stream with unget().

8. The newline character, which corresponds to the user pressing Enter.

9. The answers are as follows:

   a. Valid.

   b. Valid.

   c. Valid.

   d. Not valid. There is not an identifier of q.

   e. Valid.

   f. Valid.

10. stderr cannot be redirected; it always prints to the screen. stdout can be redirected to somewhere other than the screen.

Exercises

Answers are not provided for exercises 6, 8, or 9.

1. `printf( "Hello World" );`

2. The code is as follows:

```
fprintf( stdout, "Hello World" );
puts( "Hello World");
```

3. `fprintf( stdaux, "Hello Auxiliary Port" );`

4. The code is as follows:

```
char buffer[31];
scanf( "%30[^*]", buffer );
```

5. The code is as follows:

```
printf( "Jack asked, \"What is a backslash\?\"\nJill said, \
        \"It is \'\\\'\"");
```

7. Hint: Use an array of 26 integers. To count each character, increment the appropriate array element for each character read.

10. Hint: Get a string at a time, and then print a formatted line number followed by a tab and the string.

Answers for Day 15, "More on Pointers"

Quiz

1. The code is as follows:

```
float x;
float *px = &x;
float **ppx = &px;
```

2. The error is that the statement uses a single indirection operator, and as a result, assigns the value 100 to px instead of to x. The statement should be written with a double indirection operator.

```
**ppx = 100;
```

3. array is an array with two elements. Each of those elements is itself an array that contains three elements. Each of these elements is an array that contains four type int variables.

4. array[0][0] is a pointer to the first four-element int array.

5. The first and third comparisons are true; the second is not true.

6. `void func1(char *p[]);`

7. It has no way of knowing. This value must be passed to the function as another argument.

8. A pointer to a function is a variable that holds the address where the function is stored in memory.

9. `char (*ptr)(char *x[]);`

10. If you omit the parentheses surrounding *ptr, the line is a prototype of a function that returns a pointer to type char.

Exercises

1. The answers are as follows:

   a. var1 is a pointer to an integer.

   b. var2 is an integer.

   c. var3 is a pointer to a pointer to an integer.

2. The answers are as follows:

   a. `a` is an array of 36 (3×12) integers.

   b. `b` is a pointer to an array of 12 integers.

   c. `c` is an array of 12 pointers to integers.

3. The answers are as follows:

   a. `z` is an array of 10 pointers to characters.

   b. `y` is a function that takes an integer (field) as an argument and returns a pointer to a character.

   c. `x` is a pointer to a function that takes an integer (field) as an argument and returns a character.

4. `float (*func)(int field);`

5. An array of function pointers can be used in conjunction with a menuing system. The number selected from a menu could relate to the array index for the function pointer. For example, the function pointed to by the fifth element of the array would be executed if item 5 were selected from the menu.

   ```
   int (*menu_option[10])(char *title);
   ```

6. `char *ptrs[10];`

7. `ptr` was declared as an array of 12 pointers to integers, not a pointer to an array of 12 integers. The corrected code would be

   ```
   int x[3][12];
   int (*ptr)[12];

   ptr = x;
   ```

Answers for Day 16, "Using Disk Files"

F

Quiz

1. A text-mode stream automatically performs translation between the newline character, \n, that C uses to mark the end of a line and the carriage-return line-feed character pair that DOS uses to mark the end of a line. In contrast, a binary-mode stream performs no translations. All bytes are input and output without modification.

2. Open the file using the `fopen()` library function.

3. When using `fopen()`, you must specify the name of the disk file to open and the mode to open it in. The function `fopen()` returns a pointer to type `FILE`; this pointer is used in subsequent file access functions to refer to the specific file.

4. Formatted, character, and direct.

5. Sequential and random.

6. `EOF` is the end-of-file flag. It is a symbolic constant equal to –1.

7. `EOF` is used with text files to determine when the end of the file has been reached.

8. In binary mode you must use the `feof()` function. In text mode you can look for the `EOF` character or use `feof()`.

9. The file position indicator indicates the position in a given file where the next read or write operation is to occur. You can modify the file position indicator with `rewind()` and `fseek()`.

10. The file position indicator points to the first character of the file, or offset 0. The one exception is if you open an existing file in Append mode, in which case the position indicator points to the end of the file.

Exercises

1. `fcloseall();`

2. `rewind(fp);` and `fseek(fp, 0, SEEK_SET);`

3. You cannot use the `EOF` check with a binary file. You should use the `feof()` function instead.

Answers for Day 17, "Manipulating Strings"

Quiz

1. The length of a string is the number of characters between the start of the string and the terminating null character (not counting the null character). You can determine the length of the string with the `strlen()` function.

2. You must be sure to allocate sufficient storage space for the new string.

3. Concatenate means to join two strings, appending one string onto the end of another.

4. When you compare strings, "greater than" means that one string's ASCII values are larger than the other string's ASCII values.

5. `strcmp()` compares two entire strings. `strncpy()` only compares a specified number of characters within the string.

6. `strcmp()` compares two strings, considering the case of letters. (`'A'` and `'a'` are different.) `strcmpi()` ignores case. (`'A'` and `'a'` are the same.)

7. `isascii()` checks the value passed to see whether it is a standard ASCII character between 0 and 127. It does not check for extended ASCII characters.

8. `isascii()` and `iscntrl()` both return TRUE; all others return FALSE. Remember, these macros are looking at the character value.

9. 65 is equivalent to the ASCII character A. The following macros return TRUE: `isalnum()`, `isalpha()`, `isascii()`, `isgraph()`, `isprint()`, and `isupper()`.

10. The character-test functions determine whether a particular character meets a certain condition, such as whether it is a letter, punctuation mark, or something else.

Exercises

1. TRUE (1) or FALSE (0)

2. The answers are as follows:
   a. 65
   b. 81
   c. −34
   d. 0
   e. 12
   f. 0

3. The answers are as follows:
   a. 65.000000
   b. 81.230000
   c. −34.200000
   d. 0.000000
   e. 12.000000
   f. 1000.000000

4. `string2` was not allocated space before it was used. There is no way of knowing where `strcpy()` copies the value of `string1`.

Answers for Day 18, "Getting More from Functions"

Quiz

1. Passing by value means that the function receives a copy of the value of the argument variable. Passing by reference means that the function receives the address of the argument variable. The difference is that passing by reference allows the function to modify the original variable, whereas passing by value does not.

2. A type `void` pointer is a pointer that can point to any type of C data object (a generic pointer).

3. By using a `void` pointer, you can create a "generic" pointer that can point to any object. The most common use of a `void` pointer is in declaring function parameters. You can create a function that can handle different types of arguments.

4. A type cast provides information about the type of the data object that the `void` pointer is pointing to at the moment. You must cast a `void` pointer before dereferencing it.

5. A function that takes a variable argument list must be passed at least one fixed argument. This is done to inform the function of the number of arguments being passed each time it is called.

6. `va_start()` should be used to initialize the argument list. `va_arg()` should be used to retrieve the arguments. `va_end()` should be used to clean up once all the arguments are retrieved.

7. Trick question! `void` pointers cannot be incremented because the compiler would not know what value to add.

8. Yes, a function can return a pointer to any of the C variable types. A function also can return a pointer to such storage areas as arrays, structures, and unions.

Exercises

1. `int function( char array[] );`

2. `int numbers( int *nbr1, int *nbr2, int *nbr3);`

3. The code is as follows:
   ```
   int number1 = 1, number2 = 2, number3 = 3;
   numbers( &number1, &number2, &number3);
   ```

4. Although the code might look confusing, it is perfectly correct. This function takes the value being pointed at by `nbr` and multiplies it by itself.

5. When using variable parameter lists, you should use all the macro tools. This includes `va_list`, `va_start()`, `va_arg()`, and `va_end()`. See Listing 18.3 for the correct way to use variable parameter lists.

Answers for Day 19, "Exploring the Function Library"

Quiz

1. Type `double`.

2. On most compilers it is equivalent to a `long`; however, this is not guaranteed. Check the TIME.H file with your compiler or your reference manual to find out what variable type your compiler uses.

3. The `time()` function returns the number of seconds that have elapsed since midnight, January 1, 1970. The `clock()` function returns the number of 1/100 seconds that have elapsed since the program began execution.

4. Nothing at all. It simply displays a message that describes the error.

5. Sort the array into ascending order.

6. 14

7. 4

8. 21

9. `0` if the values are equal.

   `>0` if the value of element 1 is greater than element 2.

   `<0` if the value of element 1 is less than element 2.

10. NULL

Exercises

1. The code is as follows:
   ```
   bsearch( myname, names, (sizeof(names)/sizeof(names[0])),
            sizeof(names[0]), comp_names);
   ```

2. There are three problems. First, the field width is not provided in the call to `qsort()`. Second, the parenthesis should not be added to the end of the function name in the call to `qsort()`. Third, the program is missing its comparison function. `qsort()` uses `compare_function()`, which is not defined in the program.

3. The compare function returns the wrong values. It should return a positive number if element1 is greater than element2 and a negative number if element1 is less than element2.

Answers for Day 20, "Working with Memory"

Quiz

1. The malloc() function allocates a specified number of bytes of memory, whereas calloc() allocates sufficient memory for a specified number of data objects of a certain size. calloc() also sets the bytes of memory to 0, whereas malloc() does not initialize them to any specific value.

2. To preserve the fractional part of the answer when dividing one integer by another and assigning the result to a floating point variable.

3. The answers are as follows:

    a. long

    b. int

    c. char

    d. float

    e. float

4. Dynamically allocated memory is memory that is allocated at runtime—while the program is executing. Dynamic memory allocation permits you to allocate exactly as much memory as is needed, only when it is needed.

5. memmove() works properly when the source and destination memory regions overlap, whereas memcpy() does not. If the source and destination regions do not overlap the two functions are identical.

Exercises

1. The code is as follows:

```
long *ptr;
ptr = malloc( 1000 * sizeof(long));
```

2. The code is as follows:

```
long *ptr;
ptr = calloc( 1000, sizeof(long));
```

3. Using a loop and assignment statement:

```
int count;
for (count = 0; count < 1000; count++)
    data[count] = 0;
```

Using the `memset()` function:

```
memset(data, 0, 1000 * sizeof(float));
```

4. The given example will compile and run without error; however, the results will be incorrect. Because `number1` and `number2` are both integers, the result of their division will be an integer, thus losing any fractional part of the answer. In order to get the correct answer you need to cast the expression to type `float`:

```
answer = (float) number1/number2;
```

5. Because `p` is a type `void` pointer, it must be cast to the proper type before being used in an assignment statement. The third line should be as follows:

```
*(float*)p = 1.23;
```

Answers for Day 21, "Taking Advantage of Preprocessor Directives and More"

Quiz

1. Modular programming refers to the program development method that breaks a program into multiple source-code files.

2. The main module contains the `main()` function.

3. To avoid unwanted side effects by ensuring that complex expressions passed as arguments to the macro are fully evaluated first.

4. Compared to a function, a macro results in faster program execution but larger program size.

5. The `defined()` operator tests to see whether a particular name is defined, returning `TRUE` if the name is defined and `FALSE` if it isn't.

6. You must use `#endif`.

7. Compiled source files become object files with a .OBJ extension.

8. `#include` copies the contents of another file into the current file.

9. An `include` statement with double quotes looks in the current directory for the include file. An `include` statement with <> searches the standard directory for the include file.

F

10. `--DATE--` is used to place into the program the date that the program was compiled.

11. A string containing the name of the current program, including path information.

Answers for Bonus Day 1, "Coding Styles"

Quiz

1. `mlpp` stands for "maximum lines per page" but it is too cryptic—nobody but you will know what it means

   `MaximumNumberOfPrintLinesPerPage` is certainly descriptive, but it is much longer than needed.

   `MaxLinesPerPage` is just right, fully descriptive of the variable's function but not too long.

2. There are two methods. One, called *camel* notation, uses uppercase for the first letter of each word (`MaxLinesPerPage`, for example). The other method separates words with underscores (`max_lines_per_page`). Use whichever you prefer, but be consistent.

3. It is a pointer (the `p`) to an array (the `a`) of characters (the `ch`).

4. The first thing to try is to reduce the indent size. Indents of 3 or 4 characters are usually ideal. If your indent size is 8 or more, it's too much. Even with small indents, some lines of code are just too long. Remember that you can break a line of C code with a hard return (press Enter) anywhere except within a string constant. The technique can be particularly useful with long function calls. Here's an example:

```
printf("The first 5 values are %d, %d, %d, %d, and %d\n",
        data_array[1],
        data_array[2],
        data_array[3],
        data_array[4],
        data_array[5]);
```

   You can see that this call to `printf()` would be too long to fit on a single line. By breaking it up as shown here, it's a lot easier to read.

Exercise

1. The answer is as follows:

A pointer to type `long`	`plTotal`
A type `int`	`iCount`
An array of type `char`	`achData`
An index into an array of zero-terminated strings	`iachNames`

Answers for Bonus Day 2, "Portability"

Quiz

1. It depends on the overall requirements of the program you are creating. Most times, maintainability will be more important. Efficiency is only important with a program that is time-critical. The most costly part of a program is the time the programmer spends maintaining it.

2. If you are using the ASCII character table, it is 97; however, it could be any other value. A character's numeric value is based on the character set being used.

3. The largest unsigned character value will be defined within the numeric constant `UCHAR_MAX`.

4. American National Standards Institute

5. Most C compilers are case sensitive. For most compilers, each of the variables would be treated as different. These variable names would not be portable since some compilers don't differentiate case.

6. The `isalpha()` function is an ANSI function that determines if a character is a letter of the alphabet. It's better to use this function than a function that checks to see if the character is between a and z.

7. The `isdigit()` function checks to see if a character is a number (0, 1, 2, 3, 4, 5, 6, 7, 8, and 9). This is an ANSI function. It is better to use `isdigit()` than to check to see if a character is greater than or equal to 0 and less than or equal to 9.

8. As stated in the answers to quiz questions 6 and 7, the functions are ANSI compatible. Using these functions will produce portable code. Because there isn't a proprietary character set for the C language, there is no guarantee what numeric values will represent characters. By using the `is...()` functions, you gain portability.

F

9. No. Generally, when working with data files and structures, you must ensure that all things are consistent. Issues such as word alignment must be known. Because one compiler may have word alignment on and another may not, portability may be lost.

10. No. The predefined constants are replaced at compile-time, not run-time. --TIME-- will be replaced with the time the program was compiled.

Exercises

1. This program uses ctr and CTR. These are two separate variables if your compiler is case-sensitive. If you are considering portability, you should rename one of these two variables to allow something other than the case to differentiate them.

2. Following is a function that verifies the that a character is a vowel.

```
/*   Function to verify vowel. */
/*   All checks are equality, so code will be portable. */

int verify_vowel( int ch )
{
   int rv = 0;
   switch( ch )
   {
      case 'a':
      case 'e':
      case 'i':
      case 'o':
      case 'u':
      case 'a':
      case 'A':
      case 'E':
      case 'I':
      case 'O':
      case 'U':   rv = 1;
                  break;
      default:    rv = 0;
                  break;
   }
   return( rv );
}
```

3. One of many possible answers:

```
int character_case( int ch )
{
   int rv = 0;
   if ( isalpha( ch ) )
   {
      if ( isupper( ch ) )
         rv = 1;
      else
         rv = 2;
   }
   else
   {
```

```
        rv = 0;
    }
    return( rv );
}
```

4. This exercise is one for you to do on your own! Check your compiler's manual for this information.

5. No. This program uses `system()`. This function calls an operating system specific command—in this case `TYPE`. This means that your program isn't portable to other operating systems.

6. No. This is quite similar to a program shown in today's materials. The following would be much more portable:

```
int to_upper( int x)
{
    if( isalpha( x ) && islower( x )
    {
        toupper( x );
    }
    return( x );
}
```

Answers for Bonus Day 3, "Working with Bits"

Quiz

1. By defining a bit field member with a size of three bits. Since 2^3 is equal to 8, such a field is sufficient to hold values 1 through 7.

2. Two bytes. Using bit fields, you could declare a structure as follows:

```
struct date{
    unsigned month : 4;
    unsigned day   : 5;
    unsigned year  : 7;
}
```

This structure stores the date in two bytes (16 bits). The 4-bit `month` field can hold values from 0–15, sufficient for holding 12 months. Likewise, the 5-bit day field can hold values from 0–31, and the 7-bit year field can hold values from 0–127. We assume that the year value will be added to 1900 to permit year values from 1900 to 2027.

3. 00100000

4. 00001001

5. The two expressions evaluate to the same result. Using Exclusive OR with 11111111 is the same as using the complement operator—each bit in the original value is reversed.

Exercise

1. No. When using bit fields, you must place them first within a structure. The following is correct:

```
struct quiz_answers {
    unsigned answer1    : 1;
    unsigned answer2    : 1;
    unsigned answer3    : 1;
    unsigned answer4    : 1;
    unsigned answer5    : 1;
    char student_name[15];
}
```

Answers for Bonus Day 4, "Working with Different Number Systems"

Quiz

1. Number systems are important because a computer works with numbers. All characters and symbols are converted to numeric values.

2. For IBM Compatible PCs, the ASCII Standard specifies the conversion values.

3. A decimal value is a base 10 number. Decimal numbers are the numbers that we use to count with every day. Because decimal stands for 10, only 10 numbers are used.

4. The computer stores information in bits. A bit can have one or two states, on or off. Binary numbers are base 2. This means they can use two digits, 0 and 1, to represent all numbers. These two digits can be used to represent the on and off state of the computer's information.

5. A computer stores information in bytes. A byte is 8 bits. To look at the binary representation of data means looking at eight digits for a maximum value of 256 (decimal). By using hexadecimal, these 256 possible numbers can be represented in two digits. In addition, the two hexadecimal digits can easily be converted to binary since the first digit represents the left four binary digits and the second hexadecmial digit represents the right four binary digits.

6. Although there could be many reasons for wanting to look at the numeric values of data, there is one reason that is most often given. Many characters appear as spaces when viewed as common text. In many cases, the "spaces" may be something quite different. For example, to know where a string ends, you look for the terminating NUL character. You cannot see this character in a normal text editor. In a debugger it generally shows up as a space. By looking at the numeric value, you know a NUL is equal to 0 where as a space is equal to 32 (decimal). 0 and 32 are very different!

SAMS
Sams
Learning
Center
SAMS
PUBLISHING

7. Binary: 0 and 1

8. Decimal: 0, 1, 2, 3, 4, 5, 6, 7, 8 and 9

9. Octal: 0, 1, 2, 3, 4, 5, 6, and 7

10. Hexadecimal: 0, 1, 2, 3, 4, 5, 6, 7, 8, 9, A, B, C, D, E, and F

Exercises

1. The code is as follows:

   ```
   Binary:      01000011
   Octal:       103
   Decimal:     67
   Hexadecimal: 43
   ```

2. The code is as follows:

   ```
   Binary:      11
   Octal:       3
   Decimal:     3
   Hexadecimal: 3
   ```

3. The answers are as follows:

   a. 32

   b. 89

   c. 121

   d. 57

   e. 43

4. The answers are as follows:

   a.]

   b. <

   c. ♠

   d. \

   e. 2

5. The number of marked days is 21 decimal, 10101 binary, 15 hexadecimal, or 25 octal.

6. The following is one possible answer:

   ```
   1:   /* Program:  EXERB406.c
   2:    * Book:     Teach Yourself C in 21 Days
   3:    * Purpose:  Print numeric values of an entered character.
   4:    *=========================================================*/
   5:
   6:   #include <stdio.h>
   7:   #include <stdlib.h>
   8:
   ```

F

```
 9:    int main(void)
10:    {
11:       int ch;
12:
13:       printf("\n\nEnter a character ==>" );
14:       ch = getchar();
15:
16:       printf("\n\nYour character:     %c", ch );
17:       printf("\n\n Decimal value:     %d", ch );
18:       printf("\n Octal value:        %o", ch);
19:       printf("\n Hexadecimal value: %x", ch );
20:
21:       return 0;
22:    }
```

7. The following is a complete program:

```
 1:    /* Program:  ExerB406.c
 2:     * Book:      Teach Yourself C in 21 Days
 3:     * Purpose:   convert the case of a letter.
 4:     *=========================================================*/
 5:
 6:    #include <stdio.h>
 7:
 8:    unsigned char switch_case( unsigned char );
 9:
10:    int main(void)
11:    {
12:       unsigned char letter1 = 'c',
13:                     letter2 = 'Y',
14:                     converted1,
15:                     converted2;
16:
17:       printf("\n\nThe first letter is %c", letter1);
18:       converted1 = switch_case(letter1);
19:       printf("\n\n%c is now %c", letter1, converted1);
20:
21:       printf("\n\nThe second letter is %c", letter2);
22:       converted2 = switch_case(letter2);
23:       printf("\n\n%c is now %c", letter2, converted2);
24:
25:       return 0;
26:    }
27:
28:
29:    unsigned char switch_case( unsigned char ch )
30:    {
31:       /* if lowercase, make uppercase */
32:
33:       if( ch >= 97 && ch <= 122 )   /* is letter from a to z */
34:       {
35:          ch -= 32;          /* change number by subracting 32 */
36:       }
37:       else
38:       {
39:          if( ch >= 65 && ch <= 90 )
40:          {
```

```
41:            ch += 32;          /* change number by adding 32 */
42:        }
43:    }
44:
45:    return(ch);
46: }
```

8. **BUG BUSTER:** The letter 'a' has a decimal value of 97 while the letter 'Z' has a value of 90. Since the conditional portion of the for statement is to print x while it is less than 'Z', nothing will ever print. The uppercase 'Z' is less than the lowercase 'a'. Either print only uppercase or lowercase letters, or print from 'A' to 'z'. If you select to print from 'A' to 'z', you will have a few extra characters print.

9. The following is only one of many possible answers. This is a program that you will find to be more useful. It does have one flaw. It does not print the last few characters of the file.

You also should notice that the new lines and other special characters are printed as single characters with no special processing. This means that the output is an actual representation of what is in the file. The hexadecimal numbers in the output are grouped in sets of four. Every two characters is an individual hexadecimal number. The break between every four is simply for readability.

```
1:  /* Program:  hex.c  (exercise 8)
2:   * Book:     Teach Yourself C Programming in 21 Days.
3:   * Purpose:  This program types a file to the screen.
4:   *           The information is presented in its regular
5:   *           form and its hexadecimal equivalent.
6:   * Notes:    This program has an imperfection. The last
7:   *           23 or fewer characters in the file will not
8:   *           be printed.
9:   *=======================================================*/
10:
11: #include <stdio.h>
12: #include <string.h>
13: #include <stdlib.h>
14:
15: main(int argv, char *argc[])
16: {
17:    int  ch,
18:         ctr;
19:    char buffer[24];
20:
21:    FILE *fp;
22:
23:    if( argv != 2 )
24:    {
25:        printf("\n\nOops!  Proper usage is:");
26:        printf("\n\n%s in_file ", argc[0]);
27:        printf("\n\nOriginal file will be printed in HEX.");
28:        return(1);
29:    }
30:
```

```
31:     /***  Open the file  ***/
32:     if (( fp = fopen( argc[1], "r" )) == NULL )
33:     {
34:        printf( "\n\nOops!  Error in opening file: %s\n\n",
35:                    argc[1]);
36:        exit(99);
37:     }
38:
39:     fread(buffer, 24, sizeof(char), fp );
40:
41:     while( !feof(fp))
42:     {
43:        for( ctr = 0; ctr < 24; ctr++ )
44:        {
45:           if( (ctr % 4) == 0 )
46:               printf(" ");
47:           printf("%02X", buffer[ctr] );
48:        }
49:
50:        printf( "  " );
51:
52:        for( ctr = 0; ctr < 24; ctr++ )
53:        {
54:           if( buffer[ctr] == '\n' )
55:               buffer[ctr] = '.';
56:
57:           printf("%c", buffer[ctr] );
58:        }
59:
60:        printf("\n");
61:
62:        fread(buffer, 24, sizeof(char), fp );
63:     }
64:
65:     fclose( fp );
66:
67:     return(0);
68: }
```

Answers for Bonus Day 5, "Advanced Structures: Linked Lists"

Quiz

1. 0

2. There is nothing in the list.

3. You use a pointer to the same data type as the linked structure.

4. A stack is a single-linked list that is always accessed from the top. New elements are added to the top. If an item is removed, it is also taken from the top. It is because of this that a stack is referred to as having LIFO (Last In First Out) access order.

5. A queue is a single-linked list that has new elements added to the top. When elements are removed, they always are taken from the bottom (or tail). A queue has a FIFO (First In First Out) access order.

6. A tail pointer is a separate pointer that always points to the last element in a linked list. A top pointer or head pointer is a separate point that always points to the first element in a linked list.

7. A tail pointer is generally not needed for a single-linked list. In some cases they are needed. For example, a singly-linked queue needs a tail in order to know where to remove elements from.

8. A double-linked list has a pointer to the previous element. This is in addition to the pointer to the next element that both a double and single-linked list have. Because there is a pointer to the previous element, a double-linked list can be traversed either forward or backward.

9. The malloc() function does not initialize where as the calloc() function initialize the new elements to zero.

10. A binary tree has a much quicker access time when looking for specific elements.

Exercises

1. Following is one of many possible solutions:

```
struct friend {
    char name[35+1];
    char street1[30+1];
    char street2[30+1];
    char city[15+1];
    char state[2+1];
    char zipcode[9+1];
    struct friend *next;
};
```

2. Following is one of many possible solutions:

```
struct trekkie {
    char series_code;
    unsigned int episode;
    char character[35+1];
    struct trekkie *next_trekkie;
};
```

3. Following is one of many possible solutions:

```
struct entry {
    char name[35+1];
    char phone[14+1];
    struct entry *next;
};
```

4. The structure should contain a pointer to the next client. The corrected structure is:

```
struct client {
    char name[35+1];
    char ssn[11+1];
    int  age;
    struct client *next;
};
```

5. See answer to exercise 7.

6. See answer to exercise 7.

7. The following listing contains the functions for exercises 5 and 6.

```
/* Program:  Stack.c
 * Purpose:  Demonstration of a stack.  (LIFO)
 * Note:     Program assumes that malloc() is successful.
 *           You should not make this assumption!
 *==========================================================*/
#include <stdio.h>
#include <stdlib.h>

#define NULL 0

struct stack
{
    int    value;
    struct stack *next;
};

typedef struct stack LINK;

typedef LINK *LINK_PTR;

/*** prototypes ***/
void push_stack( LINK_PTR *link1, int val );
void pop_stack( LINK_PTR *link1, int *val );
int is_stack_empty( LINK_PTR link1 );
int get_stack_data( LINK_PTR link );


int main( void )
{
    LINK_PTR first = NULL;

    int ctr,
        nbrs[10];

    for( ctr = 0; ctr < 10; ctr ++ )
    {
      nbrs[ctr] = ctr;
      printf("\nPush # %d, nbrs[ctr] = %d", ctr, nbrs[ctr]);
      push_stack(&first, nbrs[ctr]);
    }

    printf("\n---------------------");
```

```
    for( ctr = 0; ctr < 10; ctr ++ )
    {
      pop_stack(&first, &nbrs[ctr]);
      printf("\nPop # %d, nbrs[ctr] = %d", ctr, nbrs[ctr]);
    }

    return(0);
}

/*-------------------------------------------------------*
 * Name:    push_stack()
 * Purpose: Places a value into a new link on the stack.
 *          Returns the value of the data stored.
 * Params:  link = the next field from the previous link
 *          val  = value being placed on the stack.
 * Return:  None
 *-------------------------------------------------------*/

void push_stack( LINK_PTR *link1, int val )
{
    LINK_PTR tmp_link;

    tmp_link = (LINK_PTR) malloc( sizeof(LINK) );
    tmp_link->value = val;
    tmp_link->next  = *link1;
    *link1 = tmp_link;
}

/*-------------------------------------------------------*
 * Name:    pop_stack()
 * Purpose: Removes a link from the stack.
 *          Returns the value of the data stored.
 * Params:  link = the current link that is to be removed.
 *          val  = value of the removed link
 * Return:  None
 *-------------------------------------------------------*/

void pop_stack( LINK_PTR *link1, int *val )
{
    LINK_PTR first = *link1;

    if ( is_stack_empty(first) == 0 )   /* if not empty */
    {
      *val   = first->value;
      *link1 = first->next;
      free( first );
    }
    else
    {
      printf("\n\nStack is empty");
    }
}

/*-------------------------------------------------------*
 * Name:    is_stack_empty()
 * Purpose: Checks to see if a link exists.
```

```
 * Params:    link1 = pointer to links
 * Return:    0 if the stack is not empty
 *            1 if the stack is empty
 *---------------------------------------------------*/

int is_stack_empty( LINK_PTR link1 )
{
  int rv = 0;

  if( link1 == NULL )
     rv = 1;

  return( rv );
}

/*---------------------------------------------------*
 * Name:      get_stack_data()
 * Purpose:   Gets the value for a link on the stack
 * Params:    link = pointer to a link
 * Return:    value of the integer stored in link
 *---------------------------------------------------*/

int get_stack_data( LINK_PTR link )
{
  return( link->value );
}
```

Answers for Bonus Day 6, "Variable-Length Structures"

Quiz

1. The basic data types are char, int, long, double, float, and their unsigned equivalents.

2. Three ways of grouping data are arrays, structures, and unions.

3. It allows you to store information more efficiently. You only need to use the space necessary.

4. BMP graphics files, icon files, cursor files, word processor files, and more.

5. No. You cannot read a variable length structure with a single read. You don't know how long the structure is, so you need to read the initial part of the structure in order to determine how large the variable section is.

Exercises

1. The following creates a data type for declaring an SSN:

```
typedef struct {
   char first[3];
   char breaker1;
   char middle[2];
   char breaker2;
   char last[4];
} SSN;
```

2. The following is one of many possible answers:

```
struct employee_rec_tag {
   char first_name[15+1];
   char last_name[20+1];
   char child1[25+1];
   char child2[25+1];
}
```

3. The following is one of many possible answers:

```
struct employee_rec_tag {
   char first_name[15+1];
   char last_name[20+1];
   char nbr_of_children;
   char child_name[];
}
```

4. This exercise was for you to work out on your own. The answer to this exercise is simply an expansion of the listings in the chapter. Instead of two reads to pull in a structure you will have to do three reads. The first read will state how many records are on a page. You will then use this to create a loop to read the journal entries.

5. This exercise is for you to work out on your own. All the information you need was in the previous 26 days!

F

Index

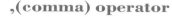

Symbols

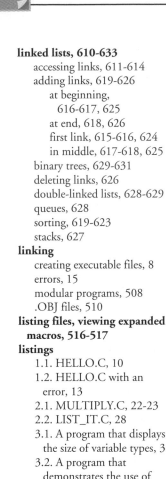

linked lists

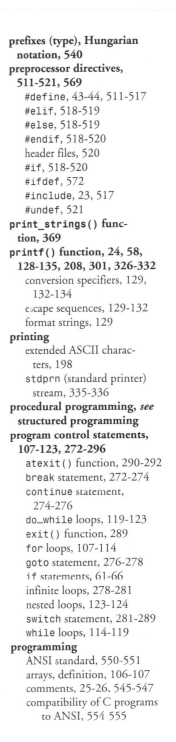

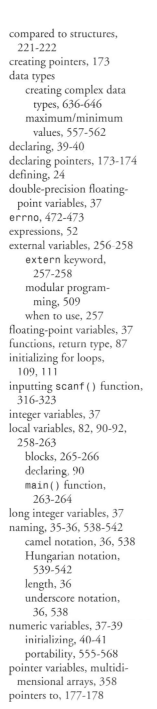

Add to Your Sams Library Today with the Best Books for Programming, Operating Systems, and New Technologies

The easiest way to order is to pick up the phone and call

1-800-428-5331

between 9:00 a.m. and 5:00 p.m. EST.
For faster service please have your credit card available.

ISBN	Quantity	Description of Item	Unit Cost	Total Cost
0-672-30471-6		Teach Yourself Advanced C in 21 Days	$34.95	
0-672-30080-X		Moving from C to C++	$29.95	
0-672-30287-X		Tom Swan's Code Secrets (Book/Disk)	$39.95	
0-672-30363-9		Your Borland C++ Consultant	$29.95	
0-672-30327-2		Moving from COBOL to C	$24.95	
0-672-22660-X		The Waite Group's Turbo C Programming for the PC, Revised Edition	$29.95	
0-672-30561-5		C Programming: Just the FAQs	$25.00	
0-672-30286-1		C Programmer's Guide to Serial Communications, Second Edition	$39.95	
0-672-48518-4		C Programming for UNIX	$29.95	
❏ 3 ½" Disk		Shipping and Handling: See information below.		
❏ 5 ¼" Disk		TOTAL		

Shipping and Handling: $4.00 for the first book, and $1.75 for each additional book. Floppy disk: add $1.75 for shipping and handling. If you need to have it NOW, we can ship product to you in 24 hours for an additional charge of approximately $18.00, and you will receive your item overnight or in two days. Overseas shipping and handling adds $2.00 per book and $8.00 for up to three disks. Prices subject to change. Call for availability and pricing information on latest editions.

201 W. 103rd Street, Indianapolis, Indiana 46290

1-800-428-5331 — Orders   1-800-835-3202 — FAX   1-800-858-7674 — Customer Service

Book ISBN 0-672-30736-7

PLUG YOURSELF INTO...

THE MACMILLAN INFORMATION SUPERLIBRARY™

Free information and vast computer resources from the world's leading computer book publisher—online!

FIND THE BOOKS THAT ARE RIGHT FOR YOU!

A complete online catalog, plus sample chapters and tables of contents give you an in-depth look at *all* of our books, including hard-to-find titles. It's the best way to find the books you need!

- **STAY INFORMED** with the latest computer industry news through our online newsletter, press releases, and customized Information SuperLibrary Reports.

- **GET FAST ANSWERS** to your questions about MCP books and software.

- **VISIT** our online bookstore for the latest information and editions!

- **COMMUNICATE** with our expert authors through e-mail and conferences.

- **DOWNLOAD SOFTWARE** from the immense MCP library:
  - Source code and files from MCP books
  - The best shareware, freeware, and demos

- **DISCOVER HOT SPOTS** on other parts of the Internet.

- **WIN BOOKS** in ongoing contests and giveaways!

TO PLUG INTO MCP: →

GOPHER: gopher.mcp.com
FTP: ftp.mcp.com

WORLD WIDE WEB: **http://www.mcp.com**

DISK AVAILABLE

You can save yourself lots of tedious typing by ordering the *Teach Yourself C Programming in 21 Days* program disk. This disk contains all the source code in the book. The time you save will be well worth the $19.95 cost. Use this form, or a photocopy, to place your order. This offer is made directly by the author, not by Sams Publishing.

Please send me _____ copies of the *Teach Yourself C Programming in 21 Days,* Premier Edition program disk.

United States: $19.95 each _____

Foreign: $24.95 each (disk will be sent airmail) _____

Total Enclosed: _____

Note: Foreign orders must be paid by credit card, or in U.S. dollars by postal money order or a check drawn on a U.S. bank.

Diskette size: _____5-1/4" (360KB) _____3-1/2" (720KB)

Name _____

Address _____

City_____State_____ZIP _____

_____Check   _____Money order   _____Visa   _____MasterCard

Credit Card # _____ Exp date _____

Signature _____ (credit card orders only)

Send your order to:
Peter Aitken, P.O. Box 3214, Durham, NC 27715
Please allow 3–4 weeks for delivery